John Maclean

Canadian Savage Folk

The Native Tribes Of Canada

I0085942

John Maclean

Canadian Savage Folk
The Native Tribes Of Canada

ISBN/EAN: 9783741186943

Manufactured in Europe, USA, Canada, Australia, Japa

Cover: Foto ©Lupo / pixelio.de

Manufactured and distributed by brebook publishing software
(www.brebook.com)

John Maclean

Canadian Savage Folk

;ANADIAN SAVAGE FOLK

THE NATIVE TRIBES OF CANADA.

BY

JOHN MACLEAN, M.A., Ph.D.,

Author of "The Indians of Canada," "The Hero of the Saskatchewan," "James Evans,
Inventor of the Cree Syllabic System," etc., etc.

Member of the American Society for the Advancement of Science, the American
Folk-Lore Society, and Corresponding Member of the Canadian
Institute and Manitoba Historical Society.

ILLUSTRATED.

TORONTO:

WILLIAM BRIGGS,

WESLEY BUILDINGS.

MONTREAL: C. W. COATES.   HALIFAX: S. F. HUESTIS.

1896.

PREFACE.

HIDDEN in the memories of the Red Men of Canada, there lie weird legends and strange stories of bygone years. Pictures and poems wrought by the fancy of the native historians and medicine men, bring home to us the primitive civilization which still lingers at our doors. The customs of our savage folk and the wealth of their languages and literature are interesting to us, as belonging to a people who were the pioneers of our land, and they open up a new world of myth, religion and native culture. Close contact with our native tribes shows us the mistake we have been making in deciding that ignorance, superstition and cruelty belong to these people, and that there is no wisdom, truth or beauty in their belief and manner of life. A faithful study of the languages and customs compels us to acknowledge that there are deeper truths than facts, and under the blanket and coat of skin there beats a human heart, as there is beauty, sweetness and wisdom in their traditions and courage, liberty and devotion in their lives. We have been looking at the red men from our own point of view, and the Canadian Indian judges the white man and his customs from the standpoint of life and training in the camp. Put yourself in his place and the verdict will be different. This work is an attempt to reach the meaning of the life of our savage folk. It was not possible to bring within the compass of a single volume all the native tribes of Canada, or to review all the languages or customs, which would take a series of volumes, and a selection had therefore to be made. Even the treatment of the subject is not exhaustive, as I have not written for the specialist, but for the general public, still, I hope that each will find a suitable portion worthy of study.

JOHN MACLEAN.

February, 1896.

CONTENTS.

CHAPTER VI.

RACES AND LANGUAGES.

CHAPTER VII.

ON THE TRAIL.

ILLUSTRATIONS.

CANADIAN SAVAGE FOLK.

CHAPTER I.

SOME QUEER FOLK.

THE SARCEES.

THE Sarcees are a branch of the Beaver or Castor tribe of Indians of the great Athapascan stock, which extends over the north of British America in scattered bands, through Oregon and California into Northern Mexico, and includes the Umpquas, Apaches, and other tribes. At some period beyond the recollection of the oldest members of the Sarcee tribe, it came under the protection of the Blackfoot Confederacy, and was united with it. The Beaver Indians still live in the district of Athabasca, where are found the Chippewayan, Slave, Dog Rib, and other Indian tribes.

Only in the traditions of the people can we learn anything of this strange isolation of the Sarcees from their kindred in the far northern country. Tradition says that in the distant past a young Beaver chief shot his arrow through a dog of one of his fellow braves, who was deeply enraged, and vowed vengeance. His friends rallied to his assistance, and eighty men fell dead as the result of the quarrel. Great was the sorrow in the camp, and a temporary truce was arranged, but sixty people who were friends of the chief who had killed the dog agreed to separate from the tribe and seek a home in another part of the land. They journeyed southward by the shores of the Lesser Slave Lake until they reached the plains and valleys of the Great Saskatchewan.

More than a century passed by, and no tidings were ever
received from this exiled band. A young Beaver Indian
accompanied a white fur hunter southward, and on their journey they camped at one of the forts in the valley of the
Saskatchewan, where strange Indians were seen loitering about
the palisades. They were members of the great Blackfoot
Confederacy. Among them were some braves who spoke a
language different from the Blackfoot tongue, and as the
Beaver Indian listened he recognized his own language, for in
these men he found the descendants of the long lost band of
the Beaver tribe. These are the Sarcee Indians of the present
day.

In the summer of 1880, when the writer reached Fort
Macleod, he found the Sarcee Indians camped upon the Old
Man's River, along with some Blackfoot and Blood Indians,
where they were being supplied with rations by the Government—the buffalo having left the plains and gone south to the
plains and valleys of the Missouri and Yellowstone rivers.
The majority of the Bloods and Blackfeet were in Montana
hunting the buffalo, and did not return till late in the fall of
that year. Some of the Sarcee children attended the day
school taught in Macleod by my wife, along with Bloods, Blackfeet and half-breed children. It was then estimated that the
Sarcees numbered about seven hundred, although the Government agent thought that there were not more than three or
four hundred.

Sir John Franklin's estimate in 1820 was that there were
one hundred and fifty lodges, with an average of eight persons
to each lodge, or a total of twelve hundred persons. Rowand,
an old trader, in 1843 counted forty-five lodges, or three hundred and fifty persons.[*] Sir George Simpson reckoned fifty
lodges and three hundred and fifty persons in the year 1841.[†]
An old friend of the writer, who has lived for fifty years in the
country, told him that during the year of the small-pox he had
counted at the Marias' River not less than one hundred "dead

* *Canadian Journal,* 1853, page 194.
† "Overland Journey Around the World," Vol. I., page 102.

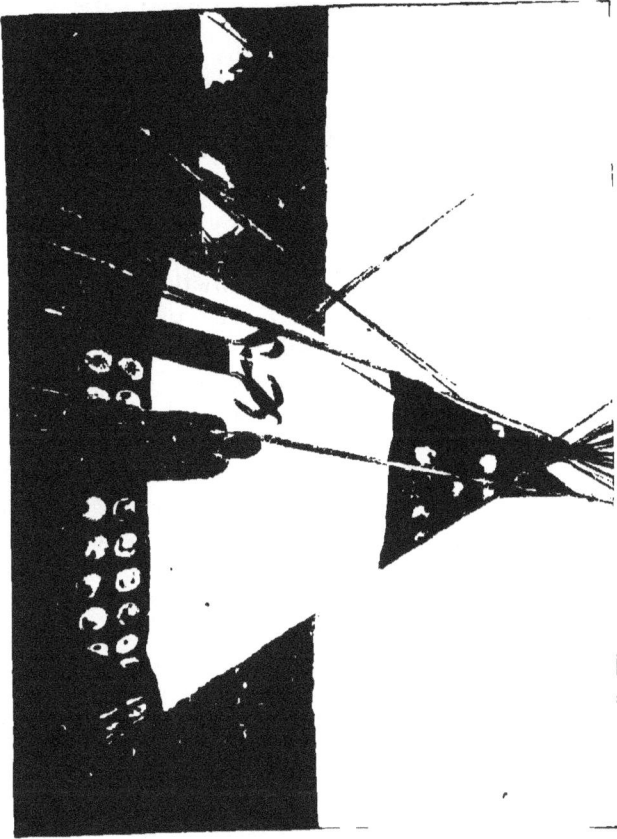

SARCEE INDIAN CAMP.

lodges," in which there was an average of ten bodies. It is, therefore, difficult to make a correct estimate of this tribe with such conflicting testimony, but there is no doubt that the population must have been quite numerous, lessened at times through the depopulating ravages of war. They were said to be "the oldest of all the tribes that inhabit the plains," and those who have come in contact with them in these later years can add to this testimony, that they are the most saucy, independent and impudent tribe of Indians that dwell in North-western Canada. They have ever been friends and allies of the Blackfeet, and enemies of the Crees. At times they have protected solitary Crees against the evil intentions of the Piegans and Blackfeet.

The Sarcees are of medium height, very few tall men being among them : the women, especially, being small. During the old buffalo days they exhibited their pride in beautiful dresses and fine buffalo-skin lodges, but the departure of the buffalo reduced them to poverty, the lodges were used for moccasins, and many of their horses were sold to obtain food and clothing. The traders and the "old timers" in the country were ever suspicious of these people, believing them to be deceitful, and consequently were ever on their guard against treachery. Like the other plain tribes, they were good hunters, delighting in hunting the buffalo, and when they had secured an abundance of food, spent their days and nights feasting and gambling.

Alexander Henry's journal says of the people : "The Sarcees are a distinct nation, and have an entirely different language from any other nation of the plains, and very difficult to acquire from the many guttural sounds it contains. Their land was formerly on the north side of the Saskatchewan, but they have now removed to the south side, and dwell commonly on the southward of the Beaver Hills, near the Slave Indians (Blackfoot Confederacy), with whom they are at peace. They have the name of being a brave and warlike people, whom the neighboring nations always appear desirous of being on amicable terms with. Their customs and manners seem to be nearly the same as the Crees, and their dress is the same. Their language bears a great resemblance to that of the Chippewayans; many words are exactly the same, from which their apparent emigration from the northward gives every cause to suppose them of that nation. They affect to despise the Slave Indians for their brutish and dastardly manners, and although comparatively few in number, frequently set them at defiance. They form ninety tents, containing about one hundred and fifty men bearing arms."*

According to Henry's estimate there would be more than seven hundred Sarcees in the years 1801-1806. In the year 1877 these Indians were included in Treaty number seven, which embraced Blackfeet, Bloods, Piegans, Stoneys and Sarcees, which was arranged by Lieutenant-Governor Laird and Lieut.-Col. J. F. Macleod, at the Blackfeet Crossing of Bow River. The Blackfeet, Bloods and Sarcees were allowed a Reservation along the north and south sides of the Bow and South Saskatchewan rivers, part of which was for ten years only, and the rest in perpetuity. Annuities of money and ammunition were agreed upon, clothing for the chiefs once in three years, a certain number of cattle and farming implements were to be supplied, and teachers sent to teach their children. The head chief of the Sarcees, Bull's Head, on behalf of his tribe, signed the treaty.

The Blackfeet settled gradually upon their Reserve, but the Bloods and Sarcees became dissatisfied and would not locate at Blackfoot Crossing. Finally the Bloods located on a Reservation which was allotted them on Belly River, south of Macleod. A few months after our arrival at Macleod the Sarcees were sent to Blackfoot Crossing under the charge of "Piscan" Munro, but they remained dissatisfied, as they alleged that the Blackfeet were domineering and looked upon them as intruders. They were removed to Fish Creek Indian Farm, where they remained for about a year, and at last they were located on their present Reservation, about eight miles south of Calgary. In 1889 the Sarcee population numbered three hundred and

---

* Henry's " Journal," by C. N. Bell.   Rev. E. F. Wilson, in " British Association Fourth Report on the North-western Tribes of Canada."

thirty-six, and the outlook is dark indeed, pointing toward
their extinction, although the Government is aiding them
materially, striving by means of agent, farm instructor, and
rations to train them to become self-supporting.

Their language is a very deep guttural, the sounds emanating
from the throat, which renders it difficult for a white man to
understand or learn. The writer has known several persons
who have attempted to learn it, not one of them having been
able to acquire the power to speak it with precision. The
people speak their own language amongst themselves, but in
conversation with others use the Cree or Blackfoot languages.
Owing to their relationship to the Blackfoot Confederacy, and
their proximity to the members of it, they use the Blackfoot
language more than the Cree, and seem to be perfectly at home
when using it. The following vocabulary, gathered from the
Sarcees, will give a slight idea of the language :

Man, kateni.	Book or paper, tetlesi.	My eye, minola.
Woman, tzika.	Church, tekaqale, tze-	My nose, mitse.
Boy, tzita.	teia nasaga.	My foot, suus.
Girl, tzitatza.	Missionary, tekaqale	My elbow, tzitzses.
Water, to.	tzeteta.	My mouth, misaka.
River, tziska.	Turnip, etzaka.	My son, tzega.
House, nasaga.	Oats, etraka.	My daughter, tzetza.
Axe, tzilq.	Flour, netziltasi.	My father, eta.
Window, misatztzetin.	Wheat, netziltasitraka	My mother, ina.
Glass, esteni.	composed of words	Large, nitcha.
Sack, altaga.	for oats and flour).	Small, nitzekla.
Waggon, masikleqoko.	Tobacco, katcina.	Fish, kluka.
Horse, eskle.	Tea, taseto.	Door, tumali.
Cow, kanamaka.	Sugar, klikani or teka-	A lodge, krawa.
Cattle, kauleklisata.	halenegur.	Day, tzines.
Dog, kle.	Beef, elene.	Night, eklage.
Boat, kanakasi.	Bacon, klikra.	Sun, tzataga.
Steamboat,kotranakasi.	Moccasin, ka.	Moon, ilnaga.
Locomotive, metakok-	Fire, ko.	Stars, so.
seskani.	Light, kokoneti.	Summer, ama.
Town, nasoenkuk.	Darkness, koilkrasi.	Winter, okrasi.
School, tetlesira.	Lamp, ikatoteskani.	A month, klikesatza-
School teacher, kork-	Pipe, mistole.	taga.
wineqi.	My head, titse.	A year, klikesasoska.

Warm, trakoilkez.	Seven, tzistete.	Fifteen, kwiltrametra.
Cold, koskasi.	Eight, klastetza.	Sixteen, kostrametra.
One, kliketza.	Nine, klagoega.	Seventeen, tzistetzeme-
Two, akwie.	Ten, koenesnani.	tra.
Three, take.	Eleven, klikimetra.	Eighteen, klastezemetra.
Four, tatetza.	Twelve, kametra.	Nineteen, klagoemetra.
Five, kwilta.	Thirteen, takimetrar.	Twenty, ekate.
Six, kostreni.	Fourteen, tatetremetra.	Mine, aselqina.

Mackenzie, in his "Voyages," says: "The Sarcees, who are but few in number, appear from their language to come, on the contrary, from the north-westward, and are of the same people as the Rocky Mountain Indians, . . who are a tribe of the Chippewayans."

In Bancroft's "Native Races" we learn that "Umfreville, who visited these people, compares their language to the cackling of hens, and says that it is very difficult for their neighbors to learn it;" that Richardson compares some of the sounds to the Hottentot cluck; and Isbister calls them "harsh and guttural, difficult of enunciation, and unpleasant to the ear."

Horatio Hale, in his "Ethnology in the United States Exploring Expedition," says the Sarcees speak a dialect of the Chippewayan (Athapascan) allied to the Tahkali: and Latham classes the Beaver language as transitional to the Slave and Chippewayan proper. Mr. Howse, who spent several years in the northern country, and published a grammar of the Cree language, says of the Indian tongue: "As the Indian languages are numerous, so do they greatly vary in their effect upon the ear. We have the rapid Cootoonay of the Rocky Mountains and the stately Blackfoot of the plains, the slow, embarrassed Flathead of the Mountains; the smooth-toned Pierced-nosed, the difficult Sussee (Sarcee) and Chippewayan; the sing-song Assiniboine, the deliberate Cree, and the sonorous, majestic Chippeway." The writer can corroborate these statements from his association with the tribes mentioned. Oftentimes has he tried to understand the Sarcee tongue, as he has conversed with the natives in the Blackfoot tongue, but the clicking sound of many of their words and the double

2

SARCEE INDIAN.

guttural made it impossible. The whole of their language seems to consist of clicks and gutturals, that it is difficult to distinguish one syllable from another, and the study of the language had to be given up in despair. The women and children invariably speak the Sarcee language, but the men use in addition the Blackfoot and Cree.

The writer does not know of any literature in the Sarcee language, but in the parent Beaver and Chippewayan tongues there exists quite an extensive list of vocabularies and religious works; most of them, however, are small. In the Chippewayan tongue there have been translated the New Testament, the Ten Commandments, hymns, prayers and catechisms. Translations of legends and songs of the people have been made. Small grammatic treatises and a syllabary, tribal names, and vocabularies have been also arranged. Missionaries, traders and travellers have done considerable work in the language of the Chippewayans. The Beaver language has some translations of the same character, though not so numerous. The Sarcees have, in a great measure, been overshadowed by the tribes in their vicinity, and less attention has been paid to them by travellers and missionaries than to their kindred in the far North, and consequently they have no printed works in their language.

They are similar in their political and social organization to the Blackfeet, having a head chief over the tribe and a minor chief over each band. They have also an annual sun dance, which cannot be of Athapascan origin, but must have been learned from the Blackfeet. Indeed, in all their social customs, they are essentially members of the Blackfoot Confederacy. They are sun worshippers, whose religious ideas have been modified through contact with the white people. Dancing and singing, and throwing the wheel and arrows are native amusements, to which they have added card playing, which they have learned from the white people.

The boys run naked in early childhood, having occasionally a garment or cloth around their loins. The girls are always dressed, although the raiment is oftentimes scanty. At the early age of twelve or thirteen the girls are sold in marriage; sometimes to an old man, who may have several wives. Polygamy is practised amongst them, although not to so great a degree as in times of war, when the men were slain and the women compelled to marry members of their own tribe. In the long winter evenings they will gather in their lodges, or in their modern log houses, and, with drum and song, have a tea dance, where tea is drunk in profusion and the well-filled pipe is passed around. Stories of the old buffalo days are told, wherein the narrator has been one of the principal actors, and as the aged man tells vividly of battles, scalps, hairbreadth escapes, horses, and women captured, and glorious wounds, the hearts of the young men are thrilled, and they long for the time when they may follow in the footsteps of their forefathers; but when they step beyond the lodge they see the agent's house, and they are at once confronted with the fact that the pale-face dwells in the land, and he has come to rule. Thoughts too deep for words rankle in their breasts, and fain would they live a hunter's life and taste the sweets of war. Brought into contact with civilization their native customs are dying out.

The Government is seeking to teach them agriculture, which is a difficult thing to do, as they are by nature hunters. Yet they are progressing slowly, as can be seen by the fields of grain and roots which they cultivate upon their Reservation. The children attend the Government school, and an English Church missionary ministers unto them in spiritual things. The influence of the sun dance is passing away, and the war instinct is being suppressed through their inability to contend with their enemies. Their close proximity to Calgary is injurious to the morals of the white people and Indians, as the natives of the plains always find the lower stratum of society ready to teach the willing learner lessons of immorality, and degradation is sure to follow any close relationship of Indians with white people in the early stages of their training. Because of this expression of immorality and a longing on the part of some people for their fine tract of land, there has arisen an agitation for the removal of the Sarcees, but as the Canadians have ever been lovers of fair play, the better class of people will not listen to any question of removal except upon conditions agreeable to the treaty and British law.

The outlook for these Indians is not very bright, yet we are unable to predict their ultimate condition, as they are still in a transition state. The sudden appearance of a contagious disease would sweep them off the face of the earth, while care may preserve them as a remnant of a powerful tribe, transformed through stages of civilization from a bold, independent and war-like race, into a thriftless number of serfs, without ambition or manhood. Education, training in the arts of peace, and the Gospel may do much to enlighten and inspire them with an earnest desire to attain a position of respectability, and this is the hope of those who have the welfare of the Sarcees at heart. They are well cared for, but they feel keenly their changed condition, which is seen in their tawdry dress and habits of uncleanliness, and without hope they cannot succeed. A pang of sorrow comes to the heart in contrasting the former and latter conditions of this tribe. Let us hope for a solution of the Indian problem in its relation to the Sarcees.

THE STONEY INDIANS.

The Stoney Indians are a branch of the great Dakota or Siouan Confederacy. They are Assiniboines, of which Stoney is the English translation. According to Dr. Riggs, who spent forty years among the Sioux Indians, Assiniboine means Stone Sioux, and is a compound of French and Ojibway. "Bwan" is the name given by the Ojibways to the Sioux ; "assin" is the Ojibway for a stone. Baraga and other authorities on the Ojibway and Sioux give this translation of Assiniboine. The derivation of the name is said to come from the fact that the Assiniboines cooked their food on heated stones, and from this custom they received this name, which was translated by the white people into the Stone People, and finally into Stoney Indians. We often meet with the names, Stone People and Stone Indians. in

the old books treating of the history of North-western Canada.
We have therefore some branches of the tribe called Assiniboines, and others Stoney Indians. The Blackfeet call the
Stoneys, Suqseoisokituki, which, however, is not a Blackfoot
word. Suqseo must be a Sarcee word, and is the name given
by the Blackfeet to the Sarcees. The full word would therefore be a combination of Sarcee and Blackfoot, and the meaning
in full is Sarcee-Sioux, the latter part of the word referring to
the Sioux, who are called by the Blackfoots, "Cut-throats." In
the Cree language, Asini means a stone, and Asinipwat a Stone
Indian. The adjective "Stoney" is Asoniweo, and Asinipwatiwio
means he is a Stone Indian. Here we see the relation of the
Ojibway to the Cree, both languages belonging to the Algonquin stock of languages. In David Thompson's field book of
his "Explorations in the North-West," there is mentioned one of
the trading-posts belonging to the North-West Company, called
Upper House on Stone Indian River, which is now named the
Assiniboine.* The Sioux were called by the Ojibways, Nadowessi.

As early as 1660, the Assiniboines were living in the vicinity of
Grand Portage, beyond the north-west shore of Lake Superior.
They were at that time called Poualak, or Assinipoualaes, and
were dreaded by the Upper Algonquins as a warlike band of
Indians, who lived in skin lodges and made fire of coal, as wood
was scarce in the prairie region where they dwelt. In the
early maps of that period, a lake intended for Nepigon is called
"Assiniboines." In 1679 Du Lhut held a conference with the
Assiniboines at Kaministiquia, the site of Fort William of the
old North-West Company.† In large numbers they roamed all
over Manitoba and that portion of the North-West Territory
now known as the southern parts of Assiniboia and Alberta.
Alexander Henry, in his "Journal of Adventures," in 1809 gives

* Dr. Bryce's " The Assiniboine River and its Forts," in " Transactions
Royal Society of Canada," Vol. X., Sec. 2., pages 69, 70. Dr. Rigg's "Forty
Years with the Sioux," page 305. Tucker's " Rainbow in the North,"
page 48.
† Winsor's " Critical History of America," Vol. IV., pages 169, 171, 182,
249, 252. Butler's "Great Lone Land," pages 278-280.

the location of the Assiniboines as follows: "The Assiniboines are
from the Sioux. Their lands may be said to commence at the
Hair Hills (Pembina Mountains) near the Red River, then run-
ing in a western direction along the Assiniboine River, and
from that to the junction of the north and south branches of
the Saskatchewine, and up the former branch as far as Fort
Vermilion, then due south to the Battle River, and then south-
east until it strikes upon the Missouris, and down that river
until near the Mandan villages, then a north-east course until it
reached the Hair Hills. All this space of open meadow country
may be called the lands of the Assiniboines. A few tents of
straggling trees occasionally intermixed among them."

The territory of the Assiniboines became circumscribed by
the advent of white settlers, so that no longer did they roam
over this large extent of country, and finally the Government
made treaties with the Indians by which they were located
upon Reserves. They are still widely scattered upon Reserves,
having been assigned to agencies with other Indian tribes,
though with separate Reserves, in the sections of country sometimes selected by themselves, near where they had made their
homes at the time they made the treaty with the Government.
This explains their separation as bands of Assiniboines and
Stoneys in different parts of the North-West, instead of being
located as a united tribe on one Reservation. They are found
at the present time as separated bands of this tribe at Moose
Mountain and Indian Head, in Assiniboia; Eagle Hills, Lac Ste.
Anne, White Whale Lake, and Morleyville, in Alberta. During
the early and middle parts of the present century the tribe
was known as Strongwood or Wood Assiniboines, and Plain
Assiniboines, which distinctions have been changed into Assiniboines, a term applied to those dwelling on the Reserves in
Assiniboia, Mountain Stoneys at Morleyville, and Wood Stoneys
in Northern Alberta. A considerable number of Assiniboines
are resident in the United States.

In the beginning of the present century, Henry estimated
about two thousand fighting men in all the Assiniboine camps,
which would make the total population number at least ten

STONEY INDIAN.

thousand people. A naturalist, named Cuthbertson, travelling
for the Smithsonian Institution, in 1850 gives the probable
number of the Assiniboines in the Upper Missouri and its
tributaries as four thousand eight hundred. Mr. Harriet, an
old trader, who had spent his life among the Blackfeet, stated
that there were, in 1842, eighty lodges of Strongwood Assiniboines, equal to six hundred and forty persons, and Mr.
Rowand, for the same date, gave for the Plain Assiniboines three hundred
lodges, equal to two thousand four hundred, or a total population of Assiniboines in North-western Canada of three thousand
and forty persons. Mr. Lefroy estimated them, at the same
time, as three thousand six hundred, and Mr. Shaw, at four
thousand persons. These men had travelled in the country and
knew a great deal about the Indians. The change in the
population is due no doubt to the fact that their estimate had
reference to the Saskatchewan country, which is borne out by .
the fact that Sir George Simpson, in his " Overland Journey,"
gave for the Assiniboines in the Saskatchewan district in 1841
four thousand and sixty persons. The entire population of
Stoney and Assiniboine Indians for the year 1890 in North-western Canada, as given in the Dominion Blue Book, is one thousand three hundred and forty-two. The cause of this decrease
arises principally from two causes, tribal wars and the plague
of small-pox, which swept them away in large numbers.

Traces of the residence of these people in Manitoba in the
early ·part of the present century are found in the fact that
Alexander Henry states that, when returning from a visit to
the Mandans and other Tribes on the Upper Missouri River in
1806, he came to the Tete-de-Beuf region, where there was a
hill, recognised by some at the present day as Calf Mountain,
upon the top of which, the Assiniboines and Crees made sacrifices of tobacco and other trifles, and collected a certain number
of bulls' heads, which they daubed over with red earth, depositing them on the summit, with the nose always pointing toward
the east.

Instead of continually using the terms, Stoney and Assiniboine the writer will employ the former name as applicable to

all the people. The Stoney Indians are of medium height, a few of the men being of massive proportions, but the average being rather below medium stature. They are well-formed, of pleasing countenance and, the Mountain Stoneys especially, active in their movements and fleet of foot. It is not too much to say that they are the most energetic of all the tribes of the North-West, well disciplined, inured to the hardships of prairie and mountain, and of industrious habits. They are comely in their dress, which has changed through advancing civilization: the painted faces, hair besprinkled with red earth and twisted into a sugar-loaf bunch on the top of the head having been discarded. The native costume of well-tanned deer-skin, beautifully ornamented by the women, was changed into garments made from blankets, but many of them are now dressed in modern apparel. The Mountain Stoneys cut their hair, and their light copper-colored complexion is attractive. In former years the men wore a profusion of dress ornaments, like all the other Indian tribes, consisting of rings on each finger, ear-rings and necklaces, coat and leggings, with colored porcupine quill or bead ornamentation, and their war accoutrements, with figures wrought or painted upon them. They were very particular about dressing their hair, especially the young men. They are none the less careful about their dress, and more cleanly in their habits at the present time, but they are more plain in their style, and not so anxious for display.

The women are small, but active, neat in their dress and cleanly in their habits. Their dress is similar to that of the women of the other tribes, although many of them are imitating their pale-faced sisters. Some of the bands are not far removed from their old-time modes of dress and habits, but those who have been brought under the influence of the missionary have advanced rapidly, and are now models of neatness and activity to the other tribes.

Before the advent of civilization, they dwelt in tents made from the hides of the buffalo, upon the sides of which hung the scalp-locks which they had taken in war, and around each tent were painted figures, representing the famous deeds of the master of the lodge. They were famous hunters of the buffalo, and those dwelling near the mountains and in the woods, pursued the deer, goat, sheep, and bear, followed the moose, or fished in the lakes. The babes were snugly shrouded in their moss-bags, and carried on the back of the mother, whether walking on the prairie or riding upon a horse. In many of their customs the Stoney Indians were similar to the Crees and Blackfeet. Their food consisted of buffalo meat principally, in the winter, and deer, except those in the North who lived on fish. In the summer they partook of wild roots and berries. They were excellent horsemen, and had the reputation of being great horse thieves. Their utensils of the lodge were made principally of wood. The women were very unchaste, induced by their customs of marriage. Polygamy was practised among them, and women were bartered for trifles.

The men were inveterate smokers (a habit in which the women also indulged), and they exhibited their skill in the manufacture of beautiful pipes. Of their ability in this direction Sir Daniel Wilson says: " Among the Assiniboine Indians a material is used in pipe manufacture altogether peculiar to them. It is a fine marble, much too hard to admit of minute carving, but taking a high polish. This is cut into pipes of graceful form, and made so extremely thin as to be nearly transparent, so that when lighted the glowing tobacco shines through, and presents a singular appearance when in use at night or in a dark lodge. Another favorite material employed by the Assiniboine Indians is a coarse species of jasper, also too hard to admit of elaborate ornamentation. This also is cut into various simple, but tasteful designs, executed chiefly by the slow and laborious process of rubbing it down with other stones. The choice of the material for fashioning the favorite pipe is by no means invariably guided by the facilities which the location of the tribe affords. A suitable stone for such a purpose will be picked up and carried hundreds of miles. Mr. Kane informs me that in coming down the Athabasca River, when drawing near its source in the Rocky Mountains, he observed his Assiniboine guides select the favorite blueish jasper from among the water-worn stones in the bed of the river to carry home for the purpose of pipe manufacture, although they were then fully five hundred miles from their lodges. Such a traditional adherence to a choice of material peculiar to a remote source may frequently prove of considerable value as a clue to former migrations of the tribe."

Some years ago the writer saw, at Morley, some beautiful specimens of sculpture, executed with a pocket-knife by a Stoney boy: among them a moose, buffalo and dog. They were remarkable exhibitions of native skill, as perfect in detail as any ever seen. The accurate measurements of the horns of the moose, and the attitude of the animal in the act of leaping, were astonishing, considering the age of the sculptor, a youth of not more than twelve years, his lack of training, and the tools with which he wrought. His work attracted considerable notice from travellers, and Senator Hardisty offered to educate the youth at his own expense, but the offer was refused by the boy's father, who preferred the money obtained from the sale of the articles to the advancement of his son.

In the early days the dead were buried in a sitting posture, with the face toward the East, but now they follow the custom of their white brethren. The people believed in the transmigration of souls. Charles N. Bell, in his Notes on Henry's "Journal," states that they believed that sometimes after death the spirit goes to a river, which has to be crossed on the way to the happy hunting grounds, where it is met by a fierce red buffalo bull, who drives it back and compels it to re-enter the body.

The Stoneys have several games similar to the Blackfeet, including the hoop and arrow game and the "odd-and-even" game, which is played with small sticks or goose-quills.

The tribe has its own system of government, consisting of chiefs and councillors, who compose their council, at which all questions affecting the welfare of the people are discussed and settled. They made the laws by which they are governed, and through the wise administration of the chiefs and council peace is maintained in the camp. In common with other

Indian tribes, they have a system of telegraphy, consisting of signals by means of fire at night, and in the day certain movements of their blankets, different motions of men on horseback, such as riding backward or forward, riding in a circle, or the rider sitting with his back toward the horse's head. By the use of a looking-glass they are able to communicate with each other at a distance of three or four miles. The writer was in the Stoney camp on a Sunday, conducting service, when an Indian was seen riding at a distance of two or three miles. One of the chiefs stepped aside, drew forth his looking-glass, which is carried by every Indian, and holding it so that the sun would shine upon it, sent a flash toward the rider. The Indian stopped upon his course, waited a moment or two, as the chief sent his message to him, and then rode toward us. This tribe had many famous warriors, and so great was the prowess of the people that, though less in number than the Crees or Blackfeet, these tribes were afraid of them. They were brave and skilful in the use of the bow and arrow, and no less expert in later years with the rifle. Famous as scouts, they were employed during the Riel Rebellion of 1885 in that capacity, and faithful were they in the performance of their work. Alike were they noted as hunters on the plains in the days of the buffalo, and in the mountains, spending the greater part of the year in the pursuit of game.

The old-time custom of naming their children from some physical characteristic or peculiar circumstance at the time of birth, and changing them at different periods in life, as expressive of some great deed or mean action, has passed away in a great measure, and many of them, through the missionary's influence, have adopted Christian names. Contact with white people and religious influence has caused many of them to reject the old tent-life of the camps, and erect good log-houses, with many of the conveniences of modern civilization. They still retain their love for dogs, although they are not used as beasts of burden to any extent, which was a custom of the old times. The mountain Stoneys have acted as guides to hunting parties, and during the explorations for the route of the

Canadian Pacific railroad, many of them were employed,
rendering excellent service.   During the construction of the
railroad they got out of the woods large quantities of ties.

The native religion, with its belief and ceremonies, has disappeared.   Their traditions consisted of an admixture of the
Sioux and Cree traditions, caused by their relation to the
former and contact with the latter tribe.

They have, in common with the other Indian tribes, a sign
language.   The spoken language is a dialect of the Siouan
language, which the following words, collected among the
Stoneys, will give the reader a slight idea of its construction
and significance :

Cold, wasnitz.	Lucifer match, unktu	Ten, wunkjabna.
Moose, ta.	towambin.	Eleven, aga wazi.
Cattle, tatunga; i.e., large	Good day, amba	Twelve, aga num.
moose.	wastej.	Snow, wa.
Horse, suntunga.	I, miye.	Large, tunga.
Fish, pahundo.	One, wazi.	Bad, iningite.
Good, wastej.	Two, num.	Lodge, tibi.
That's true, wim jakate.	Three, yamni.	River, wapta.
Who, tawe.	Four, tosa.	Door, tiuba.
Water, mini.	Five, sapta.	Book, waba.
House, ti.	Six, shakbi.	Iron, soda.
Stove, soda unktu.	Seven, shagoi.	Day, amba.
Fire, unktu.	Eight, shaknoi.	Night, ahe.
Sun, wahiamba.	Nine, nimtcunk.	He, iyc.

The literature of the Stoney Indians is very meagre, owing,
no doubt, to the fact that they are able to read the books
printed in the Syllabic characters of the Cree language.   A
few vocabularies have been printed in books treating of the
Hudson's Bay country and the fur trade, some personal names,
the numerals, and the Lord's Prayer.

The Jesuit missionaries were the first religious teachers
who came in contact with these people, and they remained
alone in the field, meeting them occasionally as these nomads
of the plains visited the missions.   In 1840, the Rev. Robert
Terrill Rundle, Methodist missionary, went to the North-West
and began operations among the Indian tribes of the Saskat-

chewan. Frequently he conversed with the Stoneys at Fort Edmonton, and accompanied them in their hunting expeditions, teaching and preaching. He enjoyed some measure of success, the people learned to sing hymns in the Cree language, and were instructed in the truths of the Christian religion. After laboring eight years in the Saskatchewan, at Edmonton, Pigeon Lake, and on the plains, he was compelled to return to England, because of injury received through a fall from his horse.* His brother-in-law, the Rev. Thomas Woolsey, succeeded him in this work among the Crees, Stoneys and Blackfeet, and through the labors of these devoted men, a band of faithful local preachers was raised, who preached to the people as they travelled upon the plains or roamed through the mountains in search of food. The hymns taught the people in these early years are still remembered, but the tunes have undergone a change, a peculiar Indian turn having been given to them, so that they have become essentially Indian tunes, founded upon their English predecessors.

In 1885, Rev. Thomas Woolsey wrote: "Many of the Cree and Stone Indians were members of our Church in 1864." Woolsey was stationed at Edmonton the year previous when Rev. George McDougall and his family arrived at Victoria from Norway House. The Mountain Stoneys were sought out, and the work of evangelization continued among them. A fuller account of the doings of these men 'can be found in the works of the writer, "The Hero of the Saskatchewan," "The Indians of Canada," and "James Evans." The mission among the Mountain Stoneys at Morley was begun in the autumn of 1873, by Rev. John McDougall, who still remains at his post. Visitors to Morley cannot fail to be deeply impressed with the attitude of reverence manifested by the people as they assemble for service in hundreds, filling the commodious church, drawn together by the sound of the bell, whose peals

---

*The Rev. John McDougall, in a letter to me, says, "I have made particular inquiry, and all the old Indians are unanimous in asserting that the Rev. Robert Rundle was the first missionary of any Church to reach the Saskatchewan and Rocky Mountains in British Territory."

are heard far down the beautiful valley of the Bow River. The singing is hearty, the attention given to the preacher, who may be the missionary himself or one of the native local preachers, is deep, and the whole service is so earnest, reverential and true that the pale face receives impressions which he can never forget. There is an orphanage at the Mission, two good schools upon the Reserve, and a faithful band of men and women striving to lead these people to imitate the life of the Man of Nazareth.

Deep was the sorrow of these people at the loss of Rev. George McDougall, who was frozen to death a few miles north of Calgary. When the writer lived at Macleod, some Stoney Indian women visited the mission-house, and during the conversation they drew from under their blankets the Bible in the Evan's Cree Syllabic characters, with their Methodist class tickets. During a tour of visitation in the Porcupine Hills, the writer met a Stoney Indian who recognized him, and together they called at a friend's house for a night's shelter. When shown the place where he was to sleep, an adjoining building to the house, which was not very clean, he turned to the rancher and said, as he stood in his native dignity, " I am not a dog, I am a man."

When the school teacher's wife died at Morley, the Indians, who had been absent on their hunting trips, upon their return repaired to the cemetery, and as they looked at the grave, cast small twigs and flowers upon it, saying, with deep emotion, " She was a good woman. She was a good friend to us."

Shortly after the rebellion of 1885, Mr. McDougall accompanied three Indian chiefs to Ontario and Quebec. One of these men was Chief Jonas, of the Mountain Stoneys. He is reported to have said, among many of the addresses which he gave to the white people, that he was glad to see so many people worshipping the Great Spirit, for it strengthened him. At one time he thought that those who believed in Christ were few, and those who did not follow Him were numerous, but now he had seen for himself that the Christian people were a great multitude. He would go back and tell his people that they were in the right way, for there were multitudes believing in the same Christ. He would tell his people of the cities he had seen and the multitudes praising God. He wished the white people to help him keep the fire-water out of the country. "At home the railroad came to us, and I thought that was a wonderful power. But, then, when I reached the steamboat I found another great wonder to my mind. All that has been surpassed since I came to the city (Toronto) this evening. I don't know how to describe the great big buildings and the multitudes of people, and the lights, which are like lightning. I shall be happy if I and my people, in even a humble way, will be able in our future to emulate this progress." Schools have been established among the Stoney and Assiniboine Indians on all the Reserves and the children are making good progress in their studies.

Presbyterian, Roman Catholic and Methodist missions are maintained among the Stoneys in the Edmonton district, where there is a Reserve on Sandy Lake, about sixteen miles west of Edmonton. The Government assists the bands, providing farm instructors and agents to teach them farming and look after their interests. As they are generally an industrious people, they are progressing favorably and raise good crops. The women are experts at knitting gloves and mittens on the Reserve near Indian Head, and find a ready sale for all they make. Upon the other reserves they are also industrious. The Mountain Stoneys have some fine bands of cattle, of which they are legitimately proud. As treaty Indians they have always been friendly to the white people, a fact noted by Lord Southesk and other travellers, who have visited their camps or met with them in their travels. Despite the decrease of the native population, there is hope in their progress in agricultural and industrial pursuits, and their independent spirit, that they will ultimately maintain a place among the white people, as a remnant of a powerful tribe of a great confederacy, which once roamed the western plains.*

---

*See John McDougall's "George M. McDougall."

3

THE MOUND-BUILDERS.

Many centuries before the Pilgrim Fathers landed in New England, or Columbus planted the standard of the Spanish crown on the soil of the New World, there lived and perished a race of people on our continent, concerning whom very little is known. They were men and women of like passions to the dwellers of the villages of the nineteenth century, possessed of a worthy civilization, peaceable, affectionate and intensely religious. Their villages have been destroyed; nothing of their literature is known; not a single trace of their language is in existence, and even the name of this strange people is lost to us. Search the histories of the nations of the world, and not a kindly pen is found that can tell us the name of this mysterious people who came to our land, became a large and prosperous nation, and then passed away, leaving only their cities of the dead to tell us in voiceless language the story of their life. We call them Mound-Builders, because of the monuments they have left us—the stately empire of the spirit king. Humboldt says: "The Mound-Builders were eminently a water people," and Ignatius Donnelly tells us that they were wanderers from a large continent that existed in the Atlantic ocean, called "Atlantis," but many eminent scientists hold theories at variance with these opinions. Evidence has been adduced by scholars to show that they crossed the Atlantic and settled in Mexico, and again others testify to their migration from China and Japan by the Behring straits. There were men in China who built mounds, as is learned from the fact that about ten miles from the city of Kalgan there is a cluster of over forty mounds, one of them being thirty feet high, and four hundred and twenty feet in circumference at the base, and an oval mound forty-eight feet in length at the summit. Before Julius Cæsar invaded Britain, the Nahuas entered Mexico, and made their houses there, becoming a great people. These were followed by the Toltecs, who left architectural monuments, significant and beautiful. The Mound-Builders also went to Mexico, and stamped the impress of their existence, but it is impossible at this distant date and with our present knowledge of facts to identify them as the Nahuas or Toltecs. The book of Mormon states that the Indians are the descendants of a Hebrew immigration, and some writers believe that the Indians are the offspring of the Mound-Builders; and, again, others say that the Mound-Builders are the direct lineage of the ten lost tribes of Israel. The leanings of evidence are in favor of the Toltec relationship, and still we cannot press any theory, for the path we tread is a hazy labyrinth, and not a single voice or pen is raised that can show us the way. Along the rivers and lakes they travelled as a peaceful race of nomads, erecting mounds for observation in time of war; burial mounds, in which to place their dead; sacrificial mounds; symbolical mounds, for performing the rites and ceremonies of their native worship; enclosures for defence; and sacred enclosures for religious purposes. Mounds are found in great abundance in Ohio, Wisconsin, Indiana, Missouri, Arkansas, Louisiana, Mississippi, Alabama, Georgia, Arizona, New Mexico and Florida. There are none found in New England, but westward toward the Rocky Mountains, in the Yellowstone country and Manitoba, there have been some discovered. Groups of mounds have been opened at various places in Manitoba, including the parish of St. Andrew's, near Winnipeg, the Souris river, Riding Mountain and Rainy River. Over twenty mounds having been discovered at the last-mentioned place.

The centuries have come and gone since these strange people lived in the land and made the mounds. Heavy forests have grown around the mounds, hiding them from view, and destroying their usefulness for observation in times of war; massive trees have even grown upon the top of them, and along the river banks, where many of them are seen, the river has cut a new channel and left the mounds "high and dry" since the last mound was built.

In the burial mounds have been found stone implements of peace and war, as arrow-heads, spear-heads, axes, knives, hatchets, rimmers, spades, chisels, pendants, gorgets, pipes, shuttles, badges of authority, mauls or hammers, pestles, tubes, hoes, copper ornaments, bone implements, articles of pottery and cloth have been taken from them. The skeletons taken from the mounds of sepulture have been incomplete, owing to their great age. Very few skulls have been found worthy of preservation.

In an age when there was no machinery in the land, the work of these people are in many instances gigantic. There is a notable fortification in Warren County, Ohio, about thirty-three miles north-east of Cincinatti, called Fort Ancient. This defensive enclosure has a wall five miles in extent, encircling an area of one hundred acres. The embankment is built of tough clay, from five to twenty feet in height, with an average of nine feet, and containing six hundred and twenty-eight thousand eight hundred cubic yards of excavation. There are over seventy gateways in the embankment, from ten to fifteen feet wide, and within the works are twenty-four reservoirs.

Still more elaborate and complicated are the Newark works, near Newark, Ohio, consisting of an extensive series of square, circular and polygonal enclosures, with mounds, ditches and connecting avenues, extending over about four square miles.

The great Cahokia mound, seven miles east of St. Louis, comprises a parallelogram, with sides measuring seven hundred and five hundred feet, respectively, and rising to the height of ninety feet. It covers an area of six acres, and its estimated solid contents amount to twenty million cubic feet. There is a terrace reached by a graded way, one hundred and sixty by three hundred feet, and the summit of the pyramid being truncated, made a platform two hundred by four hundred and fifty feet, upon the top of which stood a conical mound ten feet high. Dr. Forster has expressed the probability that upon this platform stood a capacious temple, within whose walls the high priests performed their mysterious rites at stated seasons in the year, as the vast multitude in the plain below gazed in wonder and waited with holy reverence the completion of the religious ceremonial.

The Grave Creek mound, near Wheeling, is nearly one thousand feet in circumference at the base, and seventy feet high.

It was excavated in 1838, and within it were found two sepulchral chambers, containing three skeletons.

The wonderful temple mounds are distinguished from the other classes of mounds by regularity of form, greater size and graded ways leading to the summit. Aroused by religious sentiments and impulses the Mound-Builders no doubt erected these mounds as sites for temples, a striking example of which is seen in the temple mounds at Marietta, Ohio, and there, in answer to the cry of the soul, sought guidance and peace in sacrifice to their spirit guides.

There are mounds of observation placed upon high hills, that signals might be transmitted from one place to another and a watch kept. One of these observation mounds is situated at Miamisburg, Ohio, and commands a view of the valley of the Great Miami.

Symbolical mounds abound chiefly in Ohio and Wisconsin. The mounds represent foxes, lizards, buffalo, bear, raccoon, otter, elk and many other kinds of animals and birds. The most significant of all the symbolical mounds is the great Serpent Mound in Adams County, Ohio, which is seven hundred feet long, five feet high and thirty-six feet wide at the centre ; and the Elephant Mound in Grant County, Wisconsin, which is about one hundred and thirty-five feet long, thirty-six feet wide and five feet high. This mound represents an elephant, or ancient mastodon of the American continent, and the existence of this representation reveals the fact that the Mound-Builders have seen the animal or they could not have made this· mound. From the contents of the mounds ethnologists form their opinions relating to the Mound-Builder as a man. From the existence of pottery, cloth, arrow-heads, hoes, fishing-spears, sinkers for sinking the seines, pipes and many other relics, ethnologists would make the Mound-Builder to be a man of peace, devoted to raising corn and fishing, possessed of artistic ability, as evidenced by the beautiful arrow-heads and the ornamented pottery found. The tiny childrens' stone hatchets and other playthings discovered beside the skeletons, show the affection of the people for their offspring. Moral and religious in their life, as manifested by the representations of their deity, the sun, and the existence of only a single specimen of obscene art in the thousands discovered, they looked for an immortality and a sensual heaven, as shown by the relics in the graves.

When the Mound-Builders were at the height of their power invaders came from the north, as learned from the situation of the mounds, and harassed these people in their fortifications and observation mounds, overthrowing them completely, so that they were compelled to flee to Mexico, where finally they passed away without leaving any record of their fate. The people of the northern mounds in Canada may have followed their brethren, as a remnant of a great nation, or the last of the Mound-Builders may have lingered on, a stranger among the red men, until he perished without a grave. It is a sad and voiceless story these mounds have to tell us, of a people who were dwellers in our land in the days of yore, and we confess that we have been touched with sympathy and our interest has deepened as we have followed the story until the end.

THE NEZ PERCE INDIANS.

The Nez Perce Indians are a tribe belonging to the Sahaptin family, a large and interesting stock. The tribe is sometimes called the Sahaptin, but the Nez Perces are one of the branches of this family. They do not derive their name from the fact that they pierce their noses, but they were so named by some of the early travellers who classed them along with others of the Sahaptin family, who pierce their noses.[*] The early travellers and traders called them Nez Perces, but the Indians called themselves Chopunnish.[†] They are not strictly a Canadian Indian tribe, as they dwelt chiefly in the early years in Idaho, Oregon and Washington Territory, but as they were frequently found upon the boundary, and I have met and often conversed with a small band of these people, who still make their home in the Pincher Creek country in the district of

[*] Fourth Annual Report, "Bureau of Ethnology," page 121.
[†] Washington Irving's "Captain Bonneville," page 54.

Alberta, I thought a short sketch of this interesting tribe might be acceptable to my readers.

It was in the summer of 1880 that I met among the foothills of the Rocky Mountains a Umattilla Indian and some of the Nez Perces, who had crossed the mountains from the Walla Walla country, and were hunting and trading horses. From the year 1843, when we first learn anything about these people, through the official records of the United States Government, and before that period, as shown by the writings of travellers, they roamed throughout Idaho, Washington and Oregon, hunting and fishing. Not until after the outbreak under Chief Joseph did any of them seek a refuge in Canada.

Amongst the numerous tribes of Oregon they were the noblest, richest and most gentle ; a typical race, noted for strength of body and mind, native prowess, heroic virtues and gentle manners. They were a powerful tribe, owning many horses, and esteemed highly as expert horsemen. They were far removed from the common idea held concerning the red men, as they had good minds and thought well on all matters affecting their interests as individuals and as a tribe. Chief Joseph, the leader of the Nez Perces, during their contest with the Government of the United States, has been described as " the ablest, uneducated chief the world ever saw." When these people were removed from their home and sent to another Reservation, as they were being taken down the Missouri river, the people who lived upon the banks of the river and had been accustomed to Indians all their lives, remarked : " What fine-looking men!" " How clean they are !" " How dignified they appear ! "

The homes of these people were similar to that of the other tribes, consisting of lodges, ornamented according to the taste, dignity and valor of the owners. Life in the camp was similar to that of adjacent tribes. Dogs were numerous, and hated the white man ; children roamed abroad at their own sweet will, unencumbered with much clothing, satisfied with nature's provision as to dress, and happy amid all their wild surroundings. Maidens were few, as they were married at an early age, and

passed from childhood into womanhood without the intervening
years which their pale-face sisters enjoy. So soon as a young
or old man desired a wife, and had settled upon the maiden he
delighted in, the parties assembled with their friends, and after
the bridegroom and all the relatives and friends had filled a
large peace pipe, and each had smoked it, the bride was
addressed as to her duties, the nuptial gifts provided by the
bridegroom were delivered to the friends, and the married pair
retired to their lodge. Polygamy prevailed among the people,
but the first wife had the pre-eminence, and exercised her
authority in the lodge, much to the confusion and sometimes to
the injury of the other members of the family.

The Nez Perce chiefs were a notable class of men, well skilled
in all the arts of diplomacy, firm in the exercise of their
authority, and generally just in all their dealings, their loyalty
to their tribe compelling them to seek the interest of their
people in preference to their own personal concerns. If at any
time a stranger of importance was introduced to the chiefs and
leading men of the tribe, the head chief, in introducing the
members of his tribe, would discriminate between them, by forbidding any who came forward to shake hands with the
stranger, simply signifying his disapproval by a motion of the
hand, which was instantly obeyed, without any sign of retalia-
tion.

These were valiant men in times of war, able to cope with the
strongest and most daring of their enemies, yet never resorting
to any foul methods whereby they might take advantage of
them and gain a victory. The usual war customs were followed
by them in the early days, when they united with the Flatheads
and Pend Oreilles against their foes, but after coming in contact with the nobler elements of the civilization of the white
men, they were not slow to perceive their superiority, and consequently adopted them in preference to some of those which
belonged to the tribes. The Nez Perces were the inveterate
enemies of the Blackfeet, and a match for them in fighting
when they were aroused, which was sometimes difficult to do,
as they delighted in peace and not in war, loving to follow some

of the arts of industry, rather than wholly depend upon the precarious livelihood of the chase. On the warpath the aged warrior wore his amulet to protect his body from the bullets of his foes, and so long as he carried this with him he believed that he was invulnerable, and his constant preservation as well as success in war gave force to his belief. If the Nez Perce war party met a band larger than their own, or were decoyed into the region of an opposing tribe, they would sell their lives dearly, rather than retreat. It has been written of the Nez Perces that they form "an honorable exception to the general Indian character—being more noble, industrious, sensible, and better disposed toward the whites, and their improvements in the arts and sciences, and though brave as Cæsar, the whites have nothing to dread at their hands in case of their dealing out to them what they conceive to be right and equitable."

Chief Joseph, whom I have already mentioned as one of the bravest and most skilful in statesmanship amongst all the leaders of the Indian tribes, stood forth unrivalled for his magnanimity, eloquence, military ability and firmness, shown in his famous retreat after the uprising of the nation.[*] When the promises made by the Government commissioners had for several years been broken, the moneys due the Indians not being paid, and efforts made to remove them from their Reservation, he was unable to restrain his people from rising, but heroically he placed himself at the head of his native troops, and conducted a campaign, distinguished for the absence of cruelty and the exhibition of talents worthy of a Roman military leader. When the American troops were aided by their bloodthirsty Bannacks, who were enemies of the Nez Perces, cruel modes of warfare were introduced, the Bannacks scalping their fallen foes, maltreating their captives, and subjecting the Nez Perce women to every indignity. The Nez Perce refused to retaliate. They did not scalp their fallen enemies, and the white women taken captive by them were dismissed unharmed. When they were defeated they made preparations for their famous retreat, covering a

* Helen Hunt Jackson's "Century of Dishonor," pages 103-135.

CHIEF JOSEPH THE NEZ PE

distance of a thousand miles, over rugged defiles and mountainous pathways, pursued by the hostile Bannacks. The military ability of Chief Joseph was displayed in the famous march homeward. Gathering the women and children, the whole members of his tribe, old and young, protected by mounted warriors, he fought his way through the ranks of his enemies, defeating them on several occasions, although he was hard pressed and they were fresh and able to obtain help to intercept him in his march. So successfully was the retreat managed that not until they were within one day's march from home were they overpowered, and then it was through a large force of infantry, cavalry and artillery from Fort Keogh effectually barring their advance. Courageous to the last, they made preparations to withstand the attacks of the American soldiers, determined to secure justice at all hazards, and humane thoughts and feelings prevailed, for they surrendered on terms satisfactory to themselves. The Nez Perces of Chief Joseph's band surrendered to General Mills in 1877, and were removed to Fort Leavenworth, Kansas, to the number of four hundred and thirty-one, where there was great mortality among them. In 1879, they were removed to their Reserve of forty thousand seven hundred and thirty-five acres, adjoining the Poncas, and situated on both sides of Salt Fork of the Arkansas. General Sherman, in his report of the Nez Perce war, said: "Thus has terminated one of the most extraordinary Indian wars of which there is any record. The Indians throughout displayed a courage and skill that elicited universal praise; they abstained from scalping, let captive women go free, did not commit indiscriminate murder of peaceful families, which is usual, and fought with almost scientific skill, using advance and rear guards, skirmish lines and field fortifications."

These people were sympathetic and respectful, their love for their own reaching beyond death, as is shown by their mortuary customs. Many of the Indian tribes are afraid of the spirits of the dead, and resort to different methods of warding off the attacks of their deceased foes. Sometimes they believe that those who were formerly their relatives are now antagonistic to them, which may arise from their belief that they will repay them for any slight done upon earth, and now that they dwell in the spiritual world, they are able to inflict injuries upon them which the living cannot well ward off. As the Nez Perces roamed over the mountains and prairies, they frequently passed the graves of their friends, and always with respect, though sometimes with fear. When they came near to a grave which they had not visited for a long time, the women and children would gather around it and wail bitterly for the dead, and the men, silent and sad, mourning their loss, would stand at a short distance in communion with the loved and lost.

Two years ago, in the Pincher Creek country in Southern Alberta, a Nez Perce Indian was condemned to death for the murder of another member of his tribe, a medicine man. There was some excitement over the occurrence, happening, as it did, not far from a white settlement; yet the native belief seemed to point to the fact that the medicine man had used his power for causing the death of a patient, a relative of the murderer. Amongst the Indian tribes the medicine man is an influential personage, using hypnotic means for destroying his foes, and curing those favorable to him, or who paid him well. The tahmanous of the shaman or medicine man have destroyed many persons who might have lived. Among some of the native tribes of the south, especially the Papagos, the medicine man, failing to cure a leading chief when he has died from any disease, instead of being killed in battle, is taken out before the whole camp and shot. Among the Nez Perce and other tribes of the north, he exercises great power over the people, and it is seldom that anyone becomes courageous enough to retaliate, believing that the shaman is powerful, and will inflict some injury upon them unless they submit to his will.

The Nez Perce women are industrious, neat in their dress, active in their habits, and when pressed in time of war heroic in defence of their husbands, children, or friends. What exciting times the natives have at lacrosse, horse racing, shooting, running on foot, guessing, and throwing the arrow and wheel. The Nez Perces have a game which I have oftentimes seen played among the Blackfeet, although not in the same fashion, which is guessing with a small piece of wood. Instead of a single pair, as amongst the Blackfeet, the Nez Perces arrange themselves in two parties, sitting opposite to each other, and a small piece of wood is passed from hand to hand of the other party, the members of which guess, until when rightly guessed, they become the possessors of the article. While the game is in motion, the parties and those not engaged in the game are betting, and some of these bets are quite large. Meanwhile the contestants sing a weird chant, beating on any article with short sticks which will produce a noise. Singing, beating time, guessing, rolling and swaying the body, in a continual state of excitement, the game proceeds until the one party defeats the other members opposed to them. The onlookers, whites and Indians, become deeply interested in the game, and share in the excitement, watching it eagerly, and animated by the furious motions of the parties in the game.

A singular instance is told of the desire of the Nez Perces for knowledge. They had heard of the superiority of the race of white men, and learning that this arose from the fact, that they had a religion that was better than that of the Indians, they despatched a delegation of two of their chief men, named " Rabbit-Skin-Leggings " and " No-Horns-on-his-Head," to St. Louis to inquire concerning the truth of the report. The object of their journey was made known through Mr. Catlin, the artist, which was " to inquire for the truth of a representation which they said some white men had made among them, that our religion was better than theirs, and that they would all be lost if they did not embrace it."

These men were entertained by the people of St. Louis, some of whom wondered at the intense eagerness of the men, who had made a long journey, to learn something of the Christian's God, and the peculiar religion of the white man. On their journey homeward, one of these men died, but the other lived to tell his friends that the report they had heard was true, and in a short time white men would come to tell them the truths of the wonderful Book, and the story of the blessed Christ.

The story of this delegation, sent by the Nez Perces upon such
a long journey, produced a deep impression upon the minds of
the Indians, and induced the white people to think seriously of
their duty to care for them. Within two years after the visit
of the Nez Perces to St Louis, the American Board and the
Methodist Episcopal Missionary Society sent missionaries to
Oregon to teach the people the truth of the Gospel.

Some years previous to this visit, some of the Hudson's Bay
Company's employees, residing at Fort Walla-Walla, had introduced some of the truths and forms of the Roman Catholic
religion amongst these natives, and the influence of these
things had exerted a decided change amongst some of the bands.
They gave up in a great measure the practice of polygamy, and
sought to live moral lives. The Christian ceremonies had
become Indianized, yet some of the people strove to practice
the precepts they had been taught. Some of the Shoshonees
observed the change which had been affected through following the white man's religion, and they began to imitate the
Nez Perces. They observed Sunday, engaged in devotional
dances and chants, and followed the other ceremonials of the
Nez Perces. This imitation sprang from a desire to gain superiority over their rival tribes, believing that in this form of
religion lay the secret of the white man's power. Some years
ago I met an intelligent Nez Perce chief, named Johnson, and
made inquiries concerning his religious belief, but found that he
still retained his native ideas, and followed not the teachings of
the Christian religion. In their native condition this tribe was
devout, always prefacing their hunts with religious rites and
prayers to the great spirit for safety and success.* Indeed, in
a starving condition they attended to their sacred days and
pious ceremonies before seeking food.

Captain Bonneville, having witnessed their piety on several
occasions, said: "Simply to call these people religious would
convey but a faint idea of the deep hue of piety and devotion

* Rev. S. D. Peet's "The Traditions of Aborigines of North America,"
in the Journal of the Victoria Institute. Vol. XXI., pages 229-247.

which pervades their whole conduct. Their honesty is immaculate, and their purity of purpose and their observance of the rites of their religion are most uniform and remarkable. They are certainly more like a nation of saints than a horde of savages." Their religion was infused with a spirit of fear, and they felt that they were surrounded by evil spirits, who sought to injure them. Their medicine men invoked the aid of their guardian spirits, and they wore on their persons amulets to protect them in time of danger.

The Protestant missionaries who went among them labored hard to teach them the doctrines of the Christian religion, and they were encouraged in their efforts by the change in the lives of the people. A sad fate befel the Rev. Dr. Whitman, who labored with success among this tribe, some of whom were aroused through false reports to rise against the white people, and this faithful missionary was stricken down by a tomahawk, in the hand of an unfriendly Indian, in the year 1849. He had labored in the country along with the Rev. Mr. Spaulding and other missionaries since 1836, and so great was his zeal on behalf of the people and the country that he said, when remonstrated with for the intensity of his labors, "I am ready, not to be bound only, but to die at Jerusalem or in the snows of the Rocky Mountains for the name of the Lord Jesus or my country."

Some years after the missionaries had begun their labors in Oregon, a traveller gave an account of his experience with a Nez Perce guide, named Creekie, which is of interest:

"Creekie was a very kind man. He turned my worn-out animal loose, and loaded my packs on his own; gave me a splendid horse to ride, and intimated, by significant gestures, that we would go a short distance that afternoon. I gave my assent, and we were soon on our way. Having ridden about ten miles we camped for the night. I noticed, during the ride, a degree of forbearance toward each other which I had never before observed in that race. When he halted for the night the two boys were behind. They had been frolicking with their horses, and as the darkness came on lost the trail. It

was a half-hour before they made their appearance, and during
this time the parents manifested the most anxious solicitude
for them. One of them was but three years old, and was
lashed to the horse he rode; the other only seven years of age
—young pilots in the wilderness at night.

"But the elder, true to the sagacity of his race, had taken
his course, and struck the brook on which we were encamped
within three hundred yards of us. The pride of the parents at
this feat, and their ardent attachment to the children, were
perceptible in the pleasure with which they received them at
their evening fire, and heard their relation of their childish
adventures. The weather was so pleasant that no tent was
spread. The willows were bent, and the buffalo robes spread
over them. Underneath were laid other robes, on which my
Indian host seated himself, with his wife and children on one
side and myself on the other. A fire burnt brightly in front.
Water was brought, and the evening ablutions having been
performed, the wife presented a dish of meat to her husband
and one to myself. There was a pause. The woman seated
herself between her children. The Indian then bowed his head
and prayed to God.

"A wandering savage in Oregon calling on Jehovah in the
name of Jesus Christ! After the prayer he gave meat to his
children and passed the dish to his wife. While eating, the
frequent repetition of the words Jehovah and Jesus Christ, in
the most reverential manner, led me to suppose that they were
conversing on religious topics, and thus they passed an hour.
Meanwhile the exceeding weariness of a long day's travel
admonished me to seek rest. I had slumbered I know not how
long, when a strain of music awoke me. The Indian family
was engaged in its evening devotions. They were singing a
hymn in the Nez Perce language. Having finished, they all
knelt and bowed their faces on the buffalo robe, and Creekie
prayed long and fervently. Afterward they sung another
hymn and retired. To hospitality, family affection and devotion, Creekie added honesty and cleanliness to a great degree,
manifesting by these fruits, so contrary to the nature and

habits of his race, the beautiful influence of the work of grace on the heart."

The Nez Perce language belongs to the Sahaptin family, of which there are two principal languages and several dialects. It is throughout an inflected language, the nouns having eight cases, and the verb surpassing in the variety of its forms and the beauty and minuteness of its distinctions the Ayran and Semitic. There are six moods and nine tenses, with many verbal forms, revealing a richness that evinces strong intellectual powers in the members of this tribe.

The following samples, taken from Horatio Hale's "Development of Language," will give the reader a slight idea of the Nez Perce language:

Nominative, Init—house.

Genitive, Ininm—of a house.

Accusative, Inina—house.

First Dative, Initph—to or for a house.

Second Dative, Initpa—in or on a house.

First Ablative, Initki—with a house (instrument).

Second Ablative, Initpkinih—from a house.

Third Ablative, Initain —for the purpose of a house.

The verb is rich in forms, the primary or simple conjugation of the verb " to see " embracing no less than forty-six pages of manuscript, and this does not include the six derived conjugations, each of which possess all the variations of the simple verb.

The following example of the first three tenses of the substantive verb, taken from the same source as those aforementioned, will suffice to show the construction of the language in its simplest forms:

PRESENT TENSE.

Wash, I am.

Awash, thou art.

Hiwash, he, she, or it is.

Washih, we are.

Athwashih, ye are.

Hiushih, they are.

PRESENT PAST TENSE.

Waka, I have just been.

Awaka, thou hast just been.

Hiwaka, he has just been.

Washeka, we have just been.

Athwasheka, ye have just been.

Hiusheka, they have just been.

4

REMOTE PAST TENSE.

Waka, I was.	Washina, we were.
Awaka, thou wast.	Athwashina, ye were.
Hiwaka, he was.	Hiushina, they were.

Far from the madding crowd in the centres of population
dwells the remnant of this powerful tribe, striving upon their
Reservation to adapt themselves to their new circumstances,
forced upon them by the greed of the white man, yet the
native ability displayed in the days of yore abides, and they
evince in their crushed condition habits of industry and a
hopefulness which few of the members of the pale-faced tribes
of men could show under oppression and the removal of incen-
tives to independence and an honorable position in life. The
silver lining to the cloud lies in the changing attitude of the
English-speaking races toward the American Indian race,
brought about through the loving energy of consecrated Christian men and women, striving to educate their fellows toward
a due appreciation of the abilities of these people, a recognition
of the rights of fellowship of the human race, and the obligations of Christian society.*

THE BLACKFOOT INDIANS.

In the ancient and happy days of yore there roamed
over the western plains, from the Red River to the Rocky
Mountains and beyond, numerous tribes of prairie Bedouins, in
quest of food and eager for war. Ojibways, Crees, Blackfeet,
Sioux, Shoshonees, Gros Ventres and other savage peoples
scoured the eastern plains with warlike intent, delighting in
their unhampered liberty, and claiming the boundless prairies
as their rightful possession. Not the least in number and
prowess was the Blackfoot Confederacy, comprising the Blackfeet, Bloods and Piegans. Frequently in these modern days

---

* J. P. Dunn's "The Massacres of the Mountains." Washington Irving's
"Astoria." Horatio Hale's "The Development of Language," pages 25-33.
Dr. W. F. Tolmie and Dr. G. M. Dawson, "Comparative Vocabularies of
the Indian Tribes of British Columbia," pages 12, 124.

have I met the aged Blood Indian warrior, with his hand upon
his mouth, singing his song of sadness; and when suddenly I
have called upon him to explain the cause of his grief, he
has ceased his monotonous plaint and turned to me, saying,
"'Niokskatas!' Where are our noble warriors of former days?
Where are the people that assembled in our camps by thousands? . Where are the buffalo that covered our plains?"
Sorrowfully was I compelled to say, "They are gone!" "See,"
said he, "the fences of the white man stopping our trails. See
the white man's cattle upon the prairies, and the towns everywhere throughont our land. Niokskatas! Our great men are
gone, our people are dying, our lands are no longer ours, and
we, too, shall soon pass away!" Resuming his song he has
continued his journey, a weary and disheartened old man.

The Blackfeet tell us in their traditional lore that they came
in the distant past from the north, from some great lake,
supposed to be Lake Winnipeg. When the Bloods, Piegans
and Blackfeet were all one people, living together, and not
separated into tribes, as at the present time, the South Piegans,
who now dwell south of the international boundary line,
preferred to live close to the mountains, which they called
their home, while the other members of the confederacy dwelt
in the north. Fifty years ago and more the Blackfoot war
parties roamed over Oregon, Idaho and Montana; but within
the past twenty years they have been confined to the southern
portion of the provisional district of Alberta.

The Blackfeet, it is said, lived for a time in that northern
portion of the country where the mud was deep and black, and
their moccasins became darkened with the soil, whence
they received the name of Siksikauo, which, being translated,
means "Blackfoot." Having taken the treaty in 1878 with the
Canadian Government, the people were given a Reservation at
Blackfoot Crossing, about sixty miles east of Calgary, and
another about twelve miles west of Fort Macleod. The Blackfeet, Bloods and Sarcees were to live on the former, and the
Piegans on the latter, but this was finally changed by the
Blackfeet remaining at Blackfoot Crossing. The Sarcees being

ENCAMPMENT OF BLACKFEET INDIANS

STEREO PLATE C.

sent to another location, within ten miles south of Calgary, and the Bloods being given a Reservation about fifteen miles south of Macleod. The population of these tribes is not as great as when first I went among them, the present number being approximately as follows : Blackfeet, one thousand five hundred ; Piegans, nine hundred ; Bloods, two thousand.

In the good old buffalo days, when the herds of buffaloes were numerous, these wild cattle of the plains roaming the country in tens of thousands, there were many old timers—trappers and traders—who lived a free and easy life, retailing whiskey, trinkets and general articles, and receiving the hides of buffaloes and other animals in trade.

Trading forts, with suggestive names, sprang up in various parts of Alberta, some of which are still in existence. The memories of days spent at Whoop-Up, Slide-Out, Stand-Off, and the Robbers' Roost still linger with me, and loath would I be to have them obliterated, though rough oftentimes were the experiences of those days; but they cannot be lived over again; and the tales which still hang around these old forts will, in a few years, have passed into oblivion. The old buffalo trails and wallows are being filled up through the action of the wind and rain driving the sand into them, and the bones of the bison, which lay scattered over the prairies for hundreds of miles, have nearly all disappeared. Here and there along the Old Man's River and the other places in Alberta and Assiniboia may be seen layers of buffalo bones, marking the spot where the Indians drove the herds over the precipices, and they perished in thousands.

Sitting in the lodges, I have listened with intense interest to the traditions of the Blackfeet, so full of beauty and morality, evincing native culture and a religious spirit. The aged men of the camps tell us of the time when there was nothing but water, and the Old Man was sitting upon a log, with four animals. Pondering over his situation, he thought that there must be something under the water, and, anxious to learn what might be there, he sent the animals down after each other, till the last to descend was the musk-rat, and he alone returned to tell the story of his explorations, bearing in his mouth some mud, which the Old Man took, and rolling it in the palm of his hand, it grew rapidly and fell into the water. Soon it assumed such dimensions that he stepped upon it, and placing there a wolf, this animal ran swiftly over the plastic matter, and wherever he stepped an indentation was made, which became a valley, and where he placed not his foot the plains and mountains appeared. The water rushed into some of the indentations, and these became lakes.

The Old Man made some women, but the first specimens of his handicraft were not satisfactory, as the mouths of the women were opened vertically, so he closed them up again and cut them anew, leaving them as they now appear. He made some men, and took them upon an excursion armed with bows and arrows. Seeing some animals upon the prairie, he told the men to shoot them, but they were afraid, whereupon he took a bow and arrow from one of the men, and, pointing it at one of the animals, sent the arrow, swiftly and surely, killing it. " There," said he, " these are buffaloes! and that is food for you." Upon another excursion they saw some other strange-looking animals, dissimilar to anything they had ever seen before, and he called to the men to go out and capture one each, but they were afraid. He went out alone and caught one of the animals, and, giving one to a man, said, " These are women, and these are to be wives for you!" So they went out, and each procured a wife by catching one.

This Old Man is not the Great Spirit, but a secondary creator, and appears in their legends as a good and bad being, sometimes as a benefactor, and again as a person full of deceit and various kinds of tricks. In the legend of the Two Brothers there is an old man with his wife and daughter and his son-in-law. This son-in-law is a lazy fellow, and treats the old man harshly. One day the daughter was cooking some meat, and some blood fell upon the floor. Picking up the clotted blood, she put it in the pot, and in a few minutes she heard a hissing sound issuing from the vessel, and, looking in, beheld a boy, begotten from the blood clot. Rapidly he grew, and he sprang from the pot a young man. The blood-clot boy was named Kutoyis, meaning "sweet grass." He was a good lad and kind to his parents, in striking contrast to his bad brother-in-law. As Kutoyis was passing his father's lodge one day he heard him wailing bitterly, and, inquiring the cause, was informed that whenever he filled his lodge with buffalo meat, wood and water the bad brother came in and took it all away, and whenever the old man complained he was beaten. Kutoyis comforted his aged parent and then departed. He returned in a short time laden with buffalo meat, which he placed in the lodge, then filled it with an abundance of wood and water. He instructed the old man, that when the bad brother came to take it away he was to point his drawn arrow at him, and threaten to kill him, and that he would be near to protect him. Not long afterward the bad brother came to seek for food, and the father did as he was told, which made the bad brother so angry that he hastened to his lodge to get his bow and arrows. He returned full-armed to take the food, and as the old man was defending himself, Kutoyis sprang from behind the lodge and engaged in the contest. In the fight he slew the bad brother, and ever afterward the father lived in peace, having abundance of food and comfort.*

Legends similar to this one appear among many Indian tribes, and the explanation given by some ethnologists is to the effect that it is a sun myth, the bad brother representing the night, darkness and storm; and the good brother representing day, light and tranquility. Darkness and storm being evil unto man, making him sad, destroying his crops, and depriving him of food; the sun, light and peace, begetting good crops and abundance of food, giving comfort and joy to man. When the sun arises there is a contention between it and the darkness, which ends in the destruction of the night and victory of the light, and with the victory comes peace and prosperity. Many beautiful legends are to be found among the Blackfeet, showing strength of intellect and imagination.

---

*Maclean's "Blackfoot Mythology," in "American Journal of Folk-Lore."

Let us enter one of the lodges in the camp, and see the people at home. The lodge itself is made of the skin of the buffalo—now unfortunately of duck or cotton—the buffalo hides being no longer obtainable. The lodge is circular, held in place by ten or twelve poles fastened at the top and spread out at the bottom, the lodge covering being also staked to the ground. In the centre of the lodge is the fire, kept from spreading by means of a circular row of stones, over which is placed a wooden tripod, tied with raw hide, from which hangs a pot or some meat. Around the lodge are placed the beds, upon which they sleep at night and serve as couches to sit upon during the day. Each has his own bed, the chief, or head of the family, occupying the place of honor, the place opposite the entrance. Around the lodge are hung guns, bags, and various articles; and behind the beds, all of which are on the ground, are bags made of skins of animals, containing berries; in fact, all that is necessary for the maintenance of the family. Visiting a lodge one day, I saw the father and one of the wives with a gruesome countenance, and upon inquiring the cause, was shown twin children in their beautiful moss bags. Twins are believed to be an omen of evil, hence the sad countenances of my friends.

When a child is born some nice, soft moss is procured, and the babe is rolled up in it, some linen or piece of blanket wrapped around, and then the moss bag, ornamented with dyed porcupine quills, various colored beads, or designs made with silk thread is brought, the little one snugly wrapped within, and laced up from bottom to top, the whole reaching to the chin. Having a loop at the bag, when the mother attends church she can hang the baby on a nail upon the wall, and when upon horseback, hang the bag with its precious contents upon the horn of the saddle. The child receives its name from the first object the mother sees after the child is born, or from something peculiar in nature, or physical characteristic of the babe.

Several times during the history of a single individual is the name changed, and in order to learn the name of anyone, a

second party must be asked. This arises from shame or
modesty. When a man or woman performs a noble deed, the
people give a new name agreeable to the action, as Heavy Gun,
symbolizing valour; Three Medicines, signifying spiritual power
or intellectual ability; and should the name describe some
physical defect, article of dress worn, or mean action performed,
the person will not proclaim his virtue, deceit, or defect by
pronouncing his name. Many of the names are compounded of
two words, as White-Calf, Black-Horse, Calf-Shirt, Red-Crow,
Medicine-Calf, North-Axe and Crow-Foot. Female names are
suggestive of sympathy, purity, and loveliness. Women
receive such names as Little Rabbit Woman, The Morning Star,
and White Antelope; the last name showing the Indian's idea
of the character of the woman, white, signifying purity, and
antelope, the tenderness of the woman's nature. An easy,
happy life is that of the red men in their camp. They eat,
drink, sleep, and amuse themselves as they feel inclined, no
settled hours of the day being set apart for this purpose.

Let us follow the young and middle-aged men at one of their
games, that of the wheel and arrows. A board, eight or ten
inches in width, is placed on its edge upon the ground, held
in place by small stakes driven into the ground; and another, in
the same fashion, about twelve feet distant. The contestants
play in pairs. Each holds in his right hand an arrow, and one
of them a small wheel, having fastened to it a bead, or special
mark placed upon it. Standing at one end and inside the
board, they run together toward the other board, the contestant
having the wheel rolls it on the ground, throwing it with such
force that it strikes the board. As the two men run they
throw their arrows against the board, and as near to the wheel
as they can. When the wheel falls, they measure the distance
between the point of the arrows and the bead or special mark
on the wheel, and the arrow which lies nearest to this point has
won the throw. They continue this running and throwing
until the one who has reached the number agreed upon as the
end of the game has won. The number of the points made by
the contestants are kept by means of small sticks held in the

hands. Several pairs of contestants sometimes play after each
other, and for days they will continue the game, surrounded
by a large number of men, old and young, who are eagerly
betting upon the result.

Tea dances are oftentimes kept up for days, the nights also
being filled with the shouts and singing of the people. The tea
is brought in pails, pots and vessels of every kind, and is passed
around, each of the guests or participants dipping a cup into
the larger vessel and drinking the tea. No food of any kind is
eaten, the tea has no sugar, and very soon tea and the pipe
passing freely around produce a state of semi-intoxication.
The whole party sings lustily, stories of the happy days of old
are told, the aged warrior recites his deeds of bravery, and
hour after hour they sing and talk, drink and smoke, until the
tea and tobacco have disappeared, and then they return to their
lodges. Sometimes the boys and young men of the camp form
themselves into a group, and play a game of guessing. Two or
more persons are opposed, each to each, or one side against the
other. A small article is selected, and one of them passing it
from one hand to the other, holds out both hands for his
opponent to guess the hand containing the article, which he
tries to do by placing in the closed hand, which he supposes is
the right one, a small piece of wood. If he has guessed rightly,
it becomes his turn to use the article to be sought. The small
sticks are kept as a record of the game, until one of the contestants has won them all from his opponent. During the
whole time of playing, the one who holds the thing to be
guessed sways his body, singing and praying for success.

The men are of medium height, well formed, but unaccus-
tomed to labor, and spending a great portion of their time on
horseback, their arms and legs are not well developed. They
have pleasing countenances, and the shape of the head shows
intellectual power. In the old days they dressed chiefly in deer
skin, or garments made of the skins of the buffalo and moose,
many of them wearing a buffalo robe as an outside covering.
With the advent of the traders, and the departure of the
buffalo, they were compelled to resort to the blanket, of which

they made leggings, with the ever present breech-cloth, a shirt of short dimensions of cotton, moccasins, and a blanket worn over the under-garments. A pair of tweezers fastened around the neck was used for pulling out the hair from the face and other parts of the body. A looking-glass for toilet purposes and signalling, and sometimes a small bag, containing an amulet, were also hung around the neck. Around the waist was fastened a belt filled with cartridges and a large knife. From two to five rings, with long appendages, hung from each ear, rings were upon each finger, except the thumb, and ornaments of various kinds were placed in the hair. The young men have beautiful hair, long and black, and of this they are very proud, sometimes spending more than an hour in arranging it. The hair of the men is more beautiful and longer than that of the women, and so vain are they of this adornment that they have oftentimes come to the mission-house requesting permission to measure the length of the hair of the lady of the mission-house, and after expressing their wonder, have eagerly · inquired the secret of the long hair worn by the white women. I have sometimes shown them the ends of their hair split, and told them to cut the ends, and with delighted hearts they have returned to their lodges to try the new plan of making the hair grow. Sometimes a head-dress was worn. The face was painted, especially in winter and in times of war, as a protection, the Indians told me, against frost bites. The people are inveterate gamblers, playing cards night and day, racing horses, and amusing themselves at various other games. They are fair riders, able to ride long distances, yet not to be compared with the cowboys as experts at horsemanship. One of their methods of breaking-in young horses is to lead the animal to a muddy spot in the river bottom, and when the horse sinks deep in the mire to mount him, or to lead him into the river and ride him when the water reaches the belly. Some of the more adventurous spirits boldly mount the animal on the prairie, while a companion leads him by a rope, thus preventing him, when the rider is thrown, from running away.

The three tribes have each a head chief; numerous bands,

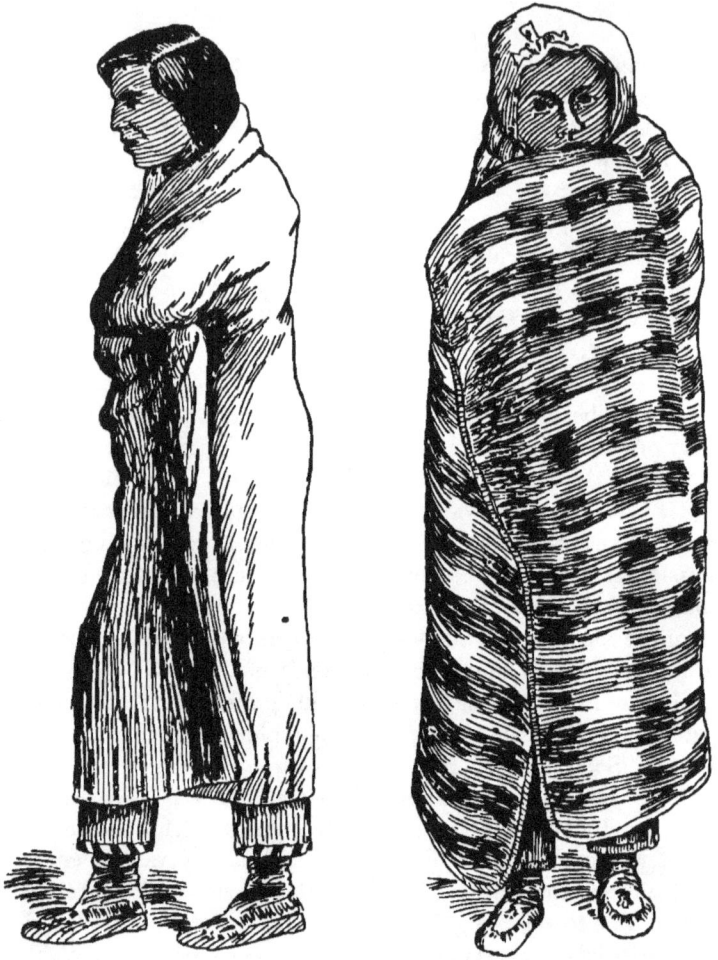

BLACKFEET INDIANS

presided over by a chief to each band, who are called in the
white man's phraseology, minor chiefs. There is a peace chief
over the whole tribe, who acts as civil officer, and a war chief,
who has command in times of war. The bands are known by
distinct native appellations, as the Tall Men, Camping in a
Bunch, Fish Eaters and similar names. The white people are
accustomed to call the bands after the name of the chief, as
Red Crow's band, but the Indians never use this method among
themselves. They have an unwritten code of laws for the
government of the people, in peace and war, regulating crime,
marriage, and applicable to social and domestic life. Secret
societies are also in existence for the training of the people.
They have also native police, called Black Soldiers, who look
after those who offend against the laws of the tribe. When
the camp is being formed each chief selects his own position,
the place of honor being given to the head-chief, and the band
collects around the lodge of the minor chief.

Calendars are kept by notching sticks, and the months have
names, as the Moon when the Geese Come, the Moon when the
Geese Go Away, and the Moon of the Big Snow. When any
important gathering is to be held, as in the event of some
notable stranger having come to the camp, the election of a
chief, or the discussion of some question affecting the interests
of the tribe, camp criers, who are generally aged men, go around
the camp calling aloud for the male members of the tribe to
assemble, and mentioning, at the same time, the object of the
meeting. Always when holding service in the camps, the
owner of the lodge where the service was held, or some one
designated by him, stood outside the lodge and called aloud,
"Niokskatos has come. It is time for prayer. Men, women
and children come!"

Some of the chiefs are noted for their native ability as
orators. Their style of language is impressive, free from any
superfluities of style, their illustrations being drawn from
nature, and the phraseology lofty and pure. The common
language of the camp in the style of the able speaker is rejected,
and it almost seems to those conversant with the language, as

if he were speaking in another tongue, the words being far removed from the common language used in ordinary conversation.

The Blackfeet have ever delighted in war, and especially in that stage of their progress, when, through the advent of the traders, they were among the first of the tribes to receive firearms, for through this agency they were enabled to gain an easy victory over their foes, and to drive the Gros Ventres, Crow Indians and Shoshonees from the plains of Southern Alberta. When one of the Blackfeet slew one of his enemies, he sprang from his horse, and drawing his knife, grasped the scalp-lock, cut a piece of the flesh, from two to three inches in diameter, and then with a sudden wrench tore it from the head. He hung the scalp-lock to his belt and then hastened on his journey to show to his enemies his success in war.

The custom of scalping the foe arose, not from any desire to inflict cruelty, but as an evidence of prowess. It is still customary at the sun dance for the warriors to narrate their exploits, and to give representations of the battles in which they were engaged. When the warriors returned from the warpath and narrated their successes, the people would not believe the man who told of his successes unless he was able to give evidence of his valor. He might say that he had killed two or three of the enemy, but where was the evidence. He could not carry the bodies of the slain with him, nor even their heads, so he brought the scalp, which was easily carried, and strong evidence that he had been victorious. A scalp dance was held upon the return of a successful war party. After the dance was over the successful warriors hung up the scalp-locks upon the outside of their lodges, and as the people passed by they would look at the picture writing on the lodge and the scalp-locks, and say to each other: " He is a brave man. He is a great warrior. See how many enemies he has slain ! When some of the Blackfeet were killed in battle or clandestinely, there was great mourning and determination to revenge. This arose, not from anger only, but they believed that the soul of the departed could find no rest, but roamed throughout the regions of the dead unsatisfied until an equal number of the enemy were slain.

Their doctrine was a "scalp for a scalp." Hence arose the danger to the white people in the early days, for if an Indian was killed by a white man, the first white man found would, in all likelihood, be killed. Sometimes through negotiations, instead of scalps being . taken, compensation was made. Early one morning I was waiting for one of my friends, a Piegan Indian, to accompany me from Macleod to the Blood Reserve, when, as I was tying my horse outside the house, I heard the sound of a revolver, and the door opened, some women rushed out screaming, one of whom carried a child. My friend had been placing his revolver in his belt, and was in the act of examining it, when it went off, the ball lodging in the head of the child in its mother's arms. The man was imprisoned, an investigation held, and the matter settled, by giving to the bereaved parents two or three horses. Compensation is thus made between friends when death arises through an accident, and sometimes between enemies, when a third party steps in and makes the necessary negotiations.

Before a war party went on the warpath a feast was held, sacrifices made of a religious character, and prayers and vows that success might be given to the expedition. The members of the party painted their bodies in the most hideous fashion, and with a great deal of bravado started out. Except in times of danger, or when expecting opposition from their friends, they left the camp secretly. They travelled by day when in their own territory, but when they reached the enemies country they travelled by night. At the time for attacking the foe they threw off their outer garments, and appeared with nothing on their persons but a cloth around the loins and a belt filled with cartridges. Some of the warriors wore the war cap as a protection against the bullets of their foes. When a single Indian saw one of his foes approaching, and was desirous of being friendly, he took care that his gun was in readiness, and keeping his eye on the foe, filled his pipe with tobacco and kinnikinick, and after lighting it held out the long stem that the other might take a smoke. If the strange Indian smoked the pipe they became friends, the pipe being the bond of union. In the

same manner, in times of peace or danger, runners were sent to
the tribes with messages, always bearing the tobacco, which,
being accepted, was an evidence of agreement in the question
under consideration.

Some of the Indians make beautiful stone pipes, with various
designs, having nothing but a knife, an old file and an iron rod.
The aged warriors still meet in the lodges and tell with glowing
eloquence of the days of war, when they won their battles and
hunted the buffalo, and the young men often long for the days
when they, too, might be able to boast of their powers, and
listen with delight to the applause of the people. These days
have gone, and the youth must remain contented to gain honor
as farmers or mechanics.

The women of the camp are below the average height, short
and stout. In youth they are generally good-looking, some of
them having pretty countenances and small hands and feet.
Their dress consists of a loose garment, reaching from the neck
to the feet, with wide flowing sleeves and a very wide belt
around the waist, ornamented with beads, porcupine quills, or
tacks with brass heads. Fastened to the belt is a knife, a
knife sharpener, and a small bag containing a bodkin, needle
and other useful articles. Short leggings, ornamented, reach
from the knee to the moccasins ; the amulet around the neck,
rings on every finger, except the thumb, a profusion of brass
bracelets, and earrings complete the dress. An outer garment
is worn, usually a blanket. Girls are married at eleven and
twelve years.

Polygamy exists among the people, arising no doubt in the
first instance from the fact that the Blackfeet did not inter-
marry with the tribes outside their confederacy, except when,
in times of war, they made captives the women of their
enemies. The men were killed in battle with their enemies,
and thus a larger number of females were found in the camps
than males. I have never seen an old maid in the camps, and
only once have I seen a bachelor, and he was a dwarf. An old
Piegan Indian called upon me one day, and I asked him the
number of his wives. " Eight," said he. " How many children
have you ?" Without a smile he said, " Forty-three!"

Anxious to learn all I could about the marriage customs of the people, I asked one of my friends, " How many wives have you ? " " Three," said he. " How did you get them ? " " Well, I paid for the first one, a horse ; she was not very good-looking, so I got her for one horse ! The second one was good-looking and a good cook, so I paid two horses for her. The third was a beauty. She was a good cook, and she had a fine disposition ; I gave three horses and a gun and a saddle for her. She was a beauty ! " After narrating this, in a business-like fashion, he turned to me, as his male companions sat by his side, and said, " Apawakas. How many horses did you pay for her ? " Apawakas is the Indian name of my wife, and means " White Antelope." I was rather taken back to have the tables turned upon me so quickly, but determined to make the best of the situation, so proceeded to tell the Indians the white man's method of courtship, then the ceremony, when the minister joins the hands of the engaged and prays to the Great Spirit.

Afterward the explanation was given of setting up house-keeping, the mother-in-law providing pillows, blankets, and many of the necessary things for the home. When this point was reached the red men could not retain their laughter any longer, and they shook with laughing at the strange customs of the white men. After they were able to control themselves one of them said, " They paid you for taking her ! " The Indian buys his wife, but the white man gets his wife for nothing, and is paid for taking her off the mother-in-law's hands. This appeared all the more significant to the Indians, as they do not speak to the father-in-law, and seldom to the mother-in-law. Pointing to the children in the home, my friend said, " If you and your wife were to die, what would become of the children ? " I explained to him the process of making a will, stating that the executors would use my property for clothing, educating and providing for the children, and that the money obtained from the sale of the property would pay all expenses.

" The white people are savages ! " said he. " When any
5

people die in our camps and leave little children, we take
them into our lodges. The best piece of buffalo meat we give
unto them. We clothe and train them. They belong to all
the people, and we all care for them. They are bone of our
bone, and flesh of our flesh. They have no father or mother,
so we are all fathers and mothers unto them. The white
people are savages. They do not love their children. The
people have to be paid for loving orphan children."

The Blackfeet have a beautiful and expressive language of
signs, by means of which they can carry on communication with
other tribes who know not their language, and also converse
with the dumb, or at times when they do not wish to be
heard. The picture writing on the lodges expresses the life of
the owner of the lodge, detailing the greatest of his exploits,
and a brief history of his life. The spoken language has been
reduced to writing, and though I desire greatly to give some
specimens of the beauty of the grammatical forms, lack of
space forbids me. I must also pass by many of the interesting
details connected with the initiation of the medicine men, and
stories relating to their hypnotic feats, methods of practice,
sweat baths and charms, reserving a fuller account of these
interesting matters till a later time.

One of the Blood Indian chiefs went on a visit to Eastern
Ontario, and upon his return the people were anxious to learn
what he had seen in the land of the white man. Camp criers
called the people to one of the lodges, when the traveller gave
an account of his visit. He said:

"That is a wonderful country. I went to the towns of the
white men and saw the houses made of stone. The white men
live upon each other's heads, for there is not room for them to
make stone lodges for every man. One of the white chiefs
gave me a paper, and when I was hungry I showed my paper
at the white man's trading-post, and they gave me all I wanted
to eat for nothing. Whenever I wished to go anywhere I
showed a man my paper, and he took me in his waggon for
nothing. I went into a trading-post, and then got into a small
house, which went up and up, when it stopped, and I got out.

I saw so many fine things after I got out! I then went into another little house, and it went down and down. Ugh! I thought I was going down to the place where the white men say there is a great big fire, but it stopped, and then I got out. I went into a house which sat on wheels, and it ran away. Some birds came along and tried to run a race with it, but it beat the birds. There are as many white people down there as there are blades of grass upon the prairie!"

"Stop!" said one of the chiefs. "There have been some white medicine men down there, and they have been beating upon their medicine drums. They have made strong medicine and blinded your eyes, that you could not see. We do not believe you."

They believed him not, and not until others had gone east and corroborated the testimony of this man, did they believe that such things were in existence.

In the crotches of trees, or raised platforms, and in lodges were the dead buried. Articles of clothing, gun, food, tobacco and the relics of the deceased were buried with him, and no one was brave enough to desecrate the graves, as they were afraid of the spirits of the dead. Late one afternoon, as I was pursuing my way through the outskirts of the camp, I heard a low sad wail, and on looking up, saw a poor woman meanly clad, the beautiful garments of yesterday having been taken from her. Her legs from the knee to the feet had been gashed with a knife and the blood was clotted upon them. Her hair had been cut off, and one of the fingers on the left hand had been severed at the first joint. A piece of wood lay in the palm of the injured hand, the clotted blood was mingled with ashes, which had been sprinkled over it. I spoke to her and she pointed to a tree, where within the branches lay a little bundle, the darling of her bosom, recently dead. She turned from me and sang her coronach, mentioning the name of her babe and calling upon it to come back to her. Deeply and tender these Indian mothers love their children, and no suffering is too great for them to bear on their behalf.

The Blackfeet are sun worshippers. They worship Omuqkatos, the Great Sun. The strangely contorted trees, peculiar stones upon the prairie, and irregular formations of land are the stopping places of the gods. When anyone is sick a part of the garments of the sick person is placed upon the top of the lodge, that being shaken by the wind the prairie spirits may be induced to stop upon their journey, and the medicine man earnestly performs his incantations and giving of medicines, assisted by the friends of the sick person, and the gods, listening to the prayers, will aid in the overthrow of the evil genius which dwells in the body. During a severe time of sickness in one of the camps, as I sat beside the medicine man in one of the lodges, a large number of children were brought in, and the medicine man, taking the dress from the top of the lodge, rubbed the children's persons with it, as a protection against the attack of the disease. When anyone dies, he is said to have gone to the Sand Hills.

The people are afraid of the spirits of the dead, and at once . they remove the lodge, and sometimes even tear down the house, lest the spirit of the deceased return and inflict injury upon the living. They believe that the spirits of the dead hold communion with each other, and require food and clothing like the living, only as they, are spiritual, they need the spiritual part, and not the material, for their sustenance. Hence the living do not see the goods disappear, as the dead extract the spiritual part of the material things. They are thus believers in animism. Sacrifices are made to the sun; prayers for pardon, and before engaging in a special religious ceremony, the person enters a sweat lodge and takes a sweat bath, believing that he can drive out the impurity from his system by profuse perspiration. He who would be holy must have a clean body and soul, and this can be secured by rejecting evil thoughts and deeds and cleansing his body.

Farm instructors and agents have been sent by the Government to teach the Blackfeet agriculture. Schools are established, where the children are taught. A Boys' Home and an hospital have been erected on the Blood Reserve, and an Industrial Home at High river. Missionaries are working

hard for the welfare of the people on all the Reserves, and
in the coming years there is hope for the uplifting of the
people. A new era has dawned, the old-time life is fast passing
away, and we may look for the advancement through the
energetic workers who are striving to lead the people toward
a nobler life.

THE CREE INDIANS.*

The Cree Indians form one of the largest tribes of the
Algonquin nation in the Dominion, extending over the greatest
extent of territory, and including several distinct branches,
speaking different dialects of the same language.   Joseph
Howse, the eminent Indian scholar, spent twenty years among
them, and early in the present century said that they were
"dispersed over a vast extent of country, from Pennsylvania
south, to Churchill River in Hudson's Bay north, or twenty
degrees of latitude; from Labrador and the Atlantic east, to
the Mississippi west, from Hudson's Bay east to the Rocky
Mountains west—that is, in its greatest width (fifty-five to
one hundred and fifteen degrees), sixty degrees of longitude."
At the present time they are to be found in the North-West
Territory, Keewatin, and Athabasca.   In the early history of
the country they were designated by various names, including
Kristineaux or Kristnaux, Knistinaux or Knistineaux, Chris-
tineaux, Klistinos or Klistineaux, Killistine, and Crees.   The
name by which these people are known among themselves is
Nehiyowuk, meaning "Exact People."   They are divided into
three branches, distinguished more by the locality where they
reside than by the dialectical differences of their language,
although there is a slight difference in their speech.   These
branches are named Plain Crees, who reside chiefly on the
prairies of Alberta and Assiniboia; Wood Crees, inhabiting

---

* Tucker's "Rainbow in the North."   Robinson's "Great Fur Land."
Maclean's "Indians of Canada." Ballantyne's "Hudson's Bay." Ryer-
son's "Hudson's Bay." Semmen's "Mission Work in the North-West."
Tuttle's "Our North Land." Southesk's "Saskatchewan and the Rocky
Mountains." Butler's "Great Lone Land."

Northern Alberta and Athabasca; and the Swampy Crees of Keewatin. There is no definite line of territory for these branches, as they encroach upon the domain of each other, but this division is in the main correct. The Crees of the Saskatchewan district were divided by several writers fifty years ago into Strongwood and Plain Crees, which numbered from three thousand five hundred to four thousand. Rowand, Shaw, Simpson and Lefroy differ in their computation, but place the population in this district at these numbers—Lefroy gives the following estimate in 1852 of the Cree Confederacy:

Plain Crees, about three thousand; Wood Crees, in the country east of the Great Plains and south of the Churchill River, including a few who traded at Fort Chippewayan, Isle a la Crosse, and Lesser Slave Lake, about five thousand; Cumberland House, three hundred; the Pas or Basqua, one hundred and fifty; Norway House, three hundred; Oxford House, one hundred; York Factory, two hundred; Beren's River, one hundred; Red River Dependencies, two thousand; Albany River, Martin Falls, five hundred; Moose Factory and outposts, five hundred; Lake Tamiscaming, two hundred—making a total of over twelve thousand souls. This estimate appears to be large, still it has been generally believed that the Cree Confederacy comprised the greatest number of any of the tribes in the Dominion during the present century. Even this estimate seems small compared with the Iroquois in the early days of the French regime. At the present time the Cree Indians, who have entered into treaty with the Government, number over ten thousand souls.

The nomadic Cree has always been found at certain times of the year a regular visitor to the posts of the Hudson's Bay Company, and no history of the country can be written without frequent reference to these people. They were employed as hunters, boatmen, and guides. Securing an advance of provisions in the beginning of the hunting season, they started off in search of furs, remaining absent for several weeks, returning, if successful, with sufficient to maintain the family for a considerable period. Some of the bands of Wood and

Swampy Crees support themselves by fishing in the lakes and rivers, thus presenting a striking contrast to the Plain Indians, who seldom eat fish.

The male members of the tribe are of medium stature, well-formed and of pleasing countenance. In the early years of the present century they were fond of tattooing their bodies, especially their arms. The Cree women, whom I have met in the camp of the Blackfeet, and in my travels throughout Alberta and Assiniboia, had three tattoo-marks on the chin, one from each corner of the mouth, and one in the middle of the chin, consisting of lines made perpendicularly, and of a blue color.

Many interesting legends and traditions are told by the Indians, one of which I will now relate: Henry B. Steinhauer, an aged missionary, related the following legend to Dr. Sutherland as they sailed down the Saskatchewan. It is the legend of Wisukatcak, who is regarded as a supernatural being, resembling the Old Man of the Blackfeet. "Of his origin little is known, but he had a father, and a mother and one brother. In this family, as in others, there were occasional disturbances, and in one of these the old man killed his wife, and cut off her head! He then told Wisukatcak to take his little brother, and run away. He also gave him a flint, a fire steel and an awl, and said: 'If your mother's head goes after you throw first the flint, then the fire steel, and then the awl behind you, and repeat the words I tell you!' So he told him the words, and Wisukatcak took his little brother, the flint, the fire steel and the awl and went away; and sure enough, the mother's head went rolling after them, calling for her children. So Wisukatcak threw the flint behind him and cried:

"'Let a great wall of rock rise up all across the earth!'

"No sooner said than done. A great wall of rock did rise up and that is why the Rocky Mountains stretch along the continent to this day.

"When the Head came to the wall of rock it could not get over it at first; but by perseverance at last succeeded, and went rolling on as before. Then Wisukatcak threw the fire steel behind him and cried:

" 'Let a great fire rise up and stretch across the earth!' So a great fire rose up, the remains of which can be seen in the extensive volcanoes of the Sierra and Rocky Mountains. When the Head came to the fire it stopped; but after a time got through, singed and roasted, and went rolling on again, calling for her children. Then Wisukatcak threw the awl behind him and cried: 'Let a great hedge of thorns spring up, and reach across the earth!' At once the thorns sprang up, forming a seemingly impassable wall, parts of which may yet be seen in the hedges of giant cactus plants in the South. But in some way the head managed to get through, and went rolling on, calling for her children. After a time Wisukatcak and his brother came to a large river, and seeing a pelican swimming about, he said: 'Grandfather, take us across to the other side, for our mother is coming after us and will kill us.'

" So the pelican took them on his back and carried them safely to the other side.

" After a time the Head came to the river, and seeing the pelican, said: 'I am going after my children. Take me to the other side and I will marry you.'

" But the pelican did not seem to be very anxious for this, and went to work very slowly. The Head tried to hurry him up, but he said: 'You must sit still, my neck is very sore.'

" Near the middle of the river were some boulders rising above the water, and the pelican, suddenly throwing his burden upon one of these, broke the Head all to pieces, and the brains may be seen to this day floating on the river in flood time in large masses of foam. So this was the end of Wisukatcak's mother.

" Wisukatcak and his brother journeyed on till they came to a beautiful lake with a sandy beach, where they remained; and Wisukatcak did all he could to amuse his brother. Among other things he made him a ball. One day, when playing with it, the ball fell into a canoe which they had not noticed before, in which sat an old man, whose name was Wamishus. Wisukatcak called to him and said:

" 'Throw back my brother's ball. He wants to play with it.'

" But Wamishus said: 'Come into the canoe and get it yourself.'

"But Wisukatcak did not like to go. Then the old man said : ' Let your brother come and get it.'

"But the brother would not go; so Wisukatcak concluded to go himself. Then Wamishus put his paddle from the canoe to the shore and said :

"' Step on that, and you can get into the canoe.'

"Wisukatcak did so, and when he was nearly over, the old man suddenly tipped up the paddle and threw Wisukatcak into the canoe, and with a single stroke sent the canoe out into the lake. Wisukatcak's brother saw them go, and cried:

"' Brother ! brother ! come back, or I'll be changed into a wolf ! I'll be changed into a wolf ! O-o-ow-w-w !'

"And he sent forth a prolonged howl, as though he were a wolf already. But Wisukatcak could not come back. He remained away for a long time, and then came back, but no one knows when or how. When he landed he began to seek for his brother, but could find only a wolf's track on the shore. Soon he heard a wolf howl, and meeting him soon after, recognized the wolf as his brother, and thenceforth they became companions. Some time after they went to another lake, and here Wisukatcak made bows and arrows for his brother to amuse himself with, and he said to him :

"' Don't shoot your arrows into the water, or if you do, don't go after them, lest some great evil befall you.'

"But little wolves, like little boys, are sometimes very self-willed ; so, in spite of the warning, Wisukatcak's brother one day shot an arrow into the water and went after it; when he was seized and killed by one of the lions who live in the water, and his skin made into a covering for a tent door !

"Then Wisukatcak went all about the lake seeking for his brother. Seeing a Kingfisher gazing intently into the water, he said : ' What are you looking at ?'

"And the Kingfisher replied, ' I am looking at the little lions playing with the skin of Wisukatcak's brother.'

"' Do they ever go ashore ?' asked Wisukatcak.

"' Yes,' said the Kingfisher, ' they go ashore on very warm days to sun themselves on the beach.'

"Then Wisukatcak said, ' If you will tell me where they go ashore, I will paint you, and make you a very handsome bird.'

" So the Kingfisher showed him the place, and Wisukatcak painted him as he had promised, and made him a very handsome bird, putting a collar of white wampum about his neck, and a tuft of beautiful feathers on the top of his head. Then Wisukatcak took his bow and arrows and went to the place where the lions came on shore. Here he changed himself into a stump and waited. One hot day many of the lions came ashore, and seeing the stump, one of them said:

" ' Why should a stump be here where none was before ?' And another said, ' Let us go and pull it down.'

" ' So they went and began to scratch and pull at poor Wisukatcak till they had like to have torn him in pieces. But they could not pull him over. At last they got tired, and went and lay down to sleep. When Wisukatcak saw they were asleep he took his bow, and aiming at the king lion sent an arrow deep into his side, at which the lion roared, and they all hurried back into the water, while Wisukatcak went to his lodge. The next day he went back to the shore, and as he was going he met a toad, who appeared like an old woman. She was shaking a rattle and singing, ' I am the rattling quill.'

" ' Granny," said Wisukatcak, ' where are you going ? '

" ' Oh,' said she, ' I am going to conjure the king of lions, who was wounded yesterday by Wisukatcak.'

" ' Will you teach me the time and how to use the rattle ? ' said Wisukatcak.

" The old woman consented, but as soon as Wisukatcak had learned the time and how to use the rattle, he killed the old woman, and stripping off her skin, put it upon himself. He then took the rattle and went off under the water to the home of the sea lions. When he got to the lodge of the king lion he saw his brother's skin hanging over the doorway. He went in, and then told the other lions that they must put up a division in the lodge, as he must be alone when conjuring for the king lion to heal him of his wound. So they made a partition and left Wisukatcak alone with the king lion. Then Wisukatcak

began to shake his rattle and to sing, ' I am the rattling quill.'
But instead of pulling out the arrow he pushed it farther in
Then the king of the lions cried out that " Wisukatcak was
killing him," whereupon the other lions raised a great commotion
and rushed into the lodge, and Wisukatcak had only time to
snatch his brother's skin from the doorway and run for his
life; but as he ran he changed his brother into a living wolf
again. When Wisukatcak got to shore the lions sent a great
flood of water after him. It rose higher and higher, and he
climbed the highest hills to get out of the way, but still the
water rose. Then he gathered all the sticks and pieces of wood
he could find and made a raft, on which he floated. By and
by the water covered the very highest hills, and Wisukatcak
saw that the world was drowned!

"After a time he began to consider what could be done.
Looking around he saw some water animals who had not been
drowned; so he called the Beaver, the Otter and the Musk-rat,
and they came upon the raft. Then Wisukatcak said to the
Beaver, ' Go down to the bottom and see if you can bring me
a little earth.' So the Beaver went down and remained a long
time. At last he came up, but he was dead. Wisukatcak
examined his mouth and paws, but there was nothing in them.
Then he said to the Otter, ' Go down to the bottom and see if
you can bring me a little earth.' So the Otter went down, but
he, too, came up dead, and brought nothing. Last of all he sent
the Musk-rat, who stayed down a very long time, and at last
came up dead; but on examining closely, Wisukatcak found a
little mud in his paws and in his mouth.

"Then Wisukatcak took the Beaver, the Otter and the Musk-
rat, and restored them to life, after which he took the mud
which the Musk-rat had brought up, rolled it into a little ball,
laid it on his raft and began to blow upon it. As he blew it
began to get larger, and grew very large, indeed.

"Then Wisukatcak said to the Wolf, ' My brother, run around
this world that I have made and see how large it is.' So the
Wolf ran around. It took him a long time, but he came back
at last and said, ' The world was very large.'

" But Wisukatcak thought it was not large enough yet. So he blew again and made it very much larger. Then he sent out a Crow, and said, 'Fly around my world and see how large it is.' So the Crow went out, but never came back again, and Wisukatcak concluded the world was large enough. And this is the story of how Wisukatcak drowned the world and made it over again."

The Cree nation has, in the three leading sub-tribes already mentioned, bands belonging to each of them, elected chiefs and appointed councillors.

The advent of the white man and his influence has changed the style of dress worn by the men and women, who follow the fashions of the pale-faced people. Before the settlement of the country the native costume consisted of leather, made from the skins of the animals which were to be found in their locality. The men wore leather shirts, leggings of the same material reaching to the hip, and fastened to the belt which held the breech-cloth. Leather caps with the hair on, which fastened under the chin, moccasins and mitts of leather were used. The breech-cloth was made of woollen material; but when this could not be obtained, leather was substituted, and this was about nine inches wide and four feet long, the ends drawn inwards, and then allowed to hang down before and behind. A robe was worn as an outer garment, in the same manner as the modern blanket. They painted their bodies, especially the face, with vermilion, using other colors during the sacred festivities and in times of war.

Alexander Henry, describing their mode of arranging the hair as he saw them, nearly a century ago, says: "Their hair is generally divided on the crown, and fastened in large knots behind each ear, from which is generally suspended bunches of blue beads or other ingenious work of their own. Their men have their hair adjusted in various forms. Some of them have it separated on the top and tied in a tail upon each side; others form but one tail, which hangs down behind, around which is twisted a strip of otter skin or the dressed entrails of buffalo. This tail is increased in size and length, frequently by adding false hair. Others again allow it to flow in the loose lank of nature. Combs are seldom used by the men, and they never besmear the hair with grease. Red earth is sometimes rubbed upon the hair. White earth dabbed over the hair generally denotes mourning, The young men sometimes have a bunch of hair formed upon the crown of the head about the size of a small tea cup, and nearly in the shape of that vessel placed upside down, to which they fasten various ornaments of feathers, quill work, ermine tails, etc. Red and white earth and charcoal are also much used in their toilets. With the former they daub their robes and other garments, some red and others white. The women generally comb their hair and make use of grease to besmear it."

Some of these modes of arranging the hair are still in use among the people. I have seen them all used, except the white earth sprinkled upon the head and the fastenings of buffalo entrails.

Various methods of communication were used, such as fire-signals, the curling smoke conveying intelligence to some member of the tribe at a distance; even the fire was so arranged that the smoke, ascending in different forms, might give a different message. The looking-glass methods of riding on horseback, motions with blankets, and the expressive use of the sign language were efficient means of sending news, and may well be called the telegraphic system of the natives.

In states of great destitution cannibalism has existed, but only in rare instances; and the natives look with abhorrence and flee from the guilty perpetrator of such a crime. Captain Back mentions a case of cannibalism, in which an old man killed and ate his wife and children, and so great was the hatred of the people of his tribe, that he was denounced by them, and requested to leave their camp, and upon refusing to do so, was killed by his own people. About the time of our arrival in the country, a Cree Indian was found guilty of a similar deed, and was hanged by the civil authorities at Edmonton.

Although the natives love intensely all kinds of stimulants, they know their failing, and repeatedly have they appealed to the officers of the State to keep liquor out of the country. Especially did they do so at the time when they were making the treaties with the representatives of the Crown.

The natives were in the habit of burning the prairie and the woods, the former in the spring to destroy the old grass and to secure tender and early grass for their horses, and the latter for the purpose of driving the animals they were hunting into the water, where they could be more easily captured. When they were travelling long journeys, they made a cache by the way, which consisted of articles of food and other necessaries, safely hidden free from the depredations of animals, which they might find on their return journey or obtained by some members of the party who were following them, and likely to be in need. Their food consisted of berries pounded and put away in leather bags, to be cooked in grease and eaten during the winter. Large quantities of berries were gathered and kept for this purpose.

Pemmican was, however, the staple food of the Crees in the days of the buffalo, and the half-breeds were especially fond of it. It was made of the flesh of the buffalo. Buffalo meat cut into thin slices and dried was used as dried beef. The pemmican, however, was made by taking the hind-quarters of the bison, cutting the flesh into thin slices, drying it on a pole in the sun and then pounding it with stones. Two parts of the dried meat were placed in a large leather bag made of the hide of a bison, and one part of melted fat poured upon it, which was closed and allowed to cool. Generally one of these bags held the meat taken from one buffalo cow, as it weighed from ninety to a hundred pounds. In this form it was the commonest kind of pemmican. Berry pemmican was made as above, with the addition of wild cherries or Saskatoon berries. Sometimes ten pounds of sugar was added to each bag, and this increased the flavor. The best kind of pemmican was made of meat finely pounded, with the addition of marrow, berries and sugar. Two pounds were sufficient for the needs of any man per day. Sometimes it was eaten uncooked, but generally it was boiled with flour and water, oatmeal and other

ingredients, and it was then called rabibu. Mixed with flour
and fried in a pan, it was named richat. When well prepared
it could be kept for a long time in good condition. When the
fat was dirty and hairs of various kinds got mixed with it, a
very unsavory dish was it for white men or red, yet hunger
gave zest in the partaking of this dish.

In the depth of winter, amid the blinding snow, when no
trail could be seen, it was well nigh impossible for the native
to lose his way, unless the distance were too great, or he failed
through lack of food. When the storm begins and the trail is
no longer visible, the native takes his bearings, and having
made up his mind as to the course he must pursue, he observes
upon what part of his head or body the wind strikes, and then
he continues his journey, taking care to keep the wind always
on that part of his body. This is travelling by the wind, and
is resorted to in times of necessity. Of course, if the wind
changes there is danger, but even then he will likely learn
that by coming to some well-known landmark, where he can
adjust his human compass. Seldom is an Indian lost upon the
prairie or frozen to death in even the severest storm.

The Crees learned of the white man's power through the use
of firearms, and there were not a few who resorted to other
means to intimidate the red men. A small galvanic battery in
the hands of the white man, by which he could give a shock to
his red companion, greatly increased his influence; or a musical
box, placed in another room or secretly hidden, made the native
believe that his white friend was a strong medicine man, able
to hold communion with the inhabitants of the spirit world.

The beautiful skin-tents of the old days, averaging twenty
feet in diameter and perfectly white, were decorated with red
and black figures, sometimes of a legendary character or historical. The mythical figures were taken from their dreams,
or represented some land or sea monster, of which their aged
friends told them, and the historical figures were chiefly auto-
biographical. Upon the inside of the buffalo robes various
designs were made, some of which on the finest robes were
excellent specimens of native decorative art. A calendar was

6

oftentimes made, the figure of each year representing the leading event of the year. The symbols are understood by the
Indians, and serve to keep fresh in their memories the recent
history of the tribe.

One of the famous dances of the Cree Indians is the thirst
dance, which is similar to the sun dance of the Blackfeet.

The Cree women have always been workers of beautiful
porcupine quill, bead and silk designs on leather. Of course
they were unable to use beads on silk until these were introduced by the trading companies. They are generally industrious and manifest ability in the tanning of the skins of animals,
some of these being white and soft, and the ornaments worthy
of ladies who had enjoyed years of training. This is especially
noticeable among the women of the Wood and Swampy Cree
branches of the nation. Moccasins, leather shirts, smoking-caps
of leather, ottoman covers, leggings and fire bags are among the
articles they delight to make.

Some of the Cree chiefs have been famous warriors, although
in the early years, when firearms were introduced among them,
they cared so little for them that they would gladly trade their
guns for horses with the Assiniboines, and this lack of adaptation to their new circumstances gave the Assiniboines and
Blackfeet great advantage over them. They, however, proved
themselves brave and warlike, and some of them were heroic
in action. They painted their bodies in times of war. When
any of their comrades fell in battle with Indians or white men,
they took precaution to remove their bodies, so that their
enemies would not get them. They were so expert at this
during the Riel rebellion that it gave rise to the belief that
they practised the custom of other tribes, of fastening stones
to their bodies and depositing them in the river.

They always dreaded hanging, and when the treaty was
made with them by the Canadian Government, one of the chiefs
said he hoped that if anything should arise which would make
anyone worthy of death, the guilty person would not be hanged.
Again, when eight of the Indians were hanged at Battleford for
complicity in the second Riel Rebellion, some of them pleaded

to be shot, and not to be hanged. When condemned to death they sing their death song, proclaiming their lack of fear and their determination to brave death.

There is no class of persons who wield a stronger influence among the people than the medicine men. When a young man is desirous of becoming a medicine man, he separates himself from the other members of his tribe for several days, without eating or drinking anything, and during this time he is visited by the spirits who converse with him, and reveal to him the spirits who are to be his servants. These dwell in various animals, as the beaver, otter, mink, musk-rat, bear and wolf. He gains power to commune with the spirits of the wind, rain, snow, ice, and stars. There are four degrees among the Cree medicine men.

First. Wapunu, or the Conjuror of the morning, who has the power of extinguishing fire.

Second. Miteo, the man who uses the bone or shell in killing, and the birdskins. He has an extensive knowledge of roots and herbs, and knows well how to use them in curing disease. He has the power of bringing any person from a distance, if he can only get a lock of hair, or a piece of garment belonging to the person. He ties two images together with the lock of hair or piece of garment on the outside, and no matter what the circumstances are, the person will come to the place after this performance has been done.

Third degree, Kesikauiyineo, or Man-of-the-Day, is the revealer of secrets. Peter Jacobs relates the fact of a number of Ojibway Indians having become so drunk that they did not know where they had hidden a keg of whiskey, and they sought the aid of the revealer of secrets. This medicine man had a little wigwam erected, made strongly, driving about eight poles, about six feet long each, into the ground to a depth of three feet, and then bending them with two hoops into the shape of a canoe. This was enclosed with birch bark. The Man-of-the-Day entered and began to sing, so that the little spirits came. The wigwam shook with great violence, and the outsiders heard them distinctly speak to one another. The spirits inquired whether or not there were any questions to be asked, and some one outside inquired about the keg of whiskey, when the following answer was given : " You must go to a certain direction " —describing it by the course of the sun—" and you will come to an old man lying down and a young man standing over him, with one leg on either side. He stands upon the whiskey."

An old man on the outside turned to some boys and said : " The old man is an old tree fallen, the young man is a younger tree with its roots growing over the trunk of the old one."

The boys ran in the direction indicated and found the place, with the keg and some beads. Sometimes the answers given seem to be at variance with what the medicine man himself wishes, as if he were controlled by some agency of spirits.

Fourth degree is Tipiskauiyineo, who has power to nullify the evil influence of the Miteo, and even to heal those he has injured.

All these degrees are conferred by the chief medicine man, and he bestows the medicine bag upon the applicant for the degree. A striking instance of the power of a medicine man of the fourth degree to destroy the evil influence of one of the second degree was related to me by a Hudson's Bay factor. While in the city of Winnipeg he met a half-breed, an old acquaintance, whose mouth was twisted and his head drawn to one side, without the power to bring it into the natural condition. He inquired the cause of this strange freak, and was told that it was a Miteo who had done it. The factor laughed at his superstitious fears, but he received the assurance that it was true, with the additional information, that there was a Tipiskauiyineo residing at Lake Winnipeg who could cure him. The following summer the factor met his friend, who had been cured, and was informed that he had gone to Lake Winnipeg, and the strong medicine man had broken the spell. Several times have I conversed with Cree half-breeds who have told me strange tales of evil wrought upon their bodies, such as hair or warts made to appear over the whole body suddenly, and to disappear as quickly through the agency of a more powerful medicine man.

It is well known that death has been caused through the assertion of the medicine man, and the spell of death has been broken by a more powerful one. Witchcraft is supposed by the Indians to be practised amongst them by women, called wendigos. These are pursued by the Indians and killed. The medicine man has sometimes to resort to the white medicine man to extract a tooth for him.

When the Crees travel by water they sometimes resort to their native method of stilling a storm. When compelled to land because of a storm upon the lake, they may seek to appease the wrath of the spirit of the lake by a gift of tobacco, meat, or some other article, but should the storm continue they will don a medicine dress and, with rattle bags, sing and shake their rattles for hours, finishing with a speech, and a promise of a suitable sacrifice made by throwing some meat or tobacco into the fire or lake.

The native religious ideas and the mortuary customs have been changed through contact with the white man, and the influence of the Christian religion.

The Cree language belongs to the great Algic family, which extends from Labrador to the Rocky Mountains. It is a euphonious and expressive tongue, systematic in arrangement, and beautiful, though complicated, in multiplicity of its forms.

Archdeacon Hunter, in his "Grammatical Construction of the Cree Language," says: "The more familiar I have become with its grammatical construction—so peculiar and unique, and yet so regular and systematic—the more I have been impressed with the beauty, order, and precision of the language used by the Indians around us. Although they may rank low in the scale of civilization, yet they carry about with them a vocabulary and a grammar which challenge and invite and will amply repay the acumen and analytical powers of the most learned philologist. If a council of grammarians, assembled from amongst the most eminent in all nations, had, after years of labor, propounded a new scheme of language, they could scarcely have elaborated a system more regular, beautiful and symmetrical."

The Plain Crees speak the language with more elegance and purity, than either the Swampy or Wood Crees.

There are several dialects of the language, due to the locality in which the people dwell, with the difference of flora and fauna, occupation and modes of living.

A very complete syllabic system of the language was invented by James Evans, a Methodist missionary, who came to the country in 1840, and lived for six years at Norway House. By means of this syllabary a clever Indian can memorize in an hour or two all the characters, and in two or three days read the Bible or any other book in his own language.

The reader will find a full account of this missionary and the syllable system, with illustrations, in the author's work— "James Evans, Inventor of the Syllabic System of the Cree Language."

A few words of the language will suffice to illustrate its construction :

Arrow, atus.	Great Spirit, (God), Kitcimunitu.	Book, masinabigan.
Autumn, takwukin.		He breaks, pikuneo.
Bad, mayatisio.	Good, miyosio.	Canoe, osi.
Beaver, amisk.	My husband, ninapem.	My daughter, nitunis.
Bear, maskwa.	My mother, nikawi.	Duck, sisip.
Black kuskitcsio.	Night, tipiskaw.	Eye, miskisik.
Bow, atcapi.	River, sipi.	Fire, iskuteo.
He is busy, aluweo.	My son, nikosis.	Forest, sakao.
Cold, takao.	Sun, pisim.	House, waskahigan.
The devil—evil spirit, mutcimunitu.	Tobacco, tcistcma.	No, nimoya.
	Ashes, pekuteo.	Sea, kitcikumi.
Dog, utim.	Axe, tcikahigan.	Stone, asini.
Evening, otakusin.	Bag, maskimut.	Thunder, piyesiwuk.
My father, Notawi.	Beads, mikis.	Water, nipi.
Fish, kinuseo.	Bird, piyesis.	

The Government has established Reservations by treaty with the Crees, whereon reside agents and farm instructors, who teach the Indians farming, and generally care for the welfare of the people. Schools are also in existence, maintained by the joint help of the State and of the churches.

Missionary work is carried on amongst them by the Roman

Catholics, English Church, Presbyterians and Methodists. Education and religious work are prosecuted vigorously, and a large measure of success has followed the labors of devoted men and women. Books have been prepared in the native language, and few Cree Indians can be found who are not able to read the literature printed in the syllabic characters.

THE ESKIMO.*

Upon the distant northern confines of the Dominion dwell the hardy hyperborean races of whom we know so little, whose condition excites our sympathy, yet are almost beyond the reach of our love. So widely scattered are the Eskimo tribes, and so far removed from our centres of civilization, that they are the only native race belonging to the old and new world.

Eskimantzik, from which the name of this people is derived, appears to be an Abnaki term, signifying "Eaters of Raw Flesh." "Flesh-eaters," the white people call them; but naturally they designate themselves, like some of the native races, by a noble term, "innuit," signifying men. The Skraelings of the age of the Norsemen may have been the ancestors of the hardy folk who make their home in the land of desolation and snow.

The Eskimos may be divided roughly into three groups—the Eastern, Central and Western—and within each group are several divisions. From Greenland on the east to Behring Strait on the west (more than five thousand miles) the settlements of these "children of the cold" are to be found. Linked by a common language, which reveals contact with other native American tribes, and a long residence in the new world, they form a separate type of men, whose ancestors may have been the primitive people who dwelt in the early age of the world's history, if the speculating scientist is able to prove the

*Back's "Arctic Explorations," and "Life of Bishop Horden, or Forty-two Years with the Eskimos and Indians." Pilling's "Eskimo Bibliography." Dr. Franz Boaz's, "The Central Eskimos." "Blue Book on Hudson's Bay," 1886. Sir John Schultz's "The Innuits of the Arctic Coast," in "Proceedings of the Canadian Institute."

AMONG THE ESKIMOS.

existence of the Garden of Eden at the North Pole. Such a theory is very pleasing, and would prove a fascinating study, if the evidences in its favor were not wanting. So striking is the unity among this race that the Moravian missionaries, who have labored in Labrador, have been able to preach to the Eskimos of Alaska, and use the Bibles already in use among the natives in the east. Still, there are differences in language and customs amongst them, separated, as they are, into more than sixty communities, with isolated dialects, so difficult, in some instances, as to appear in mastering them like a new language.

In physical·characteristics, language and social customs the Eskimo and Indian are distinct, hating each other, and without any of the affinities so common among the red men. The Indians who dwell on the borders of the territory of the Eskimo are afraid of these daring sons of the Arctic seas, who, in turn, speak in slighting terms of the red men.

History is silent as to the origin of these people, and nothing definite has yet been ascertained regarding their advent to the northern land. Across the frozen Behring Straits their ancestors could easily travel, as some of the hunters do at certain times of the year to visit some of the trading-posts, especially when there is a scarcity of tobacco in the settlements. The drifting kayak has been carried to Europe, and has been found upon the shores of the northern isles ; and the adventurous hunters, no doubt, sought out Greenland, which they visited in the fourteenth century. Southward they roamed many centuries ago, as is shown by the innuit relics discovered, so that the home of this people was not confined to its present limits.

The Eskimo land is a dreary waste of ice and snow, with scanty vegetation and less than one hundred varieties of Eskimo flowers. The Artic explorers have described oftentimes, in language which thrills our souls, the sufferings which they endured in their earnest search for a north-west passage. The long, dreary winters were sufficient to appal the strongest hearts, and even the sunshine of the short summers seemed to

increase the cares of the travellers with its swiftly-passing joys.
The Eskimos are, in general, short in stature and stout, straight
hair, and of a Mongolian cast of countenance.

The communities have slight variations of dress, but the common fashion is for the men to wear boots, trousers and jackets.
Their stockings reach above the knee, with a slipper of birds'
skin, having the feathers next the skin and the boots over them,
reaching nearly to the knee. The trousers are double—an inside pair, with the hair next the skin, and an outside pair, having
the hair turned outward. The jacket is made of two sealskins,
and is drawn over the head, having no opening in front, and a
hood is attached which can be drawn over the head in cold or
stormy weather. Their mittens are sometimes made with two
thumbs, so that they can be turned when they are wet.

The women wear the same kind of garments—boots, trousers
and jacket, the latter with a large hood wherein the baby is
deposited for safety and warmth. The jacket has a longer tail
behind than that worn by the men, and the garments are more
neatly made, besides having ornaments suited to the taste of
the wearer.

The dress of both sexes is made of the furs of the animals,
the skin of the seal being chiefly desired.

The young children are dressed in a jacket of deerskin, with
their legs bare, until having reached their second year, they
wear trousers and boots, and when eight or nine years old, are
clothed in the same fashion as the men. Girls are dressed in
the same fashion as the boys until they are nine or ten years
old, when they are clothed like the women. The Eskimo children enjoy themselves as much in their northern home as their
more highly-favored cousins in warmer climes; from the babe,
rolling among the reindeer skins of the iglu, without almost
any clothing, while the temperature is kept below the freezing
point, to the older boys and girls, happy in sporting with their
toys, made for them by their parents.

The ivory is carved into the forms of bears, foxes, geese, gulls,
walruses, seals and whales, and although not more than three
inches long, they are good specimens of workmanship, and well
represent the animals named.

A kind providence has blessed old and young with extraordinary powers of endurance, enabling them not only to battle successfully with the cold, but to find delight within the iglu while the storm rages outside. Lieutenant Schwatka says that he has seen an Eskimo baby boy taken naked from his mother's hood, made to stand on the snow until his mother sought his reindeer skin clothing from the sledge, exposed to the wind and cold for a minute, while the thermometer was thirty-eight degrees below zero, and a stiff wind blowing, the only protection being the loaded sledge, around and over which the wind was blowing. He has seen a naked man, surprised in his iglu by a bear, rush out and pursue him for two or three hundred yards, and slay him, when the thermometer stood fifteen or twenty degrees below zero. An Eskimo traveller has been seen to throw himself in the snow and rest comfortably while the thermometer registered seventy-one degrees below zero, or one hundred and three degrees below freezing. These children of the cold are intelligent, cheerful and ambitious, and were they transported to a warmer clime would yearn after the land of the walrus and seal, unsatisfied with the adjuncts of civilization, but happy in the presence of the northern lights.

It is estimated there are eighteen thousand Eskimos in Alaska. From the western boundary of Alaska to the eastern extremity of Labrador the population is sparse and widely scattered, the total population of Baffin Land numbering little more than one thousand persons. The people are found in small settlements, consisting of from ten or a dozen souls to several hundreds.

There are no marriage customs among these people, except in the settlements where the missionary has gone. The father of a boy chooses a girl to be the wife of his son while yet the interested persons are young, and a gift of a dog, sled, snowknife, or other useful article is made to the father of the maiden, and they are betrothed. They do not live together until they are grown up, and although the betrothal is a settled matter, it may be broken. When the affianced have arrived at the time considered advisable to begin housekeeping, the young man goes to the house of the maiden and lives with her parents, where as man and wife they live together, the son-in-law helping to support the family. He does not become his own master until the death of his father-in-law, and after erecting his own iglu he may take two or three wives, the first one remaining the mistress of the home. Usually, however, he is contented with one wife; but it is not uncommon for men to exchange wives.

The women tattoo their faces, arms, legs and bodies in different colors, the prevailing color being black. When they reach the age of twelve years the skin is punctured with a needle covered with soot, and the face is especially adorned. Upon the forehead a figure is made, the two lower points beginning from the upper part of the nose, and the figure drawn upward and outward over the forehead until it reaches the hair. Two

THE CHIN ORNAMENT.

lines are drawn upon each cheek, from the lower part of the nose upward toward the cheek bone.

The chin ornaments consist of six or eight single or double lines, sometimes fretted, beginning at the corners of the mouth and covering the whole chin. The women exhibit taste in dressing their hair, parting it in the middle, and forming it at the back in the form of a knob, the sides plaited, and held in place with rings made of ivory or brass.

The Eskimo live during the summer in deer-skin tents; in the autumn in wooden huts, imbedded in part in the ground and covered with earth, when they dwell in a section of country where wood is to be found, but during half of the year their place of abode is in the iglu, a symmetrical snow-house, comfortable, though not always agreeable to men accustomed to the benefits of civilised life.

Bishop Bompas, of Mackenzie River, who has long labored

among the Indians and Eskimos, thus describes the erection of
a snow-house among these people : ." In building this snow-
house the Eskimo shows a wonderful readiness, which I can
compare to nothing but the skill of the bee in making its
honeycomb. In the Eskimo country the fallen snow on the
wide river mouths, after being driven by the wind, becomes
caked or frozen, so as to have considerable tenacity, and at the
same time it can readily be cut with the knife. The Eskimo
then, with this butcher knife, cuts out square blocks of this
frozen snow, as it lies on the surface of the river, of the size of
ordinary blocks of stone masonry, and with these he builds a
house perfectly circular, of the shape of a bee-hive. With no
tool but the knife, which is used as a trowel, he works with
surprising rapidity, and the whole is arched over without any
support from beneath, except, perhaps, a single pole, during the
construction. Any architect or mason at home would, I suppose,
be astonished to witness the work, and might fail in imitating
it, for without line or plummet, and square or measurement,
the circular span and arch is exactly preserved, and the whole
finished in the space of a single hour."

Dr. Boaz says that it takes two skilled Eskimos two hours to
build a snow-house.

Sir John Franklin spoke of the beauty of the Eskimo snow-
house as follows: " The purity of the material from which the
house is framed, the elegance of its construction, and the trans-
parency of its walls, which transmitted a very pleasant light
gave it an appearance far superior to a marble building, and
one might survey it with feelings somewhat akin to those
produced by the contemplation of a Greek temple reared by
Phidias. Both are triumphs of art inimitable in their kinds."

Sometimes these snow-houses are arranged in apartments,
with a long passage, and two or three families dwell together.

When the dreary winter passes away, the hardy Eskimo
launches his boat, which is called a " kayak," and goes off in
search of salmon, which abound in the river, or with his gun
he hunts the wild geese, or he may travel long distances to
hunt the seal and walrus. In the winter he fits out his sledge,

drawn by eight or nine dogs, and armed with knives, guns and harpoons, accompanied by a friend or relative, he travels over the frozen sea in search of bear, seal or walrus. Sometimes he will stand for hours by an air-hole, awaiting the approach of the seal which comes to blow, and cautiously as it approaches he will listen, until he dashes the harpoon into his victim, and if his aim has been good, he will be fortunate in securing it. He is in great danger, however, of being drawn into the hole as the seal rushes away with the harpoon and

AN ESKIMO DOG.

line, and in his eagerness to get the seal, and fear lest he lose his harpoon, he may hold on too long and be drowned.

The Eskimo dogs are intelligent and hardy, well cared for by their owners, and highly prized. When very young they are fed and cared for in the iglu by the mistress of the home, as they play with the children upon the reindeer skins. Fitted with a harness, and guided by the strongest and most intelligent dog, they will speed over the ice at a rapid rate. The leader is proud of his position, and will not allow any interference with his rights. He is reserved toward the rest of the team, and growls when approached by an inferior. He is fed apart from the rest, and is never subjected to any punishment. When the team is called to halt by the driver, the leader slackens his pace, and makes a curve to the right or left, and faces to the rear until the sledge is stopped. The driver carries a whip, with a lash about twenty feet long, and woe to the lazy dog in the team, for instantly he is called by name and whipped into line.

Amid the dangers of travel in that northern land much depends upon the sagacity and speed of the dogs. Lieutenant Schwatka tells of a lost sailor on the ice, after whom was sent a sled with three men and forty of the best dogs in the settlement. Men, women and children stood in front of the team until all were ready, and on the signal being given the crowd parted, the dogs dashed off, and through the fast approaching darkness pressed on until at a distance of ten miles they found the lost man. The whole distance of ten miles was covered in twenty-two minutes and a half, the returning journey being leisurely undertaken.

At one period in the history of Bishop Horden, of Moosonee, that faithful missionary nearly lost his life as he was travelling on the ice on his return journey from Rupert's House. Travelling by night to avoid becoming blind from the glare of the snow, the Bishop and his two young Indian friends made rapid progress until the warm air, indicating rain, compelled them to encamp. A strong cold wind sprang up early in the morning when they started, and swiftly they travelled until ten miles out on the bay, when one of the guides suddenly exclaimed, " What is this ! the tide is coming in, and the ice is breaking up." They looked toward the sea and they beheld the moving ice rising and falling in masses, indicating a general break-up. The guide took a small stick which he carried and struck the ice and it broke with the force of the blow. What was to be done ? Ten miles from the nearest land, and the ice breaking up, struck terror to their hearts. There was not a moment to be lost, and the guide shouted, "Get into the cariole at once, and let us hurry back. We may be saved yet!" Instantly the Bishop sprang into the cariole, and they turned to seek safety on the shore from which they had started in the morning. The guide

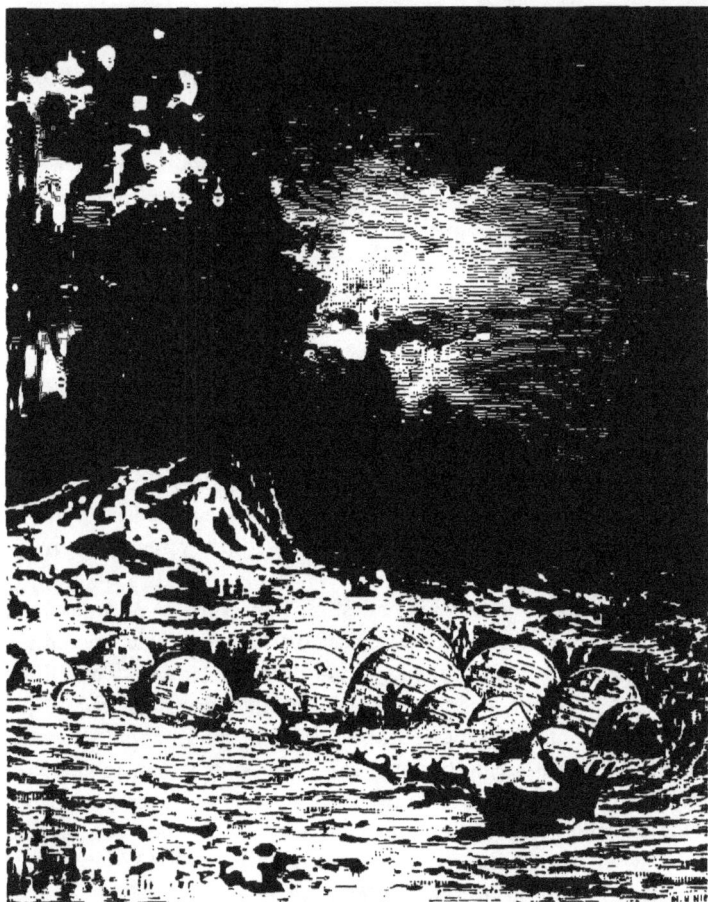

ESKIMO SNOW VILLAGE.

ran alongside, and as they pressed forward the end of the cariole broke through the ice. It was a race for life. The dogs seemed to scent the danger, and fear lent speed to their limbs. Anxiously and eagerly they rushed on, dreading every moment the breaking up of the ice. At last they reached, in the afternoon, the point from whence they started, and found the Indians delighted to welcome them in safety from the dangers of the angry waters.

The Eskimos make long journeys to visit their friends in other settlements, spending months and sometimes years in a single visit. Their mode of welcome is to rub their noses together, a performance more gratifying to them than to the civilized visitor. The loneliness of the winter is lessened by numerous games in the iglu, and when the weather is favorable they enjoy their sports in the snow.

The boys indulge in reindeer hunting, which is thus described by Lieutenant Schwatka: "Having found a long and gentle slope on a side hill, they place along the bottom of the hill a number of reindeer antlers, or as we sometimes incorrectly call them, deer-horns (for you boys must not forget that the antlers of a deer are not horn at all, but bone). These antlers of the reindeer are stuck upright in the snow, singly or in groups, in such a manner that a sled, when well-guided, can be run between them without knocking any of them down, the number of open spaces between the groups being equal to at least the number of sleds. The quantity of reindeer antlers they can thus arrange will, of course, depend upon their fathers' success the autumn before in reindeer hunting; but there are nearly always enough antlers to give two or three, and sometimes five or six, to each fearless young coaster. The boys, with their sleds, numbering from four to six in a fair-sized village, gather on the top of the hill, each boy having with him two or three spears, or a bow with as many arrows. They start together, each boy's object being to knock down as many antlers as possible, and not be the first to reach the bottom of the hill. You can see that, in such a case, the slower they go when they are passing the antlers the better. They must knock over the antlers with their spears or arrows only, as those thrown

7

down by sledge or with the bow or spear in the hand do not
count.   They begin to shoot their arrows and throw their
spears as soon as they can get within effective shooting distance,
and, even after they have passed between the rows of antlers,
the more active boys will turn around on their flying sleds and
hurl back a spear or arrow with sufficient force to bring down
an antler.   When all have reached the bottom of the hill, they
return to the rows of antlers, where each boy picks out those
he has rightfully captured, and places them in a pile by themselves.   Then those accidentally knocked over by the sledges
are again put up, and the boys return for another dash down
the hill, until all the antlers have been ' speared.'   Sometimes
there is but one antler left, and when there are five or six con-
testing sleds, the race becomes very exciting, for then speed
counts in reaching the antler first.   When all are down, the
boys count their winnings, and the victor is, of course, the one
who has obtained the greatest number of antlers."

The little children have dolls, toys resembling sleds, arrows,
and kayaks.

The Eskimos, like the red men, are inveterate gamblers.
Numerous games have they, not the least form of amusement
being story-telling, and the singing of songs.   The women and
children indulge in a game not unlike our rope skipping.

Parry describes this game in the following fashion: " This
is performed by two women holding the ends of a line and
whirling it regularly round and round, while a third jumps
over it in the middle, according to the following order: She
commences by jumping twice on both feet, then alternately
with the right and left, and next four times with the feet
slipped one behind the other, the rope passing once round at
each jump.   After this she performs a circle on the ground,
jumping about half a dozen times in the course of it, which,
bringing her to her original position, the same thing is repeated
as often as it can be done without entangling the line.   One or
two of the women performed this with considerable agility and
adroitness, considering the clumsiness of their boots and jackets,
and seemed to pride themselves in some degree on the qualifi-

cation. A second kind of this game consists in two women holding a long rope by its ends and whirling it round in such a manner over the heads of two others standing close together, near the middle of the bight, that each of these shall jump over it alternately. The art therefore, which is indeed considerable, depends more on those whirling the rope than on the jumpers, who are, however, obliged to keep exact time in order to be ready for the rope passing under their feet."

The women are very fond of making figures with strings, similar to what our girls do at home. There are games resembling dice and cup and ball, which are played with zest. Dr. Boaz's description of some of these games is so good that I insert it: "A game similar to dice, called tingmiujang—*i.e.*,

ESKIMO SLEDGE.

images of birds—is frequently played. A set of about fifteen figures belong to this game, some representing birds, others men or women. The players sit around a board or a piece of leather, and the figures are shaken in the hand and thrown upward. On falling, some stand upright, others lie flat on the back or on the side. Those standing upright belong to that player whom they face; sometimes they are so thrown that they all belong to the one who tossed them up. The players throw by turns until the last figure is taken up, the one getting the greatest number of the figures being the winner.

"A favorite game is the nuglutang. A small rhomboidal plate of ivory, with a hole in the centre, is hung from the roof, and steadied by a heavy stone or piece of ivory hanging from

its lower end. The Eskimos stand around it, and when the
winner of the last game gives a signal every one tries to hit the
hole with a stick. The one who succeeds has won. This game
is always played amid great excitement.

"The Saketan resembles a roulette. A leather cup, with a
rounded bottom and a nozzle, is placed on a board and turned
round. When it stops the nozzle points to the winner. At
present a tin cup, fastened with a nail to a board, is used for
the same purpose. Their way of managing the gain and loss
is very curious. The first winner in the game must go to his
hut and fetch anything he likes as a stake for the next winner:

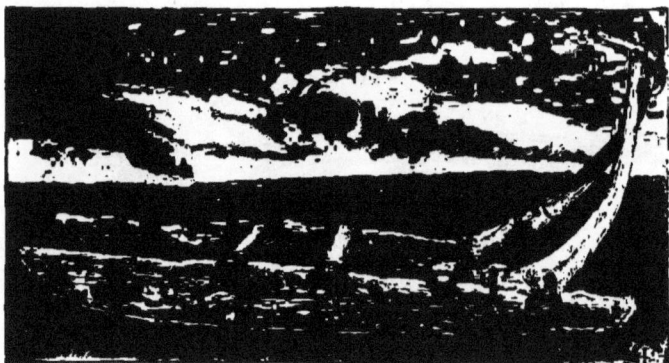

ESKIMO RAFT.

who, in turn, receives it, but has to bring a new stake in place
of this, from his hut. Thus the only one who loses anything is
the first winner of the game, while the only one who wins anything is the last winner."

The Eskimo look complacently on death, and await peacefully the dissolution of the body. The young are placed in
their graves with their feet toward the rising sun, and the
aged in the opposite direction. The deceased is borne to his
grave by relatives, who bury him in the ground, if possible, and
all the articles belonging to him, except his kayak, gun, dogs,
harpoon, and a few others are placed beside his grave. When

a woman dies some pots, lamps and knives are placed beside
her grave; and in the case of a child, some toys. For three
days the relatives must shut themselves up in their hut, where
they mourn for the deceased, and then abandon it on the expiration of that time. For some time they must cook their food
in a separate pot. When they visit the graves they deposit
articles for the use of the dead, and utter their mourning cries.

Stories of cannibalism are told of these people when in a
starving condition.

The angakoq, or medicine man, is a man of influence, who is
able to keep the people in subjection by means of his incantations and their superstitions. His power is invoked in times
of sickness or during a storm. As he enters the hut, uttering
some incoherent sounds or speaking the sacred language of the
fraternity, the lamps are made to burn low and the people
hide themselves behind screens, and seeking the back part of
the hut, he removes his outer jacket, and drawing his hood over
his head begins his incantations. In the midst of his conjurations he may fall down in a trance, or arouse the spirits to talk
with him. He is paid well for his services. Some of these
medicine men are skillful, and resort to changes of diet, cleanliness, and moral living as an aid to their incantations.

A merry group may often be seen in the snow hut in the
winter evenings, singing songs or telling stories. The story
teller turns his face to the wall and then relates with great
earnestness some of the numerous tales or fables, while the
listeners' eyes glisten with delight, and they shout with joy.

The Supreme Being of the Eskimo is a woman, named Sedna.
Hall, the Arctic explorer says : " There is one Supreme Being,
called by them Anguta, who created the earth, sea and heavenly
bodies. There is also a secondary divinity, a woman, the
daughter of Anguta, who is called Sidna. She is supposed to
have created all things having life, animal and vegetable. She
is regarded also as the protecting divinity of the Innuit people.
To her their supplications are addressed ; to her their offerings
are made ; while most of the religious rites and superstitious
observances have reference to her."

Heaven is called the "Uppermost Ones," and is above. All who live virtuous lives, helping the poor and doing good to their fellows and those who are killed by accident or commit suicide go to that happy land when they die. There they will remain forever, in that land where there is no ice or snow, no darkness or storms, but free from trouble, they will hunt the deer and always find delight.

Hell is below us, and has abodes in a descending scale, resembling Dante's "Inferno," where the wicked will remain forever. In that land of eternal darkness there is no sun, and the cold is intense, severe storms, ice, snow and trouble continually, becoming colder as the wicked descend.

ESKIMO KINDLING FIRE.

They have legends of the Man in the Moon, who makes the snow and takes care of orphans; the Three Sisters, who make the thunder, lightning and rain; and of the Great Flood, when many of the Eskimos were drowned, and a few saved by means of a boat. They believe that men are the descendants of a dog; fish were made from chips of wood; and thunder is made by rubbing a deerskin.

Long ago there lived a powerful Eskimo, a young chief, who was a conjurer, and found nothing impossible to him. He found the earth too small for him, so climbed up to the heavens, where he made the sun by means of a small fire, which he had taken with him. He took along with him his sister, who lived with him for some time in perfect harmony;

but quarrels at last arose, and he began to treat her badly. He became angry with her, and scorched her face, which was beautiful, and, unable to bear his insolence any longer, she fled from him, taking some fire, and formed the moon. He pursued; but was unable to overtake her, and he still continues the chase. When it is new moon the burnt side of her face is toward us, and when there is an eclipse he is very near to her; still, he is unable to catch her.

The stars are the spirits of the dead Eskimos, who have fixed themselves in the heavens. Within the stones in the northern land spirits reside, who are propitiated by means of sacrifices, gifts placed beside the stones, and prayers are offered unto them. The Eskimos have religious feasts and dances, and numerous native songs, tales and fables.

Ever since Hans Egede went to Greenland, missions have been in operation among the Eskimos. The Moravian missionaries have the following mission stations in Labrador: Hopedale, Zoar, Nain, Okak, Hebron and Ramah. Nain is the capital of Labrador, and there the missionaries have been laboring for nearly one hundred and fifty years. The genial agent of the Moravian Mission Rooms in Fetter Lane, London, England, showed to me, some years ago, specimens of articles of Eskimo manufacture from these distant stations, which evinced ability. As you enter the mission church you may hear the peals of the ancient-looking organ, and the intelligent congregation of nearly two hundred souls, singing: "There is a Gate that Stands Ajar," which appears in the Eskimo tongue as follows:

> "Up Kerusunanok Kilak Jesub
> Sakkyarvi a
> Jesub ikhiliksodlardub pio lu ta
> Tokkalanktub
> Napki gi jaunek o pinok apku e
> Subjandlarama uvanga
> Tank il la unanga tank.

The Moravians have now gone to Alaska to labor among the Eskimos.

In the Hudson's Bay territory and away toward the Yukon

river the Roman Catholic Church has established missions, where devoted men come in contact with these children of the cold. The Rev. Messrs. Pettitot, Morice, and other devoted men have toiled for years among the Dene Indians and Eskimos. The English Church has sent out faithful men in the persons of Bishops Bompas and Horden and Rev. Mr. Peck, who have devoted their energies for the salvation of this people.

Grammars, dictionaries and a good supply of religious literature is in existence for the Eskimos of Labrador, but the Eskimos of Hudson's Bay have only portions of the Scriptures, prayers and hymns in their language, and these have been prepared chiefly by Mr. Peck.

The natives have shown an aptitude for carving and drawing, which has been used by some of them for enlarging their geographical knowledge of Eskimo land.

A few words from the Eskimo of Hudson's Bay, by Gilder, will conclude this sketch :

Arm, teloo.	Girl, nulcuksar-wee-	River, koog.
Arrow, kakleoke.	nee.	Sea, tarreo.
Axe, oolemow,	Go, attee.	Sister, nuryearger.
Bear, nennook.	Good, mamakmut.	Skin, amingk.
Black, kernink.	Great, angewoke.	Small, mikkee.
Blood, aoonak.	Hair, nuyakka.	Smoke, eshik.
Brother, aninger.	Hand, iyreteka.	Son, earkenearar.
Cold, ikkee.	He, una.	Speak, okokpo.
Daughter, pannia.	Head, neakoke.	Spoon, allute.
Day, ogloome.	Heart, omut.	Star, ooblooriok.
Dog, kimak.	House, igloo.	Steal, tigleepoo.
Drink, emiktook.	Husband, winga.	Stone, weark.
Duck, meahtuk.	I, woonga.	Sun, neiya.
Earth, noona.	Ice, sikkoo.	Thou, ichbin.
Egg, mannig.	Iron, sowik.	To-day, oobloome.
Eskimo, innueet.	Kettle, ootkooseek.	To-morrow, okkagoo.
Eye, cieega.	Knife, panna.	Warm, oko.
Face, keenar.	Man, angoot.	White man, koblunar.
Father, atata.	Moon, anninga.	Water, emik.
Fire, ikkooma.	Morning, ooblak.	We, oobahgook.
Fish, ekkalloo.	Mother, amama.	White, kowdlook.
Flesh, neerkee:	No, nas.	Wife, nooleeanga.
Foot, issekut.	Old, ohtokok.	Wind, annoway.

Winter, okeoke.
Wolf, amaroke.
Woman, ahdenok.
Yes, armelao.
Yesterday, ikpokeyuk.
You, illeepsee.
Young, makkoke.

One, autowzig.
Two, muldelroc.
Three, pingahsuet.
Four, seetahmut.
Five, tedelemut.
Six, okbinuk.

Seven, okbinuk-moko-
   nek.
Eight, okbinuk-mok'-
   asunik.
Nine, okbinuksee-tah-
   mut.
Ten, koling.

The following is the vocabulary of John Davis, which he collected during his residence among the Eskimos in 1586:

Kesinyoh, eat some.
Madlycoyte, music.
Aginyoh, go, fetch.
Yliaoute, I mean no
   harm.
Ponameg, a boat.
Conah, leap.
Maatuke, fish.
Sambah, below.
Macoumeg, will you
   have this?
Cocah, go to him.
Paaotyck, an oar.
Asanock, a dart.

Sawygmeg, a knife.
Uderah, a nose.
Aoh, iron.
Blete, an eye.
Umvicke, give it.
Tuckloag, a stag or elan.
Panygmah, a needle.
Aob, the sea.
Mysacoah, wash it.
Lethicksaneg, a seal
   skin.
Canyglow, kiss me.
Ugnera, my son.
Acu, shot.

Aba, fallen down.
Icune, come hither.
Awennye, yonder.
Nugo, no.
Tucktodo, a fog.
Lechiksah, a skin.
Maccoah, a dart.
Sugnacoon, a coat.
Gounoh, come down.
Sasobneg, a bracelet.
Ugnake, a tongue.
Ataneg, a seal.
Macuah, a beard.
Quoysah, give it to me.

THE SIOUX INDIANS.*

The Sioux or Dakota Indians comprise a very large confederacy of tribes widely scattered over the United States and the Canadian North-West.

The meaning of Dakota,† the name which in general they give to themselves is, "Our Friends," or "Associated as Comrades," signifying their relationship as tribes. They repudiate the name by which they are known among the white people. Sioux is to them a term significant of enmity, as it means "enemies" or "hated foes," and this no doubt is the name by which they are

---

* Works of J. Owen Dorsey. S. R. Riggs' "Mary and I; or, Forty Years with the Sioux." Pilling's "Siouan Bibliography."

† Brinton's "Myths of the New World," Page 29. "Fourth Annual Report of the Bureau of Ethnology."

known among the Indian tribes foreign to themselves, as they are called generally by their enemies " Cut-throats," and in the sign language, when speaking of these people, the Algonquin family draw the finger of the right hand across the throat. The Ojibways called the Sioux Nadowessi, a contemptuous term for " rattlesnake," and after adding the French plural form to the word, it was cut down by the trappers and voyageurs to Sioux. These people were known as the Dakota family or Confederacy, but this has been changed to the Siouan family, as the earliest name by which they were known was Sioux.

The tribes and bands belonging to this confederacy are numerous, some of which are known by different names, not always correct, as travellers and students fell into error, or chose to call them by some distinctive appellation. In order to show the power of the confederacy, without certifying to the accuracy of the names in every particular, I will give the names of some of the tribes and bands by which they became known.

The Siouan family comprises the Sioux or Dakotas proper, the Tetons or Sansarc, the Santees, subdivided into the Wahpeton or Men among Leaves, and the Sisseton or Men of Prairie Marsh, the Missouris, Omahas, Ponkas, Osages, Otas or Wahtoktata, the Tutelos, Stoneys or Assiniboines, Minnitaris or Hidatsas, also called Gros Ventres, the Kansas or Kaws, Crows or Upsarokas, Iowas, Mandans or Wahtanis, Quapaws, Biloxi, Brule or Burnt Hip, Oglalas, Winnebagos, Uncpapa, Minnecowjous, Blackfoot Sioux, Yankton or Yanktonais, Two Kettle Sioux, Arickarees or Rees, Sacs, and Foxes.

There are small bands of Sioux located in Manitoba and the North-West Territories, some of whom are resident upon Reserves, but are not treaty Indians, and a few United States refugee Sioux, who are stragglers in the vicinity of the towns. There are none of these people resident in the Dominion outside of Manitoba and the North-West. They are to be found as stragglers around Portage la Prairie, Regina, Moose Jaw, Maple Creek, Swift Current, Medicine Hat and Birtle. Those resident upon Reserves, but are not treaty Indians, are located at Bird Tail Creek, Oak River, Oak Lake, Turtle Mountain, Qu'Appelle Lakes, Moose Woods, and Prince Albert. The Sioux population in Canada, not including the Stoney or Assiniboine Indians who are not classed above, is between one and two thousand.

A century ago the Sioux pursued the Crees to the borders of Southern Manitoba, and since then have roamed over Minnesota and Dakota, until they were located on Reservations. No great influx reached Manitoba or the North-West until the Minnesota Massacre and the defeat of Custer and his troops. Refugees found a home in British territory, and sought the influence of the Canadian Government to aid them in gaining a livelihood. They were not encouraged to remain, but when they had determined to make their home in Canada, and desired the protection of the Government they were allowed Reservations, and assisted to maintain themselves as farmers, without making a treaty with them.

Physically they are a dignified race, whose form and features may be known from their typical chief, Sitting Bull, as he appeared at Fort Walsh.

" Sitting Bull is about five feet ten inches in height. He wore a black and white calico shirt, black cloth leggings, magnificently embroidered with beads and porcupine quills. He held in his hand a fox-skin cap, its brush drooping to his feet. with the grace of a natural gentleman he removed it from his head at the threshold of the audience tent. His long black hair hung far down his back, athwart his cheeks, and in front of his shoulders. His eyes gleamed like black diamonds. His visage, devoid of paint, was noble and commanding; nay, it was somewhat more. Besides the Indian character given to it by high cheek bones, a broad retreating forehead, a prominent aquiline nose, there was about the mouth something of beauty, but more of an expression of exquisite and cruel irony."

Their dress consisted of the general Indian styles, each tribe, however, being distinguished by its own form of moccasins, and some of them were even known by their mode of walking, pointing the toes inward or outward, or placing ·the feet firmly

upon the ground. The tribes painted their faces in various
styles in times of war, or at sacred feasts, according to their
tribes.   Even the hair, of which the male members of the tribes
were very proud, was dressed in its own fashion, a distinguishing feature of each tribe.

The Sioux Indian mother ties her baby's feet together between pieces of wood, to give them the shape necessary for
following the mode of walking peculiar to the tribe.   The
moccasins reveal the tribe to which the wearer belongs by the
shape of the sole and the number of tags fastened behind.   So

SITTING BULL.

careful are the natives to remove any superfluous hair about
the face, that they use tweezers for plucking it out by the
roots, and when they desire to remove it from the sides of the
head, they do so by running a hot stone over the parts. Before
the introduction of mirrors, they used a clear stream for dressing themselves, and this custom is preserved in the name given
to a looking-glass, which means, " He peeped into the water at
himself."

When Catlin, the artist, travelled among the Indians, he found
the Sioux a fine-looking body of men, well dressed in their

deerskin garments, a noble type of nature's gentlemen. He has preserved for us in his striking portraits of some of the chiefs and warriors the intelligence and force of will depicted on their countenances, their taste displayed in their features, and their dignified mien in their standing and sitting attitudes.

His account of Shoodegacha, a Ponka chief, whose portrait he painted, is full of interest. " The chief, who was wrapped in a buffalo robe, is a noble specimen of native dignity and philosophy. I conversed much with him, and from his digni- fied manners, as well as from the soundness of his reasoning, I became fully convinced that he deserved to be the sachem of a more numerous and prosperous tribe. He related to me, with great coolness and frankness, the poverty and distress of his nation; and, with the method of a philosopher, predicted the certain and rapid extinction of his tribe, which he had not the power to avert. Poor, noble chief, who was equal to and worthy of a greater empire! He sat on the deck of the steamer, overlooking the little cluster of his wigwams mingled among the trees, and, like Caius Marius weeping over the ruins of Carthage, shed tears as he was descanting on the poverty of his ill-fated little community, which he told me had once been powerful and happy. That the buffaloes which the Great Spirit had given them for food, and which formerly spread all over their green prairies, had all been killed or driven out by the approach of the white men, who wanted their skins; that their country was now entirely destitute of game, and even of roots for food, as it was one continuous prairie; and that his young men, penetrating the countries of their enemies for buffaloes, which they were obliged to do, were cut to pieces and destroyed in great numbers. That his people had foolishly become fond of fire-water, and had given away everything in their country for it; that it had destroyed many of his warriors, and would soon destroy the rest; that his tribe was too small and his warriors too few to go to war with the tribes around them; that they were met and killed by the Sioux on the north, by the Pawnees on the west, by the Osages and Konzas on the south, and still more alarmed from the constant advance of the pale-faces—

their enemies from the east—with whiskey and small-pox, which already had destroyed four-fifths of his tribe, and would soon impoverish and at last destroy the remainder of them. In this way did this shrewd philosopher lament over the unlucky destiny of his tribe, and I pitied him with all my heart." The Ponkas, according to the testimony of Lewis and Clarke, at one time resided on a branch of the Red River and Lake Winnipeg. The beautiful buffalo-skin lodges of the Sioux, covered with picture writing, so full of interest to those who can read the story of the master of the lodge in these strange characters, are now replaced with small lodges of duck or cotton, among the straggling Indians of the west, and houses on the Reservation. Good houses are erected on the Reserve near Birtle, and at the Moose Wood's Reserve, near Saskatoon. The buffalo was the staple food of these people, but since they have disappeared they are following the customs of the white people in their choice of food. During the winter of 1881, when the buffaloes on the River Missouri were returning to the Chinook region of Southern Alberta, the Crow and other Sioux Indian tribes set the prairie on fire, and the herds were driven southward toward the Missouri and Yellowstone rivers, where they were corralled by the Indians and white people and exterminated.

Frequent visits made to the Sioux camp at Moose Jaw brought me into contact with these people, whom I found industrious even in their unsettled condition, the women working in the town at whatever they could find as washer-women, and the men splitting and sawing wood, or helping occasionally on the farms during harvest.

Along the line of railroad a precarious livelihood is obtained by them, in polishing buffalo horns and making moccasins, which they sell to the travelling public. The children are happy in their poverty, scantily clad, yet full of joy when they are sporting in the water, or playing at spinning top.

As the white traveller passes by their camp, the women and children seek their lodges, and peep through the holes at the stranger, and talk about him among themselves. Ask one of them his name, and he will turn to another of his friends to answer in his place. An aged chief was accustomed to spend much of his time around the stores, delighting to relate the story of his adventures and the exploits of his tribe. A genial old man was he, and yet, despite the familiarity of the two races, there was great fear manifested by some of the white people during the progress of the second Riel Rebellion, lest they should join the rebels.

The sad wails which I have heard in the Sioux camp when some little child has died has told more impressively than words could do, the depths and intensity of the mother's love. No hand is ever lifted to correct the children, and yet they are obedient to the instructions of their superiors.

The women dress in the same fashion as the other Indian tribes in the West; yet the practised eye can tell by the style of painting the face and the features, especially when they let fall a word or two of their language, the tribe to which they belong.

Polygamy has been and is still practised among them, though it is fast passing away. The girls marry when they are young, and they are sought after by the young men, who have their own method of courtship. The tribes of the Confederacy have different customs of courtship. A young man may require the services of his parents to aid him in making presents and arranging the marriage with the parents of the girl. They have no marriage ceremony, but live together as man and wife, after all the arrangements between the interested parties have been made.

The Sioux have ever been noted as warriors, having been designated as the tigers of the plains. The young man is therefore desirous of distinguishing himself by securing the scalp of an enemy, which raises him in the estimation of his tribe, and ensures him a place of honor among his people. When they go out on the warpath, they blacken their faces, hold a feast, at which they make speeches, declaring what they will do, and strike at imaginary foes. As they sing and dance within the lodge, they incite each other by their speeches, and under the influence of the excitement go to war.

Colonel Mallery, in his monograph on the "Pictographs of the American Indians," gives a striking sketch of the Dakota Count, which consists of the history of the leading events of the Sioux for the past fifty years, made by means of picture writing, and in this their battles have a leading place.

After the Sioux war, when Custer and his men were slain, Sitting Bull and his tribe fled to Canadian territory, and spent some time at Fort Walsh, one of the posts of the North-West Mounted Police. Some of the Sioux, in 1862, fled after the Minnesota massacre to Manitoba, and located at Sturgeon Creek, about six miles from Winnipeg. The Governor and Council of Assiniboia, at that time governed the Province of Assiniboia under the Hudson's Bay Company, and Mr. Dallas, the Governor-in-Chief, reported to the Council that he had visited the Sioux camp, and found about five hundred men, women and children, who were in great destitution, and after consultation with Governor McTavish, he had offered them provisions to enable them to remove to such a distance from Fort Garry as would free the settlers from any fear of danger, and provisions would be conveyed to them, along with ammunition, as would enable them to secure game, and thus support themselves. They refused to go, urging their inability to remove the old men, women and children in the winter. The Council supplied the means of transit, and they were conveyed to the White Horse Plains, distant from Fort Garry twenty miles. They were supplied with provisions, but no ammunition.

The United States authorities applied to the Governor-in-Chief of Rupert's Land and the North-West Territories, and received permission to enter Canadian territory to compel the Sioux to return to the United States, with the intention of punishing the leaders in the massacre, and giving the assurance that all others would be dealt with in a kindly manner. The troops never came, and the Sioux were allowed to remain unmolested.

In the summer of 1866 a band of Sioux came from the United States to visit their friends in the Red River Settlement, and as

hey were leaving quietly with a number of Saulteaux, they
vere attacked by a band of Red Lake Saulteaux from the
Jnited States, about a mile from Fort Garry, and five of the
Sioux were slain. Fearing an outbreak, the Council authorized
he formation of a mounted military force of from fifty to one
undred settlers to insure peace, but their services were not
equired, as the hostilities were not renewed.

The United States authorities again renewed negotiations to
nduce the Sioux to return to their own territory, and the
Council sought to secure their consent to return, offering them
he means of transit, but they refused to return, and no further
fforts were made to have them removed from the country.

When the Province of Manitoba was formed, the Sioux were
amped in the parishes of Poplar Point, High Bluff, and Portage
a Prairie, and some had gone further west into the North-
West Territories. They were quietly disposed, and became
useful helpers to the settlers. Several times they sent deputa-
ions to the Lieutenant-Governor of the Province of Manitoba
equesting the granting of Reservations, where they might live
peaceably and receive assistance in securing agricultural imple-
nents to enable them to farm. A Reservation was proposed to
hem on Lake Manitoba, but they were afraid of a renewed
onflict with the Red Lake Saulteaux, and were, therefore,
unwilling to go there. In 1874 a Reservation on the Assini-
oine River, at Oak River, and another at Bird Tail Creek were
llotted them, and the Sioux scattered throughout Manitoba
vere removed to them. In 1876 a band of Sioux, living in the
listrict of Qu'Appelle, sent a deputation of their chiefs to
ee Lieutenant-Governor Morris and the Hon. Mr. Laird at
Qu'Appelle, asking for a Reservation, and in 1877 another band
f Sioux at the Turtle Mountains sent two deputations to ask
or a Reserve in the locality where they were camped. A
Reservation was allotted them near Oak Lake, about fifty miles
orth of Turtle Mountains.

The Sioux in Canada have lived peaceably and worked hard,
emaining loyal to the authorities, and during all the time they
iave resided in the country there has been only one grave

8

offence committed, the putting to death of one of their number according to their own laws. The perpetrators of the deed escaped, and there was no further trouble.

The aged Saulteaux chief, Kouchroche, aided by messengers from the Government, visited the Sioux, and the enmity between these tribes was buried. The American Sioux sought to enlist the Canadian Sioux in the war with the United States Government, but they steadily refused, and did not in the least aid the rebels.

In 1877 Sitting Bull and his tribe fled to Canada, and much uneasiness arose among the Canadian people at their presence in the North-West. Major Crozier, commanding Fort Walsh, dealt firmly with Sitting Bull, and, along with Lieutenant-Colonel Macleod, maintained peace. The American Commissioners visited Fort Walsh, under an escort from the Mounted Police, and treated with the famous Indian chief, who refused to return to the United States.*

The chief recounted, in one of his speeches before the commissioners, the troubles which had been brought upon his people, blaming the white people as the cause of all the depredations he had committed. After stating the reason for coming to Canada, he said:

"You have got ears, and you have got eyes to see with them, and you see how I live with these people. You see me. Here I am. If you think I am a fool, you are a bigger fool than I am. This house is a medicine house. You come here to tell us lies, but we don't want to hear them. I don't wish any such language used to me—that is, to tell me lies in my Great Mother's house. This country is mine, and I intend to stay here and to raise this country full of grown people. See these people here. We were raised with them."

He shook hands with the Canadian officers, and then closed his speech with a touch of humor—"I wish you to go back, and to take it easy going back."

---

* Morris, "Treaties of Canada with the Indians of Manitoba, the North-West Territories, and Keewatin," pages 276-284.

At this conference a Santee chief said, " I will be at peace with these people as long as I live. This country is ours. We did not give it to you. You stole it away from us. You have come over here to tell us lies, and I don't propose to talk much, and that is all I have to say. I want you to take it easy going home. Don't go in a rush."

An Indian woman, named "The One that Speaks Once," said : " I was over at your country, I wanted to raise my children there, but you did not give me any time. I came over to this country to raise my children and have a little peace. That is all I have to say to you ; I want you to go back where you came from. These are the people that I am going to stay with, and raise my children with."

An Indian, named " The Crow," spoke boldly to the commissioners of the Canadians, adding : "These people that don't hide anything, they are all the people I like."*

The hatred of the Sioux toward the American soldiers was described by him in a few sentences. " Sixty-four years ago I shook hands with the soldiers, and ever since that I have had hardships. I made peace with them, and ever since then I have been running from one place to another to keep out of their way."

After Sitting Bull had contemptuously rejected the offers of the American commissioners, he made an unqualified submission to the terms proposed by the Canadian officers, which has been preserved for us by one who was present.

" My friend, and all the Queen's men whom I so respect : I have heard of your talk. I knew you would speak to me in this way. Nobody told me. I just knew it. It is right. I came to you, in the first place, because I was being hard driven by the Americans. They broke their treaties with my people, and when I rose up and fought, not against them, but for our rights, as the first people on this part of the earth, they pursued me like a dog, and would have hung me to a tree. They are not just. They drive us into war, and then seek to punish

---

* Helen Hunt Jackson, "A Century of Dishonor," pages 386-388.

us for fighting. That is not honest. The Queen would not do that. Long ago, when I was a boy, I heard of the Queen, now my Great Mother. I heard that she was just and good, now I know it. You gave me shelter when I was hard pressed. My own life is dear to me, but I did not value it when I fought the Americans, but I did value the life of my nation. Therefore, I brought my people to you. I do thank you for what you have done for them. I will go to the Red River and be at peace. Tell the Queen that. Tell her I will be a good man, that my people will be good. Tell her also that we never were bad, for she knows it is not wrong to fight for life. My people are weary and sick. I will take them to Red Deer River; and now I declare to you that I will not make trouble or annoy you, or give pain to the Queen. I will be quiet. I will never fight on your soil unless you ask me to help you, then I will fight. I wish you good. Good-bye. Place me where you like. I will be at peace in Canada. But you who are brave soldiers and not treaty-breakers, thieves and murderers, you would think me a coward if I did not die fighting the Americans. Therefore while I go to the river of the Red Deer now to live at peace, I will come back when my braves are strong; or if they will not come with me, I will come alone and fight the Americans until death. You I love and respect; them I hate; and you, Queen's soldiers, would despise me if I did not hate them. That is all. I am ready to go with you to the Red Deer river."

The Sioux under Sitting Bull ultimately left Canada and submitted to the American Government. Since that time we have not been molested by any Sioux from the United States, and the Canadian Sioux have devoted themselves to their farming operations on the Reservations. Having spent so much of their time in warlike operations, they admired bravery whenever manifested, even in the person of an enemy.

The Blood Indians relate the story of one of their young men who was desirous of distinguishing himself in war, and the opportunity of joining a small war party having come, he united with it and started on the warpath. The Bloods journeyed southward for several days, until they saw encamped in a valley a large band of Sioux, so formidable in appearance that their courage departed, and they resolved to return home. This young man determined to remain, and refused to follow his companions, who failed to persuade him to accompany them. With fears for his safety, the war party left him, and turned their faces toward home. Our youthful warrior loosened his horse, struck him with his whip, and sent him home. He hid himself until darkness rested upon the prairie, and the Sioux were fast asleep. Creeping slowly into the camp, he sought out the lodge of the chief, where a noble-looking horse was fastened in readiness for any emergency. Entering quietly he sat down by the fire, ate heartily from the contents of a pot which hung upon a tripod, and after satisfying himself, unloosed his moccasin, and left it where he sat. Leaving the lodge, he cut the horse loose which stood near by, sprang upon his back, shouted the war-cry and fled. The whole camp was roused.

The young men sprang upon their horses and followed him, but he had one of the best horses in the camp, and far ahead he rode from his pursuers. The Sioux gave up the chase reluctantly, and returned full of admiration for the young brave who had dared to perform such a feat. As they recited the heroism of the young man, whose nationality they learned from the moccasin left in the lodge, they said that such a man was too good and brave to be killed, and were they able to capture him, they would make him a chief.

The Sioux are inveterate gamblers, and in many of their forms of amusement they will join, until they have nothing left. Horse racing and card playing they frequently indulge in, spending their evenings in the lodges in the latter form of amusement. They have numerous dances, most of which are expressive of sacred things. Dancing societies exist amongst them, the members of which perform the dancing in connection with the dances.

Dr. Owen Dorsey divides the dancing societies into three classes, those which are sacred, including those connected with the practice of medicine; those connected with bravery and

war; and those merely for social pleasure. Sometimes they
dance when a patient recovers, or when they are going on the
warpath. When any of the warriors have been slain, they
sometimes place them in a sitting posture with a rattle of deer's
claws fastened to one arm, and dance over their bodies. The
men dance alone in their feasts, and the women have dancing
societies by themselves. They have their sacred tents with
men to look after them, and sacred pipes with their keepers.
They are a religious people, praying to the Great Spirit, and
looking unto him for help in their hunting or war expeditions,
and holding many things sacred to their religion. Of course
their ideas on religious matters differ from those of the white
people, yet they are sincere in their devotion. Numerous
sacred festivals have they, including the sun dance, similar to
that of the Blackfeet. They have myths of the creation of
the world, the origin of man, the flood, and the coming of a
Redeemer.*

During the spring of 1888, the son of the Sioux chief of the
band of Moose Jaw died, and the deceased was placed in a coffin
covered with red cloth and deposited upon a platform raised
about ten feet in the air, on four stout poles. When the body
was placed on the platform, a horse belonging to the deceased
was tied by the tail to one of the posts, and shot. I saw the
bones of the animal under the scaffold, the dogs having eaten
the flesh. A large and a small coffin, trimmed alike, were lying
on the scaffold. The medicine man's drum has often sounded
in my ears, and the drum and songs of the gamblers have
reminded me of the days spent among the Blackfeet. One of
the last raids made by the American Sioux in Manitoba was in
the vicinity of Pilot Mound, before that portion of the country
was settled by the white people, when they attacked the
Delorme half-breed settlement and killed several persons,
besides stealing their horses.

When the Sioux settled upon their Reservations, some of
them were anxious to have a missionary reside amongst them.

---

* "Eleventh Annual Report of the Bureau of Ethnology," pages 361-544.

Among the Canadian Sioux were some who had been Church members of the Sioux mission, under the care of Rev. Dr. John P. Williamson and Dr. S. R. Riggs. One of them was Wamdeokeya (Eagle Help), who had been Dr. Riggs' helper in his Dakota translations. These isolated native Christians corresponded with their old friends in the south, and their appeal was placed before the Presbyterian Board by Dr. Williamson, and an appropriation was made to send a native preacher among the Canadian Sioux. Solomon Toonkanshaecheye, an ordained native pastor, who was an efficient worker and had relatives in Canada, was sent in June, 1875, accompanied by Samuel Hopkins, as his assistant. They began their labors among the Sioux at Bird-Tail Creek, and travelled among the scattered bands. Owing to the poverty of the people, these two devoted men, after laboring with success for a few months, were compelled to return to the United States.

In the month of March, Henok Appearing Cloud, one of the Canadian Sioux, wrote that he had taught school during the winter and preached among the people. So great was the desire for a missionary by these people that Henok wrote: " Although I am poor and often starving, I keep my heart just as though I were rich. When I read again in the Sacred Book what Jesus the Lord has promised us, my heart is glad. I am thinking if the minister will only come this summer and stay with us a little while, our hearts will rejoice. If he comes to stay with us for a long time, we will rejoice more. But as we are so often in a starving condition, I know it will be hard for anyone to come."

The Rev. Dr. John Black, of Kildonan, heard of the strong desire of the Canadian Sioux to have a missionary, and becoming deeply interested in them, wrote to Dr. Williamson, proposing that the Presbyterian Board in Canada assume the responsibility of caring for them. Dr. Black's overtures were not entertained by the Missionary Committee, but the following year the mission was undertaken, so that in the month of October, 1877, Solomon set out for his mission at the Bird-Tail Creek Reserve.

In the summer of 1879, Solomon reported a church organized, with thirteen members, which they named Middle Hill. Solomon and Henok made a missionary tour among the scattered settlements of Sioux in Canada. They visited the people, preaching and praying, and were cheered with the results of their tour, though they met with some opposition. The church prospered under Solomon's care. Some of the people died rejoicing in the truth of the Gospel.

The missionary relates the story of the death of his son, aged seven years, in a pathetic strain : " From the time he could hear me speak I have endeavored to train him up in all gentleness and obedience, in truth and in peace. Now, for two years in this country he has been my little helper. When some could not say their letters, he taught them. He also taught them to pray, and when any were told to repeat the commandments, and were ashamed to do so, he repeated them first, for he remembered them all. Hence, I was very much attached to him. But this last winter he was taken sick, and from the first it seemed that he would not get well. But while he lived it was possible to help him, and so we did to the extent of our ability. He failed gradually. He was a long time sick. But he was not afraid to die. He often prayed. When he was dying, but quite conscious of everything that took place, then he prayed, and we listened. He repeated the prayer of the Lord Jesus audibly to the end. That was the last voice we heard from him. Perhaps when our time comes, and they come for us to climb up to the hill of the mountain of Jehovah, then we think we shall hear his new voice. Therefore, although we are sad, we do not cry immoderately."

Solomon labored faithfully for some years with great success, not only on the Reserve, but as far west as Moose Jaw, and then returned home to die. He has gone, but the work still continues.*

The English Church commenced a mission upon the Reserve at Oak River, near Griswold. This was begun shortly after the Indians located upon the Reserve.

---

* S. R. Riggs' " Forty Years with the Sioux," pages 374-381.

Some years ago I had the pleasure of visiting the Sioux school at Portage La Prairie, supported chiefly by the enterprise of the ladies of the town. The children were intelligent, and sang for their visitors very sweetly some hymns, in their own tongue. A school is maintained by the Presbyterians among the Sioux at Prince Albert, and a good work is being carried on in connection with the Methodist Mission at the Moose Wood's Reserve, near Saskatoon.

The Canadian Sioux are making progress in the art of agriculture, and advancing in civilization. The picture writing and sign language of these people present features of great interest, exhibiting intellectual power and taste.

The language of the Siouan family has several dialects. So extensive is the language, that Dr. Riggs' dictionary contains sixteen thousand words. It is a melodious tongue, has nearly one hundred primitive verbal roots, numerous separate and incorporate prepositions, three conjugations of the verb; three numbers, singular, dual and plural; three moods, indicative, infinative and imperative: and two tenses, the indefinite and future. There are several forms of the verb, named by Dr. Riggs, the frequentative, absolute, possessive, reflexive and dative, with other numerous forms. A single verb, conjugated, will show in its modifications more than five hundred changes.

The following words were collected in the lodges of the Sioux at Moose Jaw, as I visited them in the summer of 1890:

Suka, a dog.
Sukaka, a horse.
Tonga, big.
Waste, good.
Muste, it is hot.
Iqtaitoke, to-day.
Hihuna, to-morrow.
Wozila, one.
Nopa, two.
Yamina, three.
Topa, four.
Ahipe, sleep.
Ahipewozila, one sleep ;
    i.e., one night.

Ahipewi, the moon; i.e.,
    the sleep sun.
Ahipetsoka, midnight ;
    i.e., half a moon.
Tsoka, half.
Wi, the sun.
Wihenapa, sunrise.
Wetsokahia, mid-day ;
    i.e., half a sun.
Wikutcila, afternoon ;
    i.e., little sun.
Wimahia, sunset.
Tcistila, little.
Kutciala, little.

Iokapaga, night.
Kupe, come.
Iyayo, go.
Muzas kouje, one
    dollar.
Kaj papeyamina, seventy-
    five cents.
Kaj papenopa, fifty
    cents.
Kaj papewozila,
    twenty-five cents.
(Note the names of one,
    two and three in the
    last three words.)
Okise, ten cents.

Mianata, my head.	Linata, his head.	Ibalamenekete, I go.
Niandta, thy head.	Tush, tosh, and to sig-	Mie, I.
Witcanata, a man's	nify, yes.	Miwaqhataa, I laugh.
head.	Kauin, no.	Iqhataa, he laughs.

There is an extensive literature in the Sioux language, comprising the Bible, hymn-books, catechisms, "Pilgrim's Progress," grammars, dictionaries, vocabularies, and a newspaper, called the *Word-Carrier*. These belong to the American Sioux, but some of them are in use among the Canadian Sioux. Canada may well feel proud of the fact, that these aliens have ever been faithful. The late Sioux war cost the United States two million dollars, besides much anxiety and vexation, but the policy of the Canadians towards the Sioux has been to treat them justly, asking from them loyalty to the Government, and an earnest endeavor to labor for the welfare of their race.

THE MICMAC INDIANS.

In the summer of 1534, as Jacques Cartier and his associates were in search for a passage to the Indies, after having discovered Miramichi Bay, they were surrounded by a large number of canoes, containing several hundred people, who caused them so much annoyance, and foreboded danger, that the noble Frenchman was compelled to fire his cannon among them so as to disperse them. These were the Micmac Indians, a hardy coast tribe of red men, who found a livelihood in the summer as fisher-folk, and in the winter repaired to the interior, where they hunted the animals which roamed the forests during those early years in Eastern Canada.

Jacques Cartier met these people again upon the mainland after his encounter with them in their canoes, and propitiated their chief by the gift of a red hat—a precious thing always in the eyes of a Canadian red man.[*]

These Micmacs, sometimes spelled "Mikmaks," are supposed by some students of Micmac history to be related to the lost tribe of Beothuks, who formerly dwelt in Newfoundland, and of

---

[*] Winsor's "Critical History of America," Vol. IV., page 49.

whom very little is known.* The strongest evidence from the difference of language points to a hatred of each other, ending in the destruction of the Beothuks. From an examination of their mythology, Leland concludes that the Micmacs and Norsemen came in contact with each other in the prehistoric times of Canada, for in the old Norse legends there is to be found much in common with the Micmac.

Not far distant from their home were to be seen the Eskimo of Labrador, and this coast tribe of red men, in their hunting expeditions, met the hardy children of the cold, who have left the impress of their associations with them, in the stories which still linger in the memories of the aged men, and in their traditions there abides the record of a visit of some Eskimos to the land of the Micmacs.†

These people belong to the great Algonquin family, comprising one of the largest divisions of the red men on the continent. The Micmac, Penobscot, Passamaquoddy, Abnaki, and Malicete Indians call themselves the Wabanaki, which means the "People who Live in the East," or near to the rising sun.

In the maps of the eighteenth century the Micmacs are located in Nova Scotia and Prince Edward Island, while in the early records of missionaries they were found along the coast from Nova Scotia to Gaspe, and within the interior of New Brunswick, Nova Scotia, Prince Edward Island, and Newfoundland.

In the Micmac traditions we learn that before there were any white men in the country a young woman, belonging to the tribe, had a singular dream of a small island floating toward the land with tall trees upon it and human beings, and a young man dressed in rabbit-skin garments.

The wise men of the tribe were unable to interpret the young woman's dream, but next day the people saw an island float toward the land and become stationary, having trees upon

---

* A. S. Gatschet, in "Proceedings of the American Phil. Society," Vols. XXII., XXIII.

† Charles G. Leland's "Algonquin Legends of New England," pages 9-12; Winsor's "Critical History," Vol. I., page 321.

it, with bears in the branches. They seized their bows and arrows and rushed toward the shore, when they found a ship, and instead of bears on trees, men were climbing the rigging of the vessel. A canoe was lowered into the water, and several men sprang into it, having with them a man dressed in white garments, who was paddled to the shore, and went among the people speaking a strange language, but evincing by his manner his desire to be on friendly terms.

This was a priest who had come to teach them a new religion, and though the people listened to the truths he taught, the wise men opposed him, for the dream had been given to a woman, and not to a wise man.*

Since the advent of the sailors with their strange ways, the white people have mingled with the Wabanaki until the present day, sometimes on friendly terms and sometimes in war.

Within the Dominion there are about four thousand Micmacs. In 1890 there were in the provinces as follows: Quebec, six hundred and twenty; Nova Scotia, two thousand and seventy-six; New Brunswick, eight hundred and thirty-nine; Prince Edward Island, three hundred and fourteen, and a few in Newfoundland.

Dressed in the garments of primitive people, and armed with bows and arrows, they contrived to maintain themselves by the products of the sea and forest, wandering from place to place, and locating for a short period when successful in their hunt. The old-time native costume, usually worn by Indians, was kept up among the Micmacs until within the past two or three decades, but at the present day, only a few old women are to be found wearing the old-fashioned head and shoulder gear.

As the. tribe is scattered over the eastern provinces there exist difficulties in their attempts to become self-supporting, and variety as to their work. They are engaged chiefly in farming and fishing. In some places, especially on the west coast of Newfoundland, their services are sought as guides, whereas on the Lennox Island Reserve they manage to eke out a precarious living by means of the prolific oyster beds, and the

---

* "American Antiquarian," Vol. XII., page 155.

JIM GLODE, THE MIC MAC HUNTER.

STEREOPLATE Co.

manufacture of Indian goods, which they sell in the towns within easy travelling distance from their home.*

The Micmacs, despite their hard fare, were happy in their poverty, singing and dancing with great glee when nature smiled upon them. Upon the rocks of Nova Scotia may still be seen the pictographs of the Micmacs, and amongst these may be noticed the elaborate masks worn by them in their dances. They have among their dances one called the "snake dance," which, in the early history of the people, had no doubt a religious significance, but has been lost. This dance is generally performed with other dances, and is known by the tortuous performances of the dancers, resembling the motions of a snake. Another significant dance is called the "trade dance," from the fact that the dancer repairs to the lodge of a friend, and before entering sings a song. Singing his song the man enters the lodge, dancing and looking around, fixes his eyes upon something he desires, and pointing to it, offers a price for it. The owner of the article must sell this article or something else of equal value.†

The language of the Micmacs belongs to the Algonquin stock of language. It was first reduced to writing by the Recollet missionaries who dwelt among the people. When Biard, the Jesuit missionary, was living in the Micmac camp in 1611, he struggled hard to master the language, but found it lacking in many terms needful to enable him to express religious ideas. Bribing an Indian by a mouldy biscuit he sought to know the Micmac equivalents for faith, hope, charity, sacrament, baptism, and other religious terms, and with the result, as Parkman tells us, that the Indian amused himself by giving unto him unseemly words. When the missionary used these in his teaching and his Indian catechism, the effect was ludicrous, and tended not to the elevation of their minds and the growth of piety.

In 1655, Chretien Leclercq, a member of the Recollet Order

* "Department of Indian Affairs Blue Book," 1890.

† J. Walter Fewkes, in "Journal of American Folk-Lore," Vol. III., pages 257-280.

of Franciscans, was sent to Canada as a missionary, and for six years he labored among the Indians along the coast of the Island of Gaspe. During the second year of his residence among the Gaspesians, he determined to devise some easy method for teaching the people to read. Little progress had been made under the old system of using Roman characters, and by simply memorizing the prayers taught them by the missionary, the people had not been greatly enlightened. Observing some children making marks on a piece of birch bark, and after repeating a word of a prayer, pointing to the mark representing this word, the missionary thought that he might prepare such a system as would be easy for them to learn to read. Accordingly he prepared a system of hieroglyphics, which enabled the Micmacs to learn the prayers in a short time, and this syllabary, Leclercq said, was prized so much by the people that they preserved their papers in neat bark cases adorned with wampum, beads and porcupine quills.* This Micmac syllabic system is still in use. This system has been used extensively by the Roman Catholic missionaries in the preparation of religious works for the Micmacs, but the Rev. Dr. S. T. Rand, who was an eminent scholar of the Micmac and kindred languages, discarded its use, believing that it hindered the people in their progress in civilization. Several grammars and vocabularies have been prepared in the Micmac, and Dr. Rand completed a Micmac dictionary of forty thousand words.

Grammars and vocabularies in manuscript by various authors remain in the possession of individuals, or in libraries, especially in that of the Archbishopric of Quebec. The Abbe Maillard prepared a grammar of the Micmac and other works relating to the customs of the people, or as religious helps.† The most able linguist, however, was Dr. Rand, who spent over forty years among the Micmacs, laboring as a missionary, studying their language, mythology and early history, and writing

---

* Winsor's " Critical History of America," Vol. IV., pages 268, 269.

† Pilling's " Bibliography of Algonquin Languages," pages 303-306. Rev. George Patterson, D.D., in " Transactions of the Royal Society of Canada," Vol. IX., pages 168-169.

numerous works upon the Micmac tongue. He speaks of singing hymns in the mellifluous Micmac tongue, which is endless in its compounds and grammatical changes, and utterly incapable of being represented by signs. Micmac words become Anglicised, like those of other Indian languages, so that they become almost unrecognizable. As in the word Cadie or Kady-Quoddy, which simply means a "place or region," and is used in conjunction with some other noun, as Sunakady, the place of cranberries, and Pestumo-quoddy, the place of pollacks. Upon the rocks of New Brunswick and the State of Maine there have been discovered Micmac inscriptions, some of which antedate the advent of the white man, and others show the influence of the teaching of the missionaries. Colonel Mallery says these rock inscriptions can best be interpreted by means of the sign language, but as the Micmacs do. not now use this form of speech, the gestures of the other members of the Algonquin family must be applied to their interpretation. Aboriginal figures of fishes, whales, wigwams, native animals, with sketches of modern things, have been found; and Colonel Mallery was fortunate in securing impressions of a five-pointed star, an animal supposed to be a bear, an aboriginal head and bust, a very artistic moose, and a clustre of three trees, separated at the roots, conjectured to signify the first, second and third chiefs of the tribe.

During the struggle in Acadia the Micmacs were instigated by the French priest Le Loutre to fight against the English, and so determined were they to assist the French that the English were compelled to retire. They fought with great valor against their Mohawk foes, who came down upon them in great numbers. Strange tales are told of the hated Iroquois and the Micmacs in the days of war. In the quiet harbor of the picturesque village of Bic, and not far distant from Cacouna, lies L'Islet au Massacre, washed by the waters of the St. Lawrence. The centuries have come and gone since a band of three hundred Micmac men, women and children, fleeing in their canoes from the blood-thirsty Iroquois, sought, amid the darkness and the storm, rest for their weary limbs within the dark recesses of the cave upon the barren Islet beside the village of Bic. Soundly they slept, heedless, because unsuspicious, of the knowledge their foes had of the course they had taken. Guards there were none to keep a sharp look-out for the enemy, for who could find their way to this rocky speck by the sea on such a stormy night. Having dragged their boats up the steep cliffs and hidden them in the rocky recesses, daring would be the foe who would risk his life to explore this rock on such a stormy night. Asleep upon the rocky floor, secure from all alarm, the night wore on, when the Micmac warriors were aroused from their slumbers by the war-cries of the Iroquois, and the shrieks of their wounded friends.

Driven from their rocky retreat, the poisoned arrows found sure lodgment in the bodies of the Micmacs, and soon, amid the cries of the dying and the wailing of the storm, the bloody work was done. When the sun rose, five timid Micmac warriors, the last of that noble band, cautiously surveyed the scene. The bodies of their comrades lay in pools of blood, their scalps taken to grace the lodges of the Iroquois. Assured of the departure of the enemy, they sought and found some canoes which remained unharmed, and in them they sought the settlement at Bic, to relate to deeply-interested listeners the massacre of their friends. Such a tale seemed incredible, and the doubting ones sought the Islet to certify the truthfulness of the story which had filled their ears. Alas! it was too true. The Islet bore traces of a terrible struggle, and all around lay the bodies of the Micmac dead. The quaint villagers of Bic tell, with striking emphasis, the story of L'Islet au Massacre, the departure of the lonely Micmac survivors, the weird cries heard, and the strange spectres seen by their forefathers, as they gazed upon the Islet on stormy nights.

The legends of the Micmacs have furnished an interesting field for numerous explorers. Dr. S. T. Rand collected nearly one hundred Micmac tales. Charles G. Leland has written an interesting work, "The Algonquin Legends." Edward Jack, of Frederickton, has assiduously gathered many legends from the Micmacs, and other workers among the same tribe have trea-

9

sured tales of these people worthy of preservation. The Indian tribes have each a distinctive culture-hero, as Hiawatha among the Six Nations, the Old Man of the Blackfoots, and Glooscap of the Micmacs. The Blackfoot Old Man and the Micmac Glooscap performed noble and ignoble deeds, ruled as giants in their respective tribes, and although they have gone from earth, they are not dead, but live in a land unknown to the red men.

Dr. Rand related in the "American Antiquarian" some of the legends of these people, which will illustrate the mythology of the Micmacs. One of these is called "A-Cookwes," a story showing the stupidity and physical strength of the giants: "Some little boys were out hunting. A-cookwes, a giant, was prowling around watching for his prey—hunting for people. In order to attract the boys, he imitated the noise of the cock partridge, the drummer. This he did by slapping his palms upon his breast. The little boys hearing the noise were deceived by it and fell into the trap. The huge giant—they are amazingly strong, covered with hair, and are cannibals, regular gorillas—seized the boys and intended to dash their heads against a stone, but mistook an ant-hill for a stone, and so merely stunned and did not kill them, except one—one was killed. The giant then placed them all in a huge boochkajoo, a large birchen vessel, and strapped them on his back and started for home. The boys soon recovered from their stunning, and began to speculate upon their chances for escape. It certainly must have seemed rather a hopeless undertaking, but we never know what we can do till we try. One of the boys had a knife with him, and it was agreed that he should cut a hole through the boochkajoo, and that one after another they would jump out and scud for home. In order not to awaken suspicion, they waited until they heard the limbs rattling on the bark as the giant passed under the trees, before the process of cutting commenced. As soon as the hole was large enough, one slipped out, and another, and another, until all were gone but the dead one. The giant being so strong he never perceived the difference in the weight of the load. When he arrived at home he left his load outside and went into his wigwam. There he had a comrade waiting for him, to whom he communicated his good success. But on opening the cage, the birds had flown, all but one—Tokooso-goobohsijik. Then they proceeded to roast the prey, and sat down by the fire to watch and wait till it was done.

"The children soon reached their home and spread the alarm. A number of the men armed in hot haste and pursued the giant. Before the meal was cooked they reached the place. Whiz! came an arrow, and struck the one in the side who had carried off the children. He made a slight movement and complained of a stitch in the side. Soon another arrow followed, and another, but so silent and so swift that neither perceived what they were; but the fellow fell slowly over as though falling asleep. His companion rallied him on being so sleepy and going to sleep before his tender morsel had been toasted. But soon he also began to be troubled. Sharp pains began to dart through him, and sharp darts to pierce him, and he also fell dead."*

Another interesting legend is that of the Moosewood Man: "Away in the woods dwelt a young woman alone. She had to depend upon her own exertions for everything. She procured her own fuel, hunted her own food and prepared it. As she had no comrade she was often lonely and sad. One day when gathering fuel she cut and prepared a noos-a-gun, a "poker for the fire," of minkudowok—moosewood—and brought it home with her. She did not bring it in the wigwam, but stuck it up in the ground outside. Some time in the evening she heard a sound as of a human voice outside, complaining of the cold.

"'Numus, my sister, kaoochee, I am cold.'

"'Come in and warm yourself, then,' was the answer.

"'I cannot come in; I am naked,' was the reply.

"'Wait then, and I will put out some clothes,' she tells him.

"This is soon done. He dones the robes tossed out to him and walks in, a fine-looking young fellow, who takes his seat as the girl's younger brother; i.e., younger than she. (The Indians,

* "American Antiquarian," Vol. XIII., page 41. "Legends of the Micmacs," by Rev. S. T. Rand, edited by Helen L. Webster.

and it is the same with the Bannacks, have a word for a brother
older than the speaker, and another to designate a brother who
is younger than the speaker. Sisters are distinguished in the
same way). The poker she left standing outside the door had
become metamorphosed, and proves a very beneficial acquisition.
He is very affable and kind, and withal a very expert hunter,
so that all the wants of the home are bountifully supplied. He
is named Minkodowogook, from the wood from which he sprang.
After a time his female friend hints to him that it would be
well for him to seek a companion.

" ' I am lonely,' says she, 'when you are away. I want you
to fetch me a sister-in-law.'

" To this reasonable suggestion he consents, and they talk the
matter over and make arrangemants for carrying their plans
into execution.

" The sister tells him where to go and how to pass certain
dangers. 'You will have to pass several nests of serpents, but
you must not fight them nor meddle with them. Clap one end
of your bow on the ground, and use it as a pole to assist you in
jumping, and leap right straight across them.' Having received
his instructions, he starts on his journey. After a while his
sister becomes lonely from the loss of his company, and resolves
to follow him. To give him warning she sings, and he hears
and answers her in the same style, instructing her to go back
and not come after him. She does so. He goes on until he
comes to a large Indian village. He follows his sister's instructions and enters one of the lodges.

" There, as he had expected, he finds quite a bevy of girls, and
one—she is the youngest of the group—who excels in beauty.
He walks up and takes his seat by her side. This, as she
remains seated and the parents' silence, show their acquiescence,
settles the matter, and consummates the marriage. The beauty
of his countenance and his manly bearing have won the heart
of the maiden and conciliated the esteem of the father. But
the young men of the village are indignant. The young lady
has had many suitors, who have all been rejected, and now to
see her so easily won by a stranger—this is outrageous. They
determine to kill him.

" Meanwhile his father-in-law tells him to go out and try his hand at hunting. When he returns, successful, they will prepare a festival in honor of the marriage. So he takes his wife with him, and his father-in-law's canoes, and pushing up the river to the native grounds, following the directions given by the old man, they come to a steep descent and push up through the rapids, land and construct a temporary hut, and he goes into the hunting business in earnest. He is at home in that occupation, and before many days he has collected a large amount of furs and venison, and is prepared to return. But a company has been formed to cut him off and rob him of his prize. A band of young men in the village, who are skilled in magical arts have followed him, and reached the place where he has pitched his hut. But now the trouble is how to proceed. They dare not attack him openly, and as to their wiles, he may be able to outdo them. But they adopt this plan : One of them is to transform himself into a mouse and insinuate himself under the blanket while the man is asleep, and thus give him the fatal stab. But our hero is wide awake. When the mouse approaches he quietly claps his knee on him all unconsciously, as he pretends, and squeezes the little fellow most lovingly. The poor mouse cannot stand the pressure, and sings out most lustily. This arouses the wife, who, perceiving that her husband is resting his leg heavily upon some poor fellow, jogs him and tries to make him understand what is going forward. But he is wonderfully dull of comprehension, and cannot understand what she is saying, but manages, by what seems an all unconscious movement, to squeeze the wily foe—the small mouse— more affectionately, He does not design to kill him, however, but to overcome and frighten him, and send him off. So finally he releases him, and never did a poor mouse make greater speed to escape. He carries the warning to his companions, and they conclude to beat a hasty retreat.

" Minkodowogook now prepares to return. He asks his wife if she is willing to take the canoe with its load back to the village alone, and allow him to go and fetch his sister. She says she is willing, and he sees her safely off. She arrives in

due time and makes a report to her father. All are amazed at
the amount of food and fur collected in so short a time. They
convey it all up safely to the village, and then await his return.
After a few days he comes, bringing with him his sister, and
the feasts and sports commence. He is challenged to dive and
see who can remain the longest under water. He accepts the
challenge, and goes out with his antagonist.

" ' What are you ? ' asks Minkodowogook.

" ' I am a loon,' answers the other proudly.

" ' I am a Chigumoveech,' he answers.

" Down go the divers, and after a long time the poor loon
floats up to the top and drifts—dead—down the river. The
spectators wait a long while and finally the Chigumoveech
comes up, flaps his wings exultingly and comes to land in
triumph.

" ' Let us try a game of growing,' says another.

" ' What will you choose to be ? ' says Minkodowogook.

" ' I will be a pine tree.'

" ' Very well; I am the elm.'

" So at it they go. One rises a large white pine, but encum-
bered himself with branches, which exposes him to the blasts of
the hurricane. The other rises high, naked of limbs, and when
the blast comes, he always bends, but retains his hold on the
earth, while his rival is overturned and killed. The stranger
comes off victorious in every contest, and returns exultingly to
the camp. His father-in-law is proud of him, but his other
daughters, especially the eldest, are full of envy and rage.

" Meanwhile our hero is presented by his wife with a fine, little
boy. The sister pretends to be very friendly and asks to nurse
the child, but the mother declines her assistance. As she is
suspicious of the ill-suppressed jealousy of her sister. ' I can
take care of my babe myself,' she tells her. After awhile the
father-in-law advises him to move back to his own native place.
The jealousy of the hunters is deepening. He takes the advice
and departs. His father-in-law provides him with a canoe,
provisions, and weapons to defend himself with if he is attacked.
He has not gone far before he is pursued and overtaken, but he

is found to be as good in battle as in a chase. His foes are soon killed or dispersed, and he and his family return safely to his own land." *

In this story of the Moosewood Man we have the familiar myth of the Twin Brothers of the Iroquois and the Blood-Clot Boy of the Blackfeet. We observe the same contention between the Good and Bad as in this story among other Indian tribes, the minor details of the story being variable.

The story of Glooscap is like unto that of the Blackfoot Old Man. Glooscap came from the far East across the great sea, and it was he who taught the Indians all they know. He was their teacher, guide and friend, teaching them how to hunt, fish, and till the soil. He was good, kind and brave, and directed the Indians how to become wise and good. When he came to this land his boat was a granite rock, and he was accompanied by a woman, but she was not his wife, as he never had one. He put to sea in his strange canoe, taking with him a young woman who was a bad character, which was evidenced by the storm which arose, and determined to get rid of her, he sought the land, and as he sprang ashore, he pushed the craft seaward. Finally she was transformed into a ferocious fish. Glooscap went away toward the far West, telling the Indians that if they were good, they could follow him at death and make their abode with him.†

The sacred number among the Micmacs is seven, resembling that of the white man, and differing from the Dakotas and Blackfeet, whose sacred number is four.‡

The Micmacs of the present day, when brought under the civilizing influence of the Gospel, are an honest and industrious people, but in too many cases contact with the white race has induced them to manufacture goods for sale, by which they visit the villages and towns to sell their wares, and become reduced, through drink and idleness, to extreme poverty. Some of the Micmac bands are industrious and attend to farming, but others are thriftless. The Micmacs of Quebec are favorably

---

* "American Antiquarian," Vol. XIII., page 168.

† "American Antiquarian," Vol. XII., page 283.

‡ "Transactions of the Canadian Institute," Vol. III., page 203.

situated, the soil on their Reserves being good, and when they
work, a bountiful harvest rewards their labors.   They are
good trappers and fishermen, yet their progress is slow.   The
population is increasing slowly, but their love of intoxicants is
a great hindrance toward civilization.   The Micmacs of Nova
Scotia are generally self-supporting, and are reputed an honest,
industrious, and law-abiding people.

One of the agents of the Government says, concerning them :
"There is one trait in the character of the Micmacs which
cannot be too highly praised.   Living, as they do, they frequently suffer many privations.   This evening they may not
have to-morrow's breakfast in reserve for themselves and
families, and yet a case of theft from their white neighbors is,
I believe, utterly unknown.   The gradual elevation of a race
with a fair characteristic like ˙this so firmly impressed on
them ought not to be despaired of. . . . I am happy to be
able to report an unmistakable improvement in the condition
of all the Indians in my agency.   Each succeeding year shows
more clearly than the preceding one that it is only a question
of time to find them good and useful citizens, provided only
that they are well treated, and have fair opportunities of
improvement."

These people are engaged in various occupations, as fishing,
hunting coopering, basket making, cutting timber and porpoise-
shooting, while some find employment at mills, or on the railways.   Yet they are slowly decreasing in numbers.

The Micmacs of New Brunswick are engaged chiefly in
fishing and farming, and are decreasing in population, induced through the use of intoxicants.

In Prince Edward Island the Micmacs may be divided into
those who stay at home and devote themselves to agriculture,
reaping a blessing in comfort, an improved moral sentiment,
and the pleasure which arises from industrious habits, and
those who pursue a nomadic life, loitering around the towns in
poverty, with little to eat and very poorly clad.   The latter,
especially, are passing away.*

* "Department of Indian Affairs Blue Books," 1888-91.

Missionary work among the Micmacs was begun in the beginning of the seventeenth century, the rudiments of the Micmac language being collected as early as 1613. The Recollet Fathers roamed the coast of Acadia in the first years of the century. The Jesuit missionaries, Perrault and Turgis, devoted themselves to the Micmacs, itinerating among the scattered camps, caring for the sick, and suffering many hardships. Biard, Richard and Lyonne studied the language, and founded a mission among them, but few converts were won to the faith. Lyonne died in 1661, devotedly attached to his flock ; Richard continued his labors, and gained a measure of success. When Bishop Laval visited Gaspe in 1659, one hundred and forty Indians were presented for confirmation.

The Recollets took charge of the Micmac Mission, and the indefatigable Leclercq labored hard, devising his syllabary of the language, which remains till the present as an evidence of his zeal and devotion. The majority of the Micmacs have received missionary instruction from the Roman Catholic missionaries until the present day.*

The Rev. Dr. S. T. Rand was drawn toward the wandering Micmacs about 1846, and resolved to devote himself to the study of their language. Meeting with a French sailor in Charlottetown, Prince Edward Island, who had lived among the Indians, and was conversant with the French, English and Micmac language, he obtained help from him in studying the language.

Dr. Rand was a remarkable man. He began life as a poor stonemason, eager for knowledge, which he sought in various ways. One month at the Wolfville Academy studying Latin was his last effort at securing an education through an institution, for after this experience he resolved to teach himself. He mastered Syriac, Hebrew, Latin, Greek, French, German, Spanish, Italian, and the languages of the Micmac and Malisect Indians. He labored as a missionary among the Micmacs from 1846 till his death, in 1889, and for twenty years he received

* Winsor's "Critical History of America," Vol. IV., pages 266-269 ; Vol. V., page 452.

no salary from any missionary society. Legends, catechism, hymns, portions of the Bible, a Micmac grammar, and a dictionary of the same language, comprising forty thousand words, were part of the work.*

There are several religious works in the Micmac language, including hymn books, catechisms and prayer books, by Roman Catholics and Protestants. Dr. Rand translated the New Testament, some portions of the Old Testament, and tracts. Several grammars have been prepared and various vocabularies. As an illustration of the structure of the language I append Leclercq's translation of the Lord's Prayer:

" Nushinen Wajok ebin tchiptook delwigin meguidedemek Wajok n'telidanen tchiptook ignemwiek ula nemulek uledechinen Natel wajok deli chkedoolk tchiptook deli chkedulek makimiquek eimek Delamukubenigual echemieguel apch negueeh kichkook delamooktech penegunnenwin nilunen : deli abikchiktakachik wegaiwinametnik elp kel nixkam abikchiktwin elweultick melkeninrech winnchudil mu k'tygalinen keginukamkel winnchiguel twaktwin. N'delietch."

The following short vocabulary of the Micmac language will show the peculiarities of their form of speech :

Kesikwteiak, to be afraid.	Pasaalook, clouds.	Kakumik, stand.
Memaje, alive.	Temsum, cut.	Sesmogun, sugar.
Ookweioode, angry.	Piskeak, darkness.	Webetume, teeth.
Kesagawegoos, August.	Mijese, eat.	Abeesh, thread.
Mijooajeech, baby.	Booktaoo, fire.	Ebaboosowa, warm.
Mpakum, back.	Ootoogwajun, forehead.	Weisis, beast.
Winsit, bad.	Mpetun, hand.	Wokwis, fox.
Weiopak, bead.	Tumeegun, hatchet.	Wabus, hare.
Menichk, berries.	Mijooajech, Indian boy.	Abistanooch, marten.
Boochkafoo, birch bark.	Abitajeech, Indian girl.	Kitpoo, eagle.
Pakadoo, bite.	Mkusun, moccasin.	Senumkw, goose.
Maktawac, black.	Mtoon, mouth.	Abokujech, woodpecker.
Situnegoo, blow the nose.	Mkuse, nail.	Pulamook, salmon.
	Mema, oil.	Maskawe, birch tree.
Ootool, boat or canoe.	Kikpasak, rain.	Owaojit, spider.
Kwejumeak, boil.	Wiskubok, salt water.	Kuledow, raspberry.
Pegaadoo, break.	Edek, sit down.	Mooinonan, whortleberry.
	Koobech, snow.	

---

* Maclean's " Indians of Canada," page 340.

THE KOOTENAY INDIANS.*

Small parties of Kootenay Indians were sometimes met with on the eastern slope of the Rocky Mountains during my early years in the Macleod district, when they had come to trade with the white traders or barter horses with the Blood Indians. They were a noble-looking lot of men. The sounds of their deeply guttural language and the fine dresses worn made an impression not soon to be forgotten. The traders spoke of them as an honest and industrious tribe, dignified and intelligent above any of the tribes of the plains. Women belonging to the Crow and Cree tribes were found living with Blackfoot husbands, and although I have met some of these, only one Kootenay woman have I seen in the Blood Indian camp. She spoke her own language and the husband interpreted, while the children conversed in the language of their mother. The husband had lived for several years in the camp of the Kootenay Indians, and his wife had never been from the home of her own people.

The Blackfeet, in their native language, called these people Kutenae, an individual Kootenay being called Kutenaekwan. This latter word was sometimes used as a proper name, one of my Blood Indian friends being named Kutenaekwan. These people are called by various writers : Kootanie, Kootenuha, Koetenay, Cootonais, Cootanie, with other forms of the same name. They were known when De Smet was among them, in 1845, by the general name of the Skalzi, and were divided into two tribes, called the Flat Bows and the Kootenays. Flat Bow and Kootenay have been used interchangeably as names for these Indians. Dawson divides them according to the areas occupied by them, into the Upper Kootenay, Lower Kootenay, Tobacco Plains Kootenay and Flathead Kootenay. Some writers divide them into the Upper and Lower Kootenay Indians. Alexander Henry speaks of the Flat Bows or Lake Indians, and distinguishes them from the Kootenays. He made a trip to the Rocky Mountains in 1811, and came in contact with several Indian tribes. In the Kootenay Plain he found the old tents of the Kootenays made of split wood, thatched with branches and grass. In his journal he says : " Of the several tribes of Indians to the southward and westward of the Kootones we are but only just beginning to be acquainted ; those whom we now actually trade with at present are the following : The Flat Bows or Lake Indians, the Saleeish or Flatheads, the Kully-spell or Earbobs, the Skeetshues or Pointed Hearts, the Simpoils, and the Sapetens or Nez Perce. The Flat Bows dwell on a large lake on McGillivray's river, in its course to the Columbia. They have no horses, and their canoes are made of pine bark, which are very slender and weak. The Flatheads are numerous, and dwell more to the southward along the Saleeish river. They have large numbers of horses. Liquor not having been supplied to the Columbia River Indians, they were free from many of the vices common to the eastern tribes."

They speak a deep, guttural language, called by Howse " the rapid Cootonais," difficult for a stranger to learn, distinct from that spoken by any other tribe, and forming, according to Dr. Chamberlain, a stock by itself. Its grammatical construction has been studied by Drs. Boas and Chamberlain, the latter having prepared a grammar, and vocabularies of the language have been compiled by these writers and by De Smet and Dawson. Like the other Indian tribes, they have a significant sign language. The noun has no cases, the singular and plural are not distinguished by separate forms, and the adjective precedes the noun.

The construction of the language can best be seen by selections of words from those who have specially examined it, the spelling of them being given according to the methods adopted by each writer, Dr. Boas gives the personal and possessive pronouns in this manner:—

I, kamin; thou, ninko; he, ninkois; we, kamina'tla; you, niuko'nisgitl; they, ninko'isis.

My, ka; thy, nis; his, is; our, ka-na'tla; your, ni's-gitl; their, Isis.

In 1859 De Smet and Dr. G. M. Dawson in 1883 collected separate vocabularies of the language, which are worthy of comparison, and a selection from these writers is now given:

	De Smet.	Dawson.
Man,	Tittekete	Titkatth
Woman,	Pelgki	Pahtlke
Young man,	Nitstehelg	Unstautl
My father,	Kettitto	Katittoo
My mother,	Kamma	Kamma
My husband,	Kennukglakkanelg	Kanooklukunna
My wife,	Kattelgnammo	Katlnamoo
My son,	Kannagalgli	Kunhutle
My daughter,	Kessuwi	Kasoowin
Pipe,	Koos	Koos
Day,	Jaukisitnemme	Nokunmitun
Night,	Kitsilgmouiet	Tshlmitun
Morning,	Woulgnem	Witlnum
To-day,	Nowsinnemomteke	Nowsunmitka
Yesterday,	Walgkowa	Watlkoo
To-morrow,	Kannewouit	Kunmeit
Thunder,	Numma	Numa
Lightning.	Kelgglettelglig	Akutlimkooattilitlih
Water,	Woo	Wuho
Rain,	Akkeglukkekakkek	Wutlukookoot
Snow,	Akkeglo	Aakloo
Hail,	Kappekamake	Kopkoomaaka
Ice,	Akowete	Akooita
Head,	Ekkeglem	Aklamaana
Hair,	Ekkuktegle	Akukeklanena
Face,	Akkakkane	Akunkuneinna
Forehead,	Akkinnekelg	Akinkutlenam
One,	Nutkwinne	Oke
Two,	Ash	Aas
Three,	Kelgse	Katlsa
Four,	Gatse	Haalsa
Five,	Yikko	Yeko
Six,	Nmisse	Enmissa
Seven,	Wistelggle	Ustatla
Eight,	Ogwatse	Wohatsa
Nine,	Kykittowe	Kaikitoo
Ten,	Ittowe	Ittoo

	De Smet.	Dawson.
Eleven,	Ittowonglenkkwe	Klaooke
Twelve,	Ittowougleash	Klaas
Twenty,	Yowo	Aiyoowoo
Thirty,	Kattesennewe	Katltsanoo
Forty,	Gatsennowo	Kaittsaanoo
One hundred,	Ittowinnowe	Itawoonawoo
Dog,	Gelgsi	Haatltsin
Beaver,	Sinna	Sinna
Gun,	Tewwo	Tawoo
Tobacco,	Yakkyt	Yaket
House,	Kitteglana	Yakaklana

The Upper Kootenay Indians are chiefly canoe Indians, and the Lower horse Indians. This change in the Lower Kootenays has very likely taken place through their contact with the Flatheads, who owned large bands of horses. The Piegans kept up a continual feud with the Kootenays, but made peace with them, that they might be able to pass through their territory to that of the Flatheads to procure horses. When Alexander Henry went amongst them they had no horses, and the subsequent possession of these must have arisen through contact with other tribes. A singular fact is mentioned by Sir George Simpson, namely, a female chief among these people. In 1843, Rowand, an old trader, estimated the Canadian "Kooteenaies" at one hundred lodges, containing eight hundred souls. De Smet visited their camps in 1845 and 1859, and he gives the population of the "Kootenays and Flat Bows" at more than one thousand souls. The census returns for 1891, for the Kootenay Agency, which includes forty-one Shuswap Indians, give the population at six hundred and ninety-six souls. These Indians inhabit the valley of the Columbia and Kootenay rivers, west of the territory of the Blackfoot and Stoney Indians. The name of the people has been given to the valley, district, lake, river and pass in the region where they dwell, a land rich in minerals and beautiful scenery, and abounding in fish and game. Mountain sheep, goats and deer afford a supply of skins which, in former years, were made into garments, but are not used as extensively now, because of the proximity of the white people

and the tendency of the Indians to adopt the customs of their
neighbors. The lofty mountains shelter the tortuous rivulets
which flow into the valley, making numerous beautiful lakes,
and the mild climate is favorable for the growth of grasses,
capable of pasturing large herds of cattle. Amid the beauties
of their home in the valley and plains the people live happily.
Before the advent of the white man they were noted for their
industrious habits, honesty and freedom from vice. Wherever
the white race travels, however, immorality and degradation
mark their trail.

The women are industrious, and are very handy with their
needles at making shirts, moccasins, leggings, and other native
articles, ornamenting them with beads according to the custom
of the native tribes.

There is no native marriage ceremony performed by the
members of this tribe. When a young man desires a young
woman to become his wife, he makes a bargain with her parents
by giving them some presents, and when they start house-
keeping the parents give some articles to the young couple.
An old warrior generally gives a boy his name, that he may
become courageous and successful in war.

Dr. Boaz records their burial customs as he found them
during a visit made to their camps. He says the dead are
buried in an outstretched position. The head was probably
always directed eastwards. They kill the deceased's horse and
hang his property to a tree under which his grave is. The
body is given its best clothing. The mourners cut off their
hair, which is buried with the body.

When a warrior dies, they paint his face red, and bury him
between trees, which are peeled and then painted red. Before
the body is buried, they prophesy future events from the position of his hands. These are placed over the breast of the
body, the left nearer the chin than the right. Then the body
is covered with a skin, which, after a few minutes, is removed.

If the hands have not changed their position, it indicates
that no more deaths will occur in the same season. If they
are partly closed, the number of closed fingers indicates the

number of deaths. If the point of the thumb very nearly touches the point of the first finger, it indicates that these deaths will take place very soon. If both hands are firmly closed, they open the fingers one by one, and if they find beads (torn from the clothing?) in the hands, they believe that they will have good fortune. If they find dried meat in the hand, it indicates that they will have plenty of food. If both hands are closed so firmly that they cannot be opened, it indicates that the tribe will be strong and healthy and free from disease. These experiments are repeated several times.

While a few men bury the body, the mourners remain in the lodge motionless. When those who have buried the body return, they take a thorn bush, dip it into a kettle of water, and sprinkle the door of all lodges. Then the bush is broken to pieces and thrown into a kettle of water, which is drunk by the mourners. This ends the mourning ceremonies.

After the death of a woman, her children must wear, until the following spring, rings, cut out of skin, around the wrists, lower and upper arms, and around the legs. It is believed that else their bones would become weak.

Hemmed in by the mountains and unassisted by the aids of civilization, they were compelled fifty years ago to carry on their agricultural operations with implements of the most primitive kind. They scratched the earth, as I have seen the Blood Indians do, with a pointed stick, and used a piece of brushwood for a harrow. They even made their lines and hooks for fishing. Scanty oftentimes was their fare, as they dug up the wild roots, fished in the lakes and rivers, or hunted in the mountains. Without agricultural implements or firearms, they did not advance rapidly, yet were contented and happy in their poverty.

A change has taken place, and now they are blest with horses, farming implements, and fishing gear. The Lower Kootenays are principally fishermen, and the Upper, hunters. The Lower Kootenays, in their dugout canoes, navigate the lakes and rivers, pursuing their favorite occupation of fishing. The Kootenays sometimes crossed the mountains to hunt buffalo

on the plains, and I have seen them come to the camp of the
Blood Indians to trade horses, of which they have a large
number, and many of them excellent animals.

They dress in the fashion of the prairie tribes, with moccasins,
leggings, breeches, and a buckskin shirt, sometimes replaced by
a blanket coat. The white traveller to the Kootenay camps is
reminded of the camps on the plains by the presence of dogs
innumerable, who make the midnight air resound with their
howls, and steal whatever lies within their reach. They live
in lodges like the plain tribes, covered, in the buffalo days, with
the hides of the buffalo, but now replaced with canvas. Many
of the manufactured articles of these people show ability. Men
and women are skilful in making native goods, consisting of
canoes, cradles, gloves, bows and arrows, fish-spears, pipes,
moccasins, knife-sheaths, whips, necklaces, root-baskets, and
other articles.

Sitting around the old-timers' camp fires on the prairie after
a hard day's ride, a few hours were sometimes spent before
retiring to rest, wrapped up in our buffalo robes, upon the
ground, in relating stories of Indians, buffaloes, half-breeds and
camp life. At one of these camp fires I listened to the tale of
a Kootenay chief.

A priest had gone in the early days to Blackfoot Crossing to
minister to the Blackfeet, and anxious to discourse upon his
religion, had gathered the Indians around him. Whilst engaged
in this pleasant duty he was confronted by one of the Blackfeet, who told his fellows that the white man was not speaking
the truth. He said that a " Kootenay chief had died and his
spirit went to the white man's heaven, as he had accepted the
Christian faith. Upon arriving at the gate of heaven he
knocked to gain admittance, whereupon a messenger came,
inquired his name, and informed him that as he was not a
white man he could not be admitted, but must seek a heaven
elsewhere. Retracing his steps he journeyed along the path
which led toward the heaven of the Indians, and upon reaching
the gate sought admittance. The door-keeper asked his name,
and on hearing it, declared that he was not an Indian, having

10

only the skin of an Indian and the heart of a white man, as he had rejected the faith of his fathers and accepted the religion of the white man. He was told that there were two religions given by the Great Spirit unto man. One was written in a book for the guidance of the white people, who, by following the teachings of the book, would at least find a home in the heaven for the white man; and the other was given unto the Indians, and was written in their hearts, upon the sky, rocks, rivers, and mountains, so that those who follow the teachings of nature, as the Great Spirit speaks unto them, will find a home in the heaven of the Indians. When the Kootenay chief found that he was debarred from entering either heaven, and was left out in the cold, he knew not what to do: but whilst he was thinking seriously over the matter, the attendant had compassion upon him, and said that he would be given another chance of reaching his own final abode. He must return to earth, reject the faith of the white man, and instruct the Indians to retain their own religion, and not to listen to the teachings of the white men."

The Blackfoot prophet found an interested audience, and he continued: "The old Kootenay chief has returned from the dead, and is living at the Kootenay village, and he says that all the Indians are to keep their own religion, or they will not reach the Indians' heaven."

The priest listened attentively to the address of the Blackfoot, and when he had finished, announced to the red men that as it was getting late, he would reserve his reply, and he would call them together to answer the words of the prophet.

Two young men from the camp were sent out that evening stealthily to the territory of the Kootenay Indians to learn the truthfulness of the report. A long journey of two hundred miles lay before them, which they quickly passed over, and in a few days they entered the Blackfeet camp unseen, and reported themselves. A crier went through the camp calling the people together to hear the reply of the priest. Amongst the large number who assembled that day was the prophet, dignified and defiant, assured of his victory over the white teacher, and eager for the recognition of his tribe for his skill and spiritual insight. The white teacher left his lodge and came among the people to address them.   He related the circumstance of the address of the Blackfoot, the departure and return of the young men, their visit to the camps of the Kootenay Indians, where they found the chief referred to, who was alive and had never died.   No vision of heaven had ever been given unto him, and he was a faithful follower of the Great Teacher, and a firm believer in the Christian faith.

Turning toward two young men who stood near, he said:

" Here are two of the sons of the old chief who have come to our camp to corroborate the testimony of the two young men whom I sent to the Kootenay camp."

The people looked at the prophet expecting an answer, but he was silent and crest-fallen, and the words of the white teacher made an impression not easily removed from the hearts of the red men of the plains.

De Smet relates two instances of religious zeal performed by members of the tribe.   An aged chief, who was blind, was anxious to receive baptism, but for a long time had been restrained through poverty.   Guided by his son he travelled to the place where the priest was pursuing his ministrations and informed him that he owed a small debt of two beaver skins, worth about ten dollars, and not until he was able to pay this did he dare approach him for baptism.   He said:

" My poverty has always prevented me from fulfilling this obligation; and until I had done so, I dared not gratify the dearest wish of my heart.   At last I had a thought, I begged my friends to be charitable to me.   I am now in possession of a fine buffalo robe; I wish to make myself worthy of baptism."

The old man and the missionary went to the trading post to settle the debt, but the clerk could not find anything against him on the books, and refused to take the robe.   The old man insisted on giving it, and the clerk steadily refused.

At last he exclaimed: " Have pity on me, this debt has rendered me wretched long enough; for years it has weighed on my conscience.   I wish to belong to the blameless and pure prayer (religion), and to make myself worthy of the name of a child of God. This buffalo robe covers my debt."

Concluding his speech he spread the robe on the ground at the feet of the clerk and departed. Receiving the rite of baptism, he returned home happy and contented.

The other case mentioned was that of a young man who had been baptized in infancy, and removed with his parents to the territory of the Shuswaps, in the mountainous region near the Fraser River. Desiring to marry a young woman who was un-baptized, and having a sister who had not enjoyed that rite, the three persons resolved to visit the missionary that the baptism and marriage ceremony might be performed. The young man had not seen a missionary since he was a child, yet he had sub-jected himself to penance that he might be prepared for his first communion. Upon the day appointed for the consumma-tion of all the rites, he presented himself before the priest, holding in his hand some bundles of cedar chips, about the size of matches, and as he mentioned some particular sin, he handed a bundle of chips to the priest, telling him that the bundle represented the number of times he had committed it. The new method of remembering transgressions was deeply signifi-cant, and manifested sincerity and contrition.

The missionary De Smet went, in 1845, among the Kootenay Indians as their first white religious teacher. The Indians are under the care of the Roman Catholic church, which has min-istered faithfully unto them for nearly half a century. An industrial school is maintained among them by the Government, where the Kootenay youth are instructed by the principal and nuns who devote their time and talents toward the elevation of the rising generation. Good buildings have been erected, and there is no doubt but rapid progress will be made.

The Indians are directed in their efforts in agriculture by an agent of the Government with a measure of success. Good crops have been raised in the vicinity of the Columbia lakes and at Tobacco Plains; but the Lower Kootenays are not very successful in their farming operations, owing to the swampy nature of their Reserve.

Considerable uneasiness has been manifested at times through the influx of settlers, yet no serious difficulties have been experienced. Some of the native customs of these Indians correspond to those of the Blackfeet, especially in their relation to the worship of the sun. They erect a large medicine lodge in the winter, where they dance and pray for snow, that they may be able to hunt game, almost similar to the Blackfoot sun dance, which is held during the summer months. They make vows to the sun, pierce their arms and breasts, and, before going to war, have a great festival, when they make offering to the sun, praying for protection on the warpath and success in their expedition. Like the Blackfeet, they begin some of their religious gatherings by filling a pipe and then turning it toward the four points of the compass, that the sun may have a smoke, which is their consecration vow to their deity.

The medicine men are initiated in a manner almost similar to the Blackfeet. Dr. Boaz says: "The shamans of the Kutona'qa are also initiated in the woods after long fasting. They cure sick people, and prophesy the result of hunting and war parties. If this is to be done, the shaman ties a rope around his waist and goes into the medicine lodge, where he is covered with an elk skin. After a short while he appears, his thumbs firmly tied together by a knot, which is very difficult to open. He re-enters the lodge, and after a short time reappears, his thumbs being untied. After he has been tied a second time he is put into a blanket, which is firmly tied together like a bag. The line which is tied around his waist, and to which his thumbs are fastened, may be seen protruding from the place where the blanket is tied together. Before he is tied up, a piece of bone is placed between his toes. Then the men pull at the protruding end of the rope, which gives way; the blanket is removed, and the shaman is seen to lie under it. This performance is called k'eqnemna'm, "somebody cut in two."

"The shaman remains silent, and he re-enters the lodge, in which rattles, made of pieces of bone, are heard. Suddenly something is heard falling down. Three times this noise is repeated, and then singing is heard in the lodge. It is supposed

that the shaman has invoked souls of certain people whom he
wishes to see, and that their arrival produced the noise.   From
these he obtains information and instruction, which he, later on,
communicates to the people."

Amid the beauties of their mountain home these hardy sons
of the west strive to maintain themselves, but the advancing
bands of white men have made already a change in their condition, the minerals of the Kootenay district attracting the
wealthy and adventurous to seek fortunes in the foothills and
plains where the red men dwell.   Isolated they may remain for
a few years, but the time is not far distant when the railroad
will bring its thousands and the mountain torrents will be
utilized by the white men seeking the rewards of industry.
The red man fails not to mark the change, and predict the fall
of their mighty chiefs, with the departure of the glory of their
tribe.*

THE IROQUOIS INDIANS.

When the European explorers first came in contact with the
Six Nation Indians, they were formed into a confederacy of
five distinct tribes, under the general name of Iroquois.   These
are supposed to have descended from a family pair of tribes,
known as the Huron-Iroquois, of which the Hurons were the
oldest branch.   Of the early history of these tribes when
distinct, we have no records, but the language shows that the
Hurons were the oldest.   When the French explorers reached
New France, they found the Hurons separated from the

* Dr. A. F. Chamberlain, in "American Antiquarian," Vol. XV., pages
292-316 ; Vol. XVI., pages 271-274 ; Vol. XVII., pages 68-72.   Washington Irving's "Captain Bonneville," pages 121-123.   Dawson and Tolmies'
"British Columbia Indian Vocabularies," pages 79-102, 111-124.   "Cana-
dian Institute Proceedings," 1888, pages 145-160.   Pilling's "Bibliography
of Salishan Languages," pages 29-65.   Helen Hunt Jackson's "Century of
Dishonor," pages 434, 437, 438.   Rev. E. F. Wilson's "Our Forest
Children," Vol. III., pages 164-168.   Dr. A. F. Chamberlain, in "Mem.
Intern. Cong. Authr.," Chicago, 1894, pages 282-284 ; also "Journal of
American Folk-Lore," Vol. VII., pages 195-196.   Horatio Hale, in Vol.
VII. "United States Exploring Expedition," Philadelphia, 1846.

Iroquois Confederacy, and at deadly enmity with the members of it, as well they might, for they were the most terrible foes the French or Hurons met in those early years.

The name Iroquois was given to the Five Nations by the French, which Charlevoix says is derived from hiro or hero, meaning, "I have said it," a phrase which they used when they had evaded their speeches, a custom which is still employed by the Indians in the west, as they say, "I am done," or "That is all I have to say."

The French called them Iroquois, but their English name is Six Nation. The Indians, however, had two names by which they designated the confederacy. Aquanoschioni, or "United People," and Hodenosaunee, or the "People of the Long House."

Charlevoix says: "The name Iroquois is purely French, and has been formed from the word hiro, 'I have spoken,' a word by which these Indians close all their speeches, and koue, which, when long drawn out is a cry of sorrow, and when briefly uttered is an exclamation of joy."

Horatio Hale is inclined to seek the origin of their name in Ierokwa, meaning "They who Smoke," or "They who use Tobacco," or briefly, the "Tobacco People." In the sixteenth or seventeenth century, or even earlier than that, the Iroquois separated from the Hurons, and the tribes which were originally a family pair became distinct.*

The traditions of these people inform us that in the prehistoric era a famous Onondaga chief, named Hiawatha, observing that his tribe was being destroyed through continuous wars with other tribes, with skill and determination conceived the plan of uniting several tribes together in a confederacy, whereby they could present a bold front to their enemies.

Amid great opposition he formed the Iroquois League, which

*"Life of Father Isaac Jogues," by Rev. Felix Martin. "Isaac Jogues," by Rev. W. H. Withrow, D.D. Horatio Hale, "Iroquois Book of Rites," pages 9-12, 51, 171. "Life of David Zeisberger," pages 32, 54-57 (see Parkman's "Frontenac, La Salle and Pontiac," Vol. I.) Winsor's "Critical History of America," Vol. III., pages 393, 394. "Life of Peter Jones," page 5.

HURON INDIAN.

STEREO PLATE Co

was composed of Mohawks, Oneidas, Onondagas and Senecas, and became known as the Five Nations. The Tuscaroras united afterward with the confederacy, which has been called since that time the Six Nations.

This league became so powerful that the Hurons, Delawares and Ojibways dreaded the approach of these terrible foes, who roamed as far east as the territory of the Micmacs, and westward to Lake Superior. The Eries occupied a central position between the Hurons and Iroquois, which induced them to remain neutral, and the latter vowing death to all who would not unite with them, the Eries were destroyed. The native name of the confederacy is Kanousionni, meaning " A house extended."

The confederacy was compared to a house which was enlarged in the manner they employed when the families were increased by marriage, by taking out the end of the bark dwelling and making an addition, afterwards closing the end. As the confederacy increased by the addition of tribes, the house was extended, signifying that the members of the confederacy were not distinct tribes, but members of one family.

The Iroquois were known to the Delawares and southern Algonquin tribes as the Mingoes, which is the contraction of a Lenape word, meaning the "People of the Springs," from the fact that they possessed the head waters of the rivers which flowed through the country of the Delawares. This league of the Iroquois made them formidable, extending their influence throughout a great portion of Canada and the Northern States, making the interests of the tribes common, enabling them to cope successfully with their foes, and raising them in the esteem of the white race.

Morgan says : " They achieved for themselves a more remarkable civil organization and acquired a higher degree of influence than any other race of Indian lineage, except those of Mexico and Peru. In the drama of European civilization they stood for nearly two centuries, with an unshaken front, against the devastations of war, the blighting influence of foreign intercourse, and the still more fatal encroachments of a restless

and advancing border platform. Under their federal system
the Iroquois flourished in independence and capable of self-
protection long after the New England and Virginia races
had surrendered their jurisdictions and fallen into the condition of dependent nations ; and they now stand forth upon the
canvas of Indian history prominent, alike for the wisdom of
their civil institutions, their sagacity of the administration of
the league, and their courage in its defence."

The earliest home of the Iroquois was on the St. Lawrence,
from which place they wandered to the State of New York,
spreading themselves over a wide area, until they were met
with roaming through the forests or gliding over the rivers
in their canoes from the Atlantic to the Mississippi, and from
Virginia to the far northern districts of Hudson's Bay, where
the descendants of the early Iroquois voyageurs are still to be
found, speaking no longer their native tongue, but the euphonious Cree of the neighboring tribes. From the high latitudes
they journeyed toward warmer climes through a country well
adapted to their habits ; and it is a singular fact that the white
race has traversed the great highway of the Six Nations with
railways, towns and cities, once populous with the towns of the
Indian allies; but now the habitations of the progressive pale-
faces cover the territory of the adventurous tribes.

The history of the Iroquois or Six Nations has been preserved
by means of an institution peculiar to the Indian tribes, consisting of some of their greatest men being designated wampum
record keepers. When a new chief was to be elected, a
condolence ceremony was held in honor of the deceased chief,
and when the candidate for the position of chief was introduced
the induction ceremony was begun, a new name being given to
the man and the duties of his office recited in a measured chant.
After his installation he took his place among the nobles of his
nation, and then the wampum belts were brought in and the
officiating chief began the reading of the archives of the nation.
The people were conversant with the events recited, having
heard them reported oftentimes, and in this manner the history
of the nation has been preserved.

The Iroquois mythology informs us that the Indians formerly
dwelt underground, but upon learning that there was a fine
country above, they left their subterranean abode and came
upon the surface of the earth. We learn from their myths
that, in the ancient days, they had good and evil spirits, the
latter possessing great power—superhuman beings who could
not be controlled because they had an evil disposition, strong
intellectual abilities and an unconquerable will. One of these
was Atotarho, whose prowess is preserved for us in an Onondaga legend. Horatio Hale gives the substance of this legend
as follows : " Another legend, of which I have not professed to
give the origin both of the abnormal ferocity and of the preter-
human powers of Atotarho. He was already noted as a chief
and a warrior, when he had the misfortune to kill a peculiar
bird, resembling a sea-gull, which is reputed to possess poisonous qualities of singular virulence. By his contact with the
dead bird his mind was affected. He became morose and cruel,
and at the same time obtained the power of destroying men
and other creatures at a distance. Three sons of Hiawatha
were among his victims. He attended the councils which were
held and made confusion in them, and brought all the people
into disturbance and terror. His bodily presence was changed
at the same time, and his aspect became so terrible that the
story spread, and was believed, that his head was encircled by
living snakes."

There is an ancient myth of primeval days, when there
existed nothing but a vast ocean wherein dwelt great monsters
of the deep. In the heavens there abode supernatural beings,
and one of these, a woman, fell through the sky toward the
primeval waters. She found a resting-place upon the back of
a turtle, and one of the water animals having brought her some
mud, she formed the earth. She gave birth to a daughter who
grew to womanhood, and became the mother of two boys
named Juskeha and Tawiscara.

These were twins, and the young woman died in giving
birth to Tawiscara. She was buried, and from her dead body
sprang forth abundant vegetation, which clothed the earth

formed by the grandmother, Ataensic. The two boys grew to
manhood, with dispositions exactly opposite. Juskeha kind
and good, and Tawiscara ignoble and turbulent. Juskeha
found the earth dry and he made springs, rivers and lakes to
beautify and replenish it, but Tawiscara formed a large frog
which drank the water and left the earth a waste. He started
for the country of Tawiscara, and on the way saw the frog
which he pierced, and the waters again flowed over the earth.
His mother's spirit revealed to him the intent of Tawiscara to
slay him, and he accordingly prepared himself against injury.
They agreed to fight, but as they were superhuman beings
they could not kill each other, and according it was resolved
that each should tell the other the weapon which would be
effective in destruction. Juskeha revealed the fact that a
branch of the wild rose would slay him, and Tawiscara acknowledged that a deer's horn would destroy him. The battle
between the two brothers commenced, and Juskeha was
stricken down with a branch of wild rose in his brother's
hand and left for dead. In a short time he revived and struck
Tawiscara in the side with a deer's horn, making a deep wound
from which flowed blood.

He fled, besprinkling the ground with the blood issuing from
the wound, and still Juskeha pursued him as he fled and slew
him. It was impossible to slay him outright, as they were
superhuman beings who could not die, but his power was
broken, and he fled to the far West, where he became the ruler
of the realm of the dead, and there he awaits the coming of all
the Indians to preside over them in the land of spirits. Juskeha
was now free to devote himself to the good of the earth which
his grandmother made, so he stood at the mouth of a cave and
caused animals to issue from it, maiming each one as it came
out, so that it might be caught, but the wolf, by his cunning,
evaded the stroke and was not maimed, which accounts for
the difficulty experienced in catching him.

Afterward men were created, unto whom he gave life and
taught them how to make fire and cultivate the soil. He is
the master of men and of the earth, who is always ready to aid

the hunter as he goes in search of food, and the farmer as he tills the soil. He is the master of life, who helps the people when they are sick and comforts them in trouble. Tawiscara dwells in the far West, whither the Indians go at death; but Juskeha lives in the far East where he presides over the living. His old grandmother lives with him, whose work is to bring death upon all living which is her delight, and therefore men fear this aged ruler over the destinies of men.*

Of the character of the Iroquois one of the Jesuit missionaries, in 1636, said: "You will find in them virtues which might well put to blush the majority of Christians. There is no need of hospitals, because there are no beggars among them; and, indeed, none who are poor, so long as any of them are rich. Their kindness, humanity and courtesy not merely make them liberal in giving, but almost lead them to live as though everything they possess were held in common. No one can want food while there is corn anywhere in the town."

Such was the influence of this confederacy, and so striking their advancement in their savage state, that Parkman, in his work on the Jesuits in North America, said: "Among all the barbarous nations of the continent the Iroquois stand paramount. Elements which among other tribes were crude, confused and embryotic, were among them systematized and concreted into an established polity. The Iroquois was the Indian of Indians. A thorough savage, yet a finished and developed savage. He is perhaps an example of the highest elevation which man can reach without emerging from his primitive condition of the hunter." †

Faithful were they in their alliance with other tribes, but though widely separated from those who refused to co-operate with them, they pursued them with relentless fury, heedless of

---

* Pilling's "Iroquoian Bibliography," pages 93, 156, 188. Brinton's "Myths of the New World," pages 85, 87, 113, 242. "American Hero Myths," pages 53, 60. Hale's "Book of Rites," pages 75, 86. "Life of Zeisberger," pages 36, 37. Loskiel's "Mission of the United Brethren Among the Indians of North America," page 24.

† "The Jesuits in North America," page 47.

distance or danger, until they laid them low in the dust. The war cry of the Kaniounsi was heard upon the shores of Lake Superior and under the walls of Quebec.

The houses of the Iroquois in the seventeenth century were sometimes one hundred feet in length, constructed of bark, having an arched roof, the walls made of posts and poles, planted in rows, with two tiers of platforms running through the interior of the building, and a line of fires in the open space between the platforms. In the latter part of the eighteenth century these long-houses were made to accommodate a few families, a fire being placed on the ground in the middle of the house for each family. Along the top of the house was an aperture for the purpose of allowing the smoke to escape and light to enter, and from the poles of the roof hung the varied stores of the families. A number of these houses, irregularly arranged, formed a town, which was fortified by means of palisades.*

Hospitality is a common virtue among the Indian tribes, and none were more noted for this than the Iroquois, who treated strangers with great respect, preparing for them venison, maize or other native foods in great abundance. When not engaged in hunting, farming, or war, they spent their time in conversing about the great events of peace or war, or in the common affairs of the town, and in various kinds of amusements. Various native dances afforded great amusement, but some of these were used to incite the young men to deeds of bravery, as the warriors danced and sang, and then recited their exploits in war.

When the white people came in contact with the Indians they introduced cards, dice, and other forms of entertainment. The Iroquois became enamoured with card playing and dice throwing, as they lost and won numerous stakes at these games.

In times of peace and war they sang their songs with great effect, arousing or depressing the people, as the subject of the song was of love, war or death. Some of these were chanted, as we find them in the Book of Rites. Horatio Hale gives a

---

* Zeisberger, page 83 ; Loskiel, page 53.

selection from an historical chant, in the Onondaga dialect, which is as follows :

> Haihhaih ! Jiyathontek !
> Niyonkha ! Haihhaih !
> Tejoskawayenton.   Haihhaih !
> Skahentahenyon.   Hai !
> Shatyherarta—Hotyiwisahongwe—
>   Hai !
> Kayaneengoha.   Netikenen honen
> Nene kenyoiwatatye—Kayaneengowane.
>   Hai !
> Wakaiwakayonnheha.   Hai !
> Netha watyongwententhe.

The translation of this section is thus given :

> Woe ! Woe ! Harken ye !
> We are diminished ! Woe ! Woe !
> The cleared land has become a thicket.
>   Woe ! Woe !
> The clear places are deserted.   Woe !
> They are in their graves—they who established it—
>   Woe !
> The great League.   Yet they declared
> It should endure—The great League.
>   Woe !
> Their work has grown old.   Woe !
> Thus we are become miserable.

Men and women had their natural divisions of labor—the men hunting, fishing, building houses and canoes ; and the women attending to their domestic duties, dressing hides, making garments, and caring for the patch of ground containing the crops.   This division of labor, allotting the duties of farmer to the women has been the cause of the Europeans looking upon them as being overburdened and ill-treated, whereas it was their natural division of labor, the women having their rights, which were respected by the tribe.   The children belonged to the mother, and the compensation for the slaying of a woman was double that of a man, as they held that upon them devolved chiefly the continuation of the tribe. Contact with the white race has, however, modified their opinions on these matters, and individual Indians oftentimes treated their wives with coolness, and oppressed them with heavy loads, exhibiting a contemptible spirit, at variance with the teaching of the wise men of the tribe.*

The forests resounded with the war cries of the savage heroes of the confederacy, as with their flint-head lances and arrows and their stone battle-axes they fought with the Hurons or French under Champlain and his successors, or with the Delawares and other tribes. War was their pastime; and

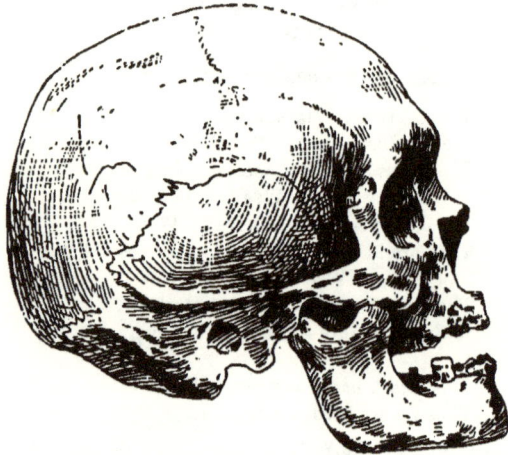

HURON-IROQUOIS SKULL.

relentless was their ferocity when pursuing their foes along the courses of the rivers or through the thickets. Whenever one of the tribe was killed by an enemy, war was declared, as each member was injured by the death of one of their number; but when a member of the confederacy was killed by another, the matter was discussed in solemn assembly, the young men not being allowed to listen, lest they might be incited to retaliate, and the unity and harmony of confederacy be endangered. Thus internal strife was not permitted, and the

* Hales' "Book of Rites," pages 64-66, 167 ; Loskiel, pages 52-60.

peace of the people was maintained. War being declared
against a common foe, preparations were made for going upon
the warpath. The captain of a war party (chosen for his
prowess and good judgment) led the warriors in their war
feast, at which they all ate and drank, smoked and sang, and
with recitals of prospective brave deeds and dancing the whole
night was spent. They painted their bodies in a hideous
fashion.

Almost exhausted with their war dance and its festivities,
they started upon their journey toward the country of the
enemy, carelessly travelling so long as there was no danger,
but so soon as they entered the territory of their foes, they
exercised great care. The records of their exploits were
sometimes painted or carved on trees or rocks, and as they
passed these places they studied them, encouraged and incited
to imitate the valor of their warriors. Amongst all the Indian
tribes prisoners were severely treated, especially if they had
been guilty of acts of cruelty or meanness. Men were burned
at the stake, but women were never treated in this fashion by
the Iroquois. Various forms of cruelty were indulged in before
the unhappy prisoners were burned.*

When peace was determined, the chiefs of the opposing tribes
smoked together the pipe of peace. Faithful have they been in
their adherence to the treaties made, the remembrance of them
being preserved by their belts of wampum, and the traditions
of the record keepers. The League of the Iroquois is an
evidence of their intelligence and faithfulness. It is a model
form of government, a native republic with good laws wisely
administered. The insignia of a chief was striking in its
import, the head-dress surmounted with horns, now disused,
indicating his position as the crown of a European queen.

The native orator in the council strode slowly to and fro as
he delivered his address in figurative, suggestive and beautiful
language, appealing to the shades of the departed, recalling the

* Sir Daniel Wilson, " The Huron-Iroquois of Canada," pages 71, 85.
" Zeisberger," pages 161, 183, 198, 199, 476. " Loskiel," pages 124, 137,
143-159. Hale's " Book of Rites," pages 17, 18, 34, 42, 68-70, 97, 167.

11

former greatness of his nation, and then, with a dignified attitude, bewailed the degeneracy of the latter days, he sought to
arouse a spirit of patriotism among the nobles of his tribe.
With a language well adapted for a patriotic address, the orator
of the Iroquois stood in the council as the prophets of ancient
days, thrilling the hearts of his audience with the recital of
brave deeds, and captivating them with the beautiful imagery
he employed.

The Jesuit Relation of 1660 placed the Iroquois population
at twenty-five thousand. Since that time they have been scattered widely, and many of them were destroyed in their wars
with the French, and in later years during the war of the
Revolution. Many of the Iroquois followed Brant to Canada
during this latter period, and their descendants still remain
with us. Less than eight thousand now dwell in Canada,
located in the Muskoka district, at Caughnawaga, St. Regis,
Oka, the Oneidas on the Thames, the Six Nations at Grand River,
and the small band near Smoking River in the Canadian North-
West. They are no longer the ferocious Iroquois of history,
but a civilized confederacy, as the visitor may easily observe
when he looks upon the homes of the people at the Grand
River or Caughnawaga.

Industrious farmers and mechanics and educated men and
women are to be found upon these Reserves, delighting in art
and literature, or pursuing quietly the various occupations of
common people. Brawny fellows at Caughnawaga astonish the
spectators with their skill at lacrosse, and expert mechanics
and farmers and industrious women take their share of prizes
at the Industrial Fair. Wherever poverty and filth is found
lurking in the homes of these self-supporting communities, the
cause is not far to seek in the drunken habits of some members
of the families.

Many famous warriors are numbered among the Iroquois,
whose memory is treasured as a precious memorial of a brave
people. Among their enemies heroic tales are told of devotion
to their cause against the hated Iroquois. The blood of the
Frenchman is stirred as he listens to the brave deed of Dollard

and his faithful band, as valiant as Leonidas and his Spartan heroes or Scotia's Wallace and his men. The struggling colony at the foot of Mount Royal, predecessor of the commercial metropolis on the St. Lawrence, was scarcely twenty years old, when brave Adam Dollard and his illustrious band of seventeen bade farewell to home and friends, and swiftly sped toward the home of the Iroquois to strike a blow for liberty and peace. The infant colony, sheltered within the recesses of the fortress, trembled at the approach of the red men who sought, by strategy, to surprise and slay the hardy poineers of New France. Frequent were the secret visits of the savages, who vowed to sweep the pale-faces from the face of the earth, and well might soldier and citizen dread the coming of the denizens of the forest, for no quarter was given to any innocent straggler from the palisades, and the peaceful arts of agriculture and commerce were injured, and the peace of the community destroyed through constant fear. None knew when retiring to rest the moment the alarm would be given that the savages were upon them, and too often had the citizens been aroused by their terrible war cry. Spring was drawing near, the time adapted for the advance of the natives, and fear was coming on apace. The future was as dark as ever, with no silver lining to the cloud which overcast the sky.

The same terrible routine of tragedy seemed inevitable, when a daring thought of revenge and peace sprang up in the heart of Adam Dollard. What could he not do with a band of young men to follow him into the heart of the Iroquois country, to strike a blow for freedom and show these cruel red men the stuff of which the pale-face was made. It was a bold thought for a young man of twenty-five, but he was no gentle courtier, fawning at court, but the gallant captain of the forces of Ville Marie, bred to military life, revealing in his stern, swarthy countenance the hardships of former days, and the courage which nestled in his soul, awaiting the hour to find a worthy foe to strike. Gathering a band of heroic men as young as he, and as devoted to their country, he made known his determination, and with one single exception they vowed allegiance to a cause so noble and a plan so fraught with danger. The citizens of Ville Marie might well rejoice at such a daring resolve, and gladly welcome the faintest ray of hope; but what could such a band of men, hardy, generous and brave though they be, perform against three hundred foes accustomed to fight in the forest depths. But Adam Dollard knew and loved the forest paths, warfare with the Indians was his delight, and he longed to do a valiant deed for home and country. Before a notary they made their wills, unburdening themselves with the entanglements of earth; and then, with firm steps and slow, they repaired to the Hotel Dieu, before whose altar they consecrated themselves anew. Tearful eyes watched the hardy band launch their canoes, following them until lost to view they passed away, never more to return. On they sped past the swift waters of Sainte Anne, across the Lake of the Two Mountains, and up the Ottawa, until within a deserted fort they sheltered themselves, awaiting the coming of the terrible foe.

Two Huron chiefs with forty braves came secretly through the forest glades as allies, to find delight in meeting a common foe. The roofless stockade afforded little comfort as they lay ready for the sound of the war-cry, but they had not long to stay, the swift gliding canoes with three hundred warriors were at hand, and the shouts of the savages evinced their joy at finding their opportunity and hope. With savage glee they rushed toward the entrenchment assured of an easy victory, but in many a redman's heart the Frenchman's bullet found its goal, and upon the sod the Iroquois fell to rise no more. Repulsed but not defeated they returned to the attack, bearing in their hands lighted torches made from the canoes of the faithful band, determined to set fire to the stockade, but the steady aim and relentless fire compelled them to desist.

Led on by a daring Seneca chief they rushed toward the fort, but the defiant leader licked the dust and his followers fled away. Bold were the hearts of the Frenchmen, and out they rushed to seize the Seneca and but a few moments elapsed till his head graced the front of the stockade. Wild with rage the Iroquois renewed the attack only to fall back upon their improvised defence. The shades of evening fell upon the combatants, but darkness brought no sleep, for the bullets whizzing as they flew past revealed the wakefulness of the savage horde. The Huron allies had weaker hearts than Dollard and his men, for in the midnight shades they sought safety in flight, leaving the leader and his heroic band alone. Morning came at last to the invaders and their enemies, but the Iroquois had met their match, for these Frenchmen would win or die in the attempt.

The invaders held a conference, unwilling to risk again the chances of defeat. Some counselled retreat, when several bundles of wood were laid on the ground, and each warrior willing to continue the battle was urged to lift one of them. One by one they advanced and lifted the bundles, some through determination and others through dread of being called cowards, until all had signified their intention of contest. Ingeniously they cut poles with their hatchets and fastened them together, making a portable defence, a shield of trees. In this fashion they advanced to the attack, protected by the wooden battery. The French were amazed, unable to comprehend the meaning of this strange proceeding; but soon they learned to their dismay the stratagem of the Iroquois. Rapidly they fired, but strategy had accomplished what valor failed to do. Onward they came, one falling here and there, until they reached the stockade, when Dollard, filling his musketoon with powder and shot, and lighting the fuse, attempted to throw it amongst the invaders, but it fell short, and bursting amongst his men, blinded them, causing such excitement that they left the loop-holes and gave the enemy an opportunity. Casting aside the trees, the Iroquois seized their hatchets and sprang within the stockade, dealing death around. Dollard bravely fought, determined in death to strike a blow for Ville Marie. Beside his comrades he fell, and none remained to tell the story of their fate. The thought of the Iroquois to save their lives that the prisoners might be subjected to a slow torture, did not bear fruit, and they were compelled to return, to tell the brave deeds of this heroic band to the warriors of their camps.

Victorious in death, the heroes of the infant colony won the

day, for the Iroquois wisely thought that if such brave men
were to be found upon the slopes of Mount Royal, no savage
horde could ever break their hearts or sweep their habitations
from their sites beside the majestic stream.

Anxiously the citizens awaited the return of brave Dollard
and the heroic seventeen, but they came not again; and not
until some Huron deserters from the Iroquois told the tale
to eager listeners at Ville Marie did they learn the fate of
their beloved band.   That noble exploit bore fruit in the
early and later days, for many years passed away before the
Iroquois dared to return, and when they mustered courage to
meet in battle the countrymen of brave Dollard, they found
them well prepared for the contest and eager to imitate the
valor of their faithful chief.

In 1642, Isaac Jogues, the Jesuit missionary and martyr, was
captured by the Iroquois and subjected to excessive torture.

During his captivity he was compelled to run the gauntlet
with his companions, became the drudge of the Indian women,
and with his fingers cut off and flesh lacerated, was scoffed at
and inhumanly treated as a sorcerer and friend of the Hurons.
At a subsequent period his flesh was torn in strips from his
body, and he fell under the blow of the tomahawk of the
savage.   During his captivity he baptized some of his enemies
and instructed others in the Christian faith.

Le Moyne, Fremin, Menard, Bruyas and other devoted missionaries toiled among the Iroquois, but with little success,
hindered by frequent wars.   They labored in the State of
New York and Canada with a heroism worthy of admiration,
enduring great hardships and in constant danger of their lives,
and ultimately were compelled to abandon the missions.   Some
of the Christian Iroquois sought instruction and protection
from their Roman Catholic guides near Montreal, where the
mission of St. Francis Xavier was founded for their benefit.
This village was moved to Sault St. Louis, and became Caughnawaga, of which St. Regis is an off-shoot.

Beside the Village of Algonquins, at the Lake of Two Mountains, is another village of Iroquois, and these comprise, with

those mentioned before, the sole remnants of the Iroquois missions of the Jesuits.

Queen Anne and her English subjects were jealous of French interference with the Iroquois, and desirous of securing them as allies in war, sought also to win them over to Protestant Christianity. Missionaries were sent from England to labor amongst them in the States of New York and Pennsylvania, who were zealous in their ministrations, but not successful in leading the natives to change their lives by following the doctrines of Christ.

The Moravians, under the eminent missionary David Zeisberger, were entreated by the American Iroquois to commence a mission amongst them after he had explained to the Sachems his deep interest in them.*

Addressing Zeisberger, in 1742, they said : " Brother, you have journeyed a long way, from beyond the sea, in order to preach to the white people and the Indians. You did not know that we were here ; we had no knowledge of your coming. The Great Spirit has brought us together. Come to our people, you shall be welcome. Take this fathom of wampum. It is a token that our words are true." The faithful missionaries of the Moravian Church met with a measure of success, but we cannot follow them in their work, as we are concerned with the Canadian Indians, and not with their brethren in the United States.

The enthusiasm of Queen Anne for the conversion of the Iroquois was manifested by the gift of a silver communion service to the Mohawks on the Grand River Reserve, bearing the following inscription :

" A. R., 1711. The gift of Her Majesty, by the grace of God, of Great Britain, France and Ireland, and of her plantations in North America, Queen ; to her Indian Chappel of the Mohawks."

Protestant missionary work among the Iroquois was begun by English Church missionaries under the auspices of the New England Company, which was established under the favor

---

* " Life of Zeisberger," pages 319, 320.

of Cromwell, " for the propagation of the Gospel in New England," and was revived on the restoration of Charles II., with the eminent philosopher, Robert Boyle, as its first Governor.

In 1714, the Book of Common Prayer with catechism, and some parts of the Bible were printed in Mohawk at New York. In 1704, the Society for the Propagation of the Gospel began work among the Mohawks in New England, by sending the Rev. Thoroughgood Moor as missionary, who remained but a short time. The Rev. Mr. Freeman, minister of the Dutch Reformed Church at Schenectady continued the work, and translated several portions of the Bible, along with the morning and evening prayers. When the Rev. Mr. Andrews came in 1712, he was given the use of the manuscript of Mr. Freeman, and by the aid of Lawrence Claesse, the interpreter, the Book of Common Prayer was completed and the whole printed. This book became scarce and a new edition was issued. Colonel Daniel Claus, Deputy-Superintendent of Indian Affairs in Canada, supervised the printing of one thousand copies. It was printed at Quebec in 1780 by William Brown, who established a press there in 1763. The publication cost the Government ninety-three pounds and ten shillings. The most of this edition was destroyed during the war, and a new edition, with the Gospel of Mark, translated by Captain Joseph Brant, appended, was published in England in 1787, the Prayer Book being revised by the Rev. Dr. Stuart, missionary to the Six Nation Indians at Grand River, who was aided in his revision by Captain Brant during the residence of the latter at Canajoharie. A later edition was printed in 1842, revised by Archdeacon Nelles, of the Grand River Reserve.

In 1783, Chief Joseph Brant came to Canada with the United Empire Loyalists, bringing with him a large number of Iroquois, who settled at Grand river. Missionary work received an impetus through the influx of Indians, and chiefly by the presence of Brant. The old Mohawk church was built, and the bell, bearing the date 1786, was hung. Ever since that period, earnest missionaries have labored there, the New England

Company spending large sums of money for the education and Christianizing of the people.

Eleven district schools are maintained, and the Mohawk Institute affords abundant educational facilities for the instruction of the youth.

The Methodist Conference sent Alvin Torry among the Iroquois in 1820, and for a long term of years, under the able leadership of William Case, the work of religious training was carried on with energy and success. But our Iroquois confreres have their religious differences, like their pale-faced brethren, and now we have Anglicans, Methodists, Baptists, Plymouth Brethren, and the Salvation Army striving to lead the descendants of savage red men toward a noble life.

The Iroquois language is represented by the separate dialects of the Six Nations. The Huron language, through the migrations of the people, became the Mohawk, which approaches nearest to the Huron speech of the present, revealing to us the fact that the Huron is the source from which all the Iroquois dialects are derived. Such is the harmony of the Mohawk, that Max Müller says: "To my mind the structure of such a language as the Mohawk is quite sufficient evidence that those who work out such a work of art were powerful reasoners and accurate reasoners."

The Mohawk speech was used as the medium of communication with the Six Nations. Yet the members of each of these tribes, when addressing the council, are easily understood by all, except the Tuscarora, which must be interpreted in one or other of the five dialects.

The Iroquois language is perfect in construction, which is seen by the study of its grammatical forms, and especially in the verb, which has nine tenses, three moods, an active and passive voice, and at least twenty forms, showing the various changes which it undergoes.

So great is the wealth of the language that Horatio Hale says: "A complete grammar of this speech, as full and minute as the best Sanscrit or Greek grammars, would probably equal

and perhaps surpass those grammars in extent. The unconscious forces of memory and of discrimination required to maintain this complicated, intellectual machine, and to preserve it
constantly exact and in good working order, must be prodigious."

The Lord's Prayer in the Mohawk tongue, from the old
prayer-book in use among the Six Nation Indians on the Grand
River will show the construction of the language: " Shoegwaniha
karonhyakonh teghsideronh wagwaghseanadokeaghdiste Say-
anertsherah aoedaweghte tsineaghsereh egh neayaweane ne-
oughweatsyake tsioni-nityonht ne-karonhyakonh takyonh ne
keagh weghniserate ne-niyadeweghneserake oegwanadarok
neoni toedagwarighwiyostea ne-tsiniyoegwatswatough tsiniy-
onht ne-oekyonhha tsitsyakhirighwiyosteanis ne-waonkhiyats-
watea neoni toghsa tagwaghsharinet tewadadeanakeraghtoeke
nok toedagwayadukoh tsinoewe niyodaxheah ikea iese saweank
ne-kayanertsherah neoni ne-kashatstenghsera neoni ne-aewese-
aghtshera tsiniyeaheawe neoni tsiniyeaheawe."

The New Testament, portion of the Old Testament, sermons,
tracts, catechisms, hymn books and prayer books have been
published in some of the dialects of the Six Nation Indians.
Grammatic treatises, dictionaries and vocabularies have also
been issued, and to the Iroquois language belongs the honor of
being the first American Indian tongue of which we have any
records.

A noble confederacy, with a beautiful language and an eventful history, has attracted many industrious men and women to
study its archives, counting themselves well repaid by having
fellowship with a people of so great renown.*

---

* Winsor's "Critical History of America," Vol. I., page 425.   Sir Daniel
Wilson's "Huron-Iroquois of Canada," pages 60, 65, 86, 87.   "Artistic
Faculty of Aboriginal Races," pages 106-117.   Horatio Hale's "Language
as a Test of Mental Capacity."   "Development of Language and Book of
Rites."   Pilling's "Iroquoian Bibliography."

THE OJIBWAY INDIANS.

The Ojibway tribe is scattered throughout the Dominion, and embraces several branches, including the Ojibways proper, Mississaugas, and Saulteaux.

The name of the tribe has been spelled in various ways, as Achipoes, Outchepoues, Otchipwes, Ojibways, Ojibwas, Chippewas, and Chippeways.

The term Ojibway, signifies "pucker," derived from the peculiar pucker of the moccasin, or to "roast till puckered up," referring to the inhuman method employed by this tribe, as well as others, of burning the captives taken in war. Some writers have sought the origin of the Ojibway, and indeed of numerous Indian tribes, from the lost tribes of Jewish history, a solution more satisfactory to their own minds than to those of their readers. When the white people first came in contact with the Ojibways, early in the seventeenth century, they found them inhabiting the south-eastern shores of Lake Superior, especially in the vicinity of Sault Ste Marie. This does not, however, appear to have been their original home, as their traditions assert that, long before the advent of the white race, they were living at the salt water in the east, probably on the St. Lawrence.

Henry Warren, a native Ojibway, relates a tradition which he heard in a speech delivered by one of the native priests wherein their religion is symbolized in the figure of a sea-shell, and the migrations of the people recorded.*

" Our forefathers were living on the great salt water toward the rising sun, the great Megis (sea shell) showed itself above the surface of the great water, and the rays of the sun for a long period were reflected from its glossy back. It gave warmth and light to the An-ish-in-aub-ag (red race). All at once it sank into the deep, and for a time our ancestors were not

* A. F. Chamberlain, "The Mississaugas." Winsor's "Critical History of America," Vol. IV., page 175. "American Antiquarian," Vol. VIII., page 388. "Annual Report of the Bureau of Ethnology," 1885-6, pages 150, 183, 184.

blessed with its light. It rose to the surface and appeared
again on the great river, which drains the water of the Great
Lakes, and again for a long time it gave life to our forefathers,
and reflected back the rays of the sun. Again it disappeared
from sight, and it rose not till it appeared to the eyes of the
An-ish-in-aub-ag on the shores of the first great lake. Again
it sank from sight, and death daily visited the wigwams of our
forefathers, till it showed its back and reflected the rays of the
sun once more at Bow-e-ting (Sault Ste Marie.) Here it remained for a long time, but once more, and for the last time, it
disappeared, and the An-ish-in-aub-ag was left in darkness and
misery, till it floated and once more showed its bright back at
Mo-ning-wun-a-kaun-ing (La Pointe Island), where it has ever
since reflected back the rays of the sun and blessed our ancestors with life, light and wisdom. Its rays reach the remotest
village of the wide-spread Ojibways."

Mr. Warren relates another tradition referring to the same
matter, only in another form : " There is another tradition told
by the old men of the Ojibway village of Fond du Lac (Lake
Superior), which tells of their former residence on the shores of
the great salt water. It is, however, so similar in character to
the one I have related that its introduction here would only
occupy unnecessary space. The only difference between the
two traditions is that the otter, which is emblematical of one
of the four Medicine Spirits who are believed to preside over
the Midáwe rites, is used in one in the same figurative manner
as the sea shell is used in the other, first appearing to the ancient
An-ish-in-aub-ag from the depths of the great salt water ; again
on the River St. Lawrence ; then on Lake Huron at Sault Ste.
Marie ; again at La Pointe ; but lastly at Fond du Lac, or end
of Lake Superior, where it is said to have forced the sandbank
at the mouth of the St. Louis River. The place is still pointed
out by the Indians where they believe the great otter broke
through."

According to tradition, the Ojibways separated into different
bands, some travelling towards the south and others westward
and northward on the shores of Lake Superior, while the main

body remained in the vicinity of the Sault. It is evident that a large band of them must have entered Pigeon River, on the north shore of Lake Superior, and travelling westward, become scattered widely throughout Algoma, locating at various points in the Thunder Bay and Rainy River districts, where their descendants still remain.

As they became known as the Bois Forts, the "Hardwood or Timber People," they must have lived for quite a long period in these districts, having entered Manitoba and the North-West Territory.

The Ojibways proper and the Saulteaux have resided in Manitoba for a long time, a large camp of the Ottawas and Ojibways having been located on the present site of the city of Winnipeg in the last decade of the eighteenth century.* From the shores of Lake Superior warriors from this tribe went in bark canoes to Georgian Bay and destroyed the Iroquois, with whom they were at war. Representatives of the tribe are to be found throughout Ontario at various points, and as far west as Fort Ellice in the North-West Territory, while away north of Winnipeg the Saulteaux are found in the hunting grounds of the Cree Indians.† The Jesuit missionaries, early in the seventeenth century, found the Saulteaux in the vicinity of Sault Ste. Marie, and the Mississagas on the River Missisauga. Eastward and westward the Ojibways travelled, until they were to be found throughout Ontario, Manitoba and the North-West. They carried on incessant war with the Sioux and Iroquois, the latter being compelled to sue for peace, and were granted tracts of land by their conquerors near Napanee and Grand River, in the Province of Ontario, and the former being driven southward, along with the Sacs and Foxes, until the Ojibways became the possessors of all the region surrounding the head-waters of the Mississippi.

---

* Dr. Bryce's " John Tanner," page 2.

† Morris' "Treaties with the Indians of Canada." " Life and Journal of Peter Jones," pages 350, 412. Brinton's " Myths of the New World," pages 27, 177. " American Antiquarian," Vols. X., page 337 ; XI., page 33 ; XIV., page 264.

Pequahkoondeba Minis or Skull Island, in Georgian Bay, received its name from the fact that a large number of the Iroquois were killed there by the Ojibways about the time the French arrived in the country.

The defiant attitude of the warrior sometimes covered a heart that was brave, kind and generous, which is sometimes forgotten when we read of their cruel treatment of the prisoners taken in war. Burning was frequently resorted to by wrapping the prisoner within the folds of birch bark, and, after setting it on fire, compelling him to run the gauntlet. The light-hearted Ojibways pursued their enemies in their swift-glancing canoes, stealing upon them and striking them down with unmerciless severity. No quarter was given to the Sioux or Foxes, whom they chased among the islands and along the courses of the rivers, driving them from their haunts toward the south. Many brave deeds were performed by the Ojibway warriors, one of which, recorded by Henry Warren, will suffice :

Biauswah was a noble chief, living with his band in the vicinity of La Pointe, by whom he was held in esteem for his prowess and wise counsel. Having gone for one day's hunt, he was surprised, and his heart filled with anguish, to find the camp destroyed, the lodges burned, and his people dead and scalped. A war party of Foxes had fallen upon his people during his absence and slain them, among whom were the members of his family.

Bent on revenge he followed the trail of his enemies and, reaching their camp, heard the yells of the people as they were rejoicing over their success. Secreting himself in the bush he awaited his opportunity for revenge. The Foxes assembled at a short distance from their camp, having with them an old man and a lad, whom they had secured as captives, and now they made preparations to subject them to torture.

The old man was enveloped in birch bark which they had set on fire, and as he run the gauntlet they beat him until he fell dead at their feet. The young lad was placed on some faggots, arranged in a long row, over which he was to run backward and forward until he was burned to death.

As Biauswah looked upon the scene from his hiding-place he recognized in the lad his own son. His heart was filled with strong affection for the youth, and knowing how helpless he was to rescue him single-handed, he stepped forth from his place of safety as the Indians were about to light the faggots. Much to the amazement of his enemies he bravely strode among them, until he stood near the lad, and then addressing them, said, "My little son, whom you are about to burn with fire, has seen but a few winters; his tender feet have never trodden the warpath, he has never injured you. But the hairs of my head are white with many winters, and over the graves of my relatives I have hung many scalps, which I have taken from the heads of the Foxes. My death is worth something to you. Let me, therefore, take the place of my child, that he may return to his people." His enemies listened in astonishment, and having long desired his death, accepted his proposal. They allowed the young lad to return to his people, and the father was burned in his stead. A terrible revenge was meted out to the Foxes when the lad told his sad tale, for a large war party fell upon the Foxes, destroying so many of them that the remainder left the district and made their home in Wisconsin.*

Proudly the warriors walked through the camp admired by the young men, women and children, wearing on their heads the eagle feather, signal tokens of their bravery. This eagle feather had significant markings, denoting the particular exploit of the warrior. An eagle feather, tipped with a piece of red flannel or horse-hair dyed red, was the privilege enjoyed by one who had killed an enemy. When split from the top toward the middle the feather denoted that the wearer had been wounded by an arrow, or if there were painted upon it a small red spot, it signified that he had been wounded by a bullet. The war bonnet having several eagle feathers was worn only by those who had killed many of his foes, the specific number not being designated.

It is estimated that there are nearly thirty-two thousand

* "Annual Report of the Bureau of Ethnology," 1885-86, pages 183, 299.

Ojibways in Canada and the United States. No definite statistics can be given of the population, as the census returns report other tribes in the same districts and members of other tribes upon the same Reservations. The following returns, taken from the report of the Department of Indian Affairs for 1891, will show the strength of the tribe within the Dominion:

Chippeways, located at the Thames, Walpole Island, Sarnia, Snake Island, Rama, Saugeen, Nawash, and Beausoliel, three thousand and forty-three; Mississaugas, at Mud Lake, Rice Lake, Scugog, Alnwick, and New Credit, seven hundred and

OJIBWAY DRUMS.

ninety. Ojibways and Ottawas of Manitoulin and Cockburn Islands, one thousand nine hundred and four; Ojibways of Lake Superior, two thousand and sixty-five; Ojibways of Lake Huron, three thousand one hundred and seventy-eight; making a total of ten thousand nine hundred and eighty. There are Ojibways and Saulteaux reported with the Cree Indians in Manitoba and the North-West, but we are unable to give any proper estimate of the number of Ojibways. The whole Ojibway population of the Dominion may be safely stated to be about twelve thousand souls.

Seated in the lodges, with a gourd filled with seeds or pebbles or a cylindrical tin box containing grains of corn, the natives sang their sacred songs, accompanied by two or three persons beating upon a drum. Songs of love and war resounded through the camp in the long evenings in which men and women joined, their sweet voices blending together in the weird musical tones, which exerted a strange influence upon the white visitors to their camp. The songs of the Mida, belonging to their sacred festivals, were recorded upon birch bark in the symbolical character of animals, and by the use of these mnemonic records the words and tunes were easily preserved. The members of the medical priesthood composed some of these songs and tunes, the manner of composing them having been taught them during the periods of their initiation to the four degrees of their Religio-Medical Fraternity. The songs of love and war were sung with spirit, according freely with the nature of the subject, and differing in a great measure with the Mida songs, the latter being sung for the purpose of impressing the people with feelings of awe and reverence. Sometimes the people will sing for hours in a lively strain, changing the words and tune.

A Mida song will occupy from fifteen minutes to half an hour in its rendition. Dr. Hoffman has given several illustrations of Mida songs set to Music, of which the following is one:

> " He-a-we-na-ne-we-do, ho,
> He-a-we-na-ne-we-do, ho,
> He-a-we-na-ne-we-do, ho,
> He-a-we-na-ne-we-do, ho,
> Ma-ni-do-we-a-ni, ni-ka-na,
> Ni-ka-na, ho, ho."

The translation of this song is: " He who is sleeping. The Spirit, I bring him, a kinsman."

Their native songs sometimes consist of a single syllable, sung indefinitely. The melodious voices of the Ojibways since they have become in a measure civilized, have been used in singing the hymns of the religious assemblies of the Christians, and their musical talent has been admired by those who have listened to the instrumental bands from Saugeen, St. Clair, Sault Ste. Marie and other Reservations.*

---

* A. F. Chamberlain, " The Mississaugas," page 159. " American Antiquarian," Vol. XI., page 338 ; Vol. XVI., page 85. " Annual Report of the Bureau of Ethnology," 1885-86.

The animated war dance of the natives deeply impressed the
beholder, as the dancers sang with great vehemence. They
danced for amusement, and at their sacred festivals dancing was
frequently indulged in, the men dancing alone. Occasionally
a woman danced in their social gatherings, but the men always,
and then singly. With head bent forward, and body in a
crouching posture the feet were lifted from the ground, keeping
time with the music, but there was no attempt at any particular
movements with the feet. The native spectators oftentimes
made a hoarse sound with their voices, something like a grunt,
at the deeper strains of the music.

The Ojibways had numerous sacred feasts. They prayed and
made sacrifices to propitiate the evil spirits which were supposed
to dwell in the caves, strangely contorted trees, peculiar looking
stones, the rapids of rivers, and indeed in any strange object in
nature. They sought to allay a storm upon the lake by sacri-
ficing a black dog, fastening a stone to his neck and casting
him into the angry waters. Offerings of tobacco, bread, clothing and trinkets were made to the spirits. They blackened
their faces and fasted to ward off the evil influence of the
avenging gods by propitiating them. When a male child was
born the friends of the family were invited to a feast, and a
Mida named as godfather, who dedicated the child to some
special pursuit in life. Stone boulders and erratic pieces of
copper were raised to the dignity of idols, and as the Ojibways
passed them on their hunting expeditions they made offerings
to them. Such stone figures were supposed to be vital, and
became fetiches, the shape having come by nature, was proof
sufficient that they were possessed by spirits.[*]

Peter Jones (Kahkewaquonaby), on one of his missionary
tours to Walpole Island, urged the Ojibways there to embrace the
Christian religion, and received a significant reply in relation
to the native religion from the head chief, Pezhekezhikquash-
kum.

---

[*] Brinton's "Myths of the New World," page 63. "American Antiquarian," Vol. XIV., page 213. "Report of the Bureau of Ethnology,"
1885-6, pages 154, 204, 207, 278.

" Brothers and friends, I arise to shake hands with you, not only with my hands, but with my heart also do I shake hands with you.

" Brothers and friends, the Great Spirit who made the earth, the waters, and everything that exists, has brought us together to shake hands with each other.

" Brothers and friends, I have listened to your words that you have spoken to us this day. I will now tell you what is in my heart.

" Brothers and friends, the Great Spirit made us all; he made the white man, and he made the Indian. When the Great Spirit made the white man he gave him his worship, written in a book, and prepared a place for his soul in heaven above. He also gave him his mode of preparing and administering medicine to the sick, different from that of the Indians.

" Brothers and friends, when the Great Spirit made the Indian he gave him his mode of worship, and the manner of administering and using medicine to the sick. The Great Spirit gave the Indian to know the virtue of roots and plants to preserve life : and by attending to these things our lives are preserved.

" Brothers and friends, I will tell you what happened to some of our forefathers that once became Christians. I have been informed that when the white people first came to this country, our fathers said to one another, ' Come, brothers, let us worship like our white brothers.' They did so, and threw away all that their fathers had told them to do, and forsook the path that their fathers had pointed out to them to walk in. When they had thrown away the religion of their fathers, sickness came among them, and most every one of them died, and but a few escaped death. Again, since my own recollection, there was one man who came among the Indians at the River Miamme, who told them the Great Spirit was angry with them on account of their witchcraft and living in the way of their forefathers. They listened to this babbler, and threw away all their medicines, all their pouches, and all their medicine bags, and everything they used in their arts into the river. They had no sooner done this than great sickness came among them also, and but few escaped death of them that had taken heed to the words of this babbler.

" Now, brothers and friends, if I should follow the example of those that once worshipped like the white man, I should expect to incur the anger of the Great Spirit, and share the same fate of them that perished. I will therefore remain as I am, and sit down alone and worship in that way that the Munedoo Spirit appointed our forefathers to do and to observe.

" Brothers and friends, how can I, who have grown old in sins and in drunkenness, break off from these things, when the white people are as bad and wicked as the Indians ? Yesterday two white men, Christians, got drunk, quarrelled and fought with one another, and one of them is now on the Island with a black eye.

" Brothers and friends, what you have said concerning the evil effects of the fire-waters is very true. Strong drink has made us poor and destroyed our lives.

" Brothers and friends, I am poor and hardly able to buy enough cloth for a pair of pantaloons to dress me like the white man, if I should become a Christian or live like the white man.

" Brothers and friends, I am glad to see you as native brethren, but will not become a Christian. This is all I have to say."*

Among the Ojibways there are several classes of mystery men, including the Wabeno, Jessakid, Herbalists and Mida. The Wabeno, or " Men of the dawn," constitute a class of men who practice mysterious rites by which they confer upon the hunter the power of securing successes in the hunting expeditions, enable men and women to exercise an unfailing influence over certain persons, such as compelling them to fall in love with them, and are able, by the use of magic medicine, to handle redhot stones, or bathe their hands in boiling water without suffering any injury or experiencing any discomfort. In their midnight orgies they dance and sing, pretending to handle fire,

---

* "Journal of Peter Jones," pages 3, 247, 248.

and by means of their superstitious craft wield a powerful influence among the people.

The Jessakid is a prophet, " a revealer of hidden truths," who has received a special gift from the thunder god, by which he performs feats of jugglery which astonish the natives, and hold them in dread of these mystery men. He possesses the power of injuring anyone, even at a distance.

A similar class of men are to be found among the Crees, and many strange stories have I heard upon the plains of the west, of persons having their bodies suddenly covered with warts, being afflicted with paralysis, palsy and other diseases one year distant to a day, according to the time pronounced by the mystery man. They can call to their aid evil spirits to aid them in their work. An empty sack will move upon the ground, a lodge on a calm night sway violently, as if shaken with a strong wind, and when tied by an Indian will unloose themselves, and the rope will be found with the numerous knots still untied in a distant lodge. They are therefore termed sorcerers, and their spiritualistic feats and seances are equal to those of any white wizard or tricks of legerdemain performed by white men.

The herbalist is skilled in the knowledge of plants of medical value, and practices the art of healing. Men and women are to be found in this class, as they are also to be met with amongst the Blackfoot and Cree Indians.

The Mida is a shaman and in his person is united the offices of priest and medical man. The term medical priesthood will appropriately apply to this class of men. There are four degrees or grades of Mida; entrance to each of which is by means of elaborate rites, feasts, special training and ability. The elaborate ceremonial, with the traditions, constitute the religion of the people.

In the seventeenth annual " Report of Bureau of Ethnology " there is a very full monograph on " The Midewiwin or Grand Medicine Society of the Ojibways," by Dr. W. J. Hoffman, which presents all the features of the medical priesthood, and will repay the careful student who desires to know accurately the ancient religious rites of these people.

HERBALIST PREPARING MEDICINE.

The rites of the Medicine Lodge of the Crees and Blackfeet, popularly called the thirst dance and the sun dance, have a striking corroboration in many of the rites of the Ghost Lodge of the Ojibways. The Mida treat the sick and act as the medical and spiritual advisers of the people.

The Ojibways, as all the other native tribes of Canada, are lovers of their pipe and tobacco. At all their social gatherings the pipe is brought out, and after mixing the tobacco with kinni-kinnic, it is lighted and passed around. In their native worship tobacco is offered to their gods, and at their sacred feasts the pipe-stem is pointed toward the sun. They have smoke ceremonies in connection with the Grand Medicine Society, and the calumet dance is a significant feature of their religious rites. When the treaty was made with the Saulteaux in 1873, at the north-west angle of the Lake of the Woods, a dance was given in honor of Lieutenant Morris, and then the pipe of peace was handed to him.* Some of the pipes were beautifully carved, and others had significant pictographs painted on them. The Indians of the Manitoulin Islands made their pipes from the black stone of Lake Huron, the white stone of St. Joseph Island and the red stone of Coteau des Prairies.†

In the early days the men were employed in hunting and fishing, and the women attended to their simple domestic duties, making in their leisure, various ornamental and useful articles. The men manufactured their axes, pipes and other necessary implements of stone, which were discarded through their influence with the white men. They still manufacture beautiful birch-bark canoes, and have added to their occupation of hunting and fishing that of farming.

Through their contact with the white people, the women have been taught basket-making and other useful manufactures. Beautiful mats and dainty articles for the home, ornamented with colored beads and dyed porcupine quills, are made by the women and sold to the white people.

* Morris' "Treaties," page 47.
† Sir Daniel Wilson's "Artistic Faculty," page 91.

The wild rice was gathered from Rice Lake by the women
for food. They went together in pairs in a birch canoe, and
raising it from the water, thrashed it into the canoe, and took
it home. A hole was dug in the ground and lined with a
deerskin, into which the rice was poured, and boys trampled it
until the chaff was removed, when it was afterward fanned,
and was then ready for use.*

Different tribes build different kinds of tents. The Ojibway
lodge was round, covered with bark. The native style of dress
has given place to that worn by the white men. They painted
their faces, fanciful at times, or as a sign of the degree held
by the person as a Mida. The special feature of the native
dress was a garter made of a band of beads from two to four
inches in width, and about twenty inches in length, to the ends
of which were fastened strands of colored wool two feet long,
which were passed round the leg and tied in a bow on the
front part of the leg. The garter was made of various designs,
according to taste, and of different colored beads. When the
Ojibways were receiving their annual distribution of presents
at Holland Landing, in 1827, Captain Basil Hall was there, and
his account of his visit shows us the style of ornaments worn
by the people at that time :

"The scene at the Holland Landing was amusing enough,
for there were collected about three hundred Indians, with
their squaws and papooses, as the women and children are
called. Some of the party were encamped under the brushwood, in birch-bark wigwams or huts, but the greater number,
having paddled down Lake Simcoe in the morning, had merely
drawn up their canoes on the grass, ready to start again as
soon as the ceremonies of the day were over. The Indian
agent seemed to have hard work to arrange the party to his
mind; but at length the men and women were placed in separate lines, while the children lay sprawling and bawling in the
middle. Many of the males, as well as the females, wore
enormous earrings, some of which I found upon admeasurement

---

* "Journal of Peter Jones," pages 181-287.

to be six inches in length; and others carried round their necks silver ornaments, from the size of a watch to that of a soup-plate. Sundry damsels, I suppose at the top of the fashion, had strung over them more than a dozen of necklaces of variously stained glass beads. One man, I observed, was ornamented with a set of bones, described to me as the celebrated wampum, of which everyone has heard; and this personage, with four or five others, and a few of the women, were wired in the nose like pigs, with rings, which dangled against their lips. Such of the papooses as were not old enough to run about and take care of themselves, were strapped up in boxes, with nothing exposed but their heads and toes. So that when the mothers were too busy to attend to their offspring, the little animals might be hooked up out of the way upon the nearest branch of a tree, or placed against a wall, like a hat or a pair of boots, and left there to squall away to their hearts' content." *

When Peter Jones was a child, a grand feast was held for the purpose of giving him a name and dedicating him to the particular care of one of the gods. He was named Kahkeway-quonabay, which means "Sacred Waving Feathers," and referred to the feathers plucked from the sacred bird, the eagle. As the eagle was the symbol of the god of thunder, he was dedicated to the god of thunder. A war-club, denoting power, and a bunch of eagle-feathers, representing the flight of the god of thunder, were given to him as a memorial of the feast, and so long as he retained these he would retain the influence conferred upon him by his god.

The Ojibways were inveterate gamblers, and were not slow to learn the games of the white people. Amongst the native forms of amusement they had a game in some respects similar to the Eskimo game, ajegaung. Peter Jones mentions this game in his book on the Ojibways. It is called Pepengunegun, which means "stabbing a hollow bone."

It consisted, according to the description given by David

---

* "Report of the Bureau of Ethnology," 1885-86, page 298.

Boyle, Curator of the Canadian Institute, of "seven conical bones strung on a leather thong about eight inches long, which has fastened to it at one end a small piece of fur, and at the other a hickory pin three and a half inches long. The game was played by catching the pin near the head, swinging the bones upwards, and trying to insert the point of the pin into one of them before they descended. Each bone is said to have possessed a value of its own; the highest being placed on the lowest bone, or the one nearest to the hand in playing. This bone has also three holes near the wide end, and to insert the pin into any of these entitled the player to an extra number of points. Above each hole is a series of notches, numbering, respectively, four, six and nine, which were, presumably, the values attached." *

Suggestive records were made by the people on birch bark. Birch-bark rolls were made containing the records of songs, traditions, religious ideas, feasts, the geographical features of the country, individual exploits, and various rites of the Grand Medicine Society. The devices of their picture writing were expressive to the minds of the natives, embodying the beginnings of literature amongst a people not blest with the privileges of civilized life.†

The Ojibway language evinces the strength of intellect possessed by the people, in its numerous forms of the verb, the nice distinctions in its grammatical constructions, and the fulness of its vocabulary. The language belongs to the Algonquin family, which includes several important languages spoken by tribes in Canada and the United States.‡

Adopting Baraga's classification the language has no articles. Gender is distinguished by different words, but has two forms, called animate and inanimate. The plural is formed by adding

---

* "Canadian Institute Archæological Report," 1890-91, page 55.

† Brinton's "Myths of the New World," pages 10, 17. "American Antiquarian," Vol. X., page 294.

‡ "Journal of Peter Jones," pages 269,. 383. Wilson's "Artistic Faculty," page 99. "Report of the Bureau of Ethnology," 1882-83, pages 17, 59, 186, 217, 218, 227. "Report of the Bureau of Ethnology," 1885-86, pages 156, 161.

a letter or syllable, without any change in the noun itself, and
there are no less than twelve different terminations for the
plural, seven for the animate, and five for the inanimate nouns.
The noun has many diminutives and four cases, and in order
that the meaning of the sentences may not be ambiguous, there
is a beautiful arrangement of three third persons. There are
five classes of pronouns, but no relatives. The language is rich
in verbs, which are divided into transitive and intransitive.
There are four classes of transitive, and six of intransitive
verbs. There is an active and passive voice, affirmative and
negative forms, four moods, six tenses, and nine conjugations.
A separate paper would be required to discuss the language, so
we shall be compelled to content ourselves with the following
short vocabulary :

Arrow, mitigwaniwi.
Axe, wagakwad.
Bad, matci.
Bag, mashkimod.
Bark (birch), wigwas.
Bear, makwa.
Beaver, amik.
Bed (my), nibigan.
Bird, bineshi.
Black, makati.
Blood, miskwi.
Bone (his), okan.
Book, masinaigan.
Canoe, tciman.
Copper, osawubik.
Darkness, kashkitibikad.
Day, gijig.
Dead, nibo.
Father, nos.
Fire, iskoti.
Fish, gigo.
Forest, mitigwaki.
Girl, ikweseus.

God, kijemunido.
Great, kitci.
Gun, pashkisigan.
Hair, Winisisima.
House, wakaigan.
Ice, mikwam.
Indian, anishinabi.
Iron, bibwybik.
Island, minis.
Knife, mokoman.
Land, aki.
Man, inini.
Moon, tibigesis.
Mother, ningi.
Mouth, odonima.
Night, okweganama.
No, ka and kawin.
Partridge, bini.
Pipe, opwagan.
Red, miskosi.
River, sibi.
Sea, kitcigami.
Sky, gijig.

Snake, ginibig.
Sun, gisis.
Tobacco, asima.
Tree, mitig.
Water, nibi.
Winter, nibon.
He loves, sagiiwi.
He loves him, sagia.
He is loved, segiigos.
I am afraid, nindagoski.
I am ashamed, nindagatc.
I am busy, nindondamita.
I come down, ninbinis-
sandawe.
I come forth, ninmokas.
I come from, nindondji.
I come here, ninbiija.
I come in, ninpindige.
I come out, ninbisagaam.
I come to him, ninbina-
sikawa.

As early as 1641 the Jesuit Fathers, Jogues and Raymbault,
visited the Ojibways at Sault Ste. Marie, to be followed by

Claude Allouez and other missionaries in later years. The Jesuit missions in Canada were confined chiefly to the Micmacs, Huron-Iroquois and Ottawas after this period, although they must have come in contact with the Ojibways without establishing any missions among them.[*]

The first Protestant missions among the Ojibways in Canada were established by the Moravians, who ministered to them when they began the Fairfield mission among the Delawares on the Thames River in 1792. About the year 1820, a strong missionary spirit was aroused among the Christian people of Ontario, and in the ten succeeding years the Ojibway bands were visited by the English Church and Methodist missionaries. Christian influences reached the Ojibways from the mission to the Iroquois on the Grand River, and some were inclined to listen to the teachings of the white men and Indians. The Government was anxious to help the Iroquois, and the churches became eager to reach the natives with the Word of Life. A great impetus was given to the work among the Ojibways by William Case, and subsequently by Peter Jones and John Sunday. Jones and Sunday were natives, who were ordained as missionaries of the Methodist Church. They made long journeys to the scattered tribes on Lake Simcoe, Georgian Bay and as far west as Sault Ste. Marie. They visited Manitoulin Island, preaching to the natives, and returned to tell to delighted audiences the story of their success. Many noble successors have followed in their footsteps, and missions are now widely scattered among the Ojibways. Deuke, among the Moravians; Baraga, of the Roman Catholics; O'Meara, of the English Church; and Hurlburt, of the Methodists, are prominent names among the Ojibway missions; but there have been numerous workers who have toiled faithfully whose names are preserved in the missionary annals and their record is on high.[†]

Wonderful legends relating to the deeds of Nanibozho, the creation of the world, the flood, the thunder god, northern

---

[*] Winsor's "Critical History of America," Vol. IV., pages 268, 286.
[†] "Journal of Peter Jones."

lights, the gift of the good things of this life, and the exploits of the gods, are full of interest, which the reader may find in special works, or sitting beside one of the wise men may listen to in a modified form.*

Since the days of Jonathan Carver many travellers have written about these people. Histories of the tribe, dictionaries and grammars have been prepared, and in the native language the Bible, hymn books, spelling books and other works have been translated. An extensive literature is now in existence for the use of the white and red men who desire to learn about things human and divine.†

A large portion of Ontario was claimed by the Ojibways, who gradually, by selling their land to the Government and by making treaties, have become dispossessed of it. They still possess lands in the Province of Ontario, and the scattered branches of the tribe are located on Reserves.

Whenever any important matters were to be discussed they held a council, and delegated their chiefs to act as spokesmen for them. The ablest men were elected chiefs, and were held in esteem, although some were jealous of their position. They have been noted for their allegiance to the Crown, despite influences which have been brought to bear upon them to beget disloyalty.

As the aged men lay in their lodges they believed that their souls would travel toward the west, and they therefore commanded their friends to deposit in their graves bows and arrows, a knife, dish, spoon, blanket and other articles for their use on the journey. The dead were buried with their heads towards the west to indicate the direction in which the departed spirit had gone. They travelled toward the "Land of the Sleeping Sun." Burial mounds are supposed to have been made by them.

* Brinton's "Myths of the New World, page 23. "American Hero Myths," page 50. "American Antiquarian," Vols. XIII., page 61 ; Vol. XIV., page 342 ; Vol. XV., page 351 ; Vol. XVI., page 31. "Report of the Bureau of Ethnology," 1885-86. Wilson's "Artistic Faculty," page 77. "Huron-Iroquois," page 62.

† Pilling's "Algonquin Bibliography."

Some of them, however, adopted a method practised among the
Blackfeet, of burying in the ground and then erecting a small
house over the grave. Feasts were given in honor of the dead,
and dishes of food brought into the "Grand Medicine Lodge"
for the departed spirits.

The Ojibways held the same animistic belief as the western
Indians, that the souls of the articles deposited in the graves
were of service to them, as being now in the spirit land, they
could live no longer on material food, but must have spiritual
food suitable to their spiritual natures.*

An old myth of these people says, "Gitci Gauzini was a chief,
who lived on the shores of Lake Superior, and once, after a few
days illness, he seemed to die. He had been a skilful hunter,
and had desired that a fine gun, which he possessed, should be
buried with him when he died. But some of his friends not
thinking him really dead, his body was not buried; his widow
watched him for four days, he came back to life and told his
story. After death, he said, his ghost travelled on the broad
road of the dead toward the happy land, passing over great
plains of luxuriant herbage, seeing beautiful groves, and hearing
the songs of innumerable birds, till at last, from the summit of
a hill, he caught sight of the distant city of the dead, far across
an intermediate space, partly veiled in mist, and spangled with
glittering lakes and streams. He came in view of herds of
stately deer, and moose and other game, which, with little fear,
walked near his path. But he had no gun, and remembering
how he had requested his friends to put his gun in his grave,
he turned back to go and fetch it. Then he met face to face
the train of men, women and children who were travelling
toward the city of the dead. They were heavily laden with
guns, pipes, kettles, meats and other articles; ornamented clubs
and their bows and arrows, the presents of their friends. Refusing a gun which an overburdened traveller offered him,

* "American Antiquarian," Vol. X., page 39 ; Vol. XI., page 384.
"Report of the Bureau of Ethnology," 1882-83, page 199 ; 1885-86, pages
171, 278-280.   "Canadian Institute Report," 1891, page 9.

the ghost of Gitci Gauzini travelled back in quest of his own, and at last reached the place where he died. There he could see only a great fire before him and around him, and finding the flames barring his passage on every side, he made a desperate leap through and awoke from his trance. Having concluded his story, he gave his auditors counsel that they should no longer deposit so many burdensome things with the dead, delaying them on their journey to the place of repose, so that almost everyone complained bitterly. It would be wiser, he said, to put such things in the grave as the deceased was particularly attached to, or made a formal request to have deposited with him."

FISHING THROUGH THE ICE.

CHAPTER II.

IN THE LODGES.

MOTHERHOOD IN THE WEST.

MOTHERHOOD in the West is as charming as it is in the East. The Canadian Occident yields not the palm to the lands of the Orient in the quaintness and beauty of its pictures and poems of domestic life.

On a beautiful summer day we wandered among the lodges of the dwellers in the wilderness, in search of health and knowledge. The buffalo-skin lodges were richly painted, and scalp-locks hung adown their sides. Indian child-life sported freely upon the green sward of the prairie, heedless of any danger, and dogs innumerable, of many breeds and colors, howled and growled at the pale-faced intruders into the privacy of their domain.

The dodging of heads and the peering of eyes through the holes in the lodges made a welcome visit somewhat uncomfortable; but there is no royal road to learning, so we must go the way of all the earth in gaining wisdom, even in an Indian camp. We might have chosen prettier spots, but we could not have found any more interesting. Upon the ground, outside of a beautifully painted buffalo-skin lodge, decorated by the hand of the Queen Mother of the lodge, sat a young woman, still under sweet sixteen, nursing a tender babe, snugly hidden within a neatly-embroidered moss-bag. With the becoming modesty of the Indian women, she hung her head as we passed by; and yet we could not help noticing the mother's smile upon her countenance, while upon ours might have been noticed a tinge of pity for the condition of bondage of one so young.

It was a chubby babe, with a fair countenance; and we could not help admiring the papoose, and secretly encouraging the pride which dwelt in the young mother's heart. She was busily plying her needle, embroidering a pair of moccasins, apparently for her lord, judging from the size of them and their shape.

Not being desirous of intruding, we journeyed on until we reached the lodge of Strangling Wolf, an old friend, and, after the usual salutations, we glanced around the lodge to secure a seat from the curling smoke, which hung low, owing to the holes in the lodge, and, from experience, we cared not to try the experiment of standing up longer than our eyes could bear the pain of the smoke. Our talk resumed the wonted strain, narrating the news of the day, and then falling back upon the wonderful days of yore, so full of the romantic deeds of the brave ancestors of the red men. While thus beguiling the time, a faint cry was emitted from a tiny bundle near at hand, and a young woman, with a rueful countenance, turned around to wait upon her babe. We had known her as a young woman of a lively disposition, and were unable to account for the sudden change in her deportment; but we were not long left in mystery, for, as we watched her tending her charge, a smile flitted over our faces, when a second parcel moved, and emitted a sound similar to the first. Ah! here was the secret of the sad countenance. An evil had befallen them in the shape of twins. What evil genius was presiding over their camp? or why should the gods thus send sorrow upon them? "Boys?" "No; worse than that, a thousandfold worse than twin boys. Twins! Girls!" The father morosely gazed upon the tiny strangers, who were unwelcome guests in that home; and not a merry heart was there in that lodge. Fain would we have lingered, but, beating a hasty retreat, we repaired homeward, musing by the way on the strange customs which prevail amongst different peoples of the earth. In a thoughtful mood we wandered, gathering the prairie flowers which grew in our path, when, upon raising our eyes, we beheld a native woman of less than thirty years, homeward

13

KAKABIKITCHIWAN FALLS, WINNIPEG RIVER.

plodding her weary way with her babe strapped upon her shoulders, as her hands were fully occupied, carrying two pails overflowing with water from the swift-flowing river. Poor drudge! And is there no help for her in this life and no hope? Trudging along, she murmured not; and yet she was a victim of premature old age. An aged woman at less than thirty years! It was she who had painted the scenes on the outside of the buffalo-skin lodge, so skilfully done, that the pale-faced stood in admiration listening to the interpretation of this book of history, which told the story of the heroism of her lord and master. It is ever thus

> " Man's work is from sun to sun,
> But woman's work is never done."

Festal songs fell upon our ears, and we turned toward the lodge from whence they proceeded, to learn that young men and old were making merry over a victory, while the mothers sat around the camp dressing hides, cooking food, and smoking their tiny pipes. These were not the peace pipes or the medicine pipes of the men, but the small pipes usually owned by the women. The children gathered near, and the urchins gently took the pipes from their mother's hands, delighted to take a whiff or two, and then to resume their sport.

And such is life!

The dull monotonous beating of the medicine man's drum awakened us from the reverie into which we had fallen, when gazing upon the scene of the camp, and we slowly wended our way toward the lodge of sorrow. A frail woman sat nursing a sick child, and sad and careworn was that gentle face of the native woman. Her mother's heart beat for her darling in his sickness, and she mourned because he rallied not. Oftentimes had the pale-faced ladies asked solemnly and sincerely, " Do the Indian mothers love their children ? " Behold, for answer, the tears trickling adown that mother's face. Soon, alas! too soon; the little form will be wrapped up in its blanket robe, and laid to rest in the crotch of a tree, mourned by the sad woman who sits in the lodge

The sun was fast sinking as we hastened homeward, anxious to cross the turbulent stream before darkness had quite fallen upon us, but we suddenly ceased our rapid pace to listen to the Indian woman's coronach, as it floated upon the evening air. A poor woman paced to-and-fro, singing a sad wailing song, in which we could detect the name of her offspring, and the pathetic words, "Come back! Come back to me!"

Slowly we approached to add our sympathy, and there stood none other than our loved friend Apawakas, with hair unkempt and cut short, bereft of her clean native dress, clothed in an old dirty garment, and without any covering for her head or feet, she stood for a moment, and then slowly paced to-and-fro, uttering the sad wail for her lost child. Her sole garment reached a little below the knee, and we saw with grief the clotted blood upon her legs.

Responsive to the customs of her people, her legs had been cut with a knife and the blood, as it trickled down, was allowed to remain. Her left hand she held transfixed, and then we saw that one of the fingers had been cut off by the first joint. Within the palm of the hand was placed a piece of wood to keep the fingers in position, and some wood ashes had been sprinkled over the bloody member. Unwashen, shunned and in deep sorrow, Apawakas sought the place where her dead child had been laid, and sang the Indian coronach.

With saddened hearts we sought repose that night, grateful that our lot had been cast in a brighter part of our fair Dominion.

HEAD GEAR.

Hats and caps are very necessary articles of clothing, worn and appreciated by all the civilized nations, and by many of the savage tribes of men. Every nation has its own peculiar style of head-dress—from the Oriental turban to the distinctive cap of the patriotic Scot.

Even different stations in life are designated by the style of hat worn. The jester's "sugar-loaf" cap with its bell, the clerical "wide awake," the military "helmet," the jolly tar's

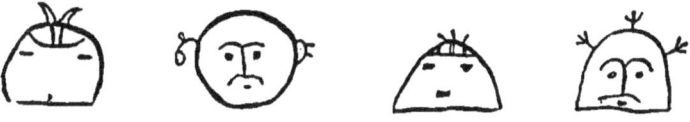

INDIAN MASKS.

"bonnet and ribbons," and the Romish "cardinal's hat," whose color denoted that he was ready to "spill his blood for the sake of Jesus Christ."

There was a period in the Roman history when the wearer of a hat was a free man, and the slave was prohibited from having any covering on his head.

Amongst the Indian tribes, the head was oftentimes uncovered, some wearing long hair, ornamented with various kinds of finery, and the scalp painted. Others did not allow the hair to grow long, but plucked it out by the roots, or rubbed a heated stone upon the scalp, destroying the hair, leaving a portion of the crown divided into two parts, which were braided and fastened with ribbons.

When going to feasts the hair was fantastically decorated, and much pride taken in having it properly arranged. Carelessness in this, however, as in other matters, was prevalent amongst the red men, as well as the more-highly privileged people of the earth.

There are chaplets, made of twigs and leaves woven together, worn by the young men undergoing torture at the sun dance of the Blackfeet. When the native priest is preparing a young man to fulfil his vow to the sun, he takes the chaplet in his left hand, and passes his right hand above and around it four times, muttering some prayers as he performs the ceremony. When he has finished this consecration of the chaplet he places it on the head of the young man. Here is a wreath for the Indian hero who has been successful in his war exploits, and has fitted himself to stand before the medicine pole to offer his sacrifice to the sun. It is not the crown of the runner in the Grecian Games, but it is as sacred, if not more so, in the eyes of the red men of the plains.

The war cap, with its long glowing pendant of eagles' feathers, and its strange besons, is a treasure that can seldom be purchased by the white man, for its proud owner boasts of his prowess, and declares with the utmost complacency, that so long as he wears this prize he is invincible in war. I have gazed upon the war bonnets of the Sioux and Blackfoot

Indians. I have wished that for a time they could speak, so
they might declare, the story of their wanderings, the history
of the wars and thrilling adventures of the people, and thus give
an insight into the customs of a race whose civilization is rapidly
passing away before the advancing strides of the white race.
The eagle feathers worn in the hair or cap were used to denote
acts of courage or success in war. They had significant markings,
designating the fact of the wearer having been wounded with
an arrow or gun, an enemy having been killed by him, and other
acts of bravery. The wearing of the feather was a privilege
enjoyed by warriors. Besons, or charms, were worn by the
Blackfeet upon the head, consisting of the heads or bodies of
birds or animals, representing the tutelary spirit of the wearer.
They were believed to afford protection in time of danger and
to ensure success.

As I sat in a lodge of one of my native friends he took out
his bonnet, placed it on my head and explained the several parts
of it. Taking from his medicine bag the head of a squirrel,
and fastening it on the front of the head-dress, he said that in
war there was given to him power, through the virtue of this
charm, which would make him invincible. The warriors might
pursue him, and his enemies discharge their rifles, but the
bullets would pass by on either side and leave him unhurt.
The tail feathers of the eagle were fastened to the pendant, as
proof of the prowess of the man. The bonnet was made to fit the
head of the wearer, and the pendant was about three feet long.
The influences of modern civilization have introduced the head
dresses of the white people. Upon the heads of the natives
may be seen the cowboy's sombrero, the soft felt hat, with the
crown cut into shreds falling over the sides of the hat, afford-
ing ventilation and adding a new style of ornament, ministering to the vanity of the brave; the "stove-pipe" hat, decked
with various colored ribbons; and the fur cap, which has in
former years covered the brain of some worthy judge in the
east.

Whilst attending an Indian feast some years ago amongst
the Piegan Indians, I could hardly retain my gravity when

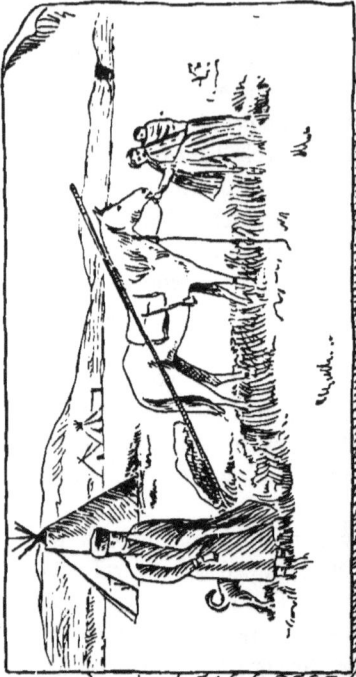

INDIANS OF THE PLAINS.

STEREO PLATE Co. Tor.

I saw an old Indian with a large Scotch cap of the Tam o' Shanter style, amongst the singers in the lodge. Instead of the gentle strains of "Ye Banks and Braes o' Bonnie Doon," there fell upon my ears the native greeting, "Hi! hi!" and the monotonous music of the camps.

Native head-dresses, made of sweet grass braided, are worn by the men. The Blackfoot and the Cree women have no covering for their heads. Within the past few years some of them wrap a handkerchief over the head, and this is the only thing which I have seen worn among them.

One of the strangest caps made came under my observation a short time ago. When I entered a chief's lodge, and had been shown my seat, there sat beside me a large goose, so life-like that I concluded a native taxidermist had arisen in the land of the lodges. Lifting it gently in my hands, I soon learned that it was a new hat, made for the chief by one of his wives!

The ladies of the towns and cities who delight to wear in their hats the feathered songsters of the woods need dote no longer on their ability to follow the fashions, for the red man can far excel in the variety of his head-dress, of which he feels proud.

The young men of the camp are very careful of their hair, often spending more than an hour combing and braiding it. They wear their hair long among the western tribes, and the front of it is cut short and combed down on the forehead, or allowed to grow upright, or rolled in a ball and fastened in front by some ornament. The ends of the plaits of hair are fastened with thread, small ribbon or a piece of fur, and ornaments, consisting of brass beads or any handy article, are placed in it. The wheels of an old brass clock, and even the disc of a pendulum, have been used for this purpose.

Horns were used among some of the tribes by the chiefs as symbolic of power. Masks were also worn resting on the head, and sometimes covering the whole face, for the purpose of amusement, as the false face of the white people, or for shamanistic purposes. The half-breeds cut their hair to half length,

between that worn by the white men and Indians, without
thinning it, so that it is very thick, and for head-dresses they
wear generally common cloth or fur caps or small felt hats.

The masks worn by the Haidas for dancing are made of
wood, ornamented with mother-of-pearl. They are fastened on
the head, and are ornamented with feathers: while from behind,
hanging down to the feet, is a strip of cloth about two feet
wide, covered with ermine skins. These masks represent the
human face and birds.

Upon ordinary occasions, when uninfluenced by civilization,
the natives of the west wear no covering on the head, but deck
their hair with the hair of animals dyed. Rapidly, however,
are they imitating the white people in their styles of head-dress.

AMULETS.

Savage tribes have ever lived in superstitious dread of the
powers of nature, afraid of spirits dwelling in stones, rivers,
caves, trees and mountains, and this fear has caused them to
resort to means of propitiating the spirits and ensuring protection in times of danger. It is but a step from security, safety
from the evils which may afflict body, mind and soul inflicted
by the spirits, to that of protection against human foes, and
obtaining power to peer into the future and find articles which
are lost. Hence arose the origin of fetiches, amulets, and
talismans.*

The fetich is generally an object in nature supposed to possess great power for good or evil, which becomes worthy of
veneration, and is therefore worshipped. Through the help of
the fetich protection against danger is secured, and assistance
given to the worshipper in the performance of certain acts.
Sometimes the fetich is a representation of some natural object,
and then it is closely allied to the amulet or charm.

The amulet is essentially a charm deposited in the home or
carried about the person, as a household god, or a tutelary
spirit.

* " Britannica Encyclopædia," Vol. I., page 781. " American Antiquarian." Vol. XVI., page 121. " Fetichism," by Dr. Fritz Schultz.

Savage people have not been alone in their attempts to invoke the aid of the dwellers in the realm of spirits, for there linger survivals of stages of savagery among the civilized races of men

The Oriental races have, from earliest times, believed in the use of charms as a preservative against evil.

The Greeks and Romans made their amulets of gems, necklaces of coral and shells, and crowns of pearls.

In Ireland the sick were passed by their friends through the "girdle of St. Bridget," that they might be healed; red thread, which is symbolic of lightning, was placed on churns to prevent the milk from being bewitched and yielding no butter.

Brand says: "About children's necks the wild Irish hung the beginning of St. John's Gospel, a crooked nail of a horseshoe, or a piece of a wolf's skin, and both the suckling child and nurse were girt with girdles, finely plaited with woman's hair."

Spells and incantations were in frequent use among the Irish, survivals lingering still in some of the country districts. The genius of Sir Walter Scott seized upon many of these survivals in Scotland, revealing superstition allied with intellectual power. As the Great Unknown lay sick, his piper, John Bruce, spent a whole Sabbath selecting twelve stones from twelve south-running streams that his master might sleep on them and be healed. Not wishing to hurt the feelings of the good man he caused him to be informed that the recipe was infallible, but that it might prove infallible, it was necessary that they be wrapped in the petticoat of a widow who wished never to marry again. The Highland piper gave up the pursuit in despair.

Medical folk-lore gives many interesting facts relating to cures effected through the superstitious belief of persons in the efficacy of harmless objects.

Lady Duff Gordon once gave an old Egyptian woman a powder wrapped up in a fragment of the *Saturday Review*. She informed her benefactress that although she had not been able to wash off all the fine writing on the paper, the small amount she had scraped off and taken had done her a great deal of good.

A NATIVE FISHING CAMP ON SLAVE RIVER.

As great faith as this was shown by a laborer who came to
Dr. John Brown, of Edinburgh, and received a prescription
from him, with the injunction, "Take that, and come back in a
fortnight, when you will be well." At the end of that time
the patient returned with a happy countenance and perfectly
well. Dr. Brown was pleased, and said, "Let me see what I
gave you."

"Oh, I took it, doctor," said the man.

"Yes, I know you did; but where is the prescription?"

"I swallowed it," he replied.

He had made a pill of the paper and taken it, with the belief
that it would cure him.

In the north-east of Scotland it is believed that you can
increase the supply of milk at your neighbor's expense, by
gathering the dew off his pasture and rinsing the milk-pans
with it.

In Shetland it is customary to call in the help of one of the
wise folk who understand the art of casting the "urested
thread," to cure a sprain. A thread spun from black wool,
having nine knots in it, is tied around the sprained leg or arm,
and while performing this act the wise person utters some
unintelligible words. In Chambers' "Fireside Stories" we read:
"During the time the operator is putting the thread around the
afflicted limb he says, but in such a tone of voice as not to be
heard by the bystanders, nor even by the person operated
upon: 'The Lord rade, and the foal slade; he lighted and he
righted; set joint to joint, bone to bone, and sinew to sinew.
Heal, in the Holy Ghost's name!'"

Witches in Scotland, it was thought, could supply themselves
with the milk of their neighbor's cows if they had a small
quantity of hair from the tail of each animal. They would
twist the hair into a rope and tie a knot on it for each animal
which had supplied some hair.

In the National Museum of the Society of Antiquaries of
Scotland is a "flat, oblong stone, four inches long by two and
three-quarters wide, and less than a quarter of an inch in
thickness, notched on the sides, and pierced with two holes, one

and a half inches apart, formerly used as a charm for the cure of diseases in Islay, Argyleshire."

Belief in charms remains in some parts of England, survivals of superstition of former days. It was believed in the north of England that the hangman's rope was a certain remedy for headache. In Hampshire a sure cure for ague was effected by running a thread through nine or eleven snails, saying as each snail was threaded, "Here I leave my ague." After being threaded the snails were held over the fire until they were frizzled, and as they were destroyed the ague disappeared. A common remedy in England for the cure of warts was to tie as many knots in a hair as there were warts, and to throw the hair away. Boys going in to swim tied the skin of an eel about the naked leg to prevent cramp.*

Belief in charms is prevalent among other tribes and races not enjoying such an advanced stage of civilization as the inhabitants of the nations mentioned. The Dutch missionaries found among the Papuans a belief in a universal spirit, represented by various malevolent powers residing in the woods, clouds, sea and storm. These lesser deities were ever ready to inflict injury on men; and the people, to secure protection against their attacks, erected rude images which represented their dead ancestors, whose spirits were supposed to reside in them. The male figures held a spear and shield, and the females a snake. These fetiches were worshipped, and the people resorted to them for safety against the attacks of their nature gods.

Medical charms are used by the Afghans. A remedy for jaundice consists of a twig from a fig tree cut into forty pieces, breathed upon by the wise men, strung together, and hung around the neck of the sick man. The patient is enjoined to abstain from food for about ten days. During a thunderstorm drums are beaten that the person sick with small-pox may not hear the thunder, lest he might become deaf. Amulets, with strange figures written upon them by the medicine men, are

---

* " Report of the Bureau of Ethnology," 1887-88, pages 556-580. " Second Annual Report of the Canadian Institute," page 13.

hung around the neck or fastened upon the bedpost, that the sickness may be driven away.

The native priest among the negroes of the Gold Coast ties a parcel of ropes, coral and other articles around the head, arms, legs and body of the new-born infant, that it may be protected against accidents and disease. The witches of Lapland sold magic cords, having a number of knots, by opening which the shipmasters could obtain, according to directions, the kind of wind they desired. They confessed that they tied a linen towel with three knots in the name of the devil, spat upon them, and then called the name of him who was doomed to destruction.

Among the American Indians, belief in amulets is universal. Sacred cords, medicine head-dresses and shirts, and various

BIRD AMULET OF STONE (HALF DIAMETER).

kinds of articles worn upon the person or applied to it, are supposed to ensure protection against enemies and disease.

During a period of sickness in our Blood Indian camp, as I sat in one of the lodges, an old medicine-man had the people send their children to him. As they stood near him, he took a garment which had been prayed over, and rubbed the body of each, omitting not a single part. They were then supposed to be fully protected from an attack of the prevailing disease. Amulets of birds and animals were fastened upon the head-dresses of the warriors, to protect them in times of danger. Men and women wore small bags around their necks, containing charms, to protect them against disease and the evil deeds of their enemies, and to help them to foretell the future, or find anything which they had lost.

Ceremonial objects of stone have been found in the Huron

ossuaries in Canada, in great abundance. A large number of them are made of Huronian slate. These ceremonial stones are shaped in the form of animals, birds, butterflies, bars, axes, and other objects in nature and art. Some of them are good specimens of native manufacture, evidencing the skill of the workers, and the value set upon these relics. Generally they have a hole in them for the insertion of a handle for suspension to some part of the person. Some of these, if not the most of them, must have been used as amulets.[*]

Visitors to the camps of the natives would never observe them, as they were, in general, worn next the skin, and hidden from view by the garments. This is the case at the present day among the Crees and Blackfoots with the personal

BIRD AMULET (FULL SIZE).

amulet, which must be distinguished from the charm used at dances, feasts, the sun dance, and in times of war and sickness.

A few personal charms have I seen during my residence among the Indians, and these were shown me by those who were my dearest friends. The amulet was carried in a small bag, or in the pocket, by women after adopting the dress of the white people. Some of the women among the tribes of British Columbia still carry about their person the amulet, which is never exposed to the gaze of another, will not be sold, or, if lost, makes the person very unhappy.

Some of the stone relics were, no doubt, used as amulets, and others for the purpose of adornment. We seldom read in books

---

[*] "Fifth Annual Report of the Canadian Institute," page 5.

written by travellers of these ceremonial stone objects, because
they would never be permitted to see them, nor make a
drawing of them. A good collection of these stone relics can
be seen in the museum of the Canadian Institute, Toronto, in
various stages of manufacture, and from different localities in
the Dominion.[*]

A pictograph, drawn by the Dakota Indians near Fort
Snelling, Minnesota, exhibits an article resembling a war-
club, with a handle, held by an Indian in an upright position in
front of another Indian, who has a drawn bow directed toward
his enemy. Evidently the ceremonial war-club was used as an
amulet to protect the possessor in the hour of danger.

Regarding this pictograph, Colonel Mallery says : " The head
of the fetich is a grooved stone hammer of moderate size,

BIRD AMULET (HALF DIAMETER).

measuring from an inch and a half to as much as five inches in
length. A withe is tied about the middle of the hammer in the
groove provided for the purpose, having a handle of from two
to four feet in length. The latter is frequently wrapped with
buckskin or rawhide to strengthen it, as well as for ornamental
purposes. Feathers attached bear mnemonic marks or designs,
indicating marks of distinction, perhaps fetichistic devices, not
understood. These objects are believed to possess the peculiar
charm of warding off an enemy's missiles when held upright
before the body. In the pictograph made by the Dakota
Indian, the manner of holding it, as well as the act of shooting

---

* "Annual Report of the Canadian Institute," 1890-91, pages 1, 45.
" Reports of the Bureau of Ethnology," 1882-83, page 202; 1887-88, pages
589, 591 ; 1889-90, pages 196-202, 275, 515.

14

an arrow by an enemy, is shown with considerable clearness. The interpretation was explained by the draftsman himself. Properties are attributed to this instrument similar to those of the small bags prepared by the shaman, which are carried suspended from the neck by means of strings or buckskin cords."

Ceremonial axes and hammers have been dug up in localities inhabited by the Indians in Canada, made of stone so fragile that they could not be used for offensive purposes. We would judge from their construction that they were employed as amulets, protecting them from the attacks of their enemies. Beads of malachite were used by the Apaches, a bead of this " blue stone," or mineral, being attached to a bow or gun, would make it shoot accurately. To it belonged also the power of bringing rain, and of helping the medicine man in his art of healing and divination. Our western Indians have been known to wear around their necks stones made of various shapes. Diseased children in Brittany were wont to be passed through the dalmeus in order to effect a cure.

Amulets were sometimes made of bone. Among the Blackfeet I have seen necklaces, made of the bones of animals, worn by the men. Necklaces were also made of bears' claws. Sometimes a child's dress was ornamented with bears' teeth, which seemed to be for the purpose of adornment, although I have sometimes thought that they might have served also as a charm. Some of the articles were used as ornaments more than amulets, as I was allowed to touch them, and they were worn on all occasions. They were not held as sacred as the amulet worn next the body or carried in the small bag. Bones are sometimes found in Indian localities in Central Ontario and in the North-West, with perforations. Some of these I have seen used among the Blackfeet for the purpose of making strings of leather. The Indian women used various implements of bone in preparing hides, making moccasins and other articles for wear. Holes were made in bone to be used as charms. Pieces of human skulls were also carried on the person, having holes made in them for suspension. As the native lover carried about with him an image of the maiden he wooed, having holes in it, and when absent in the forest took a small piece of wood, inserting it in the hole representing the heart, believing that the young woman would have her heart touched, yearning after him and returning his love, may there not have been a similar reason, said to be entertained at the present time among the Indians of Cape Croker, for the existence of these perforations in the bones, some of them believing that the holes stuffed with poisonous substances would enable the operator to generate disease or work evil upon the bodies of persons who were at enmity with him. The trepanned skulls give evidence of a belief in persons being possessed by spirits when they were sick, as in epilepsy, and the perforations were made in the skulls to permit the expulsion of the spirit. The persons who survived this treatment were looked upon as mystical people, and when they died, portions of the skull were worn as amulets. Fragments of human skulls were worn as ornaments, as well as amulets.

The Apaches made amulets of lightning-struck wood, generally pine, cedar or fir from the tops of the mountains, which was shaven fine and made to resemble the human form. These were fastened to the cradles of infants and around the necks of children, and sometimes they were carried in the phylacteries of the men. The Ojibway, Sioux and other tribes made medicine-bags of human skin and necklaces of fingers of their enemies, which they used for talismanic purposes. Lingams, made of burnt clay, are worn by the women of some of the tribes of British Columbia, who also carry on their person little images made of stone, wood or cloth, symbolic of the giver of life.*

Amulets have been made of gold and other metals among the various races of men, but iron has gained the prominence as a charm against witchcraft and disease. The Romans drove nails into the walls of their cottages as security against the plague.

Because of the popular belief in horses as luck-bringers, and

* " Report of the Bureau of Ethnology," 1887-88, pages 587-593. "American Antiquarian," Vol. IX., page 368.

the finding of old iron as a good omen, there, in all likelihood,
arose the use of the horseshoe as a talisman protecting the
home and the persons inhabiting it from the evil influences of
witches and the powers of evil. The crescent shape of the
horseshoe added to the popular belief in its virtue. During
the latter part of the last century, and the beginning of the
present, a horseshoe was nailed over the threshold of most of
the houses in the west of London, England, but most of these
had disappeared about the middle of the present century.

Lord Nelson nailed a horseshoe to the mast of the *Victory.*

This popular belief is found among the superstitious of
several countries, and has widely spread over Canada and the
United States.

Amongst the early settlers in the Bay of Quinte District,
Ontario, the fireside tales related on the long winter evenings
were oftentimes of that weird character which made the
listeners tremble as they journeyed homeward in the darkness,
through rough paths in the backwoods. The sighing of the
wind became the voice of a ghost, and the woods were peopled
with elves, which the heated imagination of the backwoodsman
saw or heard among the trees. The horseshoe was placed over
the door of the cottage of the early settler as a protection
against evil; and when some witch was injuring the health or
destroying the property belonging to himself or one of his
friends, the horseshoe was made red-hot and plunged into a
vessel containing cream ready to be churned, which was
believed to be effectual in breaking the charm. Medicine-
cords, head-dresses, bags and shirts, with symbolic designs,
were used by some of the native tribes as amulets. These
were used in religious feasts, some of them being employed in
a public manner that the spectators could see, but they were
sacred, and none but those qualified would be allowed to touch
them. Amulets were sometimes placed in the vicinity of the
lodge, as well as on the person, to afford protection from
disease.

The Rev. Mr. Cowley, Anglican clergyman, laboring among
the Cree Indians, mentions a case of this kind which came

under his observation. He says: "One day I saw something hanging on a tree, and went to look at it. It consisted of twenty small rods, peeled and painted red and black, and fastened together in a plane with cords of bark. A piece of tobacco was placed between the tenth and eleventh rods, and the whole was suspended perpendicularly from a branch of the tree. It belonged to the old chief, who told me that when he

INDIAN COPPER ORNAMENT, WITH NATIVE COPPER BEADS (FULL SIZE).

was a young man he lay down to dream, and that, in his dream, the moon spoke to him, and told him to make this charm, and to renew it every new moon, that he might have a long life. He had regularly done so ever since till the preceding summer, when he almost forgot it, and was taken so ill as to be near dying; but he remembered it, his friends did it for him, and he recovered." *

* Tucker's " Rainbow in the North," page 240.

Talismans were worn in Naples and Pompeii for the purpose
of averting the influence of the evil eye, and a red hand is
stamped on walls by the Arabs in Palestine, to the present day,
for the same purpose.

The love powder of the Ojibways was believed to possess
the power of compelling persons to love each other, and the
hunter's powder of the same people ensured success to the
native on his hunting expedition.

Charms were believed to aid the wearer in curing the sick,
enable him to find lost articles, peer into the future, foresee the
approach of an enemy, bring rain upon the parched crops, and
give strength unto the man who trusted in them. Indeed, the
faith of the natives in their amulets was so strong that they
relied upon them in almost every circumstance, assured that
they would be able to overcome any enemy, avert every danger
and live happy lives. They were unhappy when they lost
them. Many of these superstitions linger amongst all classes
in civilized and savage stages of society, showing us how
nearly we are related to each other in our popular belief
and practice.*

DREAMS.

There have been other dreamers as well as the immortal
Tinker of Bedford jail. Midnight visions have come to the
weary brain of savage and civilized men, as revelations from
the spirit land which they could not enter and live. The airy
nothings have been real things to our forefathers, and even at
the present time men of science are listening intently and striving to interpret the misty shadows of dreamland. Dreaming is
a kind of physiological delirium, which takes place when the
person is sleeping lightly, and may be induced by a train of
ideas preceding the dream. The judgment and will are held in
suspense, the most fantastic scenes passing before the mind of
the most sedate. Generally a slight impression is made upon
the memory, and not more than one dream can be remembered

* James Greenwood, " Curiosities of Savage Life," page 265. Hodder
M. Westropp, " Primitive Symbolism." pages 61-63.

which has taken place during one period of sleeping. Sometimes important problems have been solved in dreams, but
nothing ever occurs which has not in some way been the possession of the individual.

Science has overthrown many of the superstitions which lingered around dreamland, and dependence upon these dark
enchantments has been overthrown; still there remains, amid all
our unbelief, a yearning after the mysteries of the spirit realm,.
and we are sometimes influenced in a great measure by the
nature of these fancies of the brain. The dreams of the savage
intensified his belief in his nature-gods, and though many of
these might not be fulfilled, the single dream realized was sufficient to strengthen his belief. And the savage is not alone in.
giving credit to the phantasies of the brain upon the same plan;
for let a single dream be realized, and we are believers in.
dreams, no matter how many have never been fulfilled.*

The medicine man of the Apaches is believed to be in communication with spirits, who have selected him when a young
man for the position. Each of the shamans or medicine men.
has his familiar spirit, who appears to him in a dream, and becomes his counsellor and guide.

Dr. Corbusier says: "It conducts him on a long journey east
through the spirit land, in order to initiate him into its
mysteries. This journey consumed several nights, the spirit
returning night after night, providing the man be found worthy
to continue it until completed. His faith, secrecy, and endurance are tested on these occasions.

"Soon after they start, a great mountain intercepts them, and
those meet him who endeavor to turn him back by telling him,
that the journey is a perilous one, and that the mountain is too
high for him to cross, and he cannot go through it, as it is solid
rock, but the spirit encourages him and informs him it is only
earth and he can go through it. If he has faith in what the
spirit tells him, and makes the attempt, he easily penetrates the
mountain.

---

* Dr. Warfield, in *Homiletic Review*, on "Dreams and the Moral Life."
"Britannica Encyclopædia," Vol. VII., pages 61-64; Vol. XXII., page
157. Edward Clodd, in Proctor's "Nature Studies," pages 14, 22.

" Beyond it they have to cross eight parallel rivers. They then enter a delightful country, the abode of spirits, who occupy houses which face the rising sun. Farther on he visits the beautiful and silent woman, who lives alone in a round white house, the roof of which is formed of the rainbow, and the door faces the east and sparkles under the rays of the rising sun. Here he sees many beautiful rattles, and is taught the use of them. He at length reaches sunrise, and beholds the all-wise and truthful spirit, Se-ma-che, who dwells there. From him he learns how to cure pain, heal wounds, make charms, etc.

" The man is bound to secrecy until he reaches sunrise, when his journey ends, and he is at liberty to proclaim himself a medicine man or pa-semache. After this his familiar spirit visits him only when he invokes its aid in chants, accompanied by the rattling of a gourd containing some pebbles."

The spirit of the Navajo shaman, in his dreams, travels to the land of spirits where all is silent, and returns to find the world restored in beauty.*

The Blackfoot youth, impressed in his dreams with the idea that he is destined to become a medicine man, sallies forth into the recesses of the mountains, or the secluded coulees, where alone he fasts and prays until he has a vision, which reveals to him his guardian spirit, and the animal in which he dwells. Awaking from his vision he pursues the animal until he kills it, and having stuffed it, preserves it, that he may consult it in times of war and in his duties as medicine man. By the help of the guardian spirit he believes that he can find herbs to help him cure the sick, foretell the future, discover lost articles, and be successful in the art of healing.

The same custom prevails among the Cree Indians.

The Osage Indians believe that dreams are caused through the visits of invisible agents, good and evil, and they are therefore elated or depressed, according to the nature of their dream.

Hunter says that in momentous times, such as the declaration of war, the conclusion of peace and the prevalence of epidemics, the medicine men " impose on themselves long fastings and

* " American Antiquarian," Vol. VIII., page 332 ; Vol. X., page 330.

severe penance; take narcotic and nauseating drugs, envelop themselves entirely in several layers of skins, without any regard to the temperature of the season; and, in a perspiring and suffocating condition, are carried by the people into one of the public lodges, or to some sacred place, where they remain, without the slightest interruption, in a delirium or deep sleep, till the potency of the drug is exhausted. After the performance of this ceremony, while the body is much debilitated, and the mind partially deranged, they proclaim their dreams or phantasms to the astonished multitude as the will or commands of the Great Spirit, made known to them through their intercourse with his ministering agents.

"These pretended oracles are always unfolded in equivocal language, or are made to depend on contingencies; so that if they should not comport with the events which follow, they can charge it to the ignorance or misconduct of the Indians themselves; which is often done, with an assurance and cunning that secures their reputation not only against attack, but even suspicion. They usually predict such things as in the natural order of events would be most likely to take place; such, for instance, as changes in the weather, abundance or scarcity of game, visits from strangers, marriage, sickness, death, etc., and it is perfectly consistent with the doctrine of chances that they should, as they often do, turn out correct. The Indians, however, never take this view of the subject, but, in general, give full credit to the pretensions or absurdability of their prophets."[*]

The dead relations or enemies who appear to the savage in his eerie visions are real things to him. The foes he contends with, the wild animals he meets and his journey to the spirit land are actual things to him. Schoolcraft says of the Indian mind: "A dream or a fact is alike patent to it." It is his shadow, the other self of the man that engages in these conflicts and travels on these journeys to the land of spirits.

It is evident that the Mound-Builders, from the places where the dream-gods were located with the clan totems, were strong

* Hunter's "Captivity Among the Indians," pages 225-227.

believers in dreams. The belief of the savage that his other
self could leave his body in sleep was akin to the possibility of
dead friends coming to visit them in their dreams, and demons
drawn into the soul with the breath.

Sneezing and yawning were to the savage mind proofs of the
nearness of spirits, so that when they sneezed they uttered an
invocation to ward them off. The Indians of North-western
Canada are afraid of their dead relations, believing that,
although they have gone to the Sand Hills, they frequently
return.

The Blood Indians have told me that they sometimes hear
the spirits in the woods at night hooting like an owl, and they
will come to a lodge demanding a smoke. A pipe is then filled
and put outside the lodge for the spirits to smoke, and as they
are no longer material they do not consume the tobacco, but
take the spirit of the tobacco.

Some of my native friends have cautioned me to be careful
when passing trees at night where the bodies of the dead were
deposited, lest they might attack me, and in order to protect
myself have instructed me to whistle or shoot my gun that
I might frighten them away.

But the savage is not alone in his belief in dreams, as is shown
by the modern dream-books consulted by the peasantry, and
the joy experienced by us when a pleasant dream has come
to us; for, while the remembrance of it is retained, it is a real
thing to us. Most of us have apparent good faith in marvel
and myth, and the old stories of our forefathers are repeated in
new forms, although we pride ourselves in our freedom from
the power of the enchanting vision.

The youthful Ojibway blackens his face with charcoal and
builds a lodge of cedar boughs in a secluded spot, where he
fasts and prays until he is thrown into an ecstasy, and beholds
in his vision his familiar spirit.*

The desire to peer into the future and to learn the secrets of

---

* Tucker's "Rainbow in the North," page 19. "American Antiquarian,"
Vol. XI., page 48. "Britannica Encyclopædia," Vol. XV., pages 199-206.
Edward Clodd's "Childhood of the World," pages 21, 22.

the land of spirits caused the savage to betake himself to this method of sending out his other self in dreams to explore the unseen world. Among the native tribes of Canada there arose the practice of sorcery, and a class of shamans who might fitly be named dreamers, whose object was to behold in visions the mysteries forbidden to the common people. The Apaches consult their guardian spirits in dreams that they may find articles which have been lost.

Dr. Corbusier relates an instance of this kind : " A Yavape Indian related to me how one of them found for him a blanket that had been stolen from his uwah. He first presented the man with a buckskin, then described the blanket, told him where he had left it and on what night it was taken. The man went to sleep in order to question his ' familiar.' He had instructed three Indians that when he clapped his hands they must hold him to the ground, with his arms extended at right angles with his body, so that when the spirit came it could not carry him off. They did as he directed, and when he awoke he said that the blanket had been pulled out of the back of the uwah by a man, who buried it in a hole which he had dug in his own uwah, and left it there until the following night, when he dug it up and went in a roundabout way to a certain tree quite a distance off, in which he hid it among the branches. The Indian went to the tree indicated and in it found his blanket."

Charlevoix mentions the fact of some of the tribes in Canada fasting in order that they might have dreams about the animals they were going to hunt, in which they saw the animals and the place where they were to be found. When they had decided to go to war, the leader consulted his familiar spirit in dreams. After starting on the warpath, before entering the territory of the enemy, they held a great feast, and then went to sleep. Those who had dreams went from tent to tent and from fire to fire singing their death songs, in which were incorporated their dreams. After the ceremony was concluded no more fires were lighted and no one spoke except by signs.

Among the Iroquois there prevailed a belief in a race of

demons called False-faces, who possessed the power to injure
the living. In order to propitiate these evil spirits there was
formed a secret organization, called the False-face band. Any
person desirous of becoming a member of this organization
must have had a dream to that effect and then give a feast,
having informed the proper person of his dream ; and the same
things were necessary for anyone who was anxious to cease
being a member. When a sick person dreamed that he saw
a False-face, it was interpreted that it was through the agency
of the band of False-faces that he was to be cured.*

The position in sleep has something to do with the nature of
the dream. Sleeping on the back produces disagreeable dreams,
and it has been stated by observers that sleeping on the right
side begets reminiscences which are old, and the dreams are apt
to be exaggerated, full of vivacity, childish and absurd. When
verses are composed during sleep in this position, although they
may be correct in form, are lacking in sense, the moral faculties
being at work, and the intellectual faculties dormant. Sleeping
on the left side the dreams are more intelligent and are concerned with matters of recent date.

Under the influence of dreams have grown religious beliefs
and ceremonies. The natives of Canada are depressed when no
familiar spirit has been revealed to them, but so soon as there
comes a revelation of this kind they become courageous.
Among the Delawares sacrificial feasts were held, during which
one of the natives danced and sang songs, in which were
included some of his dreams. When a boy dreamed that he
had seen a large bird of prey, as large as a man, flying northward, which said to him, " Roast some meat for me," he was
under obligations to sacrifice the first bear or deer which he
killed to that bird. An elaborate ceremony was performed in
connection with this sacrifice, and men were appointed to sing
their dreams at certain times during the feast.†

The Zulu believes that when he dreams of deceased relations,

* " Third Annual Report of the Bureau of Ethnology," page 144.
† Loskiel's " Mission of the United Brethren Among the Indians," Vol.
I., pages 42, 43.

it is proof that they are alive, and it is dangerous to awaken a man in a dream, because of the possible absence of his soul, whereby he would die. The Navajo Indians believe in the necessity of having dreams to make known unto them the animals they will be able to kill in their hunting expeditions, and without these dreams they will not become successful hunters. Among the Omaha and other Indian tribes mystery songs are given in dreams.*

There have been notable dreams, which have exercised an influence on society and individuals, especially those of Joseph and Nebuchadnezzar. Through some striking dream the whole tenor of the life has been changed.

The biographer of Elizabeth Fry records the influence of a dream as follows: "A curious dream followed her almost nightly, and filled her with terror. She imagined herself to be in danger of being washed away by the sea, and as the waves approached her she experienced all the horror of being drowned. But after she came to the deciding point, or, as she expressed it, 'felt that she had really and truly got real faith,' she was lifted up in her dream above the waves. Secure upon a rock, above their reach, she watched the water as it tossed and roared, but powerless to hurt her. The dream no more recurred; the struggle was ended, and thankful calm became her portion."

Bunyan says: "For often after I had spent this and the other day in sin, I have in my bed been greatly afflicted, while asleep, with the apprehension of devils and evil spirits, who still, as I then thought, labored to draw me away with them, of which I could never be rid."

John Newton believed that God sent him the dream of a precious ring entrusted to his care, afterwards thrown away, and restored to him by a stranger, which led him to become a new man.

Dr. Legge recounts the belief of the Chinese in dreams. From the Charge to Yueh, Minister of Wuting, B.C. 1324-1264, there reads, "The king said, while I was reverently

---

* Alice C. Fletcher, in article on "Indian Music."

thinking of the right, I dreamt that God gave me a good
assistant who should speak for me. He then minutely recalled
the appearance (of the person) and caused search to be made
for him everywhere by means of a picture. Yueh, a builder in
the wild country of Fu-gen, was found like to it. On this the
king made Yueh his Prime Minister, keeping him also at his
side."

Homer said that dreams came from Jove, and Tertullian that
they were sent by God.

Some famous men have been indebted for their highest ideas
to dreams. Lawyers have written out opinions on complicated
cases which have come to them during sleep. Problems have
been solved by students of mathematics. Poets have composed
poems, and sermons have been preached in the visions of the
night.

Coleridge relates the fact of having read of a palace built by
Khan Kubla in "Purchas' Pilgrimage," and then retired to
sleep. He remained to sleep about three hours, during which
time he composed not less than two or three hundred lines.
When he awoke he sat down to write out the poem, but before
it was finished he was called away, and when he returned, the
remaining lines had utterly vanished from his memory. The
fragment of Kubla Khan remains as a marvellous poem, composed in his dream.

Sir Walter Scott mentions, in his notes to the "Antiquary,"
the case of a man who was sorely troubled about the payment
of some tithe money, which he believed was unjustly charged,
having a confused recollection that his father had discharged
the debt before he died. In his dreams he thought the shade
of his father appeared to him and inquired the cause of his
grief, whereupon he stated the facts of his case. The shade of
his father told him that the papers were in the possession of an
aged lawyer, who was living retired at Inveresk, and that he must
seek him out, but as the transaction had occurred several years
ago, he would no doubt have forgotten it. He was instructed
to call to remembrance the fact that this was the only transaction the lawyer had on his account, and to inform him of the

circumstance, that when the father went to pay the account, there was some difficulty in getting change for a Portugal piece of gold, and they repaired to a tavern and drank out the balance of the account.   He sought out the aged lawyer, who had forgotten about the affair until the Portugal gold piece was mentioned, and through this recollection the papers were found and handed over, and then carried to Edinburgh to prove the case.

The Japanese hang their dream pictures in their shrines. When a man dreams of a visit from a fox, which is the messenger of the god Inari, it means good fortune, and he expresses his gratitude by hanging up a picture of his dream.   One of these dream pictures represent a sickly woman asleep under a mattress, and a great dream proceeding from her neck.   She dreams that she sees herself sitting by her fire-box, when the paper sides are suddenly broken through by an enormous serpent, who seems about to swallow her with his gaping jaws. This woman is a worshipper of the goddess Benten, whose messenger is a snake, and in her dream the snake has swallowed her disease, and the woman is cured.*

Thus we see that civilized and savage alike are influenced by the phantasms of a weary brain.   One of the most striking dreams was that of Alexander Duff on the Judgment :

"In vision he beheld numbers without numbers summoned where the Judge was seated on the Great White Throne.   He saw the human race advance in succession to the tribunal.   He heard sentence pronounced upon men—some condemned to everlasting punishment, others ordained to everlasting life.   He was seized with indescribable terror, uncertain what his own fate would be, The doubt became so terrible as to convulse his very frame.

" When his turn for sentence drew near the dreamer awoke, shivering very violently.   The experience left an indelible

---

* " American Antiquarian," Vol. XIII., page 334.   " The Hermits," by Charles Kingsley, pages 195, 196.   Buckle's " History of Civilization," Vol. I., pages 262-274 ; Vol. II., pages 148, 149.   Dr. Abel Steven's " History of Methodism," Vol. II., pages 398, 399.

impression on his mind. It threw him into earnest prayer for
pardon, and was followed by what he long afterward described
as something like the assurance of acceptance through the
atoning blood of his Lord and Saviour Jesus Christ."

There is no class of people, however, who place such implicit
faith in dreams as the American Indians. Numerous striking
examples of the intense belief of the native tribes of Canada on
the subject of visions could be given, but one will be sufficient
for the purpose. Leland, in his "Algonquin Legends," relates a
story told him by an old Passamaquoddy Indian, to the effect
that a young man desired to become as wise and brave as his
father. His father informed him that he got all his luck from
dreams, and that it was possible for him to have such dreams
if he would marry a virgin without cohabiting with her,
and live with her for seven nights. After thinking over the
matter, he asked his father how the matter could be arranged
for him. He was told to select a beautiful young woman, and
obtain the consent of her parents to be married to him.
Having done so, he was to secure seven bear skins, and get one
man to clean one every twenty-four hours, no other person
knowing anything about the matter. After being accepted by
the parents, he sent the seven bear skins to the young woman,
and on being married, they repaired to their wigwam. He
slept on the bear skins, and directed the bride to sleep on her
own bed. Seven days he remained at home, and then suddenly
disappeared, not returning for twenty-five or thirty years, when
he came to his father, possessing the power to divine all things
by dreams. He had only to take his magic bear skin and sleep
on it to dream where good hunting or fishing was to be found.*

Joseph and Daniel were noted interpreters of dreams, and
their successors in dream interpretation are to be found in the
lodges of the red men. The desire to read the mysteries of the
spirit-land, and to know the will of heaven, called into existence,
among civilized and savage races, a class of men whose duty it
was to interpret the dreams of royal personages and people of

* Charles G. Leland's "Algonquin Legends," pages 343, 344. "Eleventh
Annual Report of the Bureau of Ethnology," pages 500, 510, 516.

lesser rank. When the red men had dreams which they could not understand they repaired to their shamans, who gave them an interpretation, upon which the dreamers relied without the least doubt. Whenever their dreams were verified, in whole or part, they generally preserved some article connected with the circumstance as a sacred thing to be used as an amulet. In the presence of our midnight visions we are all cowards, despite our protests to the contrary, and though one hundred dreams are never verified, should a single one be partially fulfilled, we are at once believers in dreams. Until the laws affecting this subject are discovered, we shall still remain in a great measure under their influence.

BACCHUS IN CAMP.

Minegeshing, the Christian Chief of the Ojibway Indians, visited some of the cities of the Eastern States a few years ago, and upon his return the minor chiefs of the tribe gathered around him and said: "Tell us what of all you saw was the most wonderful." Deeply he meditated, and then said: "When I was in the great church and heard the great organ, and all the pale-faces stood up and said, 'The Lord is in his holy temple: Let all the earth keep silent,' I thought the pale-faces have had this religion all these four hundred years, and did not give it to us, and now it is late: that is the most wondeful thing I saw." The chiefs looked upon him and said: "That is, indeed, most wonderful: Now it is late. It is, indeed, noon." The red men hate the double-tongued Indian, and when they have been taught the holier principles and nobler virtues of the Book of God, as possessed by the white man, they fail to understand the non-agreement of his principles with his practice. We do not find in all the native literature of the Indian tribes any Bacchanalian odes and songs in praise of intoxicating drinks. I have listened to Blackfoot songs of love and war, but never have my ears been filled with the maudlin strains of drunken ditties, although many have spoken in its favor and drunk freely of it. The intoxicated Blackfoot, riding

15

wildly over the prairie bereft of clothing, save the breech-cloth, his hair streaming in the wind and his horse covered with lather, has revealed the terrible results which might be expected from the use of liquor among the Indians. Some of these drunken scenes have I witnessed in the camps. When the western natives became intoxicated they began shooting their guns, endangering the lives of the people. The Indians were indebted to the white man for the rum, brandy and whiskey which they drank. The white man called it the "water of life," but the natives did not look so kindly on it, and they named it "fire water," and in a few instances "new milk." In the archives of the seminary of Quebec there is a letter on the liquor question, probably the oldest document relating to that question as it affected Canada. It was written by a French Roman Catholic missionary about 1705, and gave the history of French brandy in Canada. During Bishop Laval's life, and subsequently, there were two parties, one favoring the use of liquor and the other advocating prohibition.* The liquor party consisted of the fur traders, who were supported by the French governors : and the prohibition party, the missionaries, who were sustained in their efforts by the Church. Thus was Church and State arrayed against each other. The importers at Quebec sold the stuff to the small fur traders. The missionary making these statements say that the importers adulterated it by putting in salt and water. Modern arguments were in use in those days for the continuance of the traffic. The traders in whiskey said that the traffic in brandy was beneficial to the State on account of the revenue. Brandy was said to be good for the natives, as it protected them from the cold, and as the Dutch and English traders in New York dealt in whiskey, so the French fur traders must deal in brandy, or lose the fur trade, which would be taken up by these foreigners. When the French missionaries were laboring among the Indians, the Canadian red men argued with them in favor of using liquor. They said : " You say God made everything, if He did, then He made brandy : you say also that everything He made He made for

* "Canadian Archives," by Brymner.

men's use, hence he intended that man should drink brandy, how then dare you prohibit brandy ? "

The *Philadelphia Record* exhumed an old petition presented by the Indians to Penn's first Governor, Markham, in 1681. It is as follows : " Whereas the selling of strong liquors was prohibited in Pennsylvania and not in Newcastle, we find it a greater ill-convenience than before, our Indians going down to Newcastle, and there buying rum and making them more debauched than before in spite of prohibition ; therefore we whose names are hereunder written, do desire that prohibition may be taken off, and rum and strong liquors may be sold (in aforesaid province) as formerly until it be prohibited in Newcastle, and in that Government of Delaware.

His mark + PESEINK.
         „   „   + NAMA SEKA.
         „   „   + KEKA KAPPAN.
         „   „   + JOON GORAS.
         „   „   + ESPRA APE.

The Rev. Pere Maillard says, that during the early French regime a West India drug was largely used. When the faithful missionary arrived at a post, the trader took the adulterated liquor and, steeping tobacco in it, treated each of the Indians to a tin cup filled with the liquor, which soon caused them to demand more, and this had to be paid for in furs. The more they drank, the more they wanted, until becoming maddened under its influence they threw off their clothes and ran wildly through the camp, gashing their own bodies, and shooting and stabbing their wives, children and friends. When they had parted with all their furs they obtained more liquor on credit, to be paid in furs after their next hunt, and when unable to obtain credit they sold their wives and daughters, for immoral purposes, to the French soldiers and traders. Pere Maillard states that the Indians had no liking for brandy, as was shown when a party had only a pint or quart, they would give it all to one in order that he might get drunk. To become drunk was their desire in taking the liquor, as they would fast, so that in drinking a stronger effect might be produced.

The traders charged extortionate prices for the liquor and gave short measure. The missionary knew a trader at Three Rivers who obtained fifty bear skins for liquor sufficient to make one of the natives drunk for one evening. One trader, who took blankets and small clothes of the Indians as a pledge for debts incurred in drinking, was accustomed to make net profits above expenses of five hundred francs per month. Blankets were sold by the traders for four beaver skins each, and on the day following the purchase, they were bought back for a pint of adulterated brandy. When Bishop Laval arrived in the country in 1659, the Algonquins could muster two thousand warriors, and in 1705, chiefly through the use of brandy, they could not muster two hundred fighting men.

In the early history of the Canadian North-West liquor was used by the native population to a great extent, resulting in debauchery and crime. Henry's *Journal* says : "A common dram shop in a civilized country is a paradise in comparison to the Indian trade when two or more interests are engaged." Drinking matches were frequently held by the natives, during which serious fights took place, and some of the natives were killed. When Alexander Henry was in the west in 1801-2, stabbing affrays were of frequent occurrence. "An Indian arrived with his family in a small canoe in fifteen days from Leech lake (Minnesota), and brings intelligence from that place of several Saulteaux having murdered each other in a drinking match a few days before he left. This caused a terrible uproar in the camp here, the murdered persons being near relatives of some here. The former would insist upon retaliating, and it was with the greatest trouble that we prevented them by taking away their arms. They were all drunk, and kept up a most terrible crying, screaming, howling and lamenting the death of their relatives. The liquor only tended to augment their false grief." *

During these periods of grief at the loss of their friends liquor was frequently used. In this custom they are not alone, for in

* C. N. Bell's "Articles on Alexander Henry," in Manitoba Historical Society's Transactions.

some parts of Great Britain and Ireland, at the present day, strong drink is used at every domestic festival. Birth, marriages and deaths are occasions upon which visitors are treated to wine, whiskey and other liquors. Henry states the fact of a Saulteaux girl, aged nine years, having died, and the relatives procured a keg of whiskey to assuage their grief, a fathom of cloth to cover, and a quarter of a pound of vermilion to paint the body of the deceased. The Columbia River Indians and the tribes in the interior parts of the country were not addicted to vice as were the eastern tribes. The less the Indians came in contact with the white people the more were they noted for their morality. The chief cause of the depravity of the natives has been intoxicating drink, which was furnished them by the white people, and the example set by the vaunted civilization of the pale-faces led them on to destruction. Some of the native tribes, as the Haidas of British Columbia, have manufactured a native intoxicating drink, from the use of which there has arisen evil consequences. The literature relating to the native tribes of Canada reveals a state of degeneracy from intemperance, Invariably the strong drink has been introduced by white people, and the Indians, isolated and passionate, have drunk to excess. Crime has increased at a rapid rate, and the tribes have decreased in number.

Sometimes the chiefs have used their influence, and by force of native laws and example, the people have been saved. The strongest force on this matter which has been brought to bear on the red men has been the teaching of Christianity. The religion of the Christ has taught them principles which have liberated them from the thraldom of strong drink. Since Peter Jones remonstrated with the Ojibways at one of their annual treaty payments, the Government of the Dominion has never given liquor to them through any of its agents. Intoxicating drink was furnished to the natives at the annual meetings for the distribution of gifts by the agents of the Government, but after the remonstrances of the missionaries this custom was abandoned. In these later days the Caughnawaga Indians, numbering over one thousand seven hundred souls, have held their industrial and agricultural exhibition with the total exclusion of intoxicating drink. Some of the red men at the Pine Ridge Agency, Dakota, have asked the agent to post notices offering a reward of fifty dollars for evidence by which any person is convicted of furnishing liquor to the Indians. Prohibitory measures are the only kind that can justly be applied to the red men in relation to this question, and when these people have become citizens and are no longer the wards of the nation, they will be better prepared for a permit or license system.

OLD TIMES IN THE NORTH-WEST.

It seems but as yesterday that we went as a tenderfoot to the base of the Rocky Mountains, going from Toronto to Collingwood, then up the lakes past Prince Arthur's Landing to Duluth, across the prairies by rail to Bismarck, up the Missouri on a steamboat for ten days, to Benton, and over the plains on waggons to the old town of Fort Macleod. Travelling as fast as it was possible to go with the party, yet five weeks elapsed before we stood in the pioneer town of Southern Alberta. Anxious to begin work at once, we were soon out upon the prairie, on a good horse, looking after the welfare of Indians and old-timers. The cowboy had not made his appearance, for the buffaloes were roaming the prairies by tens of thousands. The whiskey-traders' regime had passed away, but the old whiskey forts were still in existence. The ruins of the old Bow Fort, twelve miles beyond Morley, and the Conrad Fort on High River were still standing, and as we gazed on them the thought of other days came before us. At the latter place we led a horse into a fine field of oats, the third volunteer crop in that spot. There was an old fort in the Porcupine Hills, and Fort Kipp at the junction of the Old Man and Belly rivers, better known as the Robbers' Roost, was still standing. Further up on Belly River was Slide Out, where the whiskey traders slid out when the Mounted Police came into the country, and Stand Off, where the traders kept a band of Indians at bay. In the

A PRAIRIE SCENE.

Pincher Creek district was Lee's trading-post, and near the Piegan Reservation a house where the policemen rested with their loads of hay on their way to Macleod.

Having suffered keenly in the winter from cold, it was named Freeze Out. Suggestive names were these in the early days. The most imposing of all the forts, however, was Whoop-Up, at the junction of the Belly and St. Mary rivers, kept by Dave Akers. It was a strongly built palisaded fort, with holes cut in the palisades for the insertion of rifles. The cost of building was said to be eleven thousand dollars. When last we stood within the enclosure, where we have spent some pleasant nights, entertained by our friend Akers, who came to an untimely end, the old bell still hung in its place, but the small cannon lay in a corner of the yard, no longer needed, as in the old days. It was customary to allow only a few Indians within these trading-posts at a time, as it was dangerous for many of them to be congregated together, especially after they had become maddened with liquor. Some of the traders engaged in the whiskey business because of the large profits in the trade, for the Indians having once tasted the whiskey, would give large quantities of robes for a small quantity of the stuff. There were others, however, who resorted to it for protection, asserting that they were compelled in defence to do so. An organization was formed among the whiskey traders, laws were drawn up for the regulation of their trade, and a company, named the Spitzi Cavalry, composed of the employees, for the purpose of enforcing the laws. There were many rough scenes of rioting, debauchery and killing of Indians witnessed at these places. The life of an Indian was of little worth to some of these men, and though the majority of those whom we met were generous and brave, yet the tales of other days to which we have listened revealed a state of affairs deplorable, indeed. The whiskey was of an inferior quality, and the natives, maddened with it, killed each other, and provoking the white men caused some of them to be killed. The advent of the Mounted Police put an end to the trade in whiskey among the Indians. Some left the country, but others remained and continued trading without the use of liquor. Upon the whole they were a generous lot of men, anxious to make money, and esteeming lightly the worth of an Indian.

Scattered throughout the country were a number of trappers, traders and small ranchers, who were popularly called "old-timers." Some of them were freighters, who drove the ox-trains across the prairie from Benton, on the Missouri River. A few of them wore the buckskin shirt, made by Indian or half-breed women. Three large and heavy waggons with canvas covers were fastened together, and drawn by sixteen or eighteen oxen. One of these teams was driven by one man, and several of these teams constituted a train, over which there was one "boss." Occasionally they wore their hair falling upon the shoulders, but this was not a general custom. The lowest type of the old-timer was designated a "squaw-man," from the fact that he had married an Indian woman; but this was used as a term of contempt, and was not applied generally, as all of these men lived with Indian women, and some of them were, despite their uncouth exterior, men of education and worthy of respect. They were liberal to a fault, willing to share their last cent and last crust of bread with those who needed help. The old-timers are of three classes : the first comprising the men who have raised themselves to honorable positions in the country, exerting an influence in political and social life. The second class is composed of those who have settled down to farming and cattle raising, and are hard-working and honest citizens. These still retain their independent attitude, begotten by the freedom of the country. Some of them still live with their Indian wives and a numerous progeny of half-breed children, and others have taken unto themselves wives from their homes in the east. Using the significant phraseology of the west and full of information relating to Indians, buffaloes, the country and prairie lore, they are delightful entertainers, and many a pleasant hour is spent by travellers with these worthy pioneers. The third class is found living unsettled lives in small shanties on the rivers, among the foothills, or close to the towns of the west. Occasionally engaged in trapping, loitering in the towns, working in various ways, they eke out a livelihood. Some of them are men of good education, but rovers by nature. They can tell as good a yarn as any sailor, often drawing upon their imagination for the benefit of a gaping company of tenderfeet. Oftentimes around the camp fire on the prairie and in the log shanty have we listened to humorous stories and thrilling adventures with Indians and buffaloes, related with great zest by these old-timers, and we learned to love them. Although accustomed to use strong language in common conversation, they showed such respect for others that they refrained from its use in our presence. Indeed, amongst old-timers and cowboys, only once during our residence did we hear a man deliberately swear in our company, and he was a man of low type from the Old Land. When an oath escaped unconsciously, an apology was given. Reminiscences of old times in Macleod are still vivid. The old town was built on the mainland, but the river changed its course and an island was formed, at one end of which the town stood. The Mounted Police fort and all the buildings, including the Methodist Church, were built of unhewn logs, daubed regularly once a year with mud. The daubing was quite an interesting operation to the pilgrims from the east. Shortly after our arrival in the town the primitive plastering had to be done upon the house, and the work was new to us, so we engaged a half-breed to do it. The building was a low one-storied house with a shingle roof, and was thirty-six feet long by fifteen wide. The snug sum of thirty dollars had to be paid for the job, which was finished in less than a week. A lesson had been taught which was never forgotten, and that was to give all the clean work to others and attend to the dirty jobs ourselves. The mudding operation was therefore always done by ourselves after that lesson.

Dressed in an old suit of clothes, a hole was dug with a spade and the earth made into the proper consistency, sometimes mixed with a few handfuls of prairie grass. Taking the mud in the hands without gloves, it was thrown into the interstices in the walls, filling them up, and then levelling off with the palm of the hand. Generally two coats of mud were necessary, inside and outside, the second being put on after the first had dried. The finishing operation was done with a cloth and mud made very thin, to fill up the cracks and give a smoothness to the surface. The whole was afterwards whitewashed, and the building looked very respectable, indeed. It was a serious matter to plaster a house in this primitive fashion in the winter time, for then a hole had to be dug deep enough to get below the frost, or the soil had to be carried in frozen chunks into the house, thawed out and made into aboriginal plaster with warm water. Twice we were compelled to do this in the erection of log buildings, and never afterward did we care to repeat the operation. With the exception of four or five buildings in the town all had mud roofs. The shingled buildings were as striking in comparison to the others as the city mansion to the humble workman's cottage. Poles were placed on the outside of the mud roof, and boards, cotton, whitewashed or oiled, were fastened upon the poles to carry the water off. Those who were unable to provide this luxury had to be content with erecting a trough for catching water inside. The inside of the houses were lined with "factory cotton" or any other convenient kind of stuff, stretched tightly on the walls and ceiling and then whitewashed to keep out the cold and give an appearance of comfort and respectability. What happy hours we have often spent in these old log buildings, unmindful of the joys of civilization, for which we had suppressed all desires, only eager to do the work of life, and finding in that greater pleasures than dwelling within the precincts of the great city, amid all the comforts of civilized life and the consolations of kind friends.

The two great events of the year were Christmas and the Fourth of July, the former reminding us of universal kinship through belief, and the latter that Brother Jonathan was our nearest neighbor and Canada a long way off, for although living within the Dominion, there was no communication, except by the Missouri river, all travellers preferring that route to crossing the plains. "Ontario" was a by-word. The majority of the people in the town were Americans.

Business went on as usual on Sundays, there being no Sunday

law in the Territories. The first Sunday in town was a specimen
of those which we witnessed for two or three years. An ox
train, with the bull-whackers, had arrived on Saturday night
and camped in the middle of the street. The yokes and the
harness of the oxen lay as they had been taken off, the men sat
around the fire beside their waggons cooking and eating, heedless of the passers by, except occasionally to pass a joke with
some old friend or Indian, and so soon as they had finished
their meal they entered heartily upon their work of carrying
in the freight, which they had brought for the two trading-
posts of the town. The street was crowded with Blackfeet,
Bloods, Piegans and Sarcees, and the stores were filled with
motley groups and spectators. The bowling alley and billiard
rooms were in full operation, the blacksmiths hard at work, and
all the people attending to their individual avocations. Sunday
evening found an interested congregation of men, with not more
than three women, assembled in the log church. There were
the Mounted Police in their red coats, the bull-whacker with
his leather jacket, the old-timer with an honest face, his hair
hanging down on his shoulders, half-breeds and Indians, and
three white ladies. Two or three half-breed children were
there, and one white boy, the only pale-faced child in town.

In a few weeks day and Sabbath schools were started, amid
many difficulties. Some of the scholars could not speak a
word of English, and were unable to pronounce some of the
letters of the alphabet distinctly. Two or three of the half-
breed lads could speak English, Cree and Blackfoot well, and
these were used as interpreters. Sometimes a scholar would
assert his independence, and the door had to be locked to keep
him from running away, and occasionally we had to go to
the home to bring one of them—leading him by the hand or
carrying him on the back, lest he might escape. My wife
taught the day school, and I acted as truant officer and care-
taker, sweeping out the church, kindling the fire and sawing
the wood. Some of these scholars are to-day well-educated,
and occupying good positions in the west. Only one service
could be held on Sunday, as the people lay long in bed in

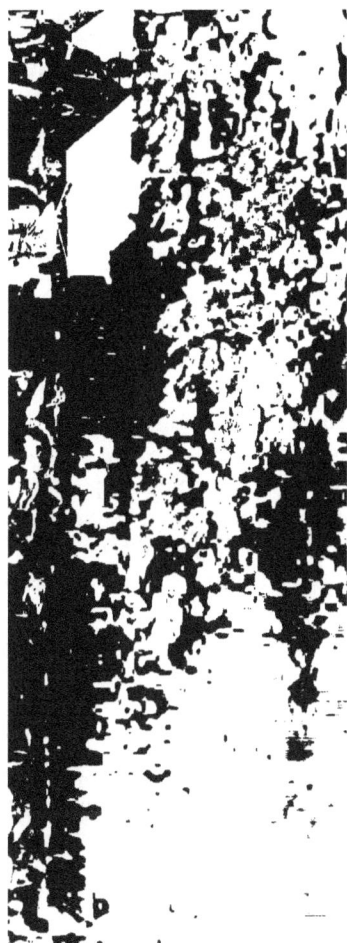

the morning, especially after the Sunday law came into force.
Two of our chief helpers in supplying wood and oil, and in
many small temporal affairs in connection with the school and
church, were a man named Johnston, better known as "Smiler,"
who had a broken nose, and loved his "cups" too well for his
own good; and Harry Taylor, known as "Kamusi," the proprietor of the hotel and billiard rooms.

Strange stuff, some would say, for helpers in religious matters, but could we refuse assistance from men who, prompted
by kindness and interest in the cause, were always willing to
lend a hand? They had no self-interest in the matter, and
though we wished that they might enjoy the strength which
comes from communion with God, we dared not refuse their
help. Indeed, we were glad to call upon them oftentimes for
a meal and shelter, when, after removing among the Indians,
we had to ride to the village in the winter. Smiler would
light the fire and attend to the lamps, and Kamusi would hurry
up his meals to his customers in time to attend service.

During a visit east, of my wife for the space of twelve
months, residence among the Indians was lonely, indeed. We
started from the Reserve for Blackfoot Crossing, one hundred
miles distant. When we arrived there, the Canadian Pacific
railroad was within ten miles east of the Crossing. Sickness
kept us three days at the Crossing, and when we were ready
for the journey by rail, we had to travel six miles west to
reach the construction train, as the road had been built that
distance during our stay. All through Sunday the men worked
hard laying rails, and it was a strange sight to see the large
number of men laying so easily upon the prairie the iron way,
keenly watched by Indians dressed in primitive fashion, who
pondered deeply upon the white man's skill in being able to
make the "fire waggon" travel swifter than the fastest horse
of the red man.

As we were driving swiftly over the prairie the axle of the
buckboard broke, and the nearest blacksmith was sixty miles
distant. Taking the axle with us we had it repaired at
Brandon. We had to pay on the construction train for riding

in a caboose, which was crowded, the snug sum of eight cents
per mile, until we reached Medicine Hat. A colonist car was
provided for, which we had to pay first-class fare until we
reached Moose Jaw, where we enjoyed the luxury of a first-class
carriage, but with definite instructions enforced not to turn the
seats. By the time we reached Winnipeg we were worn out
for the want of sleep, as it was impossible for us to lie down
since we left Blackfoot Crossing. Delightful, however, was it
for us to visit again the haunts of civilization and look into the
faces of friends of other days. Returning alone I reached
Blackfoot Crossing, and in company with a young man of
wealthy connections in England, proceeded to get ready for the
trip across the prairie to Macleod. The horses, which had been
left in charge of an Indian, had been allowed to go astray, and
there was nothing left but to hire two horses, with an Indian to
bring them back after we had reached our destination. When
putting in the mended axle we broke the boxing in the wheel,
and in this sad plight we started. As we rolled along the
prairie the axle would get heated, and then, without unhitching
the horses, we took off the wheel, filled the inside of the hub of
the wheel with axle grease, and allowed the broken box to
revolve in it. This operation had to be repeated frequently
during our journey, but we reached our destination without any
mishap.

During our solitary residence on the Reserve we had forgotten
to receive instructions about making bread, and our first
attempts were very disheartening, tending more to encourage
attacks of billiousness than afford amusement. For several
weeks, indeed for months, the bill of fare was slightly varied,
through failures at bread making, incessant toil in the camps,
and frequent visits of Indians, allowing little time for experiments in cooking. Our common resort was to make the inevitable slap-jack, better known amongst our eastern ladies by the
name of pancakes. Having made the batter and poured it into
a frying-pan, it was held over the fire until sufficiently cooked
on one side, then shaking the pan until loosened, the contents
were thrown into the air with a force that caused the cake to

turn over, and come slap down into the pan, hence the western name of slap-jacks. Well, our bill of fare for a long time consisted of slap-jacks, when we changed it to fried potatoes, and for the remaining days of enforced bachelorhood the bill of fare was as follows: Breakfast: Fried potatoes, bread and tea. Dinner: Bread, tea and fried potatoes. Supper: Tea, fried potatoes and bread.

Our first mission house on the Reserve was built of rough, unhewn logs, the walls eight feet high, a mud roof, half a window, mud floor, and a small door. The building was fifteen feet square. This single room was made to do service for kitchen, drawing-room, dining-room, and bedroom. When any of our friends came to visit us, we stretched curtains across, making temporary partitions, and slept contentedly on the floor. When it rained the water came through the roof, and it was by no means clean. It would drip through the sheets which were fastened up for a ceiling, and everywhere the water soaked through. As this was undesirable, and because lumber could not be purchased to make a floor or a roof, and therefore we could not have eavestroughs outside, the next best thing was to have an eavestrough inside. This was done by attaching a hook to the cotton ceiling with a rope, having a weight at the end. The water ran towards this point, and a vessel placed under the weight caught the water, so that the other parts of our humble habitation were kept dry. For two years we dwelt happily in this shanty, without any yearning after the comforts of civilized life, conscious of the fact that we were in the path of duty, and that was enough. We saw men greedy after filthy lucre enduring as great privations as we, and we felt that missionaries of the Christ, sustained by a great hope and engaged in an eternal work, should be able to do more than those who were seeking to nourish their flesh-garments and minister to sensual wants.

Because of the long journeys, the hard nature of the work, sleeping in lodges and shanties and on the prairie, it became necessary to lay aside the broadcloth garb of civilization, and anxious for utility and economy, the most serviceable style of

MISSIONARY COSTUME.

garment was found to be the suit of buckskin. A plain suit was therefore purchased, and with axe, spade and Bible we entered heartily upon the work of helping men toward better lives. It was sometimes our lot to be accosted by a stranger on the prairie, enquiring where our ranch was located. The men of the west designated missionaries "Sky-Pilots" and "Gospel-Grinders," and the gospel was denominated "Soul-Grub."

They were strong believers in muscular Christianity, and the missionary who was able to endure greater hardships than they, sleep on a harder bed, eat as coarse food, ride a wilder horse, and withal keep his life and language pure, was the man they delighted in, and gave to him the right hand of fellowship. They had no liking for the missionary who could smoke a cigar with them, crack a coarse joke, use the slang of the prairie, and be a "hail fellow well met." They wanted a manly man, who could lead them toward nobler things, and who was not afraid to reprove them severely for their vices. The soft-handed and smooth-tongued preacher was not the man they wished, but a wise, strong-headed and liberal-hearted man was their choice. Side by side with them on the prairie we slept, partaking of their strong coffee, rancid bacon, and slap-jacks.

On the prairie and in the log shanty, Roman Catholic and Protestant, men of every class and creed, waited until we bowed the knee to the Master of men for His kind protection and grace, and before we partook of food they sat oftentimes, hungry, indeed, until a blessing was asked. Native courtesy and goodness of heart prevented them from acting rudely in the missionary's presence, or doing anything to cast reflection upon their common faith. There is no doubt they indulged, when alone, in coarse stories, yet we never heard one during the years we spent among them. Once we remember a sportive song was being sung by an old timer in Kamusi's hotel, as he was surrounded by a number of his comrades, but as soon as we appeared the verse was unfinished and the song ended in a suppressed laugh. Farewell, my old friends, I love you all,

despite your uncouth manners, for beneath the buckskin shirts
there beat honest, manly hearts.

Anxious for the welfare of these old-timers, we started a
monthly sheet, printed on the printograph, and issued free one
hundred copies. It was named *Excelsior*, and, though unpre-
tentious, and existing for one year only, it may not be too
boastful to claim for it the place of being the third paper in
the North-West Territories. The Saskatchewan *Herald* was
in existence at Battleford, and the Edmonton *Bulletin* and
Excelsior began in the same month. The tiny sheet was
honored with notices by several Canadian papers, including
the *Globe* and *Mail*, and some English papers, including the
London *Echo*. A public reading-room was started in the little
log church, which was well supplied with papers and magazines,
and shone for a year or more as a gentle light among the
Mounted Police and civilians under the shadow of the Rocky
Mountains. During the time we were soliciting subscriptions
for the reading-room, we had occasion to call upon the
officer commanding Fort Macleod, who had an intense hatred
towards missionaries of all churches. We found him in his
room with a gentleman belonging to one of the trading-posts in
town. He offered us a twenty-five dollar subscription if we
would drink a glass of brandy with him, and, because we
refused, tried by taunts to defend his position. When he
failed, he was generous enough to give a subscription toward
the scheme. When we were busy teaching school, a plan was
set on foot by a Roman Catholic priest to establish a convent
school at Macleod, and a meeting of citizens was called to
support it. There were several speakers in favor of the scheme
who denounced the school in existence. We replied vigorously,
showing the efficiency of the school, and denouncing in turn
the methods adopted to further the opposition. An Indian
chief produced some specimens of work done at the school, and
several speakers supported the school in existence. The climax
was reached when a gentleman rose and said, "I move the
whole thing bust!" The chairman put the motion. "It is
moved and seconded that the whole thing bust!" The audience

sprang to its feet, and, waving hats, yelled, " Busted !" and
made for the door, thus ending our first and last opposition in
that matter.

Getting the mail was one of the interesting events in
the early days. Our nearest Post-office was Benton, on the
Missouri, and none but American stamps were used. Stamps
were obtained by sending for one dollar's worth, more or less,
to the Postmaster at Benton. Letters were left to be mailed at
the trading-post of I. G. Baker & Co., and, not having a three-
cent stamp, ten cents were given to the clerk for postage, being
the smallest coin used in the country at that time. When a
rancher accosted a passer-by with a request to post a letter for
him, a twenty-five cent piece was invariably given. The mail-
gig was a common spring waggon with a canvas cover, driven
by two and sometimes four horses. It was used for bringing in
the mail for the Mounted Police, and the citizens were indebted
to them for bringing in their mail. We were supposed to get
the mail once in three weeks, but, on account of swollen rivers,
storms, and the tippling propensities of the mail-driver, we
were sometimes without a mail for five and six weeks. Benton
was two hundred and twenty-five miles distant from Macleod.
Before starting out, the mail-driver drove through the town
collecting liquor permits and five-gallon kegs, until sometimes
the waggon was filled with them. There being no liquor sold
in the Territories, and the permit system being in existence, the
liquor was brought from the United States, being our nearest
point where liquor was sold.

About the time due for the arrival of the mail, the old-timers
began to come to town, and as there was not any sleeping
accommodation at Kamusi's hotel, they slept upon the counters
and floors of the trading-posts, Indian blankets being furnished
for bedding without any charge. When the mail was delayed,
a strange feeling of excitement took possession of everybody.
They all seemed riveted to the place, unable to go home and
without anything to do. Each morning and afternoon could
be seen men standing on the roofs of the houses, scanning the
prairie for any sign of an approaching waggon. Sometimes a
wag would stand on the street and shout, " Mail ! mail ! "

Doors would suddenly open and men rush out excitedly on the street, only to hear a loud laugh at their expense. The mail-fever was depressing. After four or five weeks had passed by, we have resolved to start on a journey, but it was impossible for us to tear ourselves away. We would resolve to think no more about it, but work became difficult, for every hour or oftener, we would be compelled to go to the door to look out on the prairie. The last thought at night and the first in the morning was "mail, mail!"

At last the shouts of the people announced the delayed mail, and with it came relief, for the heart-burden was removed. The Mounted Police mail was taken to the post, and the civilians' mail brought down to the store of I. G. Baker & Co. and dumped out on the floor.

Down upon our knees we fell with a will and began—a motley group—to assort it. The letters were gathered up and handed to the clerk in the store. The newspapers, magazines and books were thrown to their respective owners, and unlucky was the man who was not present to claim his illustrated magazine. Sometimes this was appropriated by another, but cases of this kind were few, as there was generally manifested a native courtesy, honesty and manliness that was creditable in a new country. It was sad to see the man who had travelled thirty or forty miles to get a letter which he expected, turn away disappointed when there was none. The tear would course down the cheek of the hardy prospector as he read a letter from home. What a luxury were letters in those days. We read them again and again, laughing and crying betimes. We carried home our sack filled with letters and papers, the religious magazines and papers smelling strongly of something that was not religious. The important letters must be answered next day, and the larger epistles were laid aside to demand a bulletin for each one. The papers were kept to be read at leisure, and although the news was old, we perused the sheets with zest, and thought we were well posted on the affairs going on in the civilized world. The old-time luxury of getting letters has gone with the advent of the railroad, and we no longer read with tears the budget of news from home, so full of charming details. That old waggon was sacred in our eyes, more beautiful as the bearer of precious memories than the stately cars of our modern mail service. Pardon the falling tear over these memories of other days, which we wish not to return, yet love them for their associations, as we sigh " for the touch of a vanished hand and the sound of a voice that is still."

THOUGHTS OF OTHER DAYS.

A few passing thoughts of men and manners in the early buffalo days are all we design to give, not because we know more than others, but to add our small portion of experience in the North-West for the entertainment of those who have not visited these scenes, and still desire to learn something of the beginnings of a people destined to play their part in the history of the West. So soon as the buffalo were driven south to the district watered by the Missouri and Yellowstone rivers, the Canadian Government began issuing rations of beef and flour to keep the Indians from dying on the prairies. These supplies necessitated a number of freighters and encouraged the raising of stock. The Mounted Police and Indians caused, through their residence in the country, the circulation of a large sum of money, which replaced the amounts lost through the extinction of the trade in buffalo robes. Money had always been plentiful in the country, and consequently labor and provisions were very dear.

The prices of goods varied in the trading-posts with the supply. During the summer coal was fifteen dollars per ton; sugar, twenty-five dollars per sack of one hundred pounds; coal oil, one dollar per gallon; flour, five dollars per sack of ninety-eight pounds; eggs, one dollar a dozen: butter, fifty cents per pound; salt, ten cents per pound; and other articles in proportion. During the winter, as the supply became scarce or one trader had the monopoly of the articles in question, the prices increased until they sold as follows: Coal, twenty dollars per ton; sugar, fifty dollars per sack; coal oil, one dollar and a half per gallon; flour, fifteen dollars per sack; eggs, two dollars a dozen; and butter, one dollar per pound. Scant sometimes was the table with provisions at these rates. We tried the experiment once of sending east for supplies, but it was not satisfactory, for they were nearly a year on the way, and we had to pay nine cents per pound for freight. Lumber cost, undressed and unsorted, ten cents per foot, and improvements were, therefore, seriously retarded.

The men were liberal to a fault, and in benevolent enterprises always ready to help. A whiteman working as cook at the Blood Indian agency, was stricken down with paralysis and taken to the Mounted Police hospital. He sent for us to request that we might raise some money to enable him to go to the Banff Hot Springs. We started through the new town of Macleod, calling at every store and billiard saloon, taking up a collection, without waiting to take down any names. Sometimes an old-timer would take the hat in a billiard saloon and pass it around, depositing the contents in our hands. Within two hours we had in dollar bills eighty dollars, which we handed over to the officer commanding Fort Macleod, and the man was subsequently sent to Banff, where he died a few weeks after his arrival. Collections were taken up in church when needed, and at no other time. We had no plates and made no previous announcement; but when the time arrived, called upon some one in the congregation to pass the hat around, and with not more than forty persons we have had placed in the hat the sum of sixteen dollars. When the new barracks of the Mounted Police was in course of erection, we called unexpectedly upon the carpenters one cold stormy evening, and held a service. Bidding them "Good night," we went to saddle the horse to return to the old town of Macleod, and while doing so, the foreman placed ten dollars in our hands, the collection having been taken up by the men after we had gone. No true value was set on money, and many used it recklessly. In the trading-posts no change was given less than a twenty-five cent piece. We have seen Indians purchase articles worth from forty to sixty cents, and after handing the clerk a dollar bill walk away,

each article representing to them one dollar. White men
received no change if an article was worth eighty-five cents.
When copper coins were brought into the country by a tenderfoot they were deposited in the safe as curiosities, and never
allowed to be put in circulation.

The dangers of travelling were great in the early years,
especially in fording the rivers. We had been in the country
only a few months when duty called us to go to Morley.
Having fallen in with an old-timer who was going to Calgary,
we journeyed together, and on arriving at Sam Livingstone's
on the Elbow river, the horse we rode could go no further.
Our old friend lent us a cart horse, and we travelled alone over
a road which was new to us. Darkness came on long before
we reached the crossing of the Bow River. We could hear the
rushing of the river, but were unable to discern the opposite
bank. We shouted, but there was no response. A boat lay
upon the shore, and we judged that we were at the ford.
Trusting to a kind Providence we entered the river, the water
rose on the sides of the horse, filled the riding boots full, yet
still we pressed on in the darkness and safely reached the
other side. The horse made his way up the steep bank, the
reins being thrown upon his neck, to follow his own sweet will.
The camp fires of the Stoney Indians were burning, and guided
by an Indian we found the mission-houses. The inmates
asked where we had come from, and when we told them we
had crossed the river, they held up their hands in amazement,
and assured us that we were the first to ford the river during
that year. Swimming the rivers on horseback was not pleasant, but duty compelled us oftentimes to do many things which
were not agreeable. When first we stood on the town site of
Calgary, there were half a dozen log-houses, one trading-post, a
small Methodist church, the Roman Catholic mission and the
Mounted Police fort. On the eastern side of the Elbow were
the Hudson's Bay post and a few log buildings. We called at
the police fort to put the horse in the stable, but the three men
stationed there had gone fishing, and the gates were locked.
We found a quiet resting-place then and subsequently, upon the

green sward where the western city now is built. Returning from Calgary with some old-timers, who had a band of horses, we found Sheep Creek swollen so badly that it was dangerous to attempt to cross. We contented ourselves by camping on the banks for two days, and then our stock of provisions ran out. Game there was none, and the alternative was to return to Calgary. After consultation, we determined to make the attempt at fording the river. Stripping ourselves to our underclothing, and fastening the bundles on our heads, and keeping on our boots because of the intense coldness of the snow-water, we drove the band of horses ahead of us, and whistling, shouting and singing plunged into the stream. Having reached the opposite shore in safety, we emptied the water out of our boots, put on our clothes, and rode on twelve miles to a ranch at High River, allowing our underclothing to dry by contact with the skin as we rode. Nature and a strong constitution favored us, so that we did not suffer from riding in our wet clothes.

Strange scenes of life and death we sometimes beheld in the western land. Life in the camp of the cowboys, especially during a round-up, was exciting, but there were hours when the halo of romance vanished. Late one evening we were called to visit an old-timer in his log shanty. When we reached the humble dwelling his comrades were sitting by his bed talking about death. As we sat down beside our old friend, who had not many hours to live, he took his pipe and other articles which he prized, and distributed them among his friends. Turning toward them he said, "Boys, it's hard to leave you, but I guess I'll have to go!" After talking with him for a short time about the great matters affecting the soul and eternity, he said, "Parson, I've done a lot of bad things in my life, and a lot of good things, and I guess my Maker will call it square!" We talked awhile and prayed, but the old-timer still felt that the good would balance the bad in his life, and he would reach home at last. Nature dealt out iron-handed justice to some of the men who acted unkindly toward their fellows. During our visits to the hospital we met a man who

A CAMP OF AXEMEN.

had murdered an old man in cold blood in Montana, and, fleeing from justice, had crossed the prairie in the depth of winter. He was picked up and brought to Macleod, where his ears, hands and feet were amputated. Apparently he had suffered deeply for his crime, and his aged father was allowed to take him away when he had sufficiently recovered.

When we began life in that new country we were pursuing a course of study in connection with the university which necessitated a trip to Morley once a year to write on examination under the supervision of a deputy examiner. When the rivers were swollen we sat by the camp fire studying Greek and algebra. A strange-looking personage was the sky-pilot dressed in his buckskin suit, with his saddle-bags. In one bag were his books, and in the other tea, sugar, bacon and biscuits. Fastened to the horn of the saddle was a small axe, frying-pan, rifle, lariat and picket-pin. Night found the student wrapped up in his saddle-blanket stretched asleep on the prairie with his saddle for a pillow and his faithful horse picketed sufficiently near as not to be stolen by an enemy or chased by wolves, and far enough away not to trample upon the sleeper. One hundred and fifty miles of a ride over the prairie, crossing several swollen rivers, was a good preparation for a college examination. There was always danger at hand through the horse straying away, and it was not safe to undertake a long journey alone. As we sat one day quietly partaking of lunch, and distant from the nearest house twelve miles, the horse suddenly bolted and left us alone. There was nothing to be done but to carry the saddle and start for home. Fortunately we met a man driving a waggon who took the saddle to the place whence we had started, and we had to walk musing by the way toward home.

At another time we were compelled to walk thirty-five miles home, ten of which were through snow almost knee deep. Without anything to eat or drink we continued the journey, which took us ten hours, and then had to wade through a river waist deep. Again duty compelling us, through losing horses, to walk fourteen miles, wade through a stream four feet deep, and cross a temporary swamp two miles wide, which was knee deep and frozen over, but not sufficiently to bear. The ice broke with every step, so that we were almost exhausted when we reached the end of the journey. Without changing our wet garments we held service with an attentive congregation, and wet and tired lay down upon the floor of the humble log church, without any bed or covering, and slept. Next day we returned on foot, avoiding the stretch of water, but when we reached the frozen river that lay between the Reserve and mission-house, we had to be carried home. Upon removing the heavy riding boots they were found to be deeply stained with blood, and our feet covered with blisters filled with blood.

A Highland Scotchman called at the old mission-house in Macleod to have the marriage ceremony performed. He was anxious to marry an Indian woman. He was told to return next day as we were not at home. Next day he had changed his mind, retaining the license and living with the woman without being married to her. The second Riel Rebellion came and found us at work among the Blood Indians; the good wife of the mission-house and the children remaining one week in Macleod, and the missionary staying at his post. All the rest of the time the entire missionary family lived among the Indians, caring for the sick, teaching and preaching, upholding the principles of true government and trusting in God. Our Indian friends came to us and said, " You need not be afraid. We will tell you when there is any danger. We will take care of you." We had implicit confidence in Red Crow, the head chief of the Blood Indians, and the Indians were loyal during the rebellion. There were some who would have enjoyed a fight, and were anxious to join the rebels, but the wisdom and tact of the chiefs prevailed, and peace was maintained.

The annual payment of the treaty moneys to the Indians was always an interesting event. The red man, with his several wives and large progeny, found himself suddenly in the possession of more than a hundred dollars, and unable to bear the strain of wealth, he started with his best wife to the town to trade. From the Reserve to town the trail was beaten by men, women and children on horseback. Some on foot and others in native conveyances, wending their way toward the trading-posts, to gaze with innocent delight upon the colored blankets, brass-wire ornaments, pipes and numerous Indian trinkets. The streets of the town were lined with the natives, sitting here and there eating bread, biscuits and candies. Horses and men were dressed in holiday attire. The stores were filled with eager buyers, each of the men having a roll of one-dollar bills. Useful articles for the home and family were purchased, and then the gee-gaws became a necessity. Vermilion for the face, rings for the ears, brass wire for finger rings and bracelets, beads to make ornaments for moccasins and blankets, strings of beads for the women and children, brass tacks for decorating the gun-stock, riding-whip handle, woman's saddle, and belt, and various other articles were included in the purchase. The young Indian strutted about in his new blanket, striped in various colors, carrying his gun just purchased, a belt well-filled with cartridges around his waist, his face painted, and numerous trinkets in his hair. In one of these stores we gazed in astonishment at the western money drawer. A large clothes basket stood in one of the rooms piled to overflowing with dollar-bills tied in small bundles. The Indians knew not the bills of different denominations, and having been frequently cheated in the early years, the Government paid them in one dollar bills.

Out upon the prairie the young men had a number of horse races, upon which they staked money, small groups were throwing the wheel and arrows (a native game), and others were playing cards. They were inveterate gamblers, and, having money, they could not resist the temptation to become suddenly rich or poor. The natives assumed an air of independence, from the fact that they were rich for a season, and withal they were liberal toward their friends. Sometimes they came to us with a gift of five dollars, which at first we refused ; but finding them not well pleased at the refusal, accepted it. Within three months they called to beg some help, always reminding us that they had proffered a gift. In a short time we had returned in money and provisions more than double the amount we had received, and then in self-defence adopted the plan of giving them money, telling them the amount, until we had repaid the gift. Whatever was afterward given was then seen to be a gift to them.

One of our Indian chiefs who knew not a word of English, having learned that sometimes we employed an interpreter to assist us in translations, thought that he was entitled to compensation when telling a native story, or explaining some peculiar phrase in his own language. We sat in his lodge conversing with him, and jotting down facts relating to the traditions, folk-lore and language of the people, when he said in his own tongue, " You owe me a dollar for that work." Without answering him we continued, and when we had finished he said, " You owe me a dollar and a half." " All right," said we, and then we began to tell him some stories of the sea, the cities of the white men, the Queen and her country, the construction of locomotives and steamboats, and numerous other facts relating to industrial arts. At the close we said, " Now, you owe us five dollars." He laughed, and then we explained to him that if he could read the English language, he would pay one dollar for a book to learn about the sea, another dollar to get some knowledge of the Queen, and some more dollars to know about the other facts about which we had told him. After he had purchased the books, it would take him several days to read them, and there would be his pay during the days he was reading them, amounting to several dollars more. " Now," said we, "instead of charging you all these dollars, we will call it five dollars." He laughed again, but not so loudly. " Come," said we, " it is time we were home, give us two dollars, and that will settle the bill." Gradually he assumed a serious look, and we persisted in pressing the claim, with the result that, although he paid nothing, he saw the ridiculousness of his claim, and was ever afterward willing to lend all the help he could in unravelling the difficulties of the language.

When the Marquis of Lorne visited the old town of Macleod, a large pool of water lay in the street in front of Kamusi's Hotel, and some wags secured a boat, drove a stake into the ground, and fastened the boat to it. Placards were placed on the walls of the log hotel announcing the name of the ferryman and prices and hours of ferriage. It was also announced that the pool was the Macleod Public Bathing Pond, stating the hours for ladies and prices of admission, and the hours and prices for the gentlemen. The Rev. Dr. Macgregor preached in the little log church, which was filled to overflowing on Sunday morning with the Governor-General and his staff, members of the police force and civilians. Sydney Hall, the artist of *Graphic* stood outside during the service and sketched the church with the Indians peering in at the windows, the sketch having the significant title, "Outside the Pale of the Church."

An unpleasant sensation is that experienced by the traveller who is lost in a snowstorm on the prairie. It has been our misfortune to endure the intense agony several times, yet happily with nothing worse than the pangs of hunger and cold, the mental strain, and being slightly frozen. Sad tales have come to us oftentimes of friends frozen severely and suffering keenly when lost in a blinding snowstorm. Blinded by the sun's glare upon the snow, the trail hidden and no landmarks to be seen, the helpless traveller wanders in a circle, thinking that he is likely to reach some settler's shanty. Happy is he, if some search party or passing traveller may find him before he lies down upon the snow to rise no more. Some strange characters have been met with in that western land. Graduates of British and Canadian universities, dressed in the meanest garb, driving an ox team, medical men on ranches, and members of the learned professions living solitary lives. Sons of titled noblemen were to be found in the Mounted Police and on ranches; ay, and even living among the Indians in their camps. During our residence at Macleod, Charles Dickens, son of the novelist, was stationed at the fort. One of the most skilful botanists and an excellent Hebrew scholar we met on the prairie dressed in humble attire. He lived in an old shanty, and his valuable library seemed out of place in such a lonely spot.

So soon as the mines were started at Lethbridge we rode to the miner's camp, holding service in the kitchen, and lecturing to the miners on popular subjects. We found them a kind-hearted lot of men, and our visits there were full of interest. In the camp of the old-timers we have listened to thrilling tales of the doings of the Vigilantes in Montana. There was a band of daring men, known as "Road Agents," who managed to secure the civil offices for themselves, and thus fustrate the ends of justice. They robbed the mail waggons, way-laid travellers, and held the law-abiding people at defiance. Montana was terror-stricken, for no man was safe. The order-loving settlers secretly formed an organization for the suppression of "Road Agents," and three thousand men were ready at a moment's call to sweep down on the offenders and hurry them into eternity. This organization was known as the Vigilantes. Without any warning the desperadoes were seized, singly or in small bands, and hung up to the nearest tree. They were pursued quietly but sternly into the gulches and deep recesses of the mountains and executed. After the slaying of more than one hundred of these desperadoes order was restored, and Montana became a peaceful territory. A gambler plying his trade on the streets would be quietly informed to give up his business in two or three significant words, and the hint was sufficient. Some of those who were gamblers in Montana have told us that frequently they have seen their comrades of yesterday, who refused to take the hint, dangling upon the trees in the morning. A temporary band of Vigilantes was organized at Edmonton for a special case. A man encroached upon the rights of one of the settlers, squatting upon his land, and erecting a house. The intruder was warned to desist, but heedless of the warning defied the citizens. The Edmonton Vigilantes came quietly one morning with ropes, and fastening them around the building, hurled it over the steep bank and dashed it to pieces, the proprietor walking out as his building went over the bank. Thus was taught a lesson to all who would interfere with the rights of the humblest settler in the land.

A few of the honest old-timers are still to be found abiding

17

peacefully in the west, but others have joined the great majority and peacefully rest in the humble God's acre on the prairie. Honest John Glenn crossed the mountains in the seventies and settled on Fish Creek, near Calgary, making an humble home, where he entertained rich and poor alike. No man was ever turned from his door. Travellers from many lands have visited his farm to witness his successful experiments in irrigation and to listen to his stories of the old days. He was a good specimen of the prairie fathers, and when his hardy frame was seen no longer among his fellows, there were many to mourn the departure of one who, despite his rough exterior, lack of education, and homely phraseology was a man among men—brave, generous and true.

A sturdy old-timer, with his keen eye, long hair falling on his shoulders, and firm, manly gait is our old friend, Sam Livingstone, who still lives in close proximity to the Sarcee Indians, within a few miles of Calgary. We first met him in the fall of 1880, and were charmed with his tales of Indians and prairie life. Sitting by his fireside we spent many happy hours in after years. Honest and resolute, he has, amid many difficulties, laid the foundation of prosperity, having faith in the country and his fellowmen. Always ready to lend a hand to the worthy settler, he set his face against shams and cant, anxious to see integrity and manhood among men.

Many honest yarns could we relate of our old friends, Kamusi, William Gladstone, in his mountain home, and Jim Scott, who drove the mail waggon from Macleod to Calgary, but we leave them as a worthy trio of the old days. They still represent the real type of the old-timer who we admired, but who must pass away with the advent of civilization. The romantic days of the west are with us no longer, railroad facilities having introduced a hard, practical life, an earnest struggle for bread, and there linger with us memories only of buffaloes, log shanties, long rides on the prairie, swimming rivers, tales of the camp fires and songs of the Indians sitting in groups on the banks of the Old Man's river. Great changes have come over the people and the country. Villages and towns, commodious dwellings and fine churches occupy the sites where the Indians pitched their camps and the red and white races chased the buffaloes. The Indian runner has given place to telegraphic communication, white children roam the streets where the papooses and native youth sported on the trails, and the busy artisan sings his song of labor on the spot where the native made his arrow and stone pipe. The footprints of the red men are being effaced by the steady tramp of the white race. It is pleasant to recall the old days, and yet sadness dwells in our hearts for the scenes which shall never return.

INDIAN PIPES.

A very insignificant subject and one without any interest, some may be apt to say, is that about which we are now going to write, and yet it is not wise to pass judgment until we have examined the facts. Almost every tribe or nation has for several centuries been addicted to the habit of smoking some stimulating herb, and for this purpose have made tubes or pipes to hold the preparation from which they drew the fumes. The discovery of clay pipes of diminutive size in the British Isles, known as " fairy pipes," in close proximity to Roman remains, has induced some observers to ascribe great antiquity to the practice of smoking, and to suggest that the habit was in use in Europe before it was introduced into England by the savages who came over in one of the vessels from Virginia, with the return of Raleigh from his first expedition. It is probable that aromatic herbs were smoked as a medicine in remote times, and this may account for the existence of tubes and pipes, but the use of tobacco among Europeans must be placed subsequent to the discovery of America by Columbus. Large numbers of clay pipes have been found near Edinburgh, Scotland, dredged from the bed of the Thames, picked up in battlefields, church-yards, and places of public resort in England and Scotland. The " Dane's Pipes " of Ireland gave rise to the belief that there were a race of elves who smoked diminutive pipes. The shape of the bowl and inscriptions on the bowl and stem indicate their modern origin, although they have been met with in strange places, beside remains of ancient date. Our Scottish forefathers used pipes made of stone, and clay; terra cotta pipes were the delight of the Swiss; and, in Holland, clay and iron pipes were used, some of which were imported into England. The pipe of the famous Miles Standish, which he brought with him in the *Mayflower* and smoked till the day of his death, was made of iron, and was no doubt exported from Holland.*

The Mexicans were not dependent upon the use of a tube or pipe, as they rolled the dried leaf of the tobacco in the form of a cigar, and smoked it, sometimes employing a boy to do the smoking for them, as the native stood in front of him, and caught the smoke in his face by holding his hands together, so that none of it could escape.

The Mound-Builders manufactured pipes, which have been discovered in the mounds; the earliest form being those carved from a single piece of stone, having "a flat curved base of variable length and width, with the bowl rising from the centre of the convex side. From one of the ends, and communicating with the hollow of the bowl, is drilled a small hole, which answers the purpose of a tube; the corresponding opposite division being left for the manifest purpose of holding the implement in the mouth." Instead, therefore, of having pipes, like the Indians or white men, with a stem, the Indian inserting the elaborately decorated stem in a large hole made in the stone or clay pipe head, the Mound-Builders used the pipe head alone, the hole in the short stem being made small for that purpose. The oldest type of the Mound-Builders' pipe was of the Monitor pattern, which consisted of a "short cylindrical urn, or spool-shaped bowl, rising from the centre of a flat and slightly curved base." The bowl and stem of the Ohio Mound-Builder's pipe was carved out of one piece of stone. The pipe of the Mound-Builder was carved in the forms of birds, animals and human beings. Otters, serpents, frogs, ducks, the manitu, toucan, woodpecker, and other animals and birds were represented in the carved figures.

* Sir Daniel Wilson, " Narcotic Usages."   Edwin A. Barber, "Antiquity of the Tobacco Pipe in Europe."   " American Antiquarian," Vol. II., pages 1-8, 117-122.

From these we learn that these people were conversant with
the habits and attitudes of the birds and animals, as can be seen
from a study of the figures. There is also embodied in them
a religious significance, showing that they were serpent worshippers, pipes having been found having a serpent coiled
around the bowl. These people made also image or idol pipes,
representing "females holding pottery vessels; others, males
holding pipes; the sex being discernable in the faces and by
the utensils used; the faces always directed toward the sun,"

INDIAN CLAY PIPE (FULL SIZE).

and from these we learn that they were sun-worshippers.
Some very interesting specimens have been found in the Gulf
States, suggesting that these people were sun-worshippers and
also idol-worshippers. From a comparison of the pattern and
the figures with those made by some Indian tribes, as, for
instance, the Cherokees, we are able to learn of the migrations
and contact of the Mound-Builders with the Indians. These
sculptured pipes transfer the practice of smoking from the
recreative plane of the white man to an elevated position

among the religious usages of the people who built the mounds,
similar to that of the native cacique who came out from his
house on the summit of the pyramid each morning to welcome
the sun, pointing his pipe toward it and then toward the four
points of the compass. When a stranger came to the village
the cacique went out to meet him, pipe in hand, addressing the
sun and pointing his pipe toward it, turning around from east
to north and from west to north, toward the four points of the
compass. The Crees and Blackfeet of the western plains have
a similar custom in their religious ceremonies, the pipe being
exalted as an implement of peace and an aid to their devotions.*

From the pipe-stone quarries of Wisconsin some of the Mound-
Builders procured the material for their pipes, as can be shown
by the pipes found in the mounds. From the famous pipe-stone
quarry of Minnesota, the Couteau des Prairies, the red men
obtained the red stone, which was highly prized because of the
beauty of its appearance and the soft nature of the material,
being easily worked and suitable for elaborate carvings. The
locality of this celebrated quarry was of traditional interest,
and seems to have been consecrated as neutral ground for all
the tribes, where they could assemble and forget awhile their
tribal feuds in the legendary history of their common origin.
Catlin relates an interesting myth relating to this pipe-stone
quarry. Here happened the mysterious birth of the red pipe
which has blown its fumes of peace and war throughout the
land, breathing through its reddened stem the oath of war and
desolation. Here was born, too, the pipe of peace, which has
soothed the wrath of the savage warrior and dispelled the
enmity of the tribes. The Great Spirit called the Indian
nations together at an ancient period, and, standing on the

* Peabody, "Museum Report," 1884, page 185. Short's "North
Americans of Antiquity," pages 37, 86. "Problem of the Ohio Mounds,"
by Cyrus Thomas, pages 38, 43. "Third Annual Report of the Bureau of
Ethnology," pages 445, 465, 469, 492. "Fifth Annual Report of the Bureau
of Ethnology," pages 38, 53, 93, 94. "American Antiquarian," Vol. VIII.,
pages 112, 131, 215, 309-313 ; VOL. IX., page 176 ; VOL. XII., page
219 ; VOL. XIII., page 350 ; VOL. XIV., pages 29, 74, 218-220, 267-
268 ; VOL. XV., pages 94, 253, 361, 362.

precipice of the red pipe-stone rock, broke a piece from its wall, making a huge pipe by turning it in his hand, which he smoked over them. He pointed it toward the north, south, east and west, telling the people that this red stone was their flesh, and they must use it for pipes of peace, that it belonged to them all, and the war-club and scalping-knife must not be raised from the ground. At the last whiff of the pipe his head

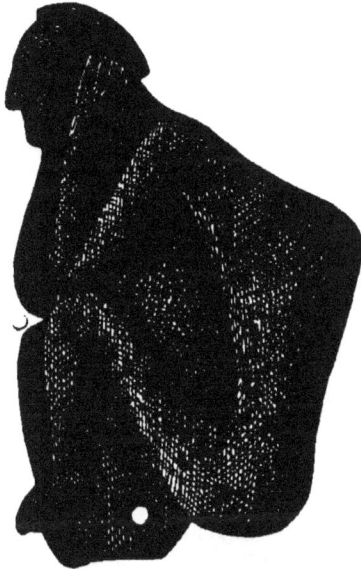

INDIAN STONE PIPE (FULL SIZE).

went into a great cloud, and the whole surface of the rock for several miles was melted and glazed.

There are other myths which speak of the red pipe-stone as the flesh of their ancestors, and because of their common origin they are to smoke the pipe, which is a symbol of peace. There is a myth of the Sioux which says: "Before the creation of man, the Great Spirit (whose tracks are yet to be seen on the stones at the red pipe-stone quarry in form of the tracks of a large bird) used to slay the buffaloes and

eat them on the ledge, and their blood running on the rocks
turned them red.   One day, when a large snake had crawled
into the nest of the bird to eat his eggs, one of the eggs
hatched out in a clap of thunder, and the Great Spirit, catching hold of a piece of the pipe-stone to throw at the snake,
moulded it into a man.   This man's feet grew fast in the
ground, where he stood for many years, like a great tree, and
therefore he grew very old.   He was older than a hundred
men at the present day.   At last another tree grew up by the
side of him, when a large snake ate them both off at the roots,
and they wandered away.   From these have sprung all the
people that now inhabited the earth."

From Catlin's relation of the myth, Longfellow wrote his
beautiful section, "The Peace Pipe," in his Indian edda
"Hiawatha,"

> " On the mountains of the prairie,
>   On the great Red Pipe-stone Quarry,
>   Gitche Manito, the mighty,
>   He the Master of Life, descending,
>   On the red crags of the quarry,
>   Stood erect, and called the nations,
>   Called the tribes of men together.
>
> .   .   .   .
>
>   From the red stone of the quarry,
>   With his hand he broke a fragment,
>   Moulded it into a pipe-head,
>   Shaped and fashioned it with figures ;
>   From the margin of the river
>   Took a long reed for a pipe-stem,
>   With its dark-green leaves upon it ;
>   Filled the pipe with bark of willow ;
>   With the bark of the red willow ;
>   Breathed upon the neighboring forest,
>   Made its great boughs chafe together,
>   Till in flame they burst and kindled ;
>   And erect upon the mountains,
>   Gitche Manito, the mighty,
>   Smoked the calumet, the peace-pipe,
>   As a signal to the nations."

The red stone has been a favorite kind of material in use among the Indians for their pipes, arising, no doubt, from the myth relating to the pipe-stone quarry. Many of this class have we seen sold by the traders to the Crees, Sarcees and Blackfeet; but, instead of a stone, a red clay was used, which

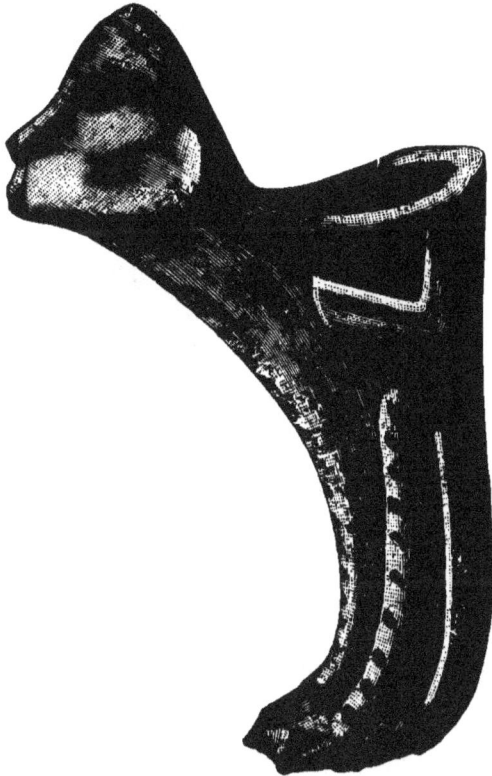

INDIAN CLAY PIPE (FULL SIZE).

was glazed, and resembled the Monitor pattern. Catlinite, or red stone, was used by the natives for pipes and various kinds of ornaments. Stone of different degrees of hardness and color was used by the tribes, some of them selecting the kind to be found in their own locality, and others travelling long

distances to procure some favored grade of stone.* Adair, in
speaking of the Cherokee stone pipes, says: " They make
beautiful stone pipes, and the Cherokees the best of any of the
Indians, for their mountainous country contains many different
sorts and colors of soils proper for such uses. They easily form
them with their tomahawks, and afterward finish them in any
desired form with their knives, the pipes being of a very soft
quality till they are smoked with and used with the fire, when
they become quite hard. They are often full a span long, and
the bowls are about half as large again as our English pipes.

INDIAN CLAY PIPE (FULL SIZE).

The fore part of each commonly runs out with a sharp peak
two or three fingers broad and a quarter of an inch thick."

Pipes were made of steatite or soapstone—white, grey, dark,
brown and black—and among the various kinds of stone used
were sandstone, limestone, gypsum, argillite and slate. Some

* Short's " North Americans of Antiquity," pages 85, 88, 528. "Smith-
sonian Anthropological Papers," page 629. Cyrus Thomas' " Problem of the
Ohio Mounds," pages 33, 35. "Annual Reports of the Bureau of Ethnology,"
Vol. III., page 439 ; Vol. IV., pages 23, 33. " Reports of Canadian Insti-
tute," Vol. I., pages 25-30 ; Vol. II., pages 23-28 ; Vol. III., pages 29-33 ;
Vol. IV., pages 35, 41 ; Vol. V., pages 13-16.

beautiful specimens of the stone pipes, as well as those made of clay and bone, are to be seen in the museum of the Canadian Institute. Indeed, the skill of the native pipe sculptor may be seen in the pipes made from serpentine marble and the beautiful white stone. From an examination of the specimens in the Institute we are able to note the ability, knowledge of the habits of the animals, and some of the customs of our savage folk.

The ancient Mexicans used paper, reed, and maize-leaf cigarettes, and wooden, metal and bamboo tubes for the purpose of smoking. Wooden pipes are seldom found among the Indians as specimens of native manufacture. Copper and iron, however, have been used. Hudson, who landed in 1609, says the natives had pipes of copper with earthen bowls. We saw a Blood Indian with a pipe made from a small hatchet, the cleft used for the insertion of the stem, and the face beaten out until it became a receptacle for the tobacco, with a small hole connecting with the stem. Whether this had been made by an Indian or not we cannot say, as we made no special inquiries at the time, but there would be no difficulty whatever in doing so, as we have known the pipe-makers spend several weeks in the preparation of a black-stone pipe. In connection with the custom of gathering catlinite from the Red Pipe-stone Quarry, Minnesota, it is stated that the Indians inscribed their totems upon the rock, either by picking or scratching it, or, if too hard, painting it in colors before venturing to quarry the stone.

The pipes of the ancient Mexicans were nearly all made of terra cotta, highly glazed or painted. Pipes of marble have been found in Tennessee and other parts of the United States, and a very fine specimen in the Canadian Institute was discovered near Richmond Hill, Ontario. The Stoney Indians of our North-West were in the habit of using a coarse species of bluish jasper procured from the shores of the Athabasca River and elsewhere in the west, and a fine grade of marble, which they made into graceful pipes, beautifully polished, but too hard for delicate carving.

Since the location of the bands of this sub-tribe on Reservations, the manufacture of these articles has become almost extinct, as the people seldom travel long distances, except during their hunting expeditions, and much of their time is spent in farming. The stone pipes of our savage folk had sometimes indentations in the form of ornaments, but seldom do we learn of a lead or pewter pipe, yet there is one to be seen in the Canadian Institute. We have seen several of the leaden

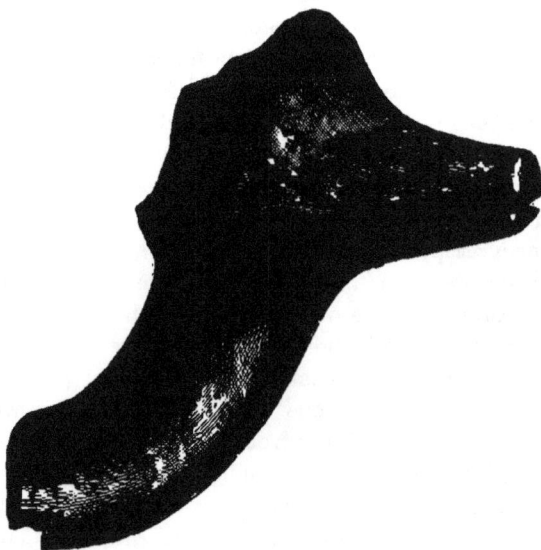

INDIAN CLAY PIPE (FULL SIZE).

ornamented pipes among the Blackfeet, the stone being cut with a knife, file or sharp piece of iron and the lead poured into the hollowed space. Pipes of obsidian have been found in the graves of the red men. Clay pipes have been found in widely scattered localities throughout the Dominion. Simcoe County has furnished the greatest number of these, and especially the classic aboriginal site of Nottawasaga. From the ancient town of Hochelaga, on the present site of Montreal, the ossuaries at Lake Medad, near Watertown, about ten miles west from Hamilton, Ontario, Brant County, and the district inhabited by the Tshimpseans of British Columbia, clay pipes of various styles have been brought, revealing the skill, taste, religious ideas and customs of the people.

From the country of the Petuns, in the County of Simcoe, the largest number of clay pipes have been brought, arising, no doubt, from the fact that this extinct tribe raised tobacco for commercial purposes, and may have made pipes also for sale. Tiny pipes of imperfect manufacture have been found, evidently the work of Indian children, which may have been used as toys. The pipe-maker moulded the plastic clay into the pattern desired, placed a twig or reed in the stem or twisted two strands of grass or fibre to make a strong cord, and the clay was fashioned around this twig, and then baked hard. Sometimes the mass was moulded with the design complete, and burned, and afterwards the bowl and hole in the stem were bored, but this was very difficult work, from the fragile nature of the native pottery, and the former method seems to have been the one most in use.

The head of the pipe was specially carved by the Mound-Builders, but among the Indians, the head and stem had their own significant uses, and both were subjected to the influences of native decorative art. The Indians regarded the pipe stem with superstitious reverence, the head of the pipe carried carefully wrapped up in a tobacco pouch. The common pipe was not so preserved, but the sacred pipe of the Crees, Blackfeet, Ojibways and Sioux had the stem decorated with paint, eagle feathers and pieces of fur, besides having in some instances elaborate carvings, and special pipe-stem bearers were appointed to guard the palladium of the tribe.

Each tribe has its own style of pipe, as well as a distinctive form of moccasin. As each white nation has a special national style of dress, so the Indian tribes had their tribal dresses, styles of wearing the hair, tattoo marks, and even a tribal gait in walking. Their houses and tents and canoes were also distinctive, so that they could be distinguished from one another. The Hochelaga potters bestowed their highest skill upon their tobacco pipes, and their class of pipes were generally of the trumpet shape. The platform pipe is supposed to have belonged to the modern Algonquin or Iroquois, and consisted of a flat platform as a substitute for a bowl, having an orifice in the centre of the plate for holding the tobacco. When the tobacco was lighted, the pipe was passed around the circle of warriors or members of the council for each to blow the smoke out as a sign of good faith and worship. The pipe-head of the savage folk of Canada was moulded or carved in various designs.

There are to be seen in the Canadian Institute, in the museum of the Manitoba Historical Society, in the collections belonging

INDIAN STONE PIPE (SEVEN-EIGHTHS DIAMETER).

to public institutions and private parties, numerous kinds of pipe sculpture. Upon these are observed the totems of the natives. Among the animals moulded and carved are the bear, panther, horse, lynx, monkey, wolf, snake and lizard; and of the bird specimens there are owls, eagles and ducks. Clay pipes had few decorations on the stem, the pipe sculptor expending his time and ability upon the bowl and base of the pipe. In the museum of the Canadian Institute there are some rare specimens of clay and stone pipes. There is one of striking design, having two snakes intertwined on the bowl, the head, mouth and eyes of both well formed, and lines made on the body to represent scales. Another snake-pipe has the snake coiled around the stem. An eagle pipe, made of a finely-veined and close-grained piece of Huronian slate, has the head and beak artistically formed, the right and left talons separated and the wings outlined. Some of the pipes have the human form represented, nearly in full, or the face alone. One design is that of a man carrying a burden on his back, another consists of a double face, one at the front and the other at the back of the bowl, and one of human form having a hat on, but whether this represents a white man or is a relic of the native costume worn before the French occupation of Canada is not known. The figures on the bowls were in general made to face the smoker. Some of the designs are essentially aboriginal, and

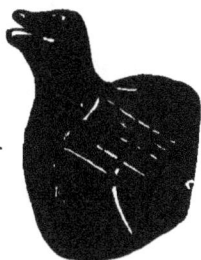

INDIAN STONE PIPE (FULL SIZE).

others, as the hatted pipe and the figure of the horse, belong to the period of the white man.

A pipe made of stone was recently found at Price's Corners, near Orillia, which has the design of an Indian woman carrying a round basket on her back, the basket forming the bowl of the pipe. The most artistic workers in pipe sculpture of all the western Indians are the Tshimpseans, who carve out of a soft blue claystone elaborate and grotesque designs, which exhibit great skill.

In the human faces on the pipes of Indians it is believed that the method practised during the past two centuries was to turn the face from the smoker, and before that period the face was turned directly toward the stem.

The earliest pipes of the western Denes consisted of a stone

bowl with a serrated base, wherein was inserted a wooden
stem. The bowl and stem were connected by a chain of den-
talium shells, alternating with colored glass beads.

The Eskimos make pipes of iron, brass, stone, reindeer antlers,
and walrus ivory, which are neatly inlaid with thin sheet copper
or brass, but the stems are made of two pieces of wood, hollowed in the centre and lashed together by a thong made of
the skin of the deer or seal. They are nearly all of the same
pattern, and have not elaborate designs, the stems being subjected to ornamentation, and that not to any great extent.*

When the Indians are in their lodges they use a common
pipe, the master of the lodge filling it, and, handing it to one
of the men in the circle, it is lighted and passed around, each
one taking a few whiffs. The smokers swallow the last whiff
of smoke and allow it to pass through the nostrils. Seldom do
they smoke alone when in company, although each man carries
his own pipe. The men never allow the women to join them
in smoking in company, but when the family is alone, husband
and wife sometimes smoke together. The pipes of the women
are small and very common, and when a company of them are
assembled they pass the pipe around, indulging in a few whiffs.
Besides these common pipes, used upon every occasion, there is
generally a sacred pipe, owned by the native, especially if he is
a chief and is in good circumstances. This is kept as a sacred
talisman, whose presence in the lodge is believed to afford
protection, and in time of sickness to exert a healing virtue.
During a period of sickness among the Blood Indians, we were
administering medicine to a child of one of the chiefs, named
Blackfoot Old Woman. It did not seem to regain its strength,
and the father was very anxious for the recovery of his child.
A change took place, and at last complete restoration to health.
As we sat in the lodge, the chief informed us that several years
ago the head chief, Red Crow, had purchased a medicine pipe
from an Indian which possessed great virtue, and he had given
ten horses for it. We were rather suspicious about the price,

* "Transactions of the Canadian Institute," Vol. VII., pages 36-38;
Sir Daniel Wilson's "Artistic Faculty," pages 81-88.

but allowed the chief to relate his story. During all the time that Red Crow owned the pipe he had been protected, and always recovered from sickness. Being anxious for the safety of his child, Blackfoot Old Woman purchased the pipe from Red Crow, and no sooner had he brought it to his lodge than his child began to recover. Pointing to the pipe, neatly

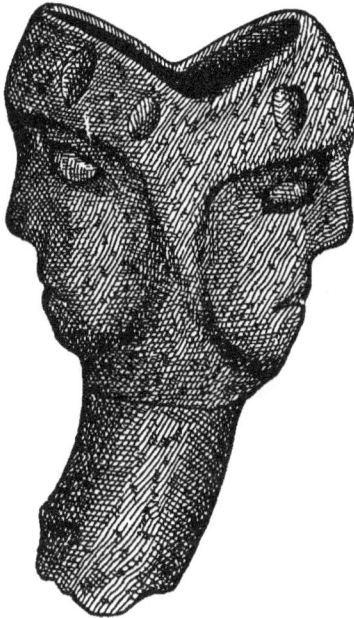

INDIAN CLAY PIPE (FULL SIZE).

enclosed in a special wrapper, he said, "That is stronger than the white man's medicine."

There are tribal pipes which are highly esteemed, and only used at the sun dance, and important political and religious gatherings. Among some of the tribes, especially the Sioux, sacred tents are provided for these pipes. The sacred tribal pipes include the war pipe and the peace pipe. When it is decided to go to war, and a large war party is desired, a large number of warriors are invited to a lodge, and, after

18

being addressed upon the subject, one of the chiefs fills the
war pipe, and all who are willing to join the party smoke the
pipe, and those who are unwilling do not put it to their lips.
The peace pipe, having a long stem decorated with eagles'
feathers, is used as a flag of truce, and the bearer is protected
by the enemy. The common people are not allowed to touch
them, and, indeed, they revere them so much that they are
afraid to desecrate them in any way. When smoked by
strangers or enemies it is a token of friendship; and even
though a great wrong may have been done to one tribe by
another, so soon as the clouds of smoke ascend from the peace
pipe there is rejoicing and peace. This is the burden of the
song of the peace pipe, as given by Longfellow:

> " Bury your clubs and your weapons,
> Break the red stone from this quarry,
> Mould and make it into peace pipes ;
> Take the reeds that grow beside you,
> Deck them with your brightest feathers ;
> Smoke the calumet together,
> And as brothers live henceforth."

Loskiel's description of the peace pipe is as follows: " The
French call it 'calumet,' and it has commonly a large head of
red marble, three inches deep and six or eight inches wide.
But the red color being the color of war, it is daubed over with
white clay or chalk. The pipe stem is made of hard, black
wood, four feet long, and wound round with a fine ribband,
neatly decorated with white corals by the women, who endeavor
to display their art to the best advantage. Sometimes ornaments are added, made of porcupine quills, with green, yellow
and white feathers." *

In the ancient rites of the Condoling Council of the Iroquois,
when opening the ceremony, a fire was kindled, a pipe lighted
and passed around among the guests with great formality,

---

*Loskiel, Vol. I., page 156 ; " Annual Report of the Bureau of Eth-
nology," Vol. III., page 332 ; Vol. IV., pages 104, 122, 221. Washington
Irving's " Astoria," pages 144, 157. " Peabody's Museum Report," 1884,
page 309. " Iroquois Book of Rites," pages 117, 121.

and the principal chief invited them to smoke together in gratitude for their safety, and to mingle their tears together in their sorrow. It is customary to pass the pipe around, each taking a few whiffs and, after going round the circle, it is returned backward, without smoking it, to the master of the lodge. The pipe plays a prominent part in the religious rites of the natives. Smoking is indulged in at the opening of nearly every ceremony of the midawin of the Ojibways, and the medicine man of the tribes east and west points his pipe to

INDIAN CLAY PIPE (FULL SIZE).

the sun or sky, and then to the four points of the compass. The mida of the Ojibways makes his smoke offering by taking a whiff, and pointing the stem of his pipe to the east; another whiff, and the stem is directed to the south; another whiff, and similar gesture in the direction of the north; a long whiff taken, with an expression of reverence, and the stem is directed forward and upward to the Great Spirit; and finally a whiff, and similar gesture forward and downward toward the earth, as an offering to Nokomis, the grandmother of the universe,

and to those who have passed to the great beyond. The pipe
stem is frequently carved and decorated with feathers, the
carvings sometimes denoting the fact that several persons
belonging to different gens live in the same house and smoke
the same pipe. Every feather is significant, and the sacred
pipes must be placed in certain definite positions, or there may
happen serious consequences to the tribe or some members of
the tribe. If the pipe stem becomes clogged in smoking, the
pipe-bearer among some of the tribes is killed; if it falls to
the ground, or is intentionally kicked about, it is believed that
the pipe-bearer or some prominent person will soon die. When
attacking a herd of buffaloes, or going out to welcome a stranger
to the camp, a man went out carrying a pipe. A sacred pipe
placed between two combatants by a proper person generally
ended a quarrel, or, if sent to a hostile tribe and smoked, secured
friendship. When two men belonging to different tribes met
on the prairie, if they smoked together, it was a token of peace.
The bearer of a sacred pipe went unarmed to the village of a
hostile tribe, taking care to reach the place in daylight, and
always was he protected and well treated. The sacred pipes
are carried around the circle of the chiefs when assembled at
their council gatherings.*

While every adult Indian is more or less a pipe maker, there
are generally a few persons who, by their skill at moulding and
carving, became known as experts, and these are employed by
their fellows to make pipes for them. Among the blood Indians a
young man, named Potaina, *alias* Joe Healey, has made some
beautiful carved black-stone pipes, with aboriginal and modern
designs. The skill shown by some of the pipe sculptors is surprising when we consider the fact that they often carve them
with a knife, an old file or a piece of iron. The pipes used by

* "Annual Report of the Bureau of Ethnology," Vol. III., pages 221-227,
342, 356-359; Vol. IV., page 129. Wilson's "Narcotic Usages," in "American Antiquarian," Vol. XIV., page 30. "Peabody Museum Report,"
1884, pages 310, 313. Fenimore Cooper's "The Pathfinder," page 37.
Hunter's "Captivity Among the Indians," pages 15, 80, 380. Brinton's
"Myths of the New World," pages 72, 183.

the Omahas in the Wawan or pipe dance can only be made by those who have given away horses, been valiant in battle or prudent in counsel. No other person can enjoy the honor of making these pipes. Dr. Wilson mentions an old Chippeway living on Great Manitoulin Island in Lake Huron, who was known as the Pipe Maker, because of his great artistic ability. With an old saw, made by himself from a bit of iron hoop, he carved some beautiful pipes, using the black pipe stone of Lake Huron, the white pipe stone of St. Joseph's Island and the red pipe stone of the famous Red Stone Quarry.

There are men specially appointed to take care of the sacred pipes, whose persons are held sacred and are entitled to privileges

INDIAN CLAY PIPE (FULL SIZE).

belonging to their office. Horses are provided by some of the tribes for transporting the pipes when the Indians are travelling. The women are not allowed to touch the pipes, nor even to witness the ceremony of uncovering them. The council is opened by the pipe-bearers filling the pipes, after repeating a formula, and handing them to the principal chiefs. If any of the laws relating to the sacred pipes are broken, the pipe-bearer will assuredly die within a short time.*

---

* Wilson's " Narcotic Usages," page 337. Contributions to " American Ethnology," Vol. VI. pages 3, 4, 471, 663. "Third Annual Report of the Bureau of Ethnology," pages 222-224, 230, 231, 239, 241, 245, 249, 363.

The tobacco pouches, sometimes called fire bags, are usually made of the skins of animals, ornamented with porcupine quills, beads and feathers, but in later years, especially among the Crees and Saulteaux of the far north, elaborate designs are sewn with silk. The Blackfeet, Crees and Ojibways make some beautiful pouches. Significant figures are drawn upon some of them. A sacred war pouch is also used as a means of making peace with a hostile tribe, and the bearer is safe even when travelling unarmed through the territory of the enemy. The Point Barrow Eskimos make their tobacco pouches of wolverine fur elaborately ornamented with borders of different colored

INDIAN STONE PIPE (HALF DIAMETER).

skin. The common pouch is fastened to the belt of the Indian and contains tobacco, pipe and stem, kinne-kinick and matches.*

Although the Indians are believed to have taught the white man the use of tobacco, many of the northern and western Indians, including the Eskimos, are indebted to the white man for its extensive use, and even for its introduction among them. The western Denes and Eskimos knew nothing of tobacco until the advent of the white man. The Petuns of Ontario and other tribes, however, had large fields of tobacco, which they grew for

† "Peabody Museum Report," 1884, pages 311, 332, 333. Loskiel, Vol. I., page 51. "Ninth Annual Report of Bureau of Ethnology," page 69.

their own use and to supply the other Indian tribes. The Indians of Puget Sound knew nothing of it till the white man brought it among them. The Ojibways, along with other tribes, appear to have used it before they came in contact with the white race. A narcotic plant was grown and in use among some tribes of Indians which they rejected when tobacco could be obtained more easily. The Haidas of British Columbia cultivated and chewed the huidakwul-ra, which they sold to neighboring tribes. Prof. Dawson says, "To prepare the plant for for use, it was dried over the fire on a little framework, finely burned in a stone mortar, and then pressed into cocks. It does not appear that they smoked it, but being mixed up with a little lime, prepared by burning clam shells, was either chewed or held in the cheek."*

When the Indians of the west are passing by a mysterious stone on the prairie, or the northern men are about to run a dangerous rapid, they make an offering of tobacco. Pipes and tobacco are placed in the lodges with the dead warriors, and sometimes a young persons will beg for a piece of bread or tobacco, that they may be taken to the friends who have joined the great majority. The Blackfeet will fill a pipe at night and hold it outside the lodge that the spirits of the dead may enjoy a smoke.

The savage folk do not use tobacco alone, but mix it with an ingredient. The Point Barrow Eskimos mix finely chopped willow twigs, in the proportion of two parts of wood to one of tobacco; the ancient Mexicans mixed liquid amber with their tobacco, and our modern Indians use the inner bark of the red willow or the leaves of cranberry or winterberry. The leaves of the winterberry are called by the Ojibways pahgezegun, which means "anything mixed," but the cranberry leaf and willow

---

* "Iroquois Book of Rites," page 171. "Smithsonian Anthropological Papers," page 699. "Annual Reports of the Bureau of Ethnology," Vol. VI., page 613; Vol. VII., pages 261, 263; Vol. IX., pages 65-72. "Transactions of the Canadian Institute," Vol. VII., pages 36-38. Hunter's "Captivity Among the Indians," pages 343, 424. "American Antiquarian," Vol. IX., page 219; Vol. XII., pages 48-50; Vol. XIII., page 328 ; Vol. XIV., page 213 ; Vol. XV., page 251.

bark are called kinne-kinick, which signifies "he mixes." The Omahas have a mixture called ninigahi, meaning "to mix with tobacco," which is "made from the inner bark of the dogwood, and dried in narrow strips over the fire, on a sieve shaped like a battle-door, and made by interlacing thin pieces of wood. The dried curled strips are powdered between the fingers." Kinne-kinick, sometimes called killikinick, is an Ojibway term, which

INDIAN CLAY PIPE (FULL SIZE).

is applied to the tobacco and ingredients by the Ojibways, and is now applied generally by white people to the ingredients alone.*

Pipe dances are performed among some of the tribes, notably the Wawan or pipe dance of the Omahas, which was an ancient custom, made for the purpose of exchanging possessions and

---

* Wilson's "Narcotic Usages," page 254. Contributions to "American Ethnology," Vol. VI., page 474. "Peabody's Museum Report," 1884, page 310. "Report of the Bureau of Ethnology," Vol. IX., pages 69-72. "American Antiquarian," Vol. IX., page 213; Vol. XI., page 349.

giving and receiving honors, a ceremony in some of its details resembling the potlach of the Indians of British Columbia and the sun dance of the Blackfeet. When Lieutenant-Governor Morris made the treaties at Forts Carleton and Pitt in 1876, there was performed by the Indians a pipe dance, or the dance of the pipe stem. The chiefs, medicine men and singers of the camp of Crees at Fort Pitt advanced toward the Governor's tent in a large semi-circle, preceded by about twenty warriors on horse-back, who sang and shouted as they went through various striking evolutions. When within fifty yards of the tent they halted, and those on foot sat down upon blankets spread on the ground for their convenience. The bearer of the stem was named " The man you strike on the back." This man carried in his hand a large and gorgeously adorned pipe stem, and walking slowly along the semi-circle, he advanced to the front, raised the stem to the sky, then slowly turned it toward the north, south, east and west. He then returned to the group seated on the ground, handed the stem to one of the young men, who commenced a low chant, at the same time performing a ceremonial dance, accompanied by the drums and singing of the men and women in the background. This dance was subsequently performed at Fort Carlton with four pipes, the singers, dancers and riders being more numerous. After the pipes were stroked by the commissioners, they were presented to each of them to be smoked, and then laid upon the table, covered with calico and cloth, and returned to the pipe-bearers. The stroking of the pipe stem by the Governor and commissioners signified that they accepted the friendship of the tribe. The pipe is a symbol of peace, and the place assigned to it in their treaties, councils and religious festivals lifts it out of the plane of recreation, which is to them not merely an agent of simulation, but a mediator and a bond of friendship among men.*

* Morris' " Indian Treaties," pages 183, 190, 198 ; " Peabody's Museum Report," 1884, page 308. "Annual Report of the Bureau of Ethnology," Vol. VII., pages 152-153. "Aboriginal Pipes," an illustrated article in Toronto *Daily Mail* Supplement, Feb. 2, 1895.

CHAPTER III.

CHURCH AND CAMP.

THE BIBLE IN THE LODGES.

THE aborigines of America have ever been impressed with religious influence. Looking out over the broad sea of the Infinite, the great questions of life have troubled their hearts. In the stillness of the forest and amid the immensity of the prairies, they have asked, "Whence came we?" and "Whither are we going?' Impressed with a sense of their dependence upon some higher power, they have sought him in the sun, and hoped to propitiate their gods who dwelt in the strangely-shaped stones that dotted the prairies, the contorted trees upon the banks of the rivers, or who presided over the boisterous rapids of the wild mountain stream.*

Devoted Christian men, filled with enthusiasm for the welfare of their fellowmen, red or white, followed in the footsteps of Champlain in their zeal for the salvation of the souls of the Indians. From the shores of Spain, France and England honest, learned and faithful teachers of righteousness found their way across the stormy Atlantic, to the shores of the new world, where the natives of America greeted them as friends, and made them welcome to their hearts and homes. Intrepid missionaries, like Brebeuf and Jogues, came to New France and following the trail of the natives of Canada, along the rivers and through the forests, sought to tell the savages the story of the ages, that they might win them from the warpath to

---

* Pilling's " American Indian Bibliographies."

become humble disciples of the Cross. Las Casas, the Roman Catholic protector of the Indians, followed the adventurous Columbus to the homes of the red men, and taught them zealously the way to life. When unable to enter the camps of the hostile Indians, he taught Indian traders the story of God's love from creation's primal day to the ascension of the Son of Man, and translating it into the tongue of the natives and setting it to music, instructed the traders to sing it in the camps. When the day's trading was over the traders sat upon the ground and sang the wondrous song, keeping time upon native instruments of music. As the Indians listened with intense earnestness they urged the singers to sing it over again, and continuously they repeated it every night for a whole week. The Bible song and story did its work effectively, for the chiefs requested Las Casas and his brother missionaries to visit them and teach the people more of these spiritual truths. Obedient to the call, they went and won the hearts of the natives for Christ and his religion.

John Eliot, the Protestant apostle of the Indians, left his English home and came to Massachusetts eleven years after the *Mayflower* landed with the noble band of pilgrim fathers. The seal of the colony was an Indian holding a label in his mouth, with the inscription, " Come over and help us."

A deep impression was made upon the mind of John Eliot on beholding the condition of the natives, and he threw himself with great energy into the work of aiding them in material and spiritual things. He studied the language of the natives, and began translating tracts and portions of the Bible. He was one of the three members chosen to prepare a new version of the Psalms of David in English metre, which was published in 1640, and, as the first book printed in the English-American colonies, is known as the Bay Psalm Book. He began his missionary labors among the Massachusetts Indians, and it was about 1643 that he earnestly set about studying their language. He translated Genesis, Matthew and a few Psalms, which were printed between 1655 and 1658. The New Testament was finished at the press in 1661, and the whole Bible in 1663. The Indians, old and young, read it with avidity. A native church was

organized, and the students from Eliot's school were so successful in declaring the Truth to their fellows that there were
fourteen praying towns in existence and more than a thousand
native Christians. A primer, grammar, catechism and several
small religious books were prepared, so that the Indians were
supplied with a native literature, and those who desired to
study the language could do so by the aid of the grammar.
War, disease and absorption swept the Indians off, the language
gave place to the use of English, until not a single descendant
remained.

Twenty-six copies of the first edition of the Bible and twenty-
eight of the second are known to be in existence, and others
may yet be traced, the sole remnant, with a few copies of his
other works, of the arduous labors of this devoted man, who
died at Roxbury in the eighty-sixth year of his age, with a
prayer on his lips for the success of the Gospel among the
Indians. To the Bible in the Massachusetts language belongs
the honor of being the first Bible printed on the American
continent.

Large portions of the Bible have been printed in many of the
native languages, and the whole Bible has been issued in the
Massachusetts, Cree, Sioux, and Greenland Eskimo languages.

Dr. S. R. Riggs labored among the Sioux for fifty years,
passing through the trying period of the Minnesota massacre,
and lived to see schools and churches established among his
people. With the assistance of his fellow-laborer, Dr. Williamson, he translated the Bible into the language of the Santee
Sioux, and its teachings have sustained and guided the people
amid the temptations and hardships of a nomadic life.

In our Canadian North-West, James Evans invented the
syllabic system of the Cree language, and H. B. Sinclair and
Henry B. Steinhauer translated the Bible into the Cree language.
Dr. Mason and his wife, assisted by Sinclair and Steinhauer,
translated the Bible which Dr. Mason took with him to England
and was published by the British and Foreign Bible Society.
Translations of the New Testament have been made for the use
of the Cree Indians by missionaries who have labored among

them, including Bishop Horden, of Moosonee, and a Roman Catholic version by Father Lacombe. Archdeacon Hunter and his wife translated the greater part of the New Testament in the same language. The different subtribes included in the Cree Confederacy are supplied with native literature to a greater extent than any of the Indian tribes in Canada.

The Ojibways have not been forgotten by those who labored among them and sought their welfare, having the New Testament in three separate translations, and a large portion of the Old Testament. There have been several zealous translators among the Ojibways since the days of Jones, Jacobs and Dr. O'Meara. As the natives sat around the camp fires in the forests of Ontario, they read and listened to the teachings of the great Book, and many a swarthy son vowed to follow the Man of Nazareth and become a new man. Touched with the sacred fire which fell upon their souls, they travelled long distances to attend camp meetings, and many notable scenes were witnessed by the worshippers who assembled in the leafy temple to sing the praises of their God.

Dr. Silas T. Rand, the eminent Micmac scholar and missionary, labored for many years among the Micmacs of Nova Scotia translating hymns, prayers, and religious tracts for the use of the Indians. He compiled an elaborate dictionary of the language, and translated a large portion of the Bible. Among the Six Nation Indians the New Testament, and a portion of the Old has been translated into the Mohawk language. Among the Indian tribes of our Dominion portions of the Bible have been translated into Seneca, Iroquois, Huron, Pottawotomi, Malicete, Abnaki, Shawnee, Blackfoot, Ottawa, Delaware and Eskimo; and in the far north, in Taculli, Tukudh, Slave, Chippewayan, Beaver and Tinne.

When Chief Joseph, of Oka, was cast into prison, he spent his solitary hours in translating the gospels and some hymns into the Iroquois tongue. Some of the Cree Indians have learned to read the Bible in a few days by the help of Evan's syllabic characters, as they sat by the camp fires when out on their hunting expeditions, taught by the members of their own

tribe, without the intervention of the white man. When they have separated to travel in different paths, they have divided their Bible in portions, that each might have a share and be able to enjoy the consolations of reading the Book in the solitude of the northern woods. They have carried these sacred books with them wherever they have gone, not as a talisman, to guard them in hours of danger, but as a guide and teacher, to lead them in the way of truth. The hardy sons of the great snowland have listened to its precepts from the lips of intrepid missionaries, who have followed the Indian trails along the Yukon and Peel rivers. In the snow hut of the Eskimo the Book has been a harbinger of peace, bringing light and joy to darkened minds. No more thrilling tales have ever been told than those we have read and listened to, of the long snow journeys of the faithful and isolated missionary toilers who have sought out the lone lodge on the prairie, and the scattered camps along the rivers and in the forests, to read to the aged savage folk the story of grace and love, unseen and sometimes forgotten by their brethren in the cities of the east, but they sought not, and indeed cared little, for the applause of men; the work was too impressive, and the intensity of their zeal sustained them, as they taught for immortality, like Apelles, the sculptor, and longed only to live and toil for men.

The influence of the Bible has been felt far and near among the wigwams and lodges of the red men, and the savage folk have learned through its teachings to forsake the dreary paths of error and superstition, rejoicing in a hope that is stronger than death, as it reaches the land beyond the river. In the home of the Northern Lights, and under the shadow of the Rocky Mountains, the light of the celestial land has dawned upon the souls that were weary of sin, and out of darkness have they been led into the light and glory of God. When the mists have rolled away we shall see the tears of thousands of American aborigines who have found their way to God through the study of the Christian revelation in the translations made into the Indian tongues.

THE DOOMED RACE.

The answer to the question of population in relation to native races is not uniform, and must be qualified, as there does not exist a pure race, for all are in a great measure mixed, changed by contact with tribes and individuals, influenced by the language and customs of other people, and therefore in a slight degree in a state of transition.

There are stages of progression and retrogression among nations and tribes, and the same is true of confederacies and races. During the spring time of a nation there is rapid development, increase in population and buoyancy of spirit, evidenced by activity in commerce or war, or the advancements of the arts of peace. So soon as a superior power breaks the spirit, by fair or foul means, the alluring fancies of a false civilization, undermining the morals of the people and destroying the patriotic zeal, the nation, or tribe, rapidly decays. There is witnessed a tendency to extinction among all savage nations, and notably amongst the American tribes who are the heirs of a deteriorating civilization.* Upon the eastern coast of Yucatan lies the Island of Cozumel, where three hundred and fifty years ago, when the Spanish conquerors arrived, the population numbered one hundred thousand, besides fifty thousand pilgrims annually visited the shrines. A mere handful of people now reside there, while vestiges of ancient dwellings are strewn among the soil.† Witness the tendency to decay amongst the aboriginal population of the State of Guatemala, which numbers now about half a million souls of pure or nearly pure blood, whereas, at the conquest the native population was denser than at present.‡ No less an observer than David Zeisberger, who spent fifty years among the Indians, believed that the struggle between civilization and barbarism would ultimately lead to the extermination of the Indians. The tribes

* Washington Irving's "Astoria," page 175. Julia McNair Wright's "Brick's from Babel," page 155.
† Alice D. le Plongeon's "Here and There in Yucatan," page 30.
‡ Brinton's "Annals of the Cakchiquels," page 21.

amongst whom he labored were not as populous in his time as in previous years, arising in a great measure from war and immorality.* The Mound-Builders and Cliff-Dwellers have disappeared. The descendants of the Pueblos are a mere handful to the numerous hosts of ancient days. The Toltecs, after having extended their sway over the remotest borders of the Anahuac, became greatly reduced by famine, pestilence, and unsuccessful wars, and finally disappeared silently and mysteriously, leaving no remains of their history, but what may be gathered from the legends of the natives which succeeded them.† Evidences of decay are seen amongst the tribes on every island and continent. Within the past hundred years every vestige of the native population of Tasmania has disappeared, and the native Australian, with the various tribes on the coasts of Australia, must soon be numbered amongst the things of the past.‡ Lady Brassey, in her "Last Voyage of the Sunbeam," says, of the natives of Australia : "The aboriginals are rapidly dying out as a pure race, and most of the younger ones are half-breeds." In 1835 the natives of Van Diemen's Land numbered two hundred and ten, and in 1848 only thirty-eight survived. The Hawaiians are doomed in a very short time to pass away, leaving a hybrid race to perpetuate their memory for a few decades, when they, too, will become absorbed by the more powerful races. When Captain Cook explored the islands he fixed the number of the people at four hundred thousand. In half a century they numbered one-half; and thirty-seven years ago, when the first accurate census was taken, there were only eighty-one thousand four hundred and fifty-three. In 1878 there were only forty-four thousand and eighty-eight natives; in 1884, only forty thousand and fourteen, and now there remain thirty-six thousand.§

The Maories of New Zealand—once a strong, healthy and manly race—and the Laplanders are on the eve of extinction.

* "Life of David Zeisberger," pages 42, 47.
 . † Prescott's "Conquest of Mexico," Vol. I., pages 34, 35.
 ‡ *The Canadian Journal*, November, 1856, page 511. .
 § G. F. Fitch, in the *Cosmopolitan*.
 19

The Fijians are declining in numbers, as shown by the greater
number of deaths than births recorded in the registers of the
little towns kept by native scribes; yet, we hope that such a fine
race of people may be saved from total extinction. The cal-
culations made by the Board of Health of several of the leading
cities upon the American continent reveal to us the fact that
the death rate amongst the negro race is very high, much
greater than amongst the white people, and unless steps are
taken to prevent this loss there must follow a slow but sure
evanishment of the colored race.

Many of the council fires of the American tribes are extinguished, the railroad traverses the sites of the Indian villages,
and the location of the mission chapel, where flocked hundreds
of red men to listen to the missionary, is now of interest to the
antiquary. "Along the Tuscarawas and the Walkosding, the
Muskingum, Hockhocking, and Sciato, not a solitary Indian
lodge remains; from the waters of Lake Erie to the bluffs of
the 'Beautiful River,' not a remnant of the Lenni-Lenape can
be found."

The towns of praying Indians in the Massachusetts and Plymouth colonies have passed away. Of the two thousand five
hundred converts, under the care of John Eliot and his co-
laborers, not a descendant of unmixed blood remains to-day.
Some of the tribes of Indians were almost exterminated during
King Philips war. Less than thirty years after John Eliot's
death, the Indian church in his beloved Natick became extinct,
and the native language was no longer used for the records of
the town.* Only a mere handful remain of the powerful
Garratine, or Penobscot, and Passamaquoddy tribes in the State
of Maine.

There are some writers who maintain that the Indians are
increasing in number. From the changed conditions of the
tribes we should naturally expect a large and steady increase.
Instead of the ravages of war, tribe fighting against tribe,
warriors continually on the warpath in quest of scalps, there
is peace. The periods of want followed by savage feasts

---

* Pilling's "Bibliographic Notes on Eliot's Indian Bible," pages 56-58.

continued day and night without cessation are now replaced by regular supplies of good food. Unskilful " medicine men " have no occupation except among the non-treaty Indians, who still wander in the unsettled parts of the country, for the practical surgeon and physician attends to the needs of the sick upon the Reservations; and where, in former years, large numbers died from the most common and simple diseases, few now fall a prey to these ailments. The records of the Indian Departments show an increase in population, and the untrained observer is apt to conclude from this, that the red men are becoming very populous. Upon the analysis of the census returns depends the answer to the question of increase or decrease.

A singular freak of nature is witnessed amongst the Seminoles, who are increasing, in the fact that although there are Indian and negro half-breeds, there are no white half-breeds, and though they are a polygamous society, there are more male children than female born, and already there are more males than females amongst them. What the effect of this will be in the future it is hard to say.*

The majority of the people in the Old and New World are in full sympathy with the growth of the red race, and are unanimous in their agreement with the sentiments of President U. S. Grant, who wrote, " I do not believe our Creator ever placed the different races of men on this earth with the view of the stronger exerting all his energies in exterminating the weaker."

There are numerous scientists and philanthropists who reiterate the utterance of Goldsmith, " It is undeniable that the American race is tending to extinction." Such a pessimistic theory as this is not pleasant to contemplate, but if it is borne out by facts, nothing but good can come from it. There must inevitably follow a change of policy in agreement with the ultimate issue which may hasten or retard the progress toward the end, as is deemed best in the interests of the race and society. What are the facts in relation to some of the United States Indians ? When Lewis and Clarke visited the Hidatsa

* " Annual Report of the Bureau of Ethnology," 1883-84, page 479.

Indians they were said to number two thousand five hundred ;
in Catlin's time, about 1830, there were only one thousand five
hundred, and in the Indian Bureau Report of 1888, there
remained, all told, five hundred and two persons.   Dr. Barrows'
estimate of a decrease of two hundred and sixty thousand since
1820, and of two thousand per annum during the past eighteen
years, appears startling.   We do not think the estimate of
five hundred and twenty-six thousand five hundred and ninety-
two in 1820 and two hundred and fifty-six thousand for the
present time can form a true comparison, because of the difficulty
in the early years of the Indian Departments obtaining a correct
census.   In the early days of missionary work among the red
men, the Methodist Episcopal Church numbered many thousands within some single tribes, and there were schools and
churches all over the land, but in 1885, there were only two
thousand four hundred members on twenty-three different
missions, and these comprised the whole field of operations, with
seven thousand five hundred in the Indian territory.

Fragments of the tribes are to be found in the Indian territory, but these represent large and powerful bodies of Indians
which once existed in the land.*   Morgan estimated the Iroquois in the seventeenth century to number not less than
twenty-five thousand souls.†   Pennsylvania was essentially the
home of the red men in the days of William Penn, where
numerous tribes dwelt, but within a few years white settlers
became numerous, purchasing land from Thomas and John
Penn, who had their land office at Philadelphia in 1745, and
toward the limits of the State there roamed broken remnants of
former nations, even dwelling together in the same wigwams.
Zeisberger found Mohicans, Shawanese and Delawares living
together on the Susquehanna.   The advance of the white man
drove the Delawares into the recesses of the western wilderness.‡
The French Colonial authorities, in a report made to the home
Government in 1736, asserted that there were no less than one
hundred and three nations, comprising sixteen thousand four

---

* *Gospel in all Lands*, July, 1885, page 324.
† Morgan's "Iroquois League."
‡ "Life of Zeisberger," page 68-72.

hundred and three warriors, and eighty-two thousand souls, under their control.*

When Principal Grant travelled over Manitoba and the North-West he wrote: "It may be said that, do what we like, the Indians, as a race, must eventually die out. It is not unlikely. Almost all the Indians in the North-West are scrofulous. But, on the other hand, in the United States and in Canada they exist, in not a few cases, as Christianized, self-supporting communities, and have multiplied and prospered."

In Alta, California, the white population in 1831 did not exceed four thousand five hundred, while the Indians of the twenty-one missions amounted to nineteen thousand, and in 1842 the white race had increased to seven thousand, and the red men had decreased to about five thousand.† The Hon. B. D. Wilson, of Los Angeles, in his report to the Interior Department in 1853, stated that "In 1830 there were living in the twenty-one missions in California some twenty thousand or thirty thousand Indians, living comfortable and industrious lives under the control of the Franciscan Fathers." There are not five thousand Indians to-day in that country.‡

There has been a great decrease among the Indians of Puget Sound since the advent of the white people amongst them.§

In 1881 there were in the United States two hundred and forty-six thousand four hundred and seventeen Indians; and in 1891 two hundred and forty-four thousand seven hundred and four, amongst whom we must class some half-breeds, as these are found generally amongst the tribes in these later days.

When we study this question among the Indian tribes of Canada, we are met with some facts not to be found in the United States, especially the antagonism of the races, the renewal or breaking of treaties, the removal of Indians from their Reservations through the demands of the white people for the fine tracts of land, the wrong treatment of the Aborigines

* Schoolcraft's "Indian Tribes," Part VI., page 198.
† Edwin Bryant's, "What I Saw in California," page 391.
‡ "Report of the United States Commissioner of Indian Affairs," 1884, pages 12, 15, 17.
§ "American Antiquarian," Vol. IX., pages 271-273.

by vicious white men, and justice not being granted the injured
in the courts of law ; but in the matter of decrease we find the
same influences at work.

Relics of the extinct race who were the Aboriginal inhabitants of Newfoundland, the Beothuks or Boethies, have been
found lately on Pilley's Island, Notre Dame Bay.   This tribe
was a branch of the powerful Algonquins, and from the remains
of skeletons, and specimens of beautifully finished arrow-heads,
axes, gouges and other stone implements, it is shown that the
Boethies were not intellectually of a low type.   They hunted
on the island for ages before the coming of Cabot, but they
found a deadly foe to aid their inveterate enemies, the Micmacs,
in the white man, and the contest waged fiercely until not a
single member of the tribe remained.   The native population
which Cartier met in 1535 is believed to have been exterminated or driven westward before the return of the French under
Champlain in 1603.   The Jesuit missionaries found the Hurons
in 1639 occupying thirty-two palisaded villages, and Brebeuf
reckoned their number in 1635 to be not less than thirty thousand.   Even at that early date the country westward from the
Ottawa to Lake Simcoe had become depopulated through the
wrath of the Iroquois.   The Eries were completely exterminated in the war with the Five Nations, which terminated in the
year 1653.   Not a member of this powerful tribe was left to
perpetuate their name.

Albanel, one of the Jesuit Fathers, states that in 1670
Tadousac was almost deserted, the Indians having decreased
through small-pox and other diseases, and through want caused
by other Indian tribes driving them from their hunting-grounds,
so that where formerly he saw from a thousand to twelve
hundred Indians, now he saw not more than one hundred.
The Attikamegues or White Fish Indians were nearly all swept
away by the Iroquois, and the Indians at Three Rivers shared
the same fate.   Montreal, in the latter part of the seventeenth
century, was a rendezvous for the Indians, but few of the
descendants of the many thousands now remain.*   The Attiwen-

* Winsor's " Critical History of America," Vol. IV., pages 271, 279.

darons or Neutrals were wholly exterminated as early as 1655, and the Hurons were almost destroyed by the powerful Iroquois. Nothing now remains of some of the British Columbia Indian villages but tombs and rotten columns.

There are some tribes in Canada which are increasing, and there are many persons, including missionaries, who believe that the red men are not doomed to extinction. The Haidas, of Queen Charlotte Island, have decreased rapidly during the present century ; but Dr. G. M. Dawson, who has been amongst them, thinks that they are not doomed to utter extinction, because of their ability to gain a good living, as they are skilful fishermen, possess a special aptitude for carving, and can perform other simple mechanical arts. We learn from the "Statistical Year Book" of 1889 that the native population is increasing. There is no doubt that some of the tribes are increasing in numbers, judging from the reports of the Department of Indian affairs. As to the actual gain or loss, we shall be able to tell more accurately when we come to examine the census returns in these reports.

Various estimates of the number of Indians in the provinces and districts have been given by different writers. Upon the American continent the entire native population three centuries ago was reckoned to be from ten to fourteen millions ; even Catlin, in his day, supposed them to be fully the latter number. In 1835, the Indians of the United States and Mexico were estimated at three hundred and thirty thousand, and on the Upper Missouri and its tributaries as late as 1850 there were said to be no less than fifty-four thousand five hundred and fifty. General Lefroy made a full investigation of this question among the Indians of Manitoba and the North-West, and concluded that in 1843 there were Crees, Blackfeet and kindred tribes numbering nearly forty thousand, while Catlin's estimate of the Crees and Blackfeet on the plains of the North-West alone was twenty-three thousand four hundred. Sir George Simpson's estimate of the Indians in the Valley of the Saskatchewan, in 1842, was about seventeen thousand, which very nearly agrees with the former, as this was one

of the most populous districts of the North-West. In 1809
Henry, an Indian trader, said the Blackfeet on the plains had
one thousand four hundred and twenty warriors. In 1857 the
Indian population of Rupert's Land—*i.e*, the territory controlled
by the Hudson's Bay Company—was supposed to be forty-three
thousand : in the Indian territory east of the Rocky Mountains,
thirteen thousand, and west of the mountains, eighty thousand.[*]

Very conflicting are these returns by traders and travellers,
and they are not to be relied upon as accurate estimates. Paul
Kane, the artist, gave the whole native population of the North-
west Coast of America at sixty-three thousand three hundred
and forty. General Lefroy believed the Indians to be decreasing rapidly. In 1852, the native population of Canada was
one hundred and twenty-four thousand five hundred and
eighteen, but Baron de la Hontan thought the Iroquois alone,
in 1690, were about half of that number.

Amongst the semi-civilized tribes of Ontario and Quebec
there is a slow but steady increase, but when we visit the tribes
which have only lately come in contact with the white people,
there is a very rapid decrease. This fact is especially noticeable among the tribes in Manitoba, the North-West Territories
and British Columbia. The Sioux at Birtle and in the North-
West, and the Indians on Muscowpetung's Reserve are decreasing. The Ojibways of Okanese seem to be stationary, a slight
increase having been reported during 1887-88, which was a
healthy year.[†] The Stoney Indians who, according to Alexander
Henry, numbered at the beginning of the present century several thousands, do not now number one thousand. The Mound-
Builders of Manitoba are gone, and some of the Indian tribes
are following them rapidly. Let us turn to the reports of the
Indian Department and read there the story of the Blue Books.

The following tabulated statement of the native population
of the Dominion is taken from the Indian reports of the years
given, the census returns relating to the years preceding :

[*] Winsor's " Critical History of America," Vol. VIII., pages, 15, 48.
[†] Rev. Dr. Bryce's " Holiday Rambles," pages 49, 64, 73, 82.

INDIAN POPULATION OF CANADA.

	1864	1869	1872	1874	1876	1878	1880	1882	1884	1886	1888	1890	1891
Ontario	9,367	13,544	12,592	14,508	15,540	15,731	15,821	17,126	16,892	17,267	17,700	17,776	17,915
Quebec	7,715	8,274	9,429	10,843	10,804	10,947	11,006	11,089	12,023	12,286	12,465	13,590	13,361
Nova Scotia	*	1,835	1,626	1,765	2,091	2,122	2,102	2,228	2,197	2,138	2,145	2,107	2,076
New Brunswick	*	1,343	1,408	1,604	1,440	1,459	1,464	1,486	1,524	1,576	1,594	1,569	1,521
Prince Edward Island	*	*	*	323	299	306	290	312	292	323	319	321	314
Manitoba & N.-W. Territory	*	*	20,998	31,808	24,547	27,204	33,787	37,044	33,959	30,578	26,368	25,743	25,195
Peace River District	*	*	*	*	*	*	*	*	2,038	2,038	2,038	2,038	2,038
†Athabasca District	*	*	*	*	2,398	2,398	2,398	2,398	8,000	8,000	8,000	8,000	8,000
†Mackenzie District	*	*	*	*	*	*	*	*	7,000	7,000	7,000	7,000	7,000
†Eastern Rupert's Land	*	*	4,370	4,370	4,370	4,370	3,770	3,770	4,016	4,016	4,016	4,016	4,016
†Labrador—Canadian Interior	*	*	*	*	*	*	*	*	1,000	1,000	1,000	1,000	1,000
†Arctic Coast	*	*	*	*	*	*	*	*	4,000	4,000	4,000	4,000	4,000
British Columbia	*	*	*	28,520	32,020	35,154	35,052	35,052	39,011	38,539	37,944	35,416	35,202
Totals	17,082	25,016	50,421	93,741	92,518	99,691	105,691	112,505	131,952	128,761	124,589	122,585	121,638

* No report. † Approximate.

The question which confronts us upon examining the figures in our statement is, Are these statistics reliable, or does there enter into them any degree of uncertainty arising from the habits of the people, their superstitions, the making of treaties, the intermarriage of tribes, or the origin of a race of hybrids? The nomadic habits of the natives is a serious hindrance towards obtaining accurate returns, and among the treaty Indians, who receive their treaty payments annually, there is a strong temptation to add to the number of persons reported, that they may receive a larger amount of money. The reports vary somewhat, large additions being made to the census returns in some years through the non-treaty Indians having made a treaty and then being enumerated. Sometimes the non-treaty Indians of a certain district are numbered with the other tribes. Thus we have the non-treaty Sioux, numbered in 1891, to the extent of nine hundred and eighty-five with the Indians of Manitoba and the North-West. Between the years 1874 and 1888 there is an increase of seventy-four thousand one hundred and sixty-eight, caused chiefly by the reports from British Columbia, Prince Edward Island, the Peace River, Athabasca and Mackenzie districts; Labrador and the Arctic Coast being furnished for the first time, the total number in 1888 amounting to seventy thousand three hundred and one.

The statistics from Peace River, Athabasca and Mackenzie districts, Labrador and the Arctic Coast are only approximate. The increase for the whole Dominion is therefore not real, but only apparent. In Nova Scotia, New Brunswick and Prince Edward Island there is apparently neither increase nor decrease: in British Columbia, Eastern Rupert's Land, Manitoba and the North-West Territories the natives are rapidly decreasing: while in Ontario and Quebec they are increasing.

The increase from 1872 to 1891 for Ontario was five thousand three hundred and twenty-three, and for Quebec three thousand nine hundred and thirty-two. Is this increase real, or is it, too, only an apparent increase? Let anyone conversant with Indian types visit the Reservations and investigate thoroughly the history of the people, and there will soon dawn

PAINTED COFFIN OF THE FLATHEADS.

upon the mind the fact that the red men of Ontario and Quebec
are a hybrid race, many of them being half-breeds and quarter-
breeds, yet these are all classed together as Indians. There
exist few pure-blood red men in these provinces. Here is
destruction through absorption, an apparent extinction only, for
some of the natives who are receiving a good education are
mingling with the white race, and standing well in the front
rank. Several notable cases have come under the writer's
notice of persons classed as Indians who have occupied good
positions amongst their white brethren. Education and intermarriage will increase this absorption. This mixed race may
linger on as a separate race, like the gypsies of Britain, through
the retention of their language and customs and the perpetuation of the Reservation system. Is the absorption a cause for
regret? We do not think so. The modern Englishman is the
descendant of the Anglo-Saxon, Dane and Norman, and the
American is a cosmopolitan, indeed. Here are cases of extinction of separate races in a defined locality through absorption.
The higher races have duties toward the lower, and both will be
benefited by the absorption.

Amongst the tribes somewhat isolated, and meeting for the
first time the strong influence of the white race, there is seen a
rapid decrease. The Chippewayans living in the district of
Isle la Crosse, in Athabasca, are decreasing, the death rate
being greater than the number of births, and there remains not
more than half the number of the people there were twenty
years ago. The Blood Indians, thirteen years ago, numbered
three thousand five hundred, and now there are not more
than half of that number. This rapid decrease is not quite correct, as there is no doubt that there were not more than three
thousand at the former date, the Indians representing that there
were more people than really existed, so that they might obtain
a larger amount of treaty money. The death rate, however, is
much greater annually than the birth rate. The Sarcee Indians
numbered, twelve years ago, seven hundred, and now there
remain not more than two hundred and fifty, with indications
of extinction in the near future.

What are the causes which bring about this rapid decrease, with apparently no means of recovery? Some of the native tribes decrease through polygamy, early marriages, intoxicating liquors and immorality. The inhabitants of the Polynesian Islands rapidly decreased through infanticide, polygamy, early marriages, labor trade and unlawful diseases;[*] the British Columbian Indians through debauchery and disease arising from immorality; the Hawaiians from leprosy, drunkenness, and the diseases arising from contact with civilization; the Indians on the Pacific Coast in the early days from war with each other;[†] the Indians of Pennsylvania and the adjoining territory through the persecution of white men whose religious belief, as they called it, demanded the extermination of the red men.[‡] Famine caused many to die, the Nanticokes, from this and other causes, being reduced to four or five families.[§] Dr. Brinton says that "the Indians have degenerated in moral sense as the result of contact with the white race;"[||] and the unanimous verdict of missionaries and travellers is that the Indians have decreased through contact with civilization, the encroachments of the people demanding their land, and eager for their extermination.[¶]

Hunter, in his narrative of his nineteen years spent among the Indians, ascribes their decrease to wars arising from trespassing on the lands belonging to other tribes in search of game, the civilization of the white people causing the Indians to indulge in luxuries, and follow the white man's vices, the destruction of the game through the white man's demand for furs, the loss of their land causing a declension of national pride, and finally, intoxicating drinks.

Paul Kane attributed the decrease of the Indians whom he

---

[*] Melbourne *Argus*. The New Westminster *Columbian*. Rev. Ebenezer Robson in "Canadian Methodist Missionary Report," 1862.

[†] G. F. Fitch in the "Cosmopolitan."

[‡] Washington Irving's "Astoria," page 126.

[§] "Life of Zeisberger," pages 72, 276, 304, 642.

[||] Brinton's "American Hero Myths," page 206.

[¶] "Life of Heckewelder," page 20. McClure's "Three Thousand Miles Through the Rocky Mountains," pages 42, 74.

visited chiefly to the indulgence in intoxicating drink. The Haidas lost three hundred people in 1868 through small-pox.[*] One or two thousand years ago the Ohio Valley was peopled by an industrious population of some Indian stock with a fair degree of civilization, who were assailed by an alliance of Hurons and Algonquins, almost wholly exterminating them. The survivors were either incorporated with the conquering tribes or fled southward and found refuge among the nations lying between the Ohio Valley and the Gulf of Mexico.[†]

The war of the Spaniards with the Indians reduced them sadly. They were beaten with the Spanish lash, brought into the most abject state of slavery, being made beasts of burden, and when their strength failed they were slain. Small-pox destroyed large numbers of them. Hispaniola had one million natives in the days of Columbus, and when this and other islands fell into the hands of the English there was no trace left of the original population. The lowest estimate made of the natives destroyed by the Spanish conquest is no less than ten million persons.[‡] War, small-pox and other diseases and immorality destroyed several of the Jesuit missions.[§] The Indians of Puget Sound have decreased through drunkenness, diseases consequent upon licentiousness, consumption, small-pox and whooping cough and measles among the children. Many have died from diseases arising from the transition from a savage to a civilized state of life, dwelling in houses instead of tents, and the wearing of European clothing, causing the accumulation of filth and, therefore, disease; whereas in the modes of savage life, with the nomadic habit of the people, the filthy camp was left, and the Indians spent much of their time in the water, which kept them in a healthy state.[‖] Amongst the natives of the Canadian North-West the changed conditions

[*] " American Antiquarian," Vol. XIII., page 53.
[†] " American Antiquarian," Vol. IX., page 378.
[‡] Mackenzie's "America," page 73.
[§] Winsor's " Critical History of America," Vol. IV., pages 271-273.
[‖] " American Antiquarian," Vol. IX , pages 271-273.

of life, fondness for unwholesome food, the filth of the houses and camp, and disease and degradation arising from immorality have been some of the chief causes of their rapid decrease.[*] General Lefroy attributed their decrease to the substitution of inferior European clothing for their robes of fur, the use of stimulants, gradual loss of native arts and appliances, abortion and sterility in females, induced by the use of potions, the deterioration of their dwellings, consciousness of decline, pressure of new necessities, and a sense of superiority of their white neighbors. Dr. J. C. Tache, late Deputy Minister of Agriculture, in his introduction to the census of 1871, made the following observations regarding this question: "The broad facts which spring from the examination of the conditions of the savage state in this country are, that the most fertile soils are not those which, in general, yield most support to those engaged in hunting; that the fisheries, and specially on the Maritime coasts, are the most abundant of the natural sources of supply found by man in a savage state. It is the Indians most favorably situated in respect to soil and climate, who supplemented the food obtained by hunting and fishing by cultivation. On the other hand, the Eskimos, whose territory is restricted to the waste and desolate shores of the frozen sea, managed to derive a rough abundance from the ice-bound waters.

"That Indian populations, living exclusively by hunting and fishing, cannot increase beyond certain very restricted limits, governed by a ratio between the number of inhabitants and the superficies inhabited. Below this ratio they descend periodically, by famine, disease, or war, oscillating in this way between an almost determinable maximum (the circumstances being known) and an indeterminable minimum. The mildness of the climate has a great bearing on this question, if not in actually adding to the natural resources, at least in lessening the wants.

"That Indian populations, keeping to the habits of hunting tribes, diminish in number in the ratio of the extent and

---

[*] Bryce's "Holiday Rambles," page 65.

frequency of their relations with civilized nations, by the
destruction of their primitive means of existence, and the introduction of vices and diseases, or by absorption in the creation
of a half-breed race."

The observations of the writer for the past twelve years,
among the Indian tribes of the Canadian North-West, have
led him to conclude that the decrease arose during the early
years before the advent of the white race from tribal wars;
but after the settlers arrived small-pox claimed a very large
number, amounting to thousands among the Crees, Blackfeet
and Sarcees.   Liquor introduced during the buffalo days,
when the traders were on the plains, aroused the Indians to
quarrel with each other, and many were killed; some died
during the famine of 1878, when the buffaloes left the country,
and since that period consumption and vice have claimed a
large number.   The new mode of life on a Reserve, dwelling in
filthy houses, badly ventilated, has induced disease; the idle
manner of living, being fed by the Government, and having
little to do; the poor clothing worn in the winter; badly
cooked food; the consciousness that as a race they are fading
away, and the increasing strength of the white race, has caused
such a depression of spirit that many of them may be said to
die of a broken heart.

The mortality among the children from diseases common to
the white children is very great.   The two chief causes, however, are immoral diseases and depression of spirit.   From our
investigation of the whole question, we have come to the conclusion that when the Indians first come into contact with
civilization they decreased rapidly, and if the tribe is numerous
it may be able to rally, and thus be saved from total extinction:
the small tribe gradually succumbing to the deteriorating
influence.   If the relations of the two races are not antagonistic,
but are of such a friendly character as to encourage the stronger
to seek the elevation of the weaker, the feeling of an exterminating influence at work entertained by the weaker will be
removed, and a recognition of equality being established,
ensuring confidence, will work so strongly upon the natives,

that the transition state being bridged over safely, a period of
increase will follow. The position of the red men will be such
that there will be an intermingling with their white neighbors, and as the result of intermarriage, according to the Indian
custom or that of the white people, there will spring up a race
of half-breeds. The slow settlement of the country will keep
this half-breed race in possession of their language, customs and
Reservation system; but so soon as there is rapid advancement,
there will follow a voluntary absorption, and this will prove to
be a benison to both races, uniting them in language, customs,
privileges and toil. Compulsory absorption is not agreeable to
our political sentiments, but as the races are drawn closer
together, they will gradually unite, and this will ultimately
solve the problem of the perpetuation of a separate race within
the bounds of the Dominion.

WHITESKINS AND REDSKINS.

When the tide of emigration reached the far west, the red
men were in a serious mood at the encroachments upon their
territory, and no longer engaged in scenes of savage warfare
with hostile tribes, they sat in their lodges during the long
evenings in groups talking about their grievances, and discussing the queer ways of the white men. The stories of brave
men and glorious deeds were forgotten for a time in the new
subjects which filled their minds, and they lent a willing ear
to the curious tales related by the adventurous warrior, who
had penetrated farther than his fellows, into the secrets of the
power and success of the men and women who were seeking
homes on the prairie land. The savage folk had come in
contact with trappers and traders, men in the employment
of the Hudson's Bay Company, miners and bull-whackers and
the Mounted Police, but the newcomers brought their wives
and children with them, determined to reside in the country,
and this compelled the Indians to ask one another what they
would do on the prairie to subsist, seeing that the buffalo had
gone to return no more. One or two of the natives had been
20

taken east on a visit before the tide of emigration set in, and
when they returned they related the most wonderful tales of
the vast populations, great wealth and skill of the white
people, but the natives did not believe them. They did not
charge them with deliberate falsehood, but asserted that they
had been enchanted by the white medicine men. Curiosity
led some of the boldest to pry into the affairs of the emigrants,
and after a while large numbers of young and old were to be
seen gathered around the primitive-looking dwelling of the
pale-face. As the busy housewife prepared the noon-day meal
or baked bread, the house suddenly became darkened by a
crowd of the natives peering in at the windows. The native
women laughed as the white woman made garments for her
children. It seemed strange to them that the cloth should be
cut into so many small pieces and then sewed together again.
The sewing machine and clothes wringer afforded much amusement. The men travelled long distances to gaze upon the fire-
waggon, their significant name for the locomotive, and when
the first steamboat sailed up the Belly River to Lethbridge, a
large number of the Blood and Piegan Indians went to satisfy
their curiosity.

Great was their astonishment at these evidences of the
ability of the white men, and whilst believing in their native
superiority, they were free to acknowledge that the white men
were superior to them in some things. They looked upon the
white men as brothers, and applied to them the same communistic belief as they obeyed and taught themselves. Whenever they asked for a gift of tea, tobacco or money, and they
were told that the individual was a poor man and had none of
these articles, the invariable answer was, " Write a letter and
I will go to the trading-post and get them."

The fact of having to pay on account never seemed to enter
their minds. They were amused when they saw potatoes cut
up and planted in the ground, and when they were learning to
farm and put the potatoes in the ground, they went day after
day looking for signs of growth, and at last getting tired
waiting, dug up the seed and ate it. One of our friends

employed some Indian families to plant his potato field, and
gave them the potatoes for that purpose. They were very
slow in getting the work done, and after being paid, the
rancher was surprised and angry to find that they had peeled
and eaten the potatoes and planted the parings. Fortunately
it was a wet season and a good crop of potatoes was the result.

The customs of the natives appear not more strange to the
white man, than do the customs of the white race to the
Indians. A village ball, where men and women danced
together, was a scene that threw the Piegan Indians, who were
spectators, into a fit of laughter. They could understand men
dancing alone and appreciate it, but to see men and women
together was to them a subject for fools. The Blood Indians
talked and laughed over the strange marriage customs of the
white people. When a detachment of infantry came to
Macleod during the second Riel Rebellion, one of the chiefs
came to the mission-house and, alternately, spoke with laughter
and scorn of the little men without horses. They could not
understand the individuality of the white men, each laboring
for himself, and apparently not caring for his brother-man, as
they were firm believers in the brotherhood of the red men,
and sought to put into practice the teachings of the wise men
of the lodges. Even the dress of the white men was a puzzle
to them. When an Indian received the present of a hat, he
cut the crown in shreds, which hung over the sides as ornaments, allowing the air to reach his head to keep it cool. A
pair of pants given to him were cut in twain and made in the
Indian fashion, and were worn with the breech cloth. The
white man was a puzzle to him, and his customs were very
queer. The savage folk ignored the customs of the white folk,
and their suspicions were aroused on many occasions. When
the native children were urged to attend school, and the adults
to assemble for religious services, they wanted to be paid for
allowing the children to be taught, as they felt that some unknown advantage was sought by the white people in the education of the children. Having an educational system of their
own, they thought that they should receive something for
allowing the white man's culture to displace their own.

KEEWATIN BAY

BOATING AT RAT PORTAGE

NEAR RAT PORTAGE

A SUMMER SCENE AT RAT PORTAGE

RAPIDS IN THE WINNIPEG RIVER NEAR RAT PORTAGE

Accustomed to war, and always expecting their enemies to take advantage of them, they could not believe that it was possible for men to leave their homes and settle among the natives to teach them without having some selfish motive, and looking for some advantage. This belief was strengthened by the first wave of emigration, when the Indians sold their beautiful moccasins and various articles of native manufacture, receiving as compensation, from despicable white men, counterfeit money, and for articles worth three and four dollars a highly-polished single cent. Sometimes they applied to the white people the terms " fools " and " white savages."

Elated by the dream of sudden wealth the white folk travelled westward, delighted with the novelty of camping out, singing as they went,

> " We'll have a tent
> Upon the banks of some wandering stream,
> Whose ripple, like the murmur of a dream,
> Shall be our music."

Some of these tenderfeet had read about Indians, and their ideas about the noble red man threw a halo of romance around the scenes of western life, and when they gazed upon the real men and women, and found the glowing descriptions of prairie life and red men did not agree with the actual vision, oftentimes there came a revulsion of feeling, and hatred dwelt where the romantic ideal had formerly reigned. The pilgrims from the east gazed in astonishment at the scantily clad wanderers from the camp, and in their ignorance concluded that these were ideal red men, and genuine specimens of the savage folk. They studied them from the standpoint of the white man, ignorant of the beautiful languages and traditions, the significant religious ideas, social and political customs, and the native independence and heroism of the dwellers in the wilderness. With childish sentimentality they treated the red men as savages, and unable to pierce the shadow of their customs, they laughed at the queer ways of the people of the lodges, concluding that wisdom was the heritage of the white race. Simple tenderfeet! Could they have reserved their verdict

until they had studied the ways of the savage folk from the
Indians' standpoint, they would have learned that native culture and independence were to be found in the lodges, and
nations and peoples are savage to one another. We are all
savages in the estimation of somebody. When we are able to
note the points of similarity, and not dwell on the differences,
we are drawn closer together, and we are able to understand
and appreciate one another.

There are no people who delight to listen to an eloquent
speaker more than the natives of the prairies and forests. The
most respectful attention is given to the person addressing the
audience, never interrupting him with manifestations of dis-
sension or applause, but they seriously listen to what he has to
say, and if deeply moved by his eloquence, they will close the
assembly after he has concluded that some time may be given
to weigh calmly the arguments set forth. The harangue of a
leader of a war party is not always so treated, but if the
speaker is a stranger, perfect stillness reigns, and all eyes are
fixed upon him, drinking deeply the truths which he is en-
deavoring to utter.   When Tecumseh, the great Shawnee
warrior visited the tribes to unite them in a grand confederacy
against the white race, he always addressed them in dignified
language, making an impassioned appeal, which touched the
hearts of his dusky audiences. As he rose to address the
people, he stood calmly for a few moments and surveyed the
audience, then, without any preliminaries, spoke to them upon
the question which had brought them together. His gestures
and language were born of the forest and the intense feelings
which moved his soul. Hunter, in his " Memoirs of a Captivity
Among the Indians," gives the substance of an address given by
Tecumseh to the Osages, which must necessarily be imperfect,
from the fact that it was written from memory some years
after it was delivered.

Tecumseh said : " Brothers, we all belong to one family ; we
are all children of the Great Spirit : we walk in the same path ;
slake our thirst at the same spring, and now affairs of the
greatest concern lead us to smoke the pipe around the same
council fire.

" Brothers,—We are friends ; we must assist each other to bear our burdens. The blood of many of our fathers and brothers has run like water on the ground to satisfy the avarice of the white men. We, ourselves, are threatened with a great evil, nothing will pacify them but the destruction of all the red men.

" Brothers,—When the white men first set foot on our ground they were hungry, they had no place on which to spread their blankets, or to kindle their fires. They were feeble, they could do nothing for themselves. Our fathers commiserated their distress and shared freely with them whatever the Great Spirit had given his red children. They gave them food when hungry, medicine when sick, spread skins for them to sleep on, and gave them grounds, that they might hunt and raise corn. Brothers, the white people are like poisonous serpents, when chilled they are feeble and harmless, but invigorate them with warmth, and they sting their benefactors to death. The white people came among us feeble, and now we have made them strong, they wish to kill us or drive us back, as they would wolves and panthers.

" Brothers,—The white men are not friends to the Indians, at first they only asked for land sufficient for a wigwam, now nothing will satisfy them, but the whole of our hunting grounds, from the rising to the setting sun.

" Brothers,—The white men want more than our hunting grounds, they wish to kill our warriors, they would even kill our old men, women, and little ones.

" Brothers,—Many winters ago there was no land, the sun did not rise and set, all was darkness. The Great Spirit made all things. He gave the white people a home beyond the great waters. He supplied these grounds with game, and gave them to his red children, and he gave them strength and courage to defend them.

" Brothers,—My people wish for peace, the red men all wish for peace ; but where the white people are there is no peace for them, except it be on the bosom of our mother.

" Brothers,—The white men despise and cheat the Indians ; they abuse and insult them ; they do not think the red men sufficiently good to live. The red men have borne many and great injuries; they ought to suffer them no longer. My people will not; they are determined on vengeance; they have taken up the tomahawk: they will make it fat with blood; they will drink the blood of the white people.

" Brothers,—My people are brave and numerous, but the white people are too strong for them alone. I wish you to take up the tomahawk with them. If we all unite, we will cause the rivers to stain the great waters with their blood.

" Brothers,—If you do not unite with us they will first destroy us, and then you will fall an easy prey to them. They have destroyed many nations of red men because they were not united, because they were not friends to each other.

" Brothers,—The white people send runners amongst us; they wish to make us enemies, that they may sweep over and desolate our hunting grounds, like devastating winds or rushing waters.

" Brothers,—Our great Father over the great waters is angry with the white people, our enemies. He will send his brave warriors against them: he will send us rifles and whatever else we want; he is our friend and we are his children.

" Brothers,—Who are the white people that we should fear them ? They cannot run fast, and are good marks to shoot at; they are only men; our fathers have killed many of them. We are not squaws, and we will stain the earth red with their blood.

" Brothers,—The Great Spirit is angry with our enemies. He speaks in thunder, and the earth swallows up villages and drinks up the Mississippi. The great waters will cover the lowlands; their corn cannot grow, and the Great Spirit will sweep those who escape to the hills from the earth with his terrible breath.

" Brothers,—We must be united, we must smoke the same pipe, we must fight each other's battles, and, more than all, we must love the Great Spirit. He is for us. He will destroy our enemies, and make all His red children happy.*

* Hunter's "Captivity Among the Indians," pages 34-35 ; "Dorsey's Omaha Sociology," page 271.

"The whiteskins, ignorant of the native customs, are apt to believe that the redskins are greedy, as they have witnessed them incessantly asking gifts from their rich neighbors; but this habit of begging arises from the fact that they are hospitable at home, and expect the same rites accorded them when they are among the white people. They are as hospitable as their white friends, if not more so, according to their wealth. When a small band of their enemies enter their camp and throw themselves upon the good-will of the natives, they will adopt them into the tribe, distributing them among the families, and afford them protection. If a young man has died or been slain another will be adopted to fill his place, who will be treated as a son, and will be expected to perform all the duties of a natural son. At meal times all the persons who may happen to be in the lodge partake, even though some of them may not be friendly to the master of the lodge. No one asks for anything, but is served as a matter of course. Should an enemy partake of food or drink, or put the pipe in his mouth, he cannot be injured by any member of the tribe; but, after leaving camp, if he is again found, he may be slain. This is the reason that travellers, having enjoyed the rites of hospitality, travel as quickly as possible in troublesome times from the camp of the red men."

As we have teachers among us to instruct us in morals, and to incite us to brave deeds by their noble examples, the sages of the camps taught the young men to be brave, generous and kind, honest and truthful in word and deed. We have listened in the lodges to these aged men, blind and covered with many scars, relating the story of their adventures to the young men, urging them always to defend their people, treat the white people as their friends, and never demean themselves by unmanly acts.*

Hunter narrates a scene similar to those we have often witnessed among the Blackfeet. The Indian warrior, addressing the youth of the camp, said, "Never steal, except it be from an enemy, whom it is just that we should injure in every possible way. When you become men, be brave and

* Dorsey's "Degiha Language," page 727.

cunning in war, and defend your hunting grounds against all encroachments. Never suffer your squaws or little ones to want. Protect the squaws and strangers from insult. On no account betray your friend. Resent insults; revenge yourself on your enemies. Drink not the poisonous strong water of the white people; it is sent by the bad spirit to destroy the Indians. Fear not death, none but cowards fear to die. Obey and venerate the old people, particularly your parents. Fear and propitiate the bad spirit, that he may do you no harm. Love and adore the good Spirit, who made us all, who supplies our hunting grounds and keeps us alive."

The privilege of greatness was conferred on those who were generous, being esteemed for their generosity as great as the man who had gained honor by his bravery in war. The man who wished to be great must not exercise his generosity toward his kindred who have a natural right to any assistance he can render them, but whenever he found any person in extreme need, especially the aged, who cannot help themselves, he was to assist them without any hope of being compensated for his gifts. Some of the tribes were noted for their generosity toward other tribes who were unfortunate in their crops, or had suffered in other ways. He was esteemed a great man who invited many people to partake of his bounty, and was not slack in showering his gifts upon the people, and who made presents of goods or horses to those he saw were in need. He was as brave as the man who feared not an enemy, for he feared not poverty, which was considered an enemy to man. Generous toward the poor, they were magnanimous toward those who were brave and upright, but unfortunately were placed within their power. When Louis XIV. desired some Iroquois Indians to be sent to France to act as galley slaves, measures were adopted to secure some captives by open hostilities, which failed, and then Lamberville, the missionary to the Onondagas, was unconsciously employed to decoy some of the Iroquois chiefs into Fort Ontario, where they were placed in irons and sent to France. The old men of the Onondagas summoned Lamberville into their presence and an aged chief addressed him:

" We have much reason to treat thee as an enemy, but we know thee too well. Thou hast betrayed us, but treason was not in thy heart. Fly, therefore, for when our young braves shall have sung their war song they will listen to no voice but the swelling voice of their anger." With a spirit of magnanimity they provided trusty guides, who conducted the missionary to a place of security. The kindness of heart shown by the natives finds expression in the death of a son, when the bereaved mother selects from among the captives taken in war a young man of about the same age as her deceased son, whom she adopts into the family. She weeps over him, makes beautiful garments, lavishes gifts and takes the greatest care of the adopted youth. Assiduous in her affectionate attendance upon him, she wins him so completely that he become devotedly attached to her.*

The red man is as earnest and sincere in his religious devotion as his brother in white, although he does not express himself in the same manner. He has his profound religious beliefs and elaborate ceremonial which make him akin to men of other nations, and as we study the man and his religion we are compelled to feel that, although we misjudge him through ignorance, he is a man, a thinker and a seer.

The same fondness for fashion which is seen among other tribes and nations is witnessed among the native tribes of our Dominion. Our brothers in white may rail at the deformities of fashion as seen in the small feet of the Chinese women and the flat heads of some of the tribes in British Columbia, and forget the deformity of the toes among themselves arising from wearing narrow-pointed boots. The Flathead matron of British Columbia would lose her reputation as a kind and dutiful mother, if she neglected to use the means for altering the shape of the head of her offspring. Fashion is a harsh ruler, and the man or woman who has not the head formed according to the custom of the tribe cannot attain a dignified position among the people. Some of them, indeed, have been sold as slaves, because they were believed to be inferior beings, lacking intelligence and unworthy of respect. The process of altering the

* " Third Annual Report of the Bureau of Ethnology," pages 280-282.

form of the head begins immediately after birth, and is continued for a period of from eight to twelve months, by which
time the head has assumed its permanent form, although it may
change slightly during subsequent growth. Some of the tribes
have their own peculiar tribal head form which distinguishes
them from one another.

The alteration of the shape of the head does not seem to
lessen the intellectual power of the individual, nor detract
from their courage, as the leaders of the tribes practising these
customs have been noted for their administrative ability and
prowess. During the flattening process there is not evident
any degree of suffering, although there might be supposed to
be pain attending the compression, but the apparent stupor of
the children is likely induced by the pressure of the bandages
on the head. There are different shapes produced by this
process of flattening the head. There is the simple frontal
depression where the forehead is compressed: the lateral form,
when the sides are flattened; the elongated form, where the
forehead and sides are flattened, so as to cause the crown of the
head to rise toward a point, and other variations made by a
combination of these forms. In some forms the back of the
head is flattened, and in others the sides of the head bulge
outward. The skull is flattened by using boards or pads made
of deerskin, stuffed with frayed cedar bark or moss, applied to
those parts which are to be compressed. The young woman is
highly complimented on the beautiful shape of her head if it
accords with the fashion of the tribe, and she is proud of this
addition to her beauty. This strange custom was a mark of
social distinction, slaves being considered unworthy of the
honor.*

If we would duly appreciate the red men in their savage
condition, not judged by the standard of modern society nor
compared with our permanent political institutions, we must
place their history and customs side by side with those of the
German tribes, who hastened the decline and fall of the Roman

* "Fashion in Deformity," in "Humboldt Science Library," pages 10,
13-16.

Empire. The savage tribes of Germany and the American continent roamed over vast districts, along the courses of rivers and in sections where game and pasture were abundant, claiming a part of the country as their tribal territory, encroaching on the territory of one another, engaging in tribal war, and uniting in a confederacy to meet a common foe. Alike were their marriage customs, in which polygamy was practised, and the bridegroom granted a dowry for his wife, inaptly termed by some writers as purchasing a wife, although the custom of giving horses and trinkets to the bride's father, and the marriage based on bargain, partook of the character of buying. Adultery was punished among the German tribes summarily by the husband cutting off the woman's hair and driving her naked through the village with many stripes; and among the Indians, by the husband cutting off her nose, beating her and driving her from his lodge. Alike the ancient and modern savages felt it to be an indispensable duty to take up the quarrels of their friends and their own tribe, and to make these their own cause. Amongst both it was no disgrace to retreat in battle, stratagem being employed in fighting, and when confronted with a superior force they held it to be the better part of valor to retire. Hospitality, a generous spirit toward friends, lack of gratitude for benefits received, and a natural inclination for stimulants are traits observed among both peoples.

They sang not of love but of war; their dances were not between the sexes, but related to war and religion, and the sages chanted their songs and told their tales of the brave deeds of their warriors. Germans and Indians scalped their enemies, painted their bodies in times of war, sang their war songs, gambled until they had lost everything, even liberty itself; followed their chiefs to death, and buried their warriors who fell in battle with such secrecy that their enemies were unable to discover the homes of the dead. Whiteskins and redskins are removed by centuries of civilization, but in the deeper instincts of human nature, and in all that relates to the best interests of the people, they are not so widely apart. When the years have rolled onward and the red men have enjoyed as expansive a course of training as the white race, the same results will follow, if they survive the absorping process which is now going on, and they abide as a permanent and enterprising race.*

THE RED PIONEERS.

Native tribes have passed away from our fair land since the day the white man stepped upon the Canadian shores, and traces of these extinct tribes are still to be seen in the names of towns, villages, lakes and rivers, the existence of mounds, and burial pits, manuscripts of missionaries and travellers, traditions, and in the relics deposited in museums. The history of races once powerful and numerous, which have disappeared, is always sad to read, yet the melancholy interest which is attached to the names of these peoples is of value to those who wish to know something of their own country in its infancy, and desire to profit by the knowledge of the belief and customs of native tribes.

When Cabot discovered Newfoundland he found a powerful and peaceable race of men, tall and dignified, of paler color than the average red man, who are known in history as the Beoths, Beothuks, or Boeothic Indians, a tribe of Algonquin origin.†
They were dressed in the skins and furs of wild animals, and used bows and arrows, spears, darts, clubs and slings as instruments of war.

Captain Richard Whitbourne, who visited Newfoundland in the seventeenth century, described them as ingenious and tractable, of a quick and lively apprehension, and willing to assist the fishermen in curing fish for small pay. They constructed

* Gibbon's "Decline and Fall of the Roman Empire," Vol. I., pages 265, 272, 277. Guizot's "History of Civilization," Vol. II., pages 156-163.

† "Transactions of the Royal Society of Canada," Vol. IX., Sec. 2, pages 123-171 ; Vol. X., Sec. 2, pages 19-32. "Transactions of Canadian Institute," October, 1890, pages 98-102. "Seventh Annual Report of Bureau of Ethnology," pages 57-58. "American Antiquarian," Vol. VIII., page 323. *Sunday School Times*, January 7th, 1893. "American Philosophical Soc. of Proc.," Vol. XXII., pages 408-424 ; Vol. XXIII., pages 411-432.

canoes of birch bark, which they sewed together and overlaid the seam with turpentine. They manufactured kettles for boiling their meat by sewing together the rinds of spruce trees.

Several attempts were made by the British Government, from 1760, to protect the Beoths, but they failed through the fear of the Indians. By means of presents and kind treatment, a few Indians who had been captured were sent back to their people, but they could not be won, owing in a great measure to their unjust treatment by the trappers and fishermen residing in the

MARY MARCH, A BEOTH WOMAN.

country. A Beoth woman was captured in 1819 and brought to St. John's, where she was known as Mary March, and after being supplied with gifts, was sent back to her people with the hope of conciliating them, but she died on the voyage, and her body being placed in a coffin, was left on the margin of a lake, where it was found by some members of the tribe and taken to their home.* All other attempts to win them failed, as the

* This portrait of Mary March is an illustration from Rev. Dr. George Patterson's paper on the "Beothic Indians," in Translations of the Royal Society of Canada, which has been kindly loaned me for this work.

natives who were seized died of consumption. Their wigwams were constructed in the form of conical lodges, the poles being snugly and tightly covered with skins or birch bark, each wigwam being large enough to accommodate from six to eighteen persons. The fire was placed in the centre of the wigwam, and a hole lined with moss was arranged for each occupant where he rested and slept.

Sweat baths, similar to those used by the Blackfeet and other Algonquin tribes, were used by them, consisting of a small lodge of boughs covered with skins, within which were introduced heated stones, upon which the patient poured water, and the vapor enveloping his naked body produced profuse perspiration. Their burial customs resembled those in use among our western Indians, four methods being employed according to the rank of the deceased. The body was placed in a hut, or laid upon a scaffold, or bent together and wrapped in birch bark and firmly secured in a wooden box which was placed on the ground, or tightly enclosed in birch bark and laid on the ground, and if the soil was not too hard a shallow grave was dug, and a cairn of stones was thrown over the corpse.

They are believed to have been sun or fire worshippers. A gentle race of people were they, delighting in fishing and hunting the deer. Their deer pounds or enclosures were similar to the buffalo pounds of the Crees and Blackfeet, but they added extensive fences and made drives to the large deer corrals, some of which can still be traced, and the skill of these hunters can well be imagined when we learn that a few of them were forty miles long. Ingenious ornaments of bone and ivory, used for decorating the hair, fastening around the neck or to other parts of the person, were made by them. Fire was produced by striking together two pieces of iron pyrites. These interesting people were exterminated by the treacherous rapacity of the white men and the cruel warfare of the Micmac Indians. Tradition says that early in the present century the last of the Beoths escaped to Labrador in two canoes, which is corroborated by the testimony of Dr. Mullock, who says, " I have slight reason to think that a

21

remnant of these people survives in the interior of Labrador.
A person told me there, some time ago, that a party of Montagnais Indians saw, at some distance (about fifty miles from
the sea coast), a party of strange Indians, clothed in long robes
or cassocks of skins, who fled from them. They lost sight of
them in a little time, but on coming up to their tracks they
were surprised to see the length of their strides, which proved
them to be of a large race, and neither Micmacs, Montagnais
nor Eskimos. I believe that these were the remains of the
Beothic nation; and as they never saw either a white or red
man but as enemies, it is not to be wondered at that they fled.
Such is the only trace I can find of the Beoths." The last of
the Beoths has no doubt disappeared, and this tribe must be
numbered among the peoples who claimed their inheritance in
Newfoundland, but remain as a name and nothing more.

It must not be supposed that the tribes which once existed,
and are now known to us in the relics which we possess, have
utterly perished, for though no longer as distinct tribes they
confront us, they remain in their descendants who have the
Iroquois name throughout Canada and the United States.
The Huron-Iroquois originally consisted of the Hurons, who
are also called Wyandots, the Tinnontates or Tobacco Nation,
the Attiwandarons or Neutral Nation, the Eries and Andastes, and the five nations of the Mohawks, Oneidas, Onondagas,
Cayugas and Senecas. These tribes spoke dialects of the
Iroquois tongue, and inhabited that portion of Canada enclosed
by Lakes Huron, Erie and Ontario, as also New York and a
part of Pennsylvania. When these tribes were conquered by
the Iroquois, and many of the people were incorporated among
the conquerors, the Iroquois became the sole representatives of
them all, and though some of them have perished as distinct
tribes, they still live in the people who bear the Iroquoian
name.

The Eries, who probably were the Carantouans mentioned
by Champlain, were an offshoot of the Seneca tribe, and dwelt
along the southern shore of Lake Erie. They perished in a
war provoked by their own cruelty. Very little is known of

this tribe, but it is believed that they were overthrown by the Iroquois early in the seventeenth century, and were incorporated among their conquerors. So little, indeed, is known of them, that they had disappeared before the French explorers knew anything of the existence of Lake Erie, for in the earliest French maps an imaginary river connects Lake Huron and Lake Ontario. They have left, as a relic of their existence, an elaborate specimen of rock-sculpture on Cunningham's Island, Lake Erie, which has attracted interest as one of the most accurate specimens of native pictorial writing found in Canada. Through the efforts of the French missionaries, Catherine Ganneaktena, an Erie captive, became a convert to Christianity, and she is remembered as the founder of a mission village on the St. Lawrence.*

The Nottawas, who were also called the "Cherohakahs," are a tribe which roamed far and wide throughout Canada, traces of their existence being found in the Nottawa River, which falls into Hudson's Bay at James' Bay, and Nottawasaga in Ontario. Their name is still retained in the Nadawas, sometimes called "Nawtowas," or "Six Nation Indians," and the tradition of "Aingolon and Naywadaha," relating to the Iroquois, is told by Schoolcraft. Small bands of the Iroquois spread toward the south, and among them were the Nottawas, who found a home in South-eastern Virginia. At the close of the seventeenth century the tribe numbered about seven hundred souls, but twenty years afterward only twenty remained. At that time two vocabularies were obtained, which furnish evidence of their relation to the Southern Iroquois tribes. The bay, river, township, and village bearing the name of Nottawasaga may furnish evidence of the migrations of the Iroquois, and not relate specially to the distinct tribe, yet in the name we have reference to a lost chapter of history, which looses none of its interest because it is unknown.†

---

* Wilson's "Huron-Iroquois," page 76. "Iroquois Book of Rites," pages 10, 15, 32, 55, 95, 178. Parkman's "Pontiac," Vol. I., page 25. Winsor's "Critical History of America," Vol. IV., page 283.

† Wilson's "Huron-Iroquois," pages 60, 90, 91, 105. Pilling's "Iroquoian Bibliography," pages 67, 104, 111.

The Tinnontates, along with other tribes, occupied that fertile section of territory which lies between Lakes Erie and Huron, where they carried on an extensive trade in growing tobacco and manufacturing clay pipes, which they sold to the other tribes. They were called the "Tobacco Nation," or " Petuns," from their cultivation and sale of tobacco.* The distinct name which belonged to this tribe seems also to have been applied to the Iroquois as a whole, for they were known as the "Tobacco People."   A large number of clay pipes from the country of the Tinnontates are preserved in the museum of the Canadian Institute.   They were an agricultural race, closely allied with the Hurons, with whom they ultimately united, retaining their own tribal organization, and preserving in their descendants the Huron or Wyandot names.

Parkman says, "In the woody valleys of the Blue Mountains, south of the Nottawasaga Bay, of Lake Huron, and two days' journey west of the Huron frontier towns, lay the nine villages of the Tobacco Nation, or Tinnontates."

The Jesuit missionaries, Garnier and Jogues, visited the towns of these people. As the missionaries formed stations and built chapels in the Huron towns, they erected, in 1639, the mission-house of St. Mary's, on the River Wye, to serve as a centre where the priests could always find refuge, and from which they could be sent to any of the towns.*

Champlain visited some of this tribe, who seem to have been located near Guelph, intending to push on to a great lake of which he had heard, beyond which, he was told, the buffaloes were to be found, whose skins he saw among the Hurons; but dissensions breaking out among his Indian allies, he was compelled to return to Quebec.

The Tinnontates celebrated their great feast of the dead, in common with the other tribes of the Huron Confederacy, by collecting the remains of their deceased friends at intervals of ten or twelve years and depositing them in one common place of sepulture, now called an ossuary, or burial pit.

---

* "Iroquois Book of Rites," pages 55, 171, 193.   "American Anti quarian," Vol. XII., page 170.

† Winsor's "Critical History of America," Vol. IV., pages 276-279.

Brebeuf has given an interesting account of this solemn feast as he witnessed it in 1636, at Ossossane or La Conception, near the modern village of Wyevale. The bodies of the dead, which lay on scaffolds or were buried in the ground, were removed, and the wrappings taken from them by official members of the tribe. The bones were laid in rows, amid the mournful wails of the populace, each family reclaiming its own, and tenderly removing the flesh which still adhered to the bones. After caressing the ghastly relics, these were wrapped in skins of varied value, according to the wealth of the family and rank of the deceased, and were borne to a large house, along with the corpses of those who had recently died. The bundles were fastened to crosspoles overhead, and a mournful feast began. The women distributed food among those assembled, while a chief addressed the concourse of people, extolling the virtues of the departed and calling upon their friends to remember and imitate them. At the close of the feast, the bundles were taken down and slung over the shoulders, the lately deceased being borne on litters, and toward the communal pit at Ossossane the sad procession went on its way. As the mourners passed through the forests they uttered weird cries, and when they drew near to a village, the inhabitants came out to meet them with sad countenances, extending to them a mournful hospitality. From the Huron towns came other processions on the same tragic errand, to celebrate the final rites of the feast of the dead at Ossossane, the chief town of the Hurons, on the Nottawasaga Bay. Upon arriving at the place, the bundles of boxes were hung upon cross-poles in bark houses, and on a scaffold erected for that purpose, as well as for supporting gifts in honor of the dead. A wide area several acres in extent had been cleared in the forest, and a pit dug about thirty feet wide and ten feet deep, with a scaffold around it, having cross-poles for supporting the bundles of gifts and the bones. The people resorted to a space close at hand, where fires were kindled and kettles hung over them in preparation for the feast. Funeral games were indulged in by men and women for prizes given in honor of the dead. At the close of the feast the bones and gifts were taken toward the communal pit, and by means of ladders were hung upon the scaffold. The ladders were removed, and several chiefs stood upon the scaffold haranguing the multitude, extolling the virtues of the dead, while several swarthy natives stood within the pit, lining it with beaver skins. Three large copper kettles were deposited in the middle of the pit, and then the bodies which remained entire were thrown into it and arranged in order by ten or twelve Indians, who were stationed within for that purpose.

Darkness coming on the multitude repaired to the village, and in the early dawn returned to the pit, where they cast the bones wildly into its mouth amid discordant shouts from the participants, the men arranging them in order with long poles. When the bones had all been deposited, logs, earth and stones were cast upon the ossuary, and the ceremony ended with a sad funeral chant. These bone pits have been opened in recent years and found to contain as many as nine hundred skeletons.

David Boyle, curator of the Canadian Institute, has located in the country of the Tinnontates, ten villages or town sites, twenty-one ossuaries, one fortified place, and three potteries.* In the Huron country one hundred and forty ossuaries have been catalogued by A. F. Hunter, and as the average ossuary contains about two hundred skeletons, the population must have been very great. From the number of communal pits containing French relics, it is evident that the feast of the dead must have taken place more frequently than every ten or twelve years.† Garnier, the devoted missionary among the Tinnontates, after toiling faithfully, was stricken down and tomahawked, as he was ministering to those wounded in their conflict with the Iroquois. The mission to the Hurons in Upper Canada begun by the Recollet missionary, LeCaron, in 1615, came to an end in 1650, through the overthrow of the Huron towns by the Iroquois and the departure of the remnant of the

---

* David Boyle's paper on "The Land of Souls," in "Canadian Institute Report."

† A. F. Hunter's "French Relics from Village Sites of the Hurons," in "Third Archæological Report (1889) of the Canadian Institute," and "National Characteristics and Migrations of the Hurons," in "Transactions of Canadian Institute," 1892. "Life of Isaac Jogues," pages, 56-58.

Tinnontates and Hurons along with the missionaries. The Tobacco Nation ceased to exist, and their descendants remain incorporated with the Hurons of Lorette.

On the fertile Niagara peninsula which lies between Lakes Erie and Ontario, and on the northern borders of these lakes dwelt the Attiwandarons or Neuters. They received the former name from the Hurons, who dwelt north of them, which signified, according to Brebeuf, " people of a speech a little different ; " and the French called them the Neutrals, from the fact that in the war between the Iroquois and Hurons they remained at peace with both parties.* They had a few towns beyond the lakes mentioned, east of Niagara and between the Iroquois and Erie tribes. It is not certain whether they were an offshoot from the Huron or Iroquois, · their language differing slightly from the Huron. They were friendly with the French and Hurons and were at peace with the Iroquois; but in the war which Champlain started against the Iroquois he had as his allies the Hurons, Neutrals, and other tribes, and with the fall of the Huron towns came the destruction of the Neutrals, large numbers of whom were incorporated with the Iroquois. They were overthrown in 1650, although Charlevoix assigns 1655 as the date of their complete destruction.† Being close neighbors to the Iroquois and Hurons, they were very demonstrative in their affection for their deceased friends, having great feasts of the dead similar to that described among the Tobacco Nation. When the Ojibways came eastward they were charmed with the rich lands, forests, rivers and lakes which formerly belonged to the Hurons and Neutrals, and they espoused the cause of the exiled Hurons and fought against the Iroquois. After many bloody battles, in which large numbers of warriors were slain, both sides became tired and a treaty was made. The territory was divided, and the south - western portion, which had been the home of the Neutrals, remained as the hunting grounds of the Iroquois;

---

* " Jesuit Relation," 1641, page 72.

† Hale's " Iroquois Book of Rites," pages 17, 55, 72, 73, 91, 95. Pilling's " Iroquoian Bibliography," page 38. " Life of Isaac Jogues," pages 235, 240.

while north and east of this, the Ojibways possessed the land. Joseph de la Roche d'Aillou, the Recollet missionary, about 1625 founded a mission among the Neutral Nation, apparently on the eastern bank of the Niagara.*

The Andastes was another Huron-Iroquois tribe which aroused the anger of the Iroquois, and were exterminated by them, the remnant of the people being incorporated with the Iroquois in the early part of the seventeenth century. The Andastes were known by several names, as Andastogues and Conestogas, the Dutch called them Minquas, and the English Susquehannocks or Susquehannahs. Dr. Shea says, concerning these people: "The Mengwe, Minquas or Mingoes were properly the Andastes or Gandastogues, the Indians of Conestoga, on the Susquehanna, known by the former name to the Algonquins and their allies, the Dutch and Sweeds; the Marylanders knew them as the Susquehannas. Upon their reduction by the Five Nations, in 1672, the Andastes were, to a great extent, mingled with their conquerors, and a party removing to the Ohio, commonly called Mingoes, was thus made up of Iroquois and Mingoes. Many treat Mingo as synonymously with Mohawk or Iroquois, but erroneously." The inland territory occupied by the tribes of the Iroquoian family stretched from North Carolina to Canada, and the Andastes, incorporated among the southern Iroquois, passed out of existence as a separate tribe.†

Beneath the wood-crowned height of Mount Royal the palisaded Indian town of Hochelaga stood, within whose safe enclosure dwelt a friendly tribe of natives, who welcomed Cartier with lavish hospitality when he came to visit them. The ancient town consisted of a triple row of palisades, having galleries with stores of stones, whereon the warriors stood in time of danger to hurl the missiles upon their enemies. In the centre of the town was an open square, around which were some fifty bark houses, made of saplings covered with bark,

* Winsor's "Critical History of America," Vol. IV., pages 265, 276, 279.
† Hale's "Iroquois Book of Rites." Winsor's "Critical History of America," Vol. V., page 484.

each house about fifty feet wide and about one hundred
and fifty feet long, and capable of accommodating several
families. On this ancient site of Montreal the natives provided
an ample feast for their white guests, the maimed and blind
and sick were brought to Cartier that he might heal them, and
moved with compassion he read to them the story of the Cross,
offered prayer for the souls and bodies of the people, and supplied them with numerous gifts of knives, beads and trinkets.
This was in the year 1535. Sometime between 1535 and 1642
Hochelaga was utterly destroyed, and the warlike attitude of
the Iroquois made the island debatable land, on which no man
lived. From an examination of the two brief vocabularies of
the Hochelagan language left by Cartier, we find that Hochelaga, which means "at the beaver dam," is Huron, and some of
the Hochalaga words agree with Huron and others with Iroquois, from which we would conclude that they belonged to the
Huron-Iroquois family; but Sir William Dawson, who has
made a special study of the history of the village, says that
the people did not belong to either the Algonquin or Iroquois,
but were a remnant of an ancient and decaying nation, which
had historical relations with the Alleghans or Mound-Builders.
He draws the line between the Alleghans and Hochelagans, but
thinks that as the Algonquins lived to the north, the Eries,
Neutrals and Hochelagans, had borrowed some of the habits of
the Mound-Builders and of the Algonquins, and were not therefore distinct in their customs.*

The relics of the Hochelagans, consisting of typical skulls,
pottery and flint implements, which are preserved in the
museum of McGill University, show no trace of contact with
the white man, but occupy a middle position between the
Mound-Builders and modern Indians. The pottery of the
Hochelagans is superior to that of the modern Indians, but not
equal to that of the Alleghans or Mound-Builders. The earth-
enware pipes of the Hochelagans were .trumpet-shaped and

* "American Antiquarian," Vol. XII., pages 260, 261. Withrow's
"History of Canada," page 30. Wilson's "Huron-Iroquois," pages 72,
80-82. Parkman's "Pioneers of New France," pages 208, 209.

agreed not with those of the Alleghans. The Alleghan copper axes, spears, knives, badges, maces or other ornaments were superior to the stone implements of the Hochelagans. Where formerly the natives raised their crops of corn, and lived in primitive simplicity, developing their savage arts, the modern city of Montreal, busy with a thousand activities of civilized life, now stand, and the traveller or citizen walking along the streets thronged with industrious men and women fails to find a trace of the people who loved ancient Hochelaga as their home, and delighted as other men in the forests and rivers of their native land.

A few years ago the last of the Tuteloes, an aged man named Nikonha, lived on the Grand River Reserve, near Brantford. The Tuteloes were absorbed in the Iroquois Confederacy. Nikonha was married to a Cayuga woman, and was the sole representative of his race. He died at the age of one hundred and six years, in February, 1871. The Tuteloes were at one time a large tribe, living in Virginia, but became greatly weakened through fighting with the Cayugas, Senecas and other tribes. They united with the Six Nations, and came with Brant to Canada after the Revolutionary War. There are still living on the Grand River Reserve several Tutelo half-breeds who speak the language, but the last full-blood Tutelo has disappeared.*

The Nanticokes were a tribe belonging to the Algonquin family, who were received into the confederacy of the Iroquois about the middle of the last century. Vocabularies of their language exist, one of which was obtained by the Rev. John Heckewelder from a Nanticoke chief in Upper Canada in the year 1785. The last of the chiefs of this tribe appears to have died in the latter part of the last century. Having been incorporated with the Six Nations they ceased to exist as a separate tribe, and were numbered among the races of bygone years.†

---

* Horatio Hale's " The Tutelo Tribe and Language." " Seventh Annual Report of the Bureau of Ethnology," pages 112-114.

† Pillings " Algonquin Bibliography," pages 227, 370, 371. " Antiquarian," Vol. IX., pages 350-354.

When the Jesuit missionaries were instructing the Indians who came to trade at Three Rivers, on the St. Lawrence, many of the natives were won to the faith. From the territory far inland there came to the mission post at Three Rivers some members of a gentle race of natives, speaking the Montagnais tongue, and requesting that a missionary be sent to their tribe to instruct them. The missionaries were delighted with their tractable disposition, and Father Buteux left in 1651 for the district in which they dwelt. These were the Attikamegues, or White Fish Indians. He ascended the river which led toward their territory, and after a weary journey of forty-three days found the people he so zealously sought. Anxiously the people had awaited his coming, and when they beheld him at last amongst them they crowded around to listen to his instructions and accept his ministrations. A rude chapel was built, where they gathered for worship. Buteux returned after this interesting visit, and the following year set out to instruct them again, but the Iroquois intercepted him while making a portage, and slew him. The Attikamegues were almost wholly exterminated, and the remnant sought refuge among the scattered Montagnais.*

Throughout the wide areas of the Dominion tribes of red men have gone forth to make homes for themselves, where they might dwell in comfort and peace; but small bands of painted savages have followed them into the deep recesses of the forest to strike them down. There is no doubt that numerous tribes have passed away of whose name or existence we know nothing, the story of these nations being unwritten, and the earth yielding no answer to the questions we repeat. Their languages, customs and civilization are shrouded in the darkness of other years, and we must await the coming of some intrepid seeker after lost races who may be able to discover some slender thread which may lead us through the labyrinthine paths to a certain knowledge of the peoples who made Canada their home in the dim past.

---

* Winsor's "Critical History of America," Vol IV., pages 265, 276, 279.

THE SYMBOL OF THE CROSS.

The cross has become so widely associated with the existence and spread of Christianity that the majority of people have ignorantly concluded that it belongs essentially to the Christian religion, whereas upon tablets, rock inscriptions, idols, buildings devoted to religious purposes among the subjects of paganism and in the manuscripts of ancient date it is sculptured and inscribed. It is a symbol of ancient date, having existed in Asia before the commencement of European civilization. It has been found in Egypt and China, Hindostan and Scandinavia. Contact with pagan nations, and the significance of the cross in its relation to the death of Christ no doubt suggested to the minds of the Christian leaders of the third century the usefulness of this system in propagating the doctrines of the Christ among the nations. It has been widely used as a symbol of paganism. Christian missionaries found it among the peoples of India, on the statues of Seva and Vishnu; on the cinerary urns of Greece and Italy; and as the hammer of Thor in the forests of barbaric Germany. The Egyptians had a similar symbol representing the flow of the Nile, and on the famous Rosette Stone it appears as equivalent to the word "life." It is found on the bricks and cylinders of Nineveh, and on the colossal tablet in the British Museum, Tiglath Pileser is represented having a cross suspended from his neck.*

The early Christian missionaries carried this symbol before them, which impressed the pagan mind and helped the natives in submitting to the faith of the new religion, as well as understanding its doctrines. When the Roman monk Augustine entered the presence of Ethelbert he carried an enormous cross before him, which impressed deeply the mind of the pagan king. The cross was raised to a position of dignity, far removed from its early barbaric use as an instrument of torture, monarchs and princes using it as part of their royal insignia, the knights who

* "American Antiquarian," Vol. X., pages 292, 297, 302; Vol. XVI., pages 178, 179.

crossed the deserts of the sacred land wearing it on their breasts and emblazoned on the hilts of their swords, and even in nature the Christian fathers saw it as an expression of their faith, so aptly expressed by Justin Martyr:

"The sign of the cross is expressed upon the whole of nature. There is hardly a handicraftsman, also, but uses the figure of it among the implements of his industry. It forms a part of man himself, as may be seen when he raises his hands in prayer."

Of crosses as the symbols of the Christian faith there are various kinds, designated the Maltese, Latin, Greek, Eleanor, Calvary and Fylfot. Designated as classes some are known as market-place, churchyard, wayside, monumental, pectoral and knightly crosses. "The English cross of St. George is a plain red cross set erect on a white ground; the Scottish cross of St. Andrew's is a plain diagonal white cross on a blue ground; and the Irish cross of St. Patrick is a plain diagonal red cross on a white ground."*

As a pagan symbol the cross became an emblem of war under the cruel customs of the Aztecs, as is shown on the Palenque tablet, where the emblems suggest that the altar was devoted to the god of war. The four gods of the winds were worshipped by the Mayas. They were supposed to support the four corners of the heavens, and to blow the winds through trumpets or wind instruments from the four cardinal points. Under the symbol of the cross they were worshipped, and this was regarded as a tree, which, in the Maya tongue, was called the "tree of life." In times of drought offerings of birds were made to it, and it was sprinkled with water. It was used as a symbol of the four cardinal points.†

The cross is the representative in Christian history of what the brazen serpent was to the Jews, and it is a suggestive fact that the serpent and cross symbols exist among the natives of the American continent as a means of expressing religious ideas. The American symbols of the cross are generally surmounted by the thunder bird and decorated with spiral ornaments, which

* "Britannica Encyclopædia," Vol. VI., page 612.
† "American Antiquarian," Vol. X., pages 312, 314.

express the ideas of the people in relation to the worship of the
sun and of nature.

In the Buddhist cave temples there was always found the
shrine with its symbol of a water bubble, to which the creed of
Buddha likened the human frame, and was intended to portray
the transient nature of earthly things.   Upon the square piers
in the Egyptian tombs, large human figures were sculptured,
invariably in a standing posture, the head decked with the lofty
priestly tiara, and the body slightly covered with the Egyptian
apron round the loins.   In the right hand of the colossal statue
was the mystic token of the Nile key in the form of a cross,
with a handle at the upper part.   Long before the cross became
the emblem of peace among Christians it was associated in
prehistoric structures with sun worship.   It exists as a religious symbol among the Ojibways without any reference to the
doctrines of Christianity.   When Marquette arrived at the
Bay of Puans he found a village inhabited by three nations,
and saw a great cross erected, which he says was "adorned with
several white skins, red girdles, bows and arrows, which that
good people had offered to the great Manitou to return him
their thanks for the care he had taken of them during the winter, and that he had granted them a prosperous hunting."   The
priest was no doubt ignorant of the exercises of the midawiwin,
as described by Dr. Hoffman, for the cross is one of the sacred
posts belonging to the Grand Medicine Society of the Ojibways,
and is the fourth degree mida post.   It is painted white with
red spots on the upper part, the lower part being squared and
painted white on the east, red on the west, black on the north
and green on the south.   In the initiation of the candidate to
the society it symbolizes the four days' struggle at the four
openings of the Medicine lodge.

The cross is the symbol for a Cheyenne Indian, and is used in
the sign language of the natives.   In the native picture writing
it stands for a Dakota lodge.   A square represents a white
man's house, and if there is a cross beside it, the signification is
that the white man is married to a Dakota woman.   It is also
used among some Indian tribes to signify "I will barter or

trade." Upon the right hand of the cross is depicted the articles
desired in exchange, and upon the left the articles offered.
The Moki maidens wear their hair in two styles, which, when
combined, become developed into the form of the Maltese Cross
which is the emblem of a virgin among these people, and this
cross appears frequently in the pottery and petroglyphs of the
Mokis. Colonel Garrick Mallery remarks that the form of a
cross was found in tattoo marks on an Arab boy, and the mother
explained its existence, "because it looked pretty." Dr. Schlei-
man, in his "Troja," presents a cross simply as a geometrical
ornamentation.

Among the Dakota Indians symbolic crosses of the Greek •
pattern are worn, representing "the four winds issuing from the
four caverns in which the souls of men existed before embodi-
ment. The top of the cross is the cold, all conquering giant,
the north wind. As worn on the body it is nearest the head,
the seat of intelligence. The top arm, covering the heart, is the
east wind, coming from the seat of life and love. The foot is
the burning south wind, indicating as it is worn the seat of
passion and fiery lust. The right is the gently west wind,
blowing from the spirit land, covering the lungs, from which at
last the breath goes out. The centre of the cross is the earth
and man, sometimes indicated at that point by a circle surrounding a dot. On the upper arm an arrow is sometimes
drawn, on the left a heart, on the right a star and on the lower
a sun."

When the Apache warriors went into a strange district they
painted a cross upon their moccasins to keep them from going
on the wrong trail. When rain was desired for their crops,
the medicine men of the Apaches bore two crosses as they led
a procession of men and women in honor of Guzanutii. The
crosses were decorated with a snake, small willow twigs, a
mirror, bell and eagles' feathers.*

---

* "American Antiquarian," Vol. X., pages 44, 80, 136, 138, 292-315.
"Annual Report of the Bureau of Ethnology," Vol. III., page 30 ; Vol. IV.,
pages 46, 132, 158, 173, 220, 232, 252, 253 ; Vol. VII., pages 155, 256 ;
Vol. IX., 479-480. Rosengarten's "Handbook of Architectural Styles,"
pages 4, 9, 29.

INDIAN GRAVE ON FRENCH RIVER.

Whenever the natives of Gaspe were troubled with a plague the medicine men had recourse to the sun, and they were instructed to make use of the cross in every period of affliction. Upon the island of Cozumel a number of oratories and temples were found, one of which was in the form of a square tower, having four openings, and within this tower was a cross made of lime, which the natives reverenced as the god of the rain. The rain-maker of the Lenni Lennape retired to a secluded spot whenever he desired to practice his art, and drawing upon the earth the form of a cross, with its arms pointing toward the cardinal points, placed upon it a piece of tobacco, a gourd, a bit of some red stuff, and then cried aloud to the spirits of the rains. Among many of the Indian tribes four was a sacred number, and the cross was used in connection with this number as a prehistoric symbol. Upon the medicine pole in the medicine lodge of the Blackfeet, we have seen the form of a cross made with twigs and the boughs of trees as a symbol of their native religion.

It was used also by some of the Blackfeet as a personal mark upon their blankets to denote their ownership. The Onondagas wore shell disks two hundred years ago, which were ornamented with crosses apparently marked out with compasses. The use of the cross among the Iroquois in late years seems to have been merely ornamental, and without any religious significance.[*] It was the custom of the brave voyageurs of Canada when death occurred among them, as they journeyed, to plant on the grave of each a low wooden cross, to mark the spot. Along the routes of the voyageurs on the Ottawa, on the shores of Lake Nippissing, and away beyond Lake Superior, these crosses were to be seen in the old days when the hardy voyageurs crossed the portages and sailed up the rivers and lakes.[†] Between Silver Islet and Nepigon, on the shores of Lake Superior, there is a pictograph known to travellers as the Jesuits' Cross.

The cross was known to the Mound-Builders, as shown by gorgets taken from the mounds in Missouri, having the form of

[*] "American Antiquarian," Vol. XI., page 3.
[†] "Journal of the Bishop of Montreal," page 17.

22

a cross to symbolize the points of the compass. An ancient monument of porphyry sculptured in bas-relief, taken from a mound in Tezcuco, had upon it an emblem suggestive of a Maltese cross. An ancient earthwork near Tarlton, Ohio, is in the form of a cross, ninety feet long and elevated three feet above the adjacent surface, the sides of the cross nearly corresponding with the cardinal points.

In the Mexican codices are found the symbol of the cross, which shows that it was used as a symbol of sun worship. Among the carved stone figures and idols is the cross of Teotihuacan, which is an altar in the shape of a cross; the idol pillar of Piaza Mayor, which is in the form of a cross; the temple of the cross on the southern slope of the pyramid of Palenque and the Lorillard tablet, which contains two figures, one representing a man holding a cross in each hand and the other a woman with a cross in her right hand.

The culture heroes of the Peruvians and other races in South America wore long robes sometimes covered with crosses. When the Spaniards arrived in Mexico, they found large stone crosses erected on the coast and in the interior, which were objects of veneration to the natives, who answered in response to the questions of the missionaries, that " one more glorious than the sun had died upon the cross."

The Spaniards found at Vera Cruz a large marble cross surmounted with a golden crown, and they were impressed with the deep reverence of the natives, who adored the cross as a symbol of the god of rain.

The existence of many of these prehistoric crosses we are unable to account for, but there may be something akin to them in the memorial and market crosses found in England. As a symbol of religious worship, the natives used the cross, but there may have been others erected as ornaments or for historic purposes. When Eleanor, wife of King Edward I., died, she was carried in a casket to London, and upon the funeral journey, wherever the casket rested, the king caused a cross to be built. There were twelve Eleanor crosses erected, three of them still remaining. Market crosses were first used in market towns,

GRAVEYARD AT OLD FORT, LAKE TEMISCAMINGUE.

for the priests went there on great market days to preach.
Boundary crosses marked the line between different places,
and preaching crosses were used as pulpits, one of which stood
in front of the old St. Paul's Cathedral, London, where some
of the Reformers preached the doctrines of the Reformation.
Pagan and Christian can lay claim to this symbol of religion as
a relic of antiquity whose origin is unknown, which has been
adopted as an expression of religious belief by many nations
and tribes, and in its use there are embodied ideas and feelings
which are sacred to all, and therefore to be treated with respect
and reverence.*

INDIAN HYMNS.

There is music in the souls of the people of every race and
tongue. It may be expressed in very weird strains, or in the
most commonplace tones, but there will be harmony, pleasant
to the ears of those whose hearts are in sympathy with the
people and the language they speak. The stolid countenance
of the red man hides the gentler passions of his nature, and we
are almost tempted to believe that the painted savage of the
warpath and the peaceful occupant of the lodge, are strangers
to the tender emotions of the singing tribes of men. But our
fears are chased away as we wander among the lodges, for
there we see the instruments of music, and can hear the shouts
of the dancers, the gay laugh of youth, and the sweet songs of
the women at their daily toil. Songs of life and death, love
and war are found in the languages of the Indians. The
Spanish conquerors listened to the natives of Mexico singing
their songs, and still we may hear the Six Nation Indians
chant the Iroquois historical song.

During several important movements in English history, and
also during the French revolution, the ballads of the people
exerted a powerful influence over the minds of the populace.

---

* Brinton's "American Hero Myths," page 122. "Smithsonian Anthro-
pological Papers," 1886-87, page 689. "American Antiquarian," Vol.
XVI., pages 20, 23, 28, 41, 73, 146, 152, 179, 249. "Canadian Methodist
Magazine," (July to December, 1886), page 35.

Recognizing this fact Christian teachers have embodied many doctrines in songs and hymns written for the Indian tribes in their own language. When Las Casas, the Roman Catholic apostle of the Indians, was laboring among the natives of Mexico he introduced the doctrines of the Christian religion among a hostile tribe by means of songs. With the help of some monks he translated into the language of the people, and in verse, a summary of the leading doctrines of the Bible. He secured the assistance of Indian traders, who occasionally visited this tribe, and taught them the song with its accompaniment on Indian instruments of music. The traders reached the tribe, made some presents to the chief, and spread their wares before the people. After the day's trading was over they called for musical instruments and began their song.

They sang of creation, the fall of man, the life, death and resurrection of Christ, and the judgment to come. The people listened with wondrous awe. Here, surely were ambassadors from the gods. The Great Spirit must have taken compassion upon them to send these teachers. Night after night for a whole week did the people ask the traders to repeat the song, so eager were they to hear and learn. The traders told them of the teachers who sang these songs, and the Indians entreated the priests to teach them more fully the doctrines of the wonderful song. Well do we remember attending an Indian camp-meeting, at Kettle Point on Lake Huron, where Shawanese, Pottawotamies and Ojibways, sang with delightful enthusiasm the songs of Zion in the Ojibway tongue. Some years ago we listened with pleasure to some Sioux children attending the Sioux school at Portage la Prairie, who sang very sweetly some hymns in the language of the Dakotas. And who that has ever gone to the Indian Reserve at Morley, nestling at the foot of the Rocky mountains, can ever forget the hearty and intelligent singing of the Stoney Indians ?

Important is all this, yet it is difficult to translate English hymns into the languages of the Indians, and make them agree with the original metre of the tunes. A thorough knowledge of the language is necessary to make a competent translation, so

that all the meaning contained in the words and ideas may be
fully and intelligently expressed in both languages. There are
a large number of hymn books in the languages of the *red
man, such as Ojibway, Mohawk, Oka, Sioux, Eskimo, Chinook,
Clallam, Cree and others.

The sacred songs, and the war and marriage songs of the
native tribes express few ideas, and consequently the hymns
translated by missionaries seem strange to the people, many of
the native songs comprising two or three words for a single
verse. The Moravian missionaries attempted to establish a
mission among the Eskimos of Labrador in 1752, but failed
through the opposition of the natives. In 1764, Jens Haven
landed on the Isle of Quirpont, off the north-east extremity of
Newfoundland, and there held his first interview with the
Labrador Eskimos. So soon as he landed he ran towards an
Eskimo, and said, in the Greenlandic dialect, " I am your friend."
From that time the work among the people of Labrador has
been continued. The following hymn, translated by the
Moravian missionaries, will reveal some of the difficulties of the
language.

It is the first verse of " There is a gate that stands ajar."

> Up Kerusunanok Kilak Jesub
> Sakkyarvi a
> Jesub ikhiliksodlardub pio lu ta
> Tokkalanktub
> Napki gi jaunck o pinok apku e
> Sutgandlarama uvanga
> Tank il la unanga tank.

One of the first hymn books issued for the Canadian Indians
was translated by Peter Jones in the Ojibway language, and
printed in 1827. It has gone through several editions, and in
a revised form is still in use. There have been several hymn
books printed for the use of the Ojibways by various translators.
Since the advent of the Rev. John West, in 1820, to the Red
River country missionary work among the Indians has been
energetically prosecuted. Earnest men and women have labored

among the Crees, Saulteaux, Sioux, Stoneys, Sarcees and Blackfeet, and away in the far north in the camps of the Athabascan
tribes, seeking to teach them the way of life. The Crees have
been favored with the greatest amount of literature, if we
except the Eskimos and Sioux.

As early as 1855 Mrs. Hunter, wife of Archdeacon Hunter,
prepared a hymn book in the Cree language, using the English
letters. Since that date several hymn books have been printed
by the missionary societies of the English and Methodist
churches, which have been translated and compiled by the
missionaries of those churches. These books have been generally printed in the Cree syllabic characters. Bishop Horden
and Drs. Mason and Mackay have been the chief translators
for the Cree Confederacy in connection with the English Church,
and Rev. Messrs. McDougall, German and Glass for the Methodist Church. The following hymn in Swampy Cree, translated
by Rev. Orrin German, will show the construction of the
language. It is the first verse of " Sweet Hour of Prayer."

Meyo ispe ayum' hayan
  Uskeh a o'che nutoomit,
Ne Manetoom hiche natul,
  'Che o'che mawimoostowuk,
Maliwach a ayimiseyan,
  Mechatwow ne nesookumah
Aka kiche mucheteyan,
  Ate we ayumehayan.

Mrs. Hunter was an excellent Cree scholar, as was also her
husband, and faithfully did she labor among the Cree Indians.
Her hymn book comprised one hundred hymns. A selection of
an old favorite , " Jesu, Lover of my soul," is here given, being
the first verse :

Jesu ! Seakehitan,
Ke ga natamoostatin,
Makwach yiskepawinik
Mena misseyootinook ;
Kasin, O tapwa kasin
Christ n'oo Pimachehewani,
Maskunow waputeyin,
O, net achak kewata.

In the province of British Columbia the Chinook jargon is
spoken by the Indians and white people as a trade language,
being easily learned and understood in a very short time.
Lacking fulness of expression, it has not been used extensively
for the purpose of religious instruction. Still there have been
published a few books dealing with the principles of the jargon,
In 1878, a small book, called " Hymns in the Chinook Jargon
Language," was published by the Rev. Marcus Eells, of
Skokomish, Washington Territory. The following hymn,
which is sung to the tune " Hold the Fort," with the translation,
is taken from this small Chinook hymn book :

1. Saghalie Tyee yaka papeh,
   Yaka Bible kloshe,
   Kopa konoway Boston tillikums
   Yaka hias kloshe.

CHORUS.

Saghalie Tyee, yaka papeh
Yaka Bible kloshe
Kopa konoway tillikums alta
Yaka hias kloshe.

2. Saghalie Tyee, yaka papeh
   Yaka Bible kloshe
   Kopa konoway Siwash tillikums
   Yaka hias kloshe.

Translation :

1. God, His paper,
   His Bible is good ;
   For all American people
   It is very good.

CHORUS.

God, His paper,
His Bible is good ;
For all people now
It is very good.

2. God, His paper,
   His Bible is good ;
   For all Indian people
   It is very good.

During our residence among the Blood Indians we translated the hymn, "Come to Jesus," into the Blackfoot language; but, as the translation will show, the idea of coming to Jesus was not clear to the native mind, besides the phrase could not be made to suit the tune, and similar ideas had to be expressed. We had first to select the tune, and then take whatever words in the language would fit the metre as nearly as the sense would permit, and thus compose a new hymn. It is not therefore a translation; indeed, few hymns are translations, but a hymn composed to suit the metre. The construction of the Indian languages make it almost impossible to translate hymns, and as the natives employ few words in their songs, when first they listen to a hymn containing words as in use by white people, they are surprised. Such a hymn as the following is more in agreement with the construction of the native songs, because of the repetition of the words and music, than those containing many words:

NOQKIMOKIT.

Tune—" Come to Jesus."

1. Jesus, Jesus, noqkimokit
   Noqkimokit anuqk,
   Jesus noqkimokit
   Noqkimokit anuqk.

2. Jesus, Jesus, Noqspumokit,
   Noqspumokit anuqk,
   Jesus noqspumokit
   Noqspumokit anuqk.

3. Jesus nitukomimoa, etc.
4. Jesus nitaikimoka, etc.
5. Jesus nitaispumoka, etc.
6. Jesus nitukomimok. etc.
7. Jesus nitaiuqsapsuk, etc.
8. Jesus Kitukomimok, etc.

Translation:

Hymn Title—" Take pity upon Me."

1. Jesus, Jesus, take pity upon me,
   Take pity upon me now.
   Jesus, take pity upon me,
   Take pity upon me now.

2. Jesus, Jesus, help me,
    Help me now.
  Jesus, help me,
    Help me now.

3. I love Jesus now.
4. Jesus takes pity upon me now.
5. Jesus helps me now.
6. Jesus loves me now.
7. Jesus is kind to me now.
8. Jesus, I love you now.

LADIES IN THE LODGES.

There have been no more devoted workers among the native tribes than the women of culture, who have consecrated their talents to the work of elevating the red men and their families in the camp. They have labored assiduously amid great privations, enduring hardships without a murmur, and though their influence has been abiding and strong, seldom have we heard their names mentioned, or read them on the printed page. We have not seen a biography of one of these saintly heroines of the lodges, though many of them have been worthy of lasting record, and this want is still more striking through the existence of numerous biographies of missionaries to the Indian tribes. Thrilling records have been published of the expeditions, sufferings and successes of the Jesuits in North America, and but faint remembrance is given to the nuns who spent many years of pious zeal at Quebec and Montreal for the education of the Indian children and the care of the sick. In 1844 the nuns reached Red River, after a long and toilsome journey in canoes, and commenced their devoted mission among Indians, half-breeds, and white people, continuing till the present day their labor of love. The wife of John Eliot, the apostle of the Indians, was in labors abundant, helping her husband in his arduous mission, and cheering him in hours of loneliness and opposition. Peter Jones found an excellent helpmate in his work among the Ojibways and Iroquois in the body of refinement whom he won from her English home, and though placed in a lowly position among the natives, she gained their hearts, and, until extreme old age, was their counsellor and guide.

There was not to be found in Ontario, during the early period of missions to the Indians, a more earnest and successful missionary than Mrs. Case, the wife of the Rev. William Case. Think of Mrs. Horden, wife of the Bishop of Moosonee, in her home in the far north, ministering to the wants of the Indians through the dreary winter, nursing the sick and caring for the poor. Mrs. A. R. McFarland, the widow of the first Presbyterian missionary in New Mexico, was induced to commence the Presbyterian mission in Alaska, and for seven months she was the only Protestant missionary in Alaska. When she went there she was the only Christian white woman in a territory as large as France. She labored alone for a whole year at Fort Wrangel, assisted by two Indians from Fort Simpson. In all their difficulties the Indians sought her counsel, having strong faith in her wisdom and sympathy. She nursed them when they were sick, arbitrated in household and tribal quarrels, acted as chairman at public meetings, and was the peacemaker and adviser of the tribe. She buried their dead, and when a white man was condemned to be hanged for murder, she became his spiritual adviser. Her fame spread far and wide among the tribes, so that great chiefs came to attend the school of " the woman that loved their people."

Helen Hunt-Jackson, the gifted friend of the Indian races, labored in another sphere, yet she was none the less a missionary. Born in 1831 at Amherst, Massachusetts, where her father was a professor in the college, she inherited from her parents literary tastes. Her early married life was spent with her husband, Major Hunt, at military posts until his death. Bereaved of her husband and children she lived for a short period at Rome, and in 1872 removed to Colorado Springs in search of health, where she married Mr. Jackson. In her mountain home she became conversant with the joys and sorrows of Indian life, and although a brilliant writer of short stories and poems, she consecrated her pen to the welfare of the Indian race. She began the study of the Indian question in earnest, and the

knowledge wrought so deeply into her soul that she longed to give utterances to the "thoughts that breathe and words that burn." Stealing away to the solitude of the mountains, she sat amid the rugged scenery of mountain, waterfall and lonely pass, and there gave birth to the sweet poetic effusions of her genius. She spent three months in Astor Library gathering facts for her famous book, "A Century of Dishonor," a work treating the question of the dealings of the Government with the Indian tribes. This faithful recital of wrong-doing against the red men caused the Government to appoint her a commissioner to investigate the condition of the Mission Indians of California. With soul aflame, the gifted authoress wrote the greatest novel relating to the Indian tribes, the "Uncle Tom's Cabin of the Red Men." "Ramona" won the hearts of the reading public, and literary men and women courted the friendship of the accomplished writer, who had so unselfishly and heroically espoused the cause of the despised race. Its thrilling scenes and faithful descriptions produced a decided change in the opinions generally held concerning the Indians, and many converts were won on their behalf.

"Ramona" was one of the chief causes of the organization and development of Indian Rights' Associations throughout the land. These associations are composed of earnest men and women, including many who are successful authors, whose names are familiar in the literature of to-day. By means of the press, and through the influence of members of Congress justice is sought for the red aliens of the west. Helen Hunt-Jackson had abundant reasons for being proud of the work she had accomplished, but she delighted more in recognizing a guiding hand directing her in her noble mission. Her articles in *The Christian Union* and *Century Magazine,* her "Bits of Travel" and "Bits of Travel at Home," sparkled with poetic inspiration, but all these must be laid aside for "Ramona." She was the sympathetic defender of the rights of the red race, and her work lives in the bills passed in Congress in favor of these people, the change of public opinion and the better condition of the western tribes. On the top of one of the lonely mountains

near Colorado Springs, where she often went with her writing
materials to seek inspiration from the beautiful scenery, she
chose a spot for her last resting-place, and there a small mound
marks the place where lie the remains of " H. H.," and near by
the enclosure grows the Indian kinni-kinnick, symbolic of the
strong attachment in life and in death between the author of
" Ramona " and the red men.

The wise women from the east, the magi of modern times,
have travelled westward with their gifts of culture, grace and
love, and laid them at the feet of the men and women who sit in
loneliness, and with depressed hearts, in the lodges widely
scattered on prairie and mountain, and in the cold and bleak
regions of the north land. They have gone forth alone as
teachers in the native schools, or as wives of missionaries, to
train the young and help the women to live useful lives. Nobly
have they toiled in the schools amid many difficulties, murmur-
ing not because of their isolation, but happy in the assurance
that they were in the path of duty, and in their vocabulary
there was not found the word "retreat." They have gathered
the women of the camp in the mission-school and taught them
how to make garments. In the mission home lessons in cooking have been given, which have added comfort and health to
the dwellers in the lodges. The people have thus been trained
in habits of industry and economy. Some have profited by
these instructions, but where the natives have been compelled
to go out on hunting expeditions, the progress has not been so
great. Frequently have we seen these queens of the mission-
houses mixing medicine and preparing a dainty dish of nourishing food for the sick children, or some helpless occupant of a
lodge. Sitting in the smoky lodges, these devoted women have
waited upon the sick and nursed them back to life. The native
girls and women have confided their heart-burdens to them, and
wise counsel has been given which has brought peace to the
home and grace to the soul.

As earnest students of science women have lived among the
lodges, studying the languages, social habits, traditions and
native religions of the Indians. Erminie Smith, Alice Fletcher,

Elaine Goodale and other women have labored among the native tribes in the United States in the interests of science, and our lack in Canada of similar workers has existed chiefly through the want of financial support from wealthy institutions to carry on such a work. Philanthropic work has, however, been carried on extensively by Women's Missionary societies, having branches in the villages, towns, and cities which help pay the salaries of women engaged in missionary work, make clothing for the poor on the Indian Reservations, and in other ways assist the work of civilizing the red men.

It is impossible for anyone who has not lived among the Indians to understand thoroughly the isolation and care which falls to the lot of the women who have so devotedly spent some of their best years in striving to elevate the Indian race. Oftentimes left alone with the care of the family, without a single servant to help in the management of the household, and with a small salary, sometimes insufficient to supply the wants of the family and the constant demands of the Indians, is it any wonder that the strain is so great that the nervous system is weakened, and after a few years the work has to be given up. The missionary enjoys relief through change of occupation, visiting the camps, undertaking long journeys and meeting with mutual friends at different times in the course of a year, but for the lady in the mission-house there is the continued isolation, toiling for years upon the same field without a single visit to friends to break the monotony and give tone to body and mind.

For such faithful workers there is no press notice, and never do we hear their names mentioned, while the husband and father receives his meed of praise for his worthy toil. Have they been forgotten, or is their work of no avail? Heroically they toil without any desire for recognition or praise. Mrs. McDougall, the aged widow of the sainted George McDougall, has spent a long life among the Indians of the Ojibway, Cree, and Stoney tribes. She became the helpmate of the faithful missionary in 1842, and from that period has been in close relations with the red men. She has tenderly cared for the

sick, counselling, teaching and nursing them. During the
winter of 1870, when residing at Victoria, on the Saskatchewan,
the dreaded plague of the small-pox reached the Indian camps,
and the inmates of the mission-house were stricken down. The
son, John McDougall, was out on the plains securing the supply
of buffalo meat for the winter, and the missionary lay at the
point of death. Two of the daughters—Flora, aged eleven,
Georgina, aged eighteen—and an adopted daughter, Anna, aged
fourteen, died within three weeks. As the dire plague passed
away, the inmates of the mission-house forgot their own
sorrows, in comforting the dwellers in the lodges. Five years
of faithful work among the Crees and Stoneys rolled past, and
then, in a blinding snowstorm, the missionary laid himself down
on the prairie and breathed out his soul to God. The earnest
woman, now a widow, murmured not, but continued to care for
the souls and bodies of the Indians. In her old age she finds
her joy in speaking words of truth and soberness to young and
old, and the Stoneys love devotedly the woman who has shared
their burdens and wept with them in their hours of sorrow.

A few months after the arrival of Archdeacon Cochran and
his wife at Red River, they were driven from their home amid
inclement weather by the swollen river. It overflowed the
banks, carrying in its course large blocks of ice, the church was
flooded, yet the mission family sought refuge on a platform
erected above the waters, and actually held service there with
some people who had sought shelter with them. Their position
was dangerous, and after three days of suspense they left in
boats, and pitched their tents on the Snake Indian Hills, where
they abode for a month. Amid the discomforts arising from
their position, Mrs. Cochran, although in a feeble state of health,
retained her accustomed cheerfulness, and manifested patience
in her work as a missionary among the native tribe.

These saintly workers in the mission field among the Canadian Indians have stood by the graves of their children and
wept, surrounded by dusky mourners, who have sympathized
with them in their hours of grief. They have lain for months
on beds of languishing pain, with no medical help at hand, save

the humble medicine chest or the care of some aged squaw of the camps. After years of suffering they have undertaken long journeys in the depth of winter to secure medical skill, and in feeble health the cariole has been the couch of the gentle patient, as the mission party halted for the night in the depth of the forest, while the blazing fire melted the snow, and the hardy pioneer prepared the hasty meal. The mission-house mother has spent sleepless nights, anxiously waiting for the return of the missionary, who has been caught in the blinding snowstorm and is fighting wind and cold with the spirit of a hero. She has listened to the howling of the blast, which aroused her fears for him who was bearing precious words of truth over the lakes to the dusky denizens along the shores. She has been aroused from her dreams by the hasty footstep of the messenger bearing sad news of death, and after hours of anguish has at last realized that far from home and friends she was a widow, and the cries of her fatherless children have pierced with intense sorrow her desolate heart. We dare not tell the tales of suffering endured by those who have devoted their lives for the welfare of the red race. It is better far to speak of hope and peace than to dwell under the shadow which has often hovered over the mission homes of the west. We would rather not speak of any suffering, for others have borne greater burdens than we; but we shall mention one of several instances, and, because we know this better than those of other mission fields, we shall select it from our old home among the Blood Indians.

Upon my return from Macleod one cold wintry day, I was surprised to find my wife suffering intense pain in the middle finger of the right hand. She was pacing the floor in agony, and there was nothing left but to take her to Macleod, a distance of twelve miles, for medical aid. As we were about to start a doctor crossed the river to the Agency, and we gladly walked across on the ice to seek his advice. Upon examination he stated that it was a felon, and must be lanced at once. There was no lance to be found, so taking a new jack knife he cut the flesh to the bone about an inch long on one side of the finger,

23

and scraped the bone. The relief expected did not come, so we returned to the Agency in about two hours, and a similar operation with the same instrument was performed upon the opposite side of the finger. Lotions and poultices were applied for several days, but without one moment's relief. Indians crowded into the house to offer sympathy, and the medicine men and medicine women prescribed remedies. In a blinding snowstorm an Indian was despatched to town for the family doctor, who speedily came, and again the finger was lanced. Several days again passed without any cessation of pain, and with the thermometer registering 36° below zero, we started through deep snow with the children for town, as it was impossible to secure a servant girl. At last a young woman was hired at twenty dollars per month, and as the pain was somewhat lessened, and it was believed that there was no longer any danger, I started for Regina to attend the meeting of the Board of Education.

I was there a few days when a telegram called me home. We were four days on the way, detained by the deep snow on the railroad. Upon reaching Macleod I found my wife there, quite contented, and was surprised at her happy countenance; but the secret was soon learned, when I saw the hand minus the finger which had caused all the trouble. Upon inquiry, I was told that after I left the pain increased, and two medical gentlemen being called in and examination made, it was found that the bones of the finger were dead. Amputation was necessary and urgent, and the finger was removed at the knuckle. The severe strain upon the nervous system was felt for months, and rest was demanded to restore the health. As great suffering has been endured by other saintly women on the mission field, and not a word has fallen from their lips to declare the agony endured. There are tales untold and biographies unwritten as great as have been heard or read by mortals, and these heroines of the Cross have borne their share in making history, yet their names are unspoken, and posterity will only know them by their influence in guiding the red men toward a nobler destiny than it was theirs to enjoy in the days of yore. Their memories are precious to the dwellers of the lodges, who remember them by the euphonic names the natives gave them in the Indian tongue ; but the white man shall never know the brave deeds enacted by his sisters in laying the foundation of an Empire in the West, yet they live in the lives of others and in the memory of God.

INDIAN NAMES.

There is a wealth of meaning in names. Races of men, who dwelt in lands now occupied by civilized nations, have disappeared, and nothing remains of their history except the names which bear the impress of their modes of life and customs. Palestine, the modern name of the Holy Land, reminds us of the ancient race of the Philistines, who made their abode in the country of sacred memories; and in the Hebrew " Pelesheth," " the land of the wanderers," and the Greek " Palaistine," we find Palestine the land of the Philistines, revealing the fact of their existence there as a people. Traces of the residence of the Celts in the English valleys are found in the names they bear. Upon the new continent the footsteps of the red men are marked in the local names of counties, towns, mountains, lakes and rivers. The extinct tribes of Eries, Nottawas, and others, have left their names in the territories in which they dwelt. The characteristics of the people are recognized in the tribal names, or in the name of the country. Wales is the land of stammerers ; Scotland, the land of the Scots ; Mexico, the sons of the war god, derived from Mexicatl, Mexitl being the war god of the Aztecs. The Eskimos are the eaters of raw flesh ; the Assiniboines are the Stoneys, or Stone People, from assin, " a stone," and bwan, " people," which is a name given to them by other tribes, from the custom of cooking their food with heated stones ; and the Senecas, who called themselves Sonontowane, meaning "great mountain," were in turn called by the Delawares " Mountain Snakes." * The Delawares were accustomed to call their enemies "snakes "; and in their own

* Hale's " Iroquois Book of Rites," page 175.

tongue sinako means "stone snakes." They employed the name common to the Iroquois tribe, "the mountain people," and added the expression of hostility, which seems to have been accepted in a measure by the Senecas themselves.

The significant names given to kings, as noted in the history of nations, tell us of their disposition and character, besides showing us in a measure the condition of the people. Only in a savage stage of society would it be possible for a king to be named, as in early English history, Ethelwulf, meaning "Noble Wolf." The English applied epithets to their kings, expressive of their character, as Alfred the Great, Edward the Confessor, William the Conqueror, and Richard the Lion-Hearted. Some of the rulers of Russia were nicknamed "Grim," "Terrible," and "Impostor," and among the other great European nations the nicknames of the kings expressed the political and religious phases of society, during the respective reigns. In the progressive stages of civilization among the Indians, there is to be noted a development in the use of names from the totemic, during the early periods of their history until they come to recognize their unity as a tribe, in which they generally designate themselves men or people, all other tribes being regarded as barbarous or inferior. The Nahuas, or Aztecs proper, who spoke the Nahuatl language, called themselves Nahuatlaca, from a sense of national pride, the meaning of the word being the "Superior People," or the "Commanding People." The sense of Nahuatl, according to Brinton, is to speak as one having authority or knowledge, and hence superior, able, astute, which is derived from Nauatile, to have "authority or command," and Nauatlato, an "expounder or interpreter." * The Dènè-Dindjié are the Athapascans of the north, who have several names. They employ a general expression for the word "people," or "men," as téné, or déné, or dindjyé, and this is the designation which they apply to themselves when they do not wish to name the district to which they belong. They generally call themselves

* "American Antiquarian," Vol. XV., page 379. "Myths of the New World," pages 80, 196.

by distinctive names, which refer to the localities in which
they dwell, and the expression téné, or déné, or the particle *ne*
is used as a suffix, meaning " people "—as Nazku'tenne, the
" People of the River Naz," which is on the Frazer River. The
Hwotsu'tinni, the " People of the River Hwotsutsən," are called
by the Kiliktons, who are of Tshimpsean parentage, Akwilgét,
" Well-dressed."

The Tsé-'kéh-ne, or " People on the Rocks," have several
tribal subdivisions in British Columbia, as the Tsé-'keh-ne-az, or
" Little People on the Rocks ; " the To-ta-t'qenne, or " People a
Little Down the River ;" the Tsé-loh-ne, or " People of the End
of the Rocks." The Dénés call all aboriginal tribes which do
not belong to them, Atna, which means " foreigner."* The Klam-
ath Indians of South-western Oregon call themselves Maklaks,
meaning " man," which is the only term employed for distinguishing this people, although there is the general expression
Lutuami, which signifies " Lake Indians." There are numerous euphonic and significant names employed for distinguishing the native tribes of Canada, some of which are used by the
people themselves, and others applied by the tribes who belong
not to the same race. The origin and meaning of the name
cannot always be given by the people, as is the case with the
Blood Indians, who use the expression Kaina, meaning " Blood
Indians," and Kainakwân a " Blood Indian." I have not been
able to obtain from any of the natives the exact meaning of
this tribal name. An old man of the camp informed me that
it was derived from Akaie, meaning "an old robe," and this
was applied to the tribe because, during one period of its
history, the people wore old robes. This tribe has two other
distinctive names. Aapaitûpi, " Blood People," from apûn, blood
and matûpe, a person ; and Sûmûkena, or Sûnûkeqtûqkûnema,
which mean that in their contests with their enemies they
fought with large knives. The Piegan Indians who, with the
Bloods, belong to the Blackfoot Confederacy, are called in the
Blackfoot tongue, Pikûne, and in the singular number, Pikûne-

* "Transactions of the Canadian Institute," October 1889, page 113;
1892-93, pages 17, 25, 27-29.

kwân, from Apikûne, meaning a "Half-dressed hide of the buffalo." The Indians say that there was a time in the history of the confederacy when the Piegans, through poverty, were compelled to dress themselves in buffalo robes which were badly tanned, and almost worthless as an article of clothing, and from this circumstance received their distinctive name The Blackfeet proper have as their distinguishing appellation Siksikauo, " Blackfeet." The singular number has always the singular termination kwân as Siksikaikwân, a Blackfoot Indian. It is a compound word, made from the adjective siksinûm, black, and oqkûts, his foot. We have the adjectival particle Siksi, the noun particles kai and kaw, and the personal termination kwân, which make the singular and plural forms of the name. There are two accounts given about the origin of the name. The Indians have informed me that the name refers to a period when the prairie was burned, leaving the ground black and dry. As the Indians travelled over the prairie their moccasins became black, and they were named by the adjacent tribes, Blackfeet. Jerry Potts, the Government guide and interpreter, who is a half-breed belonging to the Piegan tribe, and formerly a chief among them, than whom there is no more reliable authority on these questions, told me that there is another account of the origin of the name.

The tribe lived for some time in the northern part of the North-West Territories, where the soil was soft and very dark. Their moccasins were covered with the black mud as they travelled, and hence they received the name, which has been also given to the confederacy and to the language. The bands belonging to the tribes are known among the white people by the names of their respective chiefs, but among themselves there is a native name for each band. Thus we have the Siksenekaia or " Black Elk People." The legend says that a child was born which was very dark, and when he became a man he wore an elk skin. He was made a chief and the band over which he ruled were known as the " Black Elk People."

The band known as Inepoia, the " Sweating People," were named, according to the tradition of the natives, from their

ancestors having walked a long distance during sultry weather,
so that they perspired freely.   The band over which Red Crow,
the head chief of the Blood Indian tribe, presides is called
Mamyauye, "Fish-eaters," from mame, "a fish" and aouqseo "he
eats."   During an early period in their history, when the tribe
was absent on a buffalo hunting expedition, this band, on
account of sickness, remained at the mountains, fishing in the
streams, where they caught large quantities of fish, upon
which they lived.   This was a rare thing for the Indians of the
plains to do, and even at the present day they seldom eat fish.
Indeed, I have known the boys to catch fish in the rivers, which
they sold, but never have I seen a Blackfoot Indian partake
of one, except what was given him in the home of one of his
white friends.   Another name of late origin has been given to
this band.   When the brother of Red Crow was peace chief of
the tribe and the chief of this band, a friend made him a present
of a revolver having six chambers.   This circumstance was so
striking that the band was named Naâye, meaning "Six-mouthed,"
from the six chambers of the revolver.   The name is composed
of nao, six and maâye, the mouth.   The plural form of the
name, if used for the revolver itself, would be Naáyests, "Six
mouths."   The Oneidas, or "People of the Stone," in early times
planted their chief settlement near an eminence where a large
boulder of syenite lay.   The name is a corruption of a compound word formed of onenhia or onenya, stone, and kaniote,
to be upright or elevated.   Onenmiote is rendered "the project-
ing stone," and from this is formed the name Oneida.

Horatio Hale seeks the origin of the name Iroquois in the
word Ierokwa, "They who use Tobacco," or the "Tobacco People,"
which seems appropriate from the fact that these people in the
early days cultivated tobacco on an extensive scale: or in the
word for "bear," which, in the Cayuga speech, is Iakwai, and
this also seems applicable, as the Algonquins called the Iroquois
the Maquas or Bears.   Charlevoix gives the origin of the name
as follows: "The name of Iroquois is purely French, and has
been formed from the term hiro, 'I have spoken,' a word by
which these Indians close all their speeches, and koué, which,

when long drawn out, is a cry of sorrow, and when briefly uttered, is an exclamation of joy." The Delawares called them Mingo, and the readers of the works of Fenimore Cooper will recognize the people whom he called Mingoes. This is said to be a contraction of the Lenape word Mahongwi, meaning the "People of the Springs," the Iroquois having possessed the head-waters of the rivers which flowed through the Delaware country. The Caniengas or Flint People were styled by the southern Algonquins, Mowak or Mowawak, which has been corrupted into Mohawk, and when used as an appellative signifies "those who eat men," or the Cannibals. The Onondagas are the mountain people from Onontake, at the Mountain, referring to the site of their chief town. The Cree Indians call themselves Nehiyawuk, which seems to be derived from Iyiniwuk, the "True men," or the "Superior race." The Sioux were known to their foes as Nadouwe, or Nadowaessi, "Enemies" or "Snakes," a term of reproach, from which is derived the corrupted form, Sioux; but they call themselves Dakota, which signifies "friend" or "ally." Early in the seventeenth century the French missionaries frequently met with various tribes of the Algonquin stock, and among them bands of the Ojibways. One of these Ojibway bands is frequently mentioned in the "Jesuit Relations" as the Saulteurs, who were located in the vicinity of Sault Ste. Marie, and were named from their place of residence. La Hontan speaks of the "Outchepoues, *alias* Saulteurs." This name is still applied to a sub-tribe of the Ojibways scattered throughout Keewatin, Manitoba and the North-West Territories. Another sub-tribe of the Ojibways is the Mississaugas, or the Eagle tribe, from their totem. The Ojibways are known by the corrupt form of their name as Chippeways. This is said to signify "pucker," and is supposed to be derived from the peculiar pucker of the moccasin, or the custom of treating their captives by roasting them till puckered up. Along with the Ottawas, Pottowotamies and Menominies they are termed, in their traditions, Anishinabeg, meaning "Original people." The Indians dwelling on the Ottawa River were designated by the first French missionaries "The Sorcerers," from their practice

of jugglery, and the word Ottawa was loosely applied to all the
Western Algonquins, the river receiving its name from the fact
that it was the route to the country of the Ottawas. Baraga
derives the name from watawask, meaning "bulrushes." It is
said that these people called themselves Watawawininiwok, the
"Men of the bulrushes," because they dwelt upon the river where
grew a great many bulrushes. The proper pronunciation of
the name, however, ought to be Odawa. Another of the tribes,
sometimes mentioned in Canadian Indian history, are the
Epicerni or Nebicerni, better known as the Nipissings. Nibissing signifies "at the little lake," the lake bearing that name being
distinguished as one of the largest and most important in the
district. A man belonging to Nibissing, living at the little
lake, or in the surrounding country, was termed Nibissing-
dahshi-ahnine, and people dwelling there were called Nibis-
sinineyug, from which no doubt we get the corrupt form
Nebicerni. Baraga translates the name to signify, "in a little
water," or "in the leaves," but the former explanation from a
native belonging to the tribe must be accepted as more correct.

It is a prevalent custom among the native tribes of Canada
to confer names upon the white people with whom they have
dealings, or who must be distinguished in some way from the
general public. Servants of the Government, storekeepers,
teachers, missionaries, and persons residing near the Reservations, are designated by a native name. Sometimes a distinguished visitor will receive a name with a good deal of
ceremony. As the Indians cannot pronounce accurately the
common English names, and they are meaningless to them,
some Indian will point out a special characteristic of the man,
which may be a physical defect or grace, a trait in his character,
or ability displayed, and a name will be given accordingly. A
name may be conferred as an honor, with a mercenary purpose,
hoping to gain favor and receive a gift. Meaningless names
are never given. There is a distinction made between male and
female names. The names of males generally refer to power,
and the female names to gentleness and purity. These are
designated by the kind of animals chosen for the name. Most

frequently we hear of Bull's Head, a noble name, exhibiting
strength, which was given to Lieutenant-Colonel Macleod, when
acting as Indian Commissioner in the North-West Territories;
Bull's Horn, Black Bull and Buffalo Bull. The significance of
these lies in emphasizing physical or intellectual strength, wise
statesmanship and ability to rule men. Another class, relating
to power and referring to men, is that which belongs to spiritu-
ality. Power over spirits, a man powerful in prayer or eminent
in piety, may be called, Three Suns. A clever medicine man
will be known as Medicine-Calf; the word for sun being also
translated medicine. The Indian, however, has two distinct meanings for the word medicine, as used by writers about
the natives. The medicine man uses herbs as medicines, and is
in that sense a medical practitioner, but he is also a praying
man, and employs incantations for the purpose of calling his
familiar spirit to help him in healing the sick. In this sense he
has spiritual power, and the word natos, in the Blackfoot language, is translated "sun," and also "medicine." Natoapekwân
means, therefore, "medicine man," "praying man" and "missionary;" but is literally the sun man. It is not applied to the
white medical man. A missionary will be called Niokskatos,
meaning "three suns," from niokskûm, "three," and natosiks,
"suns," denoting spiritual power. Animals, birds and natural
objects are selected with qualities agreeing with the masculine
nature, as the deer, for swiftness; the eagle, for flight, and because of its sacred character among the Indians; the mountain,
suggesting massive strength; thunder, on account of its mysteri-
ousness and power of impression; and father, as a term of reverence and authority. Feminine names are selected from among
those animals suggesting innocence, purity, gentleness and goodness. The idea of power does not enter into this kind of names.
Apawakas is a woman's name, meaning "White Antelope," from
awakas, an antelope, and ap, a particle, signifying white. This
particle is seen in apio, a "white horse," and napekwân, a
"white man." The color in this name is symbolical of purity
and the animal of innocence and gentleness. Epīsoaqsĭ, the
"morning star," was a name for a little girl. Little Rabbit

Woman, the name of a young married woman. Anatcinûm, meaning "pretty," the name for a white boy of about two years of age. Names are also given from some article of dress, or striking feature about the person. They may relate to the disposition, or some notable event in the history of the individual. The names of a few of my personal friends among the Blood Indians will illustrate what I say : Calf-Shirt, Wolf-Collar, Eagle-Rib, Eagle-Shoe, Bull-Shield, Heavy-Shield, Black-Horse, Red-Crow, Low-Horn, Stolen-Person, Yellow-Snake, White-Calf, One-Spot, Bull-Back-Fat, Blackfoot-Old-Woman, Going-to-the-Bear, Father-of-Many-Children.

A child may receive its name from some circumstance in connection with its birth, and some of the children's names are very pretty. Usually among the Blackfeet young and old have two names, especially the male portion of the tribe. When teaching the Indian school I was surprised to hear the children laugh when I mentioned some of the names on the school register, and I soon learned that nearly all the children had two names, a good and a bad one. As an Indian will not tell his name, I found that some of the young folks had given me the ugly names of their companions, and it was these I was repeating when I called the roll. As they grow older the childish names are changed, and a single individual may have many names during his life time. If a man has been guilty of some mean act, a name will accordingly be given, and if he has performed a brave deed it will be remembered by a new name. This, no doubt, is the chief reason for persons not telling their names, as the mention of them will declare to his fellows the deceitfulness of the unworthy man, and the man of valor does not care to parade his heroism by telling his name. Whenever among young or old I was anxious to learn their names, it was necessary for me to ask a second party to tell me the name of the first, and *vice versa*.

Some of my native friends desired to learn somewhat of the customs of the white men, and among other things they asked the name of a farmer living near the Reservation. "John Smith," I replied. "What is the name of his oldest son?" "John Smith." They gazed at me in astonishment. "What is the name of the second boy ?" "Tom Smith." They looked again, and laughed at the strange custom of naming children, As they heard the names of each member of the family, they inquired how it was possible to distinguish them, as they all bore the surname, and the Christian name seemed to them insufficient to separate one member from another. "What is the name of the man's wife ?" "Mrs. Smith." This was too much for their gravity, and they burst into loud laughter. I had then to explain the fact that the woman lost her own surname and took that of the husband, retaining her own Christian name. With laughter, mingled with seriousness, they said, " Why don't the woman keep her own name ?" and I joined in the laughter, as I felt that they were excellent advocates of woman's rights, although they did not grant to women the freedom enjoyed among the white people. A married woman among the Indians does not change her name, and there are no surnames, each member of a family having a distinct name. They were still more puzzled when I told them of another man with a family having the same surname, and some of the young folks had the same Christian names.

As the Indians travelled through the forests, along the courses of rivers, and over the lakes they left the impress of their presence in names of beauty, suggesting legends, battles, freaks of nature, or some simple event in their nomadic life. Rivers, lakes, and mountains, and even towns and cities, bear suggestive historic facts in their names, though the corrupt forms make the hidden meaning difficult to trace.

When Captain Bienville de Celoron left Canada with French soldiers and Canadians, Iroquois and Abnaki Indians, to take possession of the Ohio country in the name of the King of France, he carried leaden plates with an inscription engraven on them, to show that the country had been claimed by the French, and these were buried at different points along his route. He coasted along the southern shore of Lake Erie, as far west as the mouth of Chautauqua Creek, where they made a portage to the Chautauqua Lake ; and for the first time, no doubt, civilized man gazed upon its placid waters and beautiful shores. On one of the leaden plates, secured surreptitiously by Sir William Johnson, the lake is called Tchadakoiu. Various forms of the name were used, arising from the inability of the French and English to catch correctly the Indian pronunciation, and spelling it phonetically as they heard it from the lips of the Indians. The tribes forming the Iroquoian Confederacy pronounced it differently from each other, and hence arose confusion in spelling it. Sir William Johnson pronounced it Jadaghque, and Cornplanter called it Chaud-dauk-wa. Several interpretations of the name have been given. It is said to mean "the foggy place," in allusion to the mists arising from the lake, "high up" referring to its elevated position; and in the Seneca tongue, Chadaqueh, which, according to Horatio Jones, who was well versed in the language, signifies "a pack tied in the middle," or two moccasins fastened together, and the lake, resembling these objects, was so named. Dr. Peter Wilson, an educated Seneca, related a tradition which made the name signify "the place where fish are taken out," or Fish Lake, derived from gajoh, "fish," and gadahgwah, "taken out." The tradition says that a party of Senecas, returning from the Ohio to Lake Erie, were passing through Chautauqua in a canoe, when they caught a strange fish, which they bore alive to Lake Erie and placed in the water, where, in after years, this kind was found in great abundance.

Another tradition says that it means "the place of easy death," or "where one vanishes away," as a young woman belonging to a party of Indians encamped on the shore, having eaten of a certain root growing on the banks of the lake, became exceedingly thirsty, and, stooping to drink of the clear water, disappeared forever.

Cornplanter alluded to this tradition in a famous speech in the following words: "In this case, one chief has said he could ask you to put him out of pain, and another, who will not think of dying by the hand of his father or his brother, has said he will retire to the Cauddaukwa, eat of the fatal root, and sleep with his fathers in peace."

In *The Allegheny Magazine* of July 4, 1816, the origin of the name has been thus explained: "The tradition among the Seneca Indians is that when their ancestors first came to the margin of this lake, and had reclined their weary limbs for the night, they were roused by a tremendous wind, which suddenly and unexpectedly brought the waves upon the shore, to the jeopardy of their lives. The aboriginal history, as handed down from father to son, further represents that in the confusion of the scene a child was swept away by the surge beyond the possibility of recovery. Hence the name of the lake, Chaud-dauk-wa, the radix from which this is formed signifying ' a child, or something respecting a child.' The word is usually spelled Chautauqua ; but, according to the pronunciation of the venerable Cornplanter, whose example is the best authority, it should be written Chaud-dauk-wa, the two first syllables of which are long, and the consonant at the end of each is to be distinctly sounded."

The native tribes of Canada have left their tribal names and others formed from their languages in every district in the Dominion. The name Canada has been variously interpreted. It has been derived from the Cree words Kanâta or Kanâtan, "something which is very neat or clean." The name, as applied to the country, first appears in " Bref Recit de la Navigation faite en," 1535-36, by Captain Jacques Cartier. Cartier, in his glossary of Indian terms, says that the Indians call their town " Canada." There is an old tradition that the Spaniards entered the country before the French, and seeing no signs of any mines had several times repeated the words *Aca nada*, meaning " nothing there." The Indians repeated this to the French, who supposed this to be the name of the country. It has also been derived from an Indian root word, which signified the " country of big lakes and rivers." Charlevoix says : " Some derive the name from the Iroquois Kannata, meaning ' a collection of cabins.'" Canada, or Kanada, seems in its original use to have been used for a village of tents or huts, and afterwards applied to the whole country.

Lake Champlain was named after the first Governor of Canada, who discovered it in 1609, and defeated the Iroquois on its banks. It was named by the Indians Patawabouque, meaning " the alternation of land and water," alluding to the numerous islands there ; and Kanaderi-quarunte, " the lips or door of the country," as it was the path from the valley of the Hudson to the St. Lawrence. Lake Simcoe was called by the Indians Ouentaron, meaning "beautiful lake." The French, however, named it Lac aux Claies, which became corrupted into Lac la Clie, and for one hundred and fifty years after the French-Huron period, it retained this name. The lake was called by Creuxius, Lacus Ouentaronius; and in some early maps the name Toronto is applied to it. As for the word Toronto, it is said to mean "the place of meeting," and in the Huron language to signify "much or multitude." A Mohawk tradition of an expedition of the Indians to the Bay at Toronto, states that as they looked around they seemed to see trees standing in the water, and the place was named in the Mohawk tongue Karonto, signifying, "trees standing in water," from which is derived the corrupted name Toronto. The name does not appear applied to its present locality till it is seen in a map illustrating the campaign which ended in Braddock's defeat in 1755, when there seems to have been a French fort located there.

Lake Ontario was known as Lake Skanadario, Lac Saint Louis, Lac Frontenac, Lac des Iroquois, and Lake Cataracoui. The name which it now bears signifies, "beautiful lake," and is so understood by an Iroquois of the present day, but its original signification was "great lake." Ontario is derived from the Huron word yontare or ontare, or the Iroquois oniatare, "lake," and the termination "io," derived from the word wiyo, which, in the Seneca dialect signifies "good," and in the Tuscarora, "great." It is also supposed to be derived from the Mohawk word Kentariyoh, meaning, "a placid sheet of water." It was called Ontario as early as 1646, Father Jogues having used that term in addressing a large gathering of Sachems and Indians at the Iroquois town of Osserion, about thirty miles distant from the Dutch town, Rensselaerswyck, now known as Albany. Having spoken to the assembly, and made some presents of wampum, he presented the Chief of the Onondagas with a thousand beads of wampum, and said, "We wish to salute you in your own country; take this present to smooth the way, and that no one may be astonished at our visit. Moreover, we have three paths to reach you—one by the Mohawk, the other by the great lake which you call Ontario, the third by the Huron country."

Ottawa is called by the Indians Kanatsio, meaning "the kettle in the water," having reference to the Chaudiere Falls. The Mohawks called the neck-like contraction between lakes Erie and Ontario, Ohnyakara, meaning "on or at the neck," derived from Onyara, "the neck or contraction between the head and trunk," and from this comes the name Niagara, which was applied to the whole stream of water between these lakes. The Ojibways have left the marks of their presence in the names beginning with Manito, "the spirit." Manitoulin is "the island of the spirit," from the Ojibway Manito and French l'île. Manitowaning is "the cave of the spirit," from Manito, "the spirit," and waning, "a hollow or cave." The Indians believed that there was a certain part of the bay which had no bottom, as they had often tried in winter to reach the bottom by letting down a decoy fish made of wood, loaded with lead, and had failed to fathom its depths, as it was inhabited by some Manito or sea-god. Manitoba is "the strait of the spirit," from Manito, "a spirit," and waba, "a strait," the lake having received its name from the strange things heard in the strait which unites the lake with another. The island of Vancouver was named after Captain Vancouver, but the Indian name is Katchutequa, meaning "the plain." Saugeen is a corrupt form of Sahging, meaning "the outlet or mouth of the river," derived from the Ottawa word, Sahkum, which signifies "to come out." Nottawasaga is also a corrupt form of an Indian word, the proper form being Nahdowa-sahging, meaning "the place where the Nahdowag used to come out." The Nahdowag were the Mohawks or Iroquois. When the Ottawas were at Manitoulin Island, the Iroquois attacked them, and they were accustomed to go out into Lake Huron or the Georgian Bay by the Nahdowa-Sahgi River. Sahgimah, the famous warrior of the Ottawas, was in the habit of watching for the Iroquois at the Blue Mountains, at the place still called Sahgimah Odahkahwahbewin, meaning "Sahgimah's watching place." There he defeated them. The last time he came out

24

to meet his enemies he found them occupying his watching place, and going alone in the evening to view their camp, he saw their arms stacked and the warriors feasting, unconscious of any danger. Returning with his warriors, he found his enemies had gone to rest, and quietly removing their arms, he fell upon the sleeping Mohawks, slaughtering all, but a few whom he saved to tell the story of their defeat. The heads of their slaughtered foes were placed upon poles with their faces turned toward the lake, and the remaining Mohawks, having been placed in a canoe loaded with provisions and ammunition, were sent home with instructions to tell their friends the story of their fate, and that similar retribution would follow every Mohawk who dared to come to the Blue Mountains. Winnipeg is derived from win, "unclean or fetid," and nipig, "water." The names of places shed light on the migrations of the native tribes, and Winnipeg is one of the suggestive names in the history of the Canadian Indians. Winnipeg means "bad smelling water." The Winnebago Indians, a branch of the Dakota or Sioux Confederacy, were called by the French, Des Puants, or the Stinkards, and in the early " Jesuit Relations " there occurs the names Ouinepeag, or Winnipeg. There was a tradition prevailing among the Winnebagoes that they came from the salt sea, or the stinking water. The name and the tradition place Winnipeg or Hudson's Bay as the original home of these people, who were driven out by the Ojibways when they entered the Red River country. The oldest village of the Winnebagoes is said to be Sturgeon Bay, a village on the St. Lawrence. The traditions of the Dakotas say that their ancestors came from the east ; *i.e.*, the Atlantic coast ; and evidence of language leads to the conclusion that the course of migration of the Indian tribes was from the Atlantic Coast, westward and southward. The traditions of the Algonquins seem to point to Hudson's Bay and Labrador as their place of origin. We cannot, however, tell the point as to the source of these tribes, whether they entered the continent from the north-east or north-west.

A Winnebago tradition says that there once appeared an eagle coming down from Manito's home in the great sky, so large that he covered the big lakes and islands, and he brooded

The bells of the Roman Mission,
That call from their turrets twain;
To the boatman on the river,
To the hunter on the plain;

over the face of the earth and waters, and then a great chief
and his wife were born. They were the first of any tribe who
came straight from heaven, and in course of time they multiplied and wandered away from the islands and shores of the
long, wide river in Canada, to the islands of the great lakes.
The waters about them they called after their own name, Bay-
des-Puans. There are several places bearing the name of this
tribe. On Sanson's map, 1656, Lake Michigan is called "Lac-
de-Puans"; the Cattaraugus Creek, near Chautauqua, on an
old French map of that region, is designated "R. a la Terre
Puante": and the Bay of Puans, or Green Bay, Wisconsin,
where Jean Nicolet visited the Winnebagoes in 1639, and
Marquette in 1673, found a village inhabited by three nations,
"Miamis," "Maskouteus," and "Kikabeux." The Winnebagoes
and the Illinois, including the Sacs and Foxes, were the original
inhabitants of Wisconsin. A tradition of the tribe seems to
suggest Winnipeg as a locality where these people dwelt in the
past. "The largest village of the Winnebagoes was at Red
Banks. It stretched both above and on the low-lands at the
foot of the cliffs. And there is a little river that cuts the low
land in two. Here was fought a great battle between the
Puants, who owned the land, and a new tribe that came in
big canoes. The blood ran in such streams that it made the
water in the little river turn red, and so the Indians gave it
the name which, in French, means 'Riviere Rouge,' after the
battles were over. The Winnebagoes, being wise and great
braves, could never be driven away by any other tribe."
Making allowance for the form of traditions by a change of
residence, through additions which are in the nature of interpretations, the evidence seems to declare in favor of Winnipeg
having received its name from the Winnebago tribe residing
on the banks of the Red River before the Ojibways entered the
country.*

* "Transactions of Canadian Institute," September, 1893, page 260. Brin
ton's "American Hero Myths," pages 103, 123. "Life of Zeisberger," pages
31, 73. "American Antiquarian," Vol. VIII., page 304; Vol. IX., pages 378,
394; Vol. X., page 83; Vol. XI., page 244; Vol. XVII., pages 219-236.
"Annual Report of Bureau of Ethnology," 1885-86, page 155. Winsor's "Critical
History of America," Vol. IV., pages 166, 167, 211.

CHAPTER IV.

NATIVE HEROES.

CROWFOOT.

THE famous chief of the Blackfeet was one of the most striking personages in the Canadian North-West. The dignified leader of his own tribe, he was also the acknowledged chief of the Blackfoot Confederacy. I was deeply impressed with his sterling qualities and abilities as a commander when first I saw him. The Bloods and Piegans always spoke in glowing terms of his eloquence and wise administration, corroborating Natosapi's (Old Sun's) opinion expressed at the making of the treaty, " Crowfoot has been called by us our Great Father." When they discussed any of his measures for the welfare of his people, they invariably finished by saying, "Crowfoot is a wise man." The father of Crowfoot was chief of the Blackfeet—a man of distinguished powers and of great influence. He was called Akautcinikasima, meaning " Many Names," a word composed of akauo, "many," and tcinikasi-mists, "names." His mother was a Blood Indian woman. Crowfoot was born near the Blackfoot Crossing, about the year 1826. Although the son of the chief, he possessed as a boy no special favors such as belong to royalty, the native laws compelling every member of the tribe to win his laurels, and permitting none to be exempt from the duties of his station. There is no social distinction in the camp, but there are civil and military positions, with their respective duties, and obedience and respect are given to those officials during the performance of their duties. The natives are a democratic people, without any faith in an aristocracy of wealth. They are, how-ever, deeply attached to an aristocracy of ability, valor and character. As a boy in the camp he felt a hereditary pride in belonging to such a warlike tribe as the Blackfeet, whose name brought terror to the Crees, Ojibways, Saulteaux and Shoshones sixty years ago, and as the member of a family of chiefs there was stirred in his bosom an ambitious desire to win a worthy place among his people.

This was the emotion which aroused the hearts of the young men in general, but this youth seemed to feel it more deeply than any other member of his race. This was shown when he was only thirteen years of age, an opportunity having occurred for him to join a party going out on a war expedition. The youthful warrior exhibited such brave qualities, and was so energetic on the warpath, that his name was changed for that of Kaiostâ, meaning "bear ghost," compounded of the words Kaio, a bear, and Stââ, a ghost or spirit. He was honored among his people for the spirit manifested, which aroused his ambition still more to merit their applause by greater deeds. He had a brother older than himself who bore the illustrious name of Crowfoot, on account of his successful expedition against the tribe of Crow Indians. The Blackfeet designed the making of a treaty with the Snake Indians, and fourteen of their bravest and wisest men were despatched for that pur-pose, Kaiostâ's brother being one of the number. The Snake Indians basely ignored the Indian laws relating to the bearers of peace, and treacherously slew them.

Chief Many Names and the tribes of the Blackfoot Con-federacy were deeply incensed at this act of cruelty in defiance of the customs of war, and determined to punish them for their cowardice and knavery. A large war party was organized and started for the country of the Snakes in Montana. Kaiostâ, aroused by fraternal love and youthful valor, joined the party. They found the Snake Indians prepared to receive them, but the Blackfeet outnumbered them, and fought so furiously that the Snakes were ignominiously defeated. So great was the bravery of the youthful son of Many Names, that again his name was changed, and he received the one belonging to his deceased brother, and that by which he was ever afterward known, namely, Crowfoot. The significance of this name is found in its allusion to the Crow Indians, who were enemies of the Blackfeet.

Esûpomûqsikaw, meaning "Crowfoot," is composed of Esûpo, the name of the Crow Indians in the Blackfoot tongue, omuqsim, "large," and oqkûts, "a foot." We have then in the name Esûpo, Crow, muqsi, large, and kaw, foot. By the euphonic laws of the language the intervening letters and syllables are elided in the composition of the name. It is composed of the word Crow, with the two words signifying the one who has a large foot. When Crowfoot reached manhood he developed striking physical characteristics, which marked him as no common man. He was above medium height, with a high forehead, thin lips firmly compressed, an aquiline nose, high cheek bones, piercing grey eyes, and a face that suggested commanding qualities. As he softly strode over the prairie, he had the dignified mien of the leader of men, a modern Roman among savages. At the sun dance he aroused the warlike emotions of young and old by the recital of his brave deeds. Foremost in the fight and the last to retreat, he led his warriors through many a successful fray, and they always returned with increased admiration for his courage and skill.

He succeeded his father as chief of the tribe, and was subsequently acknowledged as the head of the confederacy. Before being called to this position he distinguished himself at the Battle of Three Ponds, situated between the Red Deer and Battle rivers. The Crees were enemies of the Blackfeet, and seized every opportunity of attacking them. Stealthily they approached the camp of Natos (the Sun) about midnight on the 3rd of December, 1866, and attacked the people, who were few in number. In the most critical juncture, when the Crees had almost gained a victory, the voice of Crowfoot was heard shouting to his warriors as he dashed upon the Crees. His sudden appearance and great prowess renewed the courage of the Blackfeet, and the Crees were soon overcome. The

victorious Blackfeet rejoiced in the intrepid valor of Crowfoot,
who had saved them at a time when destruction stared them
in the face, and he was raised in the estimation of his people.
Only a few years later, the Blackfeet, Bloods and South
Piegans were attacked near Lethbridge, on the Belly River, by
a war party of Crees and Assiniboines. The Blackfeet and
Bloods were camped between the trading-posts called Whoop-up
and Kipp, and the South Piegans were stationed on the St.
Mary's River. The Blood camp was attacked and a few
Indians killed. The Bloods were few in number and unequal
in the contest with the combined force of Crees and Assiniboines, and runners were despatched to arouse the Piegans,
who speedily came to their aid. The Blackfeet, Bloods and
Piegans were better armed than their enemies, and having
united their forces, the Crees were compelled to retreat towards
Belly River, opposite the present site of Lethbridge. They
placed themselves in position in one of the coulees on the high
banks of the river, and the Blackfeet, with their confederates,
found a similar position in a parallel coulee about three or four
hundred yards distant. The opposing forces fought desperately
for four or five hours, when the Crees began to retreat toward
the river. Swiftly they were followed in a confused mass
down the coulee, the war cries of the pursuers mingling
with the death yells and groans of the wounded and dying.
The Crees plunged into the river still closely pursued, while
many of the victors stood upon the banks and shot down the
helpless swimmers. Almost at the base of the high bank on
the opposite side of the river the remnant made a last stand to
fight for life, and until darkness compelled them to desist the
battle continued. A formal treaty was made between the tribes
in the year following, and this has been kept until the present
time.

Crowfoot was distinguished as an orator among his people.
He was slow and deliberate in speech and a man of few words.
His language was expressive, and sometimes full of beautiful
imagery. It is impossible to gain a true idea of his power
as a speaker from his addresses to Government officials and

members of the white race, as these were harangues, and
generally dealt with questions affecting the temporal interests
of his people, these belonging to the petty concerns of everyday
life, such as food and clothing. It was when discussing grave
questions in the native council that he shone as an orator, and
his genius far surpassed the strongest intellects among his
people. I have listened to some of the native orators, and have
been charmed with the beautiful and expressive phraseology,
the dignified attitude, the piercing eye, and graceful gestures,
and the effect produced upon the people.

At the Blackfoot Treaty with the Government, made at
Blackfoot Crossing, in 1877, Crowfoot addressed Lieutenant-
Governor Laird and the Commissioners as follows: " While
I speak be kind and patient. I have to speak for my people,
who are numerous, and who rely upon me to follow that course
which in the future will tend to their good. The plains are
large and wide, we are the children of the plains, it is our home,
and the buffalo has been our food always. I hope you look
upon the Blackfeet, Bloods, and Sarcees as your children now,
and that you will be indulgent and charitable to them. They
all expect me now to speak for them, and I trust the Great
Spirit will put into their breasts to be a good people—into the
minds of the men, women, and children, and their future gen-
erations. The advice given me and my people has proved to be
very good. If the police had not come to the country, where
would we be all now ? Bad men and whiskey were killing us
so fast that very few, indeed, of us would have been left to-day.
The police have protected us as the feathers of the bird protect
it from the frosts of winter. I wish them all good, and trust
that all our hearts will increase in goodness from this time
forward. I am satisfied! I will sign the treaty." The
difficulty of presenting Crowfoot as a distinguished speaker
may be learned from the fact that in addressing those who did
not understand his native tongue, he had to speak a sentence
at a time, which was then interpreted, and consequently his
thoughts were somewhat disconnected, and his flow of language
interrupted.

When the correspondent for the *Mail* visited the Blackfoot
Crossing, Crowfoot was interviewed, and his skill in dealing
with men is seen in the manner in which he dealt with the
subjects mentioned to him. He said : " It always happens that
far-away countries hear exaggerated stories of one another. The
distance between them causes the news to grow as it circulates.
I often hear things of far-off places, but I do not believe them ;
it may be very little, and be magnified as it goes. When I
hear such news about you as you hear about me, I don't believe
it ; but I go to the Indian agent, or some one else in authority,
and ask and find out the truth. Why should the Blackfeet
create trouble ?   Are they not quiet and peaceable and
industrious ? The Government is doing well for them and
treating them kindly, and they are doing well. Why should
you kill us, or we kill you ? Let our white friends have
compassion. I have two hearts—one is like stone, and one is
tender. Suppose the soldiers come, and, without provocation,
try to kill us—I am not a child—I know we shall get redress
from the law. If they did kill us, my tender heart would
feel for my people."

When asked about his grievances, he replied : " There is no
grievance, except the burning of the grass on our Reserve by
the sparks from the railway, which has been reported by the
agent. Last year the grass was burned, and the year before,
too. Great damage was caused. Our horses lost their food,
and some were lost by going on the heated ground. The first
year we asked no recompense ; but last year we asked for
damages, and have yet received no answer. If this harm was
done in the white man's country it would be redressed. If my
people burned other people's grass, I should speak to them, and
make them give redress. Mr. Dewdney told me to tell the
agent, Mr. Begg, of any grievance, and I told him of this : but I
didn't say anything till I saw the misery and destitution the fire
had caused. It nearly burned our own houses. This is my
only grievance."

It was in the councils of the nation and in dealing with his
own people that Crowfoot's abilities as a leader were specially

een. He had a strong intellect, a good knowledge of human
nature, and was a wise and successful native diplomat. It was
he who suggested plans for bettering the condition of his
people; and, in times of difficulty, he saw a way of escape,
when others failed to provide a remedy. He was intensely
patriotic. He loved his people sincerely and the customs of his
race. Always friendly toward the white people, and never tired
of urging the natives to imitate their virtues and eschew their
vices, setting before them the benefits of industry and a wise
conformity to their changed conditions through the advent of
civilization and the departure of the buffalo, he still counselled
them to follow the native traditions, and maintain their tribal
unity. He wisely foresaw the impossibility of making
civilized white men from Indians; and he could not forget
the prestige of former days. Unto the last he remained
deeply attached to the faith of his fathers; and his people
followed him in their adherence to their native faith. The
land in which they dwelt was filled with sacred memories,
every hill and valley marking a battle field, burial place of
their loved ones, or honored with some tradition which was
dear to their hearts.

The policy of Crowfoot was peaceful, and his wise adminis-
ration revealed the consummate shrewdness and sterling character of the man. How changed was the condition of affairs
from the former days when Chief Many Names could lead his
thousands to war, and the latter days when Crowfoot, in his
old age, reigned over a few savages upon an Indian Reserve.
Small-pox had slain its hundreds, the buffalo were no more, the
white race had invaded the land, planting towns, laying rail-
roads, and with the blessings of civilization, bringing in its
train numerous diseases and deep-rooted vices, which sapped
the foundations of native morality, and sent many of the noble
sons and daughters of the red race to untimely and dishonoured
graves.

Some of the Indians entertained grave fears, and held superstitious ideas about the railroad before it reached their country;
but Crowfoot believed that it was a waggon on wheels, made

by man without any supernatural power. He stood almost alone in his belief until the people saw it for themselves. When he visited the east he was entertained at Winnipeg, Ottawa, Montreal and other important places. During his visit to Montreal, Sir Wm. VanHorne, in the name of the company, informed him that a perpetual pass would be granted him over the Canadian Pacific Railroad. This was sent him subsequently, and acknowledged by the chief. In reply to the address of the railway officials he said, " My heart has always been loyal. I love the pale-faces. They are good friends to me and to my people. I would not let my young men go on the warpath. When Indians tell me lies I shut my ears. I will only believe in wrong when the white man tells me himself. When I return my young men will protect the railway and the fire waggons."

Owing to various rumors of dissatisfaction among the Indians, it was thought wise by the Government to send some of the chiefs of the different tribes on a visit to the towns and cities of Ontario and Quebec, that they might learn something of the wealth, power, numbers and spirit of the white people. Crowfoot was one of the chiefs selected for that visit. The Mayor and Council of each of the cities received the native deputations and honorably entertained them.

As he journeyed eastward, upon learning that Lake Superior was not the sea, he christened it "The Little Brother of the Sea." Crowfoot desired the Blackfeet to be represented at the unveiling of the Brantford monument to Chief Joseph Brant, and as he was anxious to see his people, and could not wait for the ceremony, he confided to the care of Mr. L'Heureux, the interpreter, four historic arrows, to be given to the Iroquois. Mr. L'Heureux is authority for the statement that these arrows are connected with a native legend, that the earth was once covered with water, and all the tribes were gathered on a mountain. The white, black and yellow tribes were on the top of the mountain, but the red men were in the inside. After a time the wise men among the Indians bored a hole out of the side of the mountain, and, looking out, saw a white

THE BRANT MEMORIAL.

AT BRANTFORD

STEREOPLATE Co.

swan floating on the waters near the mountain. The swan
bore four arrows, pointing to the north, south, east and west
The red men killed the swan and captured the arrows, which
possess a hidden meaning for the Indians. The arrows conveyed to the Iroquois represented the captured ones of the
legend. The Iroquois received the arrows with due solemnity,
and sent to Crowfoot a small string of wampum beads. Crowfoot's influence was unlimited in his own tribe, but even beyond
the confederacy his name was honored by the members of
other tribes, The white people admired his policy in dealing
with the natives, and respected him for his abilities and his
attitude toward the white race. Some doubts were entertained
about Crowfoot's loyalty, which were, however, set at rest by
his actions during the Rebellion, and his own declarations afterward upon several occasions. When asked whether Riel had
ever asked him to join in revolt, he said, "Yes; over in Montana
in the winter of 1879 or the spring of 1880. He wanted me to
join with all the Sioux, and Crees, and half-breeds. The idea
was to have a general uprising and capture the North-West,
and hold it for the Indian race and the Metis. We were to meet
at Tiger Hills, in Montana; we were to have a government
of our own. I refused, but the others were willing; and then
they reported that already some of the English forts had been
captured. This was a lie. Riel took Little Pine's treaty paper
and trampled it under his foot, and said we should get a better
treaty from him. Riel came also to trade with us, and I told
my people to trade with him, but not to listen to his words.
Riel said he had a mighty power behind him in the east."

In 1875, Sitting Bull and ten of his chiefs, who had fought
Custer, visited Crowfoot to secure his help, but he firmly
refused. In protesting his loyalty Crowfoot concluded: "To
rise there must be an object; to rebel there must be a wrong
done; to do either, we should know how it would benefit us.
We do not wish for war. We have nothing to gain; but we
know that people make money by war on Indians, and these
people want war. If these people want to incite war, or to
steal the right of warring men—that is, to fight without the

consent or knowledge of the Government—don't let them, and when they find out that there is no profit in it, they will stop. The Queen does not want war when there is no cause. She is not in favor of war. Let the Government know that we favor peace, and want it. I have done."

Crowfoot had been failing in health for some time, and both he and his people knew that his days were numbered. The medicine men gathered around his bed, but their incantations and medicines availed not to bring relief. Everything was done by the people to minister to his wants and make him comfortable, but the end was near. He distributed his horses among his relations. The numerous gifts he had received during his visit east were given to his white friends. His brother, Three Bulls, he nominated as his successor, and with an admonition to the natives to live on good terms with the white people, on April 27th, 1890, surrounded by whites and Indians, he quietly breathed his last. Rev. Father Lacombe performed the burial service, and the great chief of the Blackfeet was laid to rest amid great lamentations from his people, and sincere sorrow among the white population. He was a noble red man, worthy the respect and grief of a great nation, which delighted to honor him in life, and now holds dear his memory as a sacred trust.

POUNDMAKER.

Poundmaker was one of the ablest chiefs of the Cree Confederacy. His father was a Cree Indian, and the early years of him who was destined to occupy a prominent place in the councils of his nation were spent in the camps of his own people. When but a youth he met Crowfoot at a trading party, and the Blackfoot chief looked kindly on him. Crowfoot had lost a son whom he tenderly loved, and mourned deeply for him, and as he gazed into the face of the Cree lad, he saw a resemblance to the son who was, no more. He told the youth that he would be a father to him, and accordingly adopted him. He went to the camp of the Blackfeet with

Crowfoot, and dwelt with him in his lodge for several years. In manhood he returned to his own people, married among them, and soon rose to distinction as a brave warrior and wise statesman.

The Cree country lies to the north of the Blackfeet, and the people, though distinct tribes and belonging to different confederacies, are members of the Algonquin stock. There have never, within the memory of man, existed cordial relations between these tribes, but they have always been most inveterate enemies toward each other. Cessation of hostilities has only been enjoyed when they have been tired of warfare and a treaty has been made. Wars were frequent between them, and they were eager for every opportunity, upon the slightest provocation, of attacking the camps. The intellectual ability of Poundmaker gave him pre-eminence, which he exerted for the purpose of securing peaceful relations between the tribes, and it was chiefly through his influence that a treaty was made between them. Little Pine, Big Bear and some other chiefs were always anxious to go on the warpath, and they seemed to have special delight in harrassing the Blackfeet.

The policy of Poundmaker, like that of Crowfoot, was peaceful, and with his influence on the side of justice, he maintained peace when others were eager for war. He was a fine specimen of the Cree Indian—tall and slender, a high forehead, a Grecian nose, intelligent countenance, free from any signs of coarseness or sensuality, and a body well formed, marked him as no common man. His dignified bearing and quiet demeanour struck the visitor to his Reserve, and these stamped him as a man wise in council, intensely devoted to his people, and strong to command the warriors who were deeply attached to him. Poundmaker's Reserve was situated about thirty miles west of Battleford, on the south side of Battle River, and its area was thirty square miles. Possessed of an independent spirit, and accustomed to a nomadic life, he did not take kindly to farming operations, and was none too submissive to the plans of the Government toward inducing the Indians to become self-supporting. He consequently was considered to be troublesome.

which arose in a great measure from failing to see the benefits
which would result from leading an agricultural life. When
once convinced that it would be beneficial to his people to adopt
the new mode of living, he was not slow to avail himself of the
helps at hand, and he worked industriously himself and encouraged his young men to forsake their roving life and follow
his example. As he was born to rule, and not to serve, and was
accustomed to dictate instead of being instructed, it was not
always easy to manage him.

The chiefs are not arbitrary leaders, working out their own
plans without consulting the people; but, in the councils, the
wishes of the people are known through the minor chiefs, and
the head chief acts as spokesman for the tribe in all important
matters. Sometimes the head chief is compelled to follow
instead of leading, and to acquiesce in plans which his own
judgment does not approve, and blame is often attached to the
chief by persons ignorant of the customs of the natives for his
attitude on public questions. Poundmaker was sometimes
placed in this anomalous position, assenting to schemes which
the people believed were right, and he was not in agreement
with them. He wavered not, however, in the performance of
his duty, when the members of his tribe through their chiefs
had come to a decision on some tribal matter, or policy of the
Government. At the Carleton treaty, made between the Crees
and the Government in the year 1876, he agreed to the proposi-
tions of the Commissioners, and signed the treaty. He said on
that occasion : " We have heard your words that you had to say
to us as the representative of the Queen. We were glad to
hear what you had to say, and have gathered together in
council and thought the words over amongst us. We were
glad to hear you tell us how we might live by our own work.
When I commence to settle on the lands to make a living for
myself and my children, I beg of you to assist me in every way
possible. When I am at a loss how to proceed I want the
advice and assistance of the Government. The children yet un-
born, I wish you to treat them in like manner as they advance
in civilization like the white man. This is all I have been told
   25

to say now. If I have not said anything in a right manner I wish to be excused. This is the voice of my people." The people agreed to all the offers of the Commissioners, but before signing the treaty, Poundmaker wished to understand everything in a definite manner, and again addressed the Commissioners: " I do not differ from my people, but I want more explanation. I heard what you said yesterday, and I thought that when the law was established in the country it would be for our good. From what I can hear and see now, I cannot understand that I shall be able to clothe my children and feed them as long as the sun shines and water runs. With regard to the different chiefs who are to occupy the Reserves, I expected they would receive sufficient for their support. This is why I speak. In the presence of God and the Queen's representative I say this, because I do not know how to build a house for myself. You see how naked I am, and if I tried to do it, my naked body would suffer. Again, I do not know how to cultivate the ground for myself; at the same time, I quite understand what you have offered to assist us in this ? "

When Governor-General Lord Lorne visited the North-West in 1881 Poundmaker expressed his loyalty, and he was honorably attached to the Viceregal party, with whom he travelled for some time, on their journey through the country. Among the chiefs who deeply impressed the members of the Viceregal party with his native eloquence, intellectual power, wisdom and dignity, was the aged Cree chief, Mistawasis (Big Child). Though small of stature, he was one of the most influential chiefs of the Cree Confederacy. His address to the Governor-General on matters relating to his Reserve and the people who acknowledged his authority reveals the mental power of the leaders among the Crees. It is as follows: " I am glad that God has permitted me to meet the Governor. I feel flattered that it was a governor who put this medal on my neck. I did not put it on myself. We are the children of the Great Mother, and we wish that through her representative, our brother-in-law, she would listen for a little while to our complaints, and sympathize with our sufferings. I have no great complaints to make, but I wish to make just a few remarks concerning our property. The kindness that has been shown to us is great: but, in our eyes, it is not enough to put us on our feet. In days gone by the buffalo was our wealth and our strength, but he has left us. In those days we used the horse with which to chase the buffaloes, and when the buffaloes left us we thought we might use the horse with which to follow after other game. But we have lost many of our ponies with the mange, and we have had to sell others; and when I look around me, and see that the buffaloes are gone, and that our ponies are no longer left to us, I think I and my people are poor, indeed. The white man knows whence his strength comes, and we know where we require more strength. The strength to harvest the crop is in animals and implements, and we have not enough of these. If our crops should be enough to keep us alive, we would not have the means with which to harvest them. We would very much like more working cattle, and more farming implements. I would beg also that, if possible, a grist-mill should be put up somewhere within our reach, so that we can have our wheat ground into flour, and our other crops ground. I do not speak for myself, but for those poor people behind me. I am very thankful that I am able to see the Governor-General in my old days. He has come just in time that I may see him before I die. Many a time have I been in terrible straits for food for myself and my people, but I have never yet been angry about it, for I knew the Indian Agent was a good friend to us, and that he always acted on the instructions left for him, which he was bound to obey. Often have I been sorely perplexed and miserable at seeing my people starving and shrunken in flesh, till they were so weak that, with the first cold striking them, they would fall off their feet, and then nothing would save them. We want teachers to instruct and educate our children; we want guns and traps and nets to help us to get ready for the winter. We try to do all that the farm instructor has told us, and we are doing the best we can; but, as I said before, we want farming implements. I do not speak for myself, as I am

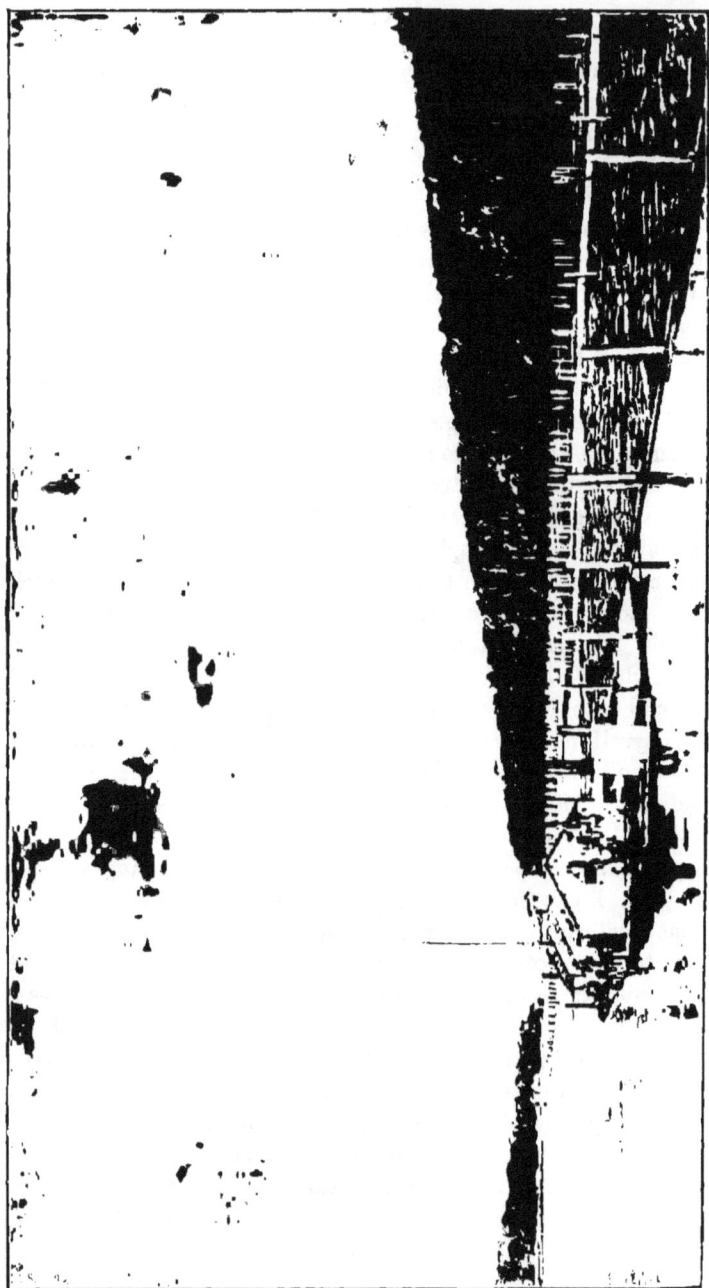

getting old, and it does not much matter for me, but I speak for my people, and for my children and grandchildren, who must starve if they do not receive the help that they so much need."

Poundmaker was intensely loyal, although his attitude at times seemed to express dissatisfaction and disloyalty; but the young men on his Reserve were athletic fellows, who loved the warpath, and the memory of the brave deeds of their forefathers kept alive their military ambition. The influence of Riel, the rebel leader, quickened the desires of the young men for power and glory, and Poundmaker was swayed by the attitude of his warriors.

The rebellion of 1885 found Poundmaker's warriors arrayed against the Government, when they pillaged Battleford and fought the soldiers at Cut Knife Hill, on his Reserve. He deeply regretted the position which he was compelled to assume, and on May 26th, 1885, he surrendered to General Middleton at Battleford. He was tried at Regina for participating in the rebellion, and, ignorant of the law, he made an eloquent appeal in self-defence. In a few dignified and manly sentences he addressed the Judge: "Everything I could do was done to stop bloodshed. Had I wanted war, I should not be here now —I should be on the prairie. You did not catch me. I gave myself up. You have got me because I wanted justice.".

Addressing the jury, in a passionate burst of eloquence he concluded with the words: "I cannot help myself, but I am a man still, and you may do as you like with me. I said I would not take long. Now I am done."

He was sentenced to three years in Stoney Mountain Penitentiary. After being conveyed to the prison, he learned with intense grief that, according to the rules of the institution, his hair would be cut. He had long, black locks, of which he was justly proud, and he besought the warden to intercede for him that these might be spared. This was done, and the imprisoned chief was allowed to retain his locks, which lent dignity to his presence when engaged in the menial duties which were imposed upon him. The leader of a savage host spent the spring

and summer months working in the garden as a common
prisoner. He felt keenly the change, and his robust constitution was sadly undermined. Brooding over his degradation
induced disease, and his condition awakened the sympathy of
his enemies.

Poundmaker was a chief of great ability. He had the skin
of a Cree Indian, the visage of a commander, and the cool and
strong judgment of a white man. He was a native Demos-
thenes in savage attire.

Upon the New Year's Day following his trip with the
Governor-General, he gave a feast to his people. Every member of his band who could possibly attend, from the missionary
to the youngest babe, was there. The feast consisted of ragout,
made of buffalo meat, bacon and berries, mixed with a little
flour, boiled buffalo meat, boiled bacon, with an abundance of
berry pies, sweet galette, and tea. There were no intoxicants
of any kind. After the feast he made the following speech to
his people :

"My Friends, Parents, Men, Women and Children,—I have
called you here together to-day because I wish to speak to you
all, and to everyone of you. It is not only to-day that I tried
to please you, to help you. In all my travels since the treaty—
but especially last summer—only one thought busies my mind :
how to support my family, and how to help you to support
yourselves and your children. While travelling this fall with
the Governor-General and Mr. Dewdney, I heard many things
that have opened my eyes Very soon the rations to the
Indians will be stopped at Eagle Hills and other Reserves ; at
least they will be greatly reduced, and we have only this winter
and next summer to receive help from the Government, so we
will have to mind ourselves and to work constantly, and make
all the preparations in our power for next spring. We must
sow as much as we can of wheat, barley, oats, potatoes, and
every kind of vegetable. We must take good care of our
cattle, that they may prosper in our hands. We can do a good
deal of work with the help we get now from the Government ;
but let us not forget it is the last year to receive rations. The

Governor-General told me so, and it will be so. Next summer, or, at the latest, next fall, the railway will be close to us, the whites will fill the country, and they will dictate to us as they please. It is useless to dream that we can frighten them, that time has passed. Our only resource is our work, our industry, our farms. The necessity of earning our bread by the sweat of our brows does not discourage me. There is only one thing that can discourage me. What is it? If we do not agree among ourselves. Let us be like one man, and work will show quick, and there will be nothing too hard. Allow me to ask you all to love one another, that is not difficult. We have faced the balls of our enemies more than once, and now we cannot bear a word from each other. Let the women mind themselves, and not carry tales from one house to another. If any persons carry stories to your houses, stop them at once. Tell them that you do not get any richer or fatter by such nonsense, and the news carrier will soon lose the bad habit. We have a missionary on our Reserve, we have a school, let us profit by them. I have given you an example. Nearly two years since I sent my son to Saint Albert, Big Lake school. My heart was sick when I saw my boy crying at his departure from me, and I find long the time of his absence, but he is at school. Some day he will be able to help himself and to help his fellowmen. He will be able to speak English and French, and he will be able to read and to write, besides know how to work like a white man. Do the same for your children if you want them to prosper and be happy."

Poundmaker had a generous heart, and the lofty traits of his nature were written on his handsome face. He was a savage statesman with an influence that reached beyond his tribe. The clemency of the Government released the chief before the expiration of his term in prison. He was baptized and admitted into the Roman Catholic church by Archbishop Tache while in prison. After his release he went to the Blackfoot Indian Reserve to pay a visit to Crowfoot, whom he still called father, in remembrance of the youthful days when the Blackfoot Chief adopted him. Great, indeed, was the rejoicing

in the camp during his residence there.   Suddenly, in peaceful
hours, the din of war no longer heard, and the prison days
ended, surrounded by friends of early days, he was stricken
down.   In the midst of the festivities of the lodge he burst a
blood vessel, and died.   Crowfoot mourned deeply for the loss
of his adopted son.   The Blackfeet honored his memory, and
the Crees heard with intense sorrow that the heroic soul was
no more.   His name will always be associated with the Rebellion in the North-West, but the nobler and truer side of his
character will best be known by his intimate relations with his
people, and his earnest struggles on their behalf.

HIAWATHA.

Longfellow's Indian Edda has made familiar to a large circle
of readers the famous exploits of the native hero and reformer,
Hiawatha.   The substance of this beautiful poem was founded
on an Indian legend found in the works of Schoolcraft, and incorporated with various native myths and customs and descriptions of scenery in the land inhabited by the Ojibway tribes.
The poet was happy in his selection of an interesting subject,
and of the form in which the poem was cast.   The metre, and
many of the forms of expression were suggested to Longfellow
by the great Epic of Finland, the "Kalevala" which reminds
one of Homer's Iliad in the simplicity of its lines, and the
beautiful imagery of the poem.*   The "Kalevala" is a description of the animal life of Finland, the manners and customs of
the early inhabitants, and is replete with the fascinating folk-
lore about the mysteries of nature.   It consists of twenty-three
thousand lines, written in the sonorous and flexible tongue of
Finland.   Whether or not it is the work of a single poet, or the
gathering together of all the traditions of the country after
they had been sung for ages by the people, no one is able to
tell.   The fragments of the poem were collected by two
learned men, Topelius and Lönnrot, and published between
1822 and 1835.   There are some striking parallelisms between
the "Kalevala" and "Hiawatha" in both incident and metre.   In

---

* Dr. J. M. Crawford's "Translation of the Kalevala."

" Hiawatha " the Indians hope to conquer a mighty fish called
Misho-Nahma, a king of fishes, and in the " Kalevala," the hero
Wainamoien, slays an immense pike, the water hound.   Here
are a few lines in the original Finnish :

> Kanteloista Kunlemahan
> Soittoa tagumahan
> Penkaloitanza pesevi
> Oravat ojentilihe
> Lehvaselta lehvasella.

A comparison between the opening lines of the prelude of
" Hiawatha " with the " Kalevala " will show the resemblance
in metre and sentiment.   The opening lines of the " Indian
Edda " are :

> Should you ask me, whence these stories ?
> Whence these legends and traditions ?
> With the odors of the forest,
> With the dew and damp of meadows,
> With the curling smoke of wigwams,
> With the rushing of great rivers,
> With their frequent repetitions,
> And their wild reverberations
> As of thunder in the mountains ?
>   I should answer, I should tell you,
>   " From the forests and the prairies,
> From the great lakes of the Northland,
> From the land of the Ojibways,
> From the land of the Dacotahs.
> From the mountains, moors, and fenlands,
> Where the heron, the Shuh-shuh-gah,
> Feeds among the reeds and rushes,
> I repeat them as I heard them
> From the lips of Nawadaha,
> The musician, the sweet singer."
>   Should you ask where Nawadaha
> Found these songs, so wild and wayward,
> Found these legends and traditions,
> I should answer, I should tell you,
>   " In the birds' nests of the forests,
> In the lodges of the beaver,
> In the hoof-prints of the bison,
> In the eyrie of the eagle !

" All the wild fowl sang them to him,
In the moorlands and the fenlands,
In the melancholy marshes :
Chetowaik, the plover, sang them,
Mahng, the loon, the wild-goose, Wawa,
The blue heron, the Shuh-shuh-gah,
And the grouse, the Mushkodasa ! "

The following, from the " Epic of Finland," may be compared
with the extract from Longfellow's poem :

These are words in childhood taught me,
Songs preserved from distant ages ;
Legends, they that once were taken
From the belt of Wainamoinen,
From the forge of Ilmarinen,
From the sword of Kaukomieli,
From the bow of Youkahainen,
From the pastures of the Northland,
From the meads of Kalevala ;
These my dear old father sang me
When at work with knife and hatchet ;
These my tender mother taught me
When she twirled the flying spindle.
When a child upon the matting
By her feet I rolled and tumbled,
Incantations were not wanting
Over Sampo and o'er Louki ;
Sampo growing old in singing,
Louki ceasing her enchantment,
In the songs died wise Wipunen,
At the games died Lemminkainen.
There are many other legends,
Incantations that were taught me,
That I found along the wayside,
Gathered in the fragrant copses,
Blown me from the forest branches,
Culled among the plumes of pine-trees,
Scented from the vines and flowers,
Whispered to me as I followed
Flocks in land of honeyed meadows,
Over hillocks green and golden,
After sable-haired Murikki,
And the many-coloured Kimmo.

> Many rhymes the cold has told me,
> Many lays the rain has brought me,
> Other songs the winds have sung me :
> Many birds from many forests,
> Oft have sung me lays in concord ;
> Waves of sea and ocean billows,
> Music from the many waters,
> Music from the whole creation,
> Oft have been my guide and master.

The legend of Hiawatha, narrated by Longfellow, was taken chiefly from the writings of Schoolcraft, and is a mass of mythical tales relating to native heroes. In Schoolcraft's volume, entitled "The Hiawatha Legends," numerous fanciful stories of the Ojibway hero, Manabozho, and his companions are related, but not a single fact or fiction about Hiawatha.* The legend was given publicity by Mr. J. H. V. Clarke in his interesting "History of Onondaga," wherein the original name of the hero is Taounyawatha, who is described as the deity who presides over fisheries and hunting grounds.

Mythological tales have become incorporated with the true story of this illustrious lawgiver and reformer of the Iroquois, which lend an appearance of fiction to his person and work. He is described as having descended to earth in a snow-white canoe, and was seen as a demigod on Lake Ontario, approaching the shore at Oswego. He reveals his divine origin to two Onondagas, who become associates in his work, and maintain the great league of peace after he has gone. He ascends the Oswego and Seneca rivers, removing obstructions and making them navigable, and destroys all his enemies, natural and preternatural. Afterward he lives peaceably among his people as a man, and begins and carries forward his great work of establishing the League of the Iroquois, and when his work is done, ascends to heaven in his human form, seated in his white canoe,

* "American Antiquarian," Vol. VIII., page 364 ; Vol. XVI., page 68. Leland's "Algonquin Legends," pages 4, 222. Hale's "Iroquois Book of Rites," pages 18, 38, 41, 53, 73. 76, 78, 85, 87, 127, 129, 150, 154, 180, 183. Wilson's "Artistic Faculty," pages 92, 100 ; (Huron-Iroquois). Brinton's "Myths of the New World," page 186.

amid "the sweetest melody of celestial music." Longfellow's "Hiawatha" is a myth without any foundation. Still that does not destroy the fact that such a person as Hiawatha lived, and executed a great work among the Iroquois. As the Indians sat around their cabin fires in the winter, narrating stories of the brave deeds of their forefathers, fact and fiction became blended, and as they delighted in mysterious tales, the simple facts of a great life became shrouded with the deeds of a god, and the wise man among his people was elevated to the rank of a deity.

Hiawatha was a brave and wise Onondaga chief, who loved peace and sought the welfare of his people. His name signifies, " He who seeks the wampum belt." Beholding the evils which befel his own and other tribes through incessant warfare, he was greatly troubled, and revolving in his mind a means of escape from the consequences of war, he set himself to the task of uniting his own nation and enlisting them in a league of peace. He was past middle life, and deeply respected for his wisdom and benevolence among his people when he assumed the position of reformer and lawgiver. As a chief of great influence, he summoned a council of the chiefs and people of the Onondaga towns, and from all parts along the creeks, they came together to the general council fire. Hiawatha had a redoubtable foe in the person of an able chief, named Atotarho, who was strongly opposed to his peaceful attitude, and gathering a number of reckless spirits who belonged to his faction, he scattered them among the vast concourse of people, so as to intimidate the chiefs, and the council came to naught. A second council was summoned, but Atotarho was there again with his foreboding countenance, and his followers were there prepared to slay any who followed not the counsel of the grim chief, so the council ended as the first, without anything being done. A third council was called by Hiawatha, who sent out his runners in every direction; but no one come, and the grave reformer was sad. Seated upon the ground in sorrow, he enveloped his head in a mantle of skins, silent in profound thought. At length he arose and departed from the homes of his people, determined to enlist other tribes in the cause which lay near to his heart. As he strode toward the forest he passed his great antagonist seated near a well-known spring, but not a word passed between them. Bent on his mission, he crossed mountains, and on the shores of a lake which he crossed he found small white shells. He gathered some of these and strung them on strings, which, he fastened on his breast as an emblem of peace. These wampum strings were a, significant token of his mission, and their use, apparently unknown to the Indians before this time, although known to the Mound-Builders, became symbolic to the natives of peaceful relations among the tribes. He floated down the Mohawk River in a canoe. He arrived at a Canienga town, whose chief was the famous Dekanawidah, and seating himself on a fallen tree beside the spring where the people came for water, he remained silent. A woman came to draw water, but spoke not to him, his appearance and attitude forbidding conversation; but when she returned to the house she said to Dekanawidah, "A man, or a figure like a man, is seated by the spring, having his breast covered with strings of white shells." The chief said to one of his brothers, " It is a guest, go and bring him in, we will make him welcome."

Dekanawidah and Hiawatha met, and the founders of the Great League took counsel together, working out their plan and securing the consent of the people. The matter was discussed in the council, and the Canienga nation decided in favor of the scheme. Dekanawidah sent ambassadors to the Oneidas, who were the nearest tribe to them, and the plan was laid before Odatsehte, the chief, whose name signifies the " Quiver-bearer." He required the ambassadors to wait a year until he had discussed the question with his council, and thought wisely over the matter. At the end of that period the Oneidas became one of the members of the league. The Onondagas were next appealed to, but the grim and haughty Atotarho still remembered his contest with Hiawatha, and he refused the application of the ambassadors. The Cayugas were entreated and their chief, Akahenyonk, whose name signifies the "Wary Spy," readily obtained the consent of his people, and united. The wisdom,

eloquence and peaceful policy of Hiawatha asserted themselves
in again approaching the Onondagas, despite the repulse of
Atotarho. It was proposed to make the Onondagas the leading
tribe of the confederacy, their chief town the place of meeting
for the league, where the records should be kept, and Atotarho
the principal chief, with the right to summon the league and
possessed of a veto power. The Onondagas were won, and
Atotarho became more zealous for extending the league than he
was formerly in opposing it. Special prerogatives were granted
the Onondagas, and Atotarho became the Emperor of the Five
Nations. The Seneca tribe was secured next, and their two
principal chiefs, Kanyadariyo, "Beautiful Lake," and Shade-
karonges, "The Equal Skies," were made military commanders
of the confederacy. The Ojibways became allies of the league ;
but after the space of two hundred years, the alliance was
broken through the influence of the French and the sympathy
of the Ojibways for the conquered Hurons. Other tribes were
appealed to by the ambassadors sent to them, urging them to
become members of the league, or allies, but without success.
The great council, composed of the representatives of the Indian
tribes was a federal assembly, and all questions brought forward
for discussion were first submitted to the tribal council, where
they were settled by a majority vote ; but, in the federal council
the vote must be unanimous, and when this failed a plan of
pacification was made, by which all became agreed. Atotarho
required not to exercise the veto, as he was virtually governed
by the wisdom of the members, who sought to follow their
policy of peace and maintain their unity. The laws which prevailed in the league manifested the sagacity and statesmanship
of Hiawatha. He was made a chief of the Caniengas, and
probably resided with that tribe until his death. It is said that
after the establishment of the Great Peace, he devoted himself
to clearing away the obstructions in the rivers throughout the
country inhabited by the tribes belonging to the confederacy. At
what time and in what manner he died is not known. Numerous
fabulous stories are related about him, some of which have
slight foundation in fact, and others are wholly fictitious. Mr.

Clarke relates the story of the marvellous bird which killed
Hiawatha's only daughter. When Hiawatha was in attendance
at the great convention summoned to form the league, he
brought with him his only daughter, aged twelve years. A loud
rushing sound was heard, and a dark spot appeared in the sky,
when Hiawatha warned his child to await her doom at the
hands of the Great Spirit, and she bowed in resigned submission. The dark spot became an immense bird, which swept
down upon her with wide extended wings and long beak and
destroyed her.

Horatio Hale made inquiries about this story among the
Canadian Onondagas, and learned that this was an actual
occurrence, though somewhat modified. Before the meeting of
the great convention, the Onondagas held a council in an open
plain, encircled by a forest, where temporary lodges had been
pitched for the councillors and their attendants. Hiawatha was
there, accompanied by his daughter, who was married, but was
still living with her father. At the close of the discussions,
which lasted until night, and as the people were in the lodges,
the women were returning from the forest laden with fuel for
cooking purposes, and among them was the daughter of Hiawatha. As she moved slowly with her burden the loud voice
of Atotarho was heard, shouting that a strange bird was in the
air, and bidding one of his archers shoot it. The bird was
killed, and the people rushed toward the spot, and in the
excitement Hiawatha's daughter was crushed to death. Atotarho
had no doubt planned this onset and this sad calamity, to
harrass his adversary, and in the intense grief which filled the
heart of Hiawatha he found delight.

The Iroquois extol the wisdom, eloquence and great virtues
of Hiawatha, and hold him in reverence, believing firmly that
he was the founder of their league. The name of Hiawatha
is borne at the present day by some of the farmer folk on the
Grand River Reservation. Horatio Hale has made a thorough
investigation of the facts relating to the league and its founder,
and has come to the conclusion that Hiawatha was a historical
personage, a grave lawgiver and reformer, and that the legend is

composed of false and true elements which must be separated
so as to be understood. Dr. Brinton says that the legend is a
myth, a preposterous tale, based on early traditions, and Dr.
Beauchamp as strongly asserts that it is a modified life of Christ.
There is no doubt the influence of the teaching of missionaries
has changed the form of the legend, which is not related by the
aged men of the tribes with uniformity, and as the traditions of
the natives are undergoing a process of transformation through
contact with the white man, it is impossible for them to keep
intact the stories told in the lodges. Thus we have the strange
bird which the archers of Atotarho slew, when Hiawatha's
daughter was trampled to death, represented as a white bird,
having the form of a cross ; and Hiawatha, stricken with grief,
is said to have lain as one dead for three days. Afterward he
arose to life, formed the League of Peace, appointed its officers,
and after setting everything in order, resumed his divinity, and
ascended to heaven in a white canoe. These are features which
suggest the influence of Christian teaching.

Divested, however, of these accretions of Christianity, and of
the supernatural elements which have been introduced by the
story tellers of the lodges, Hiawatha appears as a wise man, a
human being of more than ordinary ability, who began an era
of peace among the Indian tribes. The artist has found subjects
for his pencil in the legend. The meeting of Atotarho, Dekanawidah and Odatsehte, is the subject of a rude pictorial representation, supposed to be the work of David Cusick, the historian
of the Six Nations. Atotarho, " The Entangled," is seated, grim,
solitary and dignified, smoking a long pipe, his head and body
enveloped with angry and writhing serpents. Before him
stands Dekanawidah, as a plumed warrior, holding in his right
hand his flint-headed spear, as the representative of the
Caniengas, or " People of the Flint." Beside him stands
Odatsehte, bearing in his hand a bow with arrows, and a quiver
at his shoulder. Dekanawidah is addressing Atotarho on the
founding of the league, and the surly Onondaga chief, who is
listening to the project, reveals in his aspect his attitude toward
the scheme of Hiawatha, and in his dress his warlike character.
26

It is a semi-mythological picture, indicating the love of the natives for the mysterious. Edmonia Lewis, the sculptor, whose father was a negro, and her mother, an Ojibway Indian, spent her early years modelling beads and wampum, until she produced her two best works in marble, " Hiawatha's Wooing " and " Hiawatha's Wedding."

Hiawatha's design of a universal federation of his race was worthy of a master mind. The misery of war had probably wrought so powerfully on the minds of the natives that the future was foreboding, as predicting the extermination of the race. This Iroquois lawgiver originated the plan of a reign of peace, supported by a federation of all the tribes. Although the work of Hiawatha did not become universal, the Confederacy of the Six Nations, and the native government, as shown by the laws of the league, revealed the genius of the man. As a native statesman, an undaunted reformer, an eloquent speaker and a man of virtue, he is esteemed by the Iroquois. Though we may grieve over the loss of the historical Hiawatha in Longfellow's beautiful poem, we can admire and honor goodness and ability wherever found. Among the red men there has not appeared a greater teacher and a wiser man than Hiawatha. Such a character living four centuries ago, the reputed founder of a new era, would naturally have many strange tales told concerning him and his work, and it is because of his greatness and the age in which he lived that so many strange things are spoken about him. His name and brave deeds are preserved in the traditions of the Iroquois, his memory is revered in the " Book of Rites," his work remains in the league which he established, and his influence abides in the life of the people.

SHAWUNDAIS.

Shawundais was a Mississaga Indian. The Mississagas are a sub-tribe of the Ojibways, and are supposed to be the descendants of the Ojibways who defeated the Iroquois in 1759. They are located at the New Credit settlement, near the city of Brantford, Alnwick, Chemoug Lake, Rice Lake and Scugog.

Shawundais was known to the English-speaking people as
John Sunday, a famous missionary, who frequently appeared on
the public platform throughout Ontario, delighting large and
deeply-interested audiences with his quaint speeches and thrilling records of missionary adventures. He was born in the State
of New York about the year 1796. His boyhood was spent in
the Indian camps. The natives travelled in those days along
the courses of the rivers and through the forests, gaining a
precarious livelihood, their camps infested frequently with
white men of the lowest type, and the men and women
debauched with liquor and loose morals. They were an industrious community until the white men introduced whiskey
among them, which made them idle and dissolute. In their
industrious years the men roamed the forests for game, the
meat was retained for food, and the furs sold to procure
the lesser luxuries of life. Sugar making in the woods
in the spring was a busy season, and when that was over
they were ready to engage in the delightful occupation of
fishing. They built canoes, which were so light that two men
could carry the largest of them, and yet they were so strong
that they could surmount the heaviest billows and suffer no
harm. The childhood days of Shawundais were spent in the
filthy camps of the natives, so sadly changed by the detestable
fire-water from the cleanliness and scenes of industry of former
years. The wild revelry of drunken men and the yells of
debauched women filled the midnight air. The children were
neglected during these scenes of delirium, and numerous tales
of suffering were told in those days of sadness and sin.
The parents of Shawundais were pagans, his companions were
ignorant and degraded, and there was no man to reach forth a
helping hand or speak an inspiring word to lead the youth
toward self-improvement and civilization. Frequently he
accompanied the Indians in their begging dances to the
settlements of the white people. He attended their dog feasts,
made sacrifices to the sun, and prayed that no evil might befal
him. He belonged to the band known as the Bay of Quinte
Indians, who roamed from the County of Northumberland to

Leeds, making Kingston, Bath and Brockville their chief places of resort.

Shawundais, the name of our subject, means "Sultry Heat," which the sun gives out in summer just before a fertilizing rain. He was rather above medium height in manhood, and his physical frame was strong and well knit. In personal appearance he was unprepossessing; a simple child of the forest, trained in native lore, familiar with the birds, flowers and insects, and without anything striking in physique or intellect to arrest the stranger. He was, however, a savage mimic, and his fund of ludicrous stories seemed inexhaustible. Oftentimes groups of red and white men gathered around him to listen to his humorous tales, and every member of the circle was soon thrown into fits of laughter. In his early years he was a successful hunter and a drunkard. Naturally quiet and inoffensive, when the fire of his anger was kindled it became a roaring flame, which burned all who dared to approach. His powers as a wit won the applause of his companions and white neighbors, and this satisfied him. There were serious moments, however, in his lodge when alone, and thoughts of God and eternity filled his mind. Then would he say to himself, "Who made the trees and animals, and stars above, and what sort of a being is He? How did man come into being? What will be his destiny when he leaves this world?" He fasted and prayed, blackened his face, and waited for a vision which would disclose to him some object in nature as his personal deity. He was unhappy, yet the tears came not to bring relief to his mind.

About this time the Ojibways were brought under Christian influences, through the efficient labors of the Rev. William Case, who devoted many years in missionary work among the Indians of the Province of Ontario. In February, Mr. Case, accompanied by a young Mississaga Indian—subsequently well known throughout the Dominion—Peter Jones, started on a missionary tour to the Bay of Quinte Indians. A public service was held in the church at Belleville, which was well attended by the white people and Indians. Shawundais had heard about the missionaries, and was anxious to learn for himself some of the strange things which they related in their message to the people. Accompanied by an Indian named Moses, he started for Belleville and, upon arriving at the church, found it so crowded that it was impossible for him to enter. During the morning service the two Indians sat outside; but, at the hour for the evening service, they were determined to hear for themselves the story the missionaries had to tell, and they made their way into the church. Peter Jones addressed the Indian part of the congregation upon the two ways of life—a favorite topic with native preachers, and one which the natives appreciate. As he described the way leading to destruction and the path leading to life the heart of Shawundais was smitten, and he resolved to try to serve the God of the Christians. So deeply was he impressed, that the thoughts of the young Mississaga's discourse never left his mind. A second missionary visit was made and, at a prayer meeting held on May 27th, 1826, a large number of Indians prayed, and told in simple yet eloquent language of the great blessings they had received. Several young persons said, with tears in their eyes: " We are going to serve the Great Spirit, because we love Him with all our hearts;" and the penitent then found the peace he sought. Shawundais was unable to read or write, but his abilities were sufficient to induce him to be sent to school, with the hope that he might be trained for missionary work among the natives. His education was limited; but after he had learned to read and write, he wrote a quaint account of his conversion, which has been preserved.

Several years after his conversion he related, in forcible language, the story of his entrance into the peaceful way of God. At a camp meeting, held on Snake Island about two years after his conversion, he gave several striking addresses, clothed in the phraseology of nature and grace. Speaking of his life as a pagan, and his subsequent experience as a Christian, he said that Christians ought to be as wise as the red squirrel, who looks ahead, thinking of the approaching winter, and provides food for every contingency. They ought

JOHN SUNDAY (SHAWUNDAIS).

to imitate the red squirrel by preparing to meet God. Now is the time to lay up the good words of the Great Spirit. Where will he go who refuses to be as wise as the red squirrel? At the same meeting he related his own experience, saying, " My brothers and sisters, I have been one of the most miserable creatures on earth. I lived and wandered amongst the white people on the Bay of Quinte, and contracted all their vices, and soon became very wicked. At one time I had a beloved child, who was very ill. I tried to save the child from dying, but could not, as the child died in defiance of all that I could do for him. I was then more fully convinced that there must be some being greater than man, and that the Great Being does all things according to His own will. When I heard the missionaries preach Jesus Christ, and what we ought to do to be saved, I believed their word, and I began at once to do as they advised, and soon found peace to my soul. Brothers and sisters, I will tell you what the good missionaries are like— they are like sun-glasses, which scatter light and heat wherever they are held ; so do the ministers of Christ spread the light of truth amongst the people, which warms their hearts and makes them very happy."

Possessed of a lively imagination, apt to describe men and things in an impressive manner, his short period of training enabled him to address large audiences with pleasure and profit.. He lacked the dignity of the ideal Indian, and the stately elo-quence of the native orator belonged not to him, yet there was an irresistible charm about his speeches, with their quaint illustra-tions, which won the hearts of his hearers. Within two months. after his conversion he was impelled by love for the souls of men to accompany Peter Jones on a missionary tour, relating the story of his life and conversion. Early one morning William Case was awakened by sounds from a wigwam, evi-dently of a person in deep distress, and proceeding to the wigwam he observed an aged woman addressing some people with intense earnestness. Upon inquiry, he learned who she was, as Shawundais gladly said, " Oh! it is my mother. She so happy all night she can't sleep." Encouraged by such tokens of success in his labors, he prosecuted his work with greater zeal.

The temporal welfare of his people deeply interested him, and he sought to help them to become civilized like the white people. He was a member of a deputation of chiefs from the Ojibways who interviewed the Government on matters relating to timber and land. He told the civil authorities that a great work had been done among his people, whereby they were forsaking their pagan rites and superstitious ideas, and progress was being made among them in material things. Along the north shore of Lake Huron he visited several Indian camps, preaching the Gospel to the people.

In 1828 he visited New York, Philadelphia, and other places in the United States in the interests of the missionary work among the natives of Canada. In Duane Street Methodist Church, New York, he delivered a characteristic address in his own language which aroused the enthusiasm of the congregation. His pathetic appeals, deep sincerity and vivid gestures revealed the thrilling eloquence of the speaker, and although the language was unknown to the audience, many persons were bathed in tears. When Dr. Bangs addressed him through an interpreter, giving him, in the name of the congregation, the right hand of fellowship, and expressing the hope that they would all meet in heaven, the faithful Shawundais cried, "Amen," as the tears flowed down his cheeks, and the congregation mingled their tears with his, as they gazed upon the savage won from superstition and vice. When he returned to Canada he told his people of the religious institutions he had seen. The noble-hearted men and women he had met, and their manifestations of sympathy and deep interest in him personally, and in the tribes in the Dominion.

Shawundais became an eloquent preacher to his own people, silence reigned when he addressed them, the coldest hearts were touched, and many of the dusky worshippers wept and prayed; scoffers remained to pray. His sermons and addresses made lasting impressions on many hearts. Several times he visited the Indians at Penetanguishene and Sault Ste. Marie, and his

labors among the red men were crowned with success. He
gave an account of one of these missionary tours to Peter Jones:
" After you left us at Matchedash Bay, we came to five Indian
camps, a few miles north of Penetanguishene. Here we stopped
three days and talked to them about Jesus Christ, the Saviour
of the poor Indian. Some of the young Indians listened to our
words, but others mocked. Among this people we saw one old
man who had attended the camp meeting at Snake Island last
year. This man told us that he had prayed ever since that
camp meeting, ' But,' said he, ' I have been compelled by my
native brethren to drink the fire-water. I refused to take it
for a long time, and when they would urge me to take the cup
to drink I would pour the bad stuff in my bosom until my shirt
was wet with it. I deceived them in this way for some time,
but when they saw that I did not get drunk they mistrusted
me, and found it out, so I was obliged to drink with them. I
am now sorry for the great evil that I have done. Some of the
young people said that they would like to be Christians and
worship the Great Spirit, but their old people forbade them.
These young people were very anxious to learn to read and
sing. Thomas Biggs, my companion, tried to teach them the
alphabet. When we would sing and pray, they would join in with
us, and knelt down by our sides; but the parents of the young
people were very angry at their children for praying, and one
woman came and snatched a blanket from her child that was
kneeling down, and said, ' I will let you know that you shall
not become a Christian unless first bidden so to do by the old
Indians.' After spending three days with these people we
went on to the north on the waters of Lake Huron, as far as
Koopahoonahning, but we found no Indians at this place, they
were all gone to receive their presents at the Island of St. Joseph.
We were gone two weeks, and having got out of bread and meat,
we were obliged to gather moss, called in the Indian tongue,
wahkoonun, ' from the rocks.' This moss we boiled, which
became very slimy, but which possessed some nourishing qualities. On this we lived for several days together, with now and
then a fish that we caught in the lake. After returning to the

Matchedash Bay we saw the same Indians that we spent the three days with at Penetanguishene. We talked to them about religion. They answered, 'That they were looking at the Christian Indians and thinking about their worship. When we are convinced that they do really worship the Good Spirit and not the bad spirit, then we shall worship with them and travel together.'

"At Penetanguishene we saw about thirty Indians from Koopahoonahning, where we went, and then returned from our visit to the north. We told these people the words of the Great Spirit, and they said 'that they were glad to hear what the Great Spirit had said to His people; if we were to hear more about these things, maybe we would become Christians, too, and worship with you.' We saw one old man at Matchedash with Brother John Asance's people, who has been much afraid of the Christian Indians, and has been fleeing from them as his greatest enemy, and kept himself hid so that no Christian Indian could talk with him. This man continued hiding and running from praying Indians until he got lame in both of his hips, so that he could not run or walk, and was obliged to call to the Christian natives to help him. He now sees his folly, confesses his errors, prays to the Great Spirit to have mercy upon him, and has become tamed and in his right mind. We also visited the Roman Catholic Indians, who have lately come from Drummond's Island. We told them what the Great Spirit had done for us, and how happy we were in our hearts in worshipping the Great Spirit who had saved us from drunkenness and from all our sins. They said that they would like to see and hear for themselves how we worshipped the Lord. So they sent those that came with us to this meeting, that they might go and tell their brethren just how it was, as a great many bad things had been told them about our way of worship by the French people among them. This is all I can tell you of our travels and labors among our native brethren in the woods."

In 1832 he was appointed by the Conference missionary to the Sault Ste. Marie and other bodies of natives. He roamed the woods in search of Indian camps to preach to the natives,

and among the number of those who became converts to the
faith were some of the chiefs and medicine men, who laid aside
their medicine bags and ceased their incantations. On the
south shore of Lake Superior he visited the Ojibways, and
declared the truth with such earnestness that they forsook their
native religion. In 1834 he was ordained and settled as missionary to the Indians on Grape Island; but his missionary zeal
compelled him to seek other bands of natives beyond his own
Mission. So excessive were his labors that his strong constitution was undermined, and he was induced to visit England.
He travelled extensively in England pleading the cause of
Missions during the year 1837, and large audiences gazed in
astonishment upon him, and were enraptured with his quaint
addresses. He was presented to the Queen as the chief of his
people, who had authorized him to act on their behalf. After
his return he visited the Indians at Sault Ste. Marie, and from
1839 to 1850 he labored among his people at Rice Lake, Mud
Lake and Alderville. At missionary meetings in Canada and
the United States, among red men and white, he preached and
lectured, and so wide was his field of operations that he quaintly
said, " My family lives at Alderville, but I live everywhere."

After spending four years among the Indians at Mount
Elgin and Muncey, he labored for eleven years at Alnwick, and
then, in 1867, he was superannuated, spending the remaining
years of his life at Alderville. His last days were filled with
labor, and as oftentimes he referred to the old days of paganism, he urged his brethren to be faithful to the cause which
lay so near to his heart.

At the advanced age of eighty years he died, amid the
sympathy and honor of all the people. He died at Alderville
on December 14, 1875. Heroic in the discharge of his duties,
he was the champion of the rights of his people.

As an advocate of the cause of missions his memory still
lingers. At a missionary meeting held at Hamilton, Ontario, in
closing his address he gave his " Gold Speech," as follows:

" There is a gentleman who, I suppose, is now in this house.
He is a very fine gentleman, but a very modest one. He does

not like to show himself at these meetings. I do not know how long it is since I have seen him—he comes out so little. I am very much afraid that he sleeps a good deal of his time, when he ought to be out doing good. His name is Gold.

"Mr. Gold, are you here to-night, or are you sleeping in your iron chest? Come out, Mr. Gold, come out and help us do this great work, to preach the Gospel to every creature. Ah, Mr. Gold, you ought to be ashamed of yourself to sleep so much in your iron chest. Look at your white brother, Mr. Silver—he does a great deal of good while you are sleeping. Come out, Mr. Gold. Look, too, at your little brown brother, Mr. Copper. He is everywhere. Your poor little brown brother is running about, doing all he can to help us. Why don't you come out, Mr. Gold? Well, if you won't show yourself, send us your shirt—that is, a bank-note. That is all I have to say."

By request of the Rev. J. Scott, he wrote the substance of a discourse which he preached, in 1835, to the Indians of Grape Island; and as it is characteristic of the man, and is a specimen of the style of preaching among the Indians, it is given:

"Brother Scott he want me that I shall write a little about my sermon last Sabbath. My text is from the Epistle of Paul, Ephesians, in the 5th chapter and 14th verse.

"St. Paul says in his epistle: 'Wherefore he saith, Awake thou that sleepest, and arise from the dead, and Christ shall give thee light.'

"My dear brother, I do not know or plainly understand about sleeping, but I will tell you what I have been saying to my Indian brethren. I suppose Paul means this: Who know nothing about religion of Jesus Christ—who do not care to pray to God—who do not care to live to God—who do not want to hear the Word of God. I suppose in that time all mankind they were asleep in their sins—know nothing about their Saviour—know nothing about salvation of their souls. So St. Paul he called them dead men. When a man sleeps in the night he does nothing, nor useful, nor thinking; he makes nothing—he is like dead man. And not only that. I will tell you other things—Indians worshipping dead gods—that is, I mean, the images. You know images cannot save souls—these are dead in their sins, because they are in darkness. I suppose St. Paul take out from Isaiah, in the 26th chapter, in the 19th verse: 'Thy dead men shall live, together with my dead body shall they arise. Awake and sing, ye that dwell in dust.' And in another place, in Isaiah, 60th chapter, in the 1st verse and 3rd verse: 'Arise, shine, for thy light is come, and the glory of the Lord is risen upon thee. And the Gentiles shall come to thy light, and kings to the brightness of thy rising.'

"Now, Isaiah his word is fulfilled. Look to the Gentiles; how many now get enlightened in their minds! I suppose great many hundred thousand now enlightened. My text says, 'Awake thou that sleepest, arise from the dead, Christ shall give thee light.' I suppose St. Paul meaning a light, the Gospel, shall arise like the sun. When the sun rises little, and begin light little, so people awake up and begin work; so the Christian people worshipping true God, no matter where, or in the sea, or on the islands, or in the lakes, or in the woods. Let us think of our America. I suppose about four hundred years ago no Gospel in America, nothing but wooden gods. And now the sun begin arise here, too. Thank God that He sent the Gospel here in the America! My brethren and sisters, let us think about ten years ago we were all asleep in sins, but the good Lord He had blew with His Gospel in our ears, so we awake up; thank God. My brothers and sisters, let us love Jesus Christ, because He done great deal for us; and He sent us ministers and teachers and books for our children. Sun begin arise here in America; so the Indians now begin awake from the dead. I hope the sun will arise higher and higher every year; yes, does some now. Look to the Montreal and Quebec, light begin arise there; seven hundred and twenty people get religion there this winter. Thanks unto the name of Jesus Christ, now the light shine upon them. Not only there, look to the Lake St. Clair Indians, begin awake there, too; light shine upon them, now they worshipping true God. And let us think other places, in Asia and Africa, etc., I hope darkness will go still under and under. I hope our world will be a light more and more every year: that is, I mean the Gospel will go far off in the wilderness. Thank God what the good white people done here in America. I hope they will send still the Gospel far off in the wood. Thank God what they done here all, that is among the Indians, now awaking from sleeping in their sins.

"My brothers and sisters—Is any of us here—are we sleep yet in sin, not to think about religion of Jesus Christ? Oh! if we are, we are danger to go into hell. We do not know when our death would come upon us. Death will not say to us, 'Now, I come; be ready, now.' Death will not wait for us. My brothers and sisters, now is the time to be prepared to go into heaven. Let us commence now to seek for religion in our hearts, that we may prepare to meet our God.

"And I told my brethren and sisters this—When any man awake early in the morning, and then before noon he begin want to sleep again: and he sleep by and by, and so with the backslider. But let us try that we may not sleep again, but work all day long: that is, I mean man to be Christian all day to the end of his life. And we must be like bees; they all work in the summer time all day long for their provisions. They know the winter coming in the six months, so they all work for their victuals. If they do not work they shall surely die; and so with us all, if we do not work for that great provision from heaven for our souls. We must work long as we live. Let us think one thing more. In Proverbs, in 6th chapter and in the 6th verse: 'Go to the ant, thou sluggard; consider her ways, and be wise.' They all work in the summer time for making ant hills. If, then, enemies come to them, they will go in the ant hill, so the enemy will not destroy them. And so, all good Christians, and watch and pray. When Christian man his enemy come near in his heart, he cry out for help from God. Brothers and sisters, we ought to be wiser than they are, because ant they very small. But we are larger than they are, as much as moose, he bigger than man. Devil he watch for us. Brethren and sisters, be wise. Devil he watch for us, just as wolf he try catch deer. We must watch and not sleep. Deer never does sleep, always watch for fear of enemy; deer do not like to be killed. We ought to be more careful for our souls, because devil want to destroy our souls. Animal had no soul; but animal wiser than man. But, I think man ought to be wiser than animal, because man has soul. Brethren and sisters, let us be wise. If we do not be faithful to serving God, we shall be lost for ever and ever. One thing more I want to mention to you, that is about squirrel. Squirrel do not like to be suffer in the winter time. Squirrel knows winter come by and by; so in the fall work all the time; get acorns out of the trees, and carry into the hollow logs for winter. And all the good people, they know Jesus Christ come by and by, so Christians they pray every day. As squirrel do carry acorns into the hollow logs, so the good man he want to get great deal religion in his heart, so his soul might be saved. Look to the wild geese, while they feeding, one always watch for fear the enemies will catch them; wild geese do not like to be killed. I think man ought to be wiser than they are. We must watch and pray every day, because devil want to kill our souls every day.

"But let us love God's commandments. God can save our souls, if we only trust in Him. God done great deal for us; that is, He give us His only Son Jesus Christ, and He died for us that our souls might be saved. Brethren and sisters, I hope we shall see Jesus by-and-bye, if only we keep His commandments. This is all I say to you."

MIKASTO.

In an old log church, in the summer of 1880, in the frontier town of Macleod, there sat a strange company of red men, belonging to the tribe of Blood Indians, unto whom I was trying to explain the first principles of Christianity, by the help of my friend and interpreter, Jerry Potts. Every available spot was taken by Indians, some on seats, but the majority squatted on the floor. Unto them it seemed to be a council held for the purpose of learning something about Omuqkatos, the "Great Sun," and Apistotokio, the "Creator." Drawing their blankets around them the pipes were lighted, and, amid clouds

of smoke, I talked to them about religion. There were several
notable chiefs in the group, but the most prominent for intelligence and general ability was Mikasto. At the close of the
short service he shook hands with me and said, " I am pleased
to hear what you have been telling us, and I wish you to teach
my people more about these things." Mikasto, or Red Crow,
is the head chief of the Blood Indians, and as a native statesman has stood next in rank in the Blackfoot Confederacy to
the famous chief, Crowfoot. He is tall and thin, an aquiline
nose, small, piercing eyes, a face beaming with intelligence, and
of a mild disposition. His quiet demeanor gives no evidence
of his warlike qualities. Yet he was, in the old buffalo days,
one of the bravest warriors that lived upon the plains. I have
listened to him at the sun dance eloquently relate his military
adventures and successes; and as he narrated his tales of
personal valor, the people, old and young, cheered loudly, and
admired the prowess of their chief. He is the hero of many
battles. As he walks through the camp, arrayed in his state-
liness and adored by his followers, he bears in his attitude the
marks of a man of peace who loves his people, and is ever
studious of their welfare. Sitting in his spacious lodge with
the minor chiefs, he discourses about the necessities of his
tribe, lays plans for their progress in the arts of civilized life,
instructs them how to maintain their laws and keep inviolate
the morality of the natives. In the old days I have often
gazed in astonishment at the record of his brave deeds in the
picture writing on his lodge. It was the largest buffalo-skin
lodge in the camp, and I have counted them when grouped
together to the number of nearly three hundred. The scalp-
locks were fastened upon it, and the writing in various colors
ran around it, which detailed the history of his life.

The head chief's lodge always occupied its own special place
in the camp, according to the custom of the natives. Mikasto
is a man of intellect. keen and critical, without any of the
cunning of the low savages. His sense of honor prevents him
from doing a mean act. I have never heard of a single action
unworthy of the dignity of a statesman, who aspires to be

an example of probity to his followers, and I never expect
to hear anything detracting from the noble character of the
man. He is essentially a leader of men. Not by force of arms,
nor even through the influence of his position, does he rule,
although his official dignity is a strong factor in maintaining
his power over men ; but it is his striking personality which
enables him to command implicit obedience to the customs and
laws of the tribe. During my residence among the Indians, one
of the most influential of the minor chiefs was working secretly
to undermine the influence of Mikasto, and had been successful
in gathering some of the people under his leadership, evidently
with the intention of arousing the war-like elements of the
tribe and getting them to go on the warpath, dissatisfied
with the peace policy of the head chief. Mikasto remained
silent until the Indians began to move their lodges to another
place on the prairie, under the direction of the factious chief,
and then the peaceful ruler of his people quietly went among
them, and addressed a few words of authority and wisdom, and
the faction was at an end. Such is the implicit faith the
natives have in his good judgment and anxiety for their welfare that they gladly obey his most authoritative commands.
His influence is no less among the white people who have
learned to trust him, assured that he has always been friendly
to their interests whilst guarding the rights of his own tribe.
It is to his friendship, intelligence, and good government that
they are indebted for the peaceful relations which have existed
for many years between the white and red races in the west.

Situated, as the Blood Indians are, within a few miles of the
international boundary line, with a large number of their confreres, the Blackfeet and South Piegans in American territory,
in close proximity, it is worthy of note that few causes of
grievance have arisen among the white people on account of
Indian depredations. It is impossible for any community,
white or red, comprising more than two thousand souls, in
touch with three or four thousands of their own people, and
surrounded by an aggressive nation of different customs, language, traditions, mode of living, and tastes, to be without some
27

low-bred, idle, and dissatisfied spirits, especially when there are
dwelling in the vicinity some persons who live a kind of intermediate life, with loose morals and no ambition.   There are
always to be found on Reserves, and in the settlements close to
these Reserves, men who delight in contention, parasites of
society, who are determined to live at the expense of other
people, and who are ever ready to stir up a faction favorable
to their own interests   These are generally the cause of trouble,
promoters of Indian scares, and begetters of strife.

There have been at times small parties engaged in horse-
stealing and cattle killing, but that there have not been more
has been due to the influence of Mikasto.   Although he has
great power among his people, he cannot induce morality in
every person, and the low types of humanity among the red
and white people are beyond his control.   He is highly
respected by the white people in the west, as a man of ability,
graceful in his bearing, wise and firm in government, and
judicious in all his dealings.

Mikasto is a man of peace, and this is seen not only in his
mode of governing, but in his personal manner, and even in the
words which he uses in conversation.   When the treaty was
made with the Government at Blackfoot Crossing, the minor
chiefs of the Bloods would not do anything, or discuss the
terms of the treaty, till Mikasto arrived.   Upon his arrival, the
commissioners explained to him the text of the treaty, and,
after a short time for deliberation, he addressed them in a few
kind words and gave his assent.   When a newspaper reporter
visited the Reserve to learn the condition of the Indians, Mikasto
told him that his people were satisfied with their treatment by
the Government, and had no grievances ; that they wanted to
settle down on their Reserve and be quiet, the Government
helping them with implements to farm with, and supplying
them with rations ; that they had trouble enough many years
ago fighting their enemies, but were now tired of fighting, and
wished to live in peace ; that they wanted to live on friendly
terms with the white people, and to treat each other well ; that
he was satisfied with his Reserve, as he was born and had

always lived in that part of the country; that he had never had a cross word with the white people since they came to his country, and they had always kept their promises with him; that some people were always looking for trouble and bad news, but he always tried to treat people well, never looked for any trouble, and always expected good news. When a Cree Indian came to the camp, although he was a relative of one of the Blood Indian minor chiefs, Mikasto gave him notice to leave, and he had quietly to depart.

The animosity toward the Crees and Red River half-breeds still remains among the Bloods, and this was seen during the Rebellion, when they wanted to be allowed to go on the war-path against the Crees. They manifested pleasure when they heard that some of the Crees had been hanged at Battleford, and that Riel had been taken and was executed. When Mikasto visited Ontario he was delighted with the civilization of the white man and the manner in which he was treated. He was very observant, and quietly studied the ways of the pale-face, the evidences of power as seen in the buildings and the wealth of the cities. He visited Stoney Mountain and saw the tame buffalo, and when he learned that this was one of the evidences of the civilizing power of the white man, he said that if civilization could domesticate the buffalo, it was a lesson to them which they would not soon forget. He is a man of few words, but when he speaks, everyone listens intently, as he indulges in no mean epithets, foolish jesting, or idle gossip. Reserved in speech, his language is chaste, and the burden of his addresses is the welfare of his people. Even the common talk of the lodge is weighted with wisdom when he is present. In the council he presides with dignity, allowing the chiefs full liberty in discussing tribal affairs, and showing his mature judgment in settling difficulties In a few words he sheds light on questions affecting the camp. As a firm administrator of law he has won the admiration of his people. It matters not who breaks the native laws, punishment must be inflicted, and the chief has been disgraced before his people when he followed not the native code. The humblest member of the tribe can

appeal to him when his rights have been invaded, and justice
will be given; and the greatest of the minor chiefs must submit
to be degraded when he has done wrong. His style of oratory
is pleasing and in striking contrast with the perpetual harangue
of the average orator of the Indian camps. The war chief
loudly declaims and seeks to arouse the passions of the warriors,
but Mikasto addresses his people in eloquent phrases and gentle
words, delivered in a more subdued tone than we are accustomed to hear in native assemblies. With convincing arguments, clothed in the language of Nature, he leads his people to
the heart of his subject and sways their will to his liking, until
they cordially give their assent. The youthful warrior talks
in a louder and more boastful strain at the sun dance of his
prowess, than Mikasto, the hero of many battles; but there is
no one more loudly applauded and more universally esteemed
than this man of gentle speech, unassuming manners, and
natural goodness of heart.

When he learned that I was going to cease my labors among
the Indians he came to see me, and for a long time we sat
together, talking about the old days and the changes which had
taken place. We had been close friends for nine years, and had
not only learned to respect, but to love each other. My
heart was sad at parting with him, and I could hardly believe
it possible to become so strongly attached to a savage of the
plains. I had cared for him when he was sick, and frequently
visited him in his home. He assured me during the Rebellion
that I had nothing to fear, that if any trouble came my family
would be safe. He had taught me some things relating to the
language and customs of the people, and I had striven to instil
the principles of Christianity into his mind, and to aid and
encourage him in helping to lead his people to adopt civilized
habits and become self-supporting. We parted in sorrow, and
with words of peace and good wishes for each other's welfare.
I watched him quietly ride away from my home, and I grieved
that the man I loved should, in all likelihood, be seen no more
by me. Mikasto is a noble specimen of the red man of the west
—a faithful friend and ally; and in these days when men judge

the Indians from the standpoint of our civilization, and possess
not the knowledge of native culture, ignorant of the beauties of
language, customs and folk lore, and consequently are unable to
understand, much less know, what an ideal native is.   It is well
that we should have some native heroes who, in the possession of
those qualities which constitute true manhood, can show us
that they are not inferior as men to many members of the white
race, blest with all the advantages of education and civilization.
The head chief of the Blood Indians still dwells in peace among
his people, and long may his life be, that he may teach a lesson
to those who believe that no good thing can come out of an
Indian camp.   A native statesman he has always been in the
days of manhood, and in these trying years for his people, when
they are in a transition state, it will test his powers to save
them from destruction, and lead them toward a noble life.
May he reign in peace, and spend many years on earth—a
wise lawgiver, teacher and friend of his race.

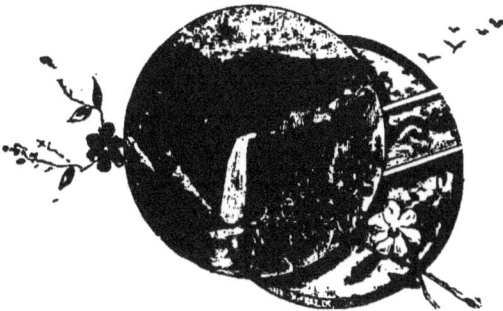

CHAPTER V.

NATIVE RELIGIONS.

SACRED NUMBERS.

THERE is a mystic charm in numbers. Odd numbers, especially, seem to have acted powerfully on the human mind, through observing their association in natural science and religion, and hence there was thrown around them a peculiar sanctity essentially their own. The untaught mind could not fail to be impressed with the frequent recurrence of certain numbers. The sexes of plants and animals suggest duality, the points of the compass and the limbs of mammals give us four, and the fingers of the hand five. In the ancient religions, especially the Jewish, three and seven were sacred numbers, which exercised a strong influence on the minds of the worshippers. The Pythagoreans developed this spiritual arithmetic in their mystic symbolism of numbers; the four of space, the seven of intelligence, the eight of love, and the ten of the universe. There is a significant law in relation to numbers in the Bible, which is applicable generally, but not universally followed, that the first mention of a place, person, or number, determines its relation to Scripture teaching and history. The unlucky number thirteen is always linked in the Old and New Testament with rebellion. The adversaries of God, and names of Satan, are numerically equivalents of thirteen or its multiples. In every list of the apostles the name of Judas is placed last, and, including Christ, he became the thirteenth member of the apostolic band. In the full list of the tribes given in the Old Testament, including

Joseph's double tribe, which was Benjamin and Manasseh, the thirteenth tribal division mentioned is Levi, and this is connected with a revolt. The influence of number is seen and felt in the laws of mechanism, and in astronomy and chemistry.

The movements of the solar system are as regular as those of a railway organization in relation to time. Nature is a mechanical factory and chemical laboratory in which every compound substance is found to be based on arithmetical laws, and every vibration of light or air is determined on length and duration with a definiteness which cannot be surpassed. The force of gravitation, the laws of planetary motion, the principles of crystallography, the classification of botany, the decorative coverings of animals, the plumage of birds, the compound eyes of bees and dragon-flies, and the symmetrical work of ants and spiders are all based on numbers.*

The natives of our forests, lakes and prairies, children of nature, ever observant in their wanderings, were unconscious students, reading the pages of the books which lay open all around them, and, by reason of their nomadic life, they became subjects of a native culture essentially their own, not understood by the white race, yet nevertheless true. I was, indeed, surprised when, through conversation with some of the members of the tribes of the Canadian North-West, I learned that they understood the sex of plants, the habits of the birds and animals, and some of the principles of astronomy. The keen powers of observation developed by the natives enabled them to grasp the truth of proportion in nature; and emphasis was laid on certain ever-recurring numbers, or numbers which were associated with their religion, and therefore became sacred. The number forty, through its relation to the sacred number four, became in a sense itself sacred. Forty "was taken as a limit to the sacred dances of some Indian tribes, and by others as the highest number of chants to be employed in exorcising

* Dr. White's "Number in Nature," page 22. President Thomas Hill's "Geometry and Faith," pages 15-19. F. W. Grant's "The Numerical Bible." "Britannica Encyclopædia," Vol. XV., page 202. Dr. Bullinger, in *Homiletic Review*, Vol. XXVIII., page 251.

diseases. Consequently, it came to be fixed as a limit in exercises of preparation or purification. The females of the Orinoco tribes fasted forty days before marriage, and those of the Upper Mississippi were held unclean the same length of time after child-birth; such was the term of the Prince of Tezcuco's fast, when he wished an heir to his throne: and such the number of days the Mandans supposed it required to wash clean the world at the deluge." *

Nineteen was a sacred number among the Druids, who had some things in common with the Indians of the American continent, as sky worship and stone structures. Stonhenge exhibits features of the sun worship of the earliest Indian tribes. It is a symbolic structure, a monument of the Stone Age, erected for sepulchral purposes. It belongs to two different periods—the inner circle of stones to the Stone Age, and the outer circle to the Bronze Age—the stones of which were brought from Wales. The outer circle consists, when entire, of sixty stones; the lesser circle, of forty smaller stones: the inner cell, of ten stones, in pairs, with imposts; and, within these, nineteen still smaller stones. The number of stones, sixty, was symbolic of the cycle; and the number of smaller stones, nineteen, was also symbolic. The whole structure was devoted to sun worship.

Dr. Peet says of the remarkable numbers, 100, 60, 30, constantly recurring, that they unavoidably bring to our recollection the great periods of astronomy—the century, the sothic cycle; the thirty years, or thirty days; and the twelve signs of the zodiac. These, and similar circular monuments, especially those made of columnal stones, were made either as representing the disc of the sun, or the sun's revolution through the twelve signs of the zodiac.†

Seven is generally regarded as the sacred number of the white man. From its frequent recurrence in the Bible and the

---

* Catlin's " Letters and Notes," Vol. I., Letter 22. L. A. Hontan's " Memoires," Vol. II., page 151. Gumilla's " History del Orinoco," page 159 ; noted by Brinton, in " Myths of the New World," page 97.

† " American Antiquarian," Vol. X., pages 138-142 ; Vol. XVI., page 229.

relation of the civilization of the white race to the doctrines and duties of Judaism and Christianity, it has become associated with the white man as if it were essentially his own; but it is a factor belonging to these religions, and not to any race. The Mosaic code was based on a septenary system. The Lord blessed the seventh day and sanctified it. The seventh month of Tizri, when the great Day of Atonement occurred, was hallowed. The seventh year was the year of release from debts and slavery, and the completed square of each seventh year led to the fiftieth year, or the Year of Jubilee. There were seven persons in the ark with Noah; and in some of the early Indian myths of the flood, exactly seven persons were saved. The influence of Sabeanism upon the Chaldeans found expression in part in the sacred number seven. This sky worship was the oldest form of nature worship, which was embodied in a measure in the Chaldean temples, constructed, as they were, according to the plan of the stars, and in the Tower of Babel. The divisions of the earth were arranged according to the geography of the heavens, and the temple was built in terraces, each terrace sacred to a planet or star, and the upper shrine sacred to the sun. The tower of Babel was called the Temple of the seven lights, or the Celestial Earth, which embodied the astronomical kingdoms of antiquity.*   The seven lights were the seven stars of the great dipper, or the seven planetary bodies, seven stages colored to represent the seven planets. This was believed to be an exact imitation of the sacred mountain, which rises in terraces, till the summit reaches the heavens, and upon the summit was a sanctuary or shrine to the sun. Among the Cherokee Indians seven is a sacred number in their ritual and mythology, but has no connection with their present calendar system, except as it is borrowed from the white race. Their medicine men suppose a sick person can be cured in seven nights. The Cherokee shaman, who wishes to destroy the life of another, conceals himself on the trail where the doomed man will pass, and secretly

---

* White's "Number in Nature," pages 23-27. Brinton's "Myths of the New World," pages 218, 243. Prescott's "Conquest of Peru," Vol. I., page 88.

follows him until he spits upon the ground. The shaman collects upon the end of a stick a little of the dust containing the spittle of his victim, which gives him power over the man. He puts the moistened clay into a tube consisting of a joint of the wild parsnip, seven earthworms beaten into a paste, and some splinters of a tree struck by lightning. Going into the forest he seeks a tree which has been struck by lightning, and digging a hole at its base, deposits a large yellow stone slab. He puts the tube, with seven yellow pebbles into the holes, fills in the earth, and builds a fire over the spot to destroy all traces of his work. The shaman and the man who has employed him fast until the completion of the ceremony. If the ceremony is successful the doomed man feels the influence, and within seven days he dies; but if it is a failure, it is believed that he has discovered the plot, and is employing counter charms, by the help of another shaman, to save himself.

The shaman and his employer then retire to a lonely spot in the mountains—in the vicinity of a small stream—and begin a new series of conjurations. A temporary bark shelter is made, and the shaman and his employer go down to the water, the shaman taking with him a piece of white cloth and a piece of black, together with seven red, and seven black beads. The shaman selects a bend in the river where his client can look toward the east while facing up stream, and he stands on the bank while his client goes into the stream, having his eyes fixed on the water, and his back to the shaman. The shaman lays the cloth on the ground, places the red beads on the white cloth, and the black beads on the black cloth, and then takes a red bead between the finger and thumb of his right hand, which represents his client; and a black bead, representing the doomed man, between the finger and thumb of his left hand. Turning toward the east, and holding up the bead in his right hand, he addresses it as the red bead, invoking blessings upon his client; and, addressing the black bead, he calls down curses upon his victim. Addressing the stream as the Long Person, he implores it to protect his client, and to raise him to the seventh heaven where he will be secure from his enemies. The man in the stream dips up water in his hand seven times, and pours it on his head, rubbing it on his breast and shoulders, or dips himself completely under seven times.   The shaman makes a hole in the ground, where he deposits the black bead, and covering it up, stamps upon it with his foot.

If the conjurations have been unsuccessful after the fourth attempt the shaman confesses that he has been defeated, but if successful the victim will die within seven nights.   The seven nights are frequently interpreted to mean seven years, and the shaman can easily escape defeat by this extension of time.*

Among the Micmacs the number seven has a mysterious significance, as a medicine compounded of seven barks or roots is very potent; but the most potent of all is a medicine compounded of seven of these compositions.

This number enters also into their mythology, as in the adventures of Aoolamsun, " Rushing Wind," and Utkoo, " Rolling Wave."   They are brothers, and as they love each other and can best work together, they perform all their astonishing feats when united.

Rushing Wind, the elder, plans an excursion with his brother, in which they will be absent for some years; but as their parents are old and infirm, and they love them, they cannot leave them without making provision for them during their absence.   Rushing Wind supplies them with a large number of animals by throwing down trees on them, and Rolling Wave brings in a large number of fish.

They leave their parents and start on their journey, coming to a village where they engage to work for a chief for a short time, and so effectually do they work, bringing in fish and fowl, that the village is well supplied, and they are dismissed, after being well paid for their services.

Before leaving the village they exhibit their powers as supernatural beings.   Rushing Wind bursts into a cyclone, scattering the tents in all directions, and Rolling Wave rushes up in a tidal wave—both of them doing more harm than all the good they had formerly done.

* "Annual Report of the Bureau of Ethnology," Vol. VII., page 395. "American Antiquarian," Vol. XVI., pages 54, 244.

Upon their journey they are absent seven years, and upon their return they bring with them as their wives, Wibbun, "Calm on the Sea," and Kogum, "Sea Foam."

The number seven again appears in some of the myths relating to Glooscap, the friend and teacher of the Micmacs. Tradition says that Glooscap dwells in a beautiful land in the west, where the Indians will go at death if they are good. The journey is long and difficult, but some of the Indians have managed to get there, and of the number were seven young men, who were successful in their attempt to reach the beautiful land in the west.

" Before reaching the place they had to pass over a mountain, the ascent of which was up a perpendicular bluff, and the descent on the other side still more difficult, for the top hung over the base. The fearful and unbelieving could not pass at all, but the good and the confident could travel it with ease and safety, as though it were a level path. Having crossed the mountain, the road ran between the heads of two huge serpents, whose heads lays opposite to each other, and they darted out their tongues so as to destroy whoever they hit. But the good and the firm of heart could dart past between the strokes of their tongues, so as to evade them. One more difficulty remained. It was a wall as of a thick, heavy cloud, that separated the present world from that beautiful one beyond. This cloudy wall rose and fell at intervals, and struck the ground with such force that whatever was caught under it would be crushed to atoms. But the good could dart under it when it rose, and come out on the other side unscathed. This our seven young heroes succeeded in doing." *

The mystic number five is the sacred number of the Athapascan Indians on the Siletz Reservation, Oregon. An infant is kept in the cradle cover four days after birth, and early on the morning of the fifth day the cradle is made and the child placed in it. This is in accordance with the command of Qawaneca, the Great Being, who made the cradle on the morning of the fifth day, after the birth of the first infant. When

* "American Antiquarian," Vol. XII., pages 9, 284.

Qawaneca made the earth he threw stones five times into the water, and nothing happened until the fifth time, when the waves arose and receded, forming the tides. Serpents were the first created animals, and these make the storms by blowing with their mouths. An enormous serpent coiled himself around the earth five times, and by this means the earth is held together.*

Four is the sacred number which is most highly esteemed by the greatest number of Indian tribes, and it was the sacred number of the Chaldeans. The four divine regions of the Chaldeans were the abodes of the gods, and the places where the gods and men met together. The Chaldean monarch was called the King of the Four Regions of Heaven.† In the Quiche cosmogony four men were created after three unsuccessful attempts, and four women were made while the men were asleep.‡ In the Maya calendar there are four different series of years, and in relation to the four cardinal points there are four dominical days, four colors, four elements, four ages, and four seasons. Among the Aztec tribes there is a myth of four brothers who were gods, born to the Great Spirit, who was eternal, infinite and without origin. These dwelt before creation, and held a council about the making of the world, which was entrusted to two of the brothers.

The Tusans rub honey mixed with saliva upon their prayer sticks, and make an offering of sugar and saliva to the four cardinal points. Schoolcraft has mentioned a myth in which four sons were born at a birth, causing their mother's death. The first was Manibozho, "The Friend of the Human Race;" the second, Chipiopos, "The Ruler of the Land of Souls;" the third, Wabosso, "The Rabbit who Rules the North;" and the fourth, Chakekenapok, the "Flint Man," who supplies fire to men from the stones scattered over the earth. Manibozho, "The Friend of Man," killed the Flint Man, and gave to the human race lances, arrows and other implements, and taught man how to make

---

* J. Owen Dorsey, in "American Anthropologist," Vol. II., page 59.
† "American Antiquarian," Vol. XVI., page 218.
‡ Baldwin's "Ancient America," page 194.

axes, traps and snares.   He placed at each of the four cardinal
points a good spirit, who ruled over the world, the spirit of the
east giving light, the spirit of the west blessing the world with
rain, the spirit of the north helping men to pursue game by
giving them snow and ice, and the spirit of the south supplying
tobacco, melons and maize.   Four is a sacred number among
the sun worshippers.   In the centre of a serpent effigy discovered in Adams County, Illinois, situated on the summit of a
hill overlooking the Mississippi, there were four large mounds,
and on the top of one of the mounds were four burial places,
the points of the compass having been observed in the burials.
Among the Dakotas there are four varieties of the bird which
symbolizes the thunder god.   When this bird flies, it is hid by
thick clouds, the lightning is the flash of its eyes, and the
thunder the echo of its voice.*   In the shell gorgets found in
Tennessee and Georgia images of serpents are engraved upon
them, evidently intended to symbolize the nature powers; and
the serpents are divided into four parts to represent the four
seasons or the four quarters of the sky.   In these shell gorgets
there are several kinds of crosses, symbolic of the number four.
In the spider gorgets, the spider is placed within four circles,
and upon its abdomen four bands; and in the bird gorgets this
sacred number four is repeated.   "There are four sides to the
quadrangle and four loops formed by four lines.   There are
four birds' heads with four stripes in the neck, and four lines
on bars in the crest.   There are four spaces in the centre of the
figure, and four bars to the cross: but in one specimen four holes
are substituted for the cross.†   The cross was a sacred symbol
to the Aztecs, representing fertility and life.   The ends of the
cross, which was of the Greek form, pointed to the four cardinal
points, the source of the winds and rains which caused the seeds
to germinate and the fruits of the earth to grow.   Here we see
the cross allied with the sacred number four, as shown in the
cardinal points.‡

* "American Antiquarian," Vol. XV., page 367.
† "American Antiquarian," Vol. X., page 307 ; XVI., page 27.
‡ Brinton's "American Hero Myths," pages 122, 123. "Myths of the
New World," pages 97-102. "American Antiquarian," Vol. X., page 307.

The sacred ash tree and the great serpent divinity were symbols of the nature powers among the Dakotas. Upon a chart descriptive of a Dakota myth there is shown a tree, representing the Tree of Life, on the bank of a river, and beneath the river the Red Morning Star. Beside this are six stars, called the elm rod, the moon, sun and seven stars, and under these are the peace pipe and war hatchet. An oak tree supports the four heavens, or upper worlds, through which the ancestors of this people passed, before they came to earth, and beside this oak tree are earth lodges and villages. Here the sacred number "four" again appears in the upper worlds. A similar idea is repeated among the Winnebagoes, Maunna, the "World Maker," sat upon a piece of earth after the creation with his face to the east, because it was the source of light, and along with him were four wolves, who were brothers and of different colors, green, black, white and grey.

When the Omahas decide to start on a hunting expedition, four men are appointed to act as directors of the hunt. Until the fourth herd of buffalo is surrounded, there is held after each hunt the feast of the hearts and tongues. When going out on the warpath, a preparatory feast is held. Sacred songs and dancing songs are sung four times, and four times the members of the party dance. When a large war party is to be organized, four men are sent around the camp to invite the guests to the lodge, where a feast is to be held. Four captains seat themselves opposite the entrance of the lodge. The feast is held to secure persons to join the war party. When it is decided to attack the enemy, sometimes the captain carries a sacred bag, which he opens four times, with its mouth toward the foe, that the wind may waft the medicine toward them, to keep them asleep. The war club is sometimes waved four times toward the foe as a sacred symbol, and the sacred bag waved four times before the scalp yell is given. The Society of Buffalo Dancers among the Omahas has four doctors.*

Four is a sacred number among the Cherokees. The medicine boiling dance was continued for four days. The chief

* Dorsey's "Omaha Sociology," pages 280, 288, 290, 316, 319, 327, 347.

ceremony in connection with it was the drinking of a strong
decoction of various herbs, which acted as a violent emetic and
purgative. The shamans have become jealous of the encroachments of the white physicians upon their rights, and the faith
of the natives in them, and consequently they assert that the
white man's medicine will prove fatal to an Indian unless
eradicated from the system by a four year's course of treatment.
In the sacred formulas of the Cherokees it is stated that rheu-
matism is caused by the spirits of slain animals, who enter the
body of the hunter thirsting for vengeance, and cause him severe
pain. These animal spirits live beyond the seventh heaven,
and are located at the four cardinal points, which have special
names and colors. The East is the Sun Land, where the red
spirits dwell, who are implored for the success of any undertaking; the North is the Frigid Land, the home of the blue gods,
who are invited to defeat the schemes of an enemy or bring
down trouble upon him; the West is the Darkening Land, the
residence of the black spirits, who cause death; and the South
is Wāhalā, a great mountain, where the white spirits make their
abode, who are besought for health, peace and other blessings.
The shaman calls upon the Red Dog in the Sun Land, who
comes to take away a portion of the disease to the uttermost
parts of the earth, then the Blue Dog of the Frigid Land, the
Black Dog of the Darkening Land, and the White Dog of
Wāhalā arrive through the entreaties of the shaman, and
depart carrying away a portion of the disease, and finally the
white terrapin of Wāhalā removes the last portion, and the
patient is cured. The sacred formulas, consisting of four paragraphs, corresponding to the four steps in the medical ceremony,
are recited four times. The shaman blows upon the patient at
the seat of the pain once at the end of each paragraph, and four
times at the end of the final repetition. The medicine consists
of a warm decoction, made from the roots of four varieties of
fern, which is rubbed on with the hand, and is applied four
times during the same morning. "Four is the sacred number
running through every detail of these formulas, there being
commonly four spirits invoked in four paragraphs; four blow-

ings, with four final blows; four herbs in the decoction; four
applications; and frequently four days, gaktunta or tabu."*

Four is a sacred number among the Ojibways. In the order
of medicine men there are four degrees. The Mide lodge of
the fourth degree has four entrances, and within the sacred
enclosure are four sacred posts, painted green, red, black and
white, which represent the four limbs and feet of the Bear
Manido. The fourth degree, Mide post, in the form of a cross,
symbolizes the four days struggle at the four entrances to the
Mide lodge. The candidate for the fourth degree must take a
sweat bath once a day for four successive days. Four priests
assist in the initiation of the candidate, and during the ceremony the number four is frequently mentioned. A bow is
shot four times at the evil spirits who are supposed to oppose
the admission of the candidate. Food is brought into the
lodge four distinct times, making four circuits of the interior.
The candidate is led around the interior of the lodge four
times, according to a prescribed order. When the participants
in the ceremony smoke in silence they present their pipe to
the four points of the compass. In a tradition of the restoring
to life of a dead boy, four Mide priests officiated. Each
chanted a Mide song four times, and then signs of life were
seen. The boy's blanket was taken off, and then he sat up.
Each of the priests gave him four pinches of powder which he
was made to swallow, and having recovered his speech he
revealed to them the grand medicine which he had learned in
the spirit land. The Jessakid has four or more tubular bones,
which he uses for extracting from the bodies of sick people the
evil spirits which are supposed to cause disease.†

Algonquin legends make their first and highest gods to consist of four brothers, born at the same time, whose names as
generally given are identical with the four points of the compass, or something relating to them. Their names usually are

* Mooney's "The Sacred Formulas of the Cherokees." "Seventh Annual
Report of the Bureau of Ethnology, pages 336, 337, 348.

† Hoffman's "The Midewin or Grand Medicine Society of the
Ojibway."

28

Wabun the " East," who is the leader, and assigns to his brother
the duty of blowing the winds: Kabun the "West," Kabibonokk
the " North," and Shawano the " South."

Four as a sacred number appears among the Indians o
British Columbia. A Tshimpsean woman, when drinking for th
first time after her marriage, must drink very little, and th
cup must be turned four times in the same direction as the su
is moving.   When a death occurs among the Tshimpsean:
Tlingits and Haidas, the relatives of the deceased cut their hai
short, blacken their faces, put ragged and soiled mats on thei
heads and walk four times around the corpse, singing mournin,
songs.   When many members of the same family die in suc
cession within a short time, the survivors lay their fourt
fingers on the edge of the box containing the corpse, and cu
off the finger by the first joint.   Among the Kwakiutls fou
boats are connected by long boards, forming a platform, upo:
which a dance is performed.   This dance is connected with th
marriage customs of the people.   When a young man is to b
married, the gens to which he belongs go out to meet his brid(
and it is during this time that the dance is performed.

The sacred number is strictly adhered to in their buria
customs.   When a husband or wife dies, the survivor must si
motionless with the knees drawn up toward the chin, for fou
days, and on the fourth day some water, heated in a wooden
kettle, is made to drip upon the head.   When tired of sittin;
motionless, he must think of his enemy, stretch his legs fou
times, and then draw them up again.   During the followin;
sixteen days he may stretch out his legs, but he must remaii
on the same spot, and after this period he may lie down, but no
stretch himself out.   For four months he must not associat
with other people.   A separate door is cut in the house for hi
use, as he must not go out the common door, and when he i
going to leave the house for the first time he must approacl
the door three times and return, and then he may leave thv
house.*   This same number is found among the Cree Indians ii

*Dr. Franz Boaz's " Report on the Indians of British Columbia," 1889
pages 41-43.

their grades of medicine men and religious ceremonies. The Blackfoot Indians, in common with other Algonquin tribes, have the same sacred number, which appears in their mythology and religion.*

INDIAN NAMES OF GOD.

It was natural for the red men in the presence of the mysterious things in nature to manifest fear, and to people the heavens with an order of beings different from themselves. The evidences of wisdom and power in the march of the stars, the regularity of the seasons, the existence of mountains and lakes, and other things in nature, independent of man, compelled the thinking savage to place a supreme being or some great deities at the head of affairs presiding over the realm of nature. The natives of Canada believed in a presiding deity, with a host of lesser gods. The Great Spirit of the Indians is not the same as the Creator of the white race. The distinction is not made clear by some of the tribes, but especially among the Algonquin family the Creator is one of the greater deities, who creates the world and peoples it with men and women. This Creator is named by the Blackfeet, Apĭstotoke the "Maker" or "Former." He is a being capable of doing good and evil ; at one time supplying man with all things needful for existence, and again performing queer pranks, which the natives laugh at when narrating his exploits.

The Blood Indians say that Apĭstotoke made the world by the help of four animals, and that lakes and valleys were formed by a wolf running over the plastic world soil, leaving indentations wherever he stepped, and the mountains mark the spot whereon he did not tread. He made some men, to whom he gave bows and arrows. He formed the buffaloes and taught the men how to hunt them. A number of women were made by him whose mouths opened vertically, and not being satisfied with the shape of them, he closed them and made them to open in their present fashion. He gave to each of the men one woman as a wife. He taught the Indians several games,

---

* " Eleventh Annual Report of the Bureau of Ethnology," page 513.

BLOOD INDIAN.

CHIEF CALF SHIRT, RATTLESNAKE CHARMER.

and that is the reason why they pray for success when they are gambling. He taught them to paint themselves, for he had a dark skin, and many of the arts of savage life were revealed to their forefathers by him. The creator of some of the tribes was a bird or animal. According to one legend the cunning coyote formed the earth and animals, and then called a council of the animals to devise some method of making man. He suggested that the new being to be formed be made according to a combination of the best characteristics of each member of the council, but this did not meet with their wishes, as each thought himself to be perfect, and man should be made according to his individual model. Acting upon his own responsibility each animal set to work to form this new being; but before the task was finished they all fell asleep, except the coyote, who toiled hard until his task was done. He then imparted life to his work, threw water upon the unfinished tasks of the others, and man became an inhabitant of the world. Before the Incas of Peru introduced the worship of the sun among their people, the Supreme Being who formed the earth was named Con, an invisible and omnipotent spirit. Kareya, the "Old Man" above, was the name given by the Karoks to the secondary creator, who sometimes comes to earth to instruct the medicine men. This is a conception similar to that of the Blackfoot Apĭstotoke. The coyote appears as one of the chief animal gods of the tribes of California, and he plays an important part in their mythology. Sometimes there seems a confusion of religious ideas among the natives, as is evident from the names sometimes given to their deities. Apĭstotoke, of the Blackfeet, is also called the Old Man, whose home was in the Rocky Mountains, near the source of the Old Man's River, in the provisional district of Alberta.

The native religion of the Cherokees is Zootheism, or animal worship, with the survival of that earlier stage called Hecasto-theism, or the worship of all things tangible, and the beginning of a higher system in which the elements and the great powers of nature are deified. The Cherokees have animal gods, as the rabbit, squirrel and dog; elemental gods, as fire, water, sun,

wind, cloud, storm and frost; inanimate gods, as the flint and
the mountain; plant gods, as the ginseng; and personal deities
as the Red Man, one of the greatest of the gods, and little
people who resemble our fairies. The sun is called Unelanuhi,
the "Apportioner," a word which has been used as synonymous
with God in the translation of the Bible, but has no relation to
the Great Spirit of the Indians.[*]

The sense of dependence on some power higher than themselves and the cry of the soul for affinity with the Great Soul
of the Universe compelled the natives to seek after a Supreme
Being, or gods presiding over different departments in the physical and spiritual worlds. Lesser deities resided in the rapids
of rivers, caves and mountains. The Thunder God spoke in the
thunder and dwelt near the bold promontories of the lakes. In
the spiritual world the presiding deity has various attributes
and names.

Rawenniio is used in various dialectical forms by Hurons and
Iroquois as the name of the deity. The modern acceptation of
the word is "He who is Master," but it had once a larger meaning, as the "Great Master." Hale says, "Its root is probably to
be found in the Iroquois kawen, or gawen, which signifies "to
belong to anyone," and yields in combination with oyata, "person," the derivatives gaiatawen to "have for subject," and gaia-
tawenston, to "subject any one." Rawenniio is the word used by
the Roman Catholic missionaries for God. It was doubtless
used from earliest times as an epithet for a great divinity. Its
use as a special name for God is doubtless due to Christian
influence.[†] The belief of the natives as to their own origin sheds
some light on their ideas of God. The Supreme Being is
believed to be over all, as when the Indians address the representatives of the Canadian Government, they invariably declare
that there is one Father common to both red and white races,
and this Being gave the land, wood and water to the red men.
When the creation of man is mentioned they somtimes maintain that the Creator made both races, but in their mythology

---

[*] "Seventh Annual Report of Bureau of Ethnology," pages 340, 341.
[†] Hale's "Iroquois Book of Rites," pages 148, 177, 208.

the creator makes the Indians of the same color and with similar tastes as Himself, and the white race is the result of a separate creation. Sometimes this creator makes each tribe separately.

Peter Jones says : " All the information I have been able to gain in relation to the question amounts to the following : Many, many years ago, the Great Spirit, Keche-Manedoo, created the Indians. Every nation speaking a different language is a second creation, but they were made by the same Supreme Being."

Hennepin, in speaking of the Indians of Algonquin stock, refers to their ideas of God as follows : " As for their opinion concerning the earth, they make use of a name of a certain Genius, whom they call Micaboche, who has covered the whole earth with water (as they imagine), and related innumerable fabulous tales, some of which have a kind of analogy with the universal deluge." * The Blood Indians, in common with other north-western tribes, pray to the sun, and offer sacrifices to it. The Cree Indians have their thirst dance, when they offer sacrifices to the sun ; but when those who have been under missionary influence pray, they address the Supreme Being, as Kĭtcĭ Mûnĭtu, the " Great Spirit."

The Ojibways believe in a large number of greater and lesser divinities, at the head of which is Kĭtcĭ Manĭdu, the " Great. Spirit ; " and the second in majesty and power is Dzhe Manĭdu, a. divinity, who has the special care of the midewiwin, or medicine. lodge, and through whom the sacred rites of the midewiwin were granted to man. The Animiki, or Thunder God, is one of the most powerful of the evil spirits, and it is from him that the Jessakid are believed to obtain their powers of doing evil. Dzhibai Manĭdu, the Shadow or Ghost Spirit, rules over the " place of shadows," or the hereafter. In the native religion of the Ojibways, the name of Kĭtchĭ Manĭdu is always mentioned with reverence, and only in connection with a sacred feast, after making an offering of tobacco, or the rite of Midewiwin.†

---

* " Peter Jones," page 31.
† "Seventh Annual Report of Bureau of Ethnology," pages 154, 163.

This is the name used by the missionaries for the Christian deity. It is pronounced by some of the Ojibways Kizhe Manĭdu, having the same meaning and form, except the hardening of the final consonants, as the same word in the Cree language.

Animal divinities were worshipped by some of the tribes, and great power attributed to them. The great raven, called by the Thlinkeets Yetl, Yesh, or Yeatl, and by the Haidas, Nekilstlus, was regarded as the creater of all things, and the benefactor of man. This was a mythical bird, possessing human attributes, and the power of changing his form into anything in the world. By him the world was peopled, and he gave to man whatever he enjoys.*

The chief divinity of some of the tribes was an animal, which presided over the territory of the tribe, and each tribe had a different name for the Creator. The Delawares called him Manibozho; the Michabo of the Algonquins, the "Great Hare," who created the earth, founded the medicine hunt, and tells the hunter in dreams where to find game. He is known among the Ojibways as Nanabozhu. The Nippissings call him Wisakedjak. The Mississaugas say Wanibozhu; and the Menominees, Manibush. The Crees call this culture hero, Wisaketcak, who is regarded as the creator of the Indians. The Saulteaux of the north call him Naniboz; and the Blackfeet, Napio, the "Old Man." The creator of the Winnebagoes was the wolf, called Maunna. The Dakotahs had numerous gods. The moving god, who holds the four winds, gave the spear and tomahawk to the Indians, makes his home in the boulders, which dot the prairies; and these stopping places of the god are worshipped as symbols of the divinity. There is the stone god, Tukan, who dwells in the round or oval stone, which is painted red, and covered with swan's down by the Indians; the god of the waters, Unktaghe, a male and female divinity, who taught the natives the use of colors. The great mystery of the Dakotas was named Taku Wakan, a great divinity, incomprehensible and yet sufficiently personal to be addressed in prayer. The Indians of Wash-

---

*"American Antiquarian," Vol. XV., page 274.

ington territory appear not to have had any idea of a great spirit before the white people went amongst them, but they believe in a culture hero, who made the world, a Supreme Being, who may come again. The Twana name for God is Wïsowulus, in Nisqually, Shuksiab; in Klallam, Tsïltsi; and in Chinook, Saghalie Tyee; all of which have the same meaning, the " Chief Above." The culture hero or creator, is named in Twana and Nisqually, Dokibatt; and in Klallam, Mikimatt, signifying the " Changer." Saghalie Tyee, the Chinook term, is used for this culture hero and the Christian Deity. The great spirit of some of the Algonquin tribes is known among the Blackfeet as Omûqkatos, the " Great Sun," and is worshipped, prayers being addressed to it and sacrifices made. The Christian Deity is known as Apïstotoke,the " Creator," and Kinon, " Our Father."

These names express the ideas of the natives relating to God, showing progress from the belief in nature powers and animal divinities, to a recognition of a Supreme Being of great wisdom, power and benevolence.

CANADIAN INDIAN THEOLOGY.

The red man of Canada is a religious being, with a distinctive religion of his own, embracing a theological system undefined, yet recognized by those who have made a special study of the native religions of the American Indians. The systems of theology held by the native tribes of Canada may be arranged according to Dr. Peets' method of classifying the Ethnographic religions : (1) Shamanism ; (2) Totemism ; (3) Sun Worship ; (4) Sabianism or Sky Worship; (5) Hero Worship; (6) Ancestor Worship.*

Shamanism is one of the lowest forms of religion, and is to be found among the Eskimos, the Tinne tribes of Athabasca, and the Tshimpsean, Kwakiutl, Tlingit, Kootaney, and other tribes of British Columbia. The shaman or medicine man is the priest of the people, possessed, as they believe, of super-natural powers, which he has gained through being in league

* " American Antiquarian," Vol. XV., pages 230-245, 272, 278 ; Vol. XVI., page 78.

with animated nature. Shamanism varies with the locality of the tribe. In British Columbia it can boast of secret societies among the tribes. Some of the religious customs of the Eskimo are degrading in the extreme. The shaman is initiated after a long period of fasting, and his supernatural power is shown in healing the sick, foretelling the events of the future, performing magical feats, and exercising an influence over people at a distance. It is believed that the shaman can gain access to and hold communion with the tribal ancestors, who are animals, and his power of doing good or evil is consequently very great. Totemism is not confined to any district, but is widely prevalent among the tribes throughout the Dominion. It prevails most extensively among the Huron-Iroquois and Algonquin families. This form of religion consists of a belief in descent from an original parent who appears in the form of an animal. This animal is so far worshipped that the skin is preserved and held sacred, and when the people journey it is their guide and protector. The food of this animal must not be eaten by the band or sub-tribe, which claims it as their ancestor. The band claiming descent from the deer will not kill or eat it, and the ancestor is worshipped in the animal. The figure of the animal is painted or carved, and placed in front of their houses as their divinity who guards them always against the malice of their enemies and the ravages of disease. Sun worship exists among the Blackfeet, Crees, Sioux and Kootaneys. The sun is worshipped as a divinity.

Sky worship is not found in a distinct form among any of the native tribes of Canada, but it has left its influence upon some of the tribes, as it has been related to sun worship. Numerous myths of the moon and stars are related by the red men, and the forces of nature are personified and worshipped. The sun god, sky gods and wind deities are revered. They people the sky with divinities like the ancient Egyptians, and worship them under different names.

Some tribes have a form of hero worship, represented by the famous lawgivers of the red race. The myth of Hiawatha among the Iroquois reveals this form of religion. A historical character may become a mythical personage endowed with supernatural powers, and adored in religious ceremonies. Another form, and the truest of hero worship, is seen in the mythical hero gods of the red race. These are the national heroes of the tribes, who are recognized as the teachers, and supreme agents in their civilization, and sometimes identified as the Creator. Among the Algonquins there is the hero god Michabo, and among the Iroquois, Ioskeha.

Ancestor worship is found chiefly among the British Columbia Indians, and is a modified form of totemism. Ancestral posts, erected by the Haidas and other tribes, contain the totem of the owner, figures suggestive of his family history, and mythologic carvings. In the system of totemism the clan is the unit, and each member of the tribe has his own place in the communistic circle; but in the system of ancestor worship, the family is the unit, and an independent attitude is maintained by the individual. The ancestor is worshipped as in totemism, under the representation of an animal or bird. There are other forms of religion held by the Indians, as the worship of stones, trees, and water; but these are only modifications of the systems already mentioned. The stone or tree is believed to be a stopping-place of the god, and some myths will gather around them in the course of time, so as to clothe them with mysterious powers. The people will then paint the stone and make offerings to it. The hunter or warrior will seek success by propitiation, and it will be a sacred stone to the worshipper. The trees, stones or rapids are not worshipped as inanimate objects, but as the abode of spirits, or as themselves possessed of life.* The Crees on the Nelson River slew their aged parents because they were a burden to them, yet the master of the lodge kept a bunch of feathers tied with a string which he reverenced, as he called it his "father's head."† This is a form

---

*Dr. Franz Boaz's, "Fifth British Association Report on the North-Western Tribes of Canada," pages 52-59. Edward Clodd's "Childhood of the World," page 24. C. F. Keary's "The Dawn of History," pages 47-53. "Britannica Encyclopædia," article, "Religion." Edward Clodd's "The Birth and Growth of Myth," pages 31-36.

†Robson's "Account of Residence in Hudson's Bay," page 48; quoted by Brinton, in "Myths of the New World," pages 274, 275.

of ancestral worship seldom found. The Blackfeet speak of
the Creator as a male personage, but they call the earth "Our
mother."

Besides the tribal gods, each of the natives believe that he is
protected by a guardian spirit, with whom he can communicate.
The Blackfoot youth, anxious to learn the name of his familiar
spirit, repairs to the ravines or secluded places on the prairie,
where he fasts and prays until the vision of his god comes to
him in a trance or dream, wherein there is revealed the name of
the animal representing his personal deity. He kills this
animal, preserves the skin, which he stuffs and always carries
with him as his guardian and guide. The Ojibway youth
blackens his face with charcoal, and in a similar fashion seeks
the vision of his god. The belief in a doctrine of sin is shown
by the religious custom of making sacrifices. The oldest rite
in all religions is sacrifice. Man feels that he has made the
gods angry, and he gives what he believes will appease their
wrath. The Blackfoot hunter or warrior, before setting out on
an expedition, will fast and make a vow that if successful he
will give a thank-offering. I have seen the young warriors
return from the south, and at the annual sun dance repair to
the medicine lodge and place his hand in that of an aged
medicine woman, who, after holding it aloft and praying to the
sun, has quickly severed a finger by the first joint by means of
a knife on a block of wood, as an offering to the sun. Sin
offerings were generally represented by tobacco. Sacrifices to
the sun were made by the Cree, Blackfoot and other tribes,
and consisted of articles of wearing apparel chiefly. Beside
the stone stopping-places of the gods were deposited by the
people, as they passed, minor articles of clothing, pipes, tobacco,
cooking utensils and trinkets of various kinds. The Tshimpseans and Kwakiutls fast for a definite period—from four to
seven days—and pray when they desire to obtain a special
object. It is believed that fasting is well pleasing to the Gods.
The Kwakiutls offer valuable burnt-offerings*. When the

* Brinton's "Myths of the New World," pages 154, 310. "Clodd's
Childhood of the World," page 27 ; and "Childhood of Religion," page 19.
Boaz's "Fifth Report of the North-Western Tribes of Canada," pages 50-52.

Kootaneys or Blackfeet are about to open a council they fill a
pipe with tobacco and present the stem to the sun, and afterwards to the four points of the compass.   The doctrine of
atonement for sin is maintained by the red men.   By means
of fasting, prayers and sacrifices the hunter, warrior and
medicine-men sought to obtain the favor of the gods.*

   In approaching the deity cleanliness of body and soul were
considered essential to an answer to prayer, and to obtain the
favor of God.   Baptism was therefore practised among some
Indian tribes.   When a young Klallam wished to obtain a
vision of his familiar spirit, he washed himself thoroughly that
he might be pure; and even the children of this tribe, anxious
to become great medicine men, bathed daily, remaining in the
water for a long time.

   The worshipper among the Blackfeet, conscious of his sin-
fulness, before engaging in any special religious ceremony,
entered a sweat bath, and drove out of his body all the un-
cleanness.   The Delawares used an emetic to rid themselves of
the guilt of sin.   The Tshimpseans, before praying, must bathe
and wash well their bodies to purify themselves, and an emetic
is taken to remove all carnal impurities, in order to please
the deity.†

   There is no devil in the native religions of the Indians in
the Christian sense.   There are spirits which work evil, and it
is in the power of many of the medicine men, as they believe,
to invoke the aid of these spirits in causing the death of their
enemies.   Sometimes the language of the Indians seems to
imply that the spirits are neither good or bad, but will protect
and guide those who have placed themselves under their care,
and will punish or destroy their enemies when propitiated.
The medicine men speak of disease as caused by the spirits of
evil dwelling in a sick person, and they invoke the help of
their familiar spirits to drive out the spirits who are causing
the disease.

   The belief in a devil has been maintained by numerous.

* " Smithsonian Anthropological Papers," 1886-87, page 678.
† Bancroft's " History of the United States," Vol. III., Chap. 22.

writers on the Indians, some agreeing with John Mecklenburg, who said of the Iroquois:

"They are entire strangers to all religion, but they have a Tharonhijouagon (which others also call Athzoockkuatoriaho); i.e., a genius which they put in the place of God, but they do not worship or present offerings to him. They worship and present offerings to the Devil, whom they call Othkon, or Aireskuoni."

The tribes do not possess any native written records of revelation, but they believe that the Creator has revealed his will to them.

When the missionaries went to the Ojibways, Delawares and Wyandots, proclaiming the Bible as the revelation of God to the human race, the natives listened attentively; and, after deliberation, said that the Bible was for the white men, because it was written in their language, and the Christian religion was for the white race.

Pointing to the skies, the Blackfeet assured me, after presenting the same argument as the tribes mentioned, that the stars were the handwriting of God, and that Nature was the book given for the red men to read, in conjunction with his conscience and his dreams.

Monuncue, the Wyandot chief, objected that the Son of God was born among the white people, and the Bible given to them; and this was the objection of the Blackfeet when they first heard the Gospel. *

The Blackfeet say that the Old Man, Napio, went away after performing great and good things for the people, but he is not dead and he may return. The Twanas and Klallams of the western coast have a myth of the coming of Dokibatt, the "Changer," who did many wonderful things, and went away and left his foot-prints on a rock. Some of the forms of the Hiawatha myth bear a striking resemblance to Christ, and although there is no definite teaching of the advent of a Redeemer, there are evident yearnings in the mythology of the Indians after a

---

* Playter's "History of Methodism in Canada," page 388.

means of escape from sin. The Tlingit hero god Yetl is expected to return, and the Twanas of Washington Territory say that Dokibatt, the Changer, will come back when the earth grows old, to make it over again.*

The red men believe in the immortality of the soul.† The Blackfeet, in common with the other tribes of Canada, placed articles upon the grave for the use of the departed. When they placed the dead in the trees, on a scaffold, or in a "dead lodge," they deposited these articles in a box or wrapped them carefully in some skins or blankets, and when they followed the customs of the white people they put them in the grave in a similar fashion to the articles in the Huron ossuaries. When asked the reason for depositing food, tobacco, bows and arrows, blankets, and numerous trinkets with the dead, they replied that the souls were not dead. They believed that the spirits of the departed returned to take the souls of the articles with them. The Huron "feast of the dead" was an expression of the belief in the immortality of the soul. It was the custom of the Sioux of the North-West to kill the horse of the deceased chief, that the soul of the animal might accompany his master to the spirit-land. Several years ago I visited the grave of a young Sioux Indian, the son of a chief, at Moose Jaw, and under the scaffold were the remains of a horse which had been killed. The Blackfeet do not slay a horse now when the owner dies, but cut off some of the hair from the forelock, mane and tail of his best animals, and these tufts of hair are deposited beside the corpse. It was the custom of some of the tribes to kill a dog, that the spirit of the dog might accompany his master to the land of souls. The Iroquois were accustomed to make a hole in the grave, and recently in the coffin, to permit the spirit to visit the body.

The Blackfeet say that the spirits of the dead return to earth, and can inflict harm to any who may have wronged them when alive. I have seen the Blood Indians tear down their

---

* "Smithsonian Anthropological Papers," page 681. Boaz's "Fifth Report on the North-Western Tribes of Canada," page 49.

† Brinton's "Myths of the New World," pages 249, 272, 273.

log house where a member of the family had died, afraid to
remain there lest the spirits of the dead would hurt them.
They have removed their camps when one of their number died
for the same reason. They believe the spirits of the dead hold
a council and feast together on the good things which have been
placed on the grave of one who has just died. The natives are
afraid of the spirits who hover near the place where their
bodies are laid. Sometimes they have warned me when travelling at night near the camps, to beware of the bodies placed in
the trees or on scaffolds, as the spirits might attack me. Dr.
Boaz says of the Kootaneys, "The dead go to the sun. One of
the important features of their religion is the belief that all the
dead will return at a future time. This event is expected to
take place at Lake Pend Oreille; therefore all Kutonaqa tribes
used to assemble there from time to time to await the dead.
On their journey they danced every night around a fire, going
in the direction of the sun. Only those who were at war with
any tribe or family, danced the opposite way. The festival at
the lake, which lasted many days, and consisted principally of
dances, was celebrated only at rare intervals."

The western tribes, including the Blackfeet, Kwakiutls,
Coast Salish, and others believe that they can see the spirits of
the dead, and to see them is a bad omen, bringing death or sickness. The Tlingits and Kwakiutls believe in the transmigration
of souls, the latter holding a special doctrine, of twins being
transformed salmon, and consequently they have control of the
weather, and must not go near the water lest they be retransformed into salmon. With this same belief in immortality, the
various tribes supposed that the soul of a slain warrior would
not rest peacefully in the spirit-land until his death was
avenged. This is the reason why Indians will sometimes slay
a stranger belonging to the white race, who has known nothing
of the Indian killed by a white man. The after life is a land
of shades, but with this belief in immortality there is the doctrine of a resurrection, shown by the care taken of the remains
of the dead. There are not any of these doctrines clearly
defined by the natives, but amid the confusion, there are

customs sufficient to determine their existence as powerful factors in the religious life of the people.*

There is not a tribe in Canada that does not believe in prayer and adhere strictly to the belief. Several of the western tribes, including the Blackfeet, Kootaneys, Tlingits, Tshimpseans, Haidas and Coast Salish pray to the sun. Some of them pray to mountains, the thunder and natural objects. They pray to mediators, who hear and help them. When the people are sick the medicine men, along with the friends of the sick person, pray to their guardian spirits to help the sick one. I have seen the old man raise his eyes to heaven and pray fervently to the sun, and the young man pray with deep sincerity at the annual sun dance, as he clasped the medicine pole when undergoing the trying ordeal of mutilation. Prayer is extemporaneous and sincere.

The medicine men of the tribes were the doctors and priests, who cared for the souls and bodies of the people. Besides administering medicine they were the protectors of the native religion and keepers of the faith. As such they opposed sternly the introduction of Christianity, sang their incantation songs, and prayed for blessings to rest upon the tribe. They fasted on behalf of the tribe, kept up communion with the spirits, and lived a separate mysterious life from the rest of the people. The Crees and Ojibways have forms of admittance into the priesthood, of which there are four grades, and the priest who attains the highest grade must be a man of wealth, ability and piety.

The journey of the spirits to the land of shadows is represented as a long and difficult road, having a river crossing it, which the Tlingits say is formed by the tears of the women weeping for the dead. The Twanas maintain that a man may be alive and his spirit in the spirit-land, as the spirits can leave their country, and returning, take with them a man's soul. The shamans pretend that they can visit the land of spirits

---

* Theo. Sagard's "Histoire du Canada," page 497. "Third Annual Report of the Canadian Institute," page 9. Charlevoix's "Nouvelle France," Vol. VI., page 78. Morgan's "League of the Iroquois," page 176.

and engage in battle with the spirits, restoring the lost souls to
their bodies on earth. The river of death, the styx of the
ancient Greeks, fabled to flow in the world of the dead, trans-
ferred to Christian literature, and used figuratively as the
Jordan which lies between earth and the heavenly Canaan, is
found in the mythology of the native tribes. The Twanas of
Washington territory, the Tlingits of British Columbia, and
the tribes which live near the sea or beside inland waters have
a fabled river lying across the pathway which souls must
travel to the other land. The passage of the dead, and the
appearance and condition of the land of the spirits are modified by the geographical conditions of the country in which the
tribes dwell. Thus the hunting tribes, living upon the prairie,
or in the forest, speak of their future abode as a place where
they will hunt, as they have done upon the earth; and the
fishing tribes believe that in the other world they will have
abundance of fish. The Ojibway, Blackfoot, Cree and other
inland tribes believe in the happy hunting ground, the Tlingits
say they will enjoy berries and salmon, the Tshimpseans and
Kwakiutls that the land of spirits is similar to the land of the
living, where there will be abundance of fish, venison and skins.

The spirit-land is for all. The native races in their primitive
theology have only one place for all the dead. There is no
distinction made between the good and the bad, and consequently no hell and heaven in accordance with the definitions
of Christian theology. A distinction is made by some natives
about the abode of suicides, but generally the native theology,
uninfluenced by Christian teaching, knows nothing of separate abodes for the good and bad in the future life. The
home of the dead, according to the Indians of Puget Sound,
is an underground world, somewhere within the earth, and yet
neither above or below. The Tlingits and Haidas, influenced,
it may be, by the Eskimos, believe that the dead live in a
country similar to the land of the living, but that those who
suffer a violent death go to the upper country, ruled by Tahit,
and those who die from sickness travel to a land beyond the

borders of the earth, but on the same level with it. They say the dead from both countries live together during the day.

Among the Eskimos there is a distinction made in man's future abode, there being an upper world where all will go who have lived righteously, been kind to the poor and hungry, and those who have been killed by accident or have committed suicide. The Eskimos' heaven is a pleasant country, where it is never dark, and in everlasting content and joy, with no storms, ice or snow to annoy them, the Eskimos spend the eternal years. To the under world the wicked and all who have been unhappy while on earth go at death. It is an eternal land of darkness, cold and dismal, terrible storms, perpetual snow and ice in abundance prevailing there.

The Peruvians believed that after a terrible famine the world would come to an end, when clouds would cover the face of the sun, and thick darkness descend upon all things. The Aztecs looked forward to the destruction of the world, the sun, and the human race. At the close of the great cycle of fifty-two years the little images of the household gods were destroyed, the holy fires were suffered to go out in the temples, and none were rekindled, and the people were in despair in expectation of a great catastrophe. On the last evening of the cycle, a procession of Aztec priests moved toward a lofty mountain, where the new fire was kindled by the friction of sticks, and the success of the operation was an assurance that the end had not yet come.* When the world will be near its end, then will Michabo destroy the nations with a dreadful pestilence, or cause the earth to be consumed; and he will, according to the Algonquins, make a new world for the faithful. That the world will be consumed by fire is the belief of the Senels, of California. In the presence of the unknown the red men sit in fear, longing for relief and hoping for the coming of the day,

---

* Prescott's "Conquest of Mexico," Vol. I., pages 64, 104-106. Eells' "Worship and Traditions of the Aborigines of America," page 29. Brinton's "Myths of the New World," pages 235, 236. "Eleventh Annual Report of the Bureau of Ethnology," pages 361-544.

THE INDIAN MESSIAH.*

The red man is superstitious, as the savage races of other lands, and none the less honest in his religious convictions. His religious belief enters into all the concerns of camp life and tinges every thought and custom in the lodge, on the warpath, and in the council. His traditions, local and general, are affected by his environment, and these again exert an abiding influence upon his religious opinions. Among the tales of the lodges, there are some which have striking resemblance to Biblical stories, some of which, no doubt, have originated indirectly through the influence of religious teachers. During my early years among the Indians in the west, whenever the aged men were asked to relate the story of the creation of the world or of man's origin, they invariably repeated the native myth. In later years, however, new stories are told, based upon the instructions given by the missionaries. The natives did not care to be singular, nor did they care to be laughed at when they told their native tales, so they repeated, as best they could, the stories told by the white men. They were neither Indian nor English, but rather Indianized stories of the Bible.

In the same way have I listened to Indian tunes sung to hymns — such weird music, so fascinating and so strange, arising perhaps from its novelty ; and these tunes had been taught them by missionaries many years ago, but having passed through the alembic of the Indian's mind, they became essentially Indian.

The Christ traditions of the Mexican Indians have no doubt arisen in a similar manner, and have spread to other tribes on the continent. There is, however, a tradition concerning the second advent of a Messiah which was believed to have been fulfilled when Cortez landed in Mexico. The traditions of the Aztec say that a saintly personage, named Quetzalcoatl—*i.e.,*" the plumed serpent "—came from the east as a divine helper to the

*"Journal of American Folk-Lore," Vol. IV., pages 57-60. *The Archæologist*, Vol. II., pages 105-111. "American Antiquarian," Vol. XIII., page 161. "Eleventh Annual Report of the Bureau of Ethnology," page 544.

nation. He was a large, well-formed white man, with a long
beard, intelligent countenance, having a mitre upon his head,
and his white garments flowing to his feet, whereon were
painted red crosses. He was a celibate, a man of peace, detest-
ing war so much that at the mention of the name he put his
fingers in his ears; an ascetic, who hated bloody sacrifices, but
delighted in fruits and flowers; a man of prayer and purity of
life, and the author of all that was good for man, producing the
arts of peace, and sending joy to the hearts and homes of the
people. He had a bitter antagonist in an evil divinity, named
Tezcatlipoca, who, by his wiles, caused him to wander from the
country. Several years after his departure, he sent back word
that he would return, and then he sailed away to the east in a
canoe of serpent skins.

When the Spaniards landed upon the new continent, Montezuma believed that the great white personage had returned, and
he sent his interpreter to Cortez welcoming him to his country
as his right, for they were all his children. After the Spaniards
had treated the natives harshly, the Indians learned, to their
sorrow, the mistake which they had made. They had eagerly
kissed the sides of the Spanish vessels as they landed upon
their shores, and received the white strangers as gods, sons and
brothers of Quetzalcoatl; but they had ultimately to bend their
necks before their mighty conquerors. General Lew Wallace, in
"The Fair God," has given a striking representation of this
tradition, and its sad consequences to the people, with the fall
of Montezuma's kingdom. Some of the native tribes have
traditions of a great teacher, changer, supreme being, a personage resembling Hiawatha or Christ, who came among men and
departed, promising to return again.

There have been shrewd, intelligent men in the Indian
camps who were subjects of apparitions and visions; and these
have exercised a strong influence over the minds of the natives.
Such have been found among the Ojibway, Sioux, Blackfoot
and other Indian tribes. These visions generally relate to
spiritual things, and especially to their own religion, but in
some instances they point to a time when the Indians shall

again be masters of the soil. Some of these prophets have
been successful in imposing upon the people of the lodges, but
the advent of the white man has brought about a change, and
the wiles of the dreamer are not as powerful as in earlier days.
The medicine men are adepts at this superstitious craze, being
able to lead the fearful and unwary through their rites of
sorcery and incantations to a firm belief in all their predictions.
The greatest medicine man of the tribe may be the most
inveterate thief or rogue in the camp, and yet they will
accept his prophecies, believe in his cures, and laugh at his
tricks of stealing and lies. The superstitious reverence of the
Indian compels him to select the strangely-shaped stones and
trees that skirt the rivers or dot the prairie as stopping places
of the gods.

The Sioux in the Minnesota massacre believed that the time
was ripe for them to rise, and their gods would give them success. Their medicine men, their makers of wakan, beat upon
their medicine drums, danced, sang and prayed, but the gods
were deaf to their entreaties, and the Indians failed. The
failure of their predictions, and the fact that their prayers
remained unanswered, influenced many to decide in favor of
Christianity. In 1890 a decided religious movement, known as
the "Messiah Craze," was witnessed among the Indians of the
north-western portion of the United States, its ulterior effects
reaching the Blackfeet, Sioux and Crees of Canada. Various
causes have been assigned for this strange movement, as the
poverty of the people arousing them to look for the advent of
the Messiah, the desire after supernatural aid, and the hatred of
the white race, compelling them to believe that Christianity, in
the form presented to them by the missionaries, was the white
man's religion; but that the Christ was the Redeemer of the
Indians as well as of the white people and the Saviour, as
taught them, was the white man's conception and untrue, as
there was an Indian Christ. The people in the valley of the
Missouri were expectant, and the hope of the advent of the
Messiah spread among the tribes.

The Sioux, Cheyennes and Arapahos heard that the Christ

had been seen, and a delegation of three Sioux and Porcupine, a Cheyenne, went to the country where it was said the Christ was living.

Good Thunder, one of the delegation, upon his return told his experience as follows: "With three others I travelled three years to the Christ. We crossed many Indian Reservations, and passed through the white man's towns. On a broad plain covered with Indians I saw him at last. I could not tell where he came from—suddenly he appeared to me—a man of surprising beauty with long, golden hair—clad in a blue robe. He did not look at me nor speak, but he read our thoughts and answered them without speech. I saw the prints of the nails in his hands and feet.

"He said that he had come upon earth once before—he had appeared to the whites and they had scorned him and slain him. Now he appeared to the Indians. He said that the crying of the Indians had sounded loud in his ears—they were dying of disease and starvation; dying of the white man's food and his strange ways. He was come to save them. He had meant to come in three days—meaning years—but the cries of the poor Indians moved his pity. He would therefore come to them to-morrow—meaning next summer. He would then gather together the souls of the Indians, and they would be in Paradise, hunting the buffalo and living in skin tents as in the old days. The souls of murderers and thieves, however, must wait for some time in outer darkness. The Indians offered Christ a pipe, tobacco pouch and moccasins, he handed the two first to others who were with him, but kept the moccasins. Three birds—the eagle, dove and hawk—attended him."

Chief Porcupine preached this new religion after his return to Pine Ridge, and as one of the delegation, he is reported to have said: "The Fisheaters, near Pyramid Lake, told me that Christ had appeared on earth again. They said Christ knew He was coming; that eleven of His children were also coming from a far land. It appeared that Christ had sent for me to go there, and that is why, unconsciously, I took my journey. It had been foreordained. They told me when I got there that my Great Father was there also, but I did not know who he was. The people assembled called a council, and the chief's sons went to see the Great Father, who sent us to remain fourteen days in that camp, and that then he would come and see us. At the end of two days, on the third morning, hundreds of people gathered at this place. They cleared a place near the agency in the form of a circus ring, and we all gathered there. Just before sundown I saw a great many people, mostly Indians, coming dressed in white men's clothes. The Christ was with them. They all formed in this ring and around it : they put up sheets all around the circle, as they had no tents.

"Just after dark some of the Indians told me that Christ had arrived. I looked around to find him, and finally saw him sitting on one side of the ring. He was dressed in a white coat with stripes. The rest of his dress was a white man's, except that he had on a pair of moccasins. Then he began our dance, everybody joining in, the Christ singing while we danced. We danced till late in the night, when he told us that we had danced enough. The next morning he told us he was going away that day, but would be back the next morning and talk to us. I heard that Christ had been crucified, and I looked to see, and I saw a scar on his wrist and on his face, and he seemed to be the man : I could not see his feet. He would talk to us all day. That evening we all assembled again to see him depart. When we were assembled he began to sing, and he began to tremble all over violently for a while, and then sat down. We danced all that night, the Christ lying down beside us, apparently dead.

"The following morning the Christ was back with us, and wanted to talk to us. He said, 'I am the man who made everything you see around you. I am not lying to you, my children. I made this earth and everything on it. I have been to heaven and seen your dead friends, and have seen my father and mother.' He spoke to us about fighting, and said that it was bad, and that we must keep from it—the earth was to be all good hereafter, that we must be friends with one another.

He said if any man disobeyed what he ordered, his tribe would be wiped from the face of the earth.

" Ever since the Christ I speak of talked to me I have thought what he said was good. I have seen nothing bad in it. When I got back, I knew my people were bad, and had heard nothing of all this, so I got them together and told them of it, and warned them to listen to it for their own good. I told them just what I have told you here to-day."

Part of the outward ceremonial of this religious movement was the ghost dance, in which men women and children clasped hands, and together danced around a sacred tree, singing native songs, as the medicine men uttered strange cries and prayers. As the dancers grew excited some fell down in a trance, and when they awoke related marvellous tales of the land of spirits, where the beautiful scenery abundance of game, and continual happiness of the dwellers delighted them so much that earth was a dreary waste, with its former pleasures all faded and gone. Although the movement was suppressed by the force of arms and the failure of the predictions of the prophets of this superstition, there are some who still believe that the Christ came at that particular period, and revealed himself as the Saviour of the Indian race.

CHAPTER VI.

RACES AND LANGUAGES.

THE LITERATURE OF EASTERN AND CENTRAL CANADA.

THE heroic age in Canada is not lacking in subjects worthy of the pen of the historian, novelist or poet, or the pencil and brush of the artist. Some of our most noted American writers explored the untrodden field of native lore for original subjects, and their laurels were won in revealing the heroism of savages, the gracefulness and beauty of swarthy maidens, the stirring deeds of a period supposed by many to be a barren waste, and the strength and purity of intellect and imagination, and the deep religious spirit of the red men hidden in their mythology and customs. Albert Gallatin laid the foundation of our study upon this continent of the Indian languages, the results of his studies being embodied in his great work, "Synopsis of the Indian Tribes of North America." He was followed by two scholars eminent in the field of native lore —Peter S. Duponceau and the Moravian missionary, John Heckewelder. The most industrious of all investigators in the study of the customs, traditions and languages of the red men was Henry B. Schoolcraft, who devoted more than thirty years to the amassing of information and the publication of works relating to the languages and folk-lore of the natives of the northern part of the continent. He published " Oneota," " Algic Researches," which was afterwards issued as "The Myth of Hiawatha," "Notes on the Iroquois," "Personal Memoirs of a Residence of Thirty Years with the Indian

RACES AND LANGUAGES. 457

Tribes," and his greatest work "History, Condition and Pro-
spects of the Indian Tribes of the United States." This last
work was published by the American Government in six quarto
volumes, and has been characterized by Parkman as "a
singularly crude and illiterate production, stuffed with blunders
and contradictions, giving evidence on every page of a striking
unfitness either for historical or scientific inquiry, and taxing
to the utmost the patience of those who would extract what is
valuable in it from its oceans of pedantic verbiage." The chief
merit of Schoolcraft's works has been the preservation of
valuable documents. He was lacking in critical power, unable
to select wisely, but was intensely in earnest in collecting facts
and fancies, which he oftentimes erroneously interpreted.

Longfellow's poem on Hiawatha was based on the myth
which Schoolcraft had dug from the folk-lore of the Ojibways,
and the success of the poem directed the reading public to the
intensely interesting character of the legendary lore of the
natives of the New Continent. Fenimore Cooper followed in
the train of these investigators, weaving facts and fancies into
stirring works of fiction, which found a numerous host of
readers in the Old and New Worlds, and seem to be as popular
as when written. The interest awakened by Heckewelder and
Cooper in the red men aroused other writers to employ their
pens in this special field of romance, and among the numerous
novels produced were Simm's stirring story, "The Yemassee,"
and the pathetic tale, "Ramona," by Helen Hunt Jackson, aptly
named the Uncle Tom's Cabin of the American Indian race.

The heroic age in Canada is not a barren period, but abounds
in subjects for the writer of prose and the maker of poetry.
The French period is prolific in materials relating to the life of
the forest rangers and voyageurs. The adventures of Du Lhut,
the Robin Hood of the Canadian greenwood, after whom the
City of Duluth is named, would make a stirring volume for the
youth of our land. Longfellow found on Canadian soil the
subject for his immortal poem "Evangeline"; and Parkman,
delving deep in our archives, resuscitated the hidden lore of
other days, and won immortal fame. Much remains to be

written of the virtues of Madame Perade, who is known as the
youthful heroine of Verchères, when, as a girl of fourteen, she
faced a band of Iroquois warriors and saved a fort by her courage and wonderful presence of mind. The pen of the ready
writer can find an appropriate subject in the legend of the death
of Father La Brosse, the devoted missionary among the Montagnais, in the Saguenay region. He died at Tadousac, and the
old folks say on that night the bells in all the mission churches
which he served, on the mainland and on the islands of the
Lower St. Lawrence, tolled of their own accord, all the people
crying, "Alas! our good missionary is dead; he warned us we
should never see him more."

Charlevoix, the famous French traveller and early historian
of Canada, in his "Histoire de la Nouvelle France," published in
1744, and "Letters to the Duchess of Lesdiguieres," gave much
valuable information relating to Canada and the Canadian
Indians. Besides treating of the French posts and settlements,
the mines, fisheries, plants and animals, the lakes, waterfalls
and rivers, and the manner of navigating them, he treated of
the character of the native tribes, their customs and traditions,
languages, government and religion. The languages of Canada
upon which he made special comments, were the Huron, Algonquin and Pottawatomi. His history was praised by scholars
and freely quoted as an authority, yet it was not until 1865 that
an English edition was published, which was issued in six
volumes at New York, by John Gilmary Shea.

Father Gabriel Sagard was one of our earliest Huron scholars.
In 1632 there was published in Paris "Le Grand Voyage du
pays des Hurons," which was followed by a dictionary of the
Huron language, and in 1636 his "Histoire du Canada et
Voyages que les frères Mineurs Recollets y ont faicts pour la
Conversion des Infidèles depuis l'an 1615." We are indebted
to Father Sagard for many facts relating to the customs of the
Hurons, their religious belief and political system. Another of
the early historians was Marc Lescarbot, who, in 1609, published
his "History of New France" in the French language. The
historians of the French period were not men of the study, who

formed their opinions by consulting manuscripts and books, but they were priests who travelled extensively among the native tribes, learning the languages and becoming conversant with the savage customs and belief of their dusky adherents, as they taught them the way of the cross; or they were soldiers and adventurers, who became enamoured of the forest life, or were aroused by a spirit of enterprise and desire for discovery; and as they travelled gathered information and formed their opinions through personal observation. Scattered throughout the pages of their books are discussions on the languages of the natives, with short vocabularies, folk-tales, traditions and recitals of religious feasts.

Lescarbot's writings were no exception, and in his pages are to be found a discussion on the languages of the natives, with short vocabularies of the Algonquin, Huron, Etchemin and Souriquois. Baron de la Hontan's "Nouveaus Voyages" were published in Paris and London in 1703. La Hontan arrived in Canada in 1683, and was stationed as a soldier at several important forts, including Frontenac, Niagara and St. Joseph. His military duties gave him opportunities of seeing the country and learning something of the natives; but truth and fiction are so blended in his writings that they have long since ceased to have any authority. The intrepid explorer and historian, Samuel de Champlain, was in the habit of keeping a journal of his observations, which was published in several volumes. In 1603, a small book of eighty pages was issued, entitled "Des Sauvages," giving an account of his voyage across the Atlantic and a description of the Gulf and River St. Lawrence, with numerous details of the scenery, the animals and birds, and the character and habits of the natives. "Les Voyages du Sieur de Champlain" was published in 1613, "Voyages et Descouvertures" in 1619, and "Les Voyages de la Nouvelle France Occidentale" in 1632. The genial Governor of New France relates, with the skill and confidence of a close observer of the ways of nature and men, his dealings with the savages, the dress, war and burial customs, feasts and religious ideas of the natives, the missions of the Recollet Fathers, his explorations

on the Ottawa, Lakes Nipissing, Huron and Ontario, with
reflections upon the Huron and neighboring Indian tribes.
Champlain's volumes are a mine of lore relating to early
Canadian history and the native tribes of Canada inhabiting
the provinces of Ontario and Quebec. Boucher, the Governor of
Three Rivers, published at Paris, in 1664, a faithful but super-
ficial account of Canada, detailing the habits of the savages and
the condition of the country. In the same year the Père du
Creux issued his tedious Latin compilation of the Jesuit Rela-
tions, with some additions from another source, bearing the
title " Historiæ Canadensis." A rare historical account of the
French colony and the missionary work of the Recollet Fathers
was given by Le Clercq in 1691, and published in two volumes,
with the title "Etablissement de la Foi," as also another work,
" Nouvelle Relation de la Gaspésie," in the same year. The
Jesuit Lafitau published at Paris, in 1724, his "Mœurs des
Sauvages Amériquains," in two volumes, with various plates.
The author had spent several years among the Iroquois, and his
work deals chiefly with the Indians. It is of great historical
value, as Lafitau was a careful observer, and narrated accurately
the results of his travels. Parkman says he is " the most satisfactory of the elder writers;" and Charlevoix said, twenty years
after the book was published, " We have nothing so exact on
the subject." Bacqueville de la Potherie published, in 1722 and
again in 1753, his " Histoire de l'Amerique Septer. rionale," in
four volumes. Although characterized by Charlevoix as an
undigested and ill-written narrative, it has been frequently
quoted, and is a respectable authority upon the French establishments at Quebec, Montreal and Three Rivers : but its chief
value lies in the faithful account of the condition of the Indians
from 1534 to 1701. In 1791 there was published in London
" Voyages and Travels of an Indian Interpreter and Trader,"
by John Long. This work gives an account of the posts on the
St. Lawrence and Lake Ontario, the fur trade, and the observations of the writer during his residence in the country. It
contains speeches in the Ojibway language, with English translations, numerals from one to one thousand in the Iroquois,

Algonquin and Ojibway languages and vocabularies of the Mohegan, Shawnee, Algonquin and Ojibway.

Among English writers on Canada and the red men in general, not including historians, poets, or essayists, who cannot be classed as producers of Canadian-Indian literature, are: Heriot, the Deputy Postmaster-General of British North America, Colonel de Peyster, Judge Haliburton, and Mrs. Jameson. George Heriot's "Travels Through the Canadas" sheds some light on the native languages, discussing the origin of language, diversity of tongues in America, grammatical notes and vocabulary of the Algonquin language, with "O ! Salutaris Hostia," in the Abnaki, Algonquin, Huron, and Illinois languages. The miscellanies of Colonel de Peyster were privately printed in 1813, at Dumfries, Scotland, and reprinted with additions at New York in 1888. Besides the original letters of De Peyster, Sir John Johnson and Colonel Guy Johnson, the work contains numerous references to the Indians, a short vocabulary of the Ottawa and Ojibway languages, and the distribution of the native tribes. The famous author of "Sam Slick," in "A General Description of Nova Scotia," gives some specimens of the Micmac language, including vocabulary, pronouns, and present and imperfect tenses of the verb *to dance*, with English translations. This work was printed at Halifax in 1823. Mrs. Jameson's "Winter Studies and Summer Rambles in Canada," discusses briefly the Ojibway language, with a few examples.

Books of travel cannot be expected to contain more than a passing reference to the Canadian Aborigines, and it is only when we turn to the works dealing with the scientific aspect of the question, that we find a full discussion of the various phases of life and thought among the natives. Fortunately we have some writers who have studied definitely, and with enthusiasm, the history, condition, languages, folk-lore, religion and government of the savage folk, from the Atlantic to the Pacific, and from the international boundary line to the Arctic Ocean. Although not emanating from Canada, yet because it treats of one of our greatest native confederacies, the famous

work "The League of the Iroquois," by the Hon. Lewis H.
Morgan, must be included in our sketch of the literature.
This is a profound study of the organization polity, customs
and character of an Indian people. Mr. Morgan was adopted a
member of the Senecas, and for nearly forty years he investigated the ancient laws and customs of the Iroquois, producing
several notable works which awakened a deeper interest in the
Indian race.

Horatio Hale, of Clinton, Ontario, is our greatest writer on
the native races. An American by birth, upon graduating at
Harvard in 1837 he was appointed philologist to the United
States Exploring Expedition under Captain Charles Wilkes. In
this capacity he studied a large number of languages in North
and South America, Australia and the Pacific Islands, and
investigated the history, traditions and customs of the people
speaking these languages. Five years were spent in preparing
his special report of the Expedition, which was published at
Philadelphia in 1846, with the title, the "Ethnography and
Philology of the United States Exploring Expedition." A large
number of memoirs on anthropology and ethnology have been
read before learned societies and published. He is a member of
many scientific societies in America and Europe, and is better
known through his writings abroad than at home. His "Iroquois Book of Rites" is a notable work, dealing with the
language, history, customs and traditions of the Iroquois. The
book is a native manuscript of a religious character, as may
be seen from its name, translated by Mr. Hale, with explana-
tory notes. The following memoirs are only a few of his
numerous publications: "Indian Migrations as Evidenced by
Language;" "Report on the Blackfoot Tribes," prepared
under the direction of the British Association;" "The Development of Language;" "Race and Language;" "Tutelo
Tribe and Language;" "The Fall of Hochelaga;" "Origin of
Languages and Antiquity of Speaking Man:" "Aryans in
Science and History:" "Language as a Political Force;"
"Huron Folk-Lore." Mr. Hale's opinions as an ethnologist
have been quoted extensively by European and American

students of anthropology. Sir Daniel Wilson published several important papers on the Canadian Indians. His notable work, "Prehistoric Man: Researches into the Origin of Civilization in the Old and New World," included investigations in modern savagery, based upon his earlier studies on the natives of our Dominion. His memoirs were read before the Canadian Institute, Royal Society of Canada, the Anthropological Institute of Great Britain and Ireland and other learned societies. Some of them were afterwards issued separately and finally incorporated in a posthumous volume, entitled, "The Lost Atlantis and other Ethnographic Studies." Relating especially to the native tribes are the essays: "The Trade and Commerce of the Stone Age," "Pre-Aryan American Man," "The Æsthetic Faculty in Aboriginal Races," and "The Huron Iroquois of Canada, a Typical Race of American Aborigines."

John Reade, our notable litterateur, wrote a few articles for *The Week* on "Nation Building," treating learnedly of the origin, tribal divisions, distribution and gradual disappearance of the natives of our Dominion. Papers, entitled "Some Wabanaki Songs" and "The Basques in North America," were read by him before the Royal Society of Canada, and published in Volumes V. and VI. of the "Proceedings and Transactions of the Society."

A. F. Chamberlain has devoted several years of intense study to the folk-lore and languages of our native tribes. Several of his papers have been read before the Canadian Institute and other societies, or published as magazine articles, and subsequently issued separately. The titles of some of his articles are as follows: "The Relationship of the American Languages," "Notes on the History, Customs, and Beliefs of the Mississauga Indians," "Tales of the Mississaugas," "The Archæology of Scugog Island," "The Eskimo Race and Language," "The Language of the Mississaugas," "The Kootenay Indians," "Contributions towards a Bibliography of the Archæology of the Dominion of Canada and Newfoundland," "Algonquin Onomatology, with some Comparisons with Basque," "The Thunder-Bird Amongst the Algonquins," "Notes on Indian Child Language," "The Aryan Element in Indian Dialects."

30

Dr. Silas T. Rand, missionary among the Micmac Indians, besides numerous translations of hymns, tracts, prayers and portions of Scripture, in the Micmac language, wrote: "A Short Statement of Facts, Relating to the History, Manners, Customs, Language and Literature of the Micmac Tribe of Indians," "First Reading Book in Micmac," in the Pitman phonetic characters, and in Roman letters; "The History of Poor Sarah, a Pious Indian Woman," in the Micmac language; and "A Short Account of the Lord's Work among the Micmac Indians." Dr. Rand was an assiduous translator, well known as an industrious student of native lore, yet excelled as a Latin and Greek scholar, the Latin versions of some of the great hymns of the Christian Church published by him showing wide culture and poetic genius.

Amongst the class of writers on our Indians who may be termed scientific are the accomplished Abbé Cuoq, missionary to the Iroquois at the Lake of Two Mountains, author of "Jugement erroné de M. Ernest Renan sur les Langues Sauvages," "Etudes Philologiques," and numerous translations in the Mohawk and Nipissing tongues; David Boyle, the indefatigable investigator of native lore, whose work as an archæologist in connection with his duties as curator of the museum of the Canadian Institute is destined to bring him prominently before the Canadian public as an enduring memorial of the heroic days of our country; Sir J. W. Dawson, and his son, Dr. G. M. Dawson, and Professor Campbell, of Montreal. Leaving the Indian literature of the western part of the Dominion to be dealt with later on, we come to the modern period of historical writings relating to the native tribes.

A reprint of John de Laet's "L'Histoire du Nouveau Monde," first published in Dutch in 1630 and 1633, and in French in 1640, was issued at Quebec in 1882.

Cadwallader Colden's "History of the Five Indian Nations of Canada" was published at New York in 1727, and in London in 1747. The native religion, customs, laws and forms of government; the wars and treaties; the condition of the trade of the Five Nations with the British, and their relation to the

French, with an account of some of the neighboring tribes, are treated in this work.

Benjamin Slight published at Montreal, in 1844, "Indian researches, or Facts Concerning the North-American Indians."

George Copway, an Ojibway Indian chief, born at the mouth of the river Trent in 1818, and known by the native name, Kagegagahbowh, left Canada when a youth, and was educated in the State of Illinois. For some years he was connected with the press of New York, and lectured extensively in Europe and the United States. After spending twelve years as a missionary to the Ojibway Indians, he published, in 1847, his "Life, History and Travels," which passed through several editions, and, in 1850, "The Traditional History and Characteristic Sketches of the Ojibway Nation." The last years of his life were spent as a missionary among his own people. He died at Pontiac, Michigan, about 1863.

Peter Jones, the famous missionary to the Ojibways of Canada, published at Toronto, in 1860, the "Life and Journals of Kahkewaquonaby (Rev. Peter Jones)," and in 1861, at London, England, his "History of the Ojibway Indians, with Especial Reference to their Conversion to Christianity."

These works contain an interesting account of the travels of the missionary among the Ojibways and neighboring tribes, the traditions, native religion, and customs of the people, with the success of missionary work among them.

Peter Dooyentate Clarke published at Toronto, in 1870, "Origin and Traditional History of the Wyandots, and Sketches of Other Indian Tribes of North America." Traditional stories of Tecumseh and his League, in the years 1811 and 1812, are given, besides an historical sketch of the Huron Indians.

The Rev. George Patterson, D.D., has written several interesting papers upon the Indians of the eastern part of the Dominion, which have been read before learned societies. Among his numerous papers, three notable ones have attracted considerable attention, namely, "The Stone Age in Nova Scotia, as illustrated by a collection of relics presented to Dalhousie College," "The Beothics or Red Indians of Newfoundland," and "Beothic Vocabularies."

A. F. Hunter, of Barrie, has devoted several years investigating the sites of the Huron villages and ossuaries in the counties of Simcoe, York, and Ontario. His papers on "National Characteristics and Migrations of the Hurons," and "French Relics from Village Sites of the Hurons," reveal the qualifications of the successful Indian scholar, original research, literary culture, intense enthusiasm, plodding industry, and the power of discrimination.

Mrs. Matilda Edgar, in 1890, published at Toronto a book of great interest to Canadian readers. "Ten Years of Upper Canada in Peace and War, 1805-1815, being the Ridout Letters, with Annotations," besides dealing with the history of the period, contains the narrative of the captivity among the Shawnee Indians, in 1788, of Thomas Ridout, afterwards Surveyor-General of Upper Canada, and a vocabulary of the Shawnee language. Mrs. Edgar is the granddaughter of Thomas Ridout, the author of the narrative and vocabulary. Her grandfather was captured by the Shawnee Indians, and spent among them the spring and summer of 1788. As an instance of the difficulties under which the captive labored in the preparation of his diary and vocabulary, he says: "I had by this time acquired a tolerable knowledge of their language, and began to understand them, as well as to make myself intelligible. My mistress loved her dish of tea, and with the tea paper I made a book, stitched with the bark of a tree, and with yellow ink of hickory ashes, mixed with a little water, and a pen made with a turkey quill, I wrote down the Indian name of visible objects. In this manner I wrote two little books, which I carried in a pocket torn from my breeches, and worn around my waist, tied by a piece of elm bark."

Mr. Ridout died at Toronto, February 8, 1829, in the seventy-fifth year of his age.

Another valuable work relating to the natives of our country, is "Ancient Lachine and the Massacre of the 5th of August, 1689." The author, D. Girouard, Q.C., M.P., is a distinguished member of the Montreal bar and parliamentarian. Early recitals of the old regime a beautiful description of the island of Montreal, personal notes on De la Salle, the founder of Lachine, the forts, Indian wars, and the trials of the early settlers are recounted in graphic style. Charts and photographs of the early military and religious habitations enliven the pages. At the time of the disaster of 1689 the population of Lachine comprised three hundred and twenty souls, not including the soldiers who kept garrison at the upper end of the village. The Iroquois were greatly embittered against the French on account of the treachery of the Marquis of Lenonville, Governor of New France, who had invited a large number of unsuspecting Indians to attend a feast at Fort Frontenac, in Cataraqui. Ninety-five accepted the Governor's invitation, and upon their arrival they were seized, put in irons and sent prisoners to Quebec. A few of them, including the famous Orcanone, chief of the Five Nations, were transported to France. No sooner had the Marquis of Lenonville left the country, and before Frontenac had reached Canada, the Indians sought a terrible revenge; falling suddenly upon Lachine, the village was reduced to ashes and many of its inhabitants were killed and scalped.

The Abbé H. R. Casgrain has been a most industrious student of Canadian history, and his works are of great interest. His best known works, having special reference to the Indians in their relations to the missionaries, the settlers and the soldiers, are "Légendes Canadiennes," 1861; "Histoire de la Mère de l'Incarnation," 1864; "Guerre du Canada, 1756-1760, Montcalm et Levis," 1891; and "Les Acadieus après leur Dispersion."

The novelist has not been wanting in our native literature. We have not been favored with a Canadian Fenimore Cooper to reveal, with cultured pen, the pathos of native life, and record the thrilling scenes of the warpath and camp. Foreign writers have sought and found subjects for their romances among our forests and lakes.

Numerous tales have been written about our forest life and the red men, and the struggles of New France. G. A. Henty's "With Wolfe in Canada" and Susanna Moodie's "Roughing it in the Bush" and "Life in the Clearings" reveal the wealth of

story in war and peace within the borders of our fair Dominion.
The Abbé Casgrain found, in his private secretary, Joseph Mar-
mette, evidences of literary ability, and encouraged him to
continue his efforts, which have been eminently successful.
The Abbé's secretary was born at St. Thomas de Montmorency
in 1844, and in his youth became enamoured of the novels of
Cooper and Scott, which aroused his imagination, and no doubt
directed his thoughts toward the romantic scenes of our own
history. Destined for the bar, he found a more congenial occupation in his leisure moments by writing historical novels. He
began his literary career with a "few unhealthy narratives,
utterly devoid of thought and equally lacking in style." His
"Charles and Eva," a tale of the taking of Schenectady,
was unfortunate, but his failure stimulated him to form
the plan "of popularizing, by means of dramatic presen-
tations, the noble and glorious deeds which every Canadian
must know." Four historical novels have firmly established
his reputation—"Francois de Bieuville," 1870; "L'Intendant
Bigot," 1872; "Le Chevalier de Mornac," 1873, and "La
Fiancée du Rebelle," 1875.

Mercer Adams' "Algonquin Maiden," Agnes Machar's "Stories
of New France," the writings of Macdonald, Oxley, Kingston,
and Mrs. Traill are intensely interesting, the habits, customs,
traditions and beliefs of the red men adding zest to the historic
scenes and general plots of the novels. Mary Hartwell Cather-
wood, although not a resident of Canada, has written several
admirable romances of the old days of New France and Acadie.
"The Romance of Dollard," 1889; "The Story of Tonty," 1890;
and "The Lady of Fort St. John," 1891. Francis Parkman has
told, in beautiful diction, the story of the long struggle between
France and England for dominance in North America. Canada
has been laid under deep obligations to Parkman for his laborious research and intense devotion to his task of unravelling
the knotted thread of our history. Stories of the Indian tribes,
their traditions and beliefs, their war-feasts and religious
festivals, their form of government and burial customs, their
languages and distributions, tales of the valor and intrigue of

their chiefs, speeches and style of oratory, their wars with
neighboring tribes and with their white enemies, the noble deeds
of the Jesuit missionaries, the prowess of the forest rangers and
fur traders, and the adventures of missionaries and laymen on
the path of exploration enliven the pages of this famous writer
on the native tribes of Canada. The volumes dealing especially
and incidentally with the red men are: "Pioneers of France
in the New World," "The Jesuits in North America," "La Salle
and the Discovery of the Great West," "The Old Regime in
Canada Under Louis XIV.," "Count Frontenac and New France
Under Louis XIV.," and "Montcalm and Wolfe."

Major G. D. Warburton's "The Conquest of Canada," 1849,
abounds in stories of Indian life fascinating and real, which
arouse the interest of the reader and maintain it to the end.
Major John Richardson's "Wacousta," Sir George Head's
"Forest Scenes and Incidents in the Wilds of North America,"
and Sellar's "Gleaner Tales" are full. of stirring incidents of
adventure among the red and white races of our own country.

Although of a religious character, the "Jesuit Relations" are the
chief source of information from 1627 to 1672 on geographical
discovery, the flora and fauna of the country, and the languages, customs, wars, and location of the Indian tribes. The
"Relations" were issued in Paris in a series of forty-one volumes,
concerning which Charlevoix said " There is no other source to
which we can apply for instruction as to the progress of
religion among the savages, or for a knowledge of these people,
all of whose languages the Jesuits spoke. The style of these
" Relations" is extremely simple; but this simplicity itself has not
contributed less to give them a great celebrity than the curious
and edifying matter they contain." Parkman's work on " The
Jesuits in North America " gives him the right to speak authori-
tatively upon the " Relations," of which he says, "Though the
productions of men of scholastic training, they are simple and
often crude in style, as might be expected of narratives hastily
written in Indian lodges or rude mission-houses in the forest,
amid annoyances and interruptions of all kinds. In respect to
the value of their contents, they are exceedingly unequal. . . .

The closest examination has left me no doubt that these missionaries wrote in perfect good faith, and that the "Relations" hold a high place as authentic and trustworthy historical documents. They are very scarce, and no complete collection of them exists in America."

Passamaquoddy and Penobscot tribes have been thoroughly treated in an instructive and entertaining volume by Charles G. Leland, with the title, "The Algonquin Legends of New England." The author spent the summer of 1882 among the Passamaquoddy Indians at Campobello, New Brunswick, and subsequently through interviewing members of the Micmac and Penobscot tribes, and the assistance of persons conversant with the Indian traditions, he gathered the materials for his interesting work, which was published at London, 1884. The Rev. W. R. Harris, Dean of St. Catharines,' issued at Toronto in 1893, "Early Missions in Western Canada," devoted to the labors of the Recollet, Jesuit and Sulpician missionaries. The labors of these devoted men are recounted with numerous stirring episodes of life among the red men, and interesting notes on the customs of the natives.

"Missionary Work among the Ojibway Indians" was published by Rev. E. F. Wilson, founder of the Shingwauk Home, Sault Ste. Marie, at London and New York in 1886, and contains many important facts relating to the language and customs of the Ojibways, with an account of the progress of religion amongst them. Interesting memoirs of Father Isaac Jogues, the Jesuit missionary martyr, have been published in English by the Rev. Dr. Withrow, the cultured editor of the *Methodist Magazine and Review*, and author of several important works relating to Canadian history and European travel, and in French by the Rev. Felix Martin. This latter work has been translated into English by Dr. John Gilmary Shea.

Dr. Withrow's "Native Races of North America" (1895) is a small volume treating of the Cliff-Dwellers, Mound-Builders and Indians of Canada and the United States. The traditional

lore, customs, social and religious burial rites, and native beliefs
of the Indians are well described, and the progress of the
Indians toward civilization, educational effort, and missionary
labors amongst them are told with the pen of a ready writer.
It is an admirable volume, fully illustrated, and cannot fail to
delight and instruct both young and old.

Some interesting monographs on the missionary martyrs of
our country and kindred subjects have also been published by
Dr. Withrow. In the study of biography, besides the works
already mentioned, the student of Canadian Indian literature
cannot afford to neglect Stone's " Life of Chief Joseph Brant "
and " Life and Times of Sir William Johnson."

Many noble poems have been written upon subjects chosen
from the forest and prairie, and the camp and warpath. Customs,
legends and stirring episodes have furnished fruitful themes
for the gifted pens of some of our Canadian poets. Charles
Mair has written an imperishable poem, " Tecumseh." It is a
historical drama, describing the stirring scenes of the war of
1812. The hero is shown to be a true lover of his people,
possessing the qualities of a great statesman, which were
exhibited by his exertions to unite the red race in a grand
federation; and though he signally failed in his patriotic
scheme, he left the impress of his thought upon the native
tribes. In the pages of " Tecumseh " there are many lessons of
patriotism, striking scenes of forest and prairie, and beautiful
lines which stir the imagination and engender thought.
Describing the primeval days of peacefulness on this continent,
the author says :

> "The passionate or calm pageants of the skies
> No artist drew ; but in the auburn west
> Innumerable faces of fair cloud
> Vanished in silent darkness with the day,
> The prairie realm—vast ocean's paraphrase—
> Rich in wild grasses numberless, and flowers
> Unnamed, save in mute Nature's inventory ;
> No civilized barbarian trenched for gain.

> And all that flowed was sweet and uncorrupt,
> The rivers and their tributary streams,
> Undammed, wound on forever, and gave up
> Their lonely torrents to weird gulfs of sea,
> And ocean wastes unshadowed by a sail."

The departure of the soldiers of York for the scene of war in 1812 recalls the Rebellion of 1885:

>   . . .   "On every hand you see
> Through the neglected openings of each house—
> Through doorways—windows—our Canadian maids
> Strained by their parting lovers to their breasts ;
> And loyal matrons busy round their lords,
> Buckling their arms on, or, with tearful eyes,
> Kissing them to the war ! "

Iena, the niece of Tecumseh, as the enemy fires, leaps forward to shield Lefroy, her lover, and is wounded to death. Lefroy expresses his impassioned grief as follows:

> "Silent forever ! Oh, my girl ! my girl !
> Those rich eyes melt; those lips are sun-warm still,
> Millions of creatures throng, and multitudes
> Of heartless beings flaunt upon the earth ;
> There's room enough for them ; but thou, dull Fate !
> Thou cold and partial tender of life's field,
> That pluck'st the flower and leav'st the weed to thrive—
> Thou hadst not room for her ! "

The poem closes with these striking lines:

> "Sleep well, Tecumseh, in thy unknown grave,
> Thou mighty savage, resolute and brave !
> Thou master and strong spirit of the woods,
> Unsheltered traveller in sad solitudes,
> Yearner o'er Wyandot and Cherokee,
> Could'st tell us now what hath been and shall be."

Seventeen pages of interesting notes explain the numerous allusions in the poem, and the impression left upon the mind by the reading of this native historical drama is vivid and abiding. Lescarbot was the earliest of our Canadian poets. In his

collection of verses, appended to his "Histoire de la Nouvelle
France," is a poem commemorating a battle fought by an Indian
chief named Memberton and a neighboring tribe. Upon our
Canadian shores Longfellow found a fitting theme for his
beautiful poem, "Evangeline," and among the Ojibway traditions, the subject matter for " Hiawatha."

J. D. Edgar, M.P., published a suggestive tale in poetic form,
"The White Stone Canoe; a Legend of the Ottawas."
"Manita," a poem based on an Indian legend of Sturgeon Point,
Ontario, was written by William McDonnell, of Lindsay, and
issued at Toronto in 1888. Charles Sangster and the Hon.
Thomas D'Arcy McGee wrote several poems of native life and
customs. The Irish patriot and poet, deeply lamented as a
Canadian statesman, stricken down in the prime of life by the
cruel hand of an assassin, laid at our feet as his homage to the
red men, poems on "The Death of Hudson," "The Launch of
the *Griffin*," "Jacques Cartier," "Jacques Cartier and the Child,"
and "The Arctic Indian's Faith." In the poem on "Jacques
Cartier," after narrating the sorrow of the people of Saint
Malo, over the supposed loss of the brave commodore, and his
return, amid the joy of his townsmen, the land of snow which
he had found in the west is thus described :

"He told them of a region hard, iron-bound, and cold ;
  Nor seas of pearls abounded, nor mines of shining gold ;
  Where the wind from Thule freezes the word upon the lip,
  And the ice in spring comes sailing athwart the early ship !
  He told them of the frozen scene until they thrilled with fear,
  And piled fresh fuel on the hearth to make him better cheer."
  .   .   .   .

"He told them of the Algonquin brave—the hunters of the wild—
  Of how the Indian mother in the forest rocks her child ;
  Of how, poor souls ! they fancy in every living thing
  A spirit good or evil, that claims their worshipping .
  Of how they brought their sick and maimed for him to breath upon,
  And of the wonders wrought for them through the Gospel of St. John."

Charles Sangster's Indian poem, "In the Orillia Woods," is a
native dirge on the departing race which peopled the County

of Simcoe and neighborhood. The poet drew his inspiration
from the great events of our history, and the striking scenery
of forest, lake and river. He published two collections of
verse, "The St. Lawrence and the Saguenay," and "Hesperus,
and other Poems and Lyrics," which were eulogized by the
Canadian press and contemporary poets. A beautiful poem,
frequently quoted, upon the names of places in Acadie and
Cape Breton, was written and published by Richard Hunting-
ton, a Nova Scotian poet and journalist. The first verse reveals
the rhythmic beauty of the poem.

> " The memory of the red men
> How can it pass away,—
> While their names of music linger
> On each mount, and stream, and bay ?—
> While Musquodoboit's waters
> Roll sparkling to the main ; ~
> While falls the laughing sunbeam
> On Chegogin's fields of grain." -

Miss E. Pauline Johnson, the gifted daughter of the late
Chief G. M. Johnson, of the Mohawks, has won favor by the
artistic rendition of her poems on the red men. She has
appeared as the poet-advocate of her race, and especially of the
Iroquois. "The White Wampum" is a quaint-looking little
volume of Indian verse, imaginative and descriptive, with a
richness and beauty that is entrancing. Some of her poems
are gems, and, when recited by Miss Johnson in her Indian
costume, produce a thrilling effect. The following poems
portray all the passion and romance of her race: "The
Avenger," "Red Jacket," and "The Cry of the Indian Woman."
The canoe-song, "In the Shadows," is a fine specimen of her
poetic utterances :

> " I am sailing to the leeward,
>   Where the current runs to seaward,
>   Soft and slow ;
>   Where the sleeping river grasses
>   Brush my paddle as it passes
>   To and fro.

PAULINE JOHNSON, IN INDIAN COSTUME.

" On the shore the heat is shaking,
All golden sands awaking
        In the cove ;
And the quaint sand-piper, winging
O'er the shallows, ceases singing
        When I move.

" On the water's idle pillow
Sleeps the overhanging willow
        Green and cool ;
Where the rushes lift their burnished
Oval heads from out the tarnished
        Emerald pool.

" Where the very water slumbers,
Water-lilies grow in numbers,
        Pure and pale ;
All the morning they have rested,
Amber-crowned and pearly-crested—
        Fair and frail.

" Here, impossible romances,
Indefinable sweet fancies,
        Cluster round ;
But they do not mar the sweetness
Of this still September fleetness
        With a sound.

" I can scarce discern the meeting
Of the shore and stream retreating,
        So remote ;
For the laggard river, dozing,
Only wakes from its reposing
        Where I float.

" Where the river mists are rising,
All the foliage baptizing
        With their spray ;
There the sun gleams far and faintly
With a shadow soft and saintly
        In its ray.

" And the perfume of some burning
Far-off brushwood, ever turning
        To exale ;

All its smoky fragrance, dying,
    In the arms of evening, lying,
        Where I sail.
            .
" My canoe is growing lazy,
    In the atmosphere so hazy,
        While I dream ;
    Half in slumber I am guiding
    Eastward, indistinctly gliding
        Down the stream."

Arthur Weir's "Champlain," "The Captured Flag," "The
Priests and the Ministers," and "L'Ordre de Bon Temps:"
Matthew Richey Knights' "Glooscap" and "The Dying Chief;"
Mrs. S. A. Curzon's "Laura Secord" and "Fort Toronto," and
George Martin's "Marguerite," "The Heroes of Ville Marie,"
and "Changes on the Ottawa," bring vividly before the mind
scenes of other days when the moccasined foot of the warrior
trod gently upon the forest trail, and he welcomed to his sorrow
the pale-faced heir of civilization, who claimed at last the red
man's heritage as his rightful possession.

Of newspapers and magazines a few have appeared in
the interest of our Canadian Indians: *Petaubun* (Peep o'
Day), a monthly periodical, was published at Sarnia in
1861 and 1862, by the Rev. Thomas Hurlburt. Three pages
were printed in the Ojibway and one in the English language. *The Pipe of Peace* was published in 1878 and 1879,
at Sault Ste. Marie, Ontario, by the Rev. E. F. Wilson, of
the Shingwauk Home. The first numbers were printed
in Ojibway and English, and the later issues in Ojibway.
After the suspension of this paper *Our Forest Children*
was begun, the first copy being issued by Mr. Wilson from
the Shingwauk Home in 1887. This also was discontinued,
but was immediately followed in 1890 by *The Canadian
Indian*, with the Rev. E. F. Wilson and Mr. H. B. Small
as editors. It was published under the auspices of the
Canadian Indian Research Society, and existed for two years.
The two latter publications were printed in English for the
purpose of awakening an interest in the Indians and aiding in

the investigation of the folk-lore, languages and customs of the natives and Canadian archæology. *The Indian* was issued as a bi-monthly paper " devoted to the Indians of America," by Chief Kahkewaquonby (Dr. P. E. Jones), in 1885. The office of publication was located at Hagersville, Ont., in close proximity to the Six Nation's Reservation on the Grand River. For a short time the paper was issued weekly, but, like all its predecessors, it ceased to exist within two years, twenty-four numbers being published.

An occasional paper, *The Aboriginal*, was published in New Brunswick, containing notes on the customs of the Indians. *The Young Canadian*, a weekly magazine, devoted to the youth of our Dominion and intended to foster a national pride in Canadian progress, history, manufactures, science, art and literature, was issued at Montreal in 1891, with Margaret Polson Murray as editor-in-chief. Interesting tales of our early history and stories of Indian life, profusely illustrated, adorned its pages, but apparently through the influence of the literature of our Great Neighbor and our limited constituency it failed to win the needful support. *Canada* was another patriotic magazine of excellent merit similar in its aims to *The Young Canadian*, whose pages were filled with tales and poems from some of our best writers. Interesting stories and essays on native life and customs have appeared frequently in the *Methodist Magazine* and *Onward*, under the able supervision of the Rev. Dr. Withrow. *The Canadian Magazine, Manitoba Free Press, Pilot Mound Sentinel*, and the Proceedings and Transactions of the Royal Society of Canada, Canadian Institute, Hamilton Association, Montreal Folk-Lore Society, Quebec Historical Society, Manitoba Historical Society, Nova Scotia Historical Society, Ottawa Literary and Scientific Society, Wentworth historical Society, Elgin Historical and Scientific Institute, Institut Canadien-Francais d'Ottawa, Société Historique de Montreal, and other societies in the Dominion supply valuable papers on the early history of the nation and on the legends, customs, languages and beliefs of the Canadian red men.

Our leading writers upon the Algonquin and Iroquoian

languages are Horatio Hale, A. F. Chamberlain and the Abbé
Cuoq. The Rev. Dr. John Campbell, of Montreal, has discussed
some of the comparative features of these languages with the
Japanese, Basque and Peninsular languages in his interesting
papers, "On the Origin of Some American Indian Tribes," "The
Hittites in America," "The Affiliation of the Algonquin Languages," "Asiatic Tribes in North America," "Some Laws of
Phonetic Change in the Khitan Languages," and "The Khitan
Language ; the Aztec and its Relations." The Abbé J. A. Cuoq
has written an appendix to his Algonquin grammar under the
title, "Anote Kekon," which appeared in the eleventh volume
of the "Proceedings and Transactions of the Royal Society of
Canada," containing valuable reflections on the folk-lore and
literature of the Algonquins, notes on the history of the mission
of the Lake of Two Mountains, and a discussion of the grammatic contents of the language, with examples of familiar
phrases, the divisions of time and natural history. There has
also appeared, in the French section of the "Transactions," his
"Algonquin Grammar." It is a compact, clear, well-arranged
and comprehensive grammar, showing the intricacies of the language in its numerous forms, sufficiently explained and definite
as to enable the student to master its difficulties. Our first
scholar of the Huron tongue was the Jesuit martyr, John
de Brebeuf. In one of his "Relations" there is a treatise on
the Huron language, which has been republished in the "Transactions of the American Antiquarian Society." He wrote a
grammar of the language, which has never been published.
Several treatises on the Micmac language have been published
separately and in conjunction with books of travel. A grammar
of the language was published in England by an unknown
French author, fragments of which have been preserved. The
Abbé Maillard left among his manuscripts a Micmac grammar,
which was published at New York in 1864. The author was
an able scholar, who came to Canada about 1738, and was
appointed Vicar-General of Acadia. He labored among the
Indian tribes and in the Acadian villages in Cape Breton and on
the coast of Miramichi. After many years of great hardship.

31

he died at Halifax, Nova Scotia, in 1768. Father Jacques Bruyas, Superior of the Iroquois mission, left among his papers "Radices Verborum Iroquæorum," containing a grammatic sketch and dictionary of the Mohawk language, written in Latin, with the meaning of the words in French. This treatise was published in 1862, in New York, and is one of the volumes of Shea's Library of American Linguistics. The author was a master of several of the dialects of the Iroquois. He came to Canada in 1666, and died at the mission of Sault St. Louis, on the St. Lawrence, in 1712. A grammar and dictionary of the Ojibway language was published at Toronto in 1874, by the Rev. E. F. Wilson, of Sault Ste. Marie. Manuscript treatises and grammars of the Micmac, Montagnais, Ojibway and Huron languages are extant, but some of the most notable manuscript volumes referred to in the writings of the early missionaries and travellers have been lost. A curious mosaic is the work of the Jesuit missionary, Stephen de Carheil. His "Radical Words of the Huron Language," forms two small duodecimo manuscript volumes in Latin, French and Huron. Of the author it is said, "As a philologist he was remarkable. He spoke Huron and Cayuga with the greatest elegance, and he composed valuable works in and upon both, some of which are extant." Chaumonot's grammar of the Huron language was found among his papers and translated by John Wilkie, from the Latin. Garnier's Huron grammar, in manuscript, is lost, as are also Lalemant's "Principles of the Huron Language," Wood's grammar of the Micmac, and Father Robert Michel Gay's "Grammar Algonquine." A "Grammaire Algonique," in manuscript, is preserved in the Biblioteca Vittorio Emmanuele, at Rome, which is the work of the Abbé Thavenet, and a manuscript translation of this work is preserved among the papers of the world's greatest linguist, Cardinal Mezzofanti, in the Biblioteca Communale, at Bologna. Potier's "Grammar of the Huron language" and other essays on the languages of the Canadian Indians are in the possession of private persons.

The first dictionary of the native languages of Canada was the Huron, prepared by Father Joseph Le Caron. Le Clercq says of this work and its author: "The dictionary of the Huron language was first drafted by Father Joseph Le Caron in 1616. The little Huron whom he took with him when he returned to Quebec, aided him greatly to extend it. He also added rules and principles during his second voyage to the Hurons. He next increased it by notes, which Father Nicolas sent him, and at last perfected it by that which that holy monk had left when descending to Quebec, and which the French placed in his hands; so that Father George, procurator of the mission in France, presented it to the king with the two preliminary dictionaries of the Algonquin and Montagnais languages in 1625." Father Gabriel Sagard's dictionary of the Huron language was published at Paris in 1632. Of the language of the Gaspesians, Christien Le Clercq, inventor of the Micmac hieroglyphics, has given some general remarks in "Nouvelle Relation de la Gaspesie," published at Paris in 1691. Father Sebastien Rasles left a valuable manuscript dictionary of the Abnaki language, which was not published till 1833. The dictionary is in French and Abnaki, and contains an introductory memoir and notes by John Pickering, A.A.S. In the supplementary notes and observations by Mr. Pickering there are extracts from Father Rasles' letters, a description of the original manuscript, the alphabet used by the author, and comments upon the Abnaki and cognate dialects. The following account of Father Rasles and his work is given in the notes and observations:

"Father Rasles, in one of his letters, dated at Nanrantsouak (Norridgwock) the 12th of October, 1723, and published in the *Lettres Edifiantes*, makes the following general remarks upon the Indian languages and his mode of studying them.

"'On the 23rd of July, 1689, I embarked at Rochelle, and after a tolerably good voyage of about three months, I arrived at Quebec the 13th of October of the same year. I at once applied myself to the study of the language of our savages. It is very difficult, for it is not sufficient to study the words and their meaning, and to acquire a stock of words and phrases, but we must acquaint ourselves with the turn and arrangement of them as used by the savages, which can only be attained by intercourse and familiarity with these people.

"'I then took up my residence in a village of the Abnaki Nation, situated in a forest, which is only three leagues from Quebec. This village was inhabited by two hundred savages, who were almost all Christians. Their huts were in regular order, much like that of houses in towns; and an enclosure of high and close pickets formed a kind of bulwark which protected them from the incursions of their enemies. . . . .

"'It was among these people, who pass for the least rude of all our savages, that I went through my apprenticeship as a missionary. My principal occupation was to study their language. It is very difficult to learn, especially when we have only savages for our teachers.

"'They have several letters which are sounded wholly from the throat, without any motion of the lips, ou, for example, is one of the number; and, in writing, we denote this by the figure 8, in order to distinguish it from other characters. I used to spend a part of a day in their huts to hear them talk. It was necessary to give the closest attention in order to connect what they said, and to conjecture their meaning. Sometimes I succeeded, but more frequently I made mistakes; because, not having been trained to the use of their gutturals, I only repeated parts of words, and thus furnished them with occasions of laughing at me. At length, after five months constant application, I accomplished so much as to understand all their terms; but that was not enough to enable me to express myself so as to satisfy their taste.

"'I still had a long progress to make in order to master the turn and genius of their language, which are altogether different from the turn and genius of our European languages. In order to save time, and to qualify myself to exercise my office, I selected some of the savages who had the most intelligence and the best style of speaking. I then expressed to them in my rude terms some of the articles in the catechism; and they rendered them for me with all the delicacy of expression of their idiom; these I committed to writing immediately, and thus in a short time I made a dictionary, and also a catechism, containing the principles and mysteries of religion.'"

The Jesuit missionary Pierre Laure prepared, in 1726, a dictionary of the Montagnais language. In recent years there have appeared an Ojibway dictionary, now out of print, by Peter York, an Indian belonging to the County of Simcoe; an Algonquin dictionary in the French language, by the Abbé J. A. Cuoq; and a Lenâpé-English dictionary, compiled from anonymous manuscripts in the archives of the Moravian Church at Bethlehem, Pennsylvania, by Dr. D. G. Brinton, of the University of Pennsylvania, and the Rev. Albert Seqaqkind Anthony, assistant to the Delawares and Six Nations in Ontario. Dictionaries in manuscript of the Huron language are to be found among the archives of Laval University, and at Lorette. One of these is attributed to Brebeuf, another to Chaumonot, and the others are by authors unknown. A Mohawk dictionary in manuscript, written by La Gallissounière, is deposited in the Bibliothèque Nationale, Paris. Dictionaries in manuscript of the Seneca, Abnaki, Algonquin, Ojibway, Ottawa and Montagnais languages are to be found among the archives of the Catholic churches at Caughnawaga, Pierville and Lake of Two Mountains; Laval University, Quebec, and McGill College, Montreal, and in the possession of private individuals.

There are extant numerous vocabularies of the native languages. Our first published vocabulary was that of Jacques Cartier, in 1545, who left us some specimens of the language of the extinct Hochelagans. Some of these vocabularies are to be found in books of travel and scientific magazines, but the greater part of them remain in manuscript deposited in the archives of churches, colleges, public libraries, historical societies and private persons. Vocabularies of the following languages spoken in the Dominion are known •to exist: Mohawk, Micmac, Seneca, Cayuga, Oneida, Onondaga, Tuscarora, Algonquin, Nanticoke, Shawnee, Abnaki, Mississauga, Ottawa, Acadian, Munsee, Nipissing, Penobscot and Pottawotomi.

Legends and folk-tales from the Cayugas, Onondagas and Tuscaroras, songs of the Abnakis, and legends of the Ojibways,

Micmacs, and Passamaquoddies have been preserved. Some of these are extant in the native tongue and others in translations.

A " Sacred History," in manuscript, in the Mohawk language is among the archives of the Roman Catholic Church, at Caughnawaga, and a " History of the People of God," in the same language, beautifully written and well preserved, in two volumes, is among the archives of the Catholic Church at the Lake of Two Mountains. Both of these works were prepared by the Abbé Terlaye, who was a missionary at La Galette and Lake of Two Mountains. He died at the latter place May 17th, 1777, and was buried here. Of lesser works in the native languages worthy of notice are the " Autobiography of Kaondinoketc," " A Nipissing Chief," " The Story of the Young Cottager," in Ojibway; "The Only Place of Safety," in Micmac: and several tracts by F. A. O'Meara and James Evans.

Nearly the whole of the Bible has been translated into the Ojibway and Micmac. The New Testament has been translated in the Ottawa and Mohawk, and portions of the scriptures in Iroquois, Delaware, Abnaki, Maliseet, Shawnee, Pottawotomi, Huron and Seneca. The leading translators of the scriptures have been Dr. S. T. Rand, Chief Joseph Brant, Chief Joseph of Oka, J. Stuart, B. Freeman, H. A. Hill, J. A. Wilkes, W. Hess, T. S. Harris, A. Wright, F. A. O'Meara, Peter Jones, James Evans, J. Lykins and C. F. Dencke.

Catechisms have been prepared for the use of the Algonquin, Ojibway, Micmac, Nipissing, Ottawa, Munsee and Abnaki Indians.

Prayer books, including the Roman Catholic and Anglican Book of Common Prayer, have been translated into the languages of the Mohawk, Algonquin, Ojibway, Ottawa, Micmac, Munsee, Nipissing, Maliseet, Penobscot and Passamaquoddy tribes.

It is a singular fact that almost the first printed book in the United States and Canada was for the use of the Indians. John Eliot issued his " Massachusetts Catechism " about 1654, and in 1767 Father de la Brosse published the " Roman Catholic Prayer Book, and " A Primer of Christian Doctrine,"

at the press of Brown and Gilmore, of Quebec, in the language
of the Montagnais Indians. "The Anglican Book of Common
Prayer" was printed at the same press, in 1780, in the lan-
guage of the Mohawk Indians, and at the expense of the
Government. The first printing press in Canada was estab-
lished by Bushel in 1751, in Halifax, Nova Scotia, who, in
January of the following year published the first *Canadian
Gazette.*

William Brown and Thomas Gilmore introduced printing into
the Province of Quebec in 1763, and on June 21st, 1764, issued
from the press at Quebec the first number of the *Quebec Gazette*
in French and English. Several little quartos on French law
were published by Brown in 1775; but the first known Canadian book was a catechism by Archbishop Languet, issued in
1765.

Hymn books have been prepared in nearly all the languages
mentioned above, which are used by the missionaries and people.
Sermons, Scripture narratives, calendars, Bible histories, reading
books and spellers, and even a work on church polity have been
translated for the use of some of the tribes. Some of these have
been published, but the most of them remain in manuscript. In
this sketch of the literature relating to the Indians of Ontario,,
Quebec and the Eastern Provinces, the reader cannot fail to be
impressed with the heroic labors of the men who have devoted
their lives to the work of elevating and saving the aborigines
of our land. Amid great privations they toiled, persecuted
sometimes by their flock, burdened with the indifference of their
dusky followers, and opposed by their white brethren, and in
the gloaming of life they were happy, if they beheld an humble
mission-house and church, and a handful of faithful disciples.
Many of them were men of great learning and of gentle birth,
who might have shone as statesmen or ruled as wealthy merchants; but they rejected wealth and fame, and labored with
intense devotion for the sake of a few red men. We have forgotten these heroes of our country, whose delight was to toil
and suffer for others, and their very names sound strangely in
our ears, but they won in life's contest, and in their death they
were more than conquerors.

THE SIGN LANGUAGE.*

Sign language is sometimes called gesture speech, as it is a method of conversing by means of gestures or signs. It is a form of speech in use among civilized and savage races, which is perfectly understood, and although greatly limited in its forms of expression by those who have a spoken language, rich in its vocabulary and possessed of an extensive literature. It is properly designated a language, as among savage races it has various conventional forms, which are in a measure definite and full. As a language it is divided into facial expression and conventional forms. The expression of the faces of individuals is sometimes concealed, as among certain tribes of Indians, by the paint which they use, but when not thus concealed the emotions can easily be detected. The movements of the face are developed by the growth of the mind, which calls new feelings into existence. These movements are the result more especially of the emotions. The instinctive or voluntary play of the features express the feelings, as is shown by babies, who are able to read the expression of the countenances of persons, and can tell their intention toward them.

Facial expression is so complete that instances are known where conversation has been carried on by its use alone. Tribes of Indians are known who are able to state clearly their ideas by means of this play of features. Corporeal motions express operations of the intellect as distinct from facial expression. These corporeal gestures are not only used by man, but are in use among animals. These gestures or signs have become conventionalized, and amongst certain tribes definite.

Animals use sign language as a mode of communication. George Romanes says: "The germ of the sign-making faculty occurs among animals as far down as the ant, and is highly developed among the higher vertebrates. Pointer dogs make

---

* W. P. Clarke, "The Indian Sign Language." Colonel Garrick Mallery, "Sign Language of the North American Indians." "Annual Reports of the Bureau of Ethnology," Vols. I. and X. "The Boys' Own Annual," Vol. XII., pages 492, 508.

signs, terriers 'beg' for food, and the cat, dog, horse and other
animals make signs. The animal is capable of converting the
logic of feelings into the logic of signs for the purpose of communication, and it is a sign language as much as that of the
deaf-mute or savages." *

Sign language is in use amongst civilized races to a limited
degree even at the present day. When we nod the head to
mean "yes" or shake it to mean "no," and when we join hands
in token of friendship, we are using gesture language. If we
were travelling among a people whose language we did not
know we should be compelled to resort to this method of
making ourselves intelligible more extensively.

In the Lowlands of Scotland the boys have a game resembling the pantomimes of the ancients, which were performed by
persons who uttered no words, but imitated the acts of the
persons represented.

In the earliest stages of the human race, when words were
short and few, sign language must have been used extensively
as an aid to the primitive form of speech ; and when tribes and
races were developed, it must have been employed in conversing
with those ignorant of each other's language †

The languages of the tribes of British Columbia and other
parts of Canada are emphasized and their meaning made clear
by the use of intonation and sign language, By laying stress
upon a syllable words are made to have different meanings. I
found a striking illustration of this when I was learning the
Blackfoot language among the Blood Indians. Being desirous
of learning the whereabouts of a friend, who was a member of
the Mounted Police, and was known among the Indians as
"the man who sews," he being by trade a tailor, I said to one
of my Indian companions, "Tcima Awatcînaké ?" but he did not
understand me. Again I essayed "Tcima Awatcînake ?" but
he only shook his head. Finally I asked "Tcima Awátcînake?"
and he smiled and gave me the needful information. The

* "Evolution of the Human Face," by A. H. Thomson, in "American
Antiquarian," Vol. XIV., pages 277-288.
† Edward Clodd's "The Story of Creation," pages 215, 216, and "Child-
hood of the World," page 12.

question I asked him was, " Where is the man who sews ?" In
the Chinook jargon not only is this expressive intonation in
use, but gesture are employed to enlarge the meaning of some
of the words. Thus " kuatan " means " a horse," but " riding
on horseback " is expressed by using the word and the gesture
sign for riding.*

Many of the gestures of the sign language are understood
by deaf mutes, but not all, as even the deaf mute language is
not definite, many conventional terms being employed in
America which are not in use in Europe ; and, indeed, differences
exist among the several institutions for deaf-mute instruction
upon the American continent. Although my personal knowledge of the sign language is quite limited, I have conversed
intelligibly for a short time with a deaf mute whom I met at
Calgary.

The language of gestures is not confined to the Indian tribes,
but traces of its existence have been found in Turkey, Sicily,
the Hawaiian and Fiji Islands, Madagascar and Japan. Collections of signs of great value have been obtained from some of
these countries. An exhaustive collection has been obtained
from Alaska. These collections go far to prove the existence
of a gesture speech of man. We are chiefly concerned, however, with this form of speech among the American Indian
tribes. It has been systematized among some tribes into pictographs, which comprise a native system of hieroglyphics. These
pictographs are the visible representation of the gestures.
These are found painted on the face of cliffs in some of the
strangest places, seldom visited by the white man, upon the
walls of caverns, on buffalo robes and the skins of other
animals, the lodges of the Plain Indians and birch-bark rolls,
and some are even carved on walrus ivory by the tribes of the
far north, especially among the Alaskan Indians. Human
figures are drawn in the attitude of making gestures. Sometimes the differences in the color of the different persons
represented is significant, and is used as an aid to the
interpretation of the gestures. For example, the symbol of

* Wilson's " Artistic Faculty," page 94.

peace is the approaching palms of two persons, and in order
to distinguish them from the approximation of the palms of
one person, the arms are painted in different colors. In a hide
painted for me by a Blood Indian, which contained the record
of the chief exploits of his career very fully depicted, and
with some degree of artistic skill, several of these signs appear.

There is a general system of gesture speech among the
Indian tribes, but it is not to be regarded as a formal or absolute
language. Whilst there exists a similarity between some signs,
and there are some that are in common use among all the tribes,
still there is a diversity which reveals centres of origin, and it
would be impossible to prepare a vocabulary that would be sufficiently definite as to be understood. As there are differences in
spoken language so are there diversities in sign language.
The investigations of Colonel Mallery and Dr. W. J. Hoffman
have been continued for several years upon this subject, and
have covered a large number of Indian tribes, and included
foreign countries, and the result of their united labors have
shown that there are certain groups of tribes which form
centres of origin of the sign language, and that some signs
have become so conventionalized as to have a definite meaning
in one group or tribe which they do not possess in another.
It is not a universal language in the sense of being understood by all the tribes, and still the ideographic signs may
be so interpreted. Gesture language has been divided into five
groups, as follows: First, the Arikara, Dakota, Mandan, Gros
Ventre or Hidatsa, Blackfoot, Crow and other tribes in Montana and Idaho; second, Arapaho, Cheyenne, Pani, Kaiowa,
Caddo, Wichita, Apache of Indian Territory, and other tribes in
the South-West as far as New Mexico, and possibly portions of
Arizona; third, Pima, Yuma, Papago, Maricopa, Hualpai (Yu-
man), and the tribes of Southern California; fourth, Shoshoni,
Banak, Pai Uta of Pyramid Lake, and the tribes of Northern
Idaho and Lower British Columbia, Eastern Washington, and
Oregon; fifth, Alaska, embracing the Southern Eskimo, Kenai,
(Athabascan), and Iakutat and Tshilkaat tribes of the T'hilin-
kit or Koloshan stock.*

* See "Annual Reports of the Bureau of Ethnology."

Sign language is used extensively by the plain tribes of our Canadian North-West. The tribes located in Ontario and Quebec seldom use it, which may arise through their contact with civilization and their imitation of the habits and customs of the white race. Indeed, the gestures employed by the Iroquois are so few that they need not be classified, and the same may be said of the tribes of British Columbia, who possess a sign language, but not sufficiently extensive for classification. Among some Indian tribes the system of gesture speech is so well defined that conversation can be carried on by means of it alone. Indeed, several instances have been known where conversation has taken place by means of the gestures of the face, and without the aid of the hands, which shows the possibilities of intellectual expressions of the face as well as emotional. The use of this language has been kept up amongst the savage tribes more than others, on account of their surroundings. Accustomed to live in situations where noise is dangerous, lest they might alarm their warlike foes, the gesture speech has been preserved as a useful adjunct to spoken language

North Axe, a Piegan Indian chief, residing on his Reserve, which is located in Southern Alberta, as he lay at the point of death unable to speak, gave instructions to the Indian agent to send his son and brother to the Brantford Institute to be educated. His wishes were conveyed by means of signs. Upon the same Reserve, during my residence in that part of the country, there lived two boys and a girl, deaf and dumb, who were able to converse with their companions and friends by signs. Kutenaekwân, a Blood Indian, was so badly shattered with gun-shot wounds that he was unable to hear or speak ; yet I have watched him for hours telling his friends the great exploits of his life. As he became excited with his narrations, his friends grew enthusiastic and encouraged him to continue his story.

A few of the gesture signs may be given to show the use made of them in expressing the ideas and emotions of the natives. Anger is almost always betrayed by the eyes, fear by the dirty greyish color of the skin, and surprise by suddenly

drawing in the breath, as if gasping. I have seen the natives
when astonished—the astonishment arising from sad news or a
message of joy—place the hand upon the mouth, covering it.
Usually, if not always, the palm of the right hand is placed
over the mouth to signify astonishment. The Apaches rarely
point to an object with the finger, but raise the chin and point
the lips toward it. In calling the attention of a person at a
distance, the right hand is raised at arm's length above the head,
with the fingers extended, and the hand moved quickly backward and forward from the wrist, the arm remaining motionless.
An Indian riding upon the prairie will stop when he sees a
man perform this sign. Should the man wish the horseman to
come to him, he will sway the hand with the palm facing the
ground, the whole arm from the shoulder performing a forward
and downward motion, till the hand reaches the knees. This
will be repeated two or three times, till the rider sees distinctly
what is intended. Walking along the Reserve one day I was
anxious to speak to a white man who was half a mile distant,
and was walking in the opposite direction, so that he was
beyond the reach of my voice. Owing to the voices of children
and the rushing of the water in the river, I could not make
myself heard by any natural or artificial call. Beyond the
white man was an Indian on foot coming toward me, and not
far from my friend. One of the Blood Indians standing beside
me came to my rescue, and making the sign to the Indian at a
distance to arrest his attention, told him in the sign language
to inform the white man that he was wanted. The Indian
meeting my white friend told him the result of the conversation, when he suddenly turned around and walked back to the
place where I was waiting for him. This is one of the methods
of what might not be inappropriately termed the native system
of telegraphy. Signal fires, different methods of riding on
horseback, signs made with blankets and stones, and the striking use of the looking-glass make up a very effective system of
communication at a distance upon the prairie. The sign for
rain is made by holding the hands in front of the shoulders,
the fingers hanging down to represent the drops. Lightning is

represented by pointing the forefinger of the right hand
upward, and bringing it down with great rapidity, with a
sinuous motion, showing the course of the lightning.

Various signs are used to distinguish the tribes. The sign
for the Blackfeet is, the right hand closed, the two forefingers
extended, and the hand pushed outward and downward over the
right foot. The sign for the Piegans is made by closing the right
hand, and the fist, with the thumb toward the face, revolving
quickly over the upper extremity of the right cheek-bone, with
an outward motion. The Blood Indians are distinguished by
the closed right hand with the two forefingers extended, pushed
horizontally across the chin close under the lip, from right to left.
The Sarcee sign is the thumb and forefinger of the right hand
brought to the right corner of the closed lip, and the points of
the finger and thumb rubbed gently together. The Dakotahs
are denoted by drawing the right hand across the throat, signifying that they cut the throats of their enemies. The Gros
Ventres, by bringing the points of the open hands toward each
other, palms toward the person and close to the breast, and then,
by an outward and downward motion, the expression of big
bellies is made. The Crow Indians are designated by the hands
held out from the sides, palms downward, raised up and down
to represent the flapping of the wings of a crow or bird; and the
gesture sign for white man is to draw the open right hand horizontally from left to right across the forehead a little above
the eyebrows, the back of the hand to be upward and the fingers
pointing toward the left; this sign may also be given by performing the same act with the forefinger of the right hand.
The sign for peace is the palms of two persons made to approach
each other. When it is intended to represent speech, the right
hand is brought toward the mouth with the palm upward and
pushed outward to mark the flow of the words. If, however,
the speech has been made by a missionary or member of the
medical priesthood, the idea of holy or supernatural must be
expressed, and this is done by holding the hand in the same
manner, or only two fingers separated and extended, and causing them to pass outward and upward from the mouth with a

wavy motion. The idea of holy or supernatural is made by
extending the forefinger, or all the fingers, of the right hand,
with the back of the hand outward, and moving the hand from
just in front of the forehead spirally upward nearly to arm's
length, from left to right. A deceitful speaker is represented
as a man with a forked tongue, and is shown by bringing the
right hand to the mouth with the back of the hand upward,
the two forefingers extended and separated, pointing outward
from the mouth. A liar is shown by causing the palm of the right
hand, with fingers pointing upward, to pass in front of the face
from right to left. A man upon whom you cannot depend is
represented as a shifting heart; the sign for this character is
the right hand held with the palm downward over the heart
and the hand swayed gently, as if unstable in motion. The
sign for shooting is the palms of the hands placed together, the
fingers of the left hand pointing outward and the fingers of the
right hand pointing toward the right; the palms are brought
down quickly several times, accompanied by an explosive action
of the mouth, to express the report of a gun. When a Plain
Indian wishes to tell one, who does not understand his language,
that he is poor, he turns his left hand closed, with the forefinger
extended toward his body, and with his right hand closed and
forefinger extended, draws the right forefinger over the top of
the left, as if he were sharpening a pencil. The Blackfoot word
to represent this sign is **Kimatapsī,** " I am poor."

The gesture sign for eating, or I am hungry, is made by
holding both hands toward the mouth with fingers pendant, and
alternately raising the hands and letting them fall as if in the
act of throwing something into the mouth. Weeping is shown
by holding the fingers of one or both hands toward the eyes,
and making a motion as if the tears were running from the
eyes down the cheeks. A long time is represented by holding
out the left arm, and drawing the point of the forefinger of the
right hand from the hand towards the shoulder. Riding on
horseback is signified by placing the two forefingers of the
right hand astride the forefinger of the left hand. The gesture
sign for buying or selling, barter or trading, is made by placing

the forefinger of the right hand over the forefinger of the left hand in the form of a cross. The written sign or pictograph for this act is a cross. Sometimes the gesture sign is made by crossing the arms. If an Indian were making a pictograph of this gesture sign, he would make a cross, and upon the left of the cross draw the animals along with several strokes, to signify the number and whatever other articles he wished to give in exchange for the articles owned by another, which are placed upon the right side of the cross. The animals would represent the skins, and if there was a gun or pipe included these would be drawn respectively upon the side of the one who owned them and wished to exchange them. Dead is shown by letting the hand fall down toward the ground; and the number of nights which a man has been travelling, or is going to travel, or the distance to any specified locality, by placing the palm of the hand upon the side of the head. The natives reckon by nights, and not by days, as the white people do, and the distance is shown by the number of times he has slept. These gesture signs might be multiplied almost indefinitely, but these will suffice to show the nature of the language of signs. It is an expressive mode of speech, useful alike to the tribes and white men who understand the meaning of the signs. As the signs do not represent letters, but words, phrases, ideas and feelings, they become very significant, and after a long period of development, so very full and clear that the natives can hold an intelligent conversation for hours without making a single mistake.*

---

* "Transactions of the Royal Society of Canada," Vol. IX., Sec. 2, page 14. Pilling's "Algonquin Bibliography," pages 255, 280, 334. "American Antiquarian, Vol. VII., page 383; Vol. VIII., pages 34, 338; Vol. IX., page 147; Vol. X., page 293; Vol. XIV., pages 277-288. *The Gospel in All Lands*, July, 1885, pages 290, 291. Edwin Bryant's "What I saw in California," pages 115, 187. Daniel Wilson's "Anthropology" (Humboldt Science Library), pages 22, 23. George F. Playter's "History of Methodism in Canada," page 392.

32

LANGUAGES AND LITERATURE OF
WESTERN CANADA.

The western part of our Dominion is rich in historical material, much of which remains unwritten, awaiting the cultured brain and pen of the future historian, poet and novelist. North and west of Lake Superior lies the land of the red man, rich in associations of the fur-trading companies, the hardy French voyageurs, the rugged prospectors and miners, where the Jesuit and Oblate fathers and the Protestant missionaries have followed the trails of the buffalo and deer, seeking the camps of the Indians and Eskimos, counting not their lives dear if permitted to win a dusky savage to the ranks of the followers of the Cross. The literature of this portion of our country is only one hundred and fifty years old, but it is crowded with facts of thrilling interest for all classes of readers. Within that short period the struggle to find a North-West passage by land or sea has been incessant, experienced travellers and navigators having dared the dangers of the Arctic winters, laying down their lives amid the dense solitudes of the far north, or returning laden with the spoils of discovery, which have delighted the hearts of men of science and enriched the world. Modest and intrepid pathfinders have hunted the buffalo and deer on the great plains of the west, crossed the mountains by the lonely passes in search of gold, and touched the confines of the territory of the Eskimo to procure the rich furs of the North Land. The missionaries have scoured the plains, climbed the Rocky Mountains, sailed along the Yukon, Mackenzie, and Peel rivers, entered the Arctic circle, and made homes upon the shores of the Pacific Ocean. In lonely mission-houses, in the native camps, or following the Indian trails, they have studied the native languages, reducing them to writing, prepared grammars and dictionaries, translated books into the native tongue, and placed the civilized world under obligation by their works on the languages. folk-lore and customs of the people among whom

⟨CQOO.⟩

No. 1. Kamloops Wawa May 2.91

Oukouk pepa iaka nem: Kamloops Wawa. Chi alta iaka chako tamas Iaka teke wawa. Kanawe Sonday, kopa kanawe klaska teke chako komtax aiak mamouk pepa Kaltash pous tekop	*(shorthand symbols)*	This paper is named Kamloops Wawa. It is born just now It wants to appear and speak, every week, to all who want to learn to write fast. No matter if they be white men,

they labored. Brave deeds have been done on the field of
battle when savage tribes met in bloody conflict, or when the
pale-face strove with dusky warriors and with men of their
own kin. The stories of other days, woven into ballads, would
rouse the heart of any people, and especially those of our own
land, whose ancestors have trod the plains, braved the field and
flood, in honest endeavor to court honor and fortune or win a
home.

This sketch of languages and literature embraces Manitoba,
Keewatin, the North-West Territories, and British Columbia,
which are included in the term North-western Canada. Within
that portion of territory east of the Rocky Mountains there are
numerous languages and dialects spoken by the tribes, in most
of which books have been translated; while travellers have
described the people and the country, and cultured men have
discussed the intricacies of the tongues of these savage folk.
The Cree language is most extensively used, being the tongue
proper to Keewatin and the Territories. The Plain Cree is
spoken by the Crees living in Alberta, and the Swampy Cree
—sometimes called Maskegon—in the north-eastern portion of
the country. There are several dialects of the language including the Moose and York District. In Southern Alberta the
Blackfoot language is spoken by the Blackfeet, Bloods and
Piegans, and in the same district the harsh, guttural Saree
tongue is spoken by the Sarcees, which is a dialect of the
Beaver language of the north. In Manitoba and the Territories the Ojibway and Sioux languages are used by the scattered remnants of the respective tribes. In the far north are
to be found tribes speaking the Saulteaux—a modified form of
Cree and Ojibway—the Chippewayan or Montagnais, and the
Tinne or Déné—sometimes called the Athapascan languages—
including the Slave, Dog Rib, Loucheux, Hare, Bad People,
Yellow Knives, Cariboo-Eaters, and Tsekehne.

In British Columbia there are seven or eight linguistic
stocks, which have numerous dialects. The Haida is spoken
by the members of the tribe who inhabit the southern end of
Prince of Wales and adjacent islands and Queen Charlotte

Islands. Dialectic differences are noted in the same language spoken by the septs or "small tribes," thus there is the Kaigani sept, the Masset, Skidegate, and Kumshewa dialects of the Haida language. The Tshimpsean stock has two principal dialects, which are spoken by numerous tribes and septs, each tribe having some peculiarity in their mode of pronouncing the language, giving it the force of a dialect. These two principal dialects are the Nasqa and the Tshimpsean proper. The people dwell upon the Naas and Skeena rivers and the adjacent islands. The Kwakiutl has numerous sub-divisions which may be included in three dialects, known as the Qāisla, the Hēiltsuk and the Kwakiutl proper. The many tribes of the group embraced in the three general divisions are widely scattered, the Qāisla being spoken by the tribes north of Grenville Channel; Hēiltsuk by the tribes from Grenville Channel to Rivers Inlet; and the Kwakiutl proper by those inhabiting the country from Rivers Inlet to the central part of Vancouver Island. The Nootka is spoken by the tribes inhabiting the west coast of Vancouver Island. The Salish stock inhabits a large part of British Columbia and the adjacent country in the United States, and has many tribes which may be divided into six groups known as the Bilqula, of Dean Inlet and Bentinck, comprising four tribes; the coast Salish having the following dialects, Catloltq or Kōmok, Sïciatl, Pentlac, Skqōmic, Kamitcin, and Lkuŋgen, the Ntlakyapamuq, the Stlatliumh, the Squapamuq, and the Okinākēn. The Kootaney stock has two dialects, known as the Upper and Lower Kootaney, besides these there are the Shahaptan, or Nez Perce tribe, speaking their own languages; the Tinne, or Dèné languages, comprising the Carriers or Takulli, the Tsilkotin and Tsekehne tribes, and the Babine sub-tribe. The Chinook jargon is also in use as an intermediary language among white men and Indians.

The literature of the period of discovery in the northern portion of the country, known as Hudson's Bay, begins about the middle of the eighteenth century. One hundred years before (1688) Groseilliers and Radisson reached a tributary of Hudson's Bay, called Rupert's River, in the ship *Nonsuch*, and two years later "The Hudson's Bay Company" was chartered. The French and English became rivals in the fur-trade, many battles being fought between the employees of the rival fur companies. The earliest published references to Hudson's Bay are to be found in that storehouse of early Canadian history, the "Jesuit Relations." In the "Relation" of 1657-1658 the routes to Hudson's Bay are mentioned, and in the "Relation" of 1660-1661 reference is made to the mission to Hudson's Bay. One year after the organization of the Hudson's Bay Company the Jesuit missionary Albanel, accompanied by the Sieur Denys de St. Simon, ascended the Saguenay, and, wintering near Lake St. John, pushed on by the Lake and River Nemiskaw until they reached the shores of Hudson's Bay, where a mission was begun. During the six- teenth and seventeenth centuries, the quest for a North-West pas- sage had been vigorously pushed by Frobisher, Davis, Hudson, and Baffin, and some lesser Arctic navigators, who left their journals, which have been published, detailing their discoveries, with an account of the Eskimos and Indians, and many important facts relating to the country. An extensive literature sprang up in connection with Arctic exploration, there having been no less than one hundred and thirty exploring expeditions to the Arctic seas from the time of Cabot to the year 1858. These expeditions have been illustrated by two hundred and fifty books and printed documents, of which one hundred and fifty have been issued in England. The "Three Voyages of Martin Frobisher;" the "Voyages and Works of John Davis, the Navigator;" the "Original Documents of Henry Hudson;" the "Voyages of William Baffin;" and "Fox from the North-West Passage," are the earliest works dealing with the earnest search after gold and a passage to the southern sea. The documentary history of the territory included in this sketch during the first hundred years of the existence of the Hudson's Bay Company is contained in the journals of the company, which were transmitted annually to the headquarters in London.

About the middle of the eighteenth century attempts were

renewed to find a passage to Asia, which naturally produced some very interesting books. "The Geography of Hudson's Bay" (1852), issued by the Hayklut Society, contains important data by Captain W. Coats, in relation to that locality, noted during his voyages between 1727 and 1751, and extracts from the log of Captain Middleton, on his voyage for the discovery of the North-West passage in H.M.S. *Furnace* in 1741-42. The *California*, commanded by Captain Frank Smith, sailed to the same region in 1746-47, upon the same mission, a detailed account of which has been given by the clerk of the vessel in the "Voyage for the Discovery of a North-West Passage by Hudson's Straits" (1748): and a similar narrative of the same voyage has been given in Henry Ellis' "Voyage to Hudson's Bay" (1748).

One of our sources for the earlier glimpses of the Hudson's Bay region, are the missionary accounts given in "Lettres Ecrites des Missions Etrangères" (1650-1750, in forty-seven volumes). Arthur Dobbs' "Account of the Countries Adjoining to Hudson's Bay" (1744), derives its special interest from the earnest support of the probability of a North-West passage and an advocacy of renewed efforts to search for it, with a severe attack upon the Hudson's Bay Company in its attempt to hinder the progress of discovery. Dobbs was followed in his attack upon the Company by Joseph Robson, who had been surveyor and supervisor of the buildings of the Company. In his "Account of Six Years' Residence in Hudson's Bay," from 1733 to 1736 and 1744 to 1747 (1752), he urges the breaking up of a rigid monopoly, which discourages the use of the rich fisheries, projects for the settlement of the country and mining enterprises. He charges the company with preventing friendly intercourse with the natives, keeping them in a barbarous condition, and hindering any attempts at the acquisition of the native languages. After showing how the French have won great prizes through the sluggishness of this vast monopoly, he says, "The Company have for eighty years slept at the edge of a frozen sea; they have shown no curiosity to penetrate further themselves, and have exerted all their art and power to crush that spirit in others."

Edward Umfreville entered the service of the Company as an apprentice, in which he continued eleven years, and upon a disagreement about his salary left it, entering a rival company, in which he remained four years. Upon his return to England he published " Present State of Hudson's Bay (1790). He was present at the surrender of Forts Churchill and York to La Perouse. Following the course of Robson and Dobbs, he attacks the Company for its greed of gain, debasing the natives with liquor, and contrasts the energy of the North-West Company in opening up the interior of the country with the lethargy of the Hudson's Bay Company, which confines itself to the dismal coast.

Samuel Hearne made some explorations for the Company in 1769-1772, an account of which was published as a "Journey from Prince of Wales' Fort to the Northern Ocean" (1795). The North-West Company followed in the line of explorations by sending Alexander Mackenzie on two tours of observation, the results of which were given in his "Voyage from Montreal to the Frozen and Pacific Oceans," 1789-1793 (1801). Alexander Henry, the famous traveller, published an account of the expedition undertaken by him between 1760 and 1766, in which he recounts his experiences as far as Lake Athabasca. His work is entitled, " Travels in Canada and the Indian Territories."

Much important information about the Indians and the country during this early period is found in the "Journal of Monsieur St. Pierre," published in the Canadian Archives in 1886, and the Field Note-books and Journals of David Thompson, which are preserved in the office of the Crown Lands Department of Ontario. An appreciative article on Thompson, giving in detail his journeys in North-western America, has been written by J. B. Tyrrell, B.A., B. Sc., in the "Proceedings of the Canadian Institute." Of this remarkable man Bancroft says, "David Thompson was an entirely different order of man from the orthodox fur-trader. Tall and fine-looking, of sandy complexion, with large features, deep-set, studious eyes, high forehead and broad shoulders, the intellectual was well-set upon the physical. His deeds have never been trumpeted as those of some of the others, but in the westward exploration of the North-West Company no man performed more valuable service, or estimated his achievements more modestly."

Alexander Henry, nephew of the traveller of the same name mentioned above, left a manuscript journal, now deposited in the Library of Parliament, Ottawa, which has been epitomized by Charles N. Bell, of Winnipeg, and contains a racy account of his experiences as a fur-trader among the Indians, from 1799 to 1811. He travelled extensively among the Indian tribes of Manitoba and the Territories, and with an observant eye, noted the customs of the people, which he jotted down in his leisure moments in the camp. Much curious information concerning the Eskimos, with accurate observations upon the Hudson's Bay country, was given by Lieutenant Edward Chappell in his "Narrative of a Voyage to Hudson's Bay" (1817), and by Thomas McKeevor in "Voyage to Hudson's Bay" (1819). McKeevor's book relates experiences of the summer of 1812 in that region, and Chappell recounts his observations upon the natives, describes the coast and river forts of the Hudson's Bay Company, commenting freely upon its illiberal policy and secret methods of dealing, keeping the real facts of the geography and condition of the country from the British Government and people. Chappell's voyage was one of investigation at the instance of the Government, still the quest for the North-West passage and the exploration of the interior kept pace with the eagerness of the people to gain a knowledge of unknown territory. Sir John Ross sought to solve the problem of a northern passage, recounting his observations in "A Voyage of Discovery" (1819), and Captain Back explored the interior, an interesting account of the expedition being given in his "Narrative of a Journey to the Shores of the Arctic Sea in 1833-4-5." Back's narrative contains numerous facts concerning the customs of the natives, the scenery, flora and fauna, and incidents of the journey. Starting from England, he went by Montreal, through the lakes to Sault Ste. Marie, Fort William, Rainy Lake and Norway House, where they began their exploration of the interior of the country. It is a very readable story of adventure, and most instructive.

ESKIMO SYLLABARY.

Previous to Back's expedition, D. W. Harmon published his "Journal of Voyages and Travels in the Interior of North America" (1820), noting his observations between the forty-seventh and fifty-eighth degrees of latitude, extending from Montreal to the Pacific Ocean, and a record of some of his experiences during nineteen years residence in the country; and Sir John Franklin's "Narrative of a Journey to the Shores of the Polar Sea in the Years 1819-1822," had been given to the public (1834). The eastern part of the country had not been neglected, for even at that early date the fact of the existence of the Selkirk Settlement and the attractions of the Lake of the Woods had reached the ears of the civilized world. About this time the controversy about the Selkirk Settlement was stirring the minds of many people, books and pamphlets being issued at intervals until the present time. Keating's "Narrative of an Expedition to the source of the Saint Peter's River, Lake Winnipeck and Lake of the Woods" (1825), revealed the experiences of a traveller in that section of country during 1823. Hardly a year passed without a book being published about Arctic discoveries or the regions farther south. Bishop George J. Mountain, in his missionary journey through the Hudson's Bay territory during the spring and summer of 1844, beguiled the tedious hours by composing poetry. The collection of poems was published, bearing the title "Songs in the Wilderness" (1846). The Bishop of Rupert's Land wrote his "Notes of the Flood of 1852," which was issued in that year. Upon the far northern shores intrepid men were eagerly exploring land and sea, with limited leisure to tell their tales of hardship to the outside world. Thomas Simpson, the brave Arctic explorer, who died so mysteriously upon the plains in 1840, left the manuscript of a work, "Narrative of the Discoveries on the North Coasts of America, Effected by the Officers of the Hudson's Bay Company," 1836-39. The account of his travels was published in 1843, having, according to the charges made by his brother Alexander, been tampered with, and not issued in the condition in which the explorer left it. Two years later Alexander Simpson, brother of the explorer, published "The Life and Travels of Thomas Simpson, the Arctic Discoverer" (1843). The brothers were related to Sir George Simpson, who was an illegitimate son of their mother's brother. Governor Simpson seems not to have shown any favor to his relations, and Thomas criticises severely the treatment received at the hands of the Government and the company.

The writers of this period were generally old employees of the Hudson's Bay Company, who spoke their minds freely, and were strongly antagonistic to this great corporation.

John McLean was a man of classical tastes, and possessed a good education, which did not hinder him from accepting the charge of solitary posts, although he felt keenly the treatment to which he was subjected. The record of his journeys and experiences as a fur-trader, his hardships and hair-breadth escapes are freely given in his "Notes of a Twenty-five Years' Service in the Hudson's Bay Territory" (1849). The promotion which was due him in the employ of the company was denied him, through the influence of Governor Simpson, and in recounting his experiences in widely separated districts, as in Labrador and New Caledonia, he charges the Governor with favoritism, which ended in his leaving the country.

In the same year a book was published in the interests of the company by R. M. Martin, entitled, "The Hudson's Bay Territories and Vancouver Island," which showed a decided bias, as many of his statements were challenged as incorrect. He describes the territories governed by the company, gives details of its constitution, and argues the special fitness of the corporation to manage the colony.

The northern seas were not left in their sullen gloom unheeded by dauntless men, for willing hearts and hands were ever ready to dare the dangers of their inhospitable shores in search of a solution of Nature's problem.

P. C. Sutherland's "Journal of a Voyage in Baffin's Bay and Barrow Straits in 1850-51" (1852), Lieutenant William Hulme Hooper's "Ten Months Among the Tents of the Tuski (1853), and J. Hayes' "Arctic Boat Journey in the Autumn of 1854" (1854), brought to light some interesting facts regarding the country and its inhabitants.

Gabriel Franchere's "Narrative of a Voyage to the North-West Coast of America in 1811-1814," first published in French (1820), appeared in an American translation in 1854. Franchere was a Frenchman from Montreal, who spent some time on the Pacific Coast in the employment of John Jacob Astor, and after enduring many privations, performed a memorable journey across the Rocky Mountains, down the Saskatchewan River, across Lake Winnipeg, through the country to Fort William, and by the lakes to Montreal. P. F. Tytler's "Northern Coasts of America and the Hudson's Bay Territories" (1854), gives impressions of that region; while Alexander Ross, in his account of "The Red River Settlement" (1856), gives the earliest history of the rise and progress of the colony. In a racy style, Ross tells of the Scotch emigrants' trip to Red River, recounts their hardships and perseverance; the progress of the settlement, and the customs of the people; the life and customs of the half-breeds; the work of the missionaries among the Indians, and many important social, religious and political features of the period. The Government was awakening to the fact that the Red River country and the Valley of the Saskatchewan were of some value, and expeditions were sent out to make explorations in these districts. George Gladman stated the results of his tour of observation in the eastern part of Manitoba and the western sections of Ontario in his "Report on the Expedition to the Country between Lake Superior and the Red River Settlement" (1858), and Henry Y. Hind's labors were recorded in his "Reports, together with a Preliminary and General Report, on the Assiniboine and Saskatchewan Exploring Expedition" (1859). Hind's report especially is important and interesting, as it deals with a part of the country little known at that time beyond its own limits, and brings into view the modes of living, superstition, social and religious customs of the Cree and other native tribes.

Following the plan of Catlin, as an artist among the Indians, Paul Kane, a Toronto artist, made a tour among the Indian tribes of Oregon, Vancouver Island, across the Rocky Mountains, along the Saskatchewan Valley and homeward to Toronto

—sketching some of the most notable chiefs and striking scenes of native life, and noting the traditions and customs of the various tribes visited by him. Some of his pictures of savage life are still in Toronto, and these give a vivid representation of the habits of the Indians of the plains, mountains and coast. His notes taken during his travels were published with the title, "Wanderings of An Artist Among the Indians of North America" (1859).

Another interesting work, prepared by an acute observer, is the "Exploration of British North America during 1857-60," by Captain John Palliser (1863), which is still of great importance, as is also Henry Youle Hind's "Narrative of the Canadian Red River Exploring Expedition of 1857." The history of the North-West Company, which was formed at Montreal, can be traced in "The Origin and Progress of the North-West Company of Canada, with a History of the Fur Trade as Connected with that Concern" (1811). This company was formed by a number of Canadian adventurers, supplemented at later dates by dissatisfied employees of the Hudson's Bay Company. It had begun operations in the Red River district in 1788, was active in exploration, sending out Alexander Mackenzie on his tours of observation, and finally united with the Hudson's Bay Company in 1804

Some knowledge of the routes of the traders and the stations of the company may be obtained from a perusal of Alexander McDonell's "Narrative of Transactions in the Red River Country" (1819), while the life of the trader, the operations of the company, and the conflict between the North-West and Hudson's Bay companies, with regard to the expulsion of the Selkirk colonists, is given by Ross Cox in his "Adventures on the Columbia River" (1831).

Captain Hall's "Life with the Esquimaux" (1864) takes us to the northern districts, and pictures the hardy natives of the Arctic regions in their daily life, quaintly describing their curious customs, and giving us a glimpse of their language. There were attractions on land which the frozen seas did not possess, and travellers were induced to seek sport and knowledge from a journey across the plains, valleys and mountains to the Pacific Ocean.

Sir George Simpson's "Narrative of a Journey Around the World" (1847) gives an interesting account of his expedition through the North-West. It is a plain record of the experiences of a traveller, shrewd and active, who visited the trading-posts and native tribes, noting the customs of Indians and half-breeds, their modes of travelling, picture writing, medicines, political life and many interesting events.

A book of more than ordinary interest is "The North-West Passage by Land" (1865), by Viscount Milton and W. B. Cheadle. These travellers crossed the continent to the Pacific Coast, and the account of what they saw by the way, the tribes visited, and the events of camp life is written with ability. Stories, scraps of native lore, bits of prairie and mountain scenery, and general notes on their expedition make a delightful book of historic value.

Archbishop Tache's long residence in the North-West, contact with the settlers, half-breeds and Indians, personally, and through the missionaries under his care, his cultured mind and library of North-West literature, specially qualified him to write his "Sketch of the North-West of America" (1868), which was published in French, with an English translation. It is a valuable work, and one to which constant reference must be made to understand the different aspects of the history of the western country.

Alexander J. Russell's "Red River Country, Hudson's Bay and North-West Territories Considered in relation to Canada" (1869), the Hon. William McDougall's "The Red River Insurrection Reviewed" (1870), Captain G. L. Huyshe's "The Red River Expedition of 1870" (1871), and Alexander Begg's "The Creation of Manitoba" (1871) deal with the affairs of the first Riel Rebellion.

"Red River" (1871), by Joseph J. Hargrave, has many interesting features in relation to the colony, and a full account of the organization and system of the Hudson's Bay Company. The history of the Red River settlement, from its origin under

Lord Selkirk, is traced by this intelligent observer. He vividly portrays the scenes of every-day life in that heterogeneous community, composed of people of various nationalities, including half-breeds and Indians. Manitoba was created a province and British Columbia incorporated with the Dominion and the project of a railroad connecting the Pacific Ocean with the railway systems of Ontario and Quebec, was the chief condition of British Columbia becoming a part of the Union.

The story of the expedition seeking a route for the continental railroad, is told with brilliancy of detail in Dr. George M. Grant's "Ocean to Ocean" (1872). Dr. Grant was the secretary of the expedition under Sanford Fleming, and a rare opportunity was given to the author of this work for giving a full account of the country on the route. The expedition started from Toronto, July 16, 1871, and on October 14th left Victoria, British Columbia, for home. During the three months' journey a diary was kept of the chief things seen and heard, and the general impressions of the country. It was published almost verbally, as it had been written, under difficulties, for the writer tells us : "Notes had to be taken sometimes in the bottom of a canoe and sometimes leaning against a stump or a tree ; on horseback in fine weather, under a cart when it was raining or when the sun's rays were fierce : at night, in the tent, by the light of the camp fire in front ; in a crowded wayside inn, or on the deck of a steamer in motion." The route traversed was up Lake Superior to Port Arthur, by the river Kaministiquia, through the lakes and rivers to Winnipeg, over the prairies, through the Qu'Appelle valley to Victoria and Edmonton, across the Rocky Mountains by the Yellow Head Pass, along the North Thompson River to Kamloops, and from thence to Yale and the waters of the Pacific. It was an eventful journey, and the descriptions of mountain, lake and prairie, visits to missions and observations thereon, and the general notes on camp life and views of the savage folk are pleasantly related. Robert Michael Ballantyne's "Hudson's Bay ; or, Everyday Life in the Wilds of North America," was published shortly after the author's return to England, in 1847. He left his Highland home in 1841, as an

apprentice clerk of the Hudson's Bay Company, and in his entertaining book he narrates, in a vivid style, the things he saw and heard during his six years' residence in the country. The forts and establishments of the company, articles of trade; the customs of the Indians, their costumes, implements and dwellings; the modes of travelling and encampment, crossing portages, canoeing, running the rapids and travelling on snow-shoes; hunting the bear, buffalo and deer; the arrival and departure of the brigades; winter sports in the woods, and Christmas festivities in the Company's posts; the gay scenes of half-breed life and many delightful stories of the North Land are charmingly described. Archibald McDonald's "Peace River" (1872) describes a canoe voyage from Hudson's Bay to the Pacific, and incidents by the way. Captain W. F. Butler went to Manitoba and the Territories in an official position in connection with the military expedition to suppress the Red River Rebellion, and at the close of the revolt, travelled in the performance of his duties through the Saskatchewan Valley to the Hudson's Bay Company post at Rocky Mountain House. In his work, "The Great Lone Land" (1873), he narrates the story of the Rebellion, describes, in an entertaining style, his varied experiences in the Territories, contact with the Indians, the hospitality of the company at the posts visited, and champions the cause of the red men of the west. One year later he published his "Wild North Land" (1874). His former journey had quickened his spirit of adventure, and wholly at his own expense he started with dogs across the country in the winter of 1872. Starting from Red River in the autumn he traversed the country by Lake Athabasca, along the Peace River to the Rocky Mountains, through the North of British Columbia and New Caledonia, down the Frazer River to the coast. Life at the company's posts, and the methods of trade, stirring adventures on the journey, and observations upon the country and its native inhabitants are described with liveliness and charming detail. "Canada on the Pacific," by Charles Horetzky (1874), who was a member of the Sandford-Fleming expedition described by Dr. George M. Grant, gives an account of the
33

journey from Edmonton to the Pacific Ocean. This narrative
recounts the route travelled with the writer's experiences, and
notes upon the Indian tribes of British Columbia.

"Saskatchewan and the Rocky Mountains" (1875) contains
the diary of the Earl of Southesk, who travelled through Manitoba and the Territories in quest of sport and adventure. Many
interesting facts are given, illustrated by his own pencil, of the
scenery of the places visited, the wild animals, plants, customs
and language of the natives, and the varied experiences of the
camp. The book is an entertaining account of what the writer
saw and heard as he hunted, fished and explored the regions he
traversed.

In J. C. Hamilton's "The Prairie Province" (1876) and Peter
O'Leary's "Travels and Experiences in Canada, the Red River,
and United States," published in the same year, we find a
narration of the impressions made upon the minds of these
travellers by their visit to Manitoba. The former work deals
with the climate, civil institutions, inhabitants, productions,
and resources of the Red River Valley. Both of them are
interesting and instructive narratives, and reveal not only the
interest awakened in the public mind about the great future
awaiting the new province in the west, but the value of the
country and its internal wealth, which impressed every impar-
tial onlooker.

Alexander Begg's "Ten Years in Winnipeg" (1879) is a lively
relation of the growth of the city, the doings of its people, and
the experiences and observations of a clever writer.

In H. M. Robinson's "Great Fur Land" (1874) are given
lively sketches of travel in the Hudson's Bay Territory. Leaving Winnipeg, the author went to Norway House and began a
winter journey among Indians, half-breeds, and Hudson's Bay
employees. In a vivacious style he describes his journey by
dog-sledge, with its enlivening incidents; travel by canoe, the
voyageurs' boat song, and shooting the rapids; the typical half-
breed, with his improvidence, social life, and mixed theology;
service in the Hudson's Bay Company; life at one of the posts,
with its daily routine of business and varied amusements; the

aboriginal voyageur; departure of a brigade of boats, and
modes of travel; the great fall hunts after the buffalo; the
fraternity of medicine men; totems; the fur hunter trapping
the beaver, with the pleasures and pains of the trapper's life;
camping out in winter; courtship among the half-breeds; and
the life of a free-trader; incidents of a half-breed ball, and
notes on the native tribes, languages, and missionary work
among them.

The historical student will find among the provincial archives
of Manitoba about a dozen manuscript books, containing the
military documents relating to the Wolseley Red River Expedition.

The Rev. Daniel M. Gordon, in the summer of 1879, accom-
panied an exploring party from Port Simpson, on the Pacific
Coast, across Northern British Columbia, travelling up the
Skeena River by boat as far as the Forks, thence on foot to
Lake Babine, and over this lake to Fort Macleod. Here the
party divided, some proceeding, under the direction of Dr. G.
M. Dawson, through the Rocky Mountains, by the Pine River
Pass; the rest of the party, including Mr. Gordon, descending
Peace River by boat until they reached Dunvegan. Various
exploring trips were made to investigate the character of the
Peace River country, and then Mr. Gordon went alone by way
of Lesser Slave Lake to Edmonton, Battleford, and thence to
Winnipeg.

In his work, "Mountain and Prairie," the author describes
Duncan's Indian Mission at Metlahkatlah, the route travelled,
the character of the country, and its resources, the manners and
customs of the Indians, the white settlers, and numerous incidents by the way.

The Honorable Alexander Morris published "The Treaties of
Canada with the Indians of Manitoba and the North-West
Territories" (1880), a work alike useful to the historical
student, statesman, missionary, and liberal-minded citizen. It
contains much useful information relating to the treaty negotiations, the location and extent of the Indian Reserves, the
education of the native youth, the training of the people in the

pursuit of agriculture, and incidental matters pertaining to
Indian customs.

In the same year Mary FitzGibbon's interesting book, " A
Trip to Manitoba," was published, and in the year following
W. Fraser Rae's " From Newfoundland to Manitoba." In that
part of the book, dealing with Manitoba, there is an entertaining chapter on the Mennonite and Icelandic colonies. The
author describes their farms, dwellings, modes of life and labor,
and their ideas on politics, education and religion. The Men-
nonites have many things in common with the Quakers, being
a peaceful and industrious people, primitive in their religious
ideas and practice. The schoolmaster and clergyman, and even
the women, toil hard in the fields during seed time and harvest;
and where fuel is scare and dear the people utilize the straw
and manure which are manufactured into pressed cakes, and
serve to burn in their clay-built fireplaces. They are an industrious class of settlers, the men making their own chairs and
tables, and the women prepare all the clothes for the family.

Professor John Macoun published a large volume, " Manitoba
and the Great North-West" (1883), of special interest to the
people of the prairie province, owing to the author's previous
knowledge of the country and his botanical reputation. It was
an exceedingly popular work in Canada and Britain, and
accomplished much in awakening an interest in the western
country, and giving enlightened views upon the great west as
an unlimited field for emigration.

W. H. Barneby's " Life and Labor in the Far, Far West "
(1884) is full of glimpses of prairie life, seen by a shrewd
traveller.

Charles R. Tuttle was a member of the Hudson's Bay Expe-
dition of 1884, under the command of Lieutenant A. R.
Gordon, R. N. The expedition left Halifax in the steamship
Neptune, chartered by the Dominion Government, skirted
Labrador, visited the Moravian mission at Nain, gazed upon
the snow-crowned hills of Nachvak, and thence into Hudson's
Strait.

In the author's " Our North Land " (1885) a detailed account is given of the expedition, with its varied experiences and interesting information gathered on the route. Life among the Eskimos is described with their habits of trading, marriage customs, villages, dwellings, dress, language and religious ideas and practice. The meteorological work done at the observing stations, the story of Marble Island, with its desolate graveyard, Fort Churchill and its inhabitants, the attractions of York Factory, bear hunting and whale fishing, the game of Hudson's Bay region, the fishes and fur-bearing animals, the navigation of Hudson's Bay and Strait, the native tribes of the north, the white settlers, the Hudson's Bay route and characteristics, and resources of the Territories and Manitoba are described in a genial mood by the author.

Sandford Fleming's " England and Canada " (1884) narrates a summer tour between Old London and the Pacific Coast, with important historical notes. The commander of the expedition described by Tuttle published an interesting " Report of the Second Hudson's Bay Expedition " (1885). Lieutenant Gordon was specially qualified by his training and experience to write an account of the expedition of more than ordinary interest, and in the pages of the report are to be found the experiences and observations of a specialist, with the work of the expedition.

Alexander S. Hill, in " From Home to Home " (1885), recounts the results of his journeys from his home in England to his stock ranche near Macleod, Alberta. Mr. Hill is a lawyer and member of Parliament in England, who organized a stock company with headquarters near Macleod, and in the interests of the company visited the ranche several times. He describes the country, stock ranching, the white settlers and Indians, and various incidents by the way. Among the most popular books of travel are Warburton Pike's " The Barren Ground of Northern Canada," and Julian Ralph's " On Canada's Frontier " (1893). Mr. Pike is an experienced sportsman, whose love of adventure led him, in the summer of 1889, to explore the almost unknown territory of the extreme north, and incidentally to hunt the musk-ox. Making his headquarters at Fort

Resolution, he remained in Northern Canada for two years.
Several expeditions were made to the barren ground from this
point, and in the autumn of 1890 he formed the intention of
crossing the Rocky Mountains to the Pacific, which proved to
be an arduous undertaking, and nearly cost the hardy adventurers their lives. Mr. Pike's record of peril is admirable in its
strength and terseness, and his descriptions of hunting the
caribou and musk-ox, and his thoughts upon the country, the
half-breeds and Indians are striking in their directness and
simplicity. Looking for the first time upon the strange land
of the north he says, " We sat down at the top of the hill and
took our last view of the Great Slave Lake. Looking southward we could see the far shore and the unknown land beyond,
rising in terraces to a considerable height and very similar in
appearance to the range we were on. Ahead of us, to the
north, lay a broken, rocky country, sparsely timbered and
dotted with lakes, the nearest of which, a couple of miles away,
was the end of our portage, a bleak and desolate country,
already white with snow, and with a film of ice over the
smaller ponds. Three hundred miles in the heart of this
wilderness, far beyond the line where timber ceases, lies the
land of the musk-ox, to which we were about to force our way,
depending entirely on our guns for food and for clothing, to
withstand the intense cold that would soon be upon us. A pair
of hawks furnished the only signs of life, and the outlook was
by no means cheerful." Julian Ralph is an experienced
traveller with the literary temperament. His book is an entertaining account of what he saw in Western Canada, in that part
which lies along the international boundary from Manitoba to
the Pacific Coast. "There is a very remarkable bit of this
continent just north of our State of North Dakota, in what the
Canadians call Assiniboia, one of the North-West provinces.
Here the plains reach away in an almost level, unbroken,
brown ocean of grass. Here are some wonderful and some
very peculiar phases of immigration and of human endeavor."
It is of these prairies and phases of human endeavor that
Julian Ralph writes in his humorous and picturesque style.

Snatches of history, adventure and sport, sketches of Indians, missionaries, traders and settlers, fact and fancy blended together, illustrated by Mr. Remington and other artists, make up an entertaining and instructive book, and show the sterling qualities of an experienced voyager.

The most prolific author on the history of Manitoba is the Rev. Dr. George Bryce, Professor in Manitoba College. His largest work on western history is " Manitoba: Infancy, Growth and Present Condition " (1882), a comprehensive and instructive volume; his lesser works consisting of numerous papers and lectures, read before the Manitoba Historical Society and Royal Society of Canada, and delivered at public assemblies. He is a member of several scientific societies at home and abroad, and has, by his writings, brought the history and progress of the country before the world to a considerable degree. An important chapter on Canada in Winsor's " Narrative and Critical History of America," " Early Days in Winnipeg," " Old Settlers of Red River," " Life of John Tanner," " Original Letters Relating to the Selkirk Settlement," " Two Provisional Governments in Manitoba," " First Recorder of Rupert's Land," " The Assiniboine River and its Forts," " Brief Outlines of the most Famous Journeys in and about Rupert's Land," " The Souris Country : Its Monuments, Mounds, Forts and Rivers," and " Holiday Rambles between Winnipeg and Victoria," comprise some of the work of this ardent advocate of the liberties of the people.

Donald Gunn's " History of Manitoba " is a work which must not be neglected by the historical student for certain phases of life in the Red River settlement and the conflict of political parties. Charles N. Bell, one of the devoted students of North-West history, who has spent much time with his confrere, Dr. Bryce, in exploring the remains of the Mound-Builders in Manitoba, has written some notable papers on the history of the country. Amongst these are included " Our Northern Waters," " The Mound-Builders," " Historical Names and Places in the North-West," " The Journal of Alexander Henry," and " Aboriginal Trade in the Canadian North-West."

Sir John Schultz, the Lieutenant-Governor of Manitoba,

found leisure, amid the duties of the State, to write several historical papers of value, whose titles are sufficient to give them a place among the lesser works of our historians, as "The Old Crow-Wing Trail," "A Long-Forgotten Fortress," "The Innuits of our Arctic Coast," "Some Old Inhabitants," and "The King's Highway." A brief statement of historical papers may be of use to the student of North-West literature, and is given for reference, that any who may desire to pursue the subject more fully will have the facts at hand.

The following papers have been published by the Manitoba Historical Society : A. Bowerman, M.A., " The Chinook Wind ;" Hon. G. McMicken, "Abortive Fenian Raid in Manitoba;" John Macbeth, " Social Customs and Amusements in the Olden Days in Red River Settlement and Rupert's Land ;" Alexander McArthur, " A Tragedy on the Plains : The Fate of Thomas Simpson, the Arctic Explorer ;" Rev. Dr. Burman, " The Sioux Language ;" Consul Taylor, " Journal of Robert Campbell," who was for over fifty years a Hudson's Bay factor; and William Dennis, journalist, " Sources of North-Western History." The Rev. Lewis Drummond, S.J., prepared a striking paper on " The French in the North-West." William Caldwell's articles in the *Manitoba Free Press* on " The Olden Days," " Fifty-one Years Ago," and " The Prairie Nimrods," present phases of life in the days gone by. Donald Gunn's " Indian Remains near Red River Settlement, Hudson's Bay Territory," in Smithsonian Report for 1867 ; A. C. Lawson, " Ancient Rock Inscriptions on the Lake of the Woods," in American Naturalist, Vol. XIX. (1885); Rev. Edward Francis Wilson's articles on the "Native Tribes of Canada" in " Our Forest Children " and " The Canadian Indian ;" Charles Mair, " The American Bison," in the " Royal Society of Canada Proceedings," Vol. VIII., Section 2 ; J. B. Tyrrell's paper, " A Brief Narrative of the Journeys of David Thompson in North-Western America," in Proceedings of the Canadian Institute, 1888 ; articles by Dr. A. F. Chamberlain on the " Kootenay Indians," in the " American Antiquarian ;" Jean l'Hereux, " The Kekip-Sesoators, or Ancient Sacrificial Stones of the North-West Tribes of Canada," in the " Journal of the Anthropo-

logical Institute of Great Britain and Ireland," Vol. XV.
(1885); John Maclean, "The Blackfoot Sun Dance and
Mortuary Customs of the Blackfeet," in "Canadian Institute Proceedings," and "Blackfoot Mythology," in "American
Journal of Folk-Lore;" Horatio Hale's interesting notes on
the "Tinneh People and their Languages," in his pamphlet
on "Languages as a Test of Mental Capacity;" George
Gibbs' "Notes on the Tinneh or Chippewayan Indians of
British and Russian America," in the Smithsonian Report for
1886; Lieut. Schwatka, "The Igloo of the Innuit," describing
the igloos and the implements used in their construction by the
Eskimos, published in "Science," Vol. II. (1883); F. F. Payne's
paper on the "Eskimo"; M. R. F. Stupart's "The Eskimo of
Stupart Bay;" and the Rev. A. G. Morice's very full in interesting monographs on "The Western Dènés: Their Manners
and Customs," "The Dèné Languages" and "Dèné Roots," in
the "Proceedings of the Canadian Institute"—are papers of
rare value to everyone interested in the history of Western
Canada.

The great North-West has abundant historical matter invit-
ing the pen of the novelist, yet the number of writers who have
been drawn toward the native life and scenery of the west has
been few, indeed. The most industrious and successful novelist
of Western life and manners is R. M. Ballantyne, who spent
several years as a clerk of the Hudson's Bay Company, and was
well qualified by his experience to depict the scenes of everyday life on the plains and in the forests of Western Canada.
Several interesting novels, written in a clear and fascinating
style, and marked by a high moral tone, were published, evidently with the intention of securing the attention of youthful
readers. The author was not disappointed in winning the
esteem of the young, who read them with avidity and delighted
in the instruction imparted in a pleasing style. "The Pioneers,"
"Over the Rocky Mountains," "The Prairie Chief," "Away in
the Wilderness," and "The Buffalo Runners," are interesting
stories of Western life. In "The Young Fur Traders," Mr.
Ballantyne has drawn largely upon his own experience, as he

says, " My desire has been to draw an exact copy of the picture which is indelibly stamped on my own memory." The story begins at Old Fort Garry, and describes the trials encountered by the Red River settlers in planting their colony, with the success attained through their indomitable courage and perseverance. "Ungava: A Tale of the Eskimo," describes the fur-trader's life in the far north, the life of the hardy voyageurs, canoeing on the great northern lakes and rivers, games and sports, feasts and fights, native camps and hunting, and numerous incidents in the life of the intrepid fur-trader.

"The Dog Crusoe and His Master" is a picture of the old buffalo days, so full of adventure, which have forever passed away. J. Macdonald Oxley is one of our popular Canadian writers, who is becoming well-known as an author of books for boys. Amongst the number of his stories are two dealing with old times in the North-West. "Archie McKenzie, the Young Nor'-Wester," and "Fergus McTavish" are lively and instructive narratives. The hero of the latter story is a courageous, strong-willed lad, who lives at the head of Lake Winnipeg, amid rough surroundings, from whose degrading influence he is preserved by the remembrance of a kind mother. In his wild environment he is influenced by the consecrated zeal of a missionary to the Indians, and he finally devotes his life as a missionary to the people he has learned to love. Incidental facts relating to early days in the service of the Hudson's Bay Company, adventures with Indians, half-breeds and Scotch settlers, and exciting times hunting the buffalo and bear, make a fascinating tale with a healthy moral tone. Captain Mayne Reid's "The Young Voyageurs," "Lake of the Woods," by A. L. O. E.; Agnes Maule Machar's "Marjories' Canadian Winter;" W. H. G. Kingston's "The Trapper's Son" and "Among the Red Skins;" Achilles Daunt's "The Three Trappers" and "In the Land of the Bear, the Moose, and the Beaver" are solid and interesting tales of life in the west. The sentimental love story, localized in the stirring times or beautiful scenery of the west, can hardly be said to have reached us, the historical novel having the pre-eminence, the material being so

abundant for the production of this class. Edmund Collins'
"Annette, the Metis Spy" and John Mackay's "The Devil's
Play-ground" and "Sinners Twain" are of the sensational type,
which find few readers in our healthy, moral communities in
the prairie land.   Egerton Ryerson Young, who spent some
few years as a missionary in the north among the lakes, rivers
and forests, where the Cree and Saulteaux Indians roamed, has
written three interesting stories of life among the natives,
which are marked by a fascinating style that has won many
readers.   "By Canoe and Dog-Train," "Stories from Indian
Wigwams and Northern Camp-Fires," and "Oowikapun; or,
How the Gospel Reached the Nelson River Indians," are tales
of missionary adventure, fact and fancy blended together for
the instruction of young and old.   Gilbert Parker wrote "The
Chief Factor," the scenes of which are laid in the North-West.
Mr. Parker spent a few years in Australia, and was connected
with the Sydney press. He returned to England, locating in
London, where he became an industrious worker in various
branches of literature, distinguishing himself by writing sketches
of Australian life.   He has recently been studying the interesting phases of French-Canadian and North-West life, and his
stories relating to Canada mark him as an author who will do
great things for himself and the land of the prairies, mountains
and lakes.

Biographical literature has not been extensively cultivated,
arising no doubt from the lack of subjects in a new country.
There has not yet appeared the life of any of our native
heroes of the plains, because the opportunity has been wanting
to give them prominence.   Excepting the "Life of Riel" there
is no biography of any of the half-breeds.   There have
been men amongst us worthy of permanent record, but the
incidents of their career have been hidden in camp life, and
when they have passed from earth, the difficulty. of securing
historical data and separating facts from traditional and mythical statements has prevented writers from exploring this field.
Two books have been published on John Tanner, who spent
thirty years among the Indians of Minnesota, Western Ontario

and Manitoba. Edwin James' "A Narrative of the Captivity
and Adventures of John Tanner" and Dr. James Macaulay's
"Grey Hawk: Life and Adventures among the Red Indians"
recount the experiences of this strange character who found
pleasure and many hardships in his singular career among the
natives of the west. John McDougall, the famous missionary
to the Stoney Indians, published "George M. McDougall" and
" Forest Lake and Prairie," the former work describing the life
and missionary career of his father, who was frozen to death
near Calgary in 1876, and the latter, an autobiography,
recounting twenty years of frontier life in Western Canada.
" Forty-two Years with the Eskimos and Indians," by Batty,
and "John Horden, Missionary Bishop; A Life on the Shores
of Hudson's Bay," by A. R. Buckland, relate the missionary
adventures and work of the courageous bishop of Moosonee.
John Maclean has published "The Hero of the Saskatchewan,"
a life of George McDougall, with sketches of the Indian missions of the Methodist Church in Manitoba and the Territories;
and "Life of James Evans," who invented the Syllabic System
of the Cree language.

Several interesting works dealing with the missions under the
care of the Roman Catholic, Anglican and Methodist churches
have been issued, which contain facts of great value relating to
the scenery, resources and geography of the country, the character of the settlers and their progress in founding colonies, the
customs, languages, folk-lore, native religions and camp life of
the Indians, the condition of the half-breeds the relation of the
Hudson's Bay Company to the natives, the rise and progress of
education among the Indians and white settlers, and the
success of missionary work in the country. The Rev. John
West's Journal (1824) contains an interesting account of his
residence at the Red River Settlement and his experiences
among the Indians and settlers. P. J. de Smet, the Jesuit missionary, wrote " Missions de l'Oregon et Voyages aux Monta-
gnes Rocheuses aux Sources de la Colombie, de l'Athabasca et
du Sascatshawin en 1845-46," relating his travels among the
Indians and sketches of missionary work. The Rev. John

Ryerson performed a missionary tour to the Methodist missions
north of Winnipeg, an account of his journey and observations
being given in "Hudson's Bay," (1855). In the following year
the gifted authoress of religious books for the young, S. Tucker,
who is better known by her *nom de plume*, A. L. O. E., published
"Rainbow in the North," (1852), a very readable record of the
English Church missions among the Indians of the north. The
Journal of Peter Jacobs, who accompanied John Ryerson on his
northern trip, gives the "Observation and Experiences of an
Indian Missionary among the Cree Indians."

Mgr. Henry J. Faraud, Apostolic Vicar of the Roman Catholic
Diocese of Mackenzie, has related his experiences in the far north-
western country in his work, "Dix-huit ans chez les Sauvages.
Voyages et Missions" (1866); and in the same year Archbishop
Tache published "Twenty Years of Missions in the North-West
of America." David Anderson, Bishop of Rupert's Land has
given some good sketches of English Church missions in his
book, "The Net in the Bay," which is a journal of his trip to
Moose and Albany in the north. A sketch of the progress of
the Gospel among the Indians will be found in "Day Spring in
the Far West" (1875).

Rev. Dr. Alexander Sutherland, General Secretary of the
Methodist Missionary Society, made a tour of the missions
of his Church in Manitoba and the Territories in 1880, and a
series of letters dealing with the country and mission work
among the Indians was written, which were gathered and
published, with the title, "A Summer in Prairie Land" (1881).
The Rev. John Semmens, a missionary for several years among
the Crees in the Norway-House District, has published some
pleasing sketches of native life, and a record of his own
experiences among the Indians in "Mission Life in the
North-West" (1884); and Bishop Bompas has written a short
but worthy "History of the Diocese of Mackenzie River"
(1888).

Such a movement as the Riel Rebellion could not pass
without some record being made by those who participated in
the stirring period; and others who were deeply moved by

patriotic feelings, or possessed a literary bent, were not slow
to avail themselves of the opportunity of expressing their
opinions, or making fame and fortune by the pen. Boulton,
Mulvaney and Mercer Adams have written books dealing with
the Rebellion of 1885. Major Boulton's work includes his
experiences during the first rebellion, which are important as
the reminiscences of one who was active in both rebellions, and
for sometime a prisoner under Riel. William Macdougall, an
enthusiastic politician, wrote a small book in a series of eight
letters to the Hon. Joseph Howe, entitled, "The Red River
Rebellion" (1870). C. R. Daoust, who accompanied the Sixty-
fifth Regiment to the front during the second rebellion, has
published a volume, giving the history of the campaign, which
is an attractive work in French, with the title, "Cent Vingt
Jours de Service Actif."

The North-West Mounted Police Force has not been
forgotten by those who have been members, and their
experiences reveal phases of life and character which are
new to the outside world, and possess a charm for those who
are conversant with the brave deeds of the riders of the plains.
Jean D'Artigue published in French a volume, which was
translated into English, "Six Years in the North-West
Mounted Police" (1882); and John G. Donkin, "Trooper and
Red Skins in the Far West" (1889). These are pleasing
reminiscences of life in a police fort, journeys across the
plains, observations of Indians, and incidents in the lives of
the authors.

There are some works of a scientific character which are
especially important, as they treat of the deeper life of the
natives, their mythology, languages, religious beliefs and
philosophy. Our greatest scientific writer on the Indians and
Eskimos is Emile Fortune Stanislas Joseph Petitot. Coming
from his home in France, in 1862, to the North-West, he
labored among the Indians and Eskimos till 1874, when he
returned to his native country for the purpose of publishing
some of his books on linguistics and geography. In 1876, he
came again to the North-West, and remained till 1882, when

he again went home, and now resides in France. He was the first missionary to the Canadian Eskimo. In his missionary work, he has endured great hardships, performing long journeys on snow-shoes to visit his people. Father Petitot has, besides other works, published the following, dealing with the tribes of Athabasca: " Etude sur la Nation Montagnaise " (1868), " Monographie des Dene-Dindijie " (1876), " Bibliotheque de Linguistique et d'Ethnographie Americaines " (1876), " Traditions Indiennes du Canada Nord-Oest " (1886), and " Accord des Mythologies dans la Cosmogonie des Danites Arctiques " (1890). Morice's monographs on the Dèné languages and customs, already noticed, places the author, with his confrere Petitot, in the front rank as writers on the natives of our country.

Newspaper literature is not confined to the haunts of civilization, but in some of the queerest places the ephemeral sheet, filled with the news of the day, has appeared. One of the strangest places for a newspaper to be sustained is in the Polar regions. The members of the Parry Arctic Expedition started the *North Georgian Gazette,* and everyone was asked to contribute to its columns. The interests of the western natives have not been forgotten by journalists, unprofessional men in this department of literature. One of the first papers devoted to the welfare of the red men in the west was issued by the author at Macleod in the autumn of 1880. It was a four-page monthly, called *Excelsior,* printed on the printograph, having no advertisements, and its circulation was limited to one hundred copies, furnished gratis to subscribers. It lived for one year, when pressing missionary duties compelled the editor to cease its publication. It was favorably noticed by the *Globe* and *Mail* and other papers in Canada, and by the *Echo* and other issues of the English press.

The following papers are published, giving special information concerning the native tribes of Manitoba and the Territories: *The Western Missionary* is the organ of the Presbyterian Synod on behalf of Home and Indian Missions, with headquarters at Manitoba College, Winnipeg. It is an interesting monthly, filled with short paragraphs relating to mission work

in the west   *The Rupert's Land Gleaner* was published in the
interests of the English Church missionary work in the diocese
of Rupert's Land and other portions of the ecclesiastical province, and gave special attention to the new settlements, the
work in the Indian Missions and St. Paul's Industrial School.
Several years ago it ceased publication.   *Progress* is the organ
of the Industrial School at Regina, which is under the care of
the Presbyterian Church.

British Columbia has its own distinctive literature, marked
by its own phases of life and character.   The beautiful province
by the western sea, with its towering forests, wide rivers teem-
ing with fish, and its majestic snow-crowned mountains, has
within its borders many tribes and languages of which little is
known.   Travellers have sought the freshening breezes of the
sea, and found health and adventure in the interior; traders
have made money at their solitary posts; prospectors have
endured great hardships in their search after gold: and missionaries have followed the Indians in their canoes along the rivers
to tell the red men of life, liberty and civilization in the Gospel.

One of the earliest works dealing with the Indian tribes of
British Columbia, is "A Narrative of the Adventures and
Sufferings of John R. Jewitt" (1815).   The narrator was a
captive for three years among the natives of Nootka Sound.
During his residence among them he studied their customs, and
in his story gives an account of what he saw and heard.

FitzGerald's "Charter and Proceedings of the Hudson's Bay
Company, with Reference to Vancouver Island" (1849), was
published in the year that Vancouver Island became a Crown
colony.   The discovery of gold in British Columbia attracted
thousands of adventurous spirits, until in 1858 there were
between twenty and thirty thousand men digging for the
precious metal on the Frazer River and its tributaries.   W. C.
Hazlett's "British Columbia and Vancouver Island" (1858) and
J. D. Pemberton's "Facts and Figures relating to Vancouver
Island and British Columbia" (1860) deal with the history of
the country, its resources and progress.   British Columbia having
become a separate Crown colony, special interest was aroused,

and several books were published in 1862, namely, R. C. Mayne's "Four Years in British Columbia and Vancouver Island;" Captain C. E. Barrett Lennard's "Travels in British Columbia;" "Cariboo, the Newly Discovered Gold Fields of British Columbia," by a Returned Digger; Dr. Charles Forbes' "Vancouver Island: Its Resources and Capabilities as a Colony;" Alexander Rattray's "Vancouver Island and British Columbia;" and D. G. F. Macdonald's "British Columbia and Vancouver Island."

The publication of so many works in one year show the deep interest awakened in the twin colonies of the west, and the consequent rapid development of the country. The history, geography, resources, geology, mining and trade interests, population and progress of the country are fully described in these books, with numerous interesting facts relating to the native tribes.

Matthew Macfie's comprehensive volume, "Vancouver Island and British Columbia" (1865) is a charming record of the past, present and future of the colonies. Savage scenes and customs, with notes on the native languages, are aptly treated in G. M. Sproat's "Scenes and Studies of Savage Life in Vancouver Island" (1868). A very full and attractive account of Lord Dufferin's tour through British Columbia in 1876 is given in two volumes by Molyneux St. John in his work, entitled "The Sea of Mountains" (1877) Charles W. Busk's "Notes of a Journey from Toronto to British Columbia" (1884) gives the reflections of the author upon what he saw and heard upon his tour. Sport and adventure in the interior, hunting in the mountains and fishing in the rivers is delightfully told in G. O. Shield's "Cruising in the Cascades" (1889), and the observations of a surveyor in the Rocky Mountains are given by W. S. Green in "Among the Selkirk Glaciers" (1890). The history of British Columbia is treated in its stirring period by Cornwallis (Kinahan) in "The New El Dorado" (1858). Hubert H. Bancroft, the noted historian of the native races of the Pacific States, has written a large work, "History of British Columbia 1792-1887" (1887), which contains nine pages of bibliography, showing how full is

34

the literature of the province by the sea; and Alexander Begg,
C.C., has published an exhaustive history of British Columbia
(1895), from its earliest discovery to the present time. This
work discusses fully the fur-trading period, with its romantic
scenes and incidents; the exploration of Vancouver; the overland journeys of Mackenzie and Sir George Simpson; the
story of the colonial and federation period; the native tribes
and mission work amongst them, and the resources of the
forests, fisheries and mines.

A charming record of the faithful missionary, Duncan, and
his successful mission among the natives in his famous native
colony at Metlakahtla is told by Henry S. Welcome, in
"The Story of Metlakahtla" (1887). This is one of the best
books ever published on missions, and is a veritable romance
by the sea.

The *Taestlaes-Nahwoelnaek* or *Carrier Review* is a native
newspaper, printed in the Dèné syllabic characters invented by
the Rev. A. G. Morice. It is an eight-page periodical, issued
solely for the use of the natives among whom Father Morice is
laboring at Stuart's Lake. Another interesting native newspaper is the *Kamloops Wawa*, published weekly in the Chinook
jargon, with stenographic characters, by the Rev. J. M. R. le
Jeune, of Kamloops. Father le Jeune adapted the Duployan
system of shorthand to the Chinook jargon with such success
that the Indians are able to read anything published in it in
three months. The *Eskimo Bulletin* is the only journal published within the Arctic circle. It is printed at Cape Prince of
Wales, Alaska, and is issued only once a year. Several interesting essays and articles on the native tribes, languages and
customs have been published by intelligent observers and
scientists which it would not be wise to pass over. Niblack's
" The Coast Indians of Southern Alaska and British Columbia,"
in the annual report of the Smithsonian Institution," is a
clear, full and striking account of the customs of the natives.
James Deans has written several interesting papers on the
Haidas and other tribes of British Columbia, which have
appeared in the " American Antiquarian."

Dr. G. M. Dawson has written some excellent essays on the Indians of British Columbia. During his explorations he visited many of the tribes, compared their languages, conversed with interpreters, missionaries, traders, and other persons who had studied the languages and customs, and in his papers numerous important facts are given of great value to the student of native lore. There is an essay of Dawson's on "The Haidas," in the "Geological Survey of Canada Report," 1878-79, "Notes on the Shuswap People of British Columbia" appears in Volume IX. of "Transactions of the Royal Society of Canada," and "Notes and Observations on the Kwakiool People," in Volume V. of the "Transactions." The following articles, by specialists, on the native races of Canada are important: Rev. A. G. Morice, "Are the Carrier Sociology and Mythology Indigenous or Exotic?" "Proceedings of the Royal Society of Canada," Volume X; Alexander Mackenzie, "Descriptive Notes on Certain Implements, Weapons, etc., from Graham Island, Queen Charlotte Islands, B.C.," "Proceedings of the Royal Society of Canada," Volume IX; Paul Kane, "The Chinook Indians," *Canadian Journal* (1854-55), Volume III., and Prof. O. T. Mason, "Basket Work of the North American Indians," describing the basket work of the Tinne, Chilkaht, Haida, Bilhoola and other native tribes; "Smithsonian Report," 1884, Part II.

Interesting papers have been read before the Natural History Society of British Columbia, on "The Bears of British Columbia," "The Crania of Certain Indian Tribes of British Columbia," "Haida Legends," and "The Preservation of the Indian Remains of British Columbia." Dr. Franz Boaz has made extensive explorations among the native tribes of British Columbia studying their languages, mythology and sociology. The results of his labors are to be found in numerous reports and papers, but many of his important notes still remain in manuscript awaiting leisure to issue them in permanent form. Amongst his publications the following bear upon the subject under consideration: "The Language of the Bilhoola in British Columbia," in "Science," Vol. VII.; "Myths and Legends of the

Catloltq," in "American Antiquarian," Vol. X. ; "The Indians of British Columbia," in " Proceedings of the Royal Society of Canada," Vol. VI. ; " Notes on the Snanaimuq," in "American Anthropologist," Vol. II. The first, second and third " General Reports of the British Association on the North-western Tribes of Canada" treat of the tribes of British Columbia, their languages and customs.

There exists a general class of books for English and French readers who desire to become conversant with the languages of the Indians and their grammatical construction. In the Cree language there have been published Lacombe's Cree Manual, Gueguen's Cree Primer, a Primer by Bishop Bompas, containing lessons, prayers, catechism and hymns, and E. B. Glass' Cree Primer and Language Lessons, and Cree Syllabic Instruction Charts. Rev. E. Pettitot has published " Monographie des Esquimaux Tchiglit du Mackenzie et de l'Anderson," and Bishop Bompas has issued a Western Eskimo Primer. These works are necessary helps to all those who wish to understand the language of the Crees and Eskimos, either for the study of comparative philology or to use in conversation with the natives. Lacombe's Blackfoot Primer is an adaptation of a part of the first reading book to the language of the Blackfoot Indians.

Grammars of the Ojibway, Cree, Blackfoot, Montagnais and Saulteaux languages have been published which compare favorably with the efforts of missionaries in this direction in civilized or savage lands. The Cree language has been chiefly studied, as there have been more missionaries laboring among the tribes comprising this confederacy, which is the most numerous in the west and north. The most comprehensive and philosophical work published on any of the western languages, except Pettitot's voluminous publication which treats of the languages of the north, is Archdeacon Hunter's "Lecture on the Grammatical Construction of the Cree Language." In his preface the author makes this suggestive remark : " Since the year 1844 my attention has been more or less directed to the Cree language, and the more familiar I have become with its grammatical construction—so peculiar and unique, and yet so regular and systematic—the more I have been impressed with the beauty, order and precision of the language used by the Indians around us. Although they may rank low in the scale of civilization, yet they carry about with them a vocabulary and a grammar which challenge and invite and will amply repay the acumen and analytical powers of the most learned philologist. If a Council of Grammarians, assembled from among the most eminent in all nations, had after years of labor propounded a new scheme of language, they could scarcely have elaborated a system more regular, beautiful and symmetrical." Such a language could not fail to attract men of culture, some of whom are found laboring among the tribes, in isolated missions, enduring great privations for the cause they so dearly love. Joseph Howse's grammar is the oldest and still remains one of the best on the language of the Cree Indians. Bishop Horden's grammar is a handy volume, well arranged and sufficiently comprehensive for everyday use. Rev. Albert Lacombe's work embraces a grammar and dictionary published in French of the language spoken by the Crees who live upon the prairies and on the margin of the lakes and forests of the, north. The Ojibway language of the Lake Superior district and Rainy Lake is treated in the grammar of Bishop Baraga. C. Lanning and Rev. J. W. Tims have each published a small grammar and vocabulary of the Blackfoot language, which are the only grammars published, although there are grammars still in manuscript, possessed by those who have lived amongst these people. A grammar of the Montagnais language of Lake Athabasca, has been published by Rev. Laurent Legoff, and one on the Saulteaux language by the Rev. George Antoine Belcourt. Besides the works already mentioned, Thomas Bowrey, nearly two hundred years ago, prepared a Cree dictionary, which has been succeeded by the Cree dictionary of the Rev. E. A. Watkins. The Rev. E. Pettitot has published a dictionary of the Montagnais or Chippewayan language and a French vocabulary of the Tchiglit ·language. A vocabulary of the language of the

Slave Indians has been prepared by Robert Kennicott, and one of the Beaver language by the Rev. A. E. Garrioch.

The natives have not been forgotten by these industrious students of the languages, who have prepared grammars, dictionaries and vocabularies as incidental to their chief work of translating books for the use of the Indians. In the Cree language E. B. Glass published Syllabic Instruction Charts, Orrin German two of Moody's Sermons, and Albert Lacombe a "Calendar for Guidance in Religious Practice and Instructions on Roman Catholic doctrine."

THE CREE SYLLABARY.

I. INITIALS OR PRIMALS.

▽	△	▷	◁
ā	ĕ	ō	ü

II. SYLLABICS.

∨	∧	>	<
pā	pĕ	pō	pä

U	∩	)	(
tā	tĕ	tō	tä

⌐	⌐	J	∪
chā	chĕ	chō	chä

q	ρ	d	b
kā	kĕ	kō	kä

⌐	⌐	⌐	L
mā	mĕ	mō	mä

⌐	σ	⌐	a
nā	nĕ	nō	nä

↘	↗	↗	↘
sā	sĕ	sō	sä

↙	↗	↙	↘
yā	yĕ	yō	yä

III. FINALS OR TERMINALS.

ᒼ = m	ᐠ = k	ᐧ = w
ᐣ = n	ᑊ = p	ᕑ = r
ᐢ = s	ᐟ = t	ᓬ = l
ᐨ = h	ᐦ = aspirate	ᐤ = ow
	ᕁ = Christ	

EXAMPLES OF WORD FORMATION.

ᒪᓂᑐ = ma-nē-tō = spirit.
ᓂᐱ = nē pē = water.
ᓂᔭ = nē-ya = I.
ᑭᔭ = kē-ya = thou.
ᓂᐸᐣ = nē-pa-n = summer.
ᒣᑕᑕᐟ = mā-ta-ta-t = ten.
ᑫᓀᐯᐠ = kā-nā-pā-k = a snake.

THE SWEET BY AND BYE.

ᐊᔩᓇᓀᐅᒥᑕᓂᐤ ᑌᐸᑯᐦᐳᓴᑊ.

---

1 ᐃᑕᑲᐧᐣ ᐁᒥᐊᐧᔨᐠ ᐊᐢᑭ
ᒪᑲᐧᐨ ᐊᐧᐦᔭᐤ ᑯᓴᐸᐦᑌᓇᐤ
ᒪᑲ ᑯᐦᑕᐃᐧᓇᐤ ᐁᑯᑌ
ᑭᐊᐧᐁᐧᔨᐢᑖᒪᑯᓈᓇᐤ.

ᐁᑯᑌ ᐹᑎᒫ
ᑭᑲᓇᑭᐢᑯᑖ ᑐᓇᓇᐤ
ᐁᑲᑌ ᐸᑎᒫ
ᑭᑲᓇᑭᐢᑯᑖᑐᓇᓇᐤ.

2 ᑭᑲᓂᑲᒧᓇᐤ ᐁᑯᑌ
ᐱᒫᒋᐦᐅᐃᐧ ᓂᑲᒧᓇ
ᐊᐦᑑˣ ᒧᓴᐠ ᑕᒥᐁᐧᔨᒧ
ᓇᒪ ᐃᐦᑲᐧᐤ ᓀᐤᑐᓯᐃᐧᐤ.

ᐁᑯᑌ ᐸᑎᒫ, &c.

3 ᑯᐦᑕᐃᐧᓇᐤ ᑭᑲᒥᔭᓇᐤ
ᔮᑭᐟᐤᑐᐃᐧ ᓇᓈᐢᑯᒧᐃᐧᐤ
ᐁᒥᔨᑯᔭˣ ᐯᒪᒋᐟᐁᐧᐟ
ᓴᐁᐧᔨᐦᑕˣ ᑕᐦᑐ ᑭᓯᑳᐤ.

ᐁᑯᑌ ᐸᑎᒪ, &c.

Bishop Bompas prepared primers in the Eskimo, Beaver, Chippewayan, Dog-Rib, Tinne and Tukudh languages. The Montagnais or Chippewayan Indians have had published for their use, by the Rev. L. Legoff, a course of religious instruction and a history of the Old Testament.

"Peep o' Day" has been translated for the Ojibways of the Diocese of Moosonee, by the Rev. John Sanders; "Readings from the Holy Scriptures" in the Blackfoot language by the Rev. J. W. Tims, and the "Sermons of Bishop Baraga" for the use of the Indians at the posts of Albany, Savern and Martin's Falls, by the Rev. A. M. Garin. In the Cree language Archdeacon Hunter has published the "Faith and Duty of a Christian," the Rev. John Semmens the "Way of Salvation," Archdeacon Vincent the "Pilgrim's Progress," and a new edition of Bunyan's immortal work is being issued by the Methodist Publishing House at Toronto.

The Cree is one of the few Indian languages in which the whole Bible has been published. The translating of the Bible has been one of the first duties of the pioneer missionaries to the Indians, and although the difficulties have been very great, they have labored hard until they were overcome. The Rev. A. G. Morice translated Genesis into Taculli; Dr. R. McDonald Genesis, Exodus and Leviticus into Tukudh; Rev. E. J. Peck portions of the Scriptures into Eskimo; and the Rev. Père Grouard an abridgment of the Bible into the Chippewayan language.

The New Testament has been translated into the Chippewayan language by the Rev. W. W. Kirby; Dr. R. McDonald translated it into Tukudh; a Roman Catholic version has been prepared in Cree by the Rev. Albert Lacombe, and a Protestant version by Bishop Horden. A Bible history in Chippewayan has been prepared by Rev. L. Legoff, and one in the Moose dialect, and another in Saulteaux by Bishop Horden. Portions of the New Testament in the languages of the Indians have been translated by these devoted laborers. The Gospels, Acts and Revelation, in the Slave dialect, have been translated by Bishop Bompas, assisted by the Rev. W. D. Reeve; Mark and John in the Tinne, by the Rev. W. W. Kirby; Luke and Revelation in Eskimo, by the Rev. E. J. Peck; Matthew, Mark and John in Cree, by Archdeacon Hunter; the First Epistle of John, by Mrs. Hunter; and the Gospel of Matthew in Blackfoot, by the Rev. J. W. Tims.

Several Roman Catholic and Protestant catechisms have been translated for the use of the natives. Mrs. Hunter, wife of Archdeacon Hunter, translated Watt's First Catechism in the Cree language, and Mrs. Mason prepared another translation of the same work. In the same language the Roman Catholic Catechism was issued by the Rev. A. M. Garin, and two separate editions, with hymns added, by the Rev. J. P. Guéguen and J. B. Thibault. Catechisms have also been published by Père Lacombe, in Saulteaux; A. G. Morice, in the Carrier tongue; Charles Ovide Perrault, in the Montagnais language; and Rev. E. J. Peck, in Eskimo.

Numerous psalm and hymn books have been translated and published for the use of the Indians in the north and west by missionaries of the Roman Catholic, Anglican, and Methodist Churches. Cree psalm and humn books have been prepared by Archdeacon Hunter and his wife, Archdeacon John A. MacKay, William Mason, William West Kirby, Orrin German, and E. B. Glass conjointly with John McDougall. A hymn book in Cree was published by the Wesleyan Methodist Missionary Society of Britain, without any author's name; a hymn book and catechism combined was published by Rev. L. M. Lebret, for the use of the Roman Catholic Indians, in the Cree language; and a hymn book for the same confederacy by Rev. A. Lacombe: a hymn and prayer book for the Slave Indians was issued by Rev. William West Kirby; Bishop Horden, assisted by Messrs. Kirby and Sanders, prepared hymn books in the Moose dialect of the Cree language, and the dialect of the York Factory District, the Saulteaux tongue, and the Ojibway Indians of the Moosonee diocese. Separate hymns in the Blackfoot language have been printed by Lacombe, Tims, and Maclean.

Prayer books in the Cree language have been prepared by Archdeacon Hunter and his wife, Bishop Horden, Archdeacon John A. Mackay; and a Roman Catholic prayer book by the Rev. Albert Lacombe. Bishop Horden has also published a prayer book in Saulteaux, and one for the use of the Ojibway Indians in his diocese. The Rev. Laurant Legoff has translated a prayer book in Montagnais, and A. M. Garin another for the indians of the posts of Albany, Savern and Martin's Falls.

The natives of British Columbia have not been forgotten by scientists and missionaries in their efforts to understand their languages and ameliorate their condition. Bancroft discusses some important features of some of the native languages in his first volume on "Native Races of the Pacific States," and the Tahkaht or Nootka Language is ably treated by the Rev. C. Knipe in his work, "Some account of the Tahkaht Language, as Spoken by Several Tribes on the Western Coast of Vancouver Island." A grammar of the Kwagiutl language, prepared by the Rev. Alfred J. Hall, was published in the "Transactions of the Royal Society of Canada," Volume VI. Several dictionaries of the Chinook jargon have been published, as it is an intermediary form of speech among the Indian tribes, and is an easy mode of communication between the natives and white men. F. N. Blanchet, Coones, Demers, Gill, Horatio Hale, Langvein, Lionnet

JAMES EVANS.

Probsch, George Gibbs, G. Stuart, J. B. Good and C. M. Tate have each published a dictionary of the jargon. Father Le Jeune has issued in the jargon a Primer and a Play, and a First Reading Book, including hymns, syllabary and vocabulary. Tolmie and Dawson's "Comparative Vocabularies of the Indian Tribes of British Columbia" is an interesting book, giving lists of words in English, with their meaning in the native languages, and important notes on the tribes and the languages spoken by them.

Dr. Franz Boaz has published in ethnological journals Chinook songs and notes on the language, and has in his possession extensive notes in manuscript on the myths, legends and grammar of the Chinookan languages.

Father Le Jeune's "Shorthand Primer for the Thompson Language" is an important help to the Indians of Thompson River, enabling them to study their own language in a very short period.

Father Morice, of Stuart's Lake, has also invented an easy method by which the Indians can gain a knowledge of their own language in a short time. Concerning his syllabary he says, in his article on "The Western Denes": "In these latter years, however, an effort has been made by the writer of this paper to teach them to read and write their own language, and the result has been really wonderful. In order to attain this satisfactory and promising result he has had to compose a syllabic alphabet, somewhat on the principle of that so suitably invented by the late Mr. Evans for the Cree language, but which he soon found to be totally inadequate to render correctly the numerous delicate sounds of the Dene dialects. Besides (why should I not say it ?) it lacks that method and logic which have been applied to the new and improved syllabics, and which have thereby simplified the acquisition of the language. I am now continually in receipt of letters from Indians whom I never taught, and who have learned to read after one or two weeks'— in some cases I might say, three or four days'—private instruction from others."

There is not, to my knowledge, any part of the Old Testa-

by J. M. R. Le Jeune. O. M. I.

PRAYERS IN THE THOMPSON TONGUE.

ment published in any of the languages of British Columbia, and the only parts of the New Testament are the Gospels of Matthew and John in the Qagutl language. Father Le Jeune has published on his mimeograph the first catechism in the Shushwap and Thompson languages.

There are several prayer books in the languages of the natives. A prayer book, in the Necklapamuk or Thompson tongue, has been prepared by the Rev. John Booth Good for the use of the Indians on the Church of England missions. Another, in the same language, for the Roman Catholic Indians has been published by the Rev. J. M. R. Le Jeune, who has also issued prayers in Shushwap: and a part of the "Book of Common Prayer" has been printed in the Kwagiutl language by the Rev. Alfred J. Hall. The native literature of Western Canada is developing slowly by the culture and energy of scientists, travellers and missionaries, who find among the savage tribes languages which are burdened with their hidden wealth, ready to yield their treasures unto those who seek.

THE CONFLICT OF RACES.

The natives of our plains, forests, rivers and mountains, uninfluenced by the civilization of the white man, believe strongly in the superiority of their race. This no doubt arises from their isolation and study of their own customs and belief, without having an opportunity of comparing them with the customs and belief of other races. During the second Riel Rebellion, a Blood Indian chief, named Bull Shield came to me and informed me that he had been to town and seen a regiment of French infantry, which had been sent from the Province of Quebec to help maintain peace in Southern Alberta. He laughed at the idea of little men on foot being able to do anything upon the prairie if the Indians should go to war. Requesting me to act the part of a sentinel, he went through a series of native military tactics to show me that the Indians could kill every man placed on guard and never be discovered. Crouching on the ground with a knife in his teeth, and his whole body covered with a blanket, he sprang unsuspectingly upon me, as I walked to and fro. "I would not shoot my gun, for that would alarm the enemy," said he, "and I would lie near at hand without any fear, until I was close enough to strike him dead." The white men seemed foolish in his eyes to send such a contingent to protect anyone. Much of this feeling, combined with anger arising from ill-treatment and the possession of native courage, has lain at the foundation of the Indian wars in the United States. The preponderance of numbers in the early days helped to sustain this feeling of superiority among the natives of Canada, as they well knew that they could easily destroy the white settlements if they chose to do so. Good treatment and the faithfulness of the Government in strictly adhering to the terms of the treaties, kept them loyal; still they always believed in their superiority. In order to give the natives a real knowledge of their position, the government sent some of the chiefs to Ontario and Quebec, and having witnessed some of the works and wealth of the white men, they returned with lasting impressions of the power of their white brethren. When, however, they turn to the peaceful arts of life they can assert their supremacy. They can tell the native names of the flowers and plants, describe their habits and medicinal properties, and the white man is a stranger to many of these things. The birds of the Rocky Mountains are their friends, and many of the plain Indians are no mean ornithologists. The animals, from the gopher on the prairie to the mountain sheep and bear, are known so well that they can speak freely of their habits, and from them learn to prognosticate the weather. They know the rivers and lakes, and although white men are frequently drowned in crossing the streams, it is a rare thing to hear of even an Indian child being drowned. Better than any white man can they track horses which are lost on the prairie, for they feel at home on the vast expanse. Nature is their teacher, and unconsciously they have learned. They have kept their eyes open and have seen wonders where the white men saw nothing. As they carve their beautiful stone pipes, which the white people eagerly buy, their belief is strengthened, for the value of the pipe as a specimen of native handicraft is often misinterpreted to mean inaptitude for the business of pipe-making. The various objects of nature, land-slides, weather-beaten cliffs, scarped mountains, deep canyons, contorted trees and strange-looking boulders are alive with mythological personages, who speak to the Indian mind a language unknown to any save the members of his race. All of these contribute their share in strengthening the belief that the white race is inferior to the natives.

When they begin to study the ways of the pioneers of civilization they are drawn toward the buildings erected by the force of intellect, and witness there a skill which they fail to understand. Patiently the Indian will follow an enemy, but patience is a virtue in the peaceful arts of life which he does not possess. The planning of the architect, the concentrated force of intellect necessary for a number of men to erect a building are to him strange things. He is willing, therefore, to accord to the white man partial superiority. He admires a good gun; a cannon raises the white men in his estimation, and when he gazes upon the feats of the cowboys in roping and tying cattle and stands beside a locomotive or steamboat, he is willing to divide the honors of supremacy.

It is perfectly legitimate for the savage of the west to be proud of his native culture, adapted as it is to his needs, and apparently better suited to him than the civilization of the white race, under whose influence he sees his fathers and brethren rapidly dwindling away. There is a native education, unsystematized it is true, yet it exists. There are lessons in the lodges from fathers, mothers, and guardians for the boys and girls. The father delights to see his boy an adept at shooting with the bow and arrow, and he is taught to ride and hunt. The youth learns the secrets of nature, the mysteries of plant life, the history of his tribe, the unwritten biographies of the great men of his race; the stars become his book of night, the old men train him in the science of politics; indeed, everything necessary to become good, great, wise and happy is taught him, and this constitutes the system of education. The girls learn to dress hides, cook the food, make moccasins and other articles of dress, and prepare themselves for all the duties of camp life. Believing firmly in the principle of adaptation, they will either object to our system of education, as reading, writing, and counting, or look upon it with an air of indifference. Naturally they wish to know how all our learning will qualify them to hunt and fight, and in any measure fit their children to become better Indians. We wish to make them white men, and they desire them to become better Indians. They believe the native culture is best suited for themselves, and having developed under it, and enjoyed it so long, they care not to give it up for an untried system. There is a danger of educating them away from their real life. When their circumstances change, and the new life does not rest upon them as a burden, they gladly accept and, indeed, desire to become possessed of the culture which will fit them for their new conditions.

The nomadic habits of the red men stand out in striking contrast with the settled life of the white men. Camp life and town life are in conflict. The one is a permanent society in a well-defined and settled condition; the other is a society governed by laws, but essentially temporary in its conditions and character. Unknown diseases to the natives seize upon their bodies with the advent of the pioneers of civilization. Different styles of dress appear which are strange, and seem to the native mind unsuited to their modes of living. The white man's food does not agree with the denizen of the prairie and forest, unlearned in the art of cooking the new materials. The class of work does not call into play the muscles, for those used by the white man are undeveloped in his red brother. Even their ideas of morality differ, and it appears as if there were a predestined antagonism of the races, but the conflict ends in the subjugation of the red man adopting the modes of life of his conqueror. It is the old story of the march of the white conquerors over the earth, and wherever they go traces of the conflict are seen in decaying and dead races of men.

35

Sometimes the conflict assumes a more determined form, and is not one solely of customs, but becomes a war of self-interest and injustice. This has evidently been the case in the contest between the red and white races in the land of our great neighbor. The sad story of the treatment of the Poncas, Winnebagoes, Sioux, and other tribes by the white race can be read in the writings of Bishop Whipple, and especially in Helen Hunt Jackson's admirable volumes, "A Century of Dishonor" and "Ramona." The Bishop says in relation to the Minnesota Massacre and the expedition of General Custer. "In 1858 the Sioux Indians of Minnesota sold us eight hundred thousand acres of their Reservation. The plea for this sale was that they needed more money to aid them in the work of civilization. This treaty provided that none of the proceeds of this sale should be paid for Indian debts, unless such debts had been recognized in an open council. No such council was ever held. The Indians waited four years They never received one penny of this money, except about fifteen thousand dollars' worth of worthless goods. All this money was taken for claims, except about eight hundred and sixty-eight dollars, which was left to their credit in Washington. In June, 1862, they came together to receive their annual payment. The annuity money had not come. The traders told the Indians that it had been stolen. They waited two months—mad, exasperated and hungry. Then came that awful massacre, in which eight-hundred of brave pioneers were murdered. No pen can describe the horrors of that desolated border. The money for the payment was sent too late. At the eleventh hour, twenty-five thousand dollars was taken from other trust funds to supply that portion of the annuities which had been paid out for claims against the Indians. The Winnebagoes lived near the Sioux. They were our friends. They refused to join in the outbreak. They even killed the Sioux messengers who asked it. They cut off their ears and sent them to the whites, to show their friendship to us and the fate of our enemies. The Winnebagoes had a goodly Reservation, which white men coveted. They were removed by force,. and were taken with the friendly Sioux to the Missouri River,

and located there at Crow Creek. Over one thousand of these
Indians died of disease and starvation that year. During that
awful winter some Indian women crossed from the Missouri to
Fairbault, my home, and God only knows how they lived, for
their only food was frozen roots which they dug on the prairie.

.   .   .   .

"I am told that when the Indian chiefs met the commissioners
at Medicine Lodge Creek they gave, as a reason for not making
another treaty with us, that three times men have come to us
and made treaties. 'They said that their Great Father sent
them. They were liars; we have not seen one thing they
promised.' After long discussion, the Indians said that 'They
believed the men who wore our uniforms had straight tongues.'
They made another treaty. One thing that they insisted upon
was that they should have a country which should not be
invaded by the whites. This pledge was made. The country
which contains the Black Hills was guaranteed to them. No
possible plea can be made against their title, except the plea of
the footpad, who places his pistol to your breast and says,
'Might makes right.' The expedition of General Custer was
made in clear violation of a nation's faith. Gold was discovered.
At first we were ashamed to violate our own treaty. The
noble man who made that treaty for us honestly tried to
keep white men out of the Indian country. It was impossible. Our only honorable course was to make such amends as
we could by purchase. The Government did send out a com-
mission, but the plea for economy was made a pretext to tie the
hands of the commissioners so that they were powerless. The
Indians wanted a fair settlement. They were ready to make a
sale. We offered them four hundred thousand dollars for the
Black Hill country. As all the Indians from the Santee
Agency to White River were to be included in this treaty, the
amount offered was only about one-fourth of our annual
expenditure for these tribes. The treaty failed. The evil has
been done. The Black Hills swarm with miners. We shall
have another Indian war, and spend some millions of dollars to
swell the hundred of millions already spent in Indian wars.

Many of our brave officers and soldiers will lose their lives in a war which brings them no glory; many a home will be destroyed and innocent people murdered by massacre."

Our Canadian Indians have beautiful languages, accurate and full in their grammatical structure, euphonious and expressive, a delight to the philologist and the pride of the natives. They will not use by compulsion another language, not even the English tongue, because they can more freely express themselves in their own form of speech, and for the same reason that an English-speaking person prefers his own language. There can be no legitimate method of stamping out the native language except by a wise policy of teaching English in the schools, and allowing the Indian tongue to die out. Prohibitory measures, compelling English alone to be used in the schools, will arouse the latent antagonism and retard progress. English must be taught. It is the desire of the Government and the missionaries that the English language should become the only medium of communication ; but this will be gained gradually, and not by the complete prohibition of the native tongue.

There exists a conflict of belief as well as language. Before the advent of the missionary the natives are deeply swayed by their own system of theology, formulated unconsciously. They have definite beliefs. They are deeply imbued with animism, which acts powerfully upon them in maintaining their own forms of religion. They have as deep a sense of God in nature as Butler and Wordsworth, and the divinity in man is as keenly felt as ever Coleridge or Carlyle taught it. Hence they are dogmatists, and believe that they are right in their belief. When the trader appears with his Christian belief and unchristian practice, they become more strongly entrenched in their dogmatic citadel, and with the advent of the missionary they are ready for an assault of their faith. It is well that the religious teacher has to spend some time in learning the native language, for then the people can observe the beauty of his life, experience his sympathy and help, and finally their opposition is thrown down by love and not by argument. The trader's belief conflicts with the native religion, and the missionary's life opens the way for the truth to gain their assent and reach their hearts. The appeal of the Cross in the hands of the Jesuits gained many converts, because the men were

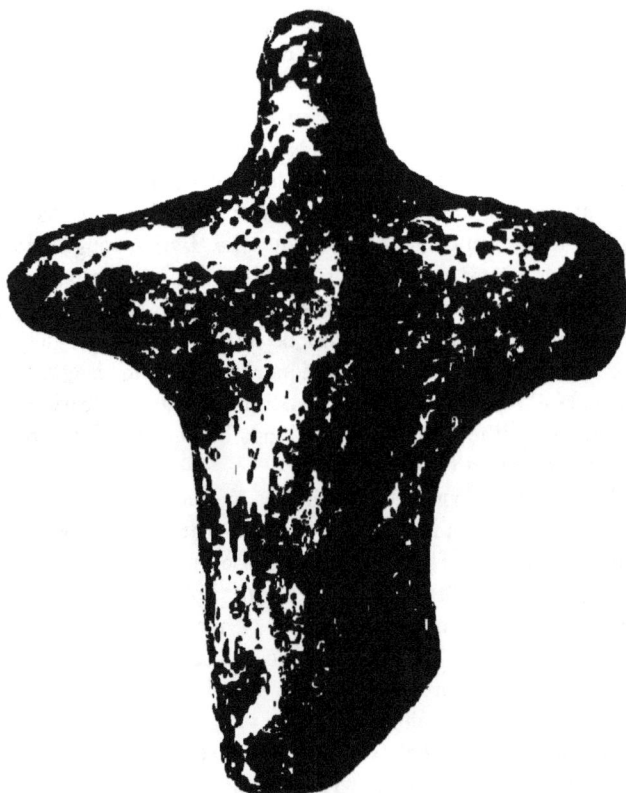

JESUIT STONE CROSS.

heroic and devoted their lives for the good of the people. Relics of the labors of these devoted men still remain among us, showing their methods of teaching and enthusiasm. A few years ago there was dug up on an old church site at Saugeen a stone cross, supposed to be two hundred years old, and to belong to the Jesuits. The illustration made from a photo of this cross gives a good idea of its shape.

In all our dealings with the Indians we have tried to win them, yet there have been many hindrances. The book of nature was the Indians guide, and he could not understand why the Bible should belong to him when it was not written in a language which he could understand and read without being taught to read. The Sabbath was new to him, but not the principle of a series of days devoted to religious purposes. He believed in prayer, sacrifice, the existence of a great nature power, if not also in a personal God, the existence of spirits, the coming of a Redeemer, the immortality of the soul and a future state. So far he was in agreement with the Christian teacher, but the lessons he learned from the society of men who were Christian only in name brought him into antagonism with the white men. Christianity exalted gentleness and humility as virtues, while the red man's graces were courage in war and supremacy in the camp. He loved and practised unbounded hospitality toward both races; but the white men were hospitable only to their own people. They saw the white men protecting their wives and daughters, and degrading the women of the camps. How could the unsophisticated red man recognize these antagonisms? They were mysteries to him, and they remain so to us.

The red man is a politician, as well as his white brother, skilful in all the arts of electioneering and the methods of statesmanship at the councils. In the election of chiefs, discussion of the civil affairs of the camp, formulation of unwritten laws and administration of justice, the natives possess wisdom and courage, and the white man might learn some good measures from their simplicity and sternness in dispensing justice and treating criminals. He can advocate the claims of his favorite candidate for political honors, and in the hidden craft of gaining support visit the lodges, and by means of criers keep his man before the minds of the people as successfully as the editors of the great newspapers of the land. When, however, he comes in contact with the new civilization his power is lost,

as he becomes a ward of the Government, and not a free man.
He enjoys the franchise of the camps, but not the franchise of
a white man. The time may soon come when the Canadian
Indian of Ontario and Quebec has ceased to be an Indian in his
belief and civilization, and is ranked with the white man in his
knowledge of the affairs of the State, that he shall exercise
the power of voting. But the man of the west will not be able
to secure this privilege until he has removed the incubus of
degraded white men and he can intelligently discuss grave
questions affecting both races, and not follow the dictates of
unprincipled men. The time has not yet come for the natives
of the west to decide for themselves on these matters, and it
would be a dangerous experiment to hurl amongst us thousands
of votes subject to the selfish interests and wily tactics of
corrupt dictators. So long as the natives must be fed at the
expense of the country, or taught to farm and engage in industrial arts and live an isolated life on Reservations, they are unfit
to stand upon an equal footing in political rights, burdens and
privileges.

In our courts of justice he is treated as a man. We respect
the treaties we have made with the tribes, and although in our
North-West a few persons, supported by one or two newspapers,
have desired the removal of a tribe of Indians from their fine
tract of land because it would be a valuable acquisition to the
white people and would help materially in the settlement of the
country, a deaf ear has been turned by our statesmen to protests
and apparent claims. We have never broken a treaty with
them, and whenever a change is desired the land is purchased
and commissioners treat with the natives at their own home.
During the present century we have not been wholly free from
arbitrary measures, yet our policy in the main has been just
and kind. An Indian is punished if he breaks the law of the
land; and if even a native woman or child has been injured by
a white man, the culprit is sought out and punished. In the
administration of the law, if we err at all, it is on the side of
leniency toward the red race.

Barbarism has rights which civilized men must respect. In

INDIAN SUMMER CAMP ON LADY EVELYN LAKE.

the struggle for supremacy the red man has not the opportunity nor has he the advantages of the centuries of experience enjoyed by the white race, consequently he must suffer in the contest. Believing and teaching the Gospel of brotherhood, we are not at liberty to kill him, nor even to pauperize him; but we may and can civilize and Christianize him. In the struggle for existence he has labored under the sternest conditions. Incessant war, continual hardship, and uncertain means of subsistence, have kept the tribes at the lowest numbers compared with the vast regions over which they roamed. Our aim must be to save the man, for he is worth saving, and to seek to solve the problem of their continuance and civilization by striving to change their social conditions and develop their latent energies. They cannot be saved in one generation. Justice and humanity compel us to treat them well, always aiming at self-support. With the watchful care of the Government and the churches during his progress from savagery to civilization, the transfer and guidance of his energies toward cattle raising and agriculture, the enlightening and strengthening of his intellect by means of schools and missionaries, and confidence in our motives and measures, we may not in our day see the native fully civilized, but we shall enjoy the consciousness of having done our duty, and some progress toward his ultimate salvation will have been gained.

CHAPTER VII.

ON THE TRAIL.

ON THE WARPATH.

WAR is the congenial occupation of the red man, as it is the delight of the white man. On the field of battle there is an outlet for ambition, and courage is seen to advantage. Every nation has its distinctive uniform and implements of warfare as well as its military tactics, and the red race is not lacking in these elements of pride and strength. The rude flint-headed arrow gave place to the flint-lock gun, and this to the later inventions of civilized life, until to-day the natives of the plains are well armed with Snider rifles, and boast of their prowess in battle. During the second Riel Rebellion the Government stopped the sale of ammunition to the western Indians, and instead of resorting to the flint arrow-head, they made the heads of their arrows from iron hoops. I have seen the old men in the camps busily engaged in this work while the young men were absent as spies.

Flint arrow-heads have been found in great abundance in the Province of Ontario, less frequently in Manitoba and the Territories, and seldom have they been discovered in British Columbia.* Only one specimen of a chipped arrow-head or spear-head having been found on the Queen Charlotte Islands, and the Haidas, to whom it was shown, expressed surprise, as they said they had never seen or heard of such a thing before. Instead of donning bright colored garments to distinguish them in the field of battle, every vestage of clothing is discarded except the

---

* "Royal Society of Canada Transactions," Vol. IX., Sec. 2, page 59.

breech-cloth, moccasins and war bonnet. The warrior paints
his body in a fantastic fashion, and there is something appalling
to the eye of civilized man on beholding a body of painted
savages. The war paint is significant. The western Indians
fought single-handed on the prairie under the direction of the
war chief or leader of the war party, spending no time in the
erection of works of defence; but upon the plain, in a river
bottom or ravine, or in any place where the combatants met
they engaged in battle. In the eastern provinces it was different, as the natives erected strong earthworks of defence, where
they were safe from the attacks of their foes.

Parkman, basing his statements upon Lafitau, says, in reference to the works of defence erected by the Iroquois: "Their
dwellings and works of defence were far from contemptible,
either in their dimensions or in their structure; and though by
the several attacks of the French, and especially by the invasion
of De Nouville in 1687, and of Frontenac nine years later, their
fortified towns were levelled to the earth, never again to reap-
pear; yet, in the works of Champlain and other early writers,
we find abundant evidence of their pristine condition. Along
the banks of the Mohawk, among the hills and hollows of Onondaga, in the forests of Oneida and Cayuga, on the romantic
shores of Seneca Lake and the rich borders of the Genesee,
surrounded by waving maize fields, and encircled from afar by
the green margin of the forest, stood the ancient strongholds
of the confederacy. The clustering dwellings were encompassed
by palisades, in single, double or triple rows, pierced with loop-
holes, furnished with platforms within for the convenience of
the defenders, with magazines of stones to hurl upon the heads
of the enemy, and with water conductors to extinguish any fire
which might be kindled from without. The area which these
defences enclosed was often several acres in extent, and the
dwellings ranged in order within were sometimes more than
a hundred feet in length."[*] The plan of the Iroquois villages
was usually circular or oval, and in one instance Frontenac
found an Onondaga village built in an oblong form, with four

---

[*] Parkman's "Pontiac," Vol. I., pages 16, 17.

bastions, having a wall formed of three rows of palisades, the outer row being forty or fifty feet high. The bastions were doubtless erected upon the advice of some European friend.

War was declared by a harangue to the assembled natives and the delivery of an axe, from which arose no doubt the figurative expression of "digging up the hatchet." A painted hatchet was sometimes used to express strong determination to fight, and to notify to their enemies their bitter enmity and resolution to destroy. It is the object of war to destroy, and the red man will seek to gain the complete overthrow of his foes by any strategy, without incurring any needless risks. He believes that all means are honorable, and he will strive to circumvent and subdue his adversary by any kind of artifice.

The causes of war between the native tribes and between the red and white races are similar to those among civilized races. The invasion of territory, hunting upon the grounds claimed by another tribe, the killing of a native in cold blood, the breaking of treaties, and the compulsory removal of the Indians (as in the case of the Nez Perces), the wholesale robbery of the Indians by the agents of the Government, and their harsh treatment by white men, the hatred of the tribes and feuds among themselves, unfulfilled promises by Government officials and the bad influence of immoral white men. The Minnesota and Custer massacres and the Riel Rebellion can be traced to some of these causes. War is not a mere pastime even among savages, for there must be some pretext, and sometimes it is a poor one, before the tribes will go on the warpath.*

Among the western tribes of our Dominion there are peace chiefs and war chiefs, the former performing the duties of civil head of the tribe, and the latter assuming the responsibilities of his office in times of war. This important military officer is elected on account of his bravery and success, and his influence is almost unlimited among his people. White Calf, the war chief of the Blood Indians, is a typical Indian, hating the

*Bryant's "California," pages 201, 223. A. K. McClure's "Through the Rocky Mountains," page 50.

FORT CHIPPEWAYAN.

language, customs and religion of the white men. As he sees
the gradual decrease of his people, and their dependence upon
the Government for support since the departure of the buffalo,
and the encroachments and haughty spirit of the white men,
remembering the freedom of the old hunting days and the
valor of the young men, and seeing them transformed into a
band of peaceful farmers, he mourns the loss of the martial
spirit and pristine liberty, and longs for the return of the heroic
days. The war chief is the native general, yet he is not absolute,
for even a chief must obey the laws of the tribe.

It was necessary to secure allies to assist the tribes in a
general war, and for the purpose of securing them, messengers
were sent by the eastern tribes to the distant tribes, bearing the
long and broad war-belt of wampum and the red-stained tomahawk. Visiting each tribe, the sachems and old men assembled
in council, when the chief of the embassy threw down the
tomahawk on the ground and delivered the speech which he
had been instructed to make. When the assemblage were in
favor of war the belt of wampum was accepted and the tomahawk snatched up as a token of their pledge. The natives
of the west sent their messengers with tobacco, and upon
addressing the council of the tribe visited, when the
warriors decided to unite in war the tobacco was accepted.
Red Crow, the peace chief of the Blood Indians, refused the
tobacco offered him by the messengers of the rebels during the
Riel Rebellion, and when Pakan, chief of the Crees, was
importuned by the messengers of Big Bear to accept the
tobacco and join the rebels, he shot one of the messengers dead.
Large war parties were not as likely to be successful as small
bodies of men, owing to their lack of discipline, individual
liberty and mode of action. The war chief could not punish
those who wished to stay at home, as they were essentially
volunteers in the service, and were bound to him by a moral
tie and an interest in the enterprise. Pride and jealousy sometimes broke out in feuds among his followers, or among the
different tribes engaged as allies, and then desertions were
frequent. The native warrior hates subordination, and delights

to gain power by means of personal bravery, so that his individuality is a barrier to concerted action, and sometimes before
the country of the enemy is reached discord has divided
the bands, and a remnant of the host is left to contend
against the foe.

When war has been declared the warriors spend a few days
singing war songs, boasting of their valor, calling upon their
gods to help them, and getting their accoutrements in readiness.
They engage in a war dance, feasting, dancing, singing and
praying; and then with their bodies painted they advance
toward the enemy's country regardless of order. Usually they
depart at night. If the distance is long they will travel by
day and rest at night, but should there be any danger they will
travel cautiously at night and rest during the day. The
western natives always take care to go upon the warpath
when there is no snow on the ground, lest they should be
tracked, and in a season when there is good feed for their
horses. If there is any chance of defeat they will make
arrangements for the safety of their women and children.
There is no likelihood of another Indian war, as there is no
refuge for the helpless folks of the camps.

Some of the natives are adepts at tracking on the prairie,
being able to tell by signs around the camping place the
number of white men and Indians in the party, whether they
are hostile or friendly, and even the names of the persons
known to them. They are experts also at concealing their
tracks by crossing, recrossing and returning upon the prints
made by the moccasin or horse-hoof, so as to baffle and
elude their pursuers, even when the snow is on the ground.
The Iroquois chiefs wore tall plumes, and arrayed themselves
in times of war in bucklers and breastplates made of cedar
wood, covered with interwoven thongs of hide; and the Hurons
carried large shields, wore greaves for the legs and cuirasses
made of twigs interwoven with cords. The scalp lock is a
thing of the past among the western warriors, if they ever
wore it, and defensive armour is unknown to them. Their
only defence is the song and divination of the medicine man
and the amulet worn on the person.

Stealing cautiously into the camp of the enemy, the single warrior enters a lodge, stirs the dying embers of the fire and quietly scans the sleeping occupants. Suddenly dealing a death-thrust to each of his victims and securing the bleeding scalps, he hurries from the scene of destruction and, elated at his success, is lost in the darkness. From our standpoint of military virtue there is no exhibition of courage, but rather an evidence of cowardice in such a dastardly feat; but the code of honor on the plains agrees with their method of fighting, which implies a wariness and coolness in the presence of danger and the defeat of their enemies by stratagem.*

Rushing suddenly upon their foes in battle, the war-whoop is given, which sends a deep thrill of excitement through the camp. White men and women who have heard it when attacked by the Blackfeet have told me, that when once it is heard it will never be forgotten. It strikes terror to the hearts of the unprotected, and men brace themselves for battle as women seek a place of refuge.

It was the custom of the natives to retain some of their prisoners to find pleasure in mutilating them, and in early Canadian history, there are sad tales of cannibalism, when the Indians, even in the presence of the French soldiers, killed their enemies, cooked and eat their flesh. Sometimes they were slain after enduring excessive tortures, but after their vengeance was appeased they would spare the remainder, and distribute them among the tribes, or allow them to be adopted by some of the families. A young man would sometimes be chosen by a native to supply the place of a dead son, and even a woman might obtain a husband for the one deceased. The Blackfeet and Crees have always spoken with intense abhorrence of cannibalism, and whenever it has been discovered, as it has in one or two instances, through starvation, the perpetrators have been ostracised. It is singular that those children who have been captured and brought up in the camp have become deeply attached to their foster parents, and have loved intensely the customs of the people, so that it was well-nigh impossible to induce them to return to

* Parkman's "Pioneers of New France," pages 342, 351.
36

civilized life or the home of their relations. John Tanner, the scout, who spent many years in Michigan, Western Ontario and Manitoba returned to his savage haunts after tasting the pleasures of civilized life. The fascination of forest and prairie and the wild ways of the red men was stronger than the joy and comfort of civilization for this strange man as it has been for other men in later years. Adoption among the Crees has been practised within the knowledge of men still living, as in the case of James Evans, the missionary. Having gone upon a missionary tour, his native companion accidentally shot himself, and the missionary returned to the family of the young man, and was adopted in his place, so that he was always recognized as the son of the parents of the deceased.

In times of peace, as well as war, the natives employ the art of signalling, in which they are very skilful. It is possible to see a long distance upon the prairie, and it is easy to send communications in times of distress. By means of lighted arrows shot through the air at night, a message can be sent and understood twenty miles away. The smoke of the fire can be so directed that it will relate its own story to anxious watchers. During the day the solitary rider will pace backward and forward upon a high bluff, or ride in a circle, or perform well-understood and significant evolutions. The single warrior will tell his tale through the sign language with his hands, or by means of his blanket, or again with a small looking-glass, he will send a flash of light across the plain, which will be easily interpreted by his people. This native system of telegraphy enables the red men to remain secluded, and yet keep one another informed on matters affecting them in times of war, by means of scouts.*

When the war expedition is ended and the warriors return home, messengers are despatched when they are approaching the camp, to inform the people of their success. The war-whoop is given a certain number of times corresponding to the number of scalps taken, and with a song of victory they enter

* Bryant's "California," page 155. McClure's "Through the Rocky Mountains," page 72.

the camp. The old men, women and children go out to meet them, and with sad wails from the women who have been bereft of husbands, fathers, sons and brothers, and shouts of victory on the part of those who have not suffered, the party is honored on account of the success of the enterprise. Since the advent of the white settlers the war expeditions have been few, and have only been undertaken to recover stolen horses. Silently they departed, and then the party was composed of only a few young men. Eight young men started about 1883, for the home of the Gros Ventre Indians in the south, to recover some horses which were stolen from the Reservation of the Blood Indians. Two of them became separated from the others, and these alone returned, the rest of them being slain and scalped by their enemies. There was great excitement in the camps for a few weeks, but the Government used its influence, and by a wise compensation to the bereaved families, a war between the two tribes was averted.

It was the custom of the Algonquins to cut off the heads of their enemies, which they carried home as trophies; and among the Indians of Nova Scotia the head was cut off and carried away and afterward scalped. The practice of scalping was in existence before the French arrived in Canada, as Jacques Cartier, in 1535, saw five scalps at Quebec, dried and stretched on hoops. Sometimes dead bodies left on the field of battle were scalped. In their anxiety to secure scalps, the conquerors did not always wait until their victims were dead, and it sometimes happened that they were only wounded slightly. Some of these persons have lived after they were scalped, which proves that scalping did not always end in death. The object of securing scalps seems not to have arisen from cruelty, but rather to give evidence of success in war. The Indian might boast in the camp of his bravery, assuring his auditors of the number of men he had slain, but there were always some who were suspicious, and believed not the statements of the young warrior. As it was not always convenient for him to secure the head of his enemy, and he could not well preserve it afterwards, the easiest way for him to substantiate his assertions was to take the scalp, which he could show to his people.[*] I have seen the lodges of half-breeds and Indians painted, having the life story of their owners depicted upon them and the scalp-locks fastened to the outside, which were tangible proofs of the military prowess of the occupants. One of my friends gave me a scalp, when it was no longer customary to hang them on the lodges, and this scalp may still be seen in the museum of the Canadian Institute, Toronto. Some of the eastern Indians were accustomed to burn their enemies at the stake, but I have never learned of this being done by the natives in the west.

During the war between the English and the French, when the Indians were engaged as allies, bounties were offered by the civilized governments for scalps, although more humane treat-ment afterward prevailed. Indeed, during this war some of the white soldiers outstripped the red men in their anxiety to secure the scalps of the Indians. It was an advantage to feign insanity among the natives who are superstitious on this matter, believing such persons as are so afflicted to be special favorites of the gods. Heckewelder mentions the case of a trader, named Chapman, who was made prisoner by the Indians at Detroit. Having determined to burn him alive, he was tied to the stake and the fire kindled. One of the Indians handed him a bowl of broth which was made scalding hot so as to give pleasure to the onlookers by the increased tortures of their victim. When the poor man placed it to his lips it produced intense pain, and in his anger he threw the bowl and its con-tents into the face of his tormentor. Instantly the crowd shouted, "He is mad! he is mad!" and as speedily as possible the fire was extinguished and the sufferer was set at liberty. Believing in destroying their enemies in any manner, the natives resorted to treachery, getting inside of forts under the pretence of friendship, and even giving pledges of protection in time of war, only to kill their foes when they had secured

* Parkman's "Frontenac," page 298. "Pioneers," page 351. *Canadian Journal*, No. 22, page 255. Guizot's "Civilization," Vol. II., page 163. "Report of the Peabody Museum," 1884, page 225. "Transactions of the Canadian Institute," Vol. III., pages 231, 237.

the advantage. There are some notable examples of honorable dealing by chiefs and warriors, who would not stoop to such acts of meanness; but when exasperated the average Indian will not in war abide by his promises, and he cannot be trusted.

The scalp dance is a significant native institution, which has passed away. The scalp having been prepared according to the native ceremonial, was fastened to a pole, which was carried through the camp, the people dancing around it, singing wildly and uttering unearthly yells.*

Upon the declaration of war black wampum belts were given by the messengers to those allies who agreed to fight, and these were pledges of unity in war, and when treaties of peace were made, belts made of white wampum were given and accepted as solemn pledges. Wampum was used by the Indians of the Eastern Provinces, especially the Six Nation Indians, but is unknown even in the traditions of the prairie tribes. At first the wampum was made of porcupine quills dyed, then of colored pieces of wood, again from the thick and blue parts of clam shells, and finally of glass beads. It was used as money by the tribes and as a pledge in solemn transactions. As late as 1844, it was extensively manufactured by the Indian women of New Jersey, who sold it to the country merchants at twelve and a half cents a string. The wampum shell beads were strung on hempen strings about a foot in length each, and one woman could make from five to ten strings a day.

At a great assembly held on July 12th, 1644, at Three Rivers, in the open square of the fort, presided over by the Governor-General, a treaty of peace was made between the Indian tribes themselves, and between the Indians and the French. There were present representatives from the Iroquois, Algonquin, Montagnais, Huron, Attikamègues and Mohawk tribes. In the middle of the open space the Iroquois planted two poles, having a cord stretched between them, upon which were placed seventeen wampum belts. Each belt was used for a specific purpose. Kiotsaeton, the famous Iroquois orator, holding the first belt of wampum, and with many significant gestures and an impressive

---

* "Eleventh Annual Report of the Bureau of Ethnology," page 526.

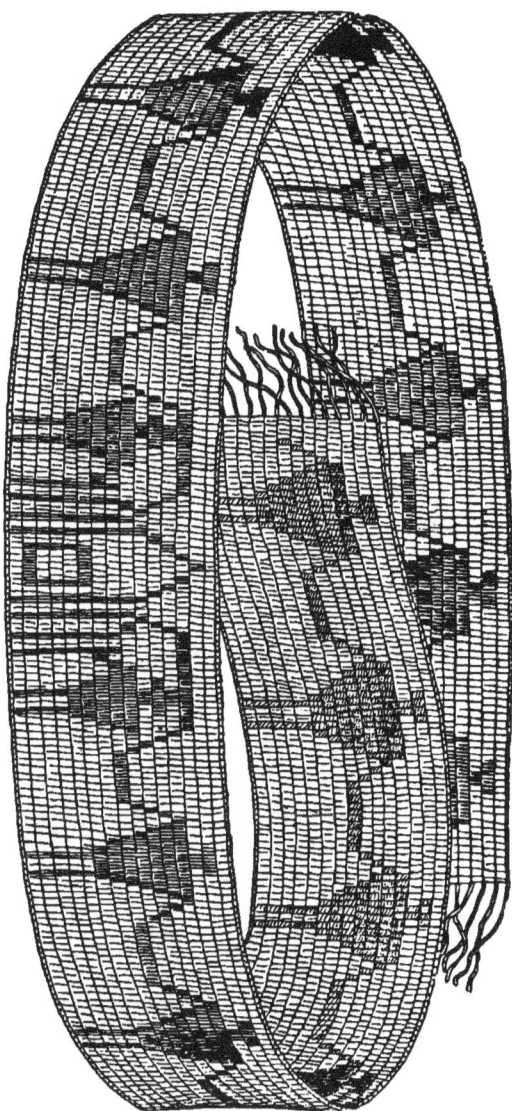

WAMPUM BELT.

speech, presented it to Onontio, the Governor-General, for rescuing Tokrahenchiaron from the Hurons. The second belt was fastened around the arm of Couture, a young Frenchman, who was a prisoner among the Iroquois, as a pledge that he was set at liberty ; the fourth belt was a pledge of peace between the Iroquois and Algonquins : the fifth belt drove the enemies' canoes away : the sixth smoothed the rapids on the way to the country of the Iroquois : the eighth was to build a road ; the tenth belt, larger and finer than the other belts, proclaimed peace between the French, Algonquins and Mohawks, and as the orator addressed the assembly he took a Frenchman and an Algonquin and bound their arms together with the belt. The eleventh belt promised hospitable board to their friends, and this part of his speech closed with the suggestive sentences, " We have fish and game in plenty ; our forests teem with stags, moose, deer, bears and beavers. Drive away the filthy hogs that defile your houses and feed only on filth." The twelfth belt banished all suspicions of deceitfulness which were ascribed to them, and as the orator beat the air, as if to scatter and drive away the clouds, he cried, " Let the sun and truth shine everywhere." The thirteenth and fourteenth belts were pledges of peace between the Iroquois and Hurons : the fifteenth was a justification of their treatment of the missionaries, Jogues and Bressani ; and the seventeenth was a present from the mother of Honateniate, who had been kept as a hostage by the Governor-General, requesting him to set her son free.*

The pipe of peace has been smoked in recent times by representatives of the tribes of the plains as a token of peaceful relations and unity, the hatchet has been buried by the eastern tribes as a pledge of friendship, and with the new conditions of existence, the progress of settlement upon the prairies, and the

---

* " Life of Isaac Jogues," page 175. "Fourth Annual Report of the Bureau of Ethnology," page 87. Parkman's " Pontiac," Vols. I. and II., has numerous references. " Old Regime," page 4, 18 ; " Pioneers," page 414. *Canadian Journal*, No. 17, page 397. " Case and His Contemporaries," Vol. IV., page 207. " American Antiquarian, Vol. VIII., page 375 ; Vol. XI., page 110-113.

growing sentiments of kindness and justice, there can never again fall upon our ears the war-whoop of the savage or the boom of cannon in the Indian camp.

RUNNING THE GAUNTLET.

The arrival of prisoners in the camps is received with great rejoicings on account of the victory, and indignities are heaped upon them by the old men, women and children, and sometimes they are subjected to excessive tortures. When they are tried for their lives by the council, and they are not adopted by any persons in the camp, or are not distributed among the tribes, but are doomed to die, they may be burned at the stake, as was customary among the Iroquois and other eastern tribes, or speedily despatched by the tomahawk. Desirous of relieving the monotony of their lives and obtaining pleasure at the expense of the sufferings of the captives, a chance was oftentimes given them of saving themselves by "running the gauntlet." Hunter, in the "Memoirs of his Captivity," says that in every native village there was a prisoner's place of refuge, designated by a post uniformly painted red in times of war, planted near the council-house. Two rows of women and children armed with clubs, switches and missiles were stationed within a short distance from the post, and the prisoners were compelled to pass between them. If they were able to run quickly and arrive in safety at the post, they were placed in charge of guards until the council decided their fate. Some were saved and became members of the tribe, but others were condemned to death. Sometimes the captives were bound hand and foot, and burned with pieces of touchwood, or whipped severely, A brave man would taunt his captors, daring them to do their utmost to injure them, and with the death song on his lips would teach them how to die. As the prisoners ran between the ranks, it sometimes happened that some of them would intentionally slacken their pace, that they might die on the way, knowing that a more cruel fate awaited them. "The return of the Kansas with their prisoners and scalps was greeted by the squaws, as is usual on such occasions, by the most extravagant rejoicings ; while every imaginable indignity was practised on the prisoners. The rage of the relict of Kiskemas knew no bounds; she, with the rest of the squaws, particularly those who had lost any connections, and the children, whipped the prisoners with green briars and hazel switches, and threw firebrands, clubs and stones at them as they ran between their ranks to the painted post, which is a goal of safety for all who arrive at it till their fate is finally determined in a general council of the victorious warriors."* The custom of compelling prisoners to run the gauntlet was enforced at two, if not all the mission villages in Canada down to the end of the French domination. Parkman says, " The practice was common, and must have had the consent of the priests of the mission." When Hannah Dustan and her nurse, Mary Neff, were taken prisoners by the Abenakis, as they journeyed toward a native village, after Hannah's infant had been dashed to death against a tree, the warriors amused themselves by telling the women that when they arrived at their destination, they would be stripped and made to run the gauntlet.

The Iroquois sometimes led their prisoners through the tribes embracing their confederacy, compelling them at every village to undergo this torture, and seldom did they escape without the loss of a hand, finger or eye, and many of them perished as they ran toward the goal. General Stark, when a young man, was captured by the Indians, and made to run the gauntlet. As he ran, he knocked down the nearest warrior, snatched the war-club from his hands, and used it so dexterously that he reached the goal in safety, while his companion was nearly beaten to death. During the Pontiac conspiracy some prisoners were taken and forced to follow this Indian custom. Parkman says : " The women having arranged themselves in two rows, with clubs and sticks, the prisoners were taken out, one by one, and told to run the gauntlet to Pontiac's lodge. Of sixty-six persons who were brought to the shore, sixty-four ran the gauntlet and all were killed. One of the remaining two, who had had his thigh broken in the firing from the shore, and who was tied

---

* Hunter's " Memoirs of Captivity among the Indians," pages 25, 328.

to his seat, and compelled to row, had became by this time so much exhausted that he could not help himself. He was thrown out of the boat and killed with clubs. The other, when directed to run for the lodge, suddenly fell upon his knees in the water, made the sign of the cross on his forehead and breast, and darted out into the stream. An expert swimmer from the Indians followed him, and having overtaken him, seized him by the hair, and crying out, ‘You seem to love water, you shall have enough of it,’ he stabbed the poor fellow, who sank to rise no more.”* .

In an old diary of colonial times, kept by the Rev. Christopher Hozen, who was the pastor of a small settlement of whites and Indians in Pennsylvania, there is an account of a novel race, suggestive of running the gauntlet, gotten up by the white settlers. In the spring of 1763 there were frequent quarrels between the Indians and white people, which culminated apparently in the murder of a white man named Murdock, with his wife and child. Upon the wall of the cabin of Ninpo, an Indian, was found the rude drawing of an arrow in blood, and at once suspicion rested upon him as the perpetrator of the murderous act. The pastor of the small community believed firmly in the innocence of his dusky friend, who was not a Christian, but a shrewd, industrious and affectionate red man. Sheinah, the Indian’s wife, was an especial favorite of Patience, the wife of the good missionary, who taught the dusky mother domestic duties, and trained her in the use of the English language. Concerning Ninpo, the pastor writes: “The young man I believe to be as innocent as my own little child of this dreadful deed. He is too shrewd a fellow, and the last person likely to sign his name to such a work of blood. I do not think either that my townspeople really believe him guilty. But they thirst for vengeance and must have a victim.” Mr. Hozen managed to put the time of trial off from month to month, while the poor man was closely guarded in the fort.

The prisoner was almost forgotten through pressure of colonial affairs, until the arrival of Judge Poindexter, a coarse,

* Parkman’s “Pontiac,” Vol. I., page 269.

burly man, with a rough voice, who hated the Indians with intense hatred. He would have hanged Ninpo without a trial,
as he did not believe in giving justice to the red skins. As the
missionary remonstrated with him in relation to the Indian
with his wife and child, the surly minister of justice replied, in
a loud tone of voice, " Better hang her and the young cub.
Stamp out a nest of snakes is my way. He is not entitled to a
trial, as you know very well, pastor. He's a red skin. He has
been kept there on our expense long enough. I mean to have
him out and put out of the way next week." When Mr. Hozen
said, " You do not believe that he murdered Mr. Murdock ? "
The judge replied, " No, I don't say that I do, but he's none
too good to do it. He's a worthless red devil, and I hold that
the sooner we put an end to him, and all of his color, the better."
One of the friends of the missionary, Seth Jarrett, knew how
to manage this strange dispenser of justice, and he suggested
that they might have some fun at the expense of Ninpo. The
young men of the village were going to have some hurdle-races
and jumping matches, and Seth proposed to the judge that the
Indian be given a chance for his life, that he be allowed to run
in the races, and if he should lose one he should be hung, but if
he won all, he should be granted his liberty. The proposal
pleased Judge Poindexter, who knew that it would suit the
rough tastes of the villagers. The day of sport came round,
and upon the field prepared for the contests were groups of
white men and women, and one solitary Indian, namely the
man who was to run for his life. The contest was hardly a fair
one, as the prisoner's joints were stiffened with three month's
confinement in prison. In the standing jump feat, an English
youth, named George Notting, defeated the Indian by three
inches, and the judge raised his rifle, when Seth interposed,
remarking that he had a chance in the race. In the dispute
which ensued, some of the villagers wishing to give him another
chance for his life, and others willing to prolong the sport, the
decision was given in favor of Ninpo. Three men stood abreast
in a hundred yards race—Ninpo, John Gabberly and Abraham
Cutting. The judge, supported by a group of men, stood with

his rifle ready to shoot the Indian as he ran. The runners
started, Cutting ahead and Ninpo close behind. Slowly the
Indian gained, and then passed Cutting, and as the people
became excited, the whizz of a bullet sped close to the ear of
Ninpo from Poindexter's rifle. With a bound the Indian rushed
to the goal, and turning swiftly struck the judge heavily in the
stomach with his head, causing the fat man to roll over on the
grass amid the laughter of the spectators. It was the work of
a moment for Ninpo to reach the wood, where unseen stood the
missionary's wife with a horse, upon which he sprang and
vanished from the presence of his persecutor. Sheinah and her
child, with the shrewd and nimble Ninpo, found a home and
safety in the western forests among their friends. A year
afterward the murderer of Murdock was discovered to be a
white man from another settlement. The bloody arrow upon
the wall of the cabin was the name of Ninpo, signifying Red
Arrow. The red man's ideas of the white man's laws and
religion could not be elevated by his treatment, and some of
these have been transmitted to posterity.

The western Indians enforced the custom of running the
gauntlet as well as the tribes of the east. The Blackfeet were
accustomed to resort to it for sport, finding pleasure in the
attempts of their prisoners to reach a place of safety. One of
the most striking instances which happened among the Blackfeet was the thrilling experience of John Colter, a trapper,
who had been a member of the Lewis and Clarke expedition.
Breaking loose from the expedition at the headwaters of the
Missouri, in the country inhabited by the Gros Ventre, Crow
and Blackfoot Indians, he began the lonely work of a trapper
with all the hardihood of this daring class of men. Meeting
another trapper named Potts, a partnership was formed, and
along the creeks and rivers they paddled, setting their beaver
traps at the fall of night and securing them before daybreak.
Hiding in the daytime and toiling during the night, they
managed to elude the craftiness of the Blackfeet. These
men were well versed in prairie craft and Indian customs;
yet they were leading a dangerous kind of life for the

572 CANADIAN SAVAGE FOLK.

sake of the peltries they could obtain. As they were paddling softly at daybreak in their canoe on a branch of the Missouri called Jefferson Fork, Colter heard the trampling of feet, and instantly gave the alarm of Indians; but Potts assured him that it was a herd of buffalo, and they continued their journey. The banks of the river were high and precipitous, and although apprehensive of danger, there was apparent safety. Suddenly, as they were stealing cautiously along the river, they were aroused with hideous yells and war-whoops from both sides of the river. They were entreated to come on shore, and as they complied, Colter stepped out of the canoe, and Potts, when about to follow, was disarmed. Colter snatched the gun from the hands of the Indian who had taken it and gave it to Potts, who now distrusted the Blackfeet and determined to run the chance of saving himself in his canoe. Pushing it from the shore, he had not gone far when he called to his companion that he was wounded. Colter entreated him to come on shore and trust to the Indians, as the only chance of safety; but he would not follow the instructions of his friend. Determined to pay the Indians for their craftiness, he levelled his gun and shot one of the Blackfeet dead. In a moment his body was pierced with many arrows. Colter was led away to the camp of the Blackfeet, about six miles distant, where the warriors deliberated as to the treatment of their captive. The poor man, having a slight knowledge of the language, listened intently to the schemes proposed which would give them the greatest amusement. Some of the natives were anxious to have him set as a mark on the prairie, at which they could test their skill in shooting. One of the chiefs, seizing the captive by the shoulder, asked him if he could run, and with the keen scent of an old trapper he knew at once the purport of the question, that he would have a chance of running for his life. Although noted among the trappers as a good runner, he felt that his life now depended upon his skill, and he informed the chief that he was a bad runner. Stripped naked, he was led out on the prairie about four hundred yards, and at the sound of the war-whoop the savages bounded after him at full speed. Colter

flew over the prairie with the speed which gives fear to man, and
although the prairie was thickly studded with the prickly-pear
cactus, which injured his feet, he left his pursuers far behind.
It was six miles to the Jefferson Fork, and toward the river he
ran with might and main. Half-way across the plain the
swiftest runners were scattered, and Colter, looking round for
a moment, saw a single warrior about one hundred yards
behind him, armed with a spear. Through the excessive
exertion the blood gushed from the mouth and nostrils of
Colter and streamed down his breast; still he ran on.
When within a mile of the river the sound of approaching
footsteps was distinctly heard, and the captive saw behind
him, not more than twenty yards, his pursuer armed with
the spear. Suddenly turning round and throwing up his

FLATHEAD MODEL CANOE.

arms he faced the savage, who became disconcerted through
this act and the bloody appearance of Colter. Stopping to hurl
the spear, he fell forward through exhaustion, the spear stuck
in the ground and the shaft broke in his hand. Colter rushed
forward, seized the pointed part and pinned the warrior to the
ground. Continuing his flight toward the river, he improved
the delay caused by the Indians, who found their companion
dead and, with horrid yells, waited for the rest of the warriors
to arrive. Fainting and exhausted, Colter succeeded in gaining
the fringe of cottonwood trees which skirted the river, through
which he ran and plunged into the stream. He swam to an
island, against the upper end of which a mass of driftwood
had lodged, forming a natural raft, under which he dived several
times until, among the floating trunks of trees, he found a
place covered over with branches and bushes several feet above
the water, which secured for him a snug place of refuge.

Scarcely had he found this temporary retreat than his pursuers arrived at the river, yelling wildly, and madly rushing into the water swam toward the raft, which they examined carefully and long. The poor man, suffering intensely, could see the Blackfeet searching for him as he watched through the chinks of the raft. The terrible thought that they were going to set the raft on fire came to his mind, and increased his torture. All through the day his pursuers searched, and not until night fell and no longer was heard the sounds of the Indians did Colter leave his place of safety. When silence reigned he dived again and came up beyond the raft, and in the darkness swam quietly down the river for a considerable distance. He landed upon the opposite bank and continued his flight during the night, anxious to get beyond the reach of the Blackfeet, and as far as possible from their country. Naked, without food or clothing, with injured feet and exhausted strength, there still lay before him several days' journey before he could reach a trading-post of the Missouri, on a branch of the Yellowstone River. With heroic endeavor he pursued his course over the prairies, his body smarting with the heat of the sun by day and chilled with the dews of night, without a companion to sustain or the means of securing game to support, living on roots or berries, which he found by the way, until, after enduring many hardships and overcoming all difficulties, he arrived at the trading-post, and found shelter, sustenance and friends. Colter lived to relate his discovery of the wonders of the famous Yellowstone Park and, like many of the trappers of the west, spent his years with the Indians, and passed away from earth " unwept, unhonored and unsung."

INDIAN CAIRNS.

Tablets of adamant! Books of stone! Is it possible that savage man could make enduring records upon materials so hard, or that facts and fancies belonged to uncultured races of so great importance as to cause the bards of the wigwams and lodges to write in characters indelible the story of bygone

years. A merry company was seated around the blazing lodge
fire in the home of Calf-Shirt as we entered, listening to stories
of valor told by the aged warriors. Old Medicine-Sun was
finishing a story which we had often heard, and after giving our quota of praise to our old friend for his loyalty
and courage, we said to the principal speaker at the lodge
fire, "Tell us the story of the writing stone." The question
remained unanswered, as some of the members of the company placed their hands upon their mouths. Unable to
gain the object of our visit, we determined to be more dis-
creet, and glean more carefully in other lodges the secrets of
the old days. A few uneventful days passed by, when, sitting
alone by a favorite mound on the prairie, we were aroused from
our meditations by the voice of Peta. He was accompanied by
a friend we had known in earlier years. Alighting from their
horses they took out their pipes and began to smoke. The
conversation turned upon the pictured rocks of the Missouri,
which my friend said were wonderful. "Many years ago," said
he, "more than any of us can tell, the spirits held a secret
meeting relating to matters affecting the welfare of the tribes.
One of their number was delegated to make known the message of the assembly of the spirits. Scattered far and wide
were the tribes over the Canadian North-West and the land of
the Big Knives, but distance was as nothing to a god. The
wise men of the tribes would, however, die, and there might
be a time when the story of the meeting of the gods would be
forgotten, and darkness would then settle upon the red men.
A more enduring record must be left to guide the children of
the wilderness, such a record as unfaithful hands could not
destroy, so, far aloft upon the rocks of the Missouri, beyond
the reach of mortals, the wisest of the gods wrote out the
divine message to all the tribes. I have gone there and gazed
upon that stone book, but could not understand it. Only a few
of the wisest men, one or two in each tribe, can interpret the
sayings of this wonderful record. They treasure its truths
carefully, as they must not be told to unwilling or immoral
ears. Whenever a wise man has received the secret of this
37

tablet of stone he becomes grave, and rises quickly in the
estimation of his tribe through the wisdom of his counsels."

Peta finished his tale, and his friend acquiesced in its truthfulness by an interjection of frequent occurrence among the
natives. The silence having been broken by this exclamation
of assent upon the part of our friend, he told us the tale of his
wanderings, how, when a youth among the Ojibways of Lake
Superior, he had travelled westward on an hunting expedition
with a few companions, but being suddenly cut off by a hostile
band, he had fled for safety to the bush, and became separated
from his companions, whom he never saw again. Several days
he journeyed, living upon roots and berries, but becoming
exhausted, he determined to enter the first camp of Indians he
could find. As he wandered along the banks of one of the
rivers, he came upon an Indian trail, which he followed until
he reached a camp of Western Indians, who treated him kindly,
and with whom he remained until he found a home among the
Blackfeet, near the Rocky Mountains. Said he, "I remember
when I was a boy, the old men of the tribe telling me the story
of the stone book on the great lake." We parted, musing upon
the fears and fancies of the red men. Gleams of fancy shot
across our path, as we wandered toward the western hills,
fragments of song and story, to which we had listened in the
early days among the lodges, and as in a vision we saw again
the writing stones of the South, which stand upon the prairie.
Strange stories have the red men told of these stones. The
wonderful writing is there, the record of the gods, and woe to
that man who goes near them, unable to interpret the strange
words. Never again shall horse and rider return to dwell in
the land of the living. Young men and middle-aged men have
gone there, through idle curiosity, but never has one returned
to tell the secret he had discovered, or to relate his story of a
visit to the land of mystery. Wonderful story! It is a land
of mystery! Man of the earth, mortal, not conversant with the
things of the spiritual world, unable to penetrate the shadows
which hide us from the invisible, beware of treading the soil of
the gods, for it is an enchanted land, and if thou utterest an

impure word, or conceivest a carnal thought, thou shalt inevitably die.

Riding carelessly over the prairie with a young man who had lately arrived from the Old World, my companion called my attention to a circle of stones. "That is a mark," said he, " placed there to commemorate a great battle that was fought between different tribes of Indians." Oftentimes had I seen these circles on the prairie, and knowing the cause of their construction, I was amused at this display of apparent wisdom. These circles are to be found on our western prairies. As the Indians travelled on their hunting expeditions, they placed stones around the edges of the lodges when they camped, to prevent the wind from overturning them, and to keep them warm. This is shown by the outer circle of stones. In the centre of the lodge the fire was made, and to keep the fire from spreading and to adapt it for cooking purposes, a small circle of stones was placed which confined the fire. When the camp was moved the circle of stones was left, and that which we saw was one of these circles. In the bush fringing the rivers of the west stone circles, deeply imbedded in the soil, are found, linking the past with the present. North-east of the cemeteries of the town of Macleod, there are several cairns erected by the Indians. I counted seven cairns of stone, one alone remaining perfect, the others being deeply imbedded in the soil, and almost level with the surface of the prairie. The Indians have not been able to give me any exact dates relating to the erection of the cairns, but native tradition asserts that Southern Alberta was the home of the Snake, Nez Perce, Crow, Flathead and Pend Oreille Indian tribes. The Cree and Stoney Indians were the first of the tribes to obtain guns and ammunition from the traders, which gave them superiority over their enemies. The tribes comprising the Blackfoot Confederacy were living in the north, and through contact with the white men they, too, become possessors of firearms, and marching southward drove the Crow and Pend Oreille tribes across the border. The Snake, Nez Perce and Flathead tribes were driven across the mountains; and then

CARVED CHEST OF THE FLATHEADS OF VANCOUVER ISLAND.

directing their attention to the Stoney and Cree tribes, they extended their domain by compelling them to retreat northward, until the district of Southern Alberta, inhabited by the buffalo, became the undisputed territory of the Blood, Piegan and Blackfoot tribes. Several great battles were fought, and these cairns were placed there to commemorate these events, and probably to mark the spot where some of their greatest warriors died. When a great chief or warrior died a lodge was placed over him, and when this was thrown down by the wind, the body of the deceased was laid upon the ground, and a cairn of stones erected over it. There is a cairn called by the Indians the " Gamblers' Cairn," near the store of I. G. Baker, in the town of Macleod. Several years ago a Piegan camp of Indians located on this spot was attacked with small-pox, and the disease proved so fatal that fifty dead lodges were left standing. Among those who died was Aikûtce ; i.e., the Gambler, head chief of the Piegan tribe. His people placed a lodge over him, and when that had been blown down by the western winds, he was reverently laid upon the ground, and the cairn of stones erected. The original cairn was three or four feet in diameter, with rows of stones between forty and fifty feet each in length, leading to the cairn. Only one row of stones remains, and the cairn is worn nearly level with the street. This simple monument is of little interest to the passing stranger ; but the Indian riding past will turn to his comrade and quietly say, " Aikûtce."

These stone monuments are to be found in widely scattered districts of the North-West, telling their own simple story of other days. There are several rows of stones several miles in length on the northern side of Belly River, near the Blood Indian Reserve, and within three miles of the Slide Out Flat, which can be seen when the prairie is burned. The Indians are unable to give any account of their history. A line of boulders may still be seen stretching from St. Mary's River northward for more than one hundred miles. In some places they are quite close together, and at intervals are separated by several miles. Some of them have been worn smooth by the action of the weather, and by the buffalo using them as rubbing-posts.

Indeed, you may see some of them lying in hollow spots on the prairie, the soil having been loosened by the tramping of the buffalo, and then blown away by the wind.

Upon the summit of a limestone hill on Moose Mountain, Assiniboia, there is a group of cairns. The central cairn is composed of loose stones, and measures about thirty feet in diameter and four feet high. This is surrounded by a heart-shaped figure of stones, having its apex toward the east, and from this radiate six rows of stones, each terminating in a small cairn. Four of these radiating lines nearly correspond with the points of the compass, and each of the lines of different lengths terminate in a smaller cairn. The Indians know nothing of the origin of these lines and cairns, but state that they were made by the spirit of the winds. In the Lake of the Woods region there are numerous boulders grooved, polished and marked by glacial action, and in the vicinity of Milk River are boulders of various shapes and sizes. Within a few miles of Toronto, in the Township of Vaughan, there was found a few years ago a flattened oval granite cobble, resembling in shape and size a shoemaker's lap-stone, having cut upon one side the date, "1641." This has been called the "Jesuit's stone." In the spring of 1641, Brebeuf and Chaumonot, Jesuit missionaries, left the country of the Neutrals for their home among the Hurons, and were compelled to remain at the Indian village of Teotongniaton, or St. Williams, where they were entertained by a woman, probably belonging to the Aondironnons, a clan of the Neutrals, for nearly a month. Dean Harris, of St. Catharines, who has investigated the matter, thinks that probably during this journey the missionaries commemorated the event by cutting the date in this stone.

Although not belonging specially to the natives of the country, nor to Indian lore, yet as it relates to the land of the red men, and is of interest to some of my readers, I cannot help referring to the amethyst mines which I lately visited. Accompanied by a few friends I had the pleasure of exploring the mines where the beautiful amethysts are found, which are located about fifteen miles east of Port Arthur and

within two miles of the bay. Some fascinating stories have
been told of the wealth of the mines, the abundance of
amethysts and the size of single amethysts, one of them
reputed to have been nearly one hundred pounds in weight,
which sold for fifteen hundred dollars. Whether the narra-
tors drew upon their imagination or not in telling these stories
I cannot say, yet the deep excavations reveal great labor
which must have repaid the workers. Numerous holes in the
ground, from twenty to thirty feet in depth, and from ten to
twelve feet wide, were partially filled with debris, rich in tiny
amethysts of purple and brown, and the sides of the rocky
caverns glistened with thousands of beautiful specimens. Those
found in the rocks were, however, of little value, as they were
destroyed in blasting, but there were layers of clay wherein
the single amethysts were found in great profusion. Some
years ago the mines were abandoned, apparently on account of
the heavy labor and the glutting of the market. Beautiful
stones of various colors are still found in abundance at Isle
Royale and along the shores of Lake Superior, which are sent
to Germany and made into ornaments. The traveller is
enraptured when he beholds their beauty and prizes them as
treasures of land and sea.

THE MOUNTED POLICE.

The southern portion of the North-West Territories in the
old buffalo days witnessed many an exciting scene when the
whiskey traders visited the Indian camps to trade their goods
for the hides of the buffalo. The trade in buffalo robes assumed
such proportions that several traders from the United States
were induced to enter the country of the Blackfeet to carry on
their trade. Some of these traders were not anxious to give or
sell whiskey to the natives, but they found others more successful in dealing with them through the gift and sale of liquor
that they felt compelled to imitate their example. In trading
with the red men the temptation proved too strong to evade
the liking for liquor shown by the men of the western lodges,

and accordingly whiskey of the worst kind was introduced, and
some terrible scenes followed. Many of the Indians drank the
liquor until they died, and murders were frequent. Fifty
thousand robes, worth two hundred and fifty thousand dollars,
constituted the annual trade, and much of the proceeds, the
greater part the missionaries said, was spent in whiskey. The
natives sold their horses to the traders, crime increased, the
native population decreased, and the Blackfeet and Crees,
beholding the fearful consequences of the traffic, became
anxious for its suppression. The missionaries, by interviews
and letters, sought the aid of the Government, and at a meet-

BADGE OF THE MOUNTED POLICE.

ing called by George McDougall and Chief Factor Christie,
of the Hudson's Bay Company, a petition was drawn up to
be sent to the Dominion authorities requesting measures to
be adopted for the overthrow of the liquor trade among
the Indians, and the maintenance of law and order, suggesting that a military force be sent to the country for that
purpose. In 1871 Mr. Christie brought this matter before
Governor Archibald, and Chief Sweet Grass, head chief of
the Crees, in his message sent to the Governor at the same
time, said, among other things, "We want you to stop the
Americans from coming to trade on our lands and giving
fire-water, ammunition and arms to our enemies, the Black-

feet." The Dominion authorities issued a proclamation pro-
hibiting the traffic in spirituous liquors to Indians and others,
and the use of strychnine in the destruction of animal life; but
the evils of the liquor traffic still existed. In 1873 the
Dominion Parliament passed an Act to establish a military
force in the North-West. This force, known as the North-West
Mounted Police, comprised three hundred men with the pro-
portionate complement of officers. In September, 1873, three
divisions of the force were organized at the Stone Fort,
near Winnipeg, and proceeded to Dufferin to await reinforcements from Montreal and Toronto. Upon the arrival of
the other three divisions from the east, the preparations for the
trip across the prairies were made, and on July 8th they left
Dufferin on the famous march of 1874, under the command of
Lieutenant-Colonel French. About the middle of September,
the main column, after many hardships, reached the Old Man's
River, near the present site of Macleod. A, B, C and F
divisions being left there under the Assistant-Commissioner,
Lieutenant-Colonel Macleod proceeded at once to erect log
buildings as a police fort, which was named Fort Macleod. A
dozen men, under Colonel Jarvis, parted from the main column
at Roche Percee for Edmonton, where they arrived on the
second day of November. The main column, under Colonel
French, crossed the plains northward to Fort Pelly by way of
Qu'Appelle, but finding their intended headquarters not ready
returned to Dufferin. In four months the main column had
travelled one thousand, nine hundred and fifty-nine miles,
besides the distance covered by detachments on special service.
Colonel Macleod succeeded Colonel French as commissioner,
and under his efficient administration law and order were
established in the country, the whiskey traffic among the
Indians wholly suppressed and life made secure. I have
listened to the genial commissioner as he related his account of
the march across the prairies, the vast herds of buffalo seen,
and adventures of great interest. The force consisted of six
divisions, named A, B, C, D, E, F. Fort Macleod was built in
the form of a square upon an island in the Old Man's River,

the buildings consisting of cotton-wood logs, filled in with mud, and subsequently with lime. It was a frail-looking structure for defence in the country of the Blackfeet, but the brave-hearted men trusted to their courage and honest dealing with the Indians to maintain order more than to works of defence. Fort Walsh was established in 1874 by Major Walsh. Considerable feeling in the east and west was manifested when it became known that a military force was being organized for the Territories. Old soldiers of the Imperial army settled in Canada, youthful aspirants to military honors, college graduates and the sons of gentlemen of wealth and political influence anxious to hunt the buffalo and take some scalps, and worthless adventurers sought admission to the ranks. It was reported that the whiskey traders were building fortifications to oppose the police and many of the people were apprehensive of danger but the whiskey traders were just as anxious as the friends of the police, for they were ever on the alert, in expectation of the coming of the force, assured that it meant the destruction of their business and, if caught, the confiscation of their property.

The force is graded as commissioner, assistant-commissioner, superintendent, inspector and constable. One half of the force was armed with Winchester carbines and Adams revolvers, and the other half with Snider carbines and the same revolver. Non-commissioned officers carried swords. The uniform was scarlet tunic and serge, faced with yellow, black breeches with wide yellow stripes and top boots. In summer white helmets and gauntlets were worn, and in winter short buffalo coats, fur caps, mitts and moccasins. The routine duties at the police forts were: Stables three times a day, one hour of artillery and another of riding drill in the morning, and one hour of riding drill in the afternoon. Men were told off as stable orderlies, regimental fatigue and room orderlies. Such a small force to maintain peace in a country as large as all our Eastern Provinces combined, inhabited by more than twenty thousand Indians and half-breeds and numerous lawless persons, had no small task before them, but their presence established order, and peaceful relations among all classes were speedily made.

OLD FORT WALSH.

Shortly after the police had stationed themselves at Fort
Macleod some of the Blackfeet paid a visit to the fort and
were kindly treated by Colonel Macleod, whom they named
"Stamiksotokan," meaning Bull's Head, significant of wise
administration and military prowess. The genial commissioner
treated them kindly and with dignity. He invited them to
inspect the cannon, and then pointing to a tree more than a
mile distant, told them to look at it. Suddenly were they
surprised as they saw the thick branch of the tree carried
away by the cannon ball, and the boom and smoke startled
them, leaving an indelible impression on their minds of the
strength and wisdom of the men who had arrived to govern
the country. From the beginning the riders of the plains
gained the respect of the natives, and ever since that period
they have retained the confidence imposed in them. It could
not but happen that hostile relations would exist at times, as
the men of the scarlet tunic enforced justice, and sought out
and punished the criminals in the camps. The feuds among the
native tribes called for the interference of the police, and they
were able by their tact, energy and courage to prevent wars
between the tribes.

An incident characteristic of this period happened at Fort
Walsh in June, 1877. A Saulteaux chief, named Little Child,
came to Fort Walsh, and reported that his people, numbering
about fifty souls, were camped with a large party of Assiniboines,
and when they decided to move their camp an Assiniboine,
named Crow's Dance, formed a war lodge with two hundred of
his warriors, and then declared that the Saulteaux would not be
allowed to leave until he gave them permission. Little Child
protested, saying that he would inform the White Mother's
chief, and upon making preparations to leave, the Assiniboines
attacked the Saulteaux, killing some of their dogs and threaten-
ing to work serious damage to the people. When the bands
separated, the Saulteaux chief went to Fort Walsh and laid a
complaint against Crow's Dance and his party. Major Walsh
started with a guide and fifteen men, at eleven o'clock in the
forenoon, and rode until three o'clock next morning, before they

reached the camp of the Assiniboines. Major Walsh, in his report of the affair, says, "The camp was formed in the shape of a war camp, with a war lodge in the centre. In the latter I expected to find Crow's Dance with his leaders. Fearing they might offer resistance (Little Child said they certainly would) I halted, and had the arms of my men inspected and pistols loaded. Striking the camp so early, I thought I might take them by surprise; so I moved west along a ravine about half a mile. This brought us within three quarters of a mile of the camp. At a short trot we soon entered the camp and surrounded the war lodge, and found Crow's Dance and nineteen warriors in it. I had them immediately moved out of camp to a small butte half a mile distant, and then arrested Blackfoot and Bear's Down, and took them to the butte. It was now 5 a.m. I ordered breakfast and sent the interpreter to inform the chiefs of the camp that I would meet them in council in an hour. The camp was taken by surprise, arrests made and prisoners taken to the butte, before a chief in the camp knew anything about it. At the appointed time the following chiefs assembled : Long Lodge, Shell King and Little Chief. I told them what I had done, and that I intended to take the prisoners to the Fort and try them by the law of the White Mother for the crime they had committed ; that they, as chiefs, should not have allowed such a crime to be committed. They replied that they tried to stop it but could not. At 10 a.m. I left council and arrived at the Fort at 8 p.m., a distance of fifty miles. If the Saulteaux, when attacked by the Assiniboines, had returned the shot, there would in all probability have been a fearful massacre." Lieutenant-Colonel Irvine, when reporting this affair to the Government, wrote : "I cannot too highly write of Inspector Walsh's prompt conduct in this matter, and it must be a matter of congratulation to feel that fifteen of our men can ride into an enormous camp of Indians, and take out of it as prisoners some of the head men. The action of this detachment will have great effect on all the Indians throughout the country." The Indians learned to trust the officers and men of the force, who won their confidence, not through a false

sentimentality or through a laxity in discipline, but by enforcing justice to red and white. During my residence at Fort
Macleod a small party of Blood Indians proceeded northward
and stole some horses from the camp of the Stoney Indians.
Returning about midnight, as the horses were being driven
across the Old Man's River, an Indian woman residing in the
town aroused William Gladstone, the interpreter, who informed
the police, and in a few moments a mere handful of the red-coats
were in hot pursuit toward the Blood Indian Reserve. The
night was dark, but they gained rapidly upon the natives, and
when they reached the band of horses the red men had disappeared. A search through the camp during the day resulted
in the capture of an Indian named Jingling Bells. He was
taken to the Fort, and at the regular session of the court was
tried by jury and sentenced. Some of the natives vowed that
he would never be taken to Stoney Mountain Penitentiary, for
Jingling Bells was a favorite in the camp. When the time
came for his removal he had to be driven across the prairie to
Fort Walsh, about three hundred miles, and the rumor from the
camp of an attempt to release the prisoner having reached the
ears of the police, they had to resort to stratagem to get him
safely out of the country. One evening a small party of police
left Fort Macleod, but this caused no surprise, as it was a circumstance of frequent occurrence. The party travelled until dark,
and then camped for the night. About midnight another party
of police left the fort with the prisoner and arrived at the
police camp at sunrise, and Jingling Bells was speedily trans-
ferred and hurried onward to prison without any delay.

The treaty at Blackfoot Crossing in 1878, between the Government and the tribes inhabiting Alberta, including the Blackfeet, Bloods, Piegans, Sarcees, and Stoneys was made successfully, and the presence of the police promoted peace, allayed the
fears and encouraged the hopes of the red men. Every year
the annual treaty payments made the transfer of a very large
sum of money in one-dollar bills a necessity, and this duty was
faithfully performed by the red-coats. During the payments
their presence was necessary on the Reserves, in the interests of

the Government, the white people and the Indians. When Sitting Bull and the hostile Sioux fled from the United States and camped in the vicinity of Fort Walsh, the energy, firmness and diplomacy of Major Crozier and his brother officers, sustained by the police, prevented serious complications. I well remember a disturbance at Blackfoot Crossing, when about a dozen men were stationed there under Captain Dickens, a son of Charles Dickens, the novelist. One of the Blackfeet had committed some depredation and the police attempted to arrest him, but the Indians fired over their heads to intimidate them, and released the prisoner. Trouble of a more serious nature was expected, and two policemen were speedily despatched during the night to Fort Macleod for reinforcements. Without a moment's delay Major Crozier, with a small detachment of police, started for the scene of the disturbance. The distance was about one hundred miles and by forced marches they arrived at Blackfoot Crossing at night. The sacks of oats were ranged inside the walls of the frail log-buildings which served as police-quarters, and works of defence were thrown up on the outside. When Crowfoot and his warriors arose from their slumbers they were surprised to see the preparations which had been made while they slept. The old chief held a conference with Major Crozier, and the brave soldier said he must have the prisoner to take to Fort Macleod. When Crowfoot asked him what he would do if he could not get him, he quietly said that then he must fight until he got him. Crowfoot saw at once the determined attitude of his friend, who now seemed his opponent, and he significantly turned to the Major and said, "We will fight, then." With these words upon this lips he retired, and the police made ready for action. It needed the utterance of a single word from Crowfoot and the entire camp would be transformed into a war camp. The wise old chief understood men and matters better than the Indians, and after weighing the circumstances with the probable effects upon his people, he concluded that discretion was the better part of valor, and in a short time he returned with the prisoner, who was handed over to the minister of justice, who took him to Fort Macleod, where he was tried and punished. I need not refer to the heroism of the riders of the plains at Duck Lake, and indeed during the whole of the rebellion. They were always ready to defend their country and were ever foremost at the call of duty when danger stared them in the face.

The police expected to find in the haunts of the whiskey traders imposing fortifications and fear was mutual, for the traders had heard of the advance of the men of the scarlet tunic. The traders had their Spitzi Cavalry organized for justice among themselves and defence against the Indians. There were forts scattered over the country—the Old Bow Fort, about twelve miles beyond Morley, in the valley of the Bow; a fort at Sheep Creek, a small trading-post in the Porcupine Hills, between Mosquito Creek and the Leavings of Willow Creek; Slide-Out, in one of the "bottoms" of the Belly River; Stand-Off, at the Junction of the Kootenay with the Belly River, and Whoop-Up, at the Junction of the Belly and St. Mary's rivers. The most formidable of these trading-posts was Whoop-Up. There was no fighting, however, to be done, as the whiskey traders quietly gave up their business and traded with the Indians without liquor. For some time the police were satisfied with the erection of large forts, which were a necessity during their first years in the country, and from these posts they kept a sharp look-out on the administration of law in the country. With the progress of settlement, consequent upon the extinction of the buffalo, the peaceful attitude of the Indians and the establishment of stock raising, it became necessary to locate small detachments in different parts of the country. Some of these posts were named after the officers, as Walsh and Macleod had been, and thus old Fort Kipp was known as Fort Winder, and after the affair at Blackfoot Crossing, the place of the parley was known amongst us as Fort Dickens. These names have passed away never to return.

Long and lonely rides over the prairie in the depth of winter were made by the members of the force. Thrilling adventures could be told by some of the men of '74, but they have made history without recording it. My first sad duty upon my

ONE OF THE RIDERS.

arrival in Macleod was to bury a young policeman named
Hooley, the son of an English Church clergyman, who was
drowned in Belly River when returning from a trip in the
discharge of his duties. I have seen the young man fresh from
the city, the child of luxury, start in the night when the thermometer was thirty degrees below zero, to bear a despatch to a
post thirty-five miles distant; but he flinched not, for underneath the red coat there beat a patriotic heart. One of these
brave men went southward, bearing an important message, but
he never returned, and some of us thought he had taken
advantage of the trust imposed in him by his officers and had
deserted. When the spring came, with its genial winds and sunshine, the body of the faithful rider was found on the shore of
the river where he had disappeared, with no friendly aid to help
in the hour of distress. In the depth of winter another brave
man, named Parker, started on his errand of justice for the post
on the St. Mary's River above the mouth of Lee's Creek. It
was an easy matter to lose the trail leading to the police
camp, and Parker missed it. He wandered around, suffering
keenly from the intense cold, and, becoming snow-blind, was
unable to reach any place of safety. For six days, without
food, he travelled aimlessly on the prairie, eating snow to
quench his thirst, and, removing the saddle from his horse, he
lay down on the bare spots made by the dumb animal pawing
the snow to obtain grass. With the instinct of a faithful friend
the horse would not leave him, although he turned it loose
that it might find its way to camp, but it stood near as if
to encourage him. After the days and nights of suspense he
was found by the stage-driver of the mail waggon, and brought
to the camp, where he was cared for until he had partially
recovered, when he was removed to the hospital in Macleod.
He was badly frozen and emaciated, but he finally regained his
strength, and his horse, Custer, became the hero of the fort.

Volumes could be written of the heroic deeds and stirring
adventures of the riders of the plains. Officers and men were
liberal in their gifts. A peculiar freak of superstition or of
self-interest was apparent in the fact that when a long journey

had to be undertaken, almost invariably they started on Sunday. Sometimes there existed a partisan feeling among the citizens and police, which broke out at the public dance at Kamusi's Hotel, in Macleod, where not a single white lady was present— as there were only five within a radius of several hundred miles— and the dancers had to find partners among the Indians and half-breed women. There was not a dressmaker or milliner in the country, and the aspirants to the honors of the ball-room would beg the white ladies to sell their dresses and bonnets, and they were quite willing to pay big prices for them.

There were clever schemers among the policemen, as might be expected where so many were located, and one of these was a sergeant who had severed his connection with the force and was engaged in farming. Driving into the fort with an empty waggon he went to the storehouse and filled his waggon with sacks of grain, and when about ready to start with his stolen goods he was confronted by the officer in charge, who asked him what he was doing. The wily ex-policeman replied that he wanted to exchange grain, as he wished to get a new kind for seed for his farm. The officer summarily ordered him away, and he coolly drove off with the load of oats.

In later years the police have aided the settlers in putting out prairie fires, and many of their horses have been recovered from the parties who stole them. Sometimes an American citizen would find his way to one of the forts, inquiring after stolen horses, and help would be given him. A civilian from Montana called upon Captain McIllree, when he was commanding officer at Fort Walsh, and informed him that a horse had been stolen from his camp, close by. His description of the horse was on this wise: "Wall, ye see, Cap, the doggoned hoss hadn't no particler color. I call him Blueskin. He ain't blue, sure; but, now I tell ye, he ain't black, and ye can't call him grey. He's a cantankerous critter; but I bet you can't beat him in those stables. Will you take me? I'll run him with anything hereabouts." The captain mildly suggested that they had better find the horse before racing him. A sergeant and four men were instructed to seek the stolen horse, and within ten minutes they were on their

OFFICER OF THE MOUNTED POLICE.

way to Assiniboine. After a ride of twenty-five miles they
found at the South Fork a camp of Cree Indians, who dis-
claimed any knowledge of the stolen animal. A search among
the Indian horses proved successful in finding the horse, and
then the police demanded the chief to give up the thief. He
said he did not know the man; but upon being told that he
would be required himself to accompany them to the fort, he
delivered the man; and within seven hours from the time of
starting the police arrived at the fort with the stolen property
and the Cree Indian, having ridden a distance of fifty miles.

The ordinary duties of the police now extend over an area
of about seven hundred and fifty miles from east to west, and
four hundred miles from north to south. Along the southern
frontier there are summer patrols, several hundred miles being
patrolled weekly. On these patrols the police horses travel
annually more than one million miles. Throughout the Territories there are about seventy detachment outposts. The
strength of the force is now about nine hundred men. Concerning the force the following tribute from Caspar W.
Whitney, in his series of articles on "Snow-Shoes to Barren
Lands," is opportune: "He has the reputation of being the
most effective arm of the Canadian Interior Department; and
he lives up to it. These 'Riders of the Plains,' as they are
called, patrol a country so large that the entire force may lose
itself within its domains and still be miles and miles apart.
Yet this comparative handful maintains order among the lawless
white men and stays discontentment among the restless red
men in a manner so satisfactorily and so unostentatiously as to
make some of our United States experiences read like those of
a tyro. The success of the North-West Mounted Police may
be accredited to its system of distribution throughout the
guarded territory. Unlike our army, it does not mass its force
in forts adjacent to Indian Reservations. Posts it has where
recruiting and drilling are constantly going forward, but the
main body of men is scattered in twos and threes over the
country, riding hither and thither—a watch that goes on relief
after relief. This is the secret of their success, and a system it

would well repay our own Government to adopt. The police
are ever on the spot to advise or to arrest. They do not wait
for action until an outbreak has occurred; they are always in
action. They constitute a most valuable peace-assuring corps,
and I wish we had one like it." They are extending their
territory and influence, a detachment being now stationed near
the boundary of Canada and Alaska. With the advance of
settlement they must still follow the Indian trail into the
Peace River district. The red-coat and the flag of the nation
give peace alike to the native tribes and the white people, and
wherever these are found there is a lessening of crime, the
establishment of order and industry, and the growth of
patriotism.

TOTEMS.

The natives of the Dominion, in common with some tribes in
the United States and other countries, have a system of kinship
which extends beyond their own family known as totemism.
The tribes are divided into clans, bands or gentes, each having
its own distinctive crest or emblem of ancestry, which constitutes a native heraldry and a bond of brotherhood. The crests
are in the form of animals, birds or fishes, which are believed
to be in a sense their ancestors, and are known as totems. The
name is derived from the Ojibway word *dodaim* or *totam.*
" A totem is a class of material objects which a savage regards
with superstitious respect, believing that there exists between
him and every member of the class an intimate and altogether
special relation. As distinguished from a fetich, a totem is
never an isolated individual, but always a class of objects, generally a species of animals or of plants, more rarely a class of
inanimate natural objects, very rarely a class of artificial
objects."*

The natives make a theoretical claim of descent from the
animals which they accept as their totems, but it cannot be

------

* J. G. Frazer, in "Britannica Encyclopædia"—article, "Totemism."
Bishop Baraga's "Ojibway Dictionary," page 301. J. Long's "Voyages
and Travels of an Indian Interpreter," 1791, page 86.

shown that this is a literal descent. Confounding the ideal with the real, they have come to speak of them as their ancestors.* In a general sense those animals which inspired fear or affection or seemed to possess a high degree of intelligence or superhuman capacities were regarded as their kindred, but those which lacked such qualities as would impress men were despised or rejected as totems.† The clan system, with its clan marks or totems, developed a clan brotherhood with very strong ties and a worship of animals. The duties of clanship consisted in making a common defence against enemies, prohibition of marriage within the clan or gens, the establishment of a common burial place, the right of electing and deposing chiefs, the bestowment of names, the adoption of strangers into the clan, attendance upon religious feasts, being represented in the tribal councils, and the mutual rights of inheritance of the property of deceased members.‡ Each of the clans is known by the name of the totem, as the clan of the wolf, bear, tortoise, deer or hawk. Different degrees of rank or dignity are attached to different totems, the bear, the tortoise, and the wolf being held in the highest rank among the Iroquois. Sometimes hereditary rights or special privileges reside in particular clans, as the furnishing of a sachem to the tribe, or performing certain religious ceremonies.§

The clan was forbidden to kill or eat the totem, and this religious ban is known as Tabooism. Although the people would not hesitate to commit grave acts of cruelty and to slay and even eat their enemies, they would not dare to kill or eat their totem, believing it to be one of their kindred or a part of themselves, and only in extreme cases of hunger or by mistake would it be eaten lest they should die. The Dakotas and other tribes believe that they are possessed by the animal whose totem they bear, and they will not eat it.|| Among some of

* Brinton's "Myths of the New World," pages 86, 248.
† Waitz's "Anthropology," Vol. III., page 192. Clodd's "Birth and Growth of Myth," pages 31-36. Schultze's "Fetichism," pages 71-73, 75-76.
‡ "American Antiquarian," Vol. IX., page 389 ; Vol. X., pages 84, 85.
§ Parkman's "Pontiac," Vol. I., page 5.
|| "American Antiquarian," Vol. XII., page 237. "Third Annual Report of the Bureau of Ethnology," 1881-82, page 215-258.

the native tribes of British Columbia, not only will a man not
kill his totem, but if he sees another slay it he will demand
compensation, and if one of the natives exhibits his totem by
painting it on his forehead or otherwise, all those belonging
to the same totem must do honor to it by casting property
before it.*

The worship of animals is based upon totemism in its religious aspect. The civilized nations of antiquity passed through
the totem stage, the members of one totem being prohibited
from eating their own, yet making a sacrificial feast of a hostile
totem. Certain kinds of food must not be eaten because of its
relation to their forms of religious worship, included in their
descent from the animal which is their totem. The totem
system was the first in all countries, even traces of its existence
being found in the symbolism of the Bible, as the lion was the
animal symbol for Judah, the ass for Issachar, the wolf for
Benjamin, the serpent for Dan, and the hind for Gad In
America the totem system was limited in general to the hunter
races, and did not go beyond the stage of savagery and barbarism. The natives protected their totems and they expected to be
protected by them. They were the divinities which guided and
protected them. Charlevoix, in speaking of our Indians going to
war, says that they were always careful to enclose in a bag the
tutelar genius or manito, and these bags were distributed among
the elders of each family. Before entering the country of an
enemy they would have a great feast and then go to sleep,
expecting to have dreams, and those who were thus privileged
would go from lodge to lodge singing their death songs, in
which were incorporated their dreams. An army of warriors,
after sending out scouts to note the presence of an enemy,
would go to sleep near their fires, believing that their totems
would protect them.†

This belief in the protective power of the totems made the
Indians of British Columbia paint or carve them upon their

* R. C. Mayne's "British Columbia," page 258.

† "American Antiquarian," Vol. X., pages 87-90; Charlevoix's "Travels
— Letters XIV.," Vol. 1., page 338.

houses, even the entrance of the house being through the body
of a fish, or the image of the thunder bird, with spreading wings,
being placed above the door. The Thlinkeet chief, lying in state,
was surrounded by his individual clan and ancestral totems, as
his guardians in death.* One of the phases of totemism was the
peopling of caves, trees, rapids of rivers, and strange-looking
stones with spirits. This is the animistic spirit which is found
so frequently upon the prairies of the west. The Crees cast a
piece of tobacco into the rapid as a sacrifice to ensure protection,
and the Blackfeet often told me of the abodes of the spirits in
the rocks which lay on the prairie. This religion of savagery

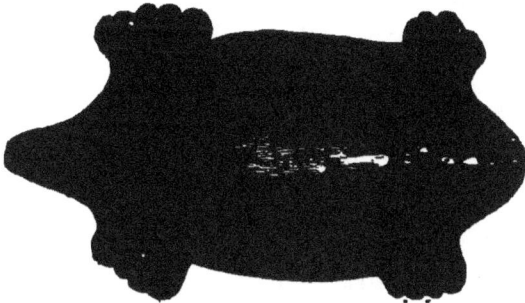

TOTEM OF TURTLE (FULL SIZE).

was a higher system than shamanism, yet, as animal worship,
found no higher personality than man.

As the primitive form of society totemism united the members of the clan as brothers and sisters, extending far beyond
the limits of family relationship, including people who spoke
different dialects and forming a clan brotherhood with ties
stronger than family life. Rival totems made war with each
other, as in Grecian mythology Lycus, the wolf, flees the
country before Ægeus, the goat, and the totem relationship
secured peace beyond the ties of the families. A husband and
wife may belong to different totems, which will divide them
when there arises a totem feud.† Intermarriage between the

* "American Antiquarian," Vol. XIV., pages 201, 202.
† " Britannica Encyclopædia "—article, " Sacrifice."

members of the same totem was forbidden. A member of the
wolf clan could not marry a wolf, but he might take a wife
from the women of the hawk clan. Such an arrangement as
this compelled the people to live together, the family ties being
scattered among the clans, and made them stronger by such a
social and religious bond. From this relationship there sprang
the custom which forbade intercourse between family relations,
especially between the husband and the parents of the wife.
This custom is followed at the present day among the Blackfeet and other tribes. By the fraternal bond every member of
the clan feels called upon to avenge the death of one of its
members by an enemy, and the hunter, warrior or wayfarer
receives a cordial welcome in the distant lodges of the clans-
men whose face he may have never seen. By the laws of
descent the children belong to the clan of the mother, and not
to the clan of the father. Among the Haidas of British
Columbia the children belong to the totem clan of the mother,
but if the clan of the father is reduced in numbers, the child
may be given to the sister of the father to suckle, and it is
then spoken of as belonging to the paternal aunt, and belongs
to the clan of the father.* Mother-right prevails among the
western Dénés, and in a general way among the northern tribes
of British Columbia, while paternal rule exists generally among
the southern tribes. Among the western Dénés titles and
landed property cannot pass by heredity into a different clan,
and the children of a noble belonging to their mother's clan
could not inherit the property of their father. If the father
had nephews by a sister one of them became his successor,
the nephews belonging to the clan of his uncle through his
mother. In order that the children of the noble might not be
wholly disinherited, one of his daughters would be united in
marriage with her inheriting maternal first cousin. Among
the Kwākiutl, matriarchate originally prevailed. The husband
becomes a member of the clan of his wife a short time after his
marriage, by assuming the name and crest of his father-in-law.
This crest descends upon his children, his daughters retaining

* " Geological Survey of Canada Report," 1878-79, page 134 B.

it, but his sons lose it as they follow their father's example, by adopting the crests of the women they marry. Patriarchal rule exists among the Salish, the children belonging to their father's gens, and the eldest son inherits his father's name and rank.* The Wyandots and Five Nations adhered strictly to the female line of descent, the office of sachem not passing to the son, but to the brother of the sachem, his sister's son, or some remoter kinsman.†

The totem is not only a clan name, denoting descent from a common ancestor, but it is also a clan symbol, constituting a conventional native heraldry. The totem marks are the native insignia, or symbols of rank or authority. Sometimes the crest refers to adventures of the ancestor. The Thlinkeets, Haidas and Tshimpseans celebrate a memorial festival and erect a

TOTEM OF BEAVER OR OTTER, MADE OF THIN SLATE (FULL SIZE).

memorial column upon the death of a man, showing the crest of the gens. The graves of great warriors are marked by a statue representing a warrior with a war club.‡ Heraldic columns are erected by the British Columbia tribes to commemorate the event of a chief taking his position in the tribe by building a house. These posts vary in length from forty to sixty feet. The general name for them among the Haidas is keeang, but each column has also an individual and distinguishing name. The keeang or lodge poles are hollowed out at the back and carved in front. When a chief decides to erect a keeang and build a lodge, invitations are sent to the tribes in

* "Proceedings of the Canadian Institute," October, 1889, page 119. "British Association Fifth Report of the North-West Tribes of Canada," 1889, page 32.

† Parkman's "Pontiac," Vol. I., pages 5, 10.

‡ Dr. Boaz, in "British Association Report of the North-West Tribes," 1889.

the vicinity to attend; who, upon their arrival, are received by dancers in costume and are hospitably entertained. At the appointed time, the Indians move the pole upon rollers to a hole previously dug, from seven to ten feet deep, long ropes are fastened to it which are grasped by gangs of men, women and children, who stand at a considerable distance, awaiting the signal to haul. The strongest men in the company raise the pole with their hands until it reaches their heads, when stout poles tied together in the form of shears are placed under it as a support. Sharp pointed poles are used to raise it to an angle of forty-five degrees, and then the signal is given for the persons at the ropes to haul it into position. With loud shouts the butt is dropped into the hole, and the column being set plumb, it is firmly set in position with earth. The crowd then repair to the

TOTEM OF WOLF OR BEAR, MADE OF THIN SLATE (FULL SIZE).

house of the owner of the column, who gives a potlach—a feast being provided of berries and grease, seaweed and other native condiments, and a distribution of all his property, consisting of blankets and numerous trinkets. These gifts are bestowed upon the members of all the gens, except the one to whom the column belongs. A pole erected by a Haida chief, named Stultah, at Masset is named Que-tilk-kep-tzoo, meaning "a watcher for arrivals." Mortuary columns erected upon the death of a chief are solid, circular poles, carved only on the base and summit. When these are erected a feast is given to the multitude, and blankets are distributed to the makers of the pole.*

The totem system introduced a lineage which united people belonging to the same clan though widely separated as kins-

* "Transactions of the Royal Society of Canada," Vol. IX., Sec. 2, pages 48, 49.

men, and when a stranger belonged to the same crest as the people he visited, he was treated as a relation. Thus a clan brotherhood existed which bound the people together. Several clans were sometimes united with a common totem, and these are known as a phratry. Four divisions are recognized in some districts by the natives: The clan or gens, the phratry or union of clans, the tribe and the confederacy or union of tribes. The phratry, with its common totem and interests, has several clans, each with its own sub-crest. There are several phratries among the tribes of British Columbia.

Totems are of three kinds: The clan totem, the personal totem, and the sex totem. The clan totem is a material object reverenced by a body of men and women who believe themselves to be of one blood, descended from the same ancestor, and bound to protect each other on account of their kinship and faith in the same totem. By means of the clan totem, the clan name was perpetuated among the Indian tribes and Mound-Builders, as shown by the totem posts, where the name of the clan generally surmounted the column, the family history and genealogical record being contained in the carvings below the clan name, and among the Mound-Builders the gigantic earth-works preserved the name of the clan. The native tribes of Canada and the United States have a large number of clan totems, estimated by Morgan to be nearly one hundred, and classified by Staniland Wake, showing a relationship between the tribes.* There cannot, however, be given any definite number of totems, as in tracing the history of the tribes some of the clan totems seem to change by the introduction of new totems and the extinction of some of the old. Different writers enumerate the clan totems for separate tribes, giving more or less for the same tribe.† The members of the same clan totem enjoyed special privileges, and were exempt from others, as upon one clan devolved the duty

* "American Antiquarian," Vol. XI., page 354.
† "Life of Zeisberger," page 78. "Proceedings of the Canadian Institute," October, 1889, page 188. "Transactions of the Royal Society of Canada," Vol. X., Sec. II., page 117. "Third Annual Report of the Bureau of Ethnology," 1881-82, pages 215-258.

of providing a sachem for the tribe, and, as has been seen, among the Haidas of British Columbia gifts were distributed at the erection of a memorial column to all the totems except the one to whom the column belonged.

Personal or individual totems are common among the native tribes of Canada. Early in life the Blackfoot seeks a lonely spot upon the prairie where he fasts and prays, until in a dream there is revealed to him his individual totem in the shape of an animal, which he kills, and preserves the skin that he may ever have it with him to protect and guide him. He must not afterward kill or eat any of its kind. Wherever he goes as a hunter or warrior, it must accompany him, and he is assured of safety in war and success in hunting. If he becomes a medicine man, it will reveal unto him some herb as medicine that the other medicine men know nothing of, and he depends upon its instruction to give him influence in his tribe. Personal totems are known among the Eastern Dènés, but not clan totems, while among the Western Dènés who were influenced through contact with the tribes from the western coast, personal and clan totems were in use.

The sex totem is generally an animal sacred to one of the sexes, each having its own special animal, which is regarded as a brother or sister, respectively, and is consequently protected. The sex totem prevails in Australia, and is not found among the native tribes of Canada.

Animals were generally chosen as totems, arising no doubt from the contact of man in his primitive condition with them, Becoming acquainted with their habits, and witnessing daily evidences of their sagacity, he learned to ascribe to them human traits, affections and superior wisdom. Among the Algonquin tribes it was believed that the Giant Rabbit shot his arrows into the soil, which became transfixed and grew up as trees, and from the dead bodies of certain animals he formed men, and these animals became the totems of the Algonquins.*

The wolf, bear, deer and buffalo prevail as animal totems among the Iroquois, Algonquins, Dakotas and their allies, the

*Brinton's "American Hero Myths," page 40.

other animals being less frequently used as totems. Among
the western Dénés, the clan totems included the toad, grouse,
crow, beaver, salmon, and other animals and birds. The hare
is found as a totemic device in Egypt and America. It appears
in the traditions of the natives as the Great Hare, Michabo, the
Hero of the Dawn in the earth effigies of the Mound-Builders,
and as a sun symbol in the stone ornaments.

Bird totems were extensively used by the Mound-Builders
and Indians, the eagle being the chief among the birds and the
most widely distributed of the bird totems; effigies of wild
geese, swallows and eagles are abundant in the Mound-Builders'
region of Wisconsin. At Muscoda there is an effigy of a bird,
with its wings spread out, measuring about one thousand feet in
length.* The dog, pheasant, snake and spider are found among
the totems, and even water, snow and ice.† A Blackfoot friend of
mine wore a bird totem on his war bonnet when he went into
battle, and he was assured that he could not be injured so long
as it remained there. Topographical names, as Red Rock, Salt
Springs and Grassy Hill ; and names of plants, as Cottonwood,
Walnut and Willow, were used by the Navajoes and Apaches of
Arizona.‡ Some of the clans of the tribe of Blood Indians
are known as Fish-Eaters, Tall Men, Camping Together, Sweaty
Feet and Black Horses, showing the absence of totems among
some of the clans, such as we understand by the use of the
word totem. Dr. Peet says that human figures were seldom
used to represent totems, although they were sometimes employed to show the mythologies which prevailed, and when it is
seen a higher type of totemism has been introduced. It
has been claimed that the monkey may be seen carved upon the
totem posts of the Haidas, but no animal figure of that kind
has been found upon the North-West coast, the figure supposed
to be that of the monkey being the bear, with the human face
and form.

* "American Antiquarian," Vol. XV., pages 94-96.
† Irving's " Astoria," page 165. Brinton's " Myths of the New World,"
page 303.
‡ "Journal of American Folk-Lore," Vol. III., page 111.

VILLAGE ON ALERT BAY, BRITISH COLUMBIA.

Various methods have been employed for exhibiting the
totems of the clans and individuals. Sometimes the totem was
beautifully carved on a stone pipe, and some fine specimens of
these totemic stone pipes may be seen in the museum of the
Canadian Institute, as well as in the archæological museums of
the United States. The British Columbia tribes tattooed it
upon their person, painted it upon their canoes and oars, placed
it upon their houses and carved it upon totem posts; the Blackfoot wore it upon his war bonnet and carried it in his medicine
bag, as the Iroquois and the Mound-Builders made earth figures
representing the totems. It was affixed to treaties, painted on
rocks, the skin of the totem was worn by the individual, the
hair was dressed to show some distinctive feature of the
animal, it was painted on the lodge, and woven into the dress
of the wearer. Stone effigies were also erected to represent the
totems.

Columns were used by the Indians of British Columbia to
inform the tribes of the movements of their enemies, as heraldic
columns, memorial posts and totem posts. Although totem posts
have prevailed among the tribes on the western coast, they were
employed by some of the eastern tribes. In the villages of the
Ottawas the different clans had separate wards, at the gates of
which were erected posts bearing the figures of the clan totems;
and near the village of Pomeiock, where the Powhattans dwelt,
were a set of carved posts, having human faces carved near the
top, which surrounded the dance circle and were used in their
sun worship. The Pacific Coast is, however, the totem post
district, more than five hundred carved columns being known
to exist in 1884 in the land of the Haidas. The age of carved
columns has passed away, many of them having fallen down,
some being cut down for firewood, and no new ones are being
erected. A few costly marble columns have been set up in
the streets and native burying-grounds, which still remain,
but the ambition of the people is to erect marble tombstones,
with an inscription giving the name and date of the death.
Some of the posts are elaborately carved, each tribe having its
own style of carving and crests. A few of them are painted,

but the majority of them are without any coloring. Strange-
looking figures are carved upon them, each figure having its
own story, embodying the myths of the people, family history,
totem and personal exploits.   The height of the column, the
variety, extent and architectural beauty displayed and the material of which it was made proclaimed the wealth of the owner.
The miniature columns made of wood and black slate, averaging
about fifteen feet in height, have taken the place of the massive
columns, and some of these cost not less than one thousand
dollars each.   The civilized stonecutter has been called in to
aid the native artist to keep alive among the people their
wonderful mythology and history, and it does seem to promise
the permanence of the totem post in another form among the
natives of the coast.   One of the wooden totem posts may be
seen standing in front of a curiosity shop in the main street of
Winnipeg, another is deposited in the museum of the Canadian
Institute, and several of them were exhibited at the World's
Fair.

James Deans, who is an authority upon the subject of carved
columns among the coast tribes, has interpreted the figures upon
the totem poles at the World's Fair.   Concerning one of these
columns, which formerly stood in an Indian town, on the Naas
River, he says: " The inscription alongside of this column reads
thus, 'Totem pole, or heraldic column, of the Tsiw Indians.'
The figures represent, counting from below upward, as follows :
First, the raven; second, dog-fish; third, man; fourth, wolf;
fifth, the killer-whale; and sixth, eagle.   On the above-mentioned
column, reading from below, the first is the carving of an Indian
with his head encircled by feathers.   This represents the party
to whom belonged the house in front of which this column
stood.   The second figure is the raven, called by these people
'caugh.'   This—the raven—is the phratry or principal crest,
along with the eagle phratry, of all these people.   The next is
the dog-fish, which, along with the raven phratry, was the
crest of the man who had this house built for himself.   The
third figure is a man, perhaps designed to represent the man
whose portrait this was, and to show that he belonged to the

tribe amongst whom the house was built. By saying this, I take a Haida standpoint; with the Sineskeans it may be different, although I hardly think so. The next or fourth figure above is a wolf. This is the crest of the wolf gens or crest. How it came to be placed there I can hardly say. This much I know, it showed a connection with that crest, or, in other words, a connection between the party who built this house and the clan bearing the wolf crest. The fifth figure is a woman with head-dress, and is evidently a figure of the housewife. Above her is a figure of a killer or fin-back whale with two young ones, one on each side of its mouth. The sixth figure is the crest of the wife. The young ones show her to have had a family, which, like herself, would have the whale crest. The next or seventh figure is that of a woman, showing that the wife was connected by birth with the tribe in which she lived. The upper or last figure is the eagle, and designates the phratry to which she belonged." *

The clan totems were sometimes tattooed on the person of the clansman. The Iroquois tattooed the totem on his body.† Indeed, the origin of tattooing seems to have had a religious significance, and is based on the totem system.‡ It was also painted upon the houses and tents. The Iroquois painted the clan totem in black or red upon the gable end of the cabin, the Thlinkeets ornamented their houses with heraldic symbols and allegorical and historical figures, the Haidas painted their totems on the front of their houses, and the posts which supported the platform upon which the houses were raised were carved and painted with totemic and historical designs, and the Nootkas followed the same custom. Among these tribes of the western coast the entrance of the house was sometimes through the body of a fish, and sometimes the image of the thunder bird, with spreading wings, was carved over the doorway. The Bella Bellas and Bella Coolas carved the entrance of their houses with

* "American Antiquarian," Vol. XV., page 281.
† "Life of Zeisberger," page 78. Parkman's "Pontiac," Vol. I., page 6.
‡ R. Fletcher's "Tattooing among Civilized Nations." Dorman's "Origin of Primitive Superstitions," page 156.

mythological figures and totemic devices; and the Kwakiutls of
Vancouver Island, instead of erecting totem posts, painted their
crests on the front of their houses. The tattoo marks of the
Haidas are skilfully done upon the bodies of men and women,
and every mark has its meaning, the designs upon the hands
and arms of the women indicating the clan to which they
belong. The simple dots and straight lines on the hands, arms
and faces of the women of the North-West coast have no particular significance, yet the more elaborate designs distinguish
the tribes. Seldom are the designs seen by white people or
understood, as the bodies of the natives are only exposed at
their festivals and masquerades, and the Haidas, as well as the
other tribes on the coast, are careful not to permit the intrusion
of white persons or strangers. Few white people have ever witnessed the extent and variety of the tattoo designs on account
of this prohibition. The Osages have a secret order, whose
members preserve some of their traditions by tattooing symbols
upon the throat and chest.*

The Indians were in the habit of signing their names to
treaties and letters by their individual totem. This can be seen
in a series of drawings in the library of the Army Medical
Museum of the United States, narrating the deeds of Sitting
Bull, and in some of the letters and picture writing of the Cree
Indians.† Rude pictographs on cliffs and in caves contained
the totems of the Indians. When the natives visited the famous
pipestone quarry of Minnesota for the purpose of securing
catlinite, they left inscriptions upon the cliffs in the vicinity,
which were probably their totems. Several caves in Minnesota
and Iowa, described by Mr. T. H. Lewis, contain inscriptions
which resemble the totems of modern tribes. Sometimes the
necklaces worn by the male members of the clans were used as
a craft symbol, an emblem of honor, or a clan totem.‡ The
clan totem was sometimes painted upon the stem of the pipe,

---

* "Fourth Annual Report of the Bureau of Ethnology," 1882-83, pages
67-71.

† Le Plongeon's "Here and There in Yucatan," page 117.

‡ "American Antiquarian," Vol. XVI., page 183.

along with other symbolic pictographs. The effigy-builders shaped their totems in extensive mounds of earth, resembling the animal or bird totem. The head-dress of the hunter or warrior might show the clan totem, the clans of the Iowas dressing their hair according to their split totem, as the Black- feet exhibited the personal totem by a bird or animal worn upon the hair or war bonnet. The Thlinkeets disguised them- selves in the form of their animal totems when they went to dance. Some tribes put the skin of their animal totem upon their lodges and others dressed themselves in it when they went to war. The Dakotas painted their clan and personal totems, as may be seen in the pictographs on the Dakota Winter Count. The Blackfeet and Dakotas made totemic figures upon the prairie of small stones, some of these covering a large area. Solitary stones were also used as clan totems, as the Onondaga stone of the Iroquois.

The use of totems is widely diffused, the ancient Egyptians and Greeks employing animal totems, and traces of totemic worship have been found in the names of Christians and pagans in the Roman catacombs.* The New Zealanders have carved posts at the eaves of their houses, and carved totemic figures covering the front of them. Totemism widely prevailed in Australia, among the Zunis, the Mound-Builders, the Iroquois, Algonquins and the tribes in British Columbia and Alaska. The Iroquois polity was based upon the totemic system and attained a high degree of perfection. It seems, however, to have been some- what modified at times, clans having been divided and new totems taken, or the clans having been absorbed by others and the totems combined. The Malicetes and Micmacs carved their clan totems on pipes made of soapstone, as well as upon other articles. A soapstone pipe carved by one of the eastern natives represented the otter, beaver and musk-rat as totems.† The Ojibways carved their totems upon blocks of wood and placed them upon the houses which covered their graves. The Ojibways had originally five totems, which have increased to twenty-one.

---

* Withrow's "The Catacombs of Rome," page 456.
† "Canadian Indian," page 335.

The Bear clan was the most numerous in the tribe. It was believed that the clans partook of the nature of the animal totems: the Bear clan being ill-tempered, the Crane clan having loud voices, and the Loon clan wearing wampum around the neck to resemble the white collar of the loon. The marten, moose and reindeer totems are included under the generic term of "Monsonceg."* The Crees, Blackfeet, Western Dénés and other tribes in Western Canada have totemic symbols, but totemism does not prevail so extensively amongst the tribes on the northern lakes and forests as among those on the north-west coast and in the east. It is in British Columbia where the totemic symbols are most extensively used, as in the carved columns, and the Haidas excel in the art of carving the totem posts. The origin of this system of perpetuating the mythology, clan name, family history and individual exploits upon the totemic columns is unknown, but it is believed that a spirit revealed to one of the chiefs, in the days when the people lived in cold huts, the plan of a house in detail. The chief and his tribe provided the necessary material for the house, when the same spirit appeared again with an addition to the plan. James Deans, in relating this tradition, says: "Just as they were about to build the same visitor appeared to the chief and again showed him the plan, with this difference: a carved column was placed in front of the house, with his crest (a raven) carved on top. Underneath the raven was a second carving, the crest of his wife, an eagle. Lower down still were the crests of his father and mother, and also those of his wife's family. While showing him the plan his adviser from the celestial sphere told him that not only was his tribe or himself to build houses like the one shown, but all the people in every village were to build the same and to set up columns. Slowly, but surely, as the old huts were pulled down, new-styled ones took their places, each one having one or more columns. One had the husband's crest and that of his parents; the other had the wife's crest and that of her parents underneath." Totem posts have been erected in great abundance in Alaska.

* Warren's "History of the Ojibways—Collections of the Minnesota Historical Society," Vol. 5.

The totems of the Indians embody some of their myths, and besides the crests which represent their mythology, there are mythological designs carved upon the heraldic columns. The totemic figures carry a story with them. This relation between the myths and totems exists among the Shoshonees, Micmacs and British Columbia tribes. The myths and the symbols served to perpetuate their remembrance among the people. As an illustration of this relationship, Dr. Boaz relates a myth of the bear gens of the Tshimpseans: "An Indian went mountain goat hunting. When he had reached a remote mountain range he met a black bear, who took him to his home, taught him how to catch salmon, and how to build boats. Two years the man stayed with the bear; then he returned to his village. All people were afraid of him, for he looked just like a bear. One man, however, caught him and took him home. He could not speak, and could not eat anything but raw food. Then they rubbed him with magic herbs, and he was retransformed into the shape of a man. Thenceforth, when he was in want he went into the woods and his friend, the bear, helped him. In winter, when the rivers were frozen, he caught plenty of salmon. He built a house and painted the bear on the front of it. His sister made a dancing blanket, the design of which represented a bear. Therefore the descendants of his sister use the bear for their crest."[*] Interesting stories of adventures as human beings are told by the Haidas about the raven, whale, wolf and salmon, which were animal totems of these people.

HUNTING THE MOOSE.

Canada is the land of sport and adventure. Its lakes and rivers teem with fish, the mountains and forests abound with animals; the climate varies from the warm and humid temperature of Ontario and British Columbia to the frigid atmosphere in the northern land of eternal ice and snow; and the scenery of the Thousand Islands, the beautiful lakes of Muskoka and the Thunder Bay district, and the grandeur of the Rocky

[*] "British Association Report of the North-West Tribes of Canada," 1889, page 24.

Mountains cannot be surpassed. Sportsmen and tourists in
search of health and recreation seek their favorite haunts in
New Brunswick and Nova Scotia, the rugged landscapes of
Muskoka attract the lovers of quiet nooks; the disciples of
Izaac Walton congregate at Nepigon and the trout streams of
Western Algoma; and the more adventurous hie away to the
Rocky Mountains or the northern districts of Manitoba, the
North-West Territories, Athabasca and British Columbia, where
they build a hut or pitch their tents and solicit pleasure in the
pursuit of the larger kinds of game. In the Rocky Mountains,
the barren grounds of Northern Canada and upon the shores of
the Arctic sea the bear seeks a secluded home, unseen by few
save the intrepid white hunter or Indian. The barren ground
bear frequents the barren grounds lying to the north of the
wooded lands, and in the summer haunts the shores of the
Arctic sea; the polar bear spends the greater part of its life in
pursuit of the different kinds of seal among the fields of ice, and
the black bear roams in the mountains and forests of the west.

The hardy trapper has followed the rivers eastward and
westward in quest of the sagacious little beaver, whose patience,
cunning and skill is the admiration of the native, as the valuable skin is highly prized by civilized man. Roasted beaver is
a prime dish for the red man. There is no animal, not even
the buffalo, which has influenced man and changed the face of
the country as this industrious worker. He has bridged rivers,
felled the trees in the forests, aroused the greed of gain, compelling men to organize companies to persecute him in driving
him from his quiet retreat. The skill and patience of the beaver
is shown in the formation of dams, and excavating vaults on
the margin of the rivers and ponds as places of safety. He is
the civil engineer among the quadrupeds, and the social leader.
Uniting in companies under the guidance of a master, from
whose ranks the lazy beaver is expelled, they formed their
colony for the purpose of building a dam to flood the stream,
so as to give them an abundant supply of water in the winter,
and to excavate the beaver-house. The white trappers and red
men have studied his habits so well that his skill was no

match for their perseverance, and in the west and east they
have become scarce; but in the district of Peace River and
along the Mackenzie they still abound in great numbers,
although nearly thirty thousand skins are annually exported.
The mountain sheep and goats roam in the recesses of the
Rocky Mountains, and these animals possess the striking
peculiarity: that the goat bears a very fine wool, well adapted
for the manufacturers of shawls; and the sheep has a close,
brittle hair, like the caribou. The sheep have such heavy horns
that when closely pursued they will dash over a precipice and
alight upon them, without breakage or harm to themselves,
and, springing upon their feet, bound away. Various kinds of
deer, including the moose, wapiti, antelope, jumping-deer and
fallow-deer range south of the barren grounds in the wooded
country, and the musk-ox and caribou find their favorite resort
in the barren grounds and northward. The wapiti, known
amongst the Cree Indians as "wawaskish," frequents the plains
of the Saskatchewan, northward and westward. The buffalo,
moose and caribou were known to the Mound-Builders, as the
grazing-places of these animals are shown by the effigies chiefly
located in the State of Wisconsin. Effigies of these animals
are found in their peculiar haunts, and game-drives have been
discovered which were erected by the Mound-Builders for hunting them. These game-drives varied for the different animals,
the moose game-drives being mainly elevated roadways on the
hills, connected by parallel walls in the bottom lands; and the
buffalo game-drives being situated on the banks of rivers near
the fords, so that the hunters could shoot them as the herds
passed down the banks.

The reindeer or caribou frequent northern Keewatin and
Athabasca, the larger variety inhabiting the mountains and
forests of the north, and the smaller kind existing on the
barren grounds, travelling to the shores and islands of the
Arctic sea in summer, and retiring to the woods in winter. The
caribou feeds upon grass and the various lichens which grow
in abundance on the barren grounds. The Eskimo and Indian
tribes—including the Chippewayans, Dog Rib, Swampy Crees.

and Copper Indians—hunt them for food and clothing, the meat being superior to the moose and buffalo. Six or seven skins sewed together make a warm blanket, suitable to ensure comfort on the coldest night in that distant region. The female has horns as well as the male, but they are not so large, and are much less palmated.

Sir John Schultz asserts that the barren ground caribou of northern Keewatin are identical with the domesticated reindeer of northern Norway, Sweden, Lapland and the Asian Arctic littoral farther east. As the United States Government have made a successful experiment of introducing among the Eskimo of Alaska eighty Russian reindeer as the nucleus of herds for the supply of food and clothing and for travelling, the intention being to distribute so soon as the herds are large enough, fifty head at each of the missionary stations, Sir John Schultz is anxious that the Canadian Government should seek to domesticate a few of our barren-ground caribou, that they might be of service to the Eskimos and Indians, and thus provide against lack of food or clothing for the dwellers in the North Land. Vast herds of caribou roam over the barren grounds of the north at the present day. Warburton Pike, in 1890, penetrated the almost unknown land of the caribou and musk-ox, and in the account of his journey he speaks of the countless herds of caribou. "Scattered bands of caribou were almost always in sight from the top of the ridge behind the camp, and increased in numbers till the morning of October 20th, when Baptiste, who had gone for firewood, woke us up before daylight with the cry of "La foule! La foule!" and even in the lodge we could hear the curious clatter made by a band of travelling caribou. La foule had really come, and during its passage of six days I was able to realize what an extraordinary number of these animals still roam in the barren ground. From the ridge we had a splendid view of the migration ; all the south side of Mackay Lake was alive with moving beasts, while the ice seemed to be dotted all over with black islands, and still away on the north shore, with the aid of glasses, we could see them coming like regiments on the march.

In every direction we could hear the grunting noise that the caribou always make when travelling; the snow was broken into broad roads, and I found it useless to try to estimate the number that passed within a few miles of our encampment."

The barren grounds lying between the sixtieth parallel and the Arctic sea is the range of the musk-ox, the hardiest of all the animals of that northern region, whose skin and horns are seldom seen by civilized man. The animal resembles in size the Highland Scotch cattle. The head is large and broad, with heavy horns which cover the crown and brow, and the body is coated with long and thick brown or black hair, curling on the shoulders and hanging down the sides and reaching half way down the legs. They are massive-looking animals, congregating in large herds, from ten to seventy in number, during April, at which time they are very wild; but in June the herds are smaller, often composed of cows and calves, and are tame even to stupidity. Unconscious of fear, apparently through their infrequent contact with man and the solitude of their range, it is sometimes possible to walk within a few yards of them, and when the herd is fired into they will run a short distance and quietly commence grazing. With head erect, clad in thickly matted hair and with short legs, the animal walks with a curious rolling motion. He is of uncertain temper, and when aroused is a formidable antagonist. When frightened he will scale the rocks and precipitous slopes with great agility, and when assembled in herds, under the leadership of two or three old bulls, their manœuvres are quick and regular as a squadron of cavalry, the horns massed together presenting a formidable front. Warburton Pike, describing his first meeting with the musk-ox, says: "After travelling about three miles through some rough hills, we caught an indistinct view of the musk-ox, fully a hundred in number, standing on a side hill from which most of the snow had drifted away; and then followed a wonderful scene, such as I believe no white man has ever looked on before. Everybody started on a run, but the dogs, which had been let out of harness, were ahead of us, and the first thing I made out clearly through the driving snow was a dense, black

TRACKING THE WAPITI.

mass galloping right at us. The band had proved too big for
the dogs to hold, and most of the musk-oxen had broken away.
I do not think they knew anything about men, or had the least
intention of charging us, but they passed within ten yards, and
so frightened my companions that I was the only man to fire at
them, rolling over a couple. The dogs, however, were still
holding a small lot at bay, and these we slaughtered without
any more trouble than killing cattle in a yard."

The male measures from base of horns to the root of the tail
generally seven feet, and the female five feet. Some of these
animals are white. Underneath the long hair there is a beautiful fine fur, softer and finer than the finest alpaca, and much
longer in the staple. As they rush down the steep declivities
they will slide on their hams, and arrest their rapid descent by
the use of their magnificent shield of horn which spreads across
their forehead. When confronted by a foe, they will pack
themselves closely together under the leadership of an old bull
and follow his directions. Captain McClintock describes the
death-struggle of one of these animals in the account of his
sledge-journey : " We saw and shot two very large musk bulls,
a well-timed supply, as the last of the venison was used this
morning. We found them to be in better condition than any
we had ever seen. I shall never forget the death-struggle of
one of the noble bulls. A Spanish bull-fight gives no idea of it,
and even the slaughter of the bear is tame in comparison. This
animal was shot through the lungs, and blood gushed from his
nostrils upon the snow. As it stood fiercely watching us, prepared to yet unable to charge; its small but fixed glaring
eyes were almost concealed by masses of shaggy hair, and
its whole frame was fearfully convulsed with agony; the trem-
ulous motion was communicated to its enormous covering of
tangled wool and hair ; even the coarse, thick mane seem to
rise indignant and slowly waved from side to side. It seemed
as if the very fury of its passion was pent up within it for
one final—a revengeful—charge. There was no roaring ; the
majestic beast was dumb; but the wild gleam of savage fire
which shot from his eyes and his menacing attitude was far

more terrible than the most hideous bellow. We watched in silence, for time was doing our work ; nor did we venture to lower our guns until, his strength becoming exhausted, he reeled and fell. I have never witnessed such an intensity of rage, nor imagined for one moment that such an apparently stupid brute, under any circumstances of pain and passion, could have presented such a truly appalling spectacle. It is almost impossible to conceive a more terrific sight than that which was presented to us in the dying moments of this matchless denizen of these northern wilds."

The moose is the largest of the American deer, and ranges on the western continent from the Atlantic to the Pacific, and in the northern districts of Keewatin and Athabasca, following the Mackenzie River to the shores of the Arctic sea, but it never enters the barren grounds. It is larger than a horse, standing five and six feet high at the shoulders, measuring about seven feet from the nose to the root of the tail, with a head resembling an enormous jackass fully two feet in length, having massive antlers from four to six feet at the widest part, broadly palmated, weighing from fifty to sixty pounds, a short stout neck and long legs which prevent it from feeding close to the ground. When full grown the animal will weigh from one thousand to twelve hundred pounds. Its brown fur is thick and coarse, and is longest at the neck and shoulders. It is an awkward, clumsy creature as it travels along with a shambling gait, yet there is a majesty about it, as it carries its antlers horizontally and so well that they are not entangled in the branches of the trees. When walking quietly it is so stealthy that it will not touch a dead twig. It can jump, trot and run easily, and when pursued is exceedingly fleet, leaving horses and dogs far behind. It can swim well, and when unable to reach the tops of the young trees as it browses in the forest, it will ride them, bearing them down with its weight. It lives chiefly on the tender buds and twigs of the willow and birch and the leaves of trees. When the snow is deep, a moose-yard is formed by treading down the snow within a small area, leaving it in a kind of wall, surrounding the family of five or six which together congregate. It is a very shy and timid creature, fleeing at the sight of man, and travels with great speed in time of danger. Possessed of an acuteness in hearing and smell, it is difficult to get near it, and the expert hunter has to exercise great care and craftiness in approaching a moose-yard or hunting in the forest, except in spring, when a crust has been formed on the snow, which is easily broken, and then as it falls repeatedly in running it can be overtaken by dogs and the Indian on his snowshoes. It can be most easily approached when sadly tormented by mosquitoes. At the rutting season the male becomes a formidable foe, attacking man or any animal that comes in his way. The flesh is the best and most juicy, except that of the reindeer, when in season, the tongue and nose especially being regarded as delicacies, and the tanned hide makes the best leather for moccasins and breeches. When caught young it can be easily domesticated, and may be used in drawing a sledge. Large numbers of them are still found in the northern portions of Manitoba and in Keewatin. In the forests that clothe the long range of mountains north of the Assiniboine River, and about the head waters of the rivers that flow north of Lake Winnipegosis they still roam in considerable numbers. The Indians located on the Reserve north of Birtle, near the spruce forests inhabited by the moose, make a business of catching the fawns. Taking a pony and cart, with a milch cow tied to the cart, the Indian starts for the forest, and when he has travelled as far as the road is passable the cart and cow are left behind, and mounting his pony he seeks the place of retreat which the female moose has selected for herself and the fawns. It is customary for the female moose, as it is with other kinds of deer and the wild cows on the ranches of the west, to hide her young while she is absent feeding, and the hunter calmly waits until evening, after finding traces of the presence of the animals, when he is awarded by hearing the mother calling her young, and discovers the place of safety. In the early dawn, before the female moose has left her retreat, an attempt is made to capture one or both of the young, and when successful, the young moose is taken to the cart, where, after the excitement is over, it is placed on a bed of soft hay, fastened simply with a strap around its neck, and it takes kindly to the cow, who suckles it as her own calf. In a short time it becomes tame enough to go at large with the cattle. A short time ago, an inspector of Indian agencies was surprised to see a full grown moose enter the home of one of the Indians, where it had been tamed and become the pet of the family.

Two years ago, as the captain of one of the fishing steamboats belonging to Rat Portage was sailing on the Lake of the

SHOOTING THE ELK.

Woods, he was surprised to see two full grown moose swimming from one island to another, and he at once gave chase. Being anxious if possible to capture them alive, the captain pursued and overtook them, and a lasso was thrown over the neck of one of them, who, on being aware of his seizure, began to bellow and lash the water at a fearful rate. His companion was making for the shore at the rate of fifteen miles an hour, but upon hearing the cries of the captured one, turned back to help him. In the desperate struggle the rope broke and the chase was continued, the moose swimming rapidly, bellowing

loudly all the time, and leaping out of the water in their efforts
to escape. They were pursued for more than half an hour,
when the captain decided to grant them their liberty, and
allowed them to reach the shore unmolested. Within one day's
drive from the city of Winnipeg the moose congregate in hundreds, passing the village of Stoney Mountain to the township
of Greenwood, where stretches of timber enclose the farms.
The moose are hunted by the farmers. Beyond this district lie
lakes Manitoba and Winnipeg, and in the forests adjacent to
them these timid creatures roam in their solitude, unrestrained
and seldom pursued. Colonel Bedson, during his residence as
warden of the Penitentiary at Stoney Mountain, domesticated
some of these animals, and a pair of two-year-old females were
broken by him to bit, bridle and harness, and were capable of
being driven like horses to a buggy or cutter. These were sent
to Montreal and daily driven in the processions connected with
the carnival.

The Indians of Round Lake sometimes hunt the moose in
the Riding Mountains with success. The animals have disappeared from the Kootenay district, but they are still abundant
in the northern part of the Territories and in Athabasca. The
annual trade in moose skins in Athabasca amounts to nearly
two thousand. Between four and five hundred moose are consumed every year at the forts of the Hudson's Bay Company
in the Peace River District, and four times that number are
consumed by the Indians who reside there, and still it is probable that there are as many moose in that district as there were
half a century ago. When Captain Back was gliding with his
companions down the Petite Rivière à Jean, the sharp sight of
the Indians detected a moose ahead of them, and La Prise, a
Chippewayan, being a skilful hunter, went in pursuit. A short
time afterwards, when the company were encamped, they were
startled by a long shrill whoop, which Louison, the interpreter,
said announced that La Prise had been successful. When the
hunter approached in his canoe the interpreter inquired if he
had been successful, and the Chippewayan answered in the
negative, " Oolah." The interpreter, in a disappointed tone,

replied: "Oolah! Monsieur, il a manqué!" ("Who ever heard the whoop without its accompanying prey ?") La Prise answered by handing him the gun from one hand, and presenting the fine tongue and nose of a moose, saying, "There; I shot it through the heart, through an opening between the trees not wider than my hand; but it was with your gun and ammunition which, according to our customs, you know, makes it your property. I thought the chief would like to have the tongue and nose, and the rest lies at the bottom of the canoe for your disposal." This adherence to custom reveals the character of the Indians, as they had hardly eaten anything for several days, and the few scraps of food which remained would scarcely suffice for a single meal, but Captain Back gave the larger portion of the animal to La Prise and his party. Moose walk at the rate of four miles an hour, even in woods so thick that it is difficult to understand how they can escape from getting their horns entangled in the branches of the trees. The Micmacs of Nova Scotia and the Indians of Keewatin and Athabasca are the best hunters of the moose. Hunting the moose is exciting and difficult, as it is impossible to see any great distance in the thick forest, and though the wind may be howling through the tree tops, and the trees rustling and groaning as they are swayed backward and forward, let the hunter tread on a rotten stick and the moose will easily detect it from other sounds and speedily depart. In creeping toward the animals, following closely the tracks in the snow, the hunter has to be exceedingly careful, as they may have doubled and got his wind, and he must study the situation by keeping to the leeward of the moose-yard, and quartering his ground against the wind. The Indians living near the Arctic sea were accustomed to place rows of moss upon the ice to keep deer in a particular direction. Sometimes the deer were caught in a pound, in much the same fashion as the tribes on the prairies entrapped and slew the buffalo before they became possessed of firearms. A well frequented deer-path was selected, which was enclosed by a stout fence of trees and brushwood, a mile or more in circumference, having within labyrinthine hedges with openings guarded with snares of twisted thongs. From the narrow entrance to the pound two

arms, several miles in length, made of trees and brushwood, gradually widening, extended. The Indians repaired to an elevated
position where they could see the deer, and when a herd was
discovered, men, women and children arranged themselves so
as to get behind them, and then with shouting and running
they were driven into the pound, where they were easily
despatched by the Indians.

The Carrier Indians usually hunt bears, caribou and moose
with dogs. Father Morice, describing the method pursued by
the Sékanais of the north in hunting the caribou, says, "They
previously set in a continuous line forty or fifty moose hide
snares in suitable defiles or passes in the mountains frequented
by the animals. Two of the most active hunters are then
deputed to watch at either end of the line, after which the
hunters, who usually number fifteen or more, drive the band
of deer or caribou to where the snares are set, and by loud
shouting and firing of guns they scare and thereby force the
reluctant game to pass through the noose, which at once con-
tracts around their necks. The deer immediately scamper
away with the moveable sticks to which the snares are
attached, and which, being soon caught among fallen or standing trees or other obstacles, cause the animal to stop suddenly
with the result of being strangled to death in a short time."
When the Eskimos desire to preserve the meat of the animals
killed they are accustomed to sink shafts or wells for that purpose. The Indians of Nova Scotia and New Brunswick prac-
tise three modes of hunting the moose, termed: Still-hunting,
fire-hunting, and calling. Still-hunting, or creeping upon the
moose, requires skill, courage and endurance, as a thorough
knowledge of the habits of the animal is needed, but it is the
most delightful, exhilarating and humane. Fire-hunting is
practised by burning bunches of birch bark in places frequented
by these animals, or by placing a torch in the bow of a canoe.
All kinds of deer are animated by curiosity to discover the
cause of anything strange to them. I have gone with the
hunter of deer into the ravines on the prairie, and upon seeing
a band of antelope beyond the range of our rifles, we have
taken a hat or handkerchief, and placing it upon the muzzle of

the gun put the butt on the ground, and the animals have ceased running and come toward us. Allured by the torchlight the moose will stand or draw near to satisfy his curiosity ; and during the moments of exploration will very likely fall a victim to the hunter's skill. Calling the moose is the Indian's prerogative, as a white man seldom acquires the art, and few among.the young men of the native tribes are successful moose callers. A moose will answer a low call much more readily at some times than others, and unsuspiciously will he come long distances. A piece of birch bark is formed into a horn, and with this simple instrument the Indian will imitate the plaintive lowing of the female moose, and the responsive bellow of the male. A low call made when the moose is pausing, uncertain whether to proceed or retreat, is a difficult thing for even an Indian, and it is a time of excitement, as a false note will be quickly detected by the acute ear of the animal. An old Indian will place the small end of his birchen horn to his lips, and the other upon the ground to deaden the sound, and with his cheeks puffed up as he pours volumes of wind into the horn, he will produce a low and far-off sounding series of grunts or calls. Only a native can detect the imitation call. If the call is successful the male will be heard crashing through the forest, rattling his horns against the trees as a challenge to his rivals, and bellowing loudly as he advances. Should the imitation be a poor one, he will not respond.

Colonel Butler, in *The Wild North Land*, touches upon moose hunting among the Indians of Peace River: "To hunt the moose requires years of study. Here is the little game which his instinct teaches him. When the early morning has come he begins to think of lying down for the day. He has been feeding on the grey and golden willow tops as he walked leisurely along. His track is marked in the snow or soft clay; he carefully retraces his footsteps, and, breaking off suddenly to the leeward side, lies down a gun shot from his feeding track. He knows he must get the wind of anyone following his trail. In the morning 'Twapoos,' or the Three Thumbs, sets forth to look for a moose ; he hits the trail and follows it, every now and again he examines the broken willow tops or the hoof marks,

when experience tells him that the moose has been feeding here
during the early night. Twapoos quits the trail, bending away
in a deep circle to leeward; stealthily he returns to the trail,
and as stealthily bends away again from it, he makes as it
were the semi-circles of the letter B, supposing the perpendicular line to indicate the trail of the moose; at each return to
it he examines attentively the willows, and judges his proximity
to the game. At last he is so near that he knows for an
absolute certainty that the moose is lying in a thicket a little
distance ahead. Now comes the moment of caution. He divests
himself of every article of clothing which might cause the
slightest noise in the forest; even his moccasins are laid aside;
and then, on a pointed toe, which even a ballot girl might
envy, he goes forward for the last stalk. Every bush is now
scrutinized; every thicket examined. See! he stops all at once!
You who follow him look, and look in vain; you can see nothing. He laughs to himself, and points to you willow covert.
No; there is nothing there. He noiselessly cocks his gun.
You look again and again, but can see nothing; then Twapoos
suddenly stretches out his hand and breaks a little dry twig
from an overhanging branch. In an instant, right in front,
thirty or forty yards away, an immense dark-haired animal
rises up from the willows. He gives one look in your direction,
and that look is his *last*. Twapoos has fired, and the moose is
either dead in his thicket or within a few hundred yards of it."

A story has been told of a white hunter on the Miramichi
who, following the track of a moose, came suddenly upon a big
one standing on the brink of a deep ravine, through which
flowed a shallow stream, known as Falls Brook. Raising his
rifle he pulled the trigger, but found that it was half-cock, and
at that moment the moose bounded down the ravine and the
hunter after him. In his haste the pursuer fell into the stream,
and besides being drenched, spoiled his cartridges. The animal
dashed past him up the stream, but his flight was hindered
by a waterfall twenty feet high, so down the stream madly he
turned and ran, only to be stopped by a fence of fallen trees.
Imprisoned in the ravine, the hunter prepared to attack him
with the stock of his gun or knife, but upon scanning his

situation, observed a long branch of water-ash stretching across the bed of the stream, under which the moose had to pass in his mad career. With a sudden resolve the hunter threw aside his gun, and grasping the ash branch swung himself outward, and as the moose passed under it he dropped upon his back and clasped him around his neck. Frantic with rage he rushed up and down the stream bearing his strange rider, until completely exhausted, when he fell, and the hunter, springing to his feet, drew his knife and killed him.

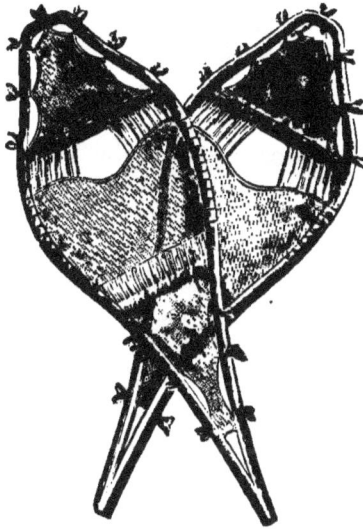

SNOWSHOES.

The white hunter is not always so fortunate, for there is great risk of life when the moose is brought to bay, for then he will use his feet and antlers in defence, and may crush his opponent to death. Two white hunters, in the depth of winter when the snow lay three feet deep, started out on foot to hunt the moose, accompanied by two strong and valuable deerhounds. With their snowshoes it did not take them long to reach the forest, and they were delighted with observing the tracks of a male and female moose and two fawns. As they were proceeding cautiously through the thicket they saw, at a distance of three hundred yards, the moose family, wholly unconscious of their presence. Letting the dogs loose they rushed after them, as they were unable at that distance in the woods to get a good shot. The hounds overtook them, owing to the heavy snow, and when the hunters arrived they found the male moose engaged fighting the hounds with his feet and antlers, the mother and fawns still in flight. The male started off in another direction upon the arrival of the hunters, who decided at once to separate, the one to seek the mother and fawns and the other to kill the male. The latter followed the tracks of the single animal for half-a-mile, when he found one of the dogs bleeding but fighting fiercely and the other lying dead, trampled under the feet of the infuriated animal. Upon seeing the man he ran for a short distance and then stood at bay, but taking a steady aim the hunter wounded him, which made him still more enraged, when suddenly he rushed at his opponent, who sought refuge behind a large tree. Attempting to reload his gun he found that he had lost his powder flask, and there he was compelled to stay, with the angry moose upon one side of the tree and he upon the other, shivering with cold, excited with fear, and impatient for the return of his companion. With knife in hand there he stood for more than an hour, the snow falling and partially obliterating the trail, and unable to decide what to do, yet resolved, if his companion did not soon extricate him, that he would dare the moose with his knife. As the infuriated animal stood upon one side of the tree, snorting and stamping his feet and ready to spring upon him at any moment, he heard the loud shout of his companion—who had killed the three moose and hung up their carcases—and relief soon came from his perilous position, as the animal fell with a bullet in his brain. The hunters had both of their dogs killed in the contest, and they were glad, indeed, when they reached home after their exciting adventure.

Moose hunting in Canada is the delight of tourists from across the sea, as well as the hunters of our own country, but with such a vast range and countless numbers of deer, there will elapse very many years before the moose become extinct.

INDEX.

41